Acts of Teaching

ACTS OF TEACHING
How to Teach Writing

A Text, A Reader, A Narrative

Joyce Armstrong Carroll
and
Edward E. Wilson
New Jersey Writing Project in Texas

With a foreword by Janet Emig

1993
Teacher Ideas Press
a Division of
Libraries Unlimited, Inc.
Englewood, Colorado

We would like to dedicate this book to our mentor, Janet Emig, and to all the teachers who have been, are, and will be a part of the New Jersey Writing Project in Texas.

TEACHER IDEAS PRESS
A Division of
Libraries Unlimited, Inc.
P.O. Box 6633
Englewood, CO 80155-6633

Library of Congress Cataloging-in-Publication Data

Carroll, Joyce Armstrong, 1937-
  Acts of teaching : how to teach writing / Joyce Armstrong Carroll
and Edward E. Wilson.
    xxi, 546 p. 19x26 cm.
    Includes bibliographical references and index.
    ISBN 1-56308-039-7
    1. English language--Composition and exercises--Study and teaching
(Elementary) 2. English language--composition and exercises--Study
and teaching (Secondary)   I. Wilson, Edward E. II. Title.
LB1576.C31717 1993
808'.042'07--dc20   93-531
                                                            CIP

CONTENTS

132689

FOREWORD

In the lost 70s, when the New Jersey Writing Project was just a whippersnapper, I received a call one morning from a state coordinator of the English-language arts. She had heard about the Project and wanted to consider offering several institutes the following summer to teachers in her state. She was however considering several other models of teacher education as well. What unique virtues did our project have?

I spoke—I thought eloquently—about writing as a process, about the highly interactive exchange between a teacher and her own writing, a teacher and her student, a teacher and her students' writing, a student with another student, and one student's writing with another student's writing. She listened thoughtfully to my highly detailed description of the Project, then asked what textbooks and other written materials I could send her to use in a comparative presentation to her board. When I said that we had none beyond a very basic brochure, there was a palpable withdrawal of interest over the miles. Then she said that her board was uncomfortable without "manipulatives" to contemplate and that she would probably recommend another heavily texted project from our region. And she did.

The incident revealed a tension those of us who espouse writing as process have experienced over the fifteen years since the Project was formed: how to honor the tenets we believe in while yet providing the specific guidelines and help that stay true to those tenets, such as proffering, when needed and when requested, appropriate readings, activities, and advice.

Through *Acts of Teaching*, Joyce Armstrong Carroll and Edward E. Wilson provide compelling solutions to this dilemma by giving just such help, advice, and solace.

The virtues of this source book are too many to catalogue, but three are especially noteworthy. First is the seamless connection between theory and practice. The classroom processes and activities they recommend are based always on the most current, valid theories of learning, writing, and thinking. They know, and appropriately apply, their Bruner, Donaldson, Murray, Vygotsky, and others.

The second is how well they know those classrooms they serve. Carroll and Wilson's advice is grounded in their almost daily observation of diverse teachers, students, and learning situations. They reveal that always discernible difference between those who spend vast amounts of time in the classroom and comprehend with sophistication what they see, like Jane Healy, Ann Dyson, and John Goodlad, and those who don't, like Tracy Kidder in *Among Schoolchildren*.

More, Carroll and Wilson can do what they say, what they recommend. Both are brilliant teachers who can cope on the spot with almost any learning challenge that greets them. Teachers consequently know that they can be trusted above the hit-and-runners who appear from academe or elsewhere and reveal immediately their own discomfort with the creative mess of daily learning and teaching.

Finally, their humanism shines through. They not only see and teach; they believe profoundly in the model of teaching writing they espouse, a model distinguished by its respect for children, for teachers, for learning, for the democratic process in and out of the classroom.

— Janet Emig

ACKNOWLEDGMENTS

- To Laurie Dudley, reference librarian at the Abilene Public Library.

- To the parents of the student authors cited in this book.

- To the many student authors who so willingly shared their writing with us so we might extend it to others.

- To the NJWPT trainers.

- To the administrators, teachers, and students in the following school districts:

  Aldine, Alief, Angleton, Austin, Belton, Boerne, Big Country (Abilene/Anson), Brower County (Florida), Birdville, Castleberry, Carroll, Cedar Hill, Colorado City, Crowley, Deer Park, Del Valle, Denton, De Soto, Ector County, Eagle Pass, Edgewood, El Campo, Edinburg, Fort Bend, Georgetown, Gilmer, Grand Prairie, Greater Longview (Kilgore, Longview, Region VII, Pine Tree), Gulf Coast (Dickinson, Clear Creek, Friendswood, Texas City), Harlandale, Hurst-Euless-Bedford, Joshua, Judson, Keller, Killeen, Klein, LaJoya, Lamar, LaPorte, Leander, Lewisville, Mansfield, McAllen, Midland, Nacogdoches, North East, Northside, Northwest, Pasadena, River Oaks Baptist School, Round Rock, Sam Houston Area (Bryan, Calvert, John Cooper School, Conroe, Corrigan-Camden, ESC Region VI, Huntsville, SHSU), San Antonio, San Marcos, SCUC (Schertz, Cibolo, Universal City), Spring, Tarleton S. U. Area (Brownwood, Cleburne, Irion County, Kerrville, Mineral Wells, Perrin-Whitt), Uvalde, Weatherford, Weslaco, and Wichita Falls.

- To Mary Howard, Jo Ann Ford, Marla Magee, and Janice Woorley for allowing us to work with their teachers on the Portfolio Profile of Student Capacities.

- To Dr. Gene Rister for his suggestion of making the teaching of the comma concrete.

- To Becky Hicks for her input on chapter 4.

- To Northside ISD, Lewisville ISD, Spring ISD, Abilene ISD, and Aldine ISD for serving as willing and gracious hosts when visitors want to observe in a demonstration site school.

- To Lee Jane Karlsson for her consistent hard work.

INTRODUCTION
A Parable

The first-graders entered the room quietly and with purpose. They rummaged in their desks; pulled out writing logs, each uniquely "loved up" with frayed, worn covers and turned-back pages; and began writing. Soon a timer bell sounded. The first-graders pushed their logs into their desks, walked to a miniature wooden house tucked in the corner of the room, and lifted the house's roof. The house held books. Each child chose a book, found a comfortable place, and began reading. Again the timer rang. The children returned the books and took their places, cross-legged, on a wonderfully inviting carpet at the front of the room. Because we were so absorbed in *kidwatching* (to use Yetta Goodman's term), we were moderately startled when the teacher appeared, book in hand, to take her place on the wooden rocker positioned at the carpet's edge.

> *Sharon Chamberlain begins school with 15 minutes of uninterrupted, sustained silent writing followed by 15 minutes of uninterrupted, sustained silent reading,* we entered into our field notes.

Sharon held up *Sylvester and the Magic Pebble*, by William Steig, for all the children to see. The students, enthralled, began making comments about their observations of the book's cover. If they strayed from the point, she gentled them back into reexamining details. She invited predictions, descriptions, and associations.

After this book talk, Sharon wrote three words from the story on the board: *perplexed, puzzled,* and *bewildered.* "These will be our spelling words, boys and girls. Listen for these big words when I read." The students, delighted with the challenge issued, readied themselves for close listening.

Sharon read *Sylvester* with all the verve associated with a first reading, although we suspected she had read it dozens of times. The students intervened, quipped, and questioned, demonstrating their involvement. When she finished, Sharon engaged the students in the spelling and meaning of the "big" words. The students evaluated their predictions and discussed the story. Finally, moving to the writing activity, Sharon produced an intriguing brown pouch from her pocket. It contained colored glass beads. Giving one bead to each child, she said, "This is your special pebble. It will help you write something wonderful when you return to your seat." Over and over she repeated those sentences like an incantation. Then the children moved into more talk, this time to help generate the writing. Among ideas about the colors and shapes and things they themselves could be changed into, the children decided they could make up how they got their pebbles, because, as one child offered, "If we all say 'teacher,' it will be *bor-r-ring.*"

> *She's doing appropriate things to prepare these diverse students for a rich language experience,* we wrote. *These students are so happy you can tell they are having fun. She is allowing them to learn through exposure to and discovery in reading and writing. Mostly, though, she is there with kind suggestions and few corrections. She is giving these students ample time to be actively creative and inventive and to be discoverers.*

And so the first-graders wrote, filling long pages with writing that told how they "found" their pebbles, what their pebbles looked like, and what happened because of their pebbles' "specialness." Then they shared.

Sitting on the "author's chair," Michael read his two-and-one-quarter pages. This was his opener:

> 🏃 I found my pebble in the flowers in spring. It is shiny yellow and orange. I found it because of the sun shining. I'd picked it up for my pebble celection, and I said I wish I had lots of pebbles like this for my pebble celection. And in a flash of litening I had lots of pebbles like the one I found. They glitered in the sun as if they were the sun themseles.

Michael's writing proved that by January of first grade he had internalized a sense of narrative and descriptive detail, at least partly due to the print-rich environment in Sharon's classroom. After this opener, Michael went on to develop a clear plot line, one obviously based on the original story, *Sylvester*.

> 🏃 I put them in a bag and took them home. When I got home I realised it was magic. One day it got mixed up with the other pebbles so I was real scared that I'd never find it again but then I remembered that I wished for lots of pebbles and said I wish I knew if this pebble works, and something said that it works. I was over joyed. I wished that my family would live in a castle, and in a flash of litening we were in a castle. I was maid king. When I was maid king I put my pebbles in the rioral treasery and I never forgot them. the end

Kyle's writing also showed the benefits of much reading and writing.

> 🏃 It all stared when I was out side playing socer with my brother. My mom Just called my brother and I in and I found a little pebble. It was cler and you could see throu it. it is chiped a little and it is relly skwigully, And it can do powers and wounders.

The powers and wonders occurring in this classroom weren't coming from any pebbles. Sharon Chamberlain created a nonthreatening environment that allowed students to connect and take risks.

The next time we visited Sharon's class, again the students wrote, read, and gathered on the rug. This time Sharon introduced *Amelia Bedelia*, and she wrote the word *idiom* on the board.

> Idiom! Idiom? We jotted humorously into our notes. Why, we taught some college freshmen who thought that was their roommate!

"This is your vocabulary word today, boys and girls. Where do we usually find the words we use for our vocabulary and spelling words?" They knew, of course, that those words came from the books they read.

"Yes, that is true, but today you must listen with different ears. Today you will not hear me read the word *idiom*. Instead, if you listen with those different ears, you will know by what Amelia Bedelia says and does what the word *idiom* means." The children couldn't wait for the story to start.

🏃 This symbol denotes student writing throughout this text.

We couldn't get enough of this class, and the children couldn't either. They were having fun, yet everything they did held meaning. Everything they did related to everything else they did. Because Sharon integrated reading and writing with listening, speaking, viewing, thinking, and skills, learning was at once cognitively appropriate and natural.

The students reveled in Sharon Chamberlain's praise and encouragement, and they grew. But one day she was absent from school. When she returned, Heather Mitchell greeted her teacher with a story she had written (figs. I.1 and I.2).

"Can you come over? You've got to see Heather's story," Sharon invited us over the phone.

When we arrived at Sharon's classroom, she thrust Heather's four pages of writing at us with no explanation. We approached Heather's writing with expectation. Her title, "The Meanis Sub," and her sense of authorship, "by Heather Mitchell," immediately caught our attention. We were hooked and quickly began reading the first page.

Fig. I.1. Heather's writing, pages 1 and 2. ♁

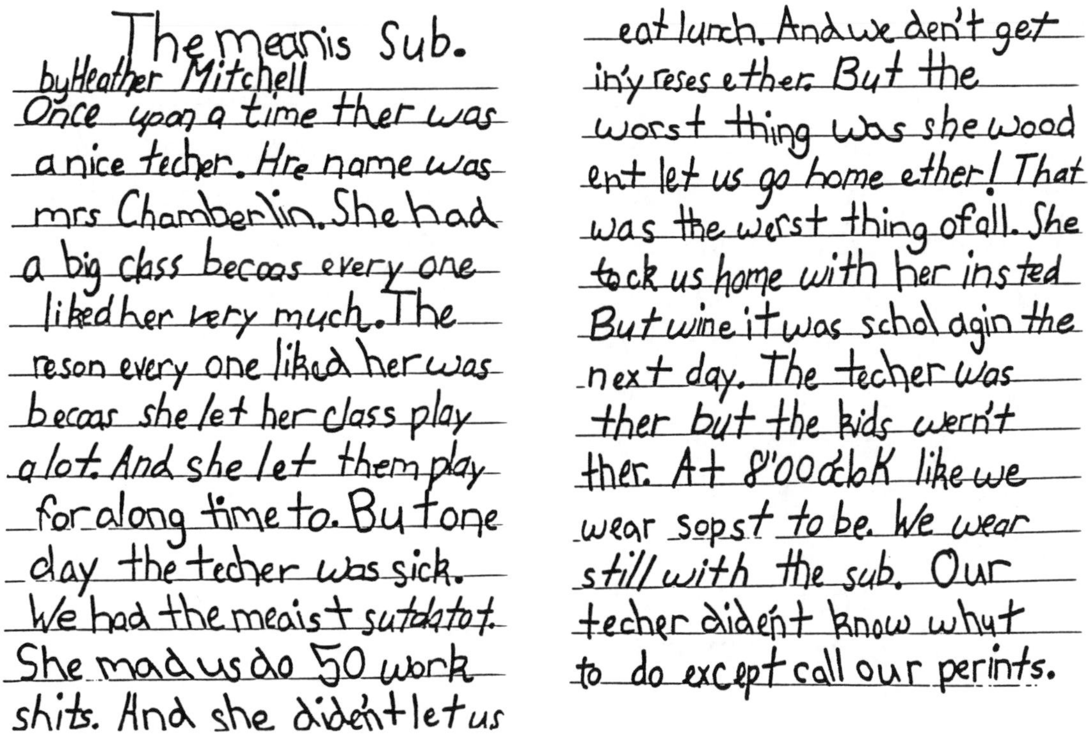

The meanis Sub.
by Heather Mitchell
Once upon a time ther was
a nice techer. Hre name was
mrs Chamberlin. She had
a big chss becoas every one
likedher very much. The
reson every one liked her was
becoas she let her class play
alot. And she let them play
for along time to. But one
day the techer was sick.
We had the meaist sutditot.
She mad us do 50 work
shits. And she dident let us

(p. 1)

eat lunch. And we den't get
in'y reses ether. But the
worst thing was she wood
ent let us go home ether! That
was the werst thing of all. She
tock us home with her insted
But wine it was schol agin the
next day. The techer was
ther but the kids wern't
ther. At 8'00 ocbK like we
wear sopst to be. We wear
still with the sub. Our
techer dident know whyt
to do except call our perints.

(p. 2)

When we read what Heather had written, which was "50 work shits," we exclaimed, "That is exactly what they are! Out of the mouths of babes...."

Indeed, Heather had written great truth. On the one hand, the mindless circling of sounds, the endless drawing of lines, the senseless coloring of pictures that match words, the isolated skills detached from anything real must have seemed mean to this six-year-old. In the hyperbolic language of childhood, Heather exaggerated what may have been 5 worksheets into 50. On the other hand, because of worksheets, Heather may have experienced what Adrienne Rich calls "psychic disequilibrium." As Rich describes it, "When someone with the authority of a teacher, say, describes the world and you are not in it, there is a moment of psychic disequilibrium, as if you looked into a mirror and saw nothing" (Rosaldo ix). Because genuine writing is an extension of self on paper, and because worksheets are not genuine writing, when doing the assigned worksheets Heather very well may have seen nothing. She was not part of the worksheet world.

As we read on, we discovered that not only did Heather have strong feelings about worksheets as opposed to the real reading and real writing she was accustomed to, but also she was able to develop those feelings into a story with characters, a plot, a conflict, and a resolution. As Jerome Bruner writes in *Acts of Meaning*, "Our capacity to render experience in terms of narrative is not just child's play, but an instrument for making meaning that dominates much of life in culture" (97). Heather tries to make meaning about someone giving first-graders "50 work shits." In her mind, it seems, that person is capable of even more dastardly deeds.

We noted the exclamation point when the sub wouldn't let the students go home. Also, we noticed the parents did not rush right out to find the children. First-graders must surely think adults do everything at night, but it is Heather's next line that remains one of our favorites—a segue with remarkable aplomb that returns her readers to the story: "Meanwhile, back with the sub...."

Fig. I.2. Heather's writing, pages 3 and 4. ⚲

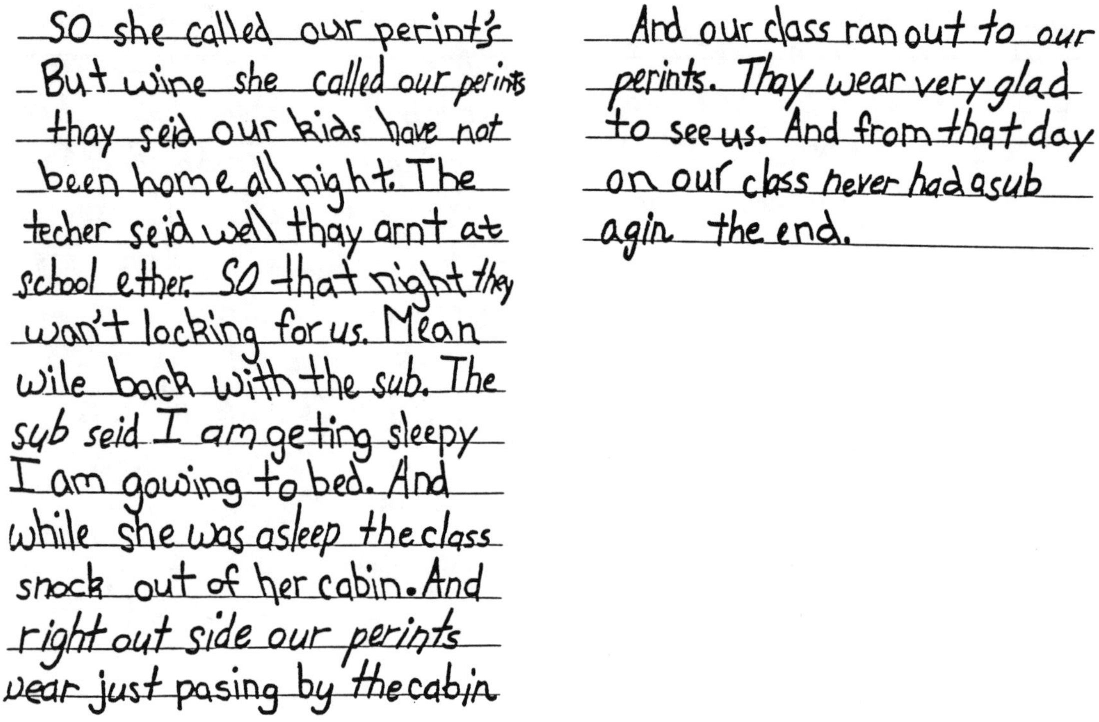

SO she called our perint's
But wine she called our perints
thay seid our kids have not
been home all night. The
techer seid well thay arnt at
school ether. SO that night they
won't locking for us. Mean
wile back with the sub. The
sub seid I am geting sleepy
I am gowing to bed. And
while she was asleep the class
snock out of her cabin. And
right out side our perints
wear just pasing by the cabin

And our class ran out to our
perints. Thay wear very glad
to see us. And from that day
on our class never had a sub
agin the end.

(p. 3)   (p. 4)

By her fourth page, Heather has delightfully, eloquently, and clearly demonstrated that she knows the elements of a story. Daily reading and writing; daily mini-lessons on various story elements; daily speaking, listening, examining, and predicting in a joyfully literate classroom have paid off. Clearly, the self-sponsored writing Heather accomplished during Sharon's absence exclaims loudly that Heather knows what writing is and is not: It is telling stories; it is not filling in worksheets.

Heather's writing shows that Sharon knows what the process of teaching writing is and is not. Writing is engaging students in grappling with words on blank pieces of paper and making those words match experiences in order to make meaning; it is not assigning worksheets. Teachers like Sharon know it takes hard work to transcribe thoughts so that they can be understood by self and others. They know they must walk alongside their students through the entire writing process. They know writing is one of our most rigorous intellectual activities. And they know how to teach in a way that helps writing happen.

Heather's writing verifies just how important this type of teaching is. This book helps teachers teach writing in a way that promotes excitement about writing. It helps teachers create a comfortable environment that encourages risk-taking in writing. It shows teachers ways to foster student writing about what they know in order to gain confidence and skill, rather than having students write simply to respond to a vague prompt that is not tied to the students' world. Heather makes her point, and the importance of being able to do that is exactly what makes this book significant.

WORKS CITED

Bruner, Jerome. *Acts of Meaning*. Cambridge, MA: Harvard University Press, 1990.

Parish, Peggy. *Amelia Bedelia*. New York: Harper & Row, 1963.

Rosaldo, Renato. *Culture and Truth: The Remaking of Social Analysis*. Boston: Beacon Press, 1989.

Steig, William. *Sylvester and the Magic Pebble*. New York: Simon & Schuster, 1969.

1

THE WORLD OF CHANGE
The Product/Process Paradigm Shift

To be accepted as a paradigm, a theory must seem better than its competitors, but it need not, and in fact never does, explain all the facts with which it can be confronted.

—Thomas S. Kuhn☐

THE SHIFTING PARADIGMS

When Kuhn defined paradigms as "achievements that for a time provide model problems and solutions to a community of practitioners" (viii), he provided a definition useful in describing the shift presently taking place in political, economic, and academic worlds. A new paradigm, according to Kuhn, presents unprecedented achievement that attracts adherents away from the competing paradigm, yet it provides an open-ended forum within which these adherents meet new and redefined challenges.

Today, some people in education look to the past and hold to the factory model for the organization and operation of schools—the product paradigm with its attendant routines, assembly lines, standardizations, top-to-bottom management systems, and either/or philosophy. Other people in education look to the future and hold to an informational model for schools—the process paradigm with its concomitant flexibility, technologies, collaborations, global empowerments, and both/all philosophy. (See figure I.1.)

Because "public education has always been tied to economic and social trends" (Caine and Caine 12), the present paradigm shift has caused a schism in public education—a schism often felt between administrators and teachers, between teachers and teachers, between parents and administrators, between administrators and boards of education, between teachers and parents—in short, between adherents to philosophically different paradigms.

In the 1968 Academy Award-winning film *Why Man Creates*, an animated sequence depicts two snails conversing. One snail says, "Have you ever thought that radical ideas threaten institutions, then become institutions, and in turn reject radical ideas that threaten institutions?"

"No."

"Gee, for a minute I thought I had something" (Sohn 39).

Indeed, the snail had something—it had encapsulated a paradigm shift. The snail could have been referring to the ideological paradigm shift from totalitarian to democratic governments; the economic shift from high-volume, standardized production to a continuous process of reinvention; or the academic paradigm shift from viewing learning as product to viewing learning as process. We have only to transpose the words *teacher centered* and *teacher/student/content centered* for *totalitarianism* and *democracy* or *boss* and *leader* to understand the range and the depth of this shift. First institutions—political, economic, and academic—are threatened by new ideas; then these new ideas become institutions.

1

Consider the ideological shifts that threatened (and continue to threaten) political institutions in Romania, Czechoslovakia, Lithuania, Latvia, Estonia, the former East Germany, South Africa, and Russia. Consider the economic shifts that threatened (and continue to threaten) organizational institutions like the Big Three auto makers, the steel producers, and the three or four major food processors. Consider the educational shifts that threatened (and continue to threaten) academic institutions, such as scope and sequence of curriculum, restructuring, and even the concept of public education itself, for example, Chris Whittle's innovative for-profit private schools (Walsh 1).

Most teachers, administrators, and board members do not want to be like the second snail, who fails to recognize a paradigm shift. These people do not want to be the dinosaurs that Janet Emig describes, with "dismaying ratio of tail to brain, awaiting only total ossification" (1983, 171). Rather, realizing that enormous change is here, such people have become what the futurist Joel Barker calls "paradigm shifters" (quoted in Sparks 22). They are innovative, they see the need for change, and they agree that "schools organized on the factory model do not open doors to the future; they imprison students in their own minds" (Caine and Caine 15). Understanding the necessity of training, retraining, and continuous learning, such people are eager paradigm pioneers, helping to restructure schools and motivate students who will soon enter the new world of change.

Fig. 1.1. The paradigm shift.

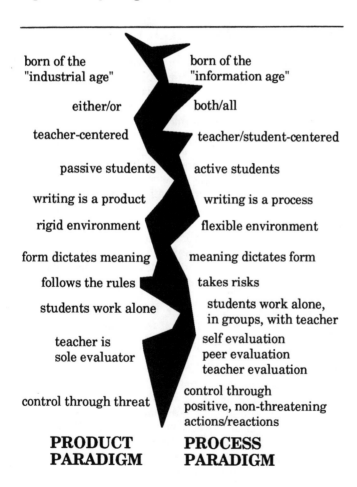

PRODUCT PARADIGM	PROCESS PARADIGM
born of the "industrial age"	born of the "information age"
either/or	both/all
teacher-centered	teacher/student-centered
passive students	active students
writing is a product	writing is a process
rigid environment	flexible environment
form dictates meaning	meaning dictates form
follows the rules	takes risks
students work alone	students work alone, in groups, with teacher
teacher is sole evaluator	self evaluation peer evaluation teacher evaluation
control through threat	control through positive, non-threatening actions/reactions

Within a few years Linda was far enough along in working toward a master's degree to receive a position as an English teacher (1990, 7-8). Today most know Rief through her readable book *Seeking Diversity*. She is a prime example of the value of retraining. In a period of eight years, she went from teacher's aide to educational consultant and author. Like Rief, students in the future will be expected to train and retrain. Like Rief, students will be expected to write apt, clear, and lively prose in the workplace. Few readers will take the time to ponder over garbled sentences or incoherent memos. Even fewer readers will have patience with inappropriate style or tone. With information bombarding the world at record rates, unwieldy writing will find no place.

> *I once heard on National Public Radio that Hewlett-Packard, with its network of over 400 offices all over the world, a network connected by computers, generates 8 million pages of discourse a day. Clearly there are those who write those pages, and just as clearly there are those who read and respond.*

THINKING

Given the massive nature of expected changes coupled with the anticipation of unexpected ones, students must learn how to think logically and creatively. They must learn how to think about thinking. Further, students will need to develop strategies to become metacognitive learners: to know what they have learned *and* how they have learned it. They must be able to think through their own learning so they can repeat the process, thereby affording them an edge over those who have no notion of their own learning processes.

Metacognitive learners, then, will be a credit both to themselves and to their employers. Already corporations are spending millions of dollars on training. "According to Roger Semerad, senior vice president at RJR Nabisco, corporations are spending $40 to $50 billion a year on training employees" (quoted in Atkins 32). Metacognitive learners will become an invaluable asset in a world where retraining and continuous learning are the norm. As Lauren Resnick, director of the Learning Research and Development Center at the University of Pittsburgh, said:

> In the old industrial model, *thinking* was left to the manager, and *doing* to the hired hands. Today, to be competitive, what seems to be required is thinking throughout the production process. Competitive high-performance work organizations seek entrants to the work force who can think their way through unfamiliar problems, who can use complex tools, and who are able to envisage the place of their own activity in the much broader activity of the workplace." (quoted in O'Neil 7)

COLLABORATING

Collaboration, another skill needed for the twenty-first century, fits the information paradigm because when used in the classroom, it alters the traditional environment and places the student in the center. Rather than each student being expected to do what every other student does, in collaborative classrooms students work together synergistically. With a goal of the whole being greater than the sum of its parts, relationships, teamwork, cooperation, and partnerships replace working alone and competition between individuals.

> Learning to collaborate suggests a different kind of education than one designed to prepare a relatively few talented young people to become professional experts.... A greater emphasis should be placed on interactive communications linked to group problem-definitions and solutions. Students should learn to articulate, clarify, and then restate for one another how to determine questions and find answers.... Students would learn how to share their understandings, and build upon each others' insights. (Reich 23)

SUMMARY

The demands of the present and the future make it clear that schools must move beyond the

> simplistic, narrow approaches to teaching and learning.... This is harsh truth telling. Educators must redefine their role and become seen as generators of meaningful, connecting, and linking knowledge, who can not only use the appropriate software but far surpass its performance in interactive questioning and exploration of information. Otherwise, the future looks bleak. (Caine and Caine vii, 22)

Full implementation of the information age paradigm is clearly needed to raise new levels of performance for the present and for a future that requires different levels of instruction. Never have reading, writing, thinking, and collaborating been more important. Yet the move from teacher-centered, authoritarian ways of teaching to student-centered instruction with teacher as facilitator, guide, or coach takes not only a deep philosophical shift but also an intense and ongoing restructuring within the theory and pedagogy of the discipline.

RESTRUCTURING SCHOOLS

Much has been written about the problems of schools and the need to change them: from school library reform (Barron and Bergen) to going beyond the rhetoric of restructuring (Tye); from articles examining alternative assessment (Maeroff) to outlines of the critical elements required for success in restructuring (David); and from examples of how specific school districts broke ground in restructuring (Caldwell and Wood) to advice from commissions such as the Commission on the Skills of the American Workforce (Magaziner and Clinton). Many have offered solutions, but ironically most of these have been top-down offerings. Little change will happen unless teachers are convinced to move away from traditional teaching. Little change will happen unless teachers understand the breadth and depth of the paradigm shift and how that shift affects the profession of teaching, education in general, and the future of students. Little change will happen until a deep philosophical paradigm shift occurs within teacher training programs. Little change will happen until school districts commit to rigorous staff development programs to retrain teachers already in the field. Until these things occur, monies will continue to be wasted on short-term, Band-Aid™ approaches to change when drastic surgery is required. Donald Graves in his 1978 report to the Ford Foundation cautioned: "Teachers do not teach a subject in which they feel unprepared, even when the subject is mandated by the school curriculum. Writing is such a subject" (15).

John I. Goodlad, director of the Center for Educational Renewal at the University of Washington, conducted a study of the education of educators in the United States. He echoes the findings of other researchers: "1) a debilitating lack of prestige in the teacher education enterprise, 2) lack of program coherence, 3) separation of theory and practice, and 4) a stifling regulated conformity" (5). Goodlad's recommendation is twofold:

1. a complete redesign of teacher education programs, and

2. a share in this redesign (although teacher educators will be most heavily involved) by a wide range of actors: policymakers (governors and legislators in particular), appointed and elected state education officials, university presidents and provosts, faculties in pedagogy representing the arts and sciences and the schools of education as well as the departments of education, administrators and teachers in the schools, parents, and a considerable portion of the general citizenry (8-9).

The New Jersey Writing Project [NJWP] began 1966-1979 as a consortium of Rutgers University, Educational Testing Service, and demographically disparate school districts across the state. The project received validation and designation in 1979 as a National Diffusion Network Project. As such, it has been in the state of Texas since 1980, where it is known as the New Jersey Writing Project in Texas. This project enjoys the reputation as the largest writing project in the state, its program is both unified and coherent, it merges theory and pedagogy, and it encourages teachers to implement its philosophy of process uniquely — according to their teaching styles and the learning styles and needs of their students.

In addition to the project's three-week basic training model, it trains teacher-trainers who then train other teachers. These trainers also model the implementation of writing as a process in their classrooms and become paradigm pioneers, helping their peers to shift philosophies from product to process. There are presently approximately 500 such trainers in the state. These trainers are certified for a period of three years, after which trainers are invited to recertify, thereby setting conditions for continued renewal and retraining.

NJWPT [i.e., NJWP-Texas] includes classroom demonstrations and classroom application. Before these sessions, there is time for teachers to share concerns; after these sessions, there is time for teachers to debrief. NJWPT is not a method, not a lock-step program; rather it is a philosophically based project that works with districts in specific and substantive ways to improve the quality of instruction through deep staff development.

Dr. D. Max McConkey, executive director of the National Dissemination Study Group (NDSG) and director of The NETWORK, Inc., praised the quality of NJWPT as its 1992 Trainers' Conference, calling it "the best statewide implementation model" he has seen. Dr. Janet Emig, keynoting the 1991 Trainers' Conference, looked out over the audience and said, "This is where true educational reform begins."

Teachers are tired of gaggles of gimmicks. They are tired of presentations by people who long ago lost touch with the inner workings of schools; but when information is relevant, interesting, and practical, when the theory is merged with the pedagogy, when teachers can see immediate ways to apply the theory in their classrooms, then they see training and retraining as effective. After a two-year research project designed to study the ability of teachers to acquire teaching skills and strategies, Bruce Joyce and Beverly Showers concluded, "Teachers are wonderful learners" (379). After more than a decade of working with teachers in writing and the integration of the language arts, NJWPT concurs.

RESTRUCTURING THE APPROACH TO TEACHING WRITING

Consider how archaic the product teacher who requires 50 or 100 note cards for an A as part of library research must look to students. Surely students wonder whether such teachers know about photocopy machines. Often such a teacher requires the note cards not because some students cannot afford photocopying but as a lesson in discipline or because it always has been done that way. Writing note cards may help students learn one way to organize data, but the truth is, most of the copying students do from book to card is mindless — a slightly more sophisticated version of a worksheet. Time would be better spent honing meaning, grappling with data, forging form, rearranging, rereading, and reformulating.

Students must become proficient in the written word—in English. As Naisbitt and Aburdene note,

> English is becoming the world's first universal language.
>
> More than 80 percent of all information stored in the more than 100 million computers around the world is in English.
>
> There are about 1 billion English speakers.
>
> English is the language of international business.
>
> English has replaced French as the language of diplomacy.
>
> English serves as a common tongue in countries where people speak many different languages, for example, India.
>
> English is the official or semiofficial language of twenty African countries.
>
> English is the ecumenical language of the World Council of Churches and the official language of the Olympics.
>
> English is the language of international youth culture.
>
> The world's most taught language, English is not replacing other languages; it is supplementing them.
>
> (139-143)

In such a world, U.S. students unable to read, write, think, communicate, and collaborate in English will be disadvantaged. Students simply disciplined for silent "sit and git" will be ill-prepared citizens in a country unwilling and eventually unable to tolerate large numbers of functional illiterates. "Most observers believe that as many as a third of our citizens do not meet present-day demands for literacy" (Bailey and Forsheim ix).

> *At a recent Houston Book and Author Dinner, one of the book reps said that 80 percent of the books are read by about 10 percent of the people.*

With many U.S. citizens sidestepping opportunities to read and write, the problem is exacerbated when applied to professionals. Donald Graves states: "As we have seen, few adults write. Teachers are no exception; they do not write either" (1978, 16).

> *On a recent visit to my dentist, I made a startling discovery. As he came at my tooth with the pneumatic drill, he stated, "I hope you don't do to your English students what my English teacher did to me." Fearful of a frontal lobotomy, I shook my head. When the drilling was done and I could talk, I asked him whatever made him make such a statement.*
>
> *"I hated English. I hated answering the questions after a story. I hated poetry. I never understood it. My interpretations never matched the teacher's. So I don't read anything now but my professional literature."*
>
> *Back at school, I rummaged around until I found May Swenson's poem "After the Dentist." I sent him a copy.*
>
> *Upon my next visit I was surprised to see it framed and hanging in his waiting room. Later he confided, "If I had read poems like that, maybe I would like poetry."*

The time has come for all teachers to bury the old paradigm. Perhaps because teachers themselves were taught and trained in the product paradigm, or perhaps because teachers generally teach the way they were taught, burying that paradigm is difficult. Yet already scholars such as Glynda Ann Hull state: "In the last 20 years, writing research and instruction have been turned on their heads.... But we've heard just half of the tale. There has been another great revolution in our thinking about writing in recent years, and it has come from learning to view writing as a process that is embedded in a context" (105, 109). Already the definition has changed from writing as a finished product to writing as a complex of cognitive processes to writing as a complex of cognitive processes embedded in a social context. Already the thinking of teachers and researchers is being restructured by the work of Scribner and Cole and Shirley Brice Heath. (The former studied literacy among the Vai, people of West Africa. The latter studied a plurality of literacies among people in the Carolina Piedmonts.) Already many are saying, "The primary goal of a pluralistic curriculum process is to present a truthful and meaningful rendition of the whole human experience" (Hilliard 1991-92, 13). All must look at teaching with eyes on those who want the freedom to know and express. As Donald Graves says, "A democracy relies heavily on each individual's sense of voice, authority, and ability to communicate desires and information" (1978, 5). He suggests that students be regarded less as receivers and more as senders. If students can only read and listen but cannot speak or write, *cannot send*, they are robbed of an essential right: the freedom of expression.

Still, students of product teachers who write only on the teacher's assigned topic most often neither send authentic messages through their writing nor receive peer-group or teacher responses. So students try at first to fit their meaning into formula, but the results usually read as utterly phony scholarship or terribly contrived trivia. Most meet deadlines, yet many continue to use poor grammar in wooden writing. Eventually they give up or content themselves with anorexic paragraphs, underdeveloped bursts of what is conventional, what is safe—paragraphs starved for substance, devoid of voice or risk or discovery. Education in the product paradigm may have once served its purpose, but it no longer works.

Results of Teaching Writing as a Process

An old adage says, "Don't take something away from someone unless you can replace it with something better." With the object of improving teaching and learning, more specifically the teaching and learning of writing, results indicate that the process paradigm offers positive results.

In a 1977-1979 study conducted through the New Jersey Writing Project of writing teachers across the state: "training in process was a potent influence on the development of writing ability. Students of teachers so trained showed statistically significant and educationally important increases in their writing performance" (Carroll 1984, 325). These data earned NJWPT its National Diffusion Network Project designation.

Interestingly, Lisa D. Delpit of the University of Alaska at Fairbanks, in the first-person article "Skills and Other Dilemmas of a Progressive Black Educator," advocates a fusion of skill-oriented and process-oriented approaches to writing. On the basis of her own product paradigm education; conversations with a person identified only as "Cathy"; and other unnamed writing project teachers, which she identifies only through a tangential reference to the Bay Area Writing Project, she espouses "'skills' *within the context of* critical and creative thinking" (384). Delpit's argument echoes Hull's call for writing as socially embedded, and the New Jersey Writing Project findings "that most dramatic drop occurred in writing on a pretest or posttest sample administered in control and project groups in the Basic Writing Skills courses where skills were taught in isolation. These data seem to indicate that the isolated teaching of basic skills might prove counterproductive, and the teaching of writing without the benefit of varying contexts and registers for stimuli might not yield desired results" (Carroll 1979, 110).

Most recently, NJWPT-site schools reported gains in students' writing scores on the Texas Assessment of Academic Skills (TAAS). These data provide convincing evidence to support teaching writing as a process within an integrated format and social context. However, to ascribe all gain to NJWPT training is generally difficult in most districts because so many variables enter into the equation. For example, all teachers in any given district may not have received NJWPT training; some may have been trained in a different program, and some may not have been trained. Data are also affected by what grade level trained teachers teach, how many years students have been taught by trained teachers, and the degree of implementation in classrooms. However, out of the more than 100 school districts with teachers who have received NJWPT training, Calvert Independent School District (ISD), a small 1-A district in central Texas, emerges as a microcosm of the macrocosm. Even recognizing that small school districts have a high degree of teacher-to-student involvement, Calvert is exemplary.

There are 135 students in grades 7-12 in Calvert ISD. Beverly Burleson and Karen Foster, an Anglo and an African-American, respectively, teach all the English classes on those levels and are responsible for preparing students for the state-mandated Texas Assessment of Academic Skills (TAAS) test. To graduate, students must pass TAAS, which is administered in Texas to all eleventh-graders. Both teachers have been trained in NJWPT; one is presently training as a trainer, and the other plans to do so sometime in the future. Demographically, Calvert is 68.3 percent African-American, 15.6 percent Anglo, and 16.1 percent Hispanic. As indicators of economic status, 84.5 percent of Calvert's student population are eligible for free lunch; 85 percent are in the Chapter I program, which means they have been identified as significantly below their grade level in reading.

In 1990-91, at the EXIT level (eleventh grade), 100 percent of Calvert's students passed the writing portion of TAAS at the first administration of the test. Thirty-eight percent received academic recognition in writing. Four percent received a score of 2, which on a 1 to 4 scale is minimally successful, 54 percent received a score of 3, and 42 percent received a score of 4 (4 being the highest). In 1991-92, at the EXIT level, after the Texas Education Agency raised the criteria, 100 percent still passed (83 percent on the first administration of the test and the remaining on the second administration). Twenty-eight percent mastered all objectives, 28 percent received the score of 2, 44 percent received the score of 3, and 11 percent received a score of 4.

So stunning were these data, surpassing many districts with what some might consider more promising demographics, that both teachers were asked what they do in their classes. "My students write every day," said Karen. "Then each chooses a paper to take through the entire process. That's when I get at those skills—when it means something to the kids." Beverly said, "We write and talk about our writing. We read and talk about the way authors write. About three weeks before the test, I take the format and do some drills on skills."

Teaching Writing as a Process

The movement from product to process demands change. Teachers cannot teach students through process unless the teachers know what the process paradigm embraces. Writing as a process means giving students time to prewrite, write, postwrite, proofread, and edit their papers. It means teaching writing, not just assigning it. It means teaching the various forms of writing so students think through their meaning, their purpose, and the needs of their audience to determine the most appropriate genre. It means encouraging students to collaborate with peers and to discuss their projects with teachers during the writing. It means permitting students to determine to some extent the schedule for completed papers to be submitted to the teacher and subsequently to be published. (At any level, students should experience the delight of publication.) It means teaching grammar and mechanics *within* the writing process. It means hard work, self-satisfaction, discovery, and making decisions. It means making classrooms joyfully literate places.

Some teachers might promptly dismiss any training in the strategies of teaching writing as a process with a decisive "No." But these teachers must think again. Process has become the prevailing paradigm. And yes, it is *radical*—radical in the best sense of the word, meaning it comes from the root or origin; it comes from teachers who have observed and recorded the way students write. It comes from teachers who have noted that the way writing happens does not match the way some textbooks say it does. It comes from teachers who have questioned, studied, and researched the way writing was handled—as if writing could happen on command. One of the first among these teachers, Janet Emig, investigated the composing processes of eight students in case studies for her 1969 dissertation at Harvard. That seminal study, *The Composing Process of Twelfth Graders*, opened the floodgates for teachers who had long verified that writing on command produced stilted, formulaic pieces of discourse and caused most students to regard writing as something you do only when someone in authority forces you. Further, Emig's work led to a field of scholarship that began to realize that teachers had not been and were not being trained in the teaching of writing.

Writing *is* a process. In a sense, there is no *process* writing, which suggests there are other appropriate adjectives. Rather the word *process* simply attaches significance to the way writing happens, the way writing has always happened when authors work. Everyone has a process, and each writer's process is idiosyncratic. Recognizing that process not only frees the writer but also frees the teacher of writing to facilitate rather than commandeer the classroom.

Soon, students discover that writing serves other functions, not the least being a look at one's self on the page in order to know one's self, to write one's meaning down to better understand that meaning. Teachers discover that writing taught as a process provides coherence for students in a fragmented world and that students who write begin to think more holistically, see patterns, work through knots, think as they write, and then share that thinking through collaboration with peers. Both discover that the entire topography of the classroom changes.

Writing to one's process this way emerges from the process paradigm. *How* the writing happens is studied as closely as the *what*, or the product, of the writing. And this *how* signals a deep and basic need for restructuring by teachers who teach writing. As we move from product to process in English language arts classes, we clearly validate Kuhn's contention that "when an individual or group first produces a synthesis able to attract most of the next generation's practitioners, the older schools gradually disappear" (18).

APPLICATION

Write a profile of a student in the twenty-first century. Include the basic corpus of knowledge that student will need to function productively in a rapidly changing world.

WORKS CITED

Atkins, Andrea. "Big Business and Education: Will Corporate Cash Aid Schools?" *Better Homes and Gardens* (March 1991): 32-34.

Bailey, Richard W., and Robin Melanie Fosheim, eds. *Literacy for Life: The Demand for Reading and Writing*. New York: Modern Language Association of America, 1983.

Barron, Daniel, and Timothy J. Bergen, Jr. "Information Power: The Restructured School Library for the Nineties." *Phi Delta Kappan* 73 (March 1992): 521-525.

Caine, Renate Nummela, and Geoffrey Caine. *Making Connections: Teaching and the Human Brain*. Alexandria, VA: Association for Supervision and Curriculum Development, 1991.

Caldwell, Sarah D., and Fred H. Wood. "Breaking Ground in Restructuring." *Educational Leadership* 50 (September 1992): 41, 44.

Carroll, Joyce Armstrong. "Process into Product: Awareness of the Composing Process Affects the Written Product." Ed.D. diss., Rutgers University, New Brunswick, NJ, 1979.

_____. "Process into Product: Teacher Awareness of the Writing Process Affects Students' Written Products." In *New Directions in Composition Research*, Richard Beach and Lillian S. Bridwell, eds. New York: Guilford Press, 1984.

Cetron, Marvin, and Owen Davies. *American Renaissance: Our Life at the Turn of the 21st Century.* New York: St. Martin's Press, 1989.

_____. "Future Trends." *Omni* (October 1989): 112-118.

David, Jane L. "What It Takes to Restructure Education." *Educational Leadership* 48 (May 1991): 11-15.

Delpit, Lisa D. "Skills and Other Dilemmas of a Progressive Black Educator." *Harvard Educational Review* 56 (November 1986): 379-385.

Doyle, Denis P. "The Challenge, The Opportunity." *Phi Delta Kappan* 73 (March 1992): 512-520.

Doyle, Denis P., and David Kearns. *Winning the Brain Race.* San Francisco: ICS, 1989.

Emig, Janet. *The Composing Process of Twelfth Graders.* Urbana, IL: National Council of Teachers of English, 1971.

_____. *The Web of Meaning.* Upper Montclair, NJ: Boynton/Cook, 1983.

Gardner, David P. *A Nation at Risk.* Washington, DC: National Commission on Excellence in Education, 1983.

Goodlad, John I. "Why We Need a Complete Redesign of Teacher Education." *Educational Leadership* 49 (November 1991): 4-10.

Graves, Donald H. *Balance the Basics: Let Them Write.* New York: Ford Foundation, 1978.

_____. *Discover Your Own Literacy.* Portsmouth, NH: Heinemann Educational Books, 1990.

Heath, Shirley Brice. *Ways with Words.* Cambridge, MA: Cambridge University Press, 1983.

Hilliard, Asa, III. "Do We Have the Will to Educate All Children?" *Educational Leadership* 49 (September 1991): 31-36.

_____. Why We Must Pluralize the Curriculum." *Educational Leadership* 49 (December 1991/ January 1992): 12-16.

Hull, Glynda Ann. "Research on Writing: Building a Cognitive and Social Understanding of Composing." In *Association for Supervision and Curriculum Development Yearbook, 1989.* Alexandria, VA: ASCD, 1989.

Hunter, Carman St. John, and David Harman. *Adult Illiteracy in the United States: A Report to the Ford Foundation.* New York: McGraw-Hill, 1979.

Joyce, Bruce, and Beverly Showers. "Improving Inservice Training: The Messages of Research." *Educational Leadership* (February 1980): 379-385.

Kuhn, Thomas. *The Structure of Scientific Revolutions.* Chicago: University of Chicago Press, 1970.

Maeroff, Gene I. "Assessing Alternative Assessment." *Phi Delta Kappan* 73 (December 1991): 272-281.

Magaziner, Ira, and Hillary Rodham Clinton. "Will America Choose High Skills or Low Wages?" *Educational Leadership* 49 (March 1992): 10-14.

Naisbitt, John, and Patricia Aburdene. *Megatrends 2000.* New York: William Morrow, 1990.

O'Neil, John. "Preparing for the Changing Workplace." *Educational Leadership* 49 (March 1992): 6-9.

Reich, Robert B. *Education and the Next Economy.* Washington, DC: National Education Association, 1988.

Rief, Linda. *Seeking Diversity.* Portsmouth, NH: Heinemann Educational Books, 1992.

Scribner, Sylvia, and Michael Cole. "Literacy Without Schooling: Testing for Intellectual Effects." *Harvard Educational Review* 48, no. 4 (1978): 448-461.

Sohn, David A. *Film: The Creative Eye.* Dayton, OH: George A. Pflaum, 1970.

Sparks, Dennis. "13 Tips for Managing Change." *Education Week* 10 (June 1992): 22.

Tye, Kenneth A. "Restructuring Our Schools: Beyond the Rhetoric." *Phi Delta Kappan* 74 (September 1992): 8-14.

Walsh, Mark. "Whittle Unveils Team to Design New Schools." *Education Week* (March 4, 1992): 1, 13.

"After the Reign of Dick and Jane"

DANIEL GURSKY

(Reprinted by permission of *Teacher Magazine*, August 1991, pages 22-29.)

Commentary

A parallel may be made between the teaching of writing as a process and the traditionalist view of teaching grammar and writing as two separate subjects. Grammar instruction centered on the drill and practice much the way reading instruction centered on drills and skills. Writing was done for the teacher, in response to the teacher's topic. Proponents of this view begin teaching the word, move to the sentence, then to the paragraph, and if students are lucky, they finish the year with an essay.

(In the white space provided, the authors invite readers to write their own comments, questions, concerns, experiences, connections, and reactions. In this way, the text becomes a dialectic.)

Children understand the structure of the narrative. Anyone who knows a four-year-old child can share the stories these children tell. Children also adore leaving marks. These marks are the child's first written symbols. Parents show off or talk about living room walls covered with these marks. Children have so much to say, to explore, to discover. Through writing, they have lasting documentation of their discoveries.

For more than 100 years, public schools in the United States have operated on the theory that children learn by mastering the component parts of complex material before grasping the entire subject. In the current system, a carefully sequenced curriculum from kindergarten to graduation is determined largely by experts outside of the schools. Within that curriculum, teachers and textbooks transmit information to students, who spend most of their time as docile recipients. They study structured textbooks containing drills and exercises that reinforce skills and knowledge they often perceive as having no relevance to the world outside the classroom. Emphasis is on the memorization of facts rather than on problem solving and creative thinking. And students are tested, drilled, and retested regularly to make sure they have learned the facts and absorbed the information.

The theory that prevails in the traditional school contends that learning is hard work and that students must be persuaded to undertake and stick with it. A system of external rewards and punishments provides the incentive for students to achieve. Learning is viewed largely as an individual activity, and students are discouraged from collaborating with each other; working together is often viewed as cheating. Since children naturally dislike hard work and would rather be playing than learning, or so the theory goes, the main challenge to the teacher in the traditional school is to maintain order and to control the students so that teaching and learning can take place.

There is a certain logic and coherence to the theory, and it has surely demonstrated a tenacity to survive and a resistance to recent research findings on how children learn. But the growing number of teachers, school administrators, and scholars who have become part of the whole language movement believe the traditional school not only doesn't encourage learning but also often obstructs it.

Proponents of whole language subscribe to the theory that children are eager to learn when they come to school, that learning is not work but rather an effortless process that goes on continuously without their even trying.

Children do not learn by first mastering the smaller parts of the whole, but by constantly developing hypotheses about the world around them and testing those hypotheses. Whole language advocates point out that children arrive at school already having learned an enormous amount without the benefit of formal schooling. The average first grader, experts say, has already acquired a vocabulary of 10,000 words and assimilated many of the rules of grammar without trying.

Whole language is an entire philosophy about teaching, learning, and the role of language in the classroom. It stresses that language should be kept whole and uncontrived and that children should use language in ways that relate to their own lives and cultures. In the whole language classroom, the final product — the "answer" — isn't as important as the process of learning to define and solve problems.

Whole language advocates believe that the ideal classroom is a child-centered one in which students enjoy learning because they perceive that the material has meaning and relevance to their lives. The teacher is not an authoritarian but a resource, coach, and co-learner who shares power with the students and allows them to make choices. Learning in such a classroom is a social act, and children learn from and help each other. The challenge to the teacher is to adapt the curriculum and activities to the interests and talents of the children, to provide a content-rich environment, and to assure that they are constantly engaged in learning. When children are not learning, whole language teachers say, they become bored and restless, and control becomes a problem. The common techniques of whole language teaching — daily journal and letter writing, a great deal of silent and oral reading of real literature, and student cooperation, to name a few — are the philosophy in action.

It is hard to imagine two schools of thought more diametrically opposed in their view of how children learn. Frank Smith, a leading authority on reading, writing, and children's literacy, finds the two views so contradictory "that they would appear to refer to two entirely different kinds of mental activity." But they share two points:

Writing as a process is also a philosophy. In that sense the word writing *embraces teaching writing as a complex of processes. Although many, as Gursky points out, rally under the label* whole language, *writing as a process enables an integrated learning of language. Integration builds upon all the theories of learning. From these theories, good educators can decide upon pedagogies and praxes.*

The product approach to writing encourages formula. Formula is the enemy of creativity. The writer Ben Shahn says it this way: "I think it can be said with certainty that the form which does emerge cannot be greater than the content which went into it. For form is only the manifestation, the shape of content." Picasso says: "A picture is not thought out and settled beforehand. While it is being done it changes as one's thoughts change. And when it is finished, it still goes on changing, according to the state of mind of whoever is looking at it." Stephen Neil, in A Genuinely Human Existence, *says, "The bad teacher imposes his ideas and his methods on his pupils, and such originality as they may have is lost in the second-rate art of imitation." And the 1976 Nobel Laureate in chemistry, William N. Lipsomb, Jr., says: "For me, the creative process, first of all, requires a good nine hours of sleep a night. Second, it must not be pushed by the need to produce practical applications" (New York Times, December 7, 1977).*

- Human learning begins with the learning of language: first, listening and speaking; then, reading and writing.

- Success in learning language is vitally important because it largely determines how well a child will do in school and in life.

Because children already know how to speak (and presumably to listen) when they come to school, their formal instruction in language begins with reading. As a result, the battles between the proponents of the divergent theories of learning are fought mainly over the way reading is taught in the primary grades.

Although teaching a child to read is certainly one of the most important acts in school, consider that a child cannot write without reading. A child can read without ever writing, however. Therefore, if we teach children to write, we also teach them to read. In this schema, writing takes on new importance and meaning.

These battles, known as "The Great Reading Debate," haven't been limited to intellectual jousting in obscure academic journals and at professional conferences. The war is regularly waged in the mass media and in statehouses and school board chambers. The adversaries skirmish in courtrooms as well as classrooms.

Although the debate is ostensibly over the most effective method of teaching reading, it goes much deeper, raising profound questions about pedagogy, the nature and purpose of schooling, and the role of teachers, students, parents, and administrators.

It follows logically that a society will establish a pedagogy, and structure its schools, to conform to the theory of learning that it subscribes to.

In the United States, the traditional theory of learning became institutionalized with the beginning of mass schooling in the nineteenth century. Its intellectual rationale was later drawn from the work of experimental psychologists such as Edward Thorndike and, subsequently, behaviorists such as B. F. Skinner. The theory is based on the belief that children learn a complex skill such as reading by first making sense of the smallest components of the language (letters) and then progressing to larger components (sound, words, and sentence). Children learn to read by learning to decode the language; understanding follows after the code is broken and the component parts are mastered.

Traditionally, school curricula starts students on the grammar ladder. First grade covers nouns and verbs. Second grade covers nouns and verbs and adjectives. Third grade covers nouns and verbs and adjectives and prepositions.... Twelfth grade covers nouns and verbs and adjectives and prepositions ... ad nauseam. Because the product was more important than the process by which we learn language, schools perpetuated this practice. No wonder students stopped listening to grammar instruction, and teachers of twelfth grade would say, "These kids don't know a noun from a verb." Possibly, they know; they just do not care. Possibly they have no need to know or care except for the Iowa Test of Basic Skills (ITBS).

Traditional American education, therefore, begins with lessons that focus on phonics (letters, combinations of letters, sounds, and rules), tightly controlled vocabulary, and short basal reading passages, followed by numerous skills exercises, each with only one correct answer, typically delivered by the teacher to a group of students using the same textbook.

Constance Weaver, a professor of English at Western Michigan University, calls this the "transmission" model of teaching, with teachers serving essentially as "scripted technicians" who pass on a curriculum established by people outside the classroom.

"Learning typically is broken down into small parts that can be taught, practiced, tested, retaught, and retested," Weaver says. "Some things can be transmitted, of course. But many things are likely to be forgotten because the learner hasn't necessarily connected to the material."

In other words—as assessments of student literacy point out all too clearly—we can't assume the student is learning just because the teacher is teaching. The 1988 National Assessment of Educational Progress found that about 70 percent of 17-year-olds could read well enough to get the overall message or specific information from a text, but only 42 percent could read and understand complicated passages, and fewer than 5 percent could comprehend the specialized material prevalent in business and higher education. Estimates of the number of functionally illiterate American adults, who read so poorly that they can't cope with the basics of everyday life, are even more shocking. Some figures range up to 60 million—more than one-third of the country's adult population.

But even allowing for the possibility of gross exaggeration, these figures show that the current system doesn't work for millions of students—and particularly for non-white and disadvantaged students. (See "Outside the Mainstream," page 26 [Daniel Gursky, *Teacher Magazine*, August 1991].) Nonetheless, inertia reinforces the dominance of the traditional model of schooling. Most people were "taught to read" that way, and most teachers have been trained to function in such a system. "It takes a revelation for teachers to even ask whether it's possible that students don't learn that way, whether language isn't acquired that way," says Patrick Shannon, head of Pennsylvania State University's language and literacy education department.

Constance Weaver also has done a great deal of research on the teaching of grammar. See chapter 6.

When we look at the writing abilities of Americans, the assessments mirror literacy rates. When test data are disaggregated, minority students suffer the poorest scores. If systems were working, then why is society plagued with high dropout rates—anywhere from 24 to 49 percent?

Training in the teaching of writing also has mushroomed. For example, in the state of Texas, the New Jersey Writing Project (NJWP —a National Diffusion Network Project) started in 1980 with 17 teachers attending a writing institute. As of 1992, NJWP in Texas had over 400 trainers and over 2,000 teachers who had attended a three-week writing institute—all grass-roots—mostly without federal or state grants and primarily funded by local districts. Districts have made a commitment to both improving and teaching writing; they are not waiting for politicians or federal programs to solve their problems. Other writing projects have experienced similar growth.

Gursky uses the term process writing. *Possibly this term is just as misunderstood by people who have not received training in the teaching of writing as* whole word *and* whole language *are misunderstood. Using the term* process writing *seems to indicate that there are different types of writing. All writing happens as a process, whether teachers teach it this way or not.* Process writing *is to the teaching of writing what processed cheese is to cheddar. Process writing is not a type of writing, a method of writing, or a genre of writing. Rhetoricians use* writing *or* writing as a process *to indicate the recursive nature of writing and the theory of process—they do not use the word* process *as an adjective for* writing. *In this text when the word* writing *is used, it is used with an understanding that processes are a vital, integral part of the act.*

But more and more teachers are asking those questions. Sometimes with the support of their administrators, but more often on their own, teachers are embracing a holistic, meaning-first learning theory. Some do it unconsciously, with a solid theoretical base, while others seek new methods out of dissatisfaction with the status quo. Whole language, which has mushroomed in popularity in recent years, is by far the most widespread manifestation of this theory.

Although the formal label only dates back a dozen years or so, whole language has deep roots both inside and outside of education. As one leading expert puts it, there have always been whole language learners—but there haven't always been whole language teachers.

Whole language owes its intellectual heritage to John Amos Comenious, a seventeenth century educator who believed that learning should be pleasurable and rooted in students' real lives; to John Dewey's theories of progressive education; to Freidrich Froebel, the founder of kindergartens, which have a lot in common with ideal whole language classrooms; to Russian psychologist Lev Vygotsky, who emphasized the social aspects of learning the role teachers and peers play in supporting or thwarting it; to Dorris Lee and Lillian Lamoreaux, whose language-experience approach encourages teachers to use students' stories as classroom reading material; and to Donald Graves, a writing scholar and pioneer of "process writing," who encouraged both teachers and students to write more. Recent theories and research in the relatively new field of psycholinguistics have provided whole language with a more scientific base.

Psycholinguists argue that, almost from birth, children engage in a search for meaning, structure, and order. They reject the idea that decoding the smallest components of written language is an effective way for children to learn to read. Instead, they argue, language proceeds from meaning as the learner draws on his or her own experience, culture, and previous knowledge to understand the text and extract information from it. Learning and understanding are inseparable.

Smith, whose 1971 book, *Understanding Reading*, was a milestone in psycholinguistic theory, says that this view of learning has been accepted as common sense for at least

2,000 years—by everyone except educators. He suggests that most learning is as inconspicuous as breathing; both teacher and student barely realize it's happening. "Learning is continuous," he says. "It requires no particular effort, attention, conscious motivation, or reinforcement." People are constantly learning without even realizing it, from street signs, conversations, headlines, movies, and other hardly noticed events in their everyday lives.

Learning only becomes difficult, Smith argues, in contrived circumstances that are disconnected from a person's immediate interests and experiences, such as teaching children to read by asking them to study and memorize individual letters that have no meaning or isolated words that lack context.

In his book *Reading Without Nonsense*, Smith makes the point by inviting readers to glance at the texts in the following boxes and ask themselves which is the easiest to understand and remember:

JLHYPAJMRWKHMYOEZSXPESLM
SNEEZE FURY HORSES WHEN AGAIN
EARLY FROSTS HARM THE CROPS

Smith and whole language advocates believe that the meaning is "in the head," not in the text. One cannot read (and learn) about a subject that one does not already understand to some degree. Baseball fans, for example, who read the morning paper to see how their team fared easily pick up the nuances of yesterday's game from the written report because they already understand the game. The same article would be almost incomprehensible to a reader who knows (or cares) nothing about baseball.

To demonstrate that meaning is in the head rather than in the surface structure of language, Smith invites the reader to determine the meaning of a number of sentences: "Visiting teachers may be boring." "The chicken was too hot to eat." "She runs through the sand and waves." "The shooting of the hunters was terrible." Obviously, all of these sentences can have more than one meaning.

The point, says Smith, is that "neither individual words, their order, nor even grammar itself can be appealed to as the source of

The writer writes best about what the writer knows. This is why when teachers give only teacher topics so many students come face to face with failure. One well-meaning teacher said she stayed up half the night trying to come up with a creative writing topic. She selected eggplant from her list of goodies. Her students were less than overwhelmed. Many had never seen an eggplant, and most had never tasted one. She wished five minutes after giving the topic she'd never seen or heard of eggplant either.

meaning in language and thus of comprehension in reading. Nor is it possible to decode from the meaningless surface structure of writing into the sounds of speech in order to find a back route into meaning. Instead, some comprehension of the whole is required before one can say how individual words should sound, or deduce their meaning in particular utterances, and even assert their grammatical function." In short, the more one knows about, or is interested in, the subject one is reading about, the more information one is likely to glean from the text.

Furthermore, Smith sees learning as social rather than solitary. "We learn from the company we keep," he explains. "We learn from the people who interest us and help us to do the things they do." As a result, children learn to read not from methods but from people. In a sense, they apprentice themselves to people who know something that they want to learn—teachers, parents, peers, and authors. Apprenticeships were a common and successful form of learning and teaching long before the advent of formal schooling.

For years, the debate over reading instruction focused on the relative merits of phonics vs. the "whole word" method, which holds that words, rather than letters, are the most effective unit for the teaching of reading. There were countless studies, and even insinuations of communist conspiracies. During the 1950s and '60s, many people came to identify phonics with political conservatives and the whole word method with liberals. The rhetoric was often malicious. Rudolph Flesch, author of the 1955 polemical best seller *Why Johnny Can't Read*, raised the stakes by blaming whole word advocates for many of America's woes, while at the same time politicizing and oversimplifying the issue of teaching reading.

In many ways, Flesch's legacy persists today, with the past attacks on the whole word methodology now aimed at whole language, whose proponents squirm with anguish at being confused with the whole word approach. They insist that the whole word method is much like the phonic approach in that it emphasizes components rather than language as a whole, memorization of individual unconnected symbols (words), and drill and practice.

Nevertheless, deliberately or inadvertently, traditionalists' attacks on whole language

Chapter 5 focuses on the social acts of writing and the reading of that writing. See also Janet Emig, "Yes, Writing and Reading Are Social Acts," Education Week, March 20, 1991.

The need for teachers who teach writing to write themselves seems evident here.

Teachers who embrace teaching writing as a process are not without their critics. Karen Jost, in an article in The English Journal, postulated, "Teachers should not have to write to teach writing." Again, the main subject the critic addresses is control: Who will control the classroom? The idea presented is that teachers who write with their students will not have time to control the bleachers or to make sure all students turn in their work and are not tardy to class. But teachers who write with their students see fallacies in these arguments.

echo Flesch's McCarthy-era tirades against the whole word method. Sidney Blumenfeld, for instance, in a recent edition of his *Education Letter*, calls whole language "an important part of the left's social agenda.... Whole language is a lot more than just a new way to teach reading. It embodies a leftist messianic vision, which may account for the fanaticism found among whole language visionaries."

In recent years, fundamentalist religious groups have latched onto phonics, with its focus on skills and literal comprehension. They denounce whole language as secular humanism, atheism, and even satanism because of its emphasis on real literature rather than value-neutral basals and because of the introspection, inquiry, and multiple interpretations of texts encouraged by whole language teachers. Not surprisingly, lobbies have sprung up around the country to influence textbook-selection committees and to persuade legislators and school boards to mandate phonics as the only acceptable method of teaching reading.

Phonics-first advocates got a boost in September 1989, when a U.S. Senate Republican Policy Committee released a document titled *Illiteracy: An Incurable Disease or Educational Malpractice?* Citing a massive study supported by the U.S. Department of Education and carried out by the Center for the Study of Reading at the University of Illinois, the document called for "the restoration of the instructional practice of intensive, systematic phonics in every primary school in America."

For whole language teachers, however, arguments about the role of phonics and other methods of reading instruction miss the point: Whole language is a *theory* about how people learn; phonics is a *method* of teaching reading based on a totally different learning theory. Whole language teachers may draw upon a number of traditional methods, including phonics, but they use them only in specific situations when they think a student would benefit; the methods are not the whole language teacher's central approach to teaching literacy. "No one's suggesting that phonics isn't involved in learning to read and write," says Kenneth Goodman, University of Arizona education professor and a leading proponent of whole language. It is the reliance on phonics as the main or sole approach to

Some people also are against writing. Writing reveals what the writer thinks. This horrifies such groups. Many educators would like to ask these groups whether they are horrified that students think, or by what students think, or by what students may think.

Teachers of writing and teachers who integrate learning understand that they are involved with teaching and learning from a theoretical basis, not from a method. No one says the teaching of grammar and mechanics is not important; it is a matter of when and how grammar and mechanics are taught.

So, too, writing as a process is about much more than instruction in writing. It empowers the self.

Writing as a process empowers students and teachers alike.

Traditionally, cultures have kept reading and writing from those within the culture who are perceived as a threat.

The question remains: Who makes these decisions?

teaching literacy, he says, that whole language proponents resist.

In fact, whole language is about much more than instruction in reading and literacy. It's about empowerment and the role of teachers, students, and texts in education. In short, it's about who controls what goes on in the classroom. Will educational decisions be made by teachers and students or by administrators, curriculum developers, textbook publishers, and policymakers?

Consequently, in addition to rethinking their attitudes about learning, many whole language teachers have found it natural—indeed necessary—to develop a broader consciousness about social and political issues. "Teachers need to think about what they're doing when they decide to teach one way or another," Penn State's Shannon says. "What does [their method of teaching] [*Gursky's brackets*] mean for teachers and their students, not just in terms of language development but in their own lives? When they ask those questions, they acknowledge the politics of their work."

John Willinsky of the University of British Columbia agrees. "To give students expression is a political move," he says. "It empowers them."

Literacy has always been about power. The way reading has been taught for the past 500 years has more to do with religious and secular authorities trying to preserve their power than with learning theories. When Johannes Gutenberg invented movable type and printed the Bible in 1455, reading was a skill largely limited to the clergy, royalty, and scribes. The authorities quickly saw the dangers inherent in widespread literacy. To prevent the spread of reading to the masses, they levied special taxes on printers, regulated the production and distribution of publications, and simply banned books and broadsides.

But even kings and popes could not withstand the inevitable, so the ruling establishment switched from trying to prevent reading to controlling it. And in some ways, as Daniel Resnick of Carnegie-Mellon University points out, the educational traditions established to control literacy during the Reformation remain stubbornly intact in modern-day American schools. Catechism-style teaching, Resnick notes, with its authoritative texts, established questions and answers, and repetitive lessons, sought to produce believers rather than thinkers. And that legacy persists. Future efforts "to move literacy expectations beyond a rudimentary ability to read, write, and calculate," he writes in the scholastic journal *Daedalus*, will be "constrained by the practice of earlier centuries: modest instructional goals, textbooks in the form of religious primers, language used primarily to create a civic culture, and mass schooling mainly for the primary years."

Basal readers, designed for specific grade levels, became the modern catechism by the 1920s, as common as pencils in the hands of primary and middle school students across the country. Shannon traces the development of the modern basal to the late 1800s when Americans' growing faith in science and industry was applied to reading. Basals were intended to "rationalize" reading instruction in order to overcome the lack of good children's literature and teachers' relatively low education levels at the time. Standardized tests, which developed roughly during the same period, reinforced the use of basals.

The belief was, Shannon says, that teachers were behaving scientifically — according to psychological "laws of learning" — if they were faithfully following the directions in the manual. At the turn of the century, he notes, basal publishers apologized for 18-page teachers' manuals that accompanied all six reading levels. Today, publishers unapologetically produce manuals the size of city telephone books for each level. Textbook publishers, editors, and authors, Shannon says, have reduced teachers to managers of commercially produced materials; the best teachers are frequently considered those who explain the material well rather than those who help their students become independent learners.

In essence, the basal system has solidified into textbook form the traditional skills-based model of learning. And if the basals are something of a modern catechism, they're followed religiously by American teachers. Surveys show that more than 90 percent of teachers use basals to teach reading, and the vast majority of their students' class work and homework comes straight from the basal. In addition, many states require the use of basals, and teachers in some districts face fines for disobeying the mandate.

Read Robert J. Connors's history of textbooks "Textbooks and the Evolution of a Discipline," College Composition and Communication 37, no. 2 (May 1986): 178-194.

A high-school English teacher facetiously suggested that her students be exempt from physical education (PE) requirements. She uses the English textbooks as her reason. The twelfth-grade literature book weighs over 5 pounds and the composition/grammar book also weighs over 5 pounds. She further states that she cannot take both teacher editions home at the same time because "They weigh more than the student editions and my arms hurt to hold them."

Why do states require certain texts? In Texas, districts do not have to adopt the basal or any of the texts approved for adoption, but they do not receive that money to purchase trade books.

It is interesting to brainstorm pros and cons on this issue.

Here the point could be made that schools should not take anything away from teachers unless they have something to put in its place. It is not enough to give teachers a new text or a one-day inservice on how to teach from a new approach. Understanding the philosophical shift from the product paradigm to the process paradigm requires intensive time and training. Teachers simply knowing the terms prewriting, rewriting, *and* revision *does not ensure that they understand or embrace the concepts or theories of the new paradigm. They need retraining about the concepts and theories. Then those who accept the new paradigm can use the recipes and use them with full knowledge of what they are doing. When these teachers have a theoretical basis from which to work, they can use almost anything from any source and synthesize the theoretical support into their pedagogy.*

A system built around basal readers and standardized textbooks takes away from teachers and students key decision making power about classroom materials. It's not surprising, then, that many teachers who are attempting to change the structure of their classes often start by limiting the use of textbooks or shelving them completely.

"For teachers," Shannon says, "whole language is about having the right and responsibility to choose what methods they use, the materials offered in class, the ways in which they assess students." Given the tradition of outside control, he argues, the thought of taking responsibility can be both frightening and exhilarating to teachers. "The possibility of control and choice has never really been offered to teachers," he says. "They thought they were supposed to fit into a scheme in which they apply someone else's material."

Weaver, of Western Michigan University, points out that many teachers prefer the safety of the basal to the unpredictable vagaries of whole language. "You can give some teachers all the power in the world and they will use the same old traditional curriculum," she says. And even if they decide to abandon their basals, it may not make a big difference. "If teachers haven't made the shift in models of learning," Weaver says, "they're going to take nice trade books and do all the awful things that have been done with basals," namely, use the literature to teach isolated skills.

The basal, skills-oriented approach is also easier for teachers. They are following a preset curriculum, their lessons are planned in advance, and they can reasonably anticipate how the class will proceed. Whole language teachers, on the other hand, are constantly adapting as classroom events unfold; they guide rather than control; they watch for teaching opportunities and improvise. Whole language teachers acknowledge that while their new role is far more fulfilling than the traditional role, it is also far more demanding.

Because there are so many teaching strategies associated with whole language — journal writing, book "publishing," free reading, etc. — some teachers simply implement a few strategies and call themselves whole language teachers. "A lot of different activities plucked out of whole language and put in traditional settings can seem to be the same," says

Goodman of the University of Arizona. "But they lose their significance when the reasons for the activities aren't there." Smith notes that many teachers mistakenly see whole language as just another method, rather than an entirely new approach to teaching. "They still do not trust children to learn unless their attention is controlled and their progress monitored and evaluated," he says.

Many publishing companies exploit teachers' misconceptions about whole language. "Publishers see the markets for traditional materials being eroded, so they start re-labeling things and saying that if you buy their materials, you're doing whole language," Goodman says. "That's predictable, and that's a danger." Some efforts by publishers to capitalize on the movement's popularity have produced seeming anomalies — whole language basals packed with skills exercises, for example, and repackaged workbooks billed as "journals."

Remember: Textbook publishing is first and foremost a business.

There are now enough committed whole language teachers in the United States to constitute a full-fledged national movement, complete with conferences, workshops, newsletters, more than 100 support groups, and a massive whole language catalog, containing information on almost every conceivable topic related to the subject.

These whole language educators take heart from the success of their counterparts abroad, particularly in New Zealand and Australia. "Essentially, what appears as a current revolution in this country," Goodman says, "was a relatively calm evolution in other countries." In New Zealand, for example, holistic theories of learning have guided many schools since before World War II. Some whole language proponents find it more than coincidental that New Zealand and Australia rank at the top of international comparisons of literacy, while the United States barely rates a spot in the top third.

Kelly Smith, a teacher/trainer for the NJWPT, recently visited a colleague in Australia. When we asked Smith what they were doing that teachers here in the United States weren't, her reply was most illuminating: "Nothing — it's just they are all doing it."

Closer to home, Canada has also become a leader in whole language, with many of the provincial educational authorities adopting the philosophy for all their schools. Extensive resources for staff development and new materials have been allocated to help with the transition.

To mandate such a system is to work from the product paradigm. Mandating all teachers to make the shift is illogical and impossible. Teachers cannot forget that making this shift changes the way a person thinks. People do not change the way they think because they are told to — they change when they see or are shown a more effective way. People elect to change; they cannot be forced to change.

Either teachers teach writing, implicit as a process, or they do not. There is only an abyss to fall into if teachers try to straddle the paradigm shift.

In the United States, whole language has been a grass-roots movement, spreading classroom by classroom, as one or two teachers — rarely more than a handful — in a school change the way they teach. One exception is Westwood, Mass., where the entire school district has completed the second year of a five-year transition to whole language in grades K-8. The switch is the direct result of a recommendation by a teacher-led reading committee, convened by Superintendent Robert Monson when he arrived in Westwood four years ago. There has been some isolated resistance among the faculty, Monson admits. But overall, he says, the transition is going smoothly as teachers move away from basals and standardized tests toward literature reading and alternative forms of assessment.

"We've put teachers in leadership roles," Monson says. "They've got the knowledge; you just have to get them away from teaching long enough to think about these questions. They invariably come up with wonderful answers."

Although the great debate over how children learn (and thus learn to read) seems destined to continue indefinitely, it hasn't really become a dominant issue of the current school reform movement. With a few notable exceptions, most of the efforts to improve the nation's schools seem to accept as a given the traditional theories of learning on which American public education is based. Those who would "fix" our schools have largely concentrated on issues such as increased teacher accountability, more high-stakes standardized tests, higher academic standards, more rigorous curricula, and more and better teacher training. In recent years, the emphasis has shifted somewhat to school restructuring, site-based management, and parental choice. But there has been little mention in the national school reform discussion about how children learn.

Whole language advocates want to change that. They would like to focus the public discussion on classroom learning and a theory of literacy that would inevitably change the way teachers teach and the way schools are organized and operated. As Jerome Harste, professor of education at Indiana University, has written: "Whole language inquirers want the politics of literacy made explicit. Politics, they argue, is the language of priorities. They understand that not to take a position is to maintain the status quo—to keep both those who are currently well-served and those not so well-served in place. From this perspective, curriculum is not just a new set of standards to be taught, nor even an unfinished agenda, but rather a vehicle for interrogating past assumptions as well as creating a better world. There is no neutral position.

Far too many educators project a neutral position.

2

AN OVERVIEW OF THE WRITING PROCESS
Prewriting, Writing, Postwriting, Editing, and Publishing

What is most powerful and persuasive, developmentally, of course, is direct, active, personal experience since only personal experience can transform into personal knowledge. And for teachers especially, personal knowledge of any process to be presented to learners is not an option; it is a requisite. Persons who don't themselves write cannot sensitively, even sensibly help others learn to write.

—Janet Emig □

Certainly since Janet Emig wrote *The Composing Process of Twelfth Graders* much has been written and documented about the writing process. Murray and Graves continue to add to the growing body of research and pedagogy. Murray, as a magazine writer and teacher, pulls the theory out of his experiences and those of his students. Graves studies children while they write. *Writing: Teachers and Children at Work* and *Build a Literate Classroom*, both by Graves, capture his keen insights. Few have affected the pedagogy as much as Cowan and Cowan. Their popular text is rich, especially with prewriting techniques, many of which are referenced in this text. Macrorie's *Telling Writing* and *Searching Writing* add to the corpus of literature about students engaged in the acts of writing. Elbow's *Writing Without Teachers* remains as fresh as it was when published in 1973. His title says what he intends: Empower students so they may become independent writers. Also, practitioners such as Atwell, Rief, and Romano continue to illuminate the praxis of student writers: their use of conventions, their habits, and their customs of writing. As classroom teachers, and in personal styles, these authors narrate stories about their students and their learning.

But still there are classrooms where writing is attacked without any real understanding of the writing process or its recursive nature. There seems to be little understanding that prewriting, writing, rewriting, and editing are ongoing and sometimes simultaneous acts. Often texts oversimplify prewriting, suggesting it as an activity undertaken only at the beginning of the process. This oversimplification belies the difficulty of how to teach the techniques of writing while at the same time allowing for the tentativeness of the act, how to provide strategies while keeping them from becoming linear stages. All too often texts extend the activity of prewriting on Monday to drafting on Tuesday, rewriting on Wednesday, editing on Thursday, and handing in the final copy on Friday. This approach does not allow students to go back to prewriting after working on a draft, nor does it encourage students to begin an entirely new portion after revising, if warranted.

A POET DESCRIBES HER WRITING PROCESS

Listening to the poet Linda Pastan, writers are struck with her idea drawer, an actual drawer in a chest standing in her writing room. She shares how leaves, especially autumn leaves, continually make their way into her poems. In her idea drawer she collects ideas, like leaves, that float in and out of her life. When a poem is in the making, she has learned to recognize its beginnings so she can work on it from its first awakening. She tells how some fragments in her idea drawer are not ready for poems. These fragments have not been fully awakened to her as poet. So she stores all of the fragments—lines written on scraps of paper, grocery cash-register slips, a page—for use when poems are not busy waking her up.

She goes to her idea drawer and stirs some fragments from their sleep. Sometimes one or two wake up, and she is busy into the making of a poem. Sometimes she puts some ideas back to sleep and coaxes others into being. Some ideas become poems that need rewriting. When she is not ready to rewrite because of other forces in her writing, she places these poems back in her drawer. The next time she pulls something from her drawer, she might find a fragment of a poem or a poem that is ready for more rewriting. Pastan understands, practices, and shares the recursive nature of her writing process.

Imagine Linda Pastan in some Magritte painting, raking leaves that are really poem fragments and poems. She writes these leaves into a giant poem. Perhaps the teaching of writing should be like the leaves of fall days moving to a wind: with all the rich metaphors of leaves and fall and wind and raking and the resurrection of spring.

PREWRITING: CREATING

When prewriting is mandated instead of introduced as a way to plumb the writer's mind for ideas or as a way to focus an idea, then any prewriting strategy becomes artificial or even detrimental to the composing process. Prewriting strategies benefit the writer because they provide a heuristic; they form the basis for inquiry that can lead the writer from the simple to the more complex and more sophisticated. Prewriting is meant to be experienced, not ordered.

George Hillocks, Jr., in his article "Synthesis of Research on Teaching Writing," found:

> The focus of instruction with the greatest power is what I have called inquiry. This approach should not be construed as discovery teaching in which students are presented with problems or tasks and set free to pursue them. On the contrary, the method involves using sets of data in a structured fashion to help students learn strategies for using the data in their writing....
> The results of these studies indicate that the process of observing and writing is far more effective in increasing the quality of student writing than the traditional study of model paragraphs that illustrate the use of strategies.... (77-78)

Effective use of prewriting also allows for connections to be made between what is being taught and what is being thought. Then students become engaged in writing rather than locked into prewriting as stage apart from anything holding meaning. Certainly prewriting taught in isolation is a carryover from product paradigm teaching. It is akin to teaching grammar as something separate from writing. Therefore, as grammar has become regarded by some teachers, prewriting may be regarded by its attributes rather than its functions. Prewriting taken out of context may foster only "pseudo-concepts," concepts that seem to be grasped abstractly but are not (Vygotsky 66). Prewriting is so much more than sitting down with paper and writing on a topic with the appropriate number of supporting details. It is a way of learning to perceive, a way of taking from the writer's life material that has potential for writing. It is living the writing. Richard Larson says it this way:

One source of help in finding this plan [heuristic] may be the psychologists who have studied the phenomenon of *creativity*, as Gordon Rohman demonstrated in the report of his experiments with *prewriting* exercises a few years ago in writing classes at Michigan State University, which were based in part on theories by Rollo May and Arthur Koestler about the process of creating. These writers argue that if a student is to create, to "bring [something new] into birth" (Rollo May's words), he must learn to understand thoroughly his experiences, the data he has to work with—what May calls his *world*. (146-147)

Prewriting strategies are tools for finding what the writer has to say.

> *My grandmother loves to garden almost as much as she loves to fish. When she gardens, she uses four tools, a spade, a shovel, a fork, and a trowel, all well worn from years of breaking the rich soil. The spade is for digging deep—getting down into the depths of the earth, turning the soil over so new nutrients can be close to tender new shoots. The shovel is for general digging. She even says, "You can use it as a hoe if you just slide the blade along the top of the ground." The fork is for breaking up the big chunks—and of course for digging up the worms she will use during the heat of the day when she leaves her garden to make her way to the tank just below the rim of the canyon. The trowel is for small chores, when she gets on her hands and knees and just turns the top soil ever so slightly to loosen it. As my grandmother readies her garden, one tool is not more important than the other—they are different. So, too, with prewriting strategies.*

Prewriting as a Manifestation of Thinking

If the writer is a random thinker, more than likely her or his prewriting will be rambling and disjointed. If the writer is a sequential thinker, more than likely her or his prewriting will resemble a shopping list. Thus, a case may be made that prewriting evidences thought. In prewriting, this thinking is recorded and thereby rendered a potential source for subsequent writing topics.

In classrooms where the prewriting is taught and practiced as an ongoing activity, as liberating, students learn its value as a collection of strategies from which to draw. They also begin to differentiate among the prewriting strategies, choosing the one most fitting for their purpose. Some prewriting activities are simply warmups, ways to get the brain in gear. Others help generate ideas, and still others assist the writer in focusing an idea. Prewriting techniques that use heuristics have the potential of being even richer sources because they aid the writer through a thinking process.

It is not enough to give a student paper and assign "writing." Nor is it enough to give a student an experience and say, "Write about it." Students need to have a repertoire of prewriting strategies to draw from just as Linda Pastan draws from her idea drawer. Then students may choose and use the appropriate prewriting strategy as a way of interpreting the world and experiencing the world as a rich rootstock.

A Student Describes His Writing Process

Jerry James, a student who had made a commitment to writing, knew and understood his writing process. He knew where and how to find ideas, how to move the ideas into drafts, and when and how to revise. He understood writing's value, and he practiced writing. He had had teachers in middle school, high school, and college who not only taught the writing process but also engaged in it themselves.

One evening in early spring, he rang his English professor's doorbell. He was delivering some posters from the college print shop. Fairly nontemporal, Jerry breezed in and out of time schedules, so the professor was not surprised when he arrived later than expected. What intrigued the professor was not what caused Jerry's lateness, but what resulted because of that lateness—an enormous web of words written on the back of one of the posters.

Jerry shared how the web came to be—the ordeal of the past several hours. Driving up a side street, he had struck a dog as it darted in front of his car. Because the animal was not dead, Jerry carried it up and down the surrounding blocks trying to find the owner, to offer assistance, and to explain. For an hour and a half he searched, yet no one knew the dog. Jerry took it to an emergency veterinary clinic, where the vet told him nothing could be done, and unless he wanted to pay to have the dog put to sleep, he could not leave the dog. Faced with a mortally injured animal, no hospice, no owner, and a student's limited budget, Jerry drove to the outskirts of town, agonized as the dog died, and then buried the animal. Afterward, trying to make sense of the episode, Jerry sat in the car writing his web.

On one part of the web he wrote the title of a poem, "Traveling Through the Dark." He said he identified with its author, William Stafford, who wrote to understand the moral dilemma of life and death. Still shaken, Jerry completed the delivery of the posters, keeping the one with the web. By midmorning the next day, Jerry had used it as prewriting for a couple of poem fragments and one letter to the editor of the local newspaper about letting dogs run free without tags. His writing reflected the anger, remorse, and pain of the episode. Although somewhat helped by what he had written, Jerry reminded himself, "I need to keep that poster. There's more there I can use."

Clearly, Jerry had internalized the potential and promise of prewriting: He wanted to keep his web on the back of that poster. He knew prewriting is a place to create, to be free with emotions and experiences. For him, prewriting provided a touchstone to his experiences. In time he completed the following poem:

I Slam the Brakes

I slam the brakes, but the car doesn't hold
spinning out like a wide roundhouse punch
crushing the dog as I come around
and stop.

When he came into the road
all I wanted was to hit my horn
and make him go away.

I pick his jerking body up
slowly, walking
daring the other cars—
wait you bastards wait.
I put him down in the grass
cold and stiff
I am sweat and confusion.

Running to doors—banging
thinking I've killed your dog
here is my poem
no one home.

One old lady
said it belonged to the people next door
They were gone
I wanted to ask her what to do
but she said she hated the dog
and thanked the Lord it was dead
"Now, don't feel bad," she said.

It hit me right then
how perfectly she would slip
into my poem.

Leaving the dog in the owner's yard
with an unheard "I'm sorry"

I screamed at my car, then stopped.
In my car, continuing my way to work
I screamed then stopped,
started to sing with the radio,
I was making myself care.

But I had a poem here
I knew I had a poem here
it sucks out life
and turns them into words.

— Jerry James

In the five years since Jerry wrote this poem, he continues to write his world, and recently the poet Walt McDonald encouraged Jerry to continue to study and submit his work for publication.

What student writers experience are echoes of what professional writers experience. For example, award-winning author Katherine Paterson describes in "Laying the First Plank" how she wrote three pages that released her three years later to write *Bridge to Terabithia* (1981, 94-98). She begins, "I am not sure I can tell this story. The pain is too fresh for it to fall into rational paragraphs, but I want to try. For David, for Lisa, for Lisa's mother, and for me" (95).

Prewriting as a Recurring Process

Because of the recursive nature of the writing process, prewriting weaves in and out of writing. Prewriting allows the writer to move in and out of experiences. The moving in, where the writer turns inward to reflect substantially on the topic, and the moving out, where the writer takes the experience from a distance to see it in a more objective light, allow for continual re-creations in the writing — re-creations of experiences, moments, hopes, dreams. Like digging in the garden soil before the sowing, during the growing, and while harvesting, prewriting happens throughout the process.

Prewriting also allows for the dormancy of writing — not just of a single piece but of myriad pieces, much like Linda Pastan's "leaves." Ideas in one piece of writing may lie dormant for years and then, when the writer rereads or reworks a piece, may awaken and present itself. An idea may even find its way into other pieces, totally different pieces, that the writer later pursues.

Although certainly not new, the film *Why Man Creates*, by Saul Bass, remains germane to the writing process, especially to prewriting. Produced in the 1960s, the film chronicles the creative processes and parallels the writing process (Carroll 1982). In it Bass defines creativity as in the film "Looking at one thing and seeing another." It could be said that prewriting is looking at one thing and seeing another.

WRITING: ORGANIZING

When writers move from prewriting to writing, they take the chaos, the fragments, the bits and pieces of prewriting and organize them. They take the unstructured and give it structure. They take what emerged in prewriting and give it form. Shaping prewriting often helps the writer uncover or "see" what is there.

> *Recently, while going through a box of old photographs taken and collected over the years, I found some shots of Yosemite. Hardly comparable to those taken by Ansel Adams, these amateur photos had a few similarities and many dissimilarities to his work. As I looked from these shots to his work, Adams's photographer's eye became apparent. He looked at a waterfall and saw the potential of a photograph. His photographs reveal how he saw the composition. He saw the light and the dark. My photos also were of a waterfall, but they were mainly — waterfall. My rocks were rocks, whereas the rocks Adams captures so magnificently seem capable of holding water and reflecting the darkness of the water's soul. Although there probably is not enough time for someone to teach me how to develop a photographer's eye, the potential does exist. It can be taught. I can learn to organize the way Adams organized. With time and practice, I might achieve a quality composition by taking lots of photographs, by looking at lots of photographs, by learning the photographer's craft.*

It is so, too, with writing. Learning to see the potential in prewriting is key to the writer. Learning to shape that prewriting is just as key. The beginning writer is sometimes tempted to say, "I don't know what to do with this stuff." More accurately, he or she might say, "I don't know how to organize this stuff."

The writing stage is characterized by organizing the details and elaborating on those details. These details are what Larson calls the "facts of writing" (147). During writing, the writer takes the ideas found in prewriting and asks questions about those ideas. This questioning is both critical and selective: critical in the sense that the writer is after all the information; selective in the sense that the writer picks and chooses what needs to be told. Somewhere in this process the writer makes the crucial decision of genre. Admittedly some writers sit down and say, "I'm going to write a novel," but implicit in this decision is that the writer's meaning (prewriting), though maybe not on paper, is already telling the writer its form. However, many writers—Doris Lessing, Nancy Willard, and Kurt Vonnegut, to name a few—have to get something down first before selecting a genre.

A writer moving from prewriting into writing is like a child moving into adolescence. One day she may play with dolls; the next she may want a boyfriend. The move through childhood to puberty is not easy, nor is it always distinctly observable. The move can be tentative or it can be forceful. Prewriting and writing are analogous. Although prewriting impels writing, the process of organizing can be tentative or forceful. Details used during writing can dismiss some of the prewriting.

Teachers of emerging writers know how writing grows and develops. They are able to guide and model, to listen and advise. Knowing the idiosyncratic processes of students allows teachers to intervene, advise, and confer during the stages most beneficial to the writer. Such teachers know how to open up the writing.

Because during writing the writer is capable of moving back and forth, to and from prewriting and postwriting, respectively, the importance of understanding this movement is crucial to the writing process. Teachers who recognize the crucial nature of both intervention and nonintervention, each at the appropriate time, act as guides for students. They provide continual and immediate assistance during the writing, yet they also yield space and time as students organize and shape their ideas. To use a garden metaphor again, anyone who has picked the persimmon before it is ripe knows the astringent puckering experienced when one bites into the succulent flesh. The teacher, like the gardener, needs to recognize the differences in the processes of students so each student's writing is able to ripen to its full potential.

POSTWRITING: POLISHING

Postwriting is when writers polish what they have written. In this book, postwriting includes correcting, revising, and reformulating, each of which is covered in detail in subsequent chapters. Briefly, correcting polishes the grammar. During postwriting, teachers teach grammar while guiding students' reentry into their writing to apply and check that grammar. Revising refines sentences. Teachers teach the appropriate sentence sense for the grade level while facilitating students' reentry into their writing to apply their sentence knowledge and check their sentences. Reformulation perfects paragraphing. During this time, teachers teach what students need to know about these larger segments of discourse. Again they shepherd students through applying the new knowledge and checking their paragraphs.

Usually writers manipulate correcting, revising, and reformulating simultaneously and throughout the process—but not necessarily. Students who are taught to correct, revise, and reformulate after they have done some prewriting and whipped that prewriting into shape generally are not stymied or hampered by obsessing over conventions too early in their process. These notions are considered again in the prewriting and revision chapters.

Correcting: Grammar

Correcting is where writers take care of what Emig calls the "stylistic infelicities" (1971, 43). Correctness is important, but it should not choke the writer.

> When I co-directed the Douglass-Cook Colleges Writing Center we were sent a student who had been identified as "remedial" based on her entry-level writing sample. Her initial writing for us was stilted. It consisted of short, choppy sentences and simplistic, almost monosyllabic, words. When I asked her about her writing, she replied with a litany of nevers: "Never have a run-on. Never have a comma splice. Never misspell a word. Never have a fragment. Never begin a sentence with and or but." Obviously, she translated those rules to her writing, for she never used a compound sentence; she never attempted to use any word she could not spell, no matter how appropriate; she never risked matching what went on in her head with what she attempted on paper. In short, she never valued what she had to say over correctness.
>
> Although she had scored quite well on her SAT, she was a crippled writer. After several sessions with a student mentor, she learned through work in sentence combining how to embed her thoughts and how punctuation could help that embedding. After her instructor modeled ways to make her writing more syntactically mature, how to avoid run-ons, and how to unsplice the comma, her writing blossomed to reveal the bright student her other scores showed her to be. This young lady was not remedial in any way. She had just been playing the correctness game.

Surely, no one expects teachers to throw rules and usage away. When teachers enable students to correct their own writing, correcting becomes part of an integrated framework. Students come closer to understanding the reasons behind rules. They fear grammar less. If students see grammar as a way to clarify thought, a way to take care of their writing problems in the context of their own writing, they will not regard grammar as the problem. The issue is not whether or not grammar should be taught, but when it should be taught. When grammar is taught at the right place, students appreciate the opportunity to make their writing better.

Revising: Sentence Sense

Here teachers work with students to help them develop sentence sense. This is a difficult task because many harbor the misconception that a sentence is simply a group of words expressing a complete thought or that a sentence always has a subject and a predicate. In truth, most good handbooks take many pages to discuss the sentence in order to include main sentence elements, secondary sentence elements, sentence classifications, and unorthodox sentences. Corder and Ruszkiewicz, in the *Handbook of Current English*, hold, "Because of their almost infinite variety, sentences are difficult to explain or define in ways that account for all the occasions of their use" (26). They also offer a realistic definition, one students would understand: "We may define a written sentence as one or more words, punctuated as an independent unit, that say something" (26).

The Little, Brown Handbook also indicates the problem with narrowly defining the sentence. The handbook suggests that knowing grammar has little to do with the proficiency of writing but is helpful "when something has gone wrong in your sentences" (Fowler 108). This handbook defines a sentence as "basic units of writing, and good writing begins with sentences that are grammatical and clear" (Fowler 109).

Yet Eugene Ehrlich, from the Department of English and Comparative Literature at Columbia University, reiterates a traditional notion of sentences as the building blocks of the paragraph, with each sentence consisting "of a number of words arranged in a grammatical relationship that gives them meaning" (84). Perhaps to avoid a definitive definition, Bonnie Carter and Craig Skates of the University of Southern Mississippi explain sentences by way of fragments: "A sentence fragment is a group of words punctuated like a complete sentence but lacking the necessary structure — at least one independent clause" (78). And Earl G. Bingham, who teaches technical writing at American River College, prefaces his handling of sentences by looking at guidelines for constructing them:

> I wish it were possible to provide every struggling writer with a magic formula for sentence construction. Someday, perhaps, some genius will invent a black box into which words can be inserted, a button pushed, and Presto! finished sentences in perfect syntax will emerge. Until that day, however, most writers will continue to struggle with words and word arrangement. (243)

Clearly, then, developing sentence sense depends less upon memorizing a definition and more upon struggling with words, arranging and rearranging words, considering the relationship of words to words, and writing and rewriting. Knowing when a sentence works is akin to knowing when training wheels are no longer needed on a bike. There is a point when the rider, ready to fly down the sidewalk, has to do it alone, has to test the balance. So, too, there is a point when students must work with their sentences, test their own ability. There is a point when writers learn how sentences work, how sentences speak to the reader, and that sentences are not spoken language transcribed. Emig says, "Examples of invalid analogies include the over-regularizing of lexical, grammatical, or rhetorical features, as well as more globally, the illogicality of proceeding as if writing were talk written down, a belief some students hold perhaps because some of their teachers have told them it is so" (1983, 143). Finally, sentences are units that mesh to make meaning for the reader. Developing sentence sense helps that meshing happen. Consider how Katherine Paterson demonstrates her sentence sense in *The Spying Heart*:

> It's sad to think that when I use the word *idea* I am using it in the weakened sense, but there you are. I do, however, have one advantage over some people. If a definition doesn't satisfy me in English, I can look it up in Japanese. And in Japanese, the word is *i*, which is made up of two characters — the character for *sound* and the character for *heart* — so an idea is something that makes a sound in the heart (the heart in Japanese, as in Hebrew, being the seat of intelligence as well as the seat of feeling). (27-28)

"But there you are" adds such voice and tone to Paterson's written word the reader almost hears her. And certainly, she doesn't worry about anything as archaic as never starting a sentence with *and*. But look at the last sentence. She connects phrases and clauses, joins them with a comma and dashes, and tucks in additional information with parentheses — all in one sentence. This may be difficult to diagram, but it is easy to understand. It works.

Reformulating: Paragraphing

Reformulating here is the word given to work done with the large hunks of discourse called paragraphs. Paragraphing is to writing what makeup is to an actor: It can do many things. Paragraphing can be topical or functional. Writers have been known to approach paragraphing intuitively or by some mathematical unit stored in some recess of their left brain. Unfortunately, if taught as a strict unit, the paragraph can become formulaic, predictable, and boring.

> *One school district has created a school culture around what they call the "box paragraph." The visual image is as comical and nonsensical as the way it is taught. A topic is assigned. Then students are given sentence checklists that contain a predetermined, specific purpose for each sentence and enumerate items each sentence should contain. Students honestly try to write according to this artificial form.*
>
> *The work of researchers the caliber of Braddock and Irmscher makes hash of this approach. The box paragraph exists only for the uninformed. When the teachers from this district began analyzing their own writing processes, they realized that what they practiced and what they taught were two different things. Somewhere in this realization they saw that paragraphing needs proper placement in the writing process and it needs to be taught realistically.*

Teachers who continue to teach *the paragraph* as if its form exists somewhere outside the realm of meaning do not understand paragraphs. Chapter 8 explains the paragraph and its history. With better understanding of the formation and the functions of paragraphs (also discussed in chapter 8), teachers can correctly teach the paragraph in its rightful place—as a part of the whole and a way to augment meaning.

Consider for a moment that the way a writer forms paragraphs is like a fingerprint. Each method uniquely marks the writer. Of course, the same could be said of style, diction, and tone. Perhaps all of these are fingerprints of the writing hand, and like fingerprints each one is different and unique to the writer. One thing is certain: A polarity exists between the way paragraphs are taught and the way they are written.

Surely the untrained eye can tell the difference between a piece of ceramic created on the wheel compared to a piece of ceramic made with a mold. One is unique, and the other is imitation—formula. The former flows from the hands of the potter to express feeling, intent, mood, meaning; the latter is a cast of the feeling, intent, mood, and meaning of someone else. When students become writers, they are like the potter, not the pourer. They prefer originality and eschew imitation. Imitation may be the highest form of flattery, but it can never bring with it the joy of discovery and creativity. They understand the maxim "Flawed brilliance is preferred to dulled perfection."

Responding to Content Versus Proofreading

"Writing and rewriting are a constant search for what one is saying," John Updike says (Murray 244). Updike, of course, pays attention to the mechanics of writing, but it is what he has to say that is important. Charles Suhor, in "Linda's Rewrite," focuses on the cost of Mrs. Blank's overcorrection. Linda suffers through rewriting session after rewriting session. Mrs. Blank's hot hand corrects, recorrects, ignores what Linda has to say, and focuses on her stylistic infelicities. Suhor ends his article with these lessons the child learns from her rewriting sessions:

1. Rules are more important than expression. Master the right forms, appearances and conventions of writing, and it won't matter if you have nothing to say.

2. Ideas and perspectives that are out of the ordinary aren't acceptable. If people before you like to feel silk, smell flowers and listen to lyric sopranos, you have no business going around listening to silk, feeling flowers or smelling lyric sopranos.

3. Writing is a tedious, demeaning and hateful task. Do it only when you must and when everything expected of you is fully explained, as on Blue Cross

forms and loan applications. Writing is, after all, a matter of satisfying the person forcing you to write. (25)

No teacher wants to be a Mrs. Blank. No teacher wants to do harm.

An editor once said, "You need to convince your reader trained to proofread that content is more important than typos." Attempting to convince this "reader" is to fall into the hands of the last temptor of T. S. Eliot's *Murder in the Cathedral*. As Eliot writes through the voice of Archbishop Thomas Beckett:

> To do the right deed for the wrong reason...
> Now my good Angel...
> ...hover over the sword's points. (Lines 664...705)

To justify the "right deed" of working with the writer's meaning over the obsessive activity of marking every error is to give credence to the "reader" who practices such activities. Instead, maybe it is such readers who should be asked to justify how mechanics supersede content. Maybe they who have done the wrong deed for the wrong reason, or for no reason, or for the reason of precedent, should face the sword's point. In *Balance the Basics: Let Them Write*, Don Graves calls the American anxiety about reading a "national neurosis" (11). Could the anxiety about mechanics be another national neurosis? In the face of all the research, all the classrooms where the teaching of writing as a process is making a difference in the lives of students who are learning to be writers, maybe these "readers" need to defend their stance that mechanics are more important than what the writer has to say.

Mina Shaughnessay, in *Errors and Expectations*, identifies "the most damaging aspect" of students' experiences with writing:

> they have lost all confidence in the very faculties that serve all language learners: their ability to distinguish between essential and redundant features of a language left them logical but wrong; their abilities to draw analogies between what they knew of language when they began school and what they learned produced mistakes; and such was the quality of their instruction that no one saw the intelligence of their mistakes or thought to harness that intelligence in the service of learning. (10-11)

Internalizing the Writer's Process

Good teachers of writing help students to internalize their processes. Processes in writing consist of the writer's inner involvement with the nature of the stimuli (self, others, environment, artifacts) as well as with all that is implicit in putting words on paper—all the stylistic infelicities, the organization, the polishing, the reformulating, the correcting, the revising. The product in writing connotes outer involvement with what has been written (correcting, revising, rewriting). Yet product is part of the process; it is culmination. The teacher who embraces writing as a process does not abandon the finished product but merely places it in its proper perspective—the end of a process. Although it is not necessary for every piece of writing to go through the entire writing process, the product cannot be ignored. The difficulties, ambiguities, and contradictions about both student writing and the teaching of writing occur because little distinction is made between process and product and because emphasis usually is placed upon the measurable product. When the teacher and the student begin to internalize their own processes, when evaluation, effort, and process take on as much emphasis in grading and classroom practice as the product, then there will be balance. Writing as a process should not be perceived as the pendulum swinging to the other side of product; rather, it is the balance between "anything goes" and product.

Students who internalize the writing process do not find the product overwhelming the process. Instead, because writing becomes something students can do, because as they internalize the process they begin to see themselves as writers, they want the product to reflect the intensity of what they know. Students who are writers care as much for the product as they do for the process. They learn about balance.

Conceptualizing the Stages

Teachers, habitually or intentionally, frequently remain on the periphery of students' writing, noting only "externals," according to Witkin (168). In discussing the process of creative expression, he suggests that this traditional concern with product may be due to the "incomprehensibility of process to the praxis of teachers" (169). He insists that involvement is so essential to the setting, making, holding, and resolving of expressive acts that teachers must "enter the creative process at the outset" (169). He reasons that to accomplish this, the teacher must have a schema for conceptualizing the structuring of the processes.

This conceptualizing is no easy task, for the teacher or the writer. The teacher of writing moves away from being the assigner of writing to being a facilitator of processes, a guide through the stages, a listener, a conferer, a discoverer, a teacher, a grammarian, and a helper. This book attempts to elaborate these different roles of the teacher, but it is the teacher who must place the information into his or her own schema. Like Jerry, earlier in this chapter, he came to write his experience in his own way. Someone else might have wanted to wait until the moment had become a distant memory. Someone else might have wanted to avoid it altogether. But when the teacher has a schema and can communicate this schema to help students find their schemata, then teacher and student alike are enriched by what writing can do.

Britton and the members of the University of London Writing Research Unit agree.

> Teachers have many reasons for being interested in writing processes. Their involvement with all the learning processes of their pupils requires that they understand how something came to be written, not just what is written. They can bring to their reading of a pupil's work all their knowledge of his [or her] life and his [or her] context, realizing, perhaps intuitively, that what they already know about a child and his [or her] thinking when they read his [or her] work enables them to understand and appreciate something that may be incomprehensible to another. In this respect, many teachers are far in advance of anything educational research has been able to offer them. (21)

A DIGRESSION

Janet Emig and Joyce Armstrong Carroll, upon being invited in 1977 by James Gray of the then-Bay Area Writing Project to start the New Jersey Writing Project, saw a need to formulate and record NJWP's premises. After analyzing what a writing project should do and could do, what they did as writers, and what they did as teachers, they developed the first premise of the project:

> Teachers who teach writing should write themselves.

Simple enough. But upon studying teachers who participated in the first New Jersey Writing Project, it was discovered that few teachers wrote on a regular basis, if at all (King). It is not enough for a teacher to be a teacher of writing; a teacher also must be a writer. This teacher may always be a teacher with an uppercase *T* and a writer with a lowercase *w*. But teachers must write. Only through falling in love with the act of writing, only through knowing the struggle of writing, can a teacher of writing really understand the writing process. Once teachers engage their own writing processes, they are better equipped to help students through their writing processes. Writing is certainly one place in this recursive process where there is much to be shared with students (Carroll 1981).

EDITING: CHECKING

One of the most difficult tasks a writer ever faces is editing his or her own work. In fact, some writers never conquer this part of the process. The acknowledgments of most books reveal expressed gratitude to editors and others who have closely read the author's work. Editing requires the writer to look at the writing with different eyes. Although some writers are able to look clearly at their work, others find editing similar to looking through a glass darkly. Learning to read as writers, to read as readers, and to write like readers is not common in most classrooms (rarely do texts or most approaches have writers read as editors, or write as editors). Reentering a text for the purpose of editing requires another protocol of strategies and method of teaching writing.

Editing requires distance from the writing. Some writers must let the writing "cool down" before they can reenter as editors. It is easy for writers who reenter their writing soon after it is written, while it is "hot," to read right through a glaring error. They read the meaning and miss the error. Then someone else reads the piece and finds the error. The lesson for classrooms seems to be that the writer, after much practice editing the writing of others, learns best how to edit his or her own work.

A first step in learning to edit is to understand what the word means. Some teachers of writing consider editing to be only the search for surface errors. They do not see editing as something substantial. Yet editing can and should be both. Again, the complexity of the processes of writing reveals a multiplicity of meaning considered in Bakhtinian terms as "the ability to see the identity of a thing not as a lonely isolate from all other categories but as a contrasting variable of all other categories which might, under different conditions, fill the same position in existence" (Clark and Holquist 7).

So, what is editing? Don Murray calls it "a continuation of the process of discovering" (100). Frank Smith says it is the "polishing of the text to make it appropriate for a reader" (127). The writer Edward Aswell, .trying to edit Thomas Wolfe's writing, made this comparison: "It was something like excavating the site of ancient Troy. One came upon evidences of entire civilizations buried and forgotten at different levels" (C-13). David Leavitt, in *The Lost Language of Cranes*, uses a simile to describe editing: "mending split infinitives and snipping off dangling participles, smoothing away the knots and bumps until the prose ... took on a sheen, like perfect caramel" (86). In this text, editing is defined not only as correcting the surface errors, but also as another opportunity to deal with meaning, clarity, and coherence.

To minimize the act of editing is to pull a trick on the writer. Possibly the worst trick is to lead the writer to believe that the work was edited by correcting misspellings, then later to point out that part of the work needs restructuring. This trick is made more cruel when the writer is never given time or instruction for that restructuring.

A corollary trick, one that wastes time and expends energy, is having students memorize and use an extensive list of proofreader's marks. Most textbooks include proofreader's marks in the section on editing. Some teachers teach these lists without a full understanding of their basic function. Historically, proofreader's marks were devised so the typographer knew where to place capitals, commas, and so on. Because some of the early editors were among the few who could read, they had to use a visual code for the less literate typographers. In time these marks became standard in print shops and publishing houses. Current editors still use these marks when editing copy. However, few students need to edit their work as if preparing a manuscript for a typographer. If they do become editors, there will be time enough to learn the proofreader's marks. The time spent having students memorize the editing marks and use them to mark up papers would be better spent getting students to edit the paper for meaning—that is where teaching plays the vital role.

Teachers need to have edited their own work so they better understand that editing is not an announced activity—"It is now time to edit." Editing is a skill that requires teaching. It requires that the writer reenter the writing not only to correct, but also to take one more opportunity to get it ready for the reader. This is difficult. Some professional writers say they never feel as if they have "gotten it." That is why they have a good editor. Although editing is difficult, students can learn how to edit by first working with someone else's writing. Eventually, at least some of that skill will be transferred to working with their own writing.

PUBLISHING: DISTRIBUTING

Naoma Huff, a drama, speech, and English teacher in Clyde ISD, Texas, said, "Writing needs some pizzazz, some zip, some zing. My speech and drama students get to show off what they have accomplished. That doesn't happen enough in writing" (Carroll 1983). Huff is correct. Teachers need to provide opportunities for students to print, to go public, to disseminate, issue, circulate—in a word, to *publish*—their work.

But who should publish, and why? What should be published, and when? Peter Elbow in *Writing with Power* states, "Writing's greatest reward, for most of us anyway, is the sense of reaching an audience.... Without having to muster all the courage it takes to stop strangers on the street, you can nevertheless find friends or make acquaintances who will *want* to read your words. In effect, publish" (212). Students fall under Elbow's category of "most of us" and are the *who* of publishing. Huff's pizzazz, zip, and zing fulfill publication's *why*. *When* to publish is best determined by the school's calendar. Students should choose *what* to publish, be it the choicest writing of a marking period, a semester, or an entire academic year or something students just want to share with others. When students select writings for publication, they should check that the language and experiences are appropriate for the audience so readers are able to interact with the meanings. In that way the experiences also become real for the readers. These are general guidelines, to be sure, but when followed, they produce apt, clear, and lively pieces for publication.

Finally, one must ask, how can student writings be published and where? The *how* of publishing varies from the stories of preschoolers drawn randomly on the back of wallpaper samples, to the work of middle-schoolers neatly photocopied and encased in plastic binders, to the typed pages of high school students. The most realistic *how* is preparing a manuscript to be sent out for publication. The *where* of publishing might be a bulletin board, a hallway, the library, or the magazines *Merlyn's Pen* or *Stone Soup*. There is no limit to where publishing can take place.

Writing should go public because publishing provides an audience. Further, publishing matters because it is the writer's solo flight; it is the writer's curtain call, recital, aria; it is the writer's exhibit, premier, trophy; it is the writer's winning basket, birdie, touchdown. And students get their applause. The applause comes in the form of responses, notes, seeing the manuscript in print, book fairs, and authors' readings.

CONCLUSION

Prewriting, writing, postwriting, editing, and publishing are common to all writers. They look different for different writers. A preschool writer might spend all of his or her time in prewriting. In fact, a preschooler's prewriting and publishing may look the same. What is important is that the writer starts to contribute to the understanding of his or her processes. Metacognitively, the writer keeps a record of what, how, and when the processes occur and do not occur. With an understanding of these processes, the writer can then duplicate, replicate, change, or abort. The writer has some control over his or her writing. Writing is, after all, fulfilling the need to express oneself. With the understanding of the processes involved in writing, the expression is meaningful and fulfills the writer's needs.

APPLICATION

Begin a writing folder where you keep all your writing. Be sure to date all entries.

WORKS CITED

Aswell, Edward. "Publishing Manuscripts Posthumously" by Edwin McDowell. *New York Times*, 10 Sept. 1984, sec. C, p. 13.

Atwell, Nancie. *In the Middle: Writing, Reading, and Learning with Adolescents*. Portsmouth, NH: Boynton/Cook and Heinemann Educational Books, 1987.

Bass, Saul. *Why Man Creates*. 25 min. 1966. Distributed by Pyramid.

Bingham, Earl G. *Pocketbook for Technical and Professional Writers*. Belmont, CA: Wadsworth, 1982.

Britton, James, et al. *The Development of Writing Abilities (11-18)*. London: Macmillan, 1975.

Carroll, Joyce Armstrong. "A Proper Commitment to Writing." *English in Texas* (Spring 1981): 57-59.

_____. "Publishing: The Writer's Touchdown." *English Journal* (April 1983): 93-94.

_____. "Visualizing the Composing Process." *English in Texas* (Spring 1982): 11-14.

Carter, Bonnie, and Craig Skates. *The Rinehart Handbook for Writers*. New York: Holt, Rinehart & Winston, 1988.

Clark, Katerina, and Michael Holquist. *Mikhail Bakhtin*. Cambridge: Belknap Press of Harvard University Press, 1984.

Corder, Jim W., and John J. Ruszkiewicz. *Handbook of Current English*. Glenview, IL: Scott, Foresman, 1985.

Cowan, Gregory, and Elizabeth Cowan. *Writing*. New York: John Wiley, 1980.

Ehrlich, Eugene. *The Bantam Concise Handbook of English*. New York: Bantam Books, 1986.

Elbow, Peter. *Writing with Power*. New York: Oxford University Press, 1981.

_____. *Writing Without Teachers*. New York: Oxford University Press, 1973.

Eliot, T. S. *Murder in the Cathedral*. New York: Harcourt Brace Jovanovich, 1964.

Emig, Janet. *The Composing Process of Twelfth Graders*. Urbana, IL: National Council of Teachers of English, 1971.

_____. "Non-Magical Thinking: Presenting Writing Developmentally in Schools." In *The Web of Meaning*. Pp. 135-144. Upper Montclair, NJ: Boynton/Cook, 1983.

Fowler, H. Ramsey. *The Little, Brown Handbook*. Boston: Little, Brown, 1980.

Graves, Donald H. *Balance the Basics: Let Them Write*. New York: Ford Foundation, 1978.

_____. *Build a Literate Classroom*. Portsmouth, NH: Heinemann Educational Books, 1991.

_____. *Writing: Teachers and Children at Work*. Exeter, NH: Heinemann Educational Books, 1983.

Hillocks, George, Jr. "Synthesis of Research on Teaching Writing." *Educational Leadership* (May 1987): 71-82.

King, Barbara. "Two Modes of Analyzing Teachers and Student Attitudes Toward Writing: The Emig Attitude Scale and the Kind Construct Scale." Ed. D. diss., Rutgers University, New Brunswick, NJ, 1979.

Larson, Richard L. "Discovery Through Questioning: A Plan for Teaching Rhetorical Invention." In *Contemporary Rhetoric: A Conceptual Background with Readings*, W. Ross Winterowd, ed. Pp. 144-154. New York: Harcourt Brace Jovanovich, 1975.

Leavitt, David. *The Lost Language of Cranes*. New York: Knopf, 1986.

Macrorie, Ken. *Searching Writing: A Contextbook*. Rochelle Park, NJ: Hayden, 1980.

_____. *Telling Writing*. New York: Hayden, 1970.

Murray, Donald M. *A Writer Teaches Writing: A Practical Method of Teaching Composition*. Boston: Houghton Mifflin, 1968.

Paterson, Katherine. *Bridge to Terabithia*. New York: Thomas Y. Crowell, 1977.

_____. *Gates of Excellence*. New York: Elsevier/Nelson Books, 1981.

_____. *The Spying Heart*. New York: E. P. Dutton and Lodestar Books, 1989.

Rief, Linda. *Seeking Diversity: Language Arts with Adolescents*. Portsmouth, NH: Heinemann Educational Books, 1992.

Romano, Tom. *Clearing the Way*. Portsmouth, NH: Heinemann Educational Books, 1987.

Shaughnessay, Mina. *Errors and Expectations: A Guide for the Teacher of Basic Writing*. New York: Oxford University Press, 1977.

Smith, Frank. *Writing and the Writer*. New York: Holt, Rinehart & Winston, 1982.

Suhor, Charles. "Linda's Rewrite." *Learning* (August/September 1975): 20-25.

Vygotsky, Lev. *Thought and Language*. Eugenia Hanfmann and Gertrude Vakar, eds. and trans. Cambridge: Massachusetts Institute of Technology, 1962.

Witkin, R. W. *The Intelligence of Feeling*. London: Heinemann Educational Books, 1974.

"The Composing Process: Mode of Analysis" and "Implications for Teaching"

JANET EMIG

Chapter 3
The Composing Process: Mode of Analysis

The purpose of this chapter is to delineate dimensions of the composing process among secondary school students, against which case studies of twelfth-grade writers can be analyzed. As with some of the accounts of the creative process in chapter 1, the premise of this chapter is that there are elements, moments, and stages within the composing process which can be distinguished and characterized in some detail.

This delineation is presented in two forms: as an outline and as a narrative. The use of an outline, which is of course linear and single layered, to describe a process, which is laminated and recursive, may seem a paradoxical procedure; but its purpose is to give a category system against which the eight case studies can be examined. The narrative portion, in contrast, is an attempt to convey the actual density and "blendedness" of the process.

Although this category system is set forth before the analysis of the data, it was derived from an extensive analysis of the eight case studies. The procedure for analyzing the data was inductive; the presentation is deductive.

Dimensions of the Composing Process among Twelfth-Grade Writers: An Outline

1. **Context of Composing**
   Community, Family, School.

2. **Nature of Stimulus**

   Registers:

   Field of Discourse—encounter with natural environment; encounter with induced environment or artifacts; human relationships; self.

   Mode of Discourse—expressive-reflexive; expressive-extensive.

   Tenor of Discourse

   Self-Encountered Stimulus

   Other-Initiated Stimulus:

   Assignment by Teacher—external features (student's relation to teacher; relation to peers

Commentary

Students of all ages have been shown to have elements, moments, and stages within the composing process. The idiosyncratic characteristics are developmentally appropriate for each grade level.

Consider the visual of placing all of these models in a three-dimensional fractal, capable of being dynamic and static at the same time. Possibly, it is akin to the quantum dot—capable of existing as a particle and wave simultaneously or separately at any given time. The quantum dot is to the silicon chip what the microwave oven is to the campfire—highly complex.

These modes of discourse strike teachers as much more workable than those of other rhetoricians, such as James L. Kinneavy in Theory of Discourse. *Could it be what strikes these teachers is the fact that Emig's classifications come inductively from student work, whereas Kinneavy's have been deductively imposed onto students' work?*

Current state competency testing seems to ignore all or most of these elements. Such tests place students, writing, and curricula in jeopardy with hidden agendas. Students spend hours trying to guess, "What do they want?" and "How do they want it?" Little attention is paid to what students have to say.

It is important to note that even in self-sponsored writing, peers and others still play a role in the contemplation of writing.

Here Emig refers to three types of planning. Clearly, the implications for the classroom point to the use of more prewriting opportunities and the use of heuristics.

Although the starting of self-sponsored and school-sponsored types of writing are the same, the results are radically different. The ownership is different. Students care far more about their own writing than they do about the writing forced upon them in schools. They keep and maintain their own writing; they seem to tolerate the school-sponsored attempts.

in classroom; relation to general curriculum and to syllabus in English; relation to other work in composition); internal features or specification of assignment (registers, linguistic formulation, length, purpose, audience, deadline, amenities, treatment of written outcome, other).

Reception of Assignment by Student — nature of task, comprehension of task, ability to enact task, motivation to enact task.

3. Prewriting

Self-Sponsored Writing:

Length of Period

Nature of Musing and Elements Contemplated — field of discourse; mode of written discourse; tenor or formulating of discourse.

Interveners and Interventions — self, adults (parents, teachers, other), peers (sibling, classmate, friend); type of intervention (verbal, nonverbal), time of intervention, reason for intervention (inferred), effect of intervention on writing, if any.

Teacher-Initiated (or School-Sponsored) Writing:

(Same categories as above)

4. Planning

Self-Sponsored Writing:

Initial Planning — length of planning; mode of planning (oral; written: jotting, informal list of words/phrases, topic outline, sentence outline); scope; interveners and interventions.

Later Planning — length of planning; mode; scope; time of occurrence; reason; interveners and intervention.

Teacher-Initiated Writing:

(Same categories as above)

5. Starting

Self-Sponsored Writing:

Seeming Ease or Difficulty of Decision

Element Treated First Discursively — seeming reason for initial selection of that element; eventual placement in completed piece.

Context and Conditions under Which Writing Began

Interveners and Interventions

Teacher-Initiated Writing:

(Same categories as above)

6. Composing Aloud: A Characterization

Selecting and Ordering Components:

Anticipation/Abeyance—what components projected; when first noted orally; when used in written piece.

Kinds of Transformational Operations—addition (right-branching, left-branching); deletions; reordering or substitution; embedding.

Style—preferred transformations, if any; "program" of style behind preferred transformations (source: self, teacher, parents, established writer, peer); (effect on handling of other components—lexical, rhetorical, imagaic).

Other Observed Behaviors:

Silence—physical writing; silent reading; "unfilled" pauses.

Vocalized Hesitation Phenomena—filler sounds (selected phonemes; morphemes of semantically low content; phrases and clauses of semantically low content); critical comments (lexis, syntax, rhetoric); expressions of feelings and attitudes (statements, expressions of emotion—pleasure/pain) toward self as writer to reader; digressions (ego-enhancing; discourse-related).

Tempo of Composing:

Combinations of Composing and Hesitational Behaviors

Relevance of Certain Theoretical Statements Concerning Spontaneous Speech

7. Reformulation

Type of Task:

Correcting; Revising; Rewriting

Transforming Operations:

Addition—kind of element; stated or inferred reason for addition.

Deletion—kind of element; stated or inferred reason for deletion.

Reordering or Substitution—kind of element; stated or inferred reason.

Embedding—kind of element; stated or inferred reason.

Many of these phenomena are what inept evaluators of writing classrooms characterize as poor learning environments or lack of teacher direction. As teachers move toward understanding the composing processes of their students, administrators will need to move toward understanding the teaching processes of teaching writing. Mindless activity in place of real thinking cannot be allowed to flourish in classrooms.

Again, the capriciousness of competency tests comes to mind. Requiring students to complete a draft of writing that shows evidence of elaboration that normally doesn't occur immediately in the writing process strikes many as unfair and as poor test construction. Performance testing appears to be the only way an accurate assessment could be made of an impromptu situation. Portfolios show a more accurate picture of students' processes.

In many classrooms the reason for stopping a piece of writing is because of the due date. In writing/reading classrooms, teachers and students are moving away from the "due date" to a "due window." Like a space shot, there are only certain days available for launching. Certain days are given for the assignment to be turned in for evaluation. The rigid "it is due today, before the end of the period" strikes teachers and students who are involved in their own processes as antiquated.

8. Stopping

Formulation:

Seeming Ease or Difficulty of Decision

Element Treated Last — seeming reason for treating last; placement of that element in piece.

Context and Conditions under Which Writing Stopped

Interveners and Interventions

Seeming Effect of Parameters and Variables — established by others; set by self.

Reformulation:

(Same categories as above)

9. Contemplation of Product

Length of Contemplation

Unit Contemplated

Effect of Product upon Self

Anticipated Effect upon Reader

10. Seeming Teacher Influence on Piece

Elements of Product Affected:

Register — field of discourse; mode of written discourse; tenor of discourse.

Formulation of Title or Topic; Length; Purpose; Audience; Deadline; Amenities; Treatment of Written Outcomes; Other.

Dimensions of the Composing Process Among Twelfth-Grade Writers: A Narrative

The first dimension of the composing process to note is the *nature of the stimulus* that activates the process or keeps it going. For students, as for any other writers, stimuli are either self encountered or other initiated. Either the student writes from stimuli with which he [or she] has privately interacted or from stimuli presented by others — the most common species of the second being, of course, the assignment given by the teacher. Both kinds of stimuli can be nonverbal or verbal, although it is an extremely rare and sophisticated teacher who can give a nonverbal writing assignment.

Linda Waitkus revealed in her study[1] that students who learned skills, mechanics, and grammar while engaged in writing reflexively retained this knowledge, whereas the information conveyed during extensive writings was not retained. Often she found students regressed in their manipulations of such skills.

---

[1]Linda Waitkus, "The Effect of Poetic Writing on Transactional Writing: A Case Study Investigating the Writing of Three High School Seniors." Ed. D. diss. (New Brunswick, NJ: Rutgers University, 1982).

All areas of experience, or fields of discourse, can provide the stimuli for writing. It is useful to pause here to present the schema of registers devised by the British linguists Halliday, McIntosh, and Stevens because of the applicability of their category-system to this inquiry.

Registers these linguists define as the varieties of language from which the user of that language makes his oral and written choices.[1] Registers are divided into the following three categories: (1) the field of discourse, or the area of experience dealt with; (2) the mode of discourse, whether the discourse is oral or written; and (3) the tenor of discourse, the degree of formality of treatment.

Although, to the investigator's knowledge, the three linguists do not attempt to specify the various fields of discourse, it seems a refinement helpful for a closer analysis of the composing process. In his essay on poetic creativity, the psychologist R. N. Wilson divides experiences tapped by writers into four categories: (1) encounters with the natural (nonhuman) environment; (2) human interrelations; (3) symbol systems; and (4) self.[2] For the analysis of student writing in this inquiry, "symbol systems" becomes "encounters with induced environments or artifacts."

Another useful refinement of the system of registers is to divide the category "the written mode of discourse" into species. In their speculations on modes of student writing, Britton, Rosen, and Martin of the University of London have devised the following schema:

Modes of Student Writing

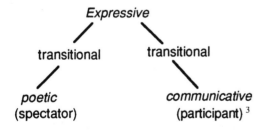

Expressive

transitional   transitional

poetic
(spectator)

communicative
(participant)[3]

They regard all writing as primarily expressive—that is, expressing the thoughts and feelings of the writer in relation to some field of discourse. But beyond sheer expressiveness, writing evolves toward, or becomes, one of two major modes: *poetic*, in which the student

Here we are reminded of Halliday's uses of language[2]:

1. instrumental—**I want**—language used for getting things done, for satisfying material needs
2. regulatory—**Do as I tell you**—language used for controlling the behavior, feelings, attitudes of others
3. interactional—**Me and you; me against you**—language used for getting along with others, for establishing status
4. personal—**Here I come**—language used to express individuality or awareness of self
5. heuristic—**Tell me why**—language used to seek and test knowledge
6. imaginative—**Let's pretend**—language used to create new worlds
7. representational—**I've got something to tell you**—language used to communicate

Frank Smith adds three of his own:

8. divertive—**Enjoy this**—language used to have fun
9. contractual—**How it must be**—language used to regulate
10. perpetuating—**How it was**—language used to preserve

To which Yetta Goodman[3] has added:

11. ritualistic—**How are you; Fine**—(phatic) language used for getting along with others
12. extending memory—**Here is what I know**—language used by authority to test knowledge

---

[2]Frank Smith, "The Uses of Language," *Language Arts* 54, no. 6 (September 1977): 638-644.

[3]Yetta Goodman, "Relating Reading and Writing," speech given at the 32d annual meeting of the Conference on College Composition and Communication, 26-28 March 1981, Dallas, Texas.

The case of language being dynamic and mutative is evidenced here; U.S. English and British English are changing denotatively and connotatively. Britton et al.'s terms do not work for us.

It is this loose and accurate terminology that makes reflexive and extensive so applicable to the classroom. In contrast, Kinneavy uses narrative, descriptive, and classificatory as his modes of writing. To these he added purposes: expressive, persuasive, and informative. Finding real writing that adheres to a strict definition for the modes and purposes is difficult, if not impossible. Real writers overlap, weave in and out of Kinneavy's divisions. Worse yet is trying to produce a piece of writing that sticks to a single mode. Emig's terms are more fluid. They come from the real writing of real students, so to find examples is easy—to produce is natural. Kinneavy's discourse is from the old paradigm—either/or. It arises from Aristotelian rhetoric. Emig's discourse is from the new paradigm—both/all. It reflects the newer philosophies of Bathkin, Richards, Langer, Derrida, and Pierce. It is a kind of abduction; it allows for the mind to range over all possibilities.

observes some field of discourse, behaving as a spectator; or *communicative*, in which the student somehow participates through his [or her] writing in the business of the world. The many exemplars of writing Britton, Rosen, and Martin regard as mid-mode they have called *transitional* writings. (One longs to give the two kinds of transitional writing exponents, as with Hayakawa's cow[1] and cow[2].)

To this investigator, the notion that all student writings emanate from an expressive impulse and that they then bifurcate into two major models is useful and accurate. Less satisfactory are the terms assigned to these modes and the implications of these terms about the relation to the writing self to the field of discourse. The terms are at once too familiar and too ultimate. Both *poetic* and *communicative* are freighted with connotations that intrude. *Poetic*, for example, sets up in most minds a contrast with prose, or prosaic, although in this schema the poetic mode includes certain kinds of prose, such as the personal fictional narrative. Second, they are too absolute: rather than describing two general kinds of relations between the writer and his [or her] world, they specify absolute states—either passivity or participation.

The following schema seems at once looser and more accurate:

Modes of Student Writing

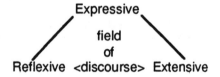

The terms *reflexive* and *extensive* have the virtue of relative unfamiliarity in discussions of modes of discourse. Second, they suggest two general kinds of relations between the writing self and the field of discourse—the *reflexive*, a basically contemplative role: "What does this experience mean?"; the *extensive*, a basically active role: "How, because of this experience, do I interact with my environment?" Note that neither mode suggests ultimate states of passivity or participation. Note too that the mid-modes or transitional writings have been eliminated from this schema as a needless complexity—at this time.

Subcategories can be established as well for the register, "tenor of discourse," which concerns the distance observed between the writing self and field of discourse, expressed by the degree of formality observed in the writing itself. Formality or decorum in written discourse can be established by one or more of the following means: lexical choices, syntactic choices, rhetorical choices. Obviously, the most formal discourse would employ all three means. The next question, of course, is what constitutes decorum for these three means.

Most past and current composition guides have been predicated upon the belief that there are established and widely accepted indices of written decorum and that student writers of all ages can learn and employ them. Levels of diction really refer to corpora of lexical items that are consigned some place on a formality continuum. Syntactically, certain orderings of words are regarded as more formal than others: the "balanced" sentence, for example, as against the "loose" sentence. Rhetorically, certain arrangements of sentences and the kinds of signals that precede and connect them are also regarded as more formal than others; for example, the use of explicit "lead sentence" and explicit transitional devices, such as *nevertheless* and *however*.

The teacher-initiated assignment as stimulus has specifiable dimensions. It occurs within a context that may affect it in certain ways. Included in this context are relationships the student writer may have with his [or her] peers or, more importantly — given the teacher-centered nature of very many American classrooms — with his [or her] teacher; the general curriculum in English being enacted, and the specific activities in composition of which the assignment is a part; and the other stimuli that have immediately accompanied the assignment, with the sequence and mode of these probably very important. As an example of the last: if a teacher shows a film as stimulus for writing, do her [or his] words precede the film, or follow it, or both? Here, as with the other dimensions specified, no research of any consequence has been undertaken.

Internal aspects of the assignment that may bear upon the student's writing process, and product, include the following specifications: (1) registers — the field of discourse, the written mode, and the tenor; (2) the linguistic

Because of the fractuality (fractual is motion) of these lexical items, their changes are varied and sometimes hurried. Teaching these to student writers can become frustrating. Because texts are often three years old before adoption, and because they stay in adoption for up to 10 years, the changes can come and go before some even have the opportunity to dismiss them as "new." So the need for teachers to maintain their own reading and writing becomes a most important task of teaching.

Joyce Carol Oates's words seem poignant here: [We] can't pretend to not know what is known....''[4]

Faulkner's career illuminates this dichotomy between what the writer wants to write and what the writer is told to write. Whereas Faulkner's novels propel readers headlong into intellectual discovery, his films sent the viewer out for popcorn. He could not write under a Hollywood system, though he could write very well what he wanted to write.

At first glance, the response to the phrase "Prewriting occurs but once" might be "I don't think so." But upon reflection, we see that a new prewriting starts a new process. Prewriting signals another start.

---

[4]Joyce Carol Oates, "Excerpts from a Journal," *The Georgia Review* XLIV, nos. 1 and 2: 121-134.

formulation of the assignment; (3) the length; (4) the purpose; (5) the audience; (6) the deadline; (7) the amenities, such as punctuation and spelling; and (8) the treatment of written outcome—that is, if the teacher plans to evaluate the product, how—by grade? comment? conference? peer response? or by some combination of these?

The reception of the assignment by the student is affected by the following: (1) the general nature of the task, particularly the registers specified; (2) the linguistic formulation of the assignment; (3) the student's comprehension of the task; (4) his [or her] ability to enact the task; and (5) his [or her] motivation to enact the task. There is now some empirical evidence that not all students can write with equal ease and skill in all modes.[4] For the less able student some species of mode present almost insuperable difficulties—for example, the impersonal argument in which the writer is to present "dispassionately" more than one side, or aspect, of a case. Consequently, if a teacher gives an assignment requiring writing in this sub-mode, certain students may be unable to complete adequately, or even to begin, such an assignment. Along with being intellectually unable to perform the assignment, the student may also be unmotivated or psychically unable to perform the assignment. Such "block" may emanate from strikingly different sources: the student may find the task too boring, or he [or she] may find the task too threatening. He [or she] may not want to write, again, about his [or her] summer vacation or the function of Banquo's ghost, or about family life, if his [or her] father has just lost his job or if his [or her] mother has just threatened divorce.

Next, there are two possible preludes to the act of writing: *prewriting* and *planning*. *Prewriting* is that part of the composing process that extends from the time a writer begins to perceive selectively certain features of his [or her] inner and/or outer environment with a view to writing about them—usually at the instigation of a stimulus—to the time when he [or she] first puts words or phrases on paper elucidating that perception.

Planning refers to any oral and written establishment of elements and parameters before or during a discursive formulation. Prewriting occurs but once in a writing process; planning can occur many times.

Whether or not a piece of writing is self- or other-initiated affects both prewriting and planning. If the piece is teacher-initiated and if the assignment is highly specific, particularly as to a fairly immediate deadline, it is likely that the prewriting period will be brief—or that the paper will be late. Planning is intricately affected by the nature of the assignment as well. One way of regarding an assignment is as the part the teacher takes in the planning of a piece of writing. If the teacher's part is extensive—as in specifying registers, length, purpose, audience—it is obvious that the part a student plays in his [or her] own planning is diminished. There seems to be some evidence that a delicate balance, if not a paradox, exists in the giving of assignments. If the teacher sets too many of the variables for a piece of writing (we need to know far more about how many are too many, and which variables are more significant than others), some students feel too confined, too constricted by the limitations to write "well." If the teacher does not specify enough variables (again, how many are enough, and for what student?), the task may daunt at least some students by its ambiguity or by its degrees of freedom. If there are individual differences here, which students learn from highly specified assignments and which from loose assignments? And if future empirical studies suggest giving more than a single assignment to accommodate these differences in responses, how can the teacher be certain there is some equality in the tasks he assigns? Again, far more research needs to be undertaken in this area of the teaching of composition.

For the phases of prewriting and planning, as in almost every other phase that follows, a category in the outline is "Interveners and Interventions." It is an extremely rare situation for writers, particularly student writers, to proceed from initial stimulus to final draft, or revision, without interruption. Rather, events and people—teachers, notably —intervene, and in major enough ways to affect the process of writing, and the product.

Interveners, for the purposes of this study, will be defined as persons who enter into the composing process of another. For student writers, interveners are most often two sorts of adults, teachers and parents, and one sort of contemporary, a friend, in self-sponsored.

Schools are still full of teachers who say, "I give my students choices," which may be translated into, "Select one of the following topics for your paper." Sure, the student has a choice—he or she gets to pick from one of the teacher's topics. And teachers wonder why students have malaise about writing.

Secondary teachers are finding that honors, gifted, and Advanced Placement students resist with fervor ambiguity or freedom. These students have learned to play a certain academic game and balk when they feel the rules have changed. Examining their writing reveals they have mastered the formula. They know what gets the A. They are not too eager to take risks in their writing for fear of a lower GPA. Curricula cannot be governed by the pressures these students and their parents can place upon them. Thinking and discovery should govern the curriculum, not the ranking of a student average.

Starting is a specifiable moment in the process of writing—and the one perhaps most resistant to logical characterization and analysis. Certain psychoanalytic or certain learning theories provide explanations as to why a writer starts to write. If one accepts the major Freudian metaphor of the tripartite self, starting can be regarded as the moment when the id, or the unconscious, is, in R. N. Wilson's terms, "the least amenable to ego mastery," and breaks through the controls usually exerted by the ego and super-ego.[5]

Because of the clearly profound, and opaque, nature of this moment, the kinds of elements that can be accurately specified, that exhibit themselves in behavior, are contextual—and, usually, trivial. Examples here are where, physically, the writer is when he [or she] begins and what habits or rituals he [or she] observes. Perhaps the most significant feature of starting that can be readily observed is what element the writer first places on paper, and where in the finished piece that element occurs, if at all.

For the purposes of this inquiry, eight twelfth graders attempt to compose aloud. The assumption here is that *composing aloud*, a writer's effort to externalize his [or her] process of composing, somehow reflects, if not parallels, his [or her] actual inner process.

At least three interesting questions can be asked about this particular, and peculiar, form of verbal behavior. First, are there recurring characteristics as one or more persons compose aloud? Second, if so, can a category-system be devised by which these behaviors can be usefully classified? Three, can provocative hypotheses be generated to account for these behaviors?

Composing aloud can be characterized as the alternation of composing behaviors that directly pertain to the selection and ordering of components for a piece of written discourse, and those which do not.

Anticipating is different from planning in the following three ways: Planning involves the projection of a total piece of discourse; anticipating, the projection of a portion of discourse. Planning does not occur in the language of the piece; anticipating often employs the exact lexicon and syntax that will appear in the finished piece of discourse.

Finally, anticipating, as Jerome Bruner notes, shuttles between the present and the future; planning does not:

Composing aloud is uniquely different from speech. Early childhood educators can attest to children "languaging" differently when they are "reading" from scribbles than when they are talking. In writing institutes we have noted a few participants who due to their writing anorexia would compose aloud in group or sharing sessions. These compositions always resemble writing more than talk.

The speaker or writer rides ahead of rather than behind the edge of his utterance. He is organizing ahead, marshaling thoughts and words and transforming them into utterances, anticipating what requires saying. If the listener is trafficking back and forth between the present and the immediate past, the speaker is principally shuttling between the present and the future.... The tonic effect of speaking is that one thrusts the edge of the present toward the future. In one case anticipation is forced into abeyance. In the other it dominates the activity.[6]

Student writers frequently demonstrate the phenomenon of anticipation in their writing as they compose aloud. They anticipate the use of a theme or of an element, then return to the present portion of discourse, to fill out the intervening matter. There are clear signs of efficiently divided attention, as they focus upon the here-and-now while at the same time considering where the future element will eventually, and best, appear.

There are other strategies a writer follows in dealing with the elements or components of discourse: he [or she] can accept, and immediately employ, an element; he [or she] can accept, then immediately abandon or delete his [or her] choice (if too much time intervenes, the action becomes reformulation or revision); or he [or she] can combine the element in some way with other elements in the discourse. (*Author's note:* The kind of self-censoring that eliminates an option before it is uttered is outside the purview of this inquiry.)

When dealing with syntactic components—and one must note at once that there are also lexical, rhetorical, and imagaic components—these actions correspond to the basic transforming operations—addition; deletion; reordering or substitution; and combination, especially embedding.[7]

In his article, "Generative Grammars and the Concept of Literary Style," Richard Ohmann gives the following definition of style: "Style is in part a characteristic way of deploying the transformational apparatus of a language."[8] As illustrations, he breaks down passages from Faulkner ("The Bear"), Hemingway ("Soldier's Home"), James ("The Bench of Desolation"), and Lawrence (*Studies*

Nancy Willard describes it this way:

The game was simple. It required two people: the teller and the listener. The teller's task was to describe a place as vividly as possible. The object of the game was to convince the listener she was there. The teller had to carry on the description until the listener said, "Stop, I'm there." ... At the height of my telling, something unforeseen happened. My sister burst into tears.

"Stop!" she cried. "I'm there!"

I looked at her in astonishment.... But to cry at a place pieced together out of our common experience and our common language, a place that would vanish the minute I stopped talking! That passed beyond the bound of the game altogether....

The joy of being the teller stayed with me, however, and when people asked me, "What do you want to be when you grow up?" I answered, "I want to tell stories." (153-154)

(Nancy Willard, "The Well-Tempered Falsehood: The Art of Storytelling." In A Nancy Willard Reader: Selected Poetry and Prose. Hanover, VT: Middlebury College Press, 1991.)

The kind of self-censoring due to lack of knowledge or interest should be acceptable, valid reasons to eliminate options, but when self-censoring occurs due to environment, prejudices, or teacher bias, students have an obligation to resist this type of censorship.

Another excellent way to see this breakdown is in William L. Stull's Combining and Creating: Sentence Combining and Generative Rhetoric *(New York: Holt, Rinehart & Winston, 1983). Two hundred and thirty-seven professional writers such as John Steinbeck, Ernest Hemingway, and William Faulkner, as well as essayists such as Joan Didion, Lewis Thomas, and Walter Lippmann make up 90 percent of the sentence-combining exercises. Examining their style becomes a natural extension of sentence combining.*

Although not the same type of silence, Tillie Olsen's Silences *(Dell, 1989) is a poetic and powerful account of the silences in the lives of writers who are women.*

John Frederick Nims writes, "According to Robert Frost, there 'are virtually but two [rhythms], strict iambic and loose iambic'." Nims also writes "Walking, too, with our legs and arms swinging in pendulum time, has developed our feeling for rhythms. Goethe composed many of his poems while walking. So, in our own day, did Voznesensky: 'I may be walking down a street or in the woods ...

in Classic American Literature*) into kernel sentences and notes that, for each, a different cluster of optional transformations is favored. The special "style" of Faulkner, for example, seems partially dependent upon his favoring three transformations: the relative, or *wh* [who, where, etc.], transformation, the conjunctive transformation, and the comparative transformation.[9]

There is no reason to believe that non-professional writers do not also have their characteristic ways "of deploying the transformational apparatus of a language," although these ways may be less striking, with less reliance on "a very small amount of grammatical apparatus."[10] (Query: When teachers or critics say that a writer has "no style," is what they mean that the writer in question has no strongly favored ways of transforming?)

The next question, of course, becomes why one favors a given cluster of transforms. One explanation seems to be that a writer is following some sort of "program" of style, a series of principles, implied or explicit, of what constitutes "good" writing. For example, he [or she] might break the concept "coherence" into a set of behavioral objectives, such as "Be clear about referents" and "Repeat necessary lexical elements."

Composing aloud does not occur in a solid series of composing behaviors. Rather, many kinds of hesitation behaviors intervene.[11] The most common of these are making filler sounds; making critical comments; expressing feelings and attitudes, toward the self as writer, to the reader; engaging in digressions, either ego-enhancing or discourse-related; and repeating elements. Even the student writer's silence can be categorized: the silence can be filled with physical writing (sheer scribal activity); with reading; or the silence can be seemingly "unfilled"—"seemingly" because the writer may at these times be engaged in very important nonexternalized thinking and composing.

The alternation of composing behaviors and of hesitation phenomena gives composing aloud a certain rhythm or tempo. It is interesting to speculate that a writer may have a characteristic tempo of composing, just as he may use a characteristic cluster of transforms.

Composing aloud captures the behaviors of planning and of writing. Partly because of the very definition of reformulation, and partly because of the attitudes of the twelfth graders toward this portion of the composing process, it does not capture reformulating.

Writing and reformulating differ in significant ways. One is in the role memory is asked to play. Another is in the nature and number of interferences in the two portions of the composing process. In writing, the memory is seldom asked to recall more than the words and the structures in the given unit of discourse upon which the writer is working and, possibly, in the unit immediately preceding. In reformulating, the memory is asked to recall larger units of discourse for longer periods of time, again the "noise" of all intervening experiences. (In writing itself, the major form of "noise" seems to be the physical act of writing, the scribal activity.)

A third way they differ is in the relative roles of encoding and decoding in the two portions of the process. In writing, encoding — the production of discourse — is clearly dominant. Decoding during the act of writing for the most part consists of rereading one's own recently formulated, and remembered, words in short, retrospective scannings. In reformulation, decoding plays a larger role because of the intervention of a longer period of time and the consequent forgetting that has occurred. One becomes more truly the reader, rather than the writer, of a given piece of discourse — that is, he [or she] views his [or her] writing from the point of view of a reader who needs all possible grammatical and rhetorical aids for his [or her] own comprehension.

Reformulation can be of three sorts: correcting, revising, and rewriting. The size of the task involved differs among the three: correcting is a small, and usually trivial, affair that consists of eliminating discrete "mechanical errors" and stylistic infelicities. Another-imposed task, correcting is synonymous with composing in the minds of many secondary and elementary school teachers of composition. Revising is a larger task involving the reformulation of larger segments of discourse and in more major and organic ways — a shift of point of view toward the material in a piece; major reorganizations and restructurings. While others may recommend correcting, the writer himself [or herself] must accede to the value of the task of revising. Rewriting is the largest of the three, often

and a rhythm starts inside, maybe connected with my breathing....' The kind of work that man and woman did for countless centuries — sowing, mowing, woodchopping, spinning, rocking the cradle — encouraged rhythmic expressions. Robert Graves believes our most vigorous rhythms originated in the ringing of hammers on the anvil and the pulling of oars through the sea."[5]

Writing takes on important implications to reading instruction. When the student writes, the student is engaged in the act of reading and rereading. Writing demands both writing and reading. Reading alone does not demand as rigorous a commitment to the mind as writing.

Many teachers mistake grading for the act of correcting. Grading means to determine the quality of, or to evaluate. Many teachers spend eons of their time correcting papers. They spend very little time grading. And to the detriment of students, they bestow grades based on the correcting.

---

[5]John Frederick Nims, *Western Wind* (New York: Random House, 1974).

involving total reformulation of a piece in all its aspects, or the scrapping of a given piece, and the writing of a fresh one.

Stopping represents a specifiable moment — rather, moments — in the writing process because, of course, a writer stops more than once although the final stopping, like the first starting — the first placement of words on a page — has special, or exaggerated, characteristics. One stops at the ends of drafts or versions of a piece of writing; he [or she] stops when he [or she] thinks the piece is finished — when he [or she] feels he [or she] has worked through or worked out the possibilities, contentive and formal, that interest him [or her] in the piece; he [or she] also stops for the purpose of presenting a piece in a given state for the reading — and, usually, evaluation — of one or more others.

These moments and motives for stopping do not necessarily coincide. Again, whether or not a piece of writing is assigned affects stopping as it affects almost every other phase in the writing process. If an imposed deadline forces the writer to submit a piece of writing for reading and evaluation before he [or she] is content with his [or her] formulation, before he [or she] experiences closure, states of tension develop that make the act of stopping painful, if not impossible. Hypothesis: Stopping occurs most "easily" when one's personal sense of closure occurs at the same time as a deadline imposed by oneself or by others.

The next moment to be noted is the *contemplation of product* — the moment in the process when one feels most godlike. One looks upon part, or all, of his [or her] creation and finds it — good? uneven? poor? If he [or she] has not steadily, or even erratically, kept his [or her] reader in mind during the process, the writer may think of him [or her] now and wonder about the reception the piece will experience in the world.

The final category concerns the *seeming influence* by a teacher or by a group of teachers upon the piece of student writing. There are five sources of information about this elusive matter of influences: student statement; student practice; teachers' written evaluations of former pieces, if available; student descriptions of composition teaching experienced; and, the most difficult information to obtain, what those composition teachers actually do in the classroom as they "teach" composition.

Maybe writing is never finished; maybe it is just abandoned.

How can teachers structure classrooms where the closure and the deadline are "easy" for the writer?

Portfolio assessment allows teachers and students to analyze and hypothesize about these influences on writing.

This chapter represents a theoretical sketch of one of the most complex processes man engages in. Although it is roughly taxonomic, it does not of course purport to be exhaustive. Nonetheless, almost every sentence contains or implies hypotheses upon which one could spend a lifetime in empirical research. Perhaps investigators other than the writer will find here materials for provocative questions and generative hypotheses about the composing process, particularly of students.

Chapter 7
Implications for Teaching

This inquiry strongly suggests that, for a number of reasons, school-sponsored writing experienced by older American secondary students is a limited, and limiting, experience. The teaching of composition at this level is essentially unimodal, with only extensive writing given sanction in many schools. Almost by definition, this mode is other-directed — in fact it is other-centered. The concern is with sending a message, a communication out into the world for the edification, the enlightenment, and ultimately the evaluation of another. Too often, the other is a teacher, interested chiefly in a product he [or she] can criticize rather than in a process he [or she] can help initiate through imagination and sustain through empathy and support.

A species of extensive writing that recurs so frequently in student accounts that it deserves special mention is the *five-paragraph theme*, consisting of one paragraph of introduction ("tell what you are going to say"), three of expansion and example ("say it"), and one of conclusion ("tell what you have said"). This mode is so indigenously American that it might be called the Fifty-Star Theme. In fact, the reader might imagine behind this and the next three paragraphs Kate Smith singing "God Bless America" or the piccolo obligato from "The Stars and Stripes Forever."

Why is the Fifty-Star Theme so tightly lodged in the American composition curriculum? The reason teachers often give is that this essentially redundant form, devoid, or duplicating, of content in at least two of its five parts, exists outside their classrooms, and in very high places — notably, freshman English classes; "business"; and in the "best

Twenty years later, school-sponsored writing is still the major experience for most secondary students. The real tragedy is not just the fact that so little change has occurred, but that the "push down" effect on middle school and elementary school curricula have younger writers experiencing more and more extensive writing. A balance is still to be found. Might the fact that 29 percent of high-school students drop out of school be attributed to the type of curriculum? Students involved in the process of learning probably stay in school. Students tested daily on the products of learning may lose interest.

Critics of writing as a process clamor over the loss of this formula. Because the only thing they understand about composition is form, they cannot imagine teaching anything else.

Teachers need to prepare students for the level they are teaching. If they do this well, then the students will be prepared for the next level, the next job, the next day.

A group of English teachers in one of the largest cities in the United States, in one of the most progressive school districts in the city, were given the opportunity to reveal what they knew about the last 20 years of Pulitzer Prize-winning poets. Out of 150 teachers, middle school and high school, only 7 knew of or recognized more than 7 of the 20 poets. Over 90 percent of the teachers admitted to never having read any of these poets. They all recognized every eighteenth-century poet and poem given. One implication might be that their knowledge of poetry is three centuries behind. By the year 2000, we may hope that such teachers will not be four centuries out of touch.

practices" of the "best writer"—that, in other words, this theme somehow fulfills requirements somewhere in the real world.

This fantasy is easy to disprove. If one takes a constellation of writers who current critical judgment would agree are among the best American writers of the sixties—Norman Mailer, Truman Capote, Philip Roth, Saul Bellow, and their juniors, Gloria Steinem and Tom Wolfe—where, even in their earliest extensive writings, can one find a single example of any variation of the Fifty-Star Theme?

As to freshman English classes, the assumption is that freshman English is a monolith, rather than a hydra-headed monster with perhaps as many curricula and syllabi as there are harassed section men [and women] and graduate assistants. In "business," where can one write the Fifty-Star Theme except as a letter to an unheeding computer or as a Pentagon memorandum?

The absence of match between what is being taught secondary—and, undoubtedly, elementary—students and the practices of the best current writers is partially attributable to teacher illiteracy: how many of the teachers described in this inquiry, would one guess, have read one or more of the writers mentioned above? Yet without such reading of wholly contemporary writers, teachers have no viable sources of criteria for teaching writing in the seventies, even in the single mode they purport to teach. No wonder that many of the students who are better- and newer-read reject models that are as old as exemplars in the secretary guides of the late eighteenth century and as divorced from the best literature of their time. (This is not to say that the only models should be works of the late twentieth century; great works from all centuries are contemporary, as the writings of Donne, Swift, Coleridge, and Carroll will attest.)

More crucial, many teachers of composition, at least below the college level, themselves do not write. They have no recent, direct experience of a process they purport to present to others. One reason may be that there are in the United States very few teacher-training institutions which have intensive and frequent composing as an organic part of the curriculum for young and for experienced teachers of English. In England, such programs seem more common, as do experiences in allied arts through creative arts workshops.[3] When, if ever, have our secondary school teachers painted, sung, or sculpted under any academic auspices?

Partially because they have no direct experience of composing, teachers of English err in important ways. They underconceptualize and oversimplify the process of composing. Planning degenerates into outlining; reformulating becomes the correction of minor infelicities.

They truncate the process of composing. From the accounts of the twelfth-grade writers in this sample one can see that in self-sponsored writing, students engage in prewriting activities that last as long as two years. In most American high schools, there are no sponsored prewriting activities: there is no time provided, and no place where a student can ever be alone, although all accounts of writers tell us a condition of solitude is requisite for certain kinds of encounters with words and concepts. (If teachers assume that the student will find elsewhere the solitude the school does not provide, let them visit the houses and apartments in which their students live.)

At the other end of the process, revision is lost, not only because it is too narrowly defined but because, again, no time is provided for any major reformulation or reconceptualization. Despite the introduction of modular scheduling in a few schools, a Carnegie-unit set toward writing, and the other arts, still prevails.

Much of the teaching of composition in American high schools is probably too abstract for the average and below-average students. This inquiry has shown that some able students can translate an abstract directive such as "Be concise" into a set of behaviors involving the selection of lexical, syntactic, and rhetorical options. But there is no indication they were taught how to make such a translation in schools. There is also no indication that less able students can do such translating on their own—at least, without constant and specific guidance by their teachers.

Much of the teaching of composition in American high schools is essentially a neurotic activity. There is little evidence, for example, that the persistent pointing out of specific errors in student themes leads to the elimination of these errors, yet teachers expend much of their energy in this futile and

Many teachers believe that knowing the terms of the writing process are the same as experiencing them. As long as they have this belief system, they will continue to underconceptualize and oversimplify.

Many secondary teachers still see themselves as "American Lit." teachers or "British Lit." teachers. They do not see their role as writing teachers. They will not be what they are not—writers.

Teachers often assign revision as a homework assignment. Consider this as precursor to failure. If a student is asked to revise without teacher intervention and assistance, how and what will the student revise?

One teacher told us that spelling tests were a part of the culture of the school and community, and the culture could not be changed.

One teacher evaluator came into the room while the teacher and students were involved in the act of writing. He said, "I'll come back when you are teaching."

Change is happening. Once a teacher understands and teaches according to learning, reading, and writing processes, she or he cannot go back to the skill and drill approach.

unrewarding exercise. Another index of neurosis is the systematic confusion of accidents and essences (one wonders, at times, if this confusion does not characterize American high schools in general). Even the student who, because of the health of his [or her] private writing life, stays somewhat whole is enervated by worries over peripherals — spelling, punctuation, length. In *The Secret Places*, as elsewhere in his writing, David Holbrook describes these emphases:

Children become so terrified of putting down a word misspelt, particularly an unfamiliar word, that they don't put down any words. I have seen it happen to a child of 8, who wrote long marvelous stories. After a year with a teacher who wrote "Please be more tidy," "Your spelling is awful," "Sloppy"—and never a good word, she stopped altogether. She wrote little lies, a sentence at a time, in a "diary." "Coming to school today I saw an elephant." It wasn't true. But that was all she was damn-well going to write— neat, complete, grammatical, well-spelt, short, and essentially illiterate lies. For her the word had been divorced from experience. The deeper effect is to make the learning process one separated from sympathy, and a creative collaborative interest in exploring the wonder of being.[4]

What is needed for the reversal of the current situation? Assuredly, frequent, inescapable opportunities for composing for all teachers of writing especially in reflexive writing, such as diaries and journals. For teachers at all levels, given the mysterious nature of learning and teaching, surely some value will adhere to having their own experiences shaped into words for pondering, perhaps into meaning and illumination.

Perhaps their students will gain benefits as well, as the result of such teacher training. Perhaps teachers will abandon the unimodal approach to writing and show far greater generosity in the width of writing invitations they extend to all students. One wonders at times if the shying away from reflexive writing is not an unconscious effort to keep the "average" and "less able" student from the kind of writing he [or she] can do best and, often, far better than the "able," since there is so marvelous a democracy in the distribution of feeling and of imagination.

Finally, a shift may consequently come in who evaluates whom, and to what end. In this inquiry we have seen that the most significant others in the private, and often the school-sponsored, writing of twelfth graders are peers, despite the overwhelming opportunity for domination teachers hold through their governance of all formal evaluation. American high schools and colleges must seriously and immediately consider that the teacher-centered presentation of composition, like the teacher-centered presentation of almost every other segment of a curriculum, is pedagogically, developmentally, and politically an anachronism.

There is too much at stake for teachers not to make this change. Failure to do so threatens the very fabric of our society. The change reflects a geopolitical shift as well as an educational one. Threatened paradigms that refuse to change are ultimately destroyed from within. Already evidence of a newer paradigm can be seen. Adherence to a dying paradigm is not productive. Emig's words hold truth—the world has little tolerance for anachronistic practices.

NOTES

Chapter 3

[1]M. A. K. Halliday, Angus McIntosh, and Peter Strevens, *The Linguistic Sciences and Language Teaching*, p. 77.

[2]Wilson, "Poetic Creativity," p. 167.

[3]Harold Rosen, Lecture, NDEA Institute in English Composition, University of Chicago, July 1968.

[4]Research of James Britton, Nancy Martin, and Harold Rosen, Institute of Education, University of London.

[5]Wilson, "Poetic Creativity," p. 168.

[6]Jerome Bruner, "Teaching a Native Language," *Toward a Theory of Instruction*, p. 103. Copyright 1966 by Belknap Press of Harvard University Press. Used by permission.

[7]For an interesting discussion of the ordering of elements, see Francis Christensen's "A Generative Rhetoric of the Sentence," *Notes Toward a New Rhetoric*, pp. 1-22.

[8]Richard Ohmann, "Generative Grammars and the Concept of Literary Style," *Word* (1964), p. 431.

[9]Ibid., p. 433.

[10]Ibid.

[11]The terminology employed in this section is, for the most part, borrowed from studies of hesitation phenomena, particularly from "Hesitation Phenomena in Spontaneous English Speech" by Howard Maclay and Charles E. Osgood, *Readings in the Psychology of Language*, pp. 305-24.

Chapter 7

[1]Kellogg Hunt, *Grammatical Structures Written at Three Grade Levels*; and Roy C. O'Donnell, William S. Griffin, and Raymond C. Norris, *Syntax of Kindergarten and Elementary School Children: A Transformational Analysis*.

[2]Kellogg Hunt et al., *An Instrument to Measure Syntactic Maturity*.

[3]See the accounts, for example, in Sybil Marshall, *An Experiment in Education*; and David Holbrook, *The Secret Places: Essays on Imaginative Work in English Teaching and on the Culture of the Child*.

[4]From *The Secret Places* by David Holbrook, p. 69. Copyright © by David Holbrook. Used by permission of the University of Alabama Press.

3

LET THE PROCESS BEGIN
Teaching Prewriting

> Get it down. Take chances. It may be bad,
> but it's the only way you can do anything really good.
>
> — William Faulkner □

Much has been written on prewriting. Some call it percolating (Romano 56); some call it rehearsal (a term Donald M. Murray attributes to Donald Graves in Murray 56); some call it creating (Cowan and Cowan 2). No matter what term is used, all agree that prewriting is intrinsic to the writing process. All agree on its idiosyncratic nature and complexity. Consider the many activities found under its heading: note taking, outlining, reading, thinking, dreaming, reverie, doodling, imagining, talking, and fooling around. Additionally, there are specific prewriting strategies, which will be defined in this chapter, such as freewriting, wet ink, trigger words, free association, writing roulette, sentence stubs, journal writing, brainstorming, listing, blueprinting, drawing, looping, dialogue, reporter's formula, the pentad, classical invention, classical invention for the contemporary student, cubing, hexagonal writing, and webbing. Because the purpose of prewriting is to find or focus a topic, most anything that gives rise to ideas constitutes prewriting.

PREWRITING PROBLEMS

Ironically, one problem with prewriting is its staying power. Some teachers and students enjoy its freedom so much they want to remain with prewriting. Such teachers point proudly to bulging writing folders filled with starts, bits, lists, loops, unfinished stories, half-written how-to's, quotations, reactions, notes, and other proof that prewriting is alive and well in their classrooms. But upon closer inspection of those folders, one sees little or no evidence of attempts at taking the prewriting any further. This ultimately leads to superficiality, lack of elaboration, or frustration because students do not experience closure on any piece or because they are expected to make a quantum leap from prewriting to what usually becomes a hastily written final copy.

Another problem is the attitude of some writers toward prewriting. Like Moses, these writers act as though their prewritings are tantamount to tablets of stone that they have brought down from a mountain. They perceive no need to change the writing in any way, nor do they have the motivation to change. These writers often quip, "But I wrote it, didn't I?" For such writers, seeing the teacher who writes, who resists the seduction of not changing anything, who accepts the challenge to reenter the piece to discover the writing's potential, becomes a powerful model and makes the reentry into their writing easier, or at least more realistic.

Then there is the phenomenon of prewriting "by grace." Some writers sit down and write a draft without seeming to have to prewrite at all. Here the prewriting has already taken place internally, perhaps, to borrow Michael Polanyi's term, "tacitly" (20). The writer comes to the task already armed with an idea or a focus, with prewriting either done in the head or completed through some substrata of the psyche. This phenomenon may happen to any writer, at any time, without warning. It may also be the modus operandi of specific writers. In either case, it is upsetting to untrained teachers who insist on evidence of prewriting, who do not themselves write, who may hold rigidly to lock-step instruction, or who may view this as the down-from-the-mountain syndrome.

The difficulty with this internalized prewriting lies in the fact that, unlike jogging or chin-ups, thinking cannot be seen. Without any physical manifestation, other than a poised pencil or furrowed brow, or until a time when classrooms are equipped with a technology that permits lights positioned above students' desks or tables to glow with the same intensity as the students' minds, teachers are left to interpret the veracity of these unseen prewrites. Because for some students prewriting happens mentally, teachers who themselves write know how to look for observable signs of mental prewriting. They note the students who stare out the window before they write, those who must talk before writing, or those who doodle through the prewriting. They become keenly aware of activities that to the untrained eye may look like off-task behavior but are really evidences of prewriting.

The actor Kevin Kline spoke to a group of business people about the boss who fired the employee for leaning back with his feet on the desk. The boss could not accept the fact that the employee was thinking. Kline's humor revealed a subtle truth: Sometimes thinkers lean back and put up their feet. In classrooms where thinking occurs, in classrooms where thinking is encouraged and nurtured, teachers find ways to allow thinkers to lean back and put up their feet. Some teachers establish thinking corners with beanbags and pillows, or they create isolated areas cordoned off with refrigerator boxes. Tracy McDonald, Keller ISD, encourages her second-graders to set cardboard lightbulbs on their desks when they are thinking so classmates do not bother them. And this concept is not exclusive to the elementary school. Linda Maxwell, Klein ISD, provides pillows and carpet squares in the back of the room for her twelfth-grade students to use when they need time to think. Trivializing what cannot be seen is like giving lip service to cognition.

FACILITATING PREWRITING

There are several ways to facilitate the process of prewriting. One way is to introduce all the prewriting techniques—freewriting, wet ink, trigger words, free association, writing roulette, sentence stubs, journal writing, brainstorming, listing, blueprinting, drawing, looping, dialogue, reporter's formula, the pentad, classical invention, classical invention for the contemporary student, cubing, hexagonal writing, and webbing—teaching one after the other like rapid fire, until all have been experienced. Students develop a repertoire of strategies, and from that point on, they choose among these strategies, try them out with different genres, or pick one they think will work best.

The second approach is to introduce an appropriate prewriting technique almost guaranteed to produce the type of writing desired. For example, if a newspaper article is the desired outcome, the reporter's formula (who? what? where? why? when? how?) would be the natural prewriting technique. If students are working on narratives, introducing dialogue as a prewriting technique might help them focus on characters.

The third way to facilitate prewriting is to teach a different prewriting technique during minilessons as part of an integrated unit of study. The techniques should be appropriate to the activities underway. For example, if the study deals with the Holocaust, several children's books or excerpts from young adult novels (see the social studies implementation model in chapter 15, pages 496-498) may be taken as prompts for prewriting. Discussion groups or class discussion followed by freewriting might be another type of prompt, and the pentad might jog still another prewriting. By generating several prewritings related to one topic, students collect many starts from which to make a commitment to a longer, sustained, more substantive paper.

PREWRITING STRATEGIES

Because prewriting is recursive, folding back upon itself if more thinking is needed, writers often prewrite several times and use different prewriting techniques pulled from a pool of strategies. If one strategy does not work, another may. Helping students build a repertoire and encouraging choice promotes a comfort zone that invites fluency and specificity. Prewriting strategies also serve varied purposes. Although the prewriting strategies listed below often may be used for purposes other than those designated — for example, freewriting may be a warmup or a way to find or focus an idea — thereby blurring purposes, this list reflects the most natural heuristic of starting with simple warmups and ending with strategies that result in text analysis.

PREWRITING WARMUPS

Freewriting, wet ink, trigger words, and free association are prewriting strategies used to stimulate the brain, to get the kinks out, to "rev up" the motor for further writing. They may be used repeatedly as anticipatory sets or as sponge activities, the latter being for those minutes of downtime that sometimes occur after a lesson but before the bell.

Freewriting

Explanation. The mother of all prewriting is freewriting because it is just that: writing freely about whatever comes to mind without regard to punctuation, spelling, mechanics, grammar, or usage. Freewriting is the mind's dictation. The point is to freely receive the mind's offerings and record them, to simply get down as quickly as possible the thoughts flowing through the brain. Because the brain works faster than the hand, many writers even abbreviate when they freewrite in an effort to write as closely as possible what the mind says. Therefore, when the mind takes a turn, the writer takes the same turn. Often in these twists and curves lies the surprising view, the intuitive leap, or the hidden memory. Think of freewriting as a dialogue between the brain and the hand.

Implementation. When implementing freewriting, 10- or 15-minute challenges work best at first. The idea is to get the juices flowing. During that time, students write freely to get down whatever comes to mind. As William Faulkner says, "Get it down. Take chances. It may be bad, but it's the only way you will get something good." Gradually increase the time period. Because freewriting is the truest, purest, and most common prewriting technique, writers usually go with its flow.

Remarks. After freewriting has been implemented, all other prewriting techniques become variations, adaptations, or extensions of that strategy, either in their call for freely getting ideas down or in their permission not to become concerned at this point in the process with what Janet Emig calls "stylistic infelicities" (43): punctuation, spelling, and other mechanics.

Wet-Ink Writing

Explanation. A close cousin to freewriting, wet-ink writing invites nonstop writing in short bursts of time. Wet-ink writing derives its name from the days when writers dipped their quill pens into ink; it is the notion of writing so quickly there is literally no time for the ink to dry on the pen. Because the hand wearies quickly when not lifted from the paper, this prewriting strategy should not last more than one or two minutes. Its purpose is to allow the subconscious to sneak in an idea.

Implementation. To implement wet-ink writing in the classroom, students begin writing at a signal and stop at a signal. Again, they do not worry about mechanics because the purpose of this warmup is to increase fluency. If they cannot think of anything to write, they are to write "I can't think of anything," or, "Nothing comes to mind," until something does (and it usually does because the brain refuses to be bored).

Remarks. Wet-ink writing allows students to measure the increasing fluency of their writing. That is, the more they engage in these short bursts of writing, the easier it becomes to get words on paper.

Trigger Words

Explanation. Trigger words combine freewriting and free association. The idea is to jog the memory with a carefully chosen word. Because the brain is capable of almost infinite connections, trigger words sometimes serve as both a warmup and a strategy for finding an idea.

Implementation. To implement trigger words, the teacher calls out a word and everyone writes words, phrases, sentences, or anything that comes to mind. A variation of this, especially for a warmup, is to invite different students on different days to call out a word for this purpose. Afterward, students volunteer to share what they have written.

Remarks. Trigger words also may be used as a mini-lesson. For example, the word *bats* may be the trigger, and when someone (predictably) writes *Batmobile*, a clear allusion to Batman, the teacher may use it to teach the purpose of allusions in writing or literature. The trigger word *bumblebee* usually results in the word *buzz* and the teacher may use this in a mini-lesson on onomatopoeia.

Further, trigger words may reinforce a skill taught earlier. For example, the trigger word *flower* may be followed by the invitation to write appropriate adjectives to describe *flower*.

Free Association

Explanation. Free association belongs in the warmup category because it gets students thinking. It does this by setting up space between two words and inviting two-way, double-level connections:

OLD _____ SHOP

Students think of a word they associate with *old*, one that would make sense following *old*, such as the word *furniture*—old furniture. Then they test that word for a connection in front of *shop*—furniture shop. Thus the association works both ways: *old* furniture, furniture *shop*.

OLD <u>FURNITURE</u> SHOP

The purpose of this prewriting strategy is to break the usual thinking patterns, to literally free students to tap the resources of their brain. Free association shows students that the mind works in myriad ways to process information and to make connections with that information. As Ornstein and Thompson say in *The Amazing Brain*, "There are perhaps about one hundred billion neurons, or nerve cells, in the brain, and in a single human brain the number of possible interconnections between these cells is greater than the number of atoms in the universe" (21).

Implementation. To encourage thinking on two levels, the connections must work after one word and before another. This process may be stretched to three, four, or more blanks between the two words. For example:

HOUSE _____ _____ _____ SINK

Someone's thinking may go like this: HOUSE boat, boat in water, water faucet, faucet part of SINK.

HOUSE <u>BOAT</u> <u>WATER</u> <u>FAUCET</u> SINK

On the other hand, another's thinking may go from HOUSE to window, window to glass, glass to porcelain, porcelain to SINK.

HOUSE <u>WINDOW</u> <u>GLASS</u> <u>PORCELAIN</u> SINK

Connections may be made by creating compound words, by associating the previous word with something (as in *boat* and *water*), by thinking whole to part (as *window glass*), or vice versa, by linking the words grammatically or sequentially, or by some other logical connection. After students share their connections, they may want to talk about how they arrived at those connections.

Remarks. Free association provides a rich and unusual way to expand vocabulary, reinforce spelling, or challenge work on parts of speech. For example, students may find synonyms or antonyms for a free association as one way to expand vocabulary.

OLD _____ _____ ANCIENT

OLD <u>ANTIQUE</u> <u>ELDERLY</u> ANCIENT

Students may choose synonyms such as *antique, elderly, antiquated, hoary*, and *aged* or antonyms such as *young, youthful, kid, baby* and so forth. Depending on their choices, the next step is to discuss connotations and look up the words and discuss their denotations. After students freely associate, they may look up the spelling of the words they choose.

As a way to work with adjectives, students may freely associate a series of adjectives before a given noun. For example:

PEPPY, _____, _____, _____, _____ DOG

PEPPY, <u>WHITE</u>, <u>EXCITABLE</u>, <u>ENERGETIC</u>, <u>ADORABLE</u> DOG

Again students may come up with any appropriate adjectives. Discussion afterward provides a vehicle for students to explain their choices.

Another implication for free association is its possible use for collaboration. In one variation, groups work their way from one word to another on long strips of cash-register tape or large pieces of butcher paper. In another variation, individual students or groups may design their own versions by giving the first and last words and any specific directions, for example, nouns. They check to make sure their challenge will work, and then they present it to another person or group.

Finally, free association is an appropriate way to begin class. It warms up the brain, sets a tone in the classroom, and readies the students for work. It also may be used to conclude class by using words from the day's lesson.

PREWRITING FOR NARRATIVES

Often, warmups produce a nugget for a story, but sometimes when asked to write a story, students will replay, "I don't know what to write." One way to break through this barrier is using collaborative narratives, or writing roulette.

Explanation. Writing roulette is a prewriting strategy undertaken by a group to produce a collaborative narrative. These group-generated stories may be shared and enjoyed, honed and polished by individuals or the group, or used for mini-lessons on the elements of a narrative. Mostly, though, they are fun and work on almost every level.

Implementation. Each student takes out a sheet of paper and writes his or her name in the top right-hand corner. After a reminder that this is prewriting, the teacher directs the students to each begin a story that will be passed on to another student. Some brainstorming may precede this activity. Students write quickly until the teacher calls time. At that signal, each student passes his or her paper to the right. The student who receives the paper reads what has been written and continues the storyline. And so it goes until the teacher tells the students that this time when they receive the story, they should bring it to a close. Then volunteers share their stories.

Remarks. Students find writing roulette enjoyable and nonthreatening. Teachers like the way it fosters fluency and provides a way into the narrative. The word *roulette* connotes chance, which makes the activity nonthreatening because each student anticipates what is coming. What results is a tangible story in a prewritten form, but it is something with which to work. There may be flat characters, hints of other elements, and little or no elaboration, yet the spontaneity yields funny, weird, sometimes poignant, and usually creative stories. The activity could end there, but the true power of this prewriting strategy lies in what it enables the teacher to do as follow-up.

Teacher and students brainstorm all the skills needed to produce this group story: everything from handwriting to reading and from following a plot line to other elements of a narrative. After the brainstorming, class discussion centers on the implications of writing roulette. What ultimately emerges are the realizations that writing and reading improve by writing and reading, and that knowledge and correct use of grammar, punctuation, and usage aid readers' understanding of what has been written.

Second, this activity supports reentry for revision by the group. For example, a mini-lesson on transitions using "signposting," John Trimble's word for transitions that signal "the kind of thought that is coming next" (51), provides an image. Students easily remember the parallel between signposts that help travelers find their way along roads and signpostings that help readers find their way through writing. Transitional words and phrases, repetitions, and rhetorical devices become important because they are immediately applicable to the group story. Signposting gives students—who have been exposed to large doses of jump cuts on television and in film and who often eschew transitions, expecting the reader to follow their thoughts—a concrete device to help the reader along. Additionally, working collaboratively on a story underscores the need for transitions because all students will not follow the connections throughout the story in the same way.

PREWRITING STRATEGIES FOR FINDING A TOPIC

One of the most obvious reasons for prewriting is to find a topic. Sentence stubs, journal writing, brainstorming, listing, blueprinting, and drawing enable students to call upon their own knowledge and experiences and those of others to find a topic. When these strategies are used in the classroom, students rarely complain, "I don't have anything to write about."

Sentence Stubs

Explanation. Sentence stubs are open-ended sentence fragments meant to be finished and meant to spark enough interest so that more writing will follow. The idea is that when the students finish that sentence stub, they continue writing out of it in an effort to find a topic.

Implementation. The teacher writes a sentence stub on the board or overhead projector and invites students to finish the sentence and continue with whatever thought the sentence generates. The teacher writes, too. A sampling of sentence stubs might read:

> Today I thought ...
>
> Once when I was little ...
>
> I like ...
>
> My wish list would include ...
>
> I wish I knew ...

Remarks. Sentence stubs are to be used sparingly, and then only as a nudge. They are short, simple, and positive, and should be kept universal so they appeal to all students regardless of background. For instance, "My favorite vacation ..." is not a good sentence stub because not all students may have had a vacation.

Journal Writing

Explanation. Writing in a journal is perhaps the most ancient of all prewriting techniques. There are records of journal keepers from antiquity; consider King Sargon of Agade (2334-2279 B.C.), who wrote detailed accounts on cuneiform tablets, as did his daughter Enheduanna (Barnstone and Barnstone 1). There are records of journals among the literati, such as *Walden* by Henry David Thoreau; there are also neophyte writers who keep journals.

> *My mother kept her journal in my dad's unused bookkeeping ledgers. Her writing extends from page edge to page edge; it ignores all lines and margins. As she approaches her eightieth birthday, she has bequeathed a legacy of over fifty of these large rectangular books filled with memories, thoughts, collected maxims, facts, speculations, poetry, stories her mother told her, and stories of her mother's mother.*

Among the first in recent years to legitimize journals as prewriting was Dorothy Lambert. Her "Keeping a Journal" (1965) was followed by Joyce Armstrong Carroll's "Journal-Making" (1972) and a spate of others. Anne Ruggles Gere extended the concept into writing to learn when she edited *Roots in the Sawdust* (1985), and Toby Fulwiler gathered much of the existing information on journals in his *The Journal Book* (1987).

Journals gain power through accumulation and connection. People who keep journals are committed to writing, usually at a certain time each day, so it becomes habitual. Over a period of time this writing takes on a life and begins to speak on its own. Earlier entries, because of time and space, are regarded with a fresh eye. They nudge their way into honed pieces, longer writing. Bits of one entry may blur into parts of another; some entries are never touched again. They may have served another purpose, perhaps "getting something out of the system," or, as Natalie Goldberg puts it, simply by "'writing down the bones,' the essential, awake speech of their minds" (4). Whatever their function, journals remain a testimony to the mysterious workings of the human mind.

Some people confuse journals kept at school with diaries kept at home. Diaries lock in the most intimate feelings and reflections—the goings and comings of family members, problems, and so on. Journals open up reflection on interesting topics and questions, not intimacies. In this world of immediacy, where quick answers, brief news reports, and instant replay are the norm, keeping a journal provides a place for students to attain depth of thought, substance, continuity, and elaboration of an idea.

Writing in journals is primarily a reflexive act—from self for self. Therefore, writing in journals is often abbreviated, fragmented, and sometimes surreal. In a sense, journals are like dreams. Susanne Langer could have been describing journals when she wrote:

> The most noteworthy formal characteristic of dream is that the dreamer is always at the center of it. Places shift, persons act and speak, or change or fade—facts emerge, situations grow, objects come into view with strange importance, ordinary things infinitely valuable or horrible, and they may be superseded by others that are related to them essentially by feeling, not by natural proximity. But the dreamer is always "there." (quoted in MacCann 201)

So it is, too, with the journal writer, who is always at the center of the entry. Consider Will Durant's description of Leonardo da Vinci's journal: "He wrote five thousand pages, but never completed one book.... They are written from right to left.... His grammar is poor, his spelling is individualistic ... he is 'a medley of brilliant fragments'" (217). Da Vinci's jumbled drawings of bones, plants, buildings, geometrical forms, airplanes, horses' heads, and organs of human beings are juxtaposed with written explorations, treatises, descriptions, vivid accounts of battles, and eloquent aggregations on science and art. But always da Vinci is center.

Implementation. Implementing journals must be accompanied by many specifics. All must be clear on the journal's purpose, the time relegated to journal keeping, the privacy of this compilation of prewriting, and how the journal is to be used. The class may brainstorm, discuss, and eventually create a list of do's and don'ts that all class members—teacher and students—are expected to uphold.

On the one hand, allow plenty of time for the habit of journal keeping to take root. At first, students may write superficially, but in time and with proper instruction and modeling by the teacher, students find their authentic voice and their own rhythm. On the other hand, if the enthusiasm for journal keeping wanes and writing deteriorates into a mundane list of daily routines, forgo journal keeping for a time. Give it a rest.

Above all, journals should not be employed simply as a classroom management tool. Too often a teacher implements journal keeping to give students something to do during roll and other housekeeping tasks. Students soon realize this, so their entries become the trivial, bland, boring: "I got up. I brushed my teeth. I went to school on the bus." If the teacher wants to underscore journal keeping as valuable and important, the teacher should keep a journal, too, and write in it during journal time.

Remarks. So common have journals become and so widely are they used in academe that misunderstandings and misconceptions have run rampant. Some people who have used the journal as a way to chronicle what they have read in literature or who have used a journal as a dialectical notebook for writing in social studies, for example, may think that keeping a journal for prewriting is a way to peek into the personal. They are misinformed. The journal as prewriting is a place to write and no one, especially not the teacher, has the right to enter that domain unless invited. Students choose sections to share. If journals are used to respond to readings or in other disciplines, discussion of what is an appropriate entry helps students understand the journal's purpose.

Often renaming school-kept journals refreshes the concept and realigns it to its classroom purpose. A more specific name can focus the objective: prewritings, daybooks, logs, learning logs, reading lots, literature logs, content journals, dialogue journals, dialectical notebooks, writers' notebooks, and notebooks. Some students name their own journals: "Prewriting Perks," "Jesse's Journal," "Notes by Nanci," or "the Log Lady."

Brainstorming

Explanation. Brainstorming is a collaborative prewriting strategy. In a sense, the class becomes a macrocosm of the microcosm of the brain because this activity works the way the brain works, with connections made among the students the way neurons make connections in the brain. The purpose of brainstorming, as with all prewriting, is to unfetter the brain and to get the ideas down. Decisions on those ideas come later.

Implementation. With brainstorming, students call out what they associate with the prompt. The teacher or a designated scribe writes all offerings on a chart or board. Brainstorming allows students to "storm their brains" aloud and listen to others storm theirs. Students freely advance their ideas, without worrying whether these ideas sound silly or unrelated. Students also piggyback on the ideas of others, listen to all offerings, and find inspiration for their own responses. After a brainstorming session, students may discuss ways to move on the ideas generated by the group.

Remarks. Because brainstorming is a group list, even the most reticent students get caught up in it. And because it is totally noncritical, wonderful ideas often present themselves. It is somewhat as Einstein explained: "As one grows older, one sees the impossibility of imposing one's will on the chaos with brute force. But if you're patient, there may come that moment, when while eating an apple, the solution presents itself politely and says, 'Here I am'" (Sohn 35).

Listing

Explanation. Listing is the most familiar of the prewriting activities. People make lists for shopping; they generate lists of "things to do," "pros and cons," "do's and don'ts"; almost everyone has written a wish list or two. Listing calls upon both the left and right sides of the brain because lists may be logical, with one thing following another in sequential order, or they may be serendipitous, with one item causing an unexpected turn, a surprising thought, or an intriguing possibility.

Implementation. The trick when implementing listing is for students not to generate one list, but several. Students take the general topic and then quickly write all the associations that come to mind. Then they use their associations as prompts for additional lists. For example, *friends* may be the general topic. This prompt may spark the associations *food, parties, school, football games*, and so forth. Each of these, in turn, may then become a prompt. After several minutes on each prompt, students study their compilations in search of connections or items that seem to go together. Then they focus on the connection, something not on the list, as they begin to freewrite.

Remarks. Often with listing, the idea does not lie in something actually listed but rather in the exploration of the connections among the words, phrases, or sentences on the lists. It is as if the idea resides in the spaces of the lists, not in the words themselves. Think of listing as an individual brainstorming session.

Blueprinting

Explanation. Blueprinting rises out of an idea in Peter Stillman's book *Families Writing* (14-16). As a prompt for finding something to write about, Stillman suggests drawing a floor plan of a house remembered.

Implementation. Implementing blueprinting is both easy and fun. First students draw a floor plan of a house or apartment they remember. They use a sheet of paper for each floor. Next they label each room with the term they comfortably called the room: kitchen, Dad's workroom, Sis's room, and so forth. Using these labels as column heads, they write as many columns as rooms.

Then they write words, phrases, sentences, names, or activities under the appropriate columns as their memory jumps from one to the other. When they feel they have exhausted their memories, they reread what they have written. Again they look for connections, things that happened in one room that connect in some way to another. They circle these items and draw the connections with a network of lines. On a fresh sheet of paper they freewrite about these connections.

Remarks. Blueprinting, which is closely tied to drawing, allows students to re-create places that hold memories that they then may choose to write about. The visualization of some remembered place catches the writer off guard sometimes, and in that instant can be clarity of perception that illuminates an idea.

> *When I tried this activity with a group of sixth-graders, I found myself drawing in detail the back porch of our house on Walling Street. There I played jacks, paper dolls, Old Maid, Uncle Wiggly, and other games during the humid, close summer days in an industrial town. I hadn't thought of that back porch in years, but as I drew it the way it came off our big kitchen, I could hear the four o'clock whistle like a shrilling hag screaming to the workmen that their day of labor was over and reminding us kids to get ready for supper. Writing from that reminder came easily then.*

Drawing

Explanation. Drawing enables students to create visual metaphors that often represent extra-ordinary ways to look at ordinary things, events, and people. Sometimes topics are lodged in a basically nonverbal mode and need to make their first escape through nonverbal means.

Implementation. After students read a story, discuss an issue, or receive some other prompt, they are invited to draw what they think or feel. It is important to distinguish this drawing from art. As a prewriting strategy, drawing is a way to release visual images from the mind, not an attempt to create art. (See "Drawing into Meaning: A Powerful Writing Tool," reprinted at the end of this chapter, pages 96-100.)

Remarks. Traditionally, teachers thought of drawing as something only primary students did. More recently, with the growing corpus of information gleaned from brain study and cognitive developmental research, more teachers on all levels consider drawing a powerful prewriting tool. In her book *Authors of Pictures, Draughtsmen of Words*, Ruth Hubbard recounts the story about e. e. cummings, who drew and painted daily. When asked once by an interviewer whether the drawing got in the way of the writing, cummings replied, "Quite on the contrary: they love each other dearly" (5-6).

PREWRITING ACTIVITIES FOR FOCUSING A TOPIC

There are times when a topic is a given and the student is expected to find a focus on that topic, or, as it is more commonly stated to students, to "narrow the topic." Looping, dialogue, and reporter's formula help students do this. Students begin with a general or broad topic and strategically progress to the specific, thereby setting a deductive line of argument or thought.

Looping

Explanation. The beauty of looping, a term coined by Peter Elbow (1981, 59), lies in the fact that students experience a prewriting strategy that not only helps them focus but also enables them to find their writing "centers of gravity," as Elbow calls them (1973, 20). These centers pull the students; they are the nuggets nestled within the writing that hold some attraction, a promise that they would be worth writing about.

Implementation. Looping begins with a topic that the students write at the top of a sheet of paper. Then the students freewrite for 5 to 10 minutes on that topic. Next they read what they have written, remaining alert to what tugs them. Finally they circle that "center of gravity." The first loop is complete. At this point in the looping experience, students may share their "centers of gravity." This helps them see that given a general topic and the opportunity to explore that topic, each person will gravitate to a different center or focus.

For the second loop, students use their centers of gravity as their prompts. Now each writer loops off in her or his own specific direction. Again students write for 5 to 10 minutes. Again they read what they have written, and again they circle their centers of gravity.

After the third loop is achieved by repeating the experience, students discuss what they have written. Some may immediately see a pattern — from the general to the specific — and feel comfortable about a deductive approach to their paper. Others may see that they need to loop further. Still others may see too much repetition. Whatever the result, the students have something to pursue.

Remarks. During the sharing times, students may see a repeated idea that is worth their concentration, or they may notice that they have strayed from the topic. Many times students do not get a choice of topics. They may be assigned an essay on a broad subject such as the Civil War. Looping helps students narrow such broad topics. They learn one way to build an organized and focused piece of writing.

Dialogue

Explanation. Dialogue works well as a prewriting activity because it is natural. Because people dialogue daily on various topics, this naturalness may be captured as potential for writing. Students take a topic and create a hypothetical conversation between two people about that topic. (See Priscilla Zimmerman's "Writing for Art Appreciation," pp. 31-45, in Anne Ruggles Gere's *Roots in the Sawdust*.) This strategy stretches students to look at the topic from more than one perspective, and often during this stretching students are surprised or intrigued, or find themselves wanting or needing more information.

Implementation. Students take a topic and quickly generate a list using the topic as a prompt. Then they circle several things on the list that suggest potential for writing. They freewrite on each of these for several minutes. Using the information generated during the freewriting, they prewrite a dialogue. Often providing the first line in the dialogue helps students get started. To avoid dialogue turning into monologue, limit the number of lines allowed each speaker. Ultimately students rework the dialogue into a draft.

Remarks. This strategy permits ancillary teaching of the various conventions for formatting, indenting, and punctuating dialogue. Dialogue invites students to hear at least two sides of a topic, gets them to use their imagination and sense of humor, and provides a way to analyze a topic.

Reporter's Formula

Explanation. Reporter's formula is a prewriting technique based on the standard journalistic approach to gathering information—who? what? where? why? when? how? By using the reporter's basic questions, a writer may plumb the depths, uncover the hidden, or startle the unexpected onto the blank page.

Implementation. One way to implement this technique in one class period, a way adapted from *Seeking Diversity* by Linda Rief, is to establish a comfort zone by using this as a get-acquainted activity.

1. Distribute three 5-by-8-inch index cards to each student as she or he enters the room.

2. Invite students to choose a partner, preferably someone they know the least about or someone they want to know better. Allot three minutes.

3. After students are settled, instruct them to fold two cards in half and number each section respectively, 1, 2, 3, 4. They number the unfolded card 5. Allot one minute.

4. In section 1, remind students of the who, what, where, why, when, and how questions. Then tell them to generate five questions they want to ask their partner. Allot five minutes.

5. Students ask their partner the questions they have generated and record answers in section 2. Allot seven minutes.

6. Students read the answers. They circle the one answer that they like best, that they want to know more about, or that surprises them. In section 3 they generate four to six more questions that focus on the circled answer. Allot five minutes.

7. In section 4, students record their partner's answers. This time they try to capture the exact words and body language of their partner. Allot seven minutes.

8. Students use the card numbered 5, both sides if needed, to write a draft based on the answers. Encourage students to hook the reader immediately with a zippy opener, to use direct quotes, and to find an "angle." Allot twelve minutes.

9. Students read their draft to their partner, who confirms or corrects the facts and points out what he or she likes. Allot three minutes.

10. Students revise, title, and put their name on the card. Allot three minutes.

11. Invite volunteers to share aloud. Allot five to six minutes. Students then give their gift of words to their partner.

12. Debrief. Allot two to three minutes.

Remarks. This activity may be used as an introduction to research. Students gather data, analyze that data, identify a focus, refocus, gather more data, synthesize, and present the data concisely and correctly. Another way to use this activity is to teach leads appropriate for what has been written on the last card.

RHETORICAL STRATEGIES

Rhetoric, *eiro* in Greek, means simply, "I say." When students practice rhetorical invention (prewriting) such as the pentad, classical invention, classical invention for the contemporary student, and cubing, they develop strategies that enable them to come closer to what they want or need to say.

The Pentad

Explanation. The pentad is an elegantly simple strategy that invites writers to examine an event, a happening, or a piece of literature as if it were a drama with actors, acts, scenes, purposes, and agencies pivoting on human motives and motifs. Adapted from Kenneth Burke's five key terms of dramatism, fully explained in "The Five Key Terms of Dramatism" (155-162) as well as in his *A Grammar of Motives*, the pentad turns the elements of the drama into generating principles or questions. By concentrating on one of these five terms, students are free not to have to write everything. What usually emerges is a depth of focus and a blend of one or two of the other elements.

For example, if students are prewriting about Robert Frost's "Out, Out!" they might be given this generic set of questions:

Actors: Who did the action?

Acts: What was done?

Scenes: When or where was it done?

Agencies: How was it done?

Purposes: Why was it done?

Several students may choose to focus on who (the boy, the sister, the doctor, the saw), whereas others may opt for where (the hills of Vermont or the yard) or why (the reason for the boy's death). Although each student may write to his or her chosen focus, all will find their writing touching upon the other elements, albeit tangentially.

Implementation. When implementing the pentad, it is helpful to first talk about the topic or read or discuss the piece of literature that students are about to explore through prewriting. Then invite students to draw a five-pointed star as their prewriting graphic. At each point on the star they write one of the elements of drama—actor(s), act(s), scene(s), agency(ies), and purpose(s). In the center of the star they write the topic or the title of the piece of literature. Finally students make a commitment to one point on the star, and they freewrite to that focus.

After the freewriting, students draw a triangle to join their focus element to one or two other points they found themselves emphasizing most—the parts they dramatized the most. That triangle becomes the focus for their paper.

Remarks. Using this prewriting strategy minimizes rambling because students focus on one element. Then they are able to dramatize or emphasize that focus, although not to the exclusion of other significant elements. Finally, the pentad helps students come closer to uncovering the human motives of the "drama."

Classical Invention

Explanation. Classical invention is an adaptation of the principles found in Aristotle's *Art of Rhetoric*, the oldest extant textbook on the subject. Aristotle believed in the practical value of rhetoric and that rhetoric is the faculty of discovery. Therefore, Aristotle developed a set of principles that he believed aided in the discovery of precepts such as truth, wisdom, and a sense of the aesthetic. If speakers defined their topic, compared and contrasted it, explained its relationship to other like topics, investigated its circumstances, and provided testimony about the topic, their speech would be thorough and well organized. Aristotle's rhetoric is still applied to speeches and also has been applied to the realm of writing.

Implementation. Implement classical invention as a heuristic: Move from the simple to the more difficult questions hierarchically. Working first as a class, let students choose an interesting topic. Guide students through the generic questions based on Aristotle's principles. These questions may be applied to a wide range of topics. If answers give rise to other questions, encourage students to follow the new line of thought. Keep in mind that classical invention is not a rigid set of rules. Aristotle's principles are:

1. Definition: Define the topic. What connotations may be applied to this topic? Can this topic be divided into parts?
Here the writer begins with the basic definition and takes into consideration connotations and any division of the topic. For example, if the topic is drugs, students use the dictionary to define drugs. They offer their definitions of drugs. They then may divide drugs into prescription drugs and street drugs.

2. Comparison: How is this topic similar to other like topics? To what degree? How is it different? To what degree?
On this level the writer thinks of the topic as similar to and different from something else. Then the writer investigates the degree of that difference. Students may, for example, compare drugs to other things that get people high, such as winning a sporting event. They may discuss degree by comparing synthetic or artificial highs to natural ones.

3. Relationship: What causes or caused this topic? What are its effects? What came before it? What are its opposites?
When writers work with relationship they are looking for cause and effect or antecedent and consequence. For example, students may research the beginnings of a specific drug, such as aspirin, and trace its effects. They may look at a consequence, such as drug abuse, and attempt to ascertain its antecedent.

4. Circumstance: What makes this topic possible? What would make it impossible? What are some past facts about this topic? What are some future predictions about it?
Circumstance in Aristotelian terms emphasizes the qualities and conditions that make something possible or impossible. Examining past conditions aids predictions. With the topic drugs, for instance, students may talk about how high technology and research monies make possible the variety and effectiveness of prescription drugs, or they may talk about how dropouts, gangs, or lack of adequate policing make possible street drugs. With either they may make predictions.

5. Testimony: Find statistics about the topic. Are there any sayings, rules, laws, precedents, or maxims about this topic? What do credible sources say about it? Have there been any testimonials about it?
Testimonials have always been part of what makes people buy into a product, an idea, or a project. Investigating what people have said about a topic provides prewriting information that may later be worked into the draft. For example, reading what the editors of *The Michigan Daily*, in their supplement *Student Life*, had to say in an editorial titled "Pot: The Newest 'U' Tradition" (Reaske and Willson 109-111), is considerably different from reading *Worst Pills Best Pills*, which was based on 1985 data from the *National Disease and Therapeutic Index* and had a medical advisory board of 18 medical doctors (Wolfe). Discerning degrees of credibility is an important discovery for students.

Susan Partida, a teacher in Killeen ISD, Texas, adapted Aristotle's classical invention for her Chapter I students. She called it "Let's Invent!" and she used it with various topics to show her students how to get information on a topic.

A. Meaning
    1. What does your topic mean?
    2. What group is your topic in?

B. Like or Different
    1. How is your topic like something else?
    2. How is your topic different from something else?
    3. Is there anything better than your topic? What?

C. Cause or Effect
    1. Why does your topic happen?
    2. What happens after your topic?

D. Talk
    1. What have I heard people say about my topic?
    2. What do my friends think about my topic?

E. Yes, No, or Maybe
    1. Is my topic possible? Why?
    2. Is my topic impossible? Why?

Rudiger, a fourth-grader, wrote:

The Key to Happiniss

The key to happiness is being able to have your own skeateboard, car, and yur own house. The first step is the gold rule treate others as you want them to treat you. Second step is to not be mean. Third step is to help others when they need help. And that will open the dorr to happines.

Cori, a second-grade student, wrote:

Happiness

Happiness is a evry special feeling. Sometime poepole make you feel glad.

Happiness mean a evry special feeling inside after the test.

Remarks. When students follow Aristotle's principles in their prewriting, they make discoveries. They may have to scramble to libraries for some answers, but the research is more organic, rising out of the questions. There is direction and organization, and when they are through, they have preliminary information to use. Perhaps, like the people of Athens—who delighted in the power of language to move minds and influence actions, considering it somewhat magical—students may begin considering what they evoke through classical invention as somewhat magical, too.

Classical Invention for the Contemporary Student

Explanation. Richard L. Larson tailored the principles of Aristotle to fit the needs of today's students. Larson's "Plan for Teaching Rhetorical Invention" constitutes a useful heuristic for writing about single items; events or processes; abstract concepts; collections of items; or completed events, propositions, or questions. This rhetorical approach is both simple and practical and provides a systematic way to approach any topic. Perhaps more important, teachers may use these heuristics to model additional questions even better suited to the needs of their curriculum and students.

Implementation. Students choose a single item to write about. The teacher introduces Larson's 15 questions that are applicable to "Writing about Single Items" (in present existence) (152). The first question, "What are its precise physical characteristics (shape, dimensions, composition, etc.)?" is a concrete one that clearly outlines for the writer a way into analyzing any item. From that point questions range from "How do the parts of it work together?" to "Who uses it? for what?" After answering all these questions as part of prewriting, students have collected information that may be useful in writing their papers.

To prewrite about events, repeat the procedure. For events, Larson offers such questions as, "Exactly what happened? What were its causes? What does its occurrence imply? What action (if any) is called for?" and, "Is it (in general) good or bad? By what standard? How do we arrive at the standard?"

When guiding students into writing about abstract concepts; collections of items; or groups of completed events, including processes, propositions, or questions, use the appropriate heuristic of questions as probes. With these rhetorical strategies, students have an organizing principle to guide them in possibly ferreting out pertinent information on any given topic. (Larson's plan in its entirety may be found on pages 152-154 in *Contemporary Rhetoric*.)

Remarks. Larson explains:

> As for invention—until very recently we have done little to help the student. When we awakened to the simple notion that we needed to help the student gain ideas, we resorted too often to what I call the "smelly-looky-feely" gimmicks that were based on the notion that if students could be brought alive to the sensual world around them, they would have things to say. Which was right, as far as it went. But rhetorical invention has a profounder meaning than awakening students to their senses and having them produce haiku about autumn leaves, sandpaper, and limburger cheese. We live not only in a sensual world but in a world of ideas and concepts, and it is to this world that rhetorical invention addresses itself. (144-145)

Cubing

Explanation. Cubing is a prewriting strategy defined by Gregory Cowan and Elizabeth Cowan in *Writing* as a technique designed to help the writer learn to look at a subject from a variety of perspectives (21). During this prewriting, students quickly shift perspectives on a topic, usually a thing, by describing it; associating it with some experience, person, or event; applying it in some way; analyzing it by breaking it into parts; comparing it to or contrasting it with something; and finally arguing for or against it—taking a stand. By writing something for each of these, the writer progresses through Bloom's taxonomy and uses higher levels of thinking.

Implementation. Implementing cubing may be done by distributing a commercially wrapped cube-shaped caramel candy. Together the class orally progresses through the six cubing levels using the caramel as the thing they are cubing. For example:

1. How would you describe the caramel you are holding to someone who is not in the room?

2. Does the caramel remind you of something you have experienced? Does it make you think of someone, something, or some event in your life?

3. What kinds of things can you do with or to the caramel?

4. Think of the caramel in parts. How would you separate the caramel into those parts?

5. What other confection is similar to the caramel? How is it like that confection? What other confection is unlike the caramel? Explain the difference.

6. Do you like caramels or not? Why or why not?

After this oral model, students may cube in writing something they have chosen. After they write to the six perspectives, they make choices about whether or not to incorporate all of the perspectives or several of them into one paper, focus on one perspective, blur two or three together, or omit one that emerges as weak or unrelated.

Remarks. Teachers sometimes make a large cube with the different perspectives written on each side to make cubing concrete. This technique is especially helpful for students needing structure.

PREWRITING ABOUT LITERATURE

Aristotle cautions, "It is not sufficient to know what one ought to say, but one must also know how to say it." Often when writing about literature (or other subjects in the curriculum), students know what to say but are at a loss for how to say it. The prewriting strategies of hexagonal writing and webbing reconcile these two aspects.

Hexagonal Writing

Explanation. Hexagonal writing is a heuristic for writing about literature. It extends the cubing concept of writing about things to literature. Based on Bloom's taxonomy and Cowan's cubing, hexagonal writing enables students to produce six perspectives on a piece of literature, which may be shaped into a unified response. In addition, it provides an inventive way to teach literature, one that engages students through its systematic movement into higher levels and challenging through. Hexagonal writing results in an authentic, layered response because it moves the reader/writer from simple plot summaries toward elaborated text analysis. Using a heuristic for responding to a literary piece, as table 3.1 shows, students move from the plot summary, which is Bloom's knowledge level, to evaluation, called the judgment level in cognitive taxonomy.

Implementation. To help students see the connections between cubing and hexagonal writing, many teachers have students make manipulatives. Because the making of this manipulative works on all levels, Marsha Lilly, mathematics coordinator for Alief ISD, uses it to reinforce higher level thinking skills. Adapted here, it serves as an English language arts manipulative that may be used again and again.

Table 3.1.

Cognitive/Prewriting Taxonomy

Cognitive Taxonomy	Cubing	Hexagonal
1. Knowledge/memory	Describe it	Literal level/plot summary
2. Comprehension	Associate it	Personal allusions
3. Application	Apply it	Theme (social/universal)
4. Analysis	Analyze it	Analyze/literary devices
5. Synthesis	Compare/contrast it	Literary allusions
6. Judgment	Argue for or against it	Evaluation

1. Take three colored strips of construction paper that measure 15 by 3 inches.

2. Measure off five 3-inch squares on each strip.

3. Leave the first square blank on one strip.

4. Write D/P (Describe/Plot) in the second square.

5. Leave the third square blank and write A/PA (Associate/Personal Allusions) in the fourth square.

6. Leave the last square on the strip blank.

7. On the second strip, write A/T (Apply/Theme) in the second square and A/A (Analyze/Analyze) in the fourth square.

8. On the third strip, write C/LA (Compare/Literary Allusions) in the second square and A/E (Argue/Evaluate) in the fourth square.

9. The final challenge is to fold the three strips on the lines and fashion them into a cube. All the letters must show, and the cube must be capable of being tossed in the air without coming apart. (Students who finish first may help others make their cubes.)

From this point on, each student has a concrete representation for the hexagonal process he or she will apply when responding to literature. As the teacher moves them through the heuristic, students turn their cubes to the appropriate letters. In time, students work this heuristic individually. It becomes internalized when students respond to literature by giving much more than a rehash of the plot.

Remarks. Hexagonal writing may be used on any level. It works equally well for the advanced high-school student prewriting for a paper on *Hamlet* and for the kindergartener who may be orally engaged in discussing *Beauty and the Beast*. Table 3.2 (see page 82) shows how a teacher might develop the hexagonal heuristic for high school or for kindergarten. The structure is the same for both levels, only the vocabulary changes.

By using hexagonal writing, teachers have at their disposal a ready way to discuss literature. For example, when approaching a short story unit in an anthology, teachers may begin with one story and invite either written or oral plot summaries as a way into the story. For the next story, students may quickly summarize and then share personal allusions. The third story in the unit may

Table 3.2.

Hexagonal Heuristics for Two Levels

Hamlet	*Beauty and the Beast*
1. Retell the plot of *Hamlet*.	1. Tell the story of *Beauty and the Beast* in your own words.
2. Does *Hamlet* remind you of anything or anyone in your life?	2. Does this story make you think of something or someone?
3. Brainstorm possible themes.	3. What is the author trying to tell you?
4. Choose a scene from *Hamlet*. Discuss the figurative language in that scene.	4. What parts of *Beauty and the Beast* are believable? What parts are unbelievable?
5. How is *Hamlet* like or unlike other pieces of literature you have studied?	5. How is this story like some other stories you have heard?
6. Answer these three questions in sentences: a. Do you like *Hamlet* or not? b. What makes you think/feel that way? c. What specifically in the play makes you think/feel that way? Quote this and explain.	6. Answer these three questions. a. Did you like the story *Beauty and the Beast* or not? b. Why do you like or not like it? c. Can you remember something in the story you especially liked or did not like?

build on the two previous approaches before students discuss its theme. The fourth story may be approached through an accumulation of the previous three plus an analysis of one or several of the story's literary devices. Students move through story five using the preceding four levels but concentrating on comparisons and contrasts with other literary works, films, song lyrics, current events, historical events, or whatever the teacher thinks appropriate. The important thing to remember is that at this level it is the thinking and connecting that are important. Finally, students evaluate the sixth story after they have taken that story through all its other levels. This heuristic serves two purposes: Students experience using all levels of cognition on one piece of literature, and they learn the importance of not making a snap judgment by jumping from a simple reading of the story or plot summary to a judgment of that story.

Generally there will be several remaining stories in the unit. The teacher may then invite the students to choose one to evaluate through hexagonal writing and eventually polish this as a final paper. The same approach may be used with younger students with trade books or selections from their language arts or reader texts.

Webbing

Explanation. Webbing, sometimes called *semantic webbing* (Freedman and Reynolds 677), *semantic mapping* (Pearson and Johnson 324), or *clustering* (Rico 10) is one of the most popular of the prewriting techniques. It enjoys this popularity for three reasons: its versatility, its controlled easiness, and its instant tapping of right and left modes of thinking and learning. Webbing may be used on any topic to generate ideas for any mode of writing, or it may be used to organize ideas related to or integrated with a core idea or topic.

Implementation. Students of any age can draw the diagram – a central circle with extending lines – because it looks so much like a sun and its rays, an image that makes sense in an archetypal way to students. The central thought, topic, or story (literature) title is written in the "sun" with tangential thoughts radiating out from the sun's center. Some versions of this technique encourage writing along the line; others terminate the line with a word that is then circled; still others use arrows to indicate the direction of the thought. Whatever the version, enacting this prewriting technique enables writers to access what Rico calls their "design mind" (28). Webbing usually results in a plethora of ideas that may be turned into writing.

Remarks. Webbing makes visible an invisible, nonlinear process of mixed and matched thought, associations, experiences, moods, dreams, imaginings, and feelings. Writers first spill out onto the page without anxiety. When they reenter the web in search of patterns, they call upon the "design mind" and then the "sign mind" (Rico 17). Rico calls this "writing the natural way"; Euclid calls it bringing order out of chaos.

CONCLUSION

Some teachers try to categorize prewriting by making it a stage, one taken on Monday and followed by a different stage each day, resulting in a finished product on Friday. In a true writing classroom, writing does not happen on command on designated days. Although time certainly may be set aside for prewriting, the process simply does not occur in clear, lock-step stages. There are times when an idea hits with such force that it is a waste to spend any more time hunting for one. When that happens, less time is needed for generating the idea and more time is needed for extending and elaborating it. At other times, several days are required to discover an idea or a focus. Still other times, what at first seemed to be a good idea or a workable focus emerges as false and needs to be scrapped. Finally, there are times when the writer returns to prewriting after several drafts or even during revising or proofreading the final copy. Thus, just as the process of writing is recursive, so is each of the processes within that process. The skilled teacher allows for these ebbs and flows, for individual rhythms, and for the turning inward and turning outward nature of writing.

APPLICATION

Divide into groups. Each group chooses one or more of the prewriting strategies to try. Afterward in a large group session, discuss findings, observations, and implications of each strategy.

WORKS CITED

Aristotle. *Art of Rhetoric.* Cambridge: Harvard University Press, 1932.

Barnstone, Aliki, and Willis Barnstone. *A Book of Women Poets from Antiquity to Now.* New York: Schocken Books, 1980.

Burke, Kenneth. "The Five Key Terms of Dramatism." In *Contemporary Rhetoric: A Conceptual Background with Readings*, W. Ross Winterowd, ed. New York: Harcourt Brace Jovanovich, 1975.

_____. *A Grammar of Motives.* Berkeley: University of California Press, 1969.

Carroll, Joyce Armstrong. "Journal-Making." *Media & Methods* (November 1972): 61-63.

Cowan, Gregory, and Elizabeth Cowan. *Writing.* New York: John Wiley, 1980.

Durant, Will. *The Renaissance.* Vol. 5, *The Story of Civilization.* New York: Simon & Schuster, 1957.

Elbow, Peter. *Writing with Power.* New York: Oxford University Press, 1981.

_____. *Writing Without Teachers.* New York: Oxford University Press, 1973.

Emig, Janet. *The Composing Process of Twelfth Graders.* Urbana, IL: National Council of Teachers of English, 1971.

Freedman, Glenn, and Elizabeth G. Reynolds. "Enriching Basal Reader Lessons with Semantic Webbing." *The Reading Teacher* (March 1980): 677-684.

Fulwiler, Toby, ed. *The Journal Book.* Portsmouth, NH: Heinemann Educational Books, 1987.

Gere, Anne Ruggles, ed. *Roots in the Sawdust: Writing to Learn Across the Disciplines.* Urbana, IL: National Council of Teachers of English, 1985.

Goldberg, Natalie. *Writing Down the Bones.* Boston: Shambhala, 1986.

Hubbard, Ruth. *Authors of Pictures, Draughtsmen of Words.* Portsmouth, NH: Heinemann Educational Books, 1989.

Lambert, Dorothy. "Keeping a Journal." *English Journal* 56, no. 2 (1967): 286-288.

Larson, Richard L. "Discovery Through Questioning: A Plan for Teaching Rhetorical Invention." In *Contemporary Rhetoric: A Conceptual Background with Readings*, W. Ross Winterowd, ed. Pp. 144-154. New York: Harcourt Brace Jovanovich, 1975.

MacCann, Richard Dyer. *Film: A Montage of Theories.* New York: E. P. Dutton, 1966.

Murray, Donald M. "Write Before Writing." In *Composition and Its Teaching*, Richard C. Gebhardt, ed. Findlay: Ohio Council of Teachers of English Language Arts, 1979.

Ornstein, Robert, and Richard Thompson. *The Amazing Brain.* Boston: Houghton Mifflin, 1984.

Pearson, David P., and Dale D. Johnson. *Teaching Reading Comprehension.* New York: Holt, Rinehart & Winston, 1978.

Polanyi, Michael. *The Tacit Dimension.* Garden City, NY: Doubleday, 1966.

Reaske, Christopher R., and Robert F. Willson, Jr. *Student Voices/One.* New York: Random House, 1971.

Rico, Gabriele Lusser. *Writing the Natural Way.* Los Angeles: J. P. Tarcher, 1983.

Rief, Linda. *Seeking Diversity.* Portsmouth, NH: Heinemann Educational Books, 1992.

Romano, Tom. *Clearing the Way: Working with Teenage Writers.* Portsmouth, NH: Heinemann Educational Books, 1987.

Sohn, David A. *Film: The Creative Eye.* Dayton, OH: Geo. A. Pflaum, 1970.

Stillman, Peter R. *Families Writing.* Cincinnati, OH: Writer's Digest Books, 1989.

Thoreau, Henry David. *Walden.* New York: Doubleday, 1960.

Trimble, John R. *Writing with Style.* Englewood Cliffs, NJ: Prentice Hall, 1975.

Wolfe, Sidney M. *Worst Pills Best Pills.* Washington, DC: Public Citizen Health Research Group, 1988.

"Write Before Writing"

DONALD M. MURRAY

(From *College Composition and Communication*, NCTE December 1978.
Copyright 1978 by the National Council of Teachers of English.
Reprinted with permission.)

We command our students to write and grow frustrated when our "bad" students hesitate, stare out the window, dawdle over blank paper, give up and say, "I can't write," while the "good" students smugly pass their papers in before the end of the period.

When publishing writers visit such classrooms, however, they are astonished at students who can write on command, ejaculating correct little essays without thought, for writers have to write before writing.

The writers were the students who dawdled, stared out windows, and, more often than we like to admit, didn't do well in English — or in school.

One reason may be that few teachers have ever allowed adequate time for prewriting, that essential stage in the writing process which precedes a completed first draft. And even the curricula plans and textbooks which attempt to deal with prewriting usually pass over it rather quickly, referring only to the techniques of outlining, note-taking, or journal-making, not revealing the complicated process writers work through to get to the first draft.

Writing teachers, however, should give careful attention to what happens between the moment the writer receives an idea or an assignment and the moment the first completed draft is begun. We need to understand, as well as we can, the complicated and intertwining processes of perception and conception through language.

In actual practice, of course, these stages overlap and interact with one another, but to understand what goes on we must separate them and look at them artificially, the way we break down any skill to study it.

First of all, we must get out of the stands where we observe the process of writing from a distance — and after the fact — and get on the field where we can understand the pressures under which the writer operates. On the field, we will discover there is one principal negative force which keeps the writer from writing and

Commentary

If published writers and students were given the opportunity to impact curricula and testing situations, how would they change them? Query: What would the impact be if these writers and students were members of curriculum meetings and testing committees? Who would be threatened by their membership? Why can't these writers and students have more to say in the way writing is practiced in classrooms and tests?

There is still the misconception that knowing the words that denote the writing process is to know the writing process. Most teachers would recognize the word angiography, but surely none would be comfortable performing an angiography. Knowing the words alone does not ensure correct praxis.

This understanding does not come from reading about these processes alone, it also comes from experiencing them.

This also applies to professors who teach and train future teachers. Periodically, and for extended time, they need to go into classrooms on all levels and teach.

four positive forces which help the writer move forward to a completed draft.

Resistance to Writing

The negative force is *resistance* to writing, one of the great natural forces of nature. It may be called the Law of Delay: that writing which can be delayed, will be. Teachers and writers too often consider resistance to writing evil, when, in fact, it is necessary.

In Tom's classroom, which is in a large urban school, a student appeared to be unengaged and disinterested with the writing being pursued. Suddenly, with apparently no prompting, he began. The results showed a deep interest. Uninformed teachers and misdirected classroom evaluators can inadvertently short-circuit the resistance to writing and allow for no writing to be produced because of their compulsion for all students to be engaged at all times. How sad it is that they do not understand the writing process enough to know this negative force is a positive, vital aspect to writing.

When I get an idea for a poem or an article or a talk or a short story, I feel myself consciously draw away from it. I seek procrastination and delay. There must be time for the seed of the idea to be nurtured in the mind. Far better writers than I have felt the same way. Over his writing desk Franz Kafka had one word, "Wait." William Wordsworth talked of the writer's "wise passiveness." Naturalist Annie Dillard recently said, "I'm waiting. I usually get my ideas in November, and I start writing in January. I'm waiting." Denise Levertov says, "If ... somewhere in the vicinity there is a poem then, no I don't do anything about it, I wait."

Even the most productive writers are expert dawdlers, doers of unnecessary errands, seekers of interruptions—trials to their wives or husbands, friends, associates, and themselves. They sharpen well-pointed pencils and go out to buy more blank paper, rearrange offices, wander through libraries and bookstores, chop wood, walk, drive, make unnecessary calls, nap, daydream, and try not "consciously" to think about what they are going to write so they can think subconsciously about it.

While the co-authors were writing this book, the Weather Channel became the diversion. When a section became troublesome, or tiring, the forecasts for cities became stopovers in the process of finding the words.

Writers fear this delay, for they can name colleagues who have made a career of delay, whose great unwritten books will never be written, but, somehow, those writers who write must have the faith to sustain themselves through the necessity of delay.

Forces of Writing

In addition to that faith, writers feel four pressures that move them forward towards the first draft.

The first is *increasing information* about the subject. Once a writer decides on a subject or accepts an assignment, information about the subject seems to attach itself to the writer. The writer's perception apparatus finds significance in what the writer observes or overhears or reads or thinks or remembers. The writer becomes a magnet for specific details, insights, anecdotes, statistics, connecting thoughts, references. The subject itself seems to take hold of the writer's experience, turning everything that happens to the writer into material. And this inventory of information creates pressure that moves the writer forward towards the first draft.

Classrooms and teachers became the magnets for this endeavor. They acted as the source on occasion. They served as confirmation at other times. But they could never be too far away.

Usually the writer feels an *increasing concern* for the subject. The more a writer knows about the subject, the more the writer begins to feel about the subject. The writer cares that the subject be ordered and shared. The concern, which at first is a vague interest in the writer's mind, often becomes an obsession until it is communicated. Winston Churchill said, "Writing a book was an adventure. To begin with, it was a toy, and amusement; then it became a mistress, and then a master. And then a tyrant."

This becomes a type of ownership for the student. Any parent who has had a child involved in soccer, drama, or the self-sponsored activities in which children involve themselves can attest to the devotion and ownership that the child displays. When students feel the same concern for their writing, teaching writing ceases to be the onerous task in a curriculum and becomes the confirmation of thinking and learning.

The writer becomes aware of a *waiting audience*, potential readers who want or need to know what the writer had to say. Writing is an act of arrogance and communication. The writer rarely writes just for himself or herself, but for others who may be informed, entertained, or persuaded by what the writer has to say.

Bob Rath, interestingly, upset the canon of the waiting audience in his research that reveals the writer only writes for himself/ herself. Self is the ultimate audience.

And perhaps most important of all is the *approaching deadline*, which moves closer day by day at a terrifying and accelerating rate. Few writers publish without deadlines, which are imposed by others or by themselves. The deadline is real, absolute, stern, and commanding.

If the deadline is unrealistic and imposing, the brain will perceive it as a threat, and this can result in downshifting. (See chapter 12.)

Rehearsal for Writing

What the writer does under the pressure not to write and the four countervailing pressures to write is best described by the word, *rehearsal*, which I first heard used by Dr. Donald Graves of the University of New Hampshire to describe what he saw young children doing as they began to write. He watched them draw what they would write and heard them, as we all have, speaking aloud what they might say on the page before

There is a significance to Murray's term rehearsal. The writer must "rehear" what he or she has chosen to say.

A teacher cannot underestimate the power of this collaboration. It gives the writer balance. It keeps the writer on track. For too long writing classrooms have been classrooms where the only voice heard was the teacher's. If students are to become writers, then they must hear their own voices.

Students will not experiment in classrooms where risk taking is not valued and rewarded. The cost is too high. Jimmie Kanning, at Marshall High School in Northside ISD, San Antonio, is an excellent example of the teacher valuing and rewarding risk taking. Working with seniors who have been disenfranchised by a system, she placed magical safety nets to catch any student who falls from academic grace. They risk under her guidance. They learn failure is just another way of signaling learning.

they wrote. If you walk through editorial offices of a newspaper city-room you will see lips moving and hear expert professionals muttering and whispering to themselves as they write. Rehearsal is a normal part of the writing process, but it took a trained observer, such as Dr. Graves, to identify its significance.

Rehearsal covers much more than the muttering of struggling writers. As Dr. Graves points out, productive writers are "in a state of rehearsal all the time." Rehearsal usually begins with an unwritten dialogue within the writer's mind. "All of a sudden I discover that I have been thinking about a play," says Edward Albee. "This is usually between six months and a year before I actually sit down and begin typing it out." The writer thinks about characters or arguments, about plot or structure, about words and lines. The writer usually hears something which is similar to what Wallace Stevens must have heard as he walked through his insurance office working out poems in his head.

What the writer hears in his or her head usually evolves into note-taking. This may be simple brainstorming, the jotting down of random bits of information which may connect themselves into a pattern later on, or it may be journal-writing, a written dialogue between the writer and the subject. It may even become research recorded in a formal structure of note-taking.

Sometimes the writer not only talks to himself or herself, but to others — collaborators, editors, teachers, friends — working out the piece of writing in oral language with someone else who can enter into the process of discovery with the writer.

For most writers, the informal notes turn into lists, outlines, titles, leads, ordered fragments, all sketches of what later may be written, devices to catch a possible order that exists in the chaos of the subject.

In the final stage of rehearsal, the writer produces test drafts, written or unwritten. Sometimes they are called discovery drafts or trial runs or false starts that the writer doesn't think will be false. All writing is experimental, and the writer must come to the point where drafts are attempted in the writer's head and on paper.

Some writers seem to work more in their head, and others more on paper. Susan Sowars, a researcher at the University of New

Hampshire, examining the writing processes of a group of graduate students found

> a division ... between those who make most discoveries during prewriting and those who make most discoveries during writing and revision. The discoveries include the whole range from insights into personal issues to task-related organizational and content insight. The earlier the stage at which the insights occur, the greater the drudgery associated with the writing-rewriting tasks. It may be that we resemble the young reflective and reactive writing. The less developmentally mature reactive writers enjoy writing more than reflective writers. They may use writing as a rehearsal for thinking just as young, reactive writers draw to rehearse writing. The younger and older reflective writers do not need to rehearse by drawing to write or by writing to think clearly or to discover new relationships and significant content.

This concept deserves more investigation. We need to know about both the reflective and reactive prewriting mode. We need to see if there are developmental changes in students, if they move from one mode to another as they mature, and we need to see if one mode is more important in certain writing tasks than others. We must, in every way possible, explore the significant writing stage of rehearsal which has rarely been described in the literature on the writing process.

The Signals Which Say "Write"

During the rehearsal process, the experienced writer sees signals which tell the writer how to control the subject and produce a working first draft. The writer Rebecca Rule points out that in some cases when the subject is found, the way to deal with it is inherent in the subject. The subject itself is the signal. Most writers have experienced this quick passing through of the prewriting process. The line is given and the poem is clear; a character gets up and walks the writer through the story; the newspaperman attends a press conference, hears a quote, sees the lead and the entire structure of the article instantly. But many times the process is far less clear. The

Teela McKee, Carroll High School, Carroll ISD, Southlake, Texas, uses students' natural interest in self to engage her students in writing. They collect old photos, stuffed animals, blankets, and other childhood memorabilia. From these, they share explorations in writing persuasively.

To recognize these signals, the teacher of writing must become a diagnostician. The teacher must learn to not only recognize but also assist the writer in knowing what to do in the writing. This is no easy task.

Lesson planning becomes a developmental process rather than a checklist of accomplishments. Although on the one hand it is important for the teacher to plan what he or she is going to do with the students who are engaged in the writing process, it is equally important to leave this planning open-ended and dynamic. Principals who want to see six-week lesson plans, semester lesson plans, or even weekly lesson plans do not want to see writers who are learners, or learners who are actively discovering what they know and need to know. This type of learning does not occur because the lesson plan says it will happen on day fourteen of the six weeks. Learning and writing happen best when facilitated. Facilitation requires planning, replanning, chance, and good teaching.

In a writing institute, one member looked somewhat surprised when another group member responded with, "I think you have the makings of a poem there." She responded, "But I didn't start out to write a poem." It is much like Einstein's "apple" quote in the film Why Man Creates.

writer is assigned a subject or chooses one and then is lost.

E. B. White testifies, "I never knew in the morning how the day was going to develop. I was like a hunter, hoping to catch sight of a rabbit." Denise Levertov says, "You can smell the poem before you see it." Most writers know these feelings, but students who have never seen a rabbit dart across their writing desks or smelled a poem need to know the signals which tell them that a piece of writing is near.

What does the writer recognize which gives a sense of closure, a way of handling a diffuse and overwhelming subject? There seem to be eight principal signals to which writers respond.

One signal is *genre*. Most writers view the world as a fiction writer, a reporter, a poet, or an historian. The writer sees experience as a plot or a lyric poem or a news story or a chronicle. The writer uses such literary traditions to see and understand life.

"Ideas come to a writer because he has trained his mind to seek them out," says Brian Garfield. "Thus when he observes or reads or is exposed to a character or event, his mind sees the story possibilities in it and he begins to compose a dramatic structure in his mind. This process is incessant. Now and then it leads to something that will become a novel. But it's mainly an attitude; a way of looking at things; a habit of examining everything one perceives as potential material for a story."

Genre is a powerful but dangerous lens. It both clarifies and limits. The writer and the student must be careful not to see life merely in the stereotype form with which he or she is most familiar but to look at life with all of the possibilities of the genre in mind and to attempt to look at life through different genre.

Another signal the writer looks for is a *point of view*. This can be an opinion towards the subject or a position from which the writer—and the reader—studies the subject.

A tenement fire could inspire the writer to speak out against tenements, dangerous space-heating systems, a fire-department budget cut. The fire might also be seen from the point of view of the people who were the victims or who escaped or who came home to find their home gone. It may be told from the point of view of a fireman, an arsonist, an insurance investigator, a fire-safety engineer, a real-estate planner, a housing inspector, a landlord, a spectator, as well as the victim. The list could go on.

Still another way the writer sees the subject is through *voice*. As the writer rehearses, in the writer's head and on paper, the writer listens to the sound of the language as a clue to the meaning in the subject and the writer's attitude toward that meaning. Voice is often the force which drives a piece of writing forward, which illuminates the subject for the writer and the reader.

A writer may, for example, start to write a test draft with detached unconcern and find that the language appearing on the page reveals anger or passionate concern. The writer who starts to write a solemn report of a meeting may hear a smile and then a laugh in his own words and go on to produce a humorous column.

News is an important signal for many writers who ask what the reader needs to know or would like to know. Those prolific authors of nature books, Lorus and Margery Milne, organize their books and each chapter in the books around what is new in the field. Between assignment and draft they are constantly looking for the latest news they can pass along to their readers. When they find what is new, then they know how to organize their writing.

Writers constantly wait for the *line* which is given. For most writers, there is an enormous difference between a thesis or an idea or a concept and an actual line, for the line itself has resonance. A single line can imply a voice, a tone, a pace, a whole way of treating a subject. Joseph Heller tells about the signal which produced his novel *Something Happened*:

> I begin with a first sentence that is independent of any conscious preparation. Most often nothing comes out of it: a sentence will come to mind that doesn't lead to a second sentence. Sometimes it will lead to thirty sentences which then come to a dead end. I was alone on the deck. As I sat there worrying and wondering what to do, one of those first lines suddenly came to mind: "In the office in which I work, there are four people of whom I am afraid. Each of these four people is afraid of five people."

Katherine Paterson says in The Spying Heart, "[A]n idea is something that makes a sound in the heart (the heart in Japanese ... being the seat of intelligence as much as the seat of feeling) (28)." The point is that writers should listen to the sound of their hearts.

In the poem "August Pickings," by Joyce Armstrong Carroll (English Journal, 1990), she starts with, "'I hear the swamp berries are ready,' Dad announced." She tells how when working with a group of teachers on prewriting techniques, she wrote the words "berry picking." She fully intended to move on from those words, but instead she felt the pull of the words compelling her to write about the times her father took her berry picking. Had she not been open to the resonance of the line, she would have missed the poem.

Many times the first line that leads the way into a writing never finds its way into the final piece. Mundo, a student in Beverly McKinley's high school class, Pasadena ISD, Texas, discovered this. His prewriting began, "Back in the 40's and 50's my father hunted as a young boy with his father." Subsequently, he scratched this line out and wrote beside it, "cheesy story." This line, however, galvanized a poignant story entitled "On the Hunt." It begins, "Long ago my father introduced hunting to his three oldest sons." The story chronicles his passage from a punk kid armed with a slingshot aimed at lizards to a responsible hunter of bigger game. Nowhere in Mundo's rather lengthy story does that original line appear. And the story is anything but "cheesy."

Immediately, the lines presented a whole explosion of possibilities and choices—characters (working in a corporation), a tone, a mode of anxiety, or of insecurity. In that first hour (before someone came along and asked me to go to the beach) I knew the beginning, the ending, most of the middle, the whole scene of that particular "something" that was going to happen; I knew about the brain-damaged child, and especially, of course, about Bob Slocum, my protagonist, and what frightened him, that he wanted to be liked, that his immediate hope was to be allowed to make a three-minute speech at the company convention. Many of the actual lines throughout the book came to me—the entire "something happened" scene with those solar plexus lines (beginning with the doctor's statement and ending with "Don't tell my wife" and the rest of them) all coming to me in that first hour on that Fire Island deck. Eventually I found a different opening chapter with a different first line ("I get the willies when I see closed doors") but kept the original, which had spurred everything, to start off the second section.

Newspapermen are able to write quickly and effectively under pressure because they become skillful at identifying a lead, that first line—or two or three—which will inform and entice the reader and which, of course, also gives the writer control over the subject. As an editorial writer, I found that finding the title first gave me control over the subject. Each title became, in effect, a pre-draft, so that in listing potential titles I would come to one which would be a signal as to how the whole editorial could be written.

Poets and fiction writers often receive their signals in terms of an *image*. Sometimes this image is static; other times it is a moving picture in the writer's mind. When Gabriel García Márquez was asked what the starting point of his novels was, he answered, "A completely visual image ... the starting point of *Leaf Storm* is an old man taking his grandson to a funeral, in *No One Writes to the Colonel*, it's an old man waiting, and in *One Hundred Years*, an old man taking his grandson to the fair to find out what ice is." William Faulkner was quoted as saying, "It begins with a character, usually, and once he stands up on his feet and begins to move, all I do is trot along behind him with a paper and pencil trying to keep up long enough to put down what he says and does." It's a comment which seems facetious—if you're not a fiction writer. Joyce Carol Oates adds, "I visualize the characters completely; I have heard their dialogue, I know how they speak, what they want, who they are, nearly everything about them."

Although image has been testified to mostly be imaginative writers, where it is obviously most appropriate, I think research would show that nonfiction writers often see an image as the signal. The person, for example, writing a memo about a manufacturing procedure may see the assembly line in his or her mind. The politician arguing for a pension law may see a person robbed of a pension, and by seeing that person know how to organize a speech or the draft of a new law.

Many writers know they are ready to write when they see a *pattern* in a subject. This pattern is usually quite different from what we think of as an outline, which is linear and goes from beginning to end. Usually the writer sees something which might be called a gestalt, which is, in the words of the dictionary, "a unified physical, psychological, or symbolic configuration having properties that cannot be derived from its parts." The writer usually in a moment sees the entire piece of writing as a shape, a form, something that is more than all of its parts, something that is entire and is represented in his or her mind, and probably on paper, by a shape.

Marge Piercy says, "I think that the beginning of fiction, of the story, has to do with the perception of pattern in event." Leonard Gardner, in talking of his fine novel *Fat City*, said, "I had a definite design in mind. I had a sense of circle ... of closing the circle at the end." John Updike says, "I really begin with some kind of solid, coherent image, some notion of the shape of the book and even of its texture. *The Poorhouse Fair* was meant to have a sort of wide shape. *Rabbit, Run* was kind of zigzag. *The Centaur* was sort of a sandwich."

We have interviews with imaginative writers about the writing process, but rarely interviews with science writers, business writers, political writers, journalists, ghost writers, legal writers, medical writers—examples

These examples of Murray's attest to the need for a variety of prewriting experiences. Not all writing for all students will come from one prewriting activity. A variety allows for student writers to find their topics and their genre and to feel success.

Although published writers see this gestalt, it is not so clear to the student writer. With practice, much practice, the student writer develops this "sight." When and how this occurs are worthy of more study and research. Marsha White, Victoria ISD, Texas, spends time in her classroom allowing students to verbalize the "how" of their gestalt. She listens to her students and offers possibilities to guide them in their discoveries.

of effective writers who use language to inform and persuade. I am convinced that such research would reveal that they also see patterns or gestalts which carry them from idea to draft.

For the new paradigm, the skill of asking questions, the right questions, will become even more valuable. With the information explosion, knowing the answers will become an impossibility, so society will need people who can ask the right questions.

"It's not the answer that enlightens but the question," says Ionesco. This insight into what the writer is looking for is one of the most significant considerations in trying to understand the freewriting process. A most significant book based on more than ten years of study of art students, *The Creative Vision, A Longitudinal Study of Problem-Finding in Art*, by Jacob W. Getzels and Mihaly Csikszentmihalyi, has documented how the most creative students are those who come up with the problem to be solved rather than a quick answer. The signal to the creative person may well be the problem, which will be solved through the writing.

See pages 76-80 on classical invention and classical invention for the contemporary student.

We need to take all the concepts of invention from classical rhetoric and combine them with what we know from modern psychology, from studies of creativity, from writers' testimony about the prewriting process. Most of all, we need to observe successful students and writers during the prewriting process, and to debrief them to find out what they do when they move effectively from assignment or idea to completed first draft. Most of all, we need to move from failure-centered research to research which defines what happens when the writing goes well, just what is the process followed by effective student and professional writers. We know far too little about the writing process.

Implications for Teaching Writing

Our speculations make it clear that there are significant implications for the teaching of writing in a close examination of what happens between receiving an assignment or finding a subject and beginning a completed first draft. We may need, for example, to reconsider our attitude towards those who delay writing. We may, in fact, need to force many of our glib, hair-trigger student writers to slow down, to daydream, to waste time, but not to avoid a reasonable deadline.

Murray advocates student responsibility. It is time for students to be the ones responsible for what goes on in classrooms. Teachers are not the only decision makers present in classrooms.

We certainly should allow time within the curriculum for prewriting, and we should work with our students to help them understand the process of rehearsal, to allow them the experience of rehearsing what they will write in their minds, on the paper, and with collaborators. We should also make our students familiar with the signals they may see during the rehearsal process which will tell them that they are ready to write, that they have a way of dealing with their subject.

The prewriting process is largely invisible; it takes place within the writer's head or on scraps of paper that are rarely published. But we must understand that such a process takes place, that it is significant, and that it can be made clear to our students. Students who are not writing, or not writing well, may have a second chance if they are able to experience the writer's counsel to write before writing.

Murray's article invites mini-lessons on the four forces of writing; increasing information, increasing concern for subject, a waiting audience, and the approaching deadline. Also, it begs for mini-lessons on rehearsal and "the signals which say 'write' ": genre (see chapter 4, pages 102-110), point of view, voice, news, line, image, and patterns.

"Drawing into Meaning: A Powerful Writing Tool"

JOYCE ARMSTRONG CARROLL

(From *English Journal* 80, no. 6 [October 1991]. Copyright 1991 by the National Council of Teachers of English. Reprinted with permission.)

"... and [he] told her she could keep it forever and ever."

"Now we're going to write," said Ms. Smith. Promptly, twenty-one kindergartners, some with crayons, some with fat or skinny pencils, began talking and turning their oversized, unlined papers this way and that. Soon the chatter generated by Joan de Hamel's *Hemi's Pet* (1985) slowed as drawings of real and make-believe animals flew, trotted, crawled, and ran across the students' papers.

Background

When we watch children in primary or elementary grades, we delight in all this drawing; we accept it as a way of meaning; we accept it as writing. "Read what you have written," we invite. So automatically playing the "believing game" (Elbow 1973, 148), they read their circles with lines radiating out as "a bright sunny day"; they read their row of stick figures as "I love my family." Yet somewhere up the ladder of academe, we educate out of students this powerful writing tool. We let middle- and high-school students know in subtle and sometimes not-so-subtle ways that drawing belongs to little kids.

I find this curious since I draw when I write. I usually line up boxes along my top margin like square soldiers. Then, apparently depending upon the nature of the writing, I fill them in with lines and shading — the more complex the piece of writing, the more intricate the details in the boxes. I don't do this consciously, perhaps because they are "fugitives of my unconscious" (Torrey 1989, 65), yet boxes always appear on my papers.

So curious (or obsessive) did I become about connections between drawing and writing, I began a quiet and admittedly unscholarly research project — no control groups, no statistics — just the random glancing at people engaged in the act of writing. I saw much drawing going on surreptitiously — clouds, smoke, flowers, houses, hands, cowboys, and cats sat side by side scribbles and squiggles on page after page. Some people even drew beautiful, suitable-for-framing designs like the elaborate mandalas a friend of mine creates before he ever writes a word.

Theory

As is usually the case when something strikes the mind, I noticed articles on this "frittering" everywhere. Obviously my curiosity was shared by readers ranging the gamut from *American Baby* (Lamme 1985) to *Omni* (Torrey), from *Psychology Today* (Winner 1986) to *College English* (Fulwiler and Petersen 1981). I wondered: if drawing, scribbling, and doodling fascinate us all, if all these loops and lines hold tacit meaning, why don't we use drawing in middle and high schools as the powerful writing tool it is?

In a jointly written article, Toby Fulwiler and Bruce Petersen validate this notion of drawing as a writing tool by not only identifying three types of doodles and suggesting doddling as analogous "to journal writing, free writing, and rough drafting" but also by explaining that doodles help "develop concrete records of otherwise incompletely synthesized intellection" (626). In other words, they believe that doodles help make visible that which might remain ethereal.

Ruth Hubbard (1989b), borrowing the terms *disigno interno* (inner languages) and *disigno esterno* (visual modes) from the Italian painter Frederico Zuccari, echoes Fulwiler and Petersen: "These final products — on the canvas or printed page — are only a representation, or perhaps interpretation, of what goes on in our minds" (134). Further, she quotes Walter Grey's study of the modes in which people communicate: "15% of the population thinks exclusively in the visual modes, another 15% thinks only in verbal terms, and the remaining 70% uses a mixture of approaches" (133-134). When I read those statistics, I began to realize why so many people naturally turn to drawing while writing.

Then I heard about Judy Skupa's dissertation (1985). In it, she analyzes the writings of three groups of elementary students: those permitted to draw and look at their drawings before writing, those permitted to draw but not look at their drawing before writing (blind drawers), and those who were not permitted to draw at all before writing. Her data show that those permitted to draw and look at their drawings wrote best.

Skupa's research supports that of psychologists James Gibson and Patricia Yonas. They recorded the delight two-year-olds took in making marks across a page, but they noted that if they replaced the child's marker with one that left no trace, the children would stop writing (Winner 25).

I am reminded here of Janet Emig's observation about Sartre's blindness and his frustration at not being able to read his own work: "The eye ... permits individual rhythms of review to be established and followed" (1978, 66). It seems obvious that the graphic symbol, born from the self for the self, different yet similar to the written one, contains its own intrinsic power, power arising from its unique ability to display a visual knowing and from its unique ability to enable a focused concentration.

Beginning to understand why drawing emerges as so powerful a writing tool, I hypothesized that meaning embodied in a graphic symbol leads to what Susanne Langer calls "symbolic expression" (Cassirer 1946, ix). Put another way, drawing provides "a cognitive economy in its metaphoric transformations, which make it possible for a seemingly limited symbol to spread its power over a range of experience" (Bruner 1971, 14).

Perhaps Betty Edwards (1986) most clearly explains it. Making a case that perceptual skills (those used when drawing) enhance *thinking* skills, she proposes that

learning to see and draw is a very efficient way to train the visual system, just as learning to read and write can efficiently train the verbal system.... And when trained as equal partners, one mode of thinking enhances the other, and together the two modes can release human creativity. (8)

That's power.

To withhold that power from middle- and high-school students—no matter how well-intentioned—to permit only elementary students access to that symbolizing system ignores the importance of drawing as a powerful preliminary of writing. Along with brainstorming, mapping, classical invention, the pentad, and other prewriting strategies, students should be encouraged to draw into meaning, whether as prewriting for their reflexive or extensive pieces or as initial responses to literature. In order to help that happen, we need to

1. Enable students to reenter texts in visual, non-threatening ways

2. Encourage drawing as a prewriting technique

3. Appropriate drawing as a springboard for further writing

4. Consider drawing an initial graphic probe, a strategy for tapping deeper or other awarenesses

Application

In an effort to capitalize on the power in drawing (as well as to test my hypothesis), I visited many middle and high schools, and through interactive inservice (teaching classes, being observed by teachers, then meeting with those teachers afterwards), I was able to invite drawing as response to literature, then to see where that response might lead.

First, I talked to the students about symbolic drawing. I explained that such drawing is a symbolizing system just as writing is a symbolizing system: the former is one of images, the latter is one of words; the former is visual, the latter is verbal. Together we talked about the cave drawings found to date back as far as 16,000 BC, to the Old Stone Age. I showed pictures of symbolic drawings taken from the caves at Altamira, Combarelles, Les Eyzies, and Font de Gaume in France. The students were hooked.

I followed with examples from the archaeological finds at Novgorod. These birchbark manuscripts show actual school exercises done by Onfim, a six- or seven-year-old boy, in the first half of the thirteenth century. Some are letters; some are syllables; some are remarkably contemporary looking "drawings of himself, battle scenes and pictures of his teacher" (Yanin 1990, 89). Onfim used letters and drawing to give form to his meaning.

Next, I showed a *pictograph* and defined pictographs as capturing the essence of what the reader knows. The one I chose was a simple stick figure of a man with twenty or so lines emanating out of each foot because three-year-old Jenny told me as she pointed to her picture, "My father's barefoot."

"She drew what she knew," I explained.

Next I showed four-year-old Derrick's map as another example of symbolic drawing, the *ideograph*, a more sophisticated visual than the pictograph since it conveys relationships. Here I pointed out the way Derrick outlined the trip from his house to the babysitter's house as well as from his house to church. As Hubbard (1989a) says,

> As each of us attempts our search for meaning, we need a medium through which our ideas can take shape. But there is not just one medium; productive thought uses many ways to find meaning. (3)

Through discussion, it was made clear that drawing as a powerful tool of writing was not the same as drawing as an art form. The students realized that such drawing gives form to thought for self then communicates that meaning to others. This got them past the reluctance to participate, even to try because of the "I-can't-draw" syndrome, meaning "I'm not an artist."

Making connections between the history of writing and the symbol system children create, the students grew more curious. They wondered whether they could still tap drawing as a medium of meaning. The students were anxious to try this "new" symbol system; they were ready to put it to use, so I placed Richard Brautigan's poem "In a Cafe" on the overhead.

> I watched a man in a cafe fold a slice of bread
> as if he were folding a birth certificate or looking
> at the photograph of a dead lover.
>   (Brautigan 1979, 46)

After reading it aloud as students followed along, I said, "Let's tackle this poem by fooling the usual and perhaps dominant hemi-

spheres of our brain. Take your pen or pencil in the hand opposite the hand with which you usually write and draw what you know." Heads down they worked. I did, too.

In about five or seven minutes, I intervened. "Switch to your comfortable hand and write what you discover in your drawing." Again heads bowed down as they worked. Mine did too.

"Let's see what happened. Who would like to share?" I invited. Many hands shot up.

Stephanie shared her drawing of an eye in the upper left corner and a tear in the upper right corner. She read,

> My Scottish grandfather wore khakis. He was a railroad man—his box house was next to the station. They were both painted railway yellow with coal black trim. I only saw him twice.

"Talk to us about any connections you see between the poem and what you drew and wrote," I invited.

"The poem made me feel sad. All of a sudden I thought about my grandfather who I only saw twice. I think I thought about him because I feel bad I only saw him twice before he died. Maybe he sat at a table alone. Maybe he thought about me."

"What did your drawing and writing tell you about the poem?" I pressed.

Stephanie thought a long while as she studied her work and Brautigan's. Finally she said, "My grandfather was a loner. When you read the poem, I felt lonely. That made me think of Papa Mac. When I thought of him, I thought of what he did and where he lived. That's what first popped into my mind. The colors came later.

"Now I think I'd add that the poet wanted to tell us not just about being lonely but also about being lonely even when you are around people, like in a cafe or by a railroad where you'd see lots of people.

"The more I think about this, it's like my mind keeps changing because now I'm thinking more of isolation than loneliness. Maybe the man in the cafe, like Papa Mac, wanted to be alone, wanted to be isolated. That piece of bread wasn't bread at all, not when he really looked at it. It became the birth certificate or the photograph. The poet could be telling us something about wanting to see something so badly you do see it. Maybe the whole poem is about our perceptions."

Stephanie's writing and subsequent telling seem to validate Lev Vygotsky's contention that drawing is not representational but rather it yields "predispositions to judgments that are invested with speech or capable of being so invested" (1978, 112). It's unlikely that if Stephanie had been given the poem in the traditional setting any mention of Papa Mac would have occurred. It's even less likely that the sequence of conjectures following that telling would have occurred. Later, when Stephanie drafted her essay about the poem, there was a quality, a depth to her writing which, according to her teacher, hitherto did not exist.

Continuing the sharing, another student held up a shaky sketch of a seated man. She read, "Withered and solitary the man sits and waits. Auschwitz thin in striped pajamas, quietly letting go."

T: How did your drawing cause that writing, Cathy?

C: Unexpectedly I thought about *The Diary of Anne Frank*, I think because we just finished reading it. When you read the poem I thought how that man in the poem could be a Jew who had been in a concentration camp. Then after the war he came to France. I thought of France because of the word "cafe." He could have trouble eating because every time he goes to eat he thinks of the concentration camp.

T: Do those thoughts help you understand the poem?

C: Well, it's awfully short — like Anne Frank's life. I think the poet wanted to condense everything like Anne had to condense everything in that tiny room.

I know poems are always condensed, but in this one it's like it shows what it means. You can get a lot of meaning into a little space if you choose carefully. I want to choose carefully. I want my life to be full even if I'm only thirteen years old.

These thoughts shared aloud echo Hubbard's own exploration of the relationship between her words and images. Here Cathy conveys the complexity of that relationship. First,

Brautigan's poem caused an association with a book Cathy had just finished, which came out through the shaky drawing and the thin man. That, in turn, caused an allusion to a concentration camp to surface in the writing. When sharing, Cathy made application to her own life, her own desire to live life to the fullest.

As with Stephanie, the tendency is to use drawing as the basic response, then to move in hierarchical, heuristical ways from the known (their graphic representation) to discoveries, to transformations, and to higher levels of knowing.

Another example comes from a twelfth grader named Raul who drew a large trash can. Bits of paper spilled over and cluttered the area around it. He wrote simply, "The man is a discard. No one cares about him." Raul didn't elaborate orally. At first blush it seemed nothing further had been triggered. However, when I revisited Raul's class several weeks later, he thrust a neatly written two-page paper at me. "Read this," he murmured, "I wrote it after your drawing class." The title "A Disenfranchised Man" promised and the prose delivered a profound look at a person living in America, homeless, without privilege, without identity.

Raul and others had used drawing as a visual probe, a method of inquiry which helped them transform the raw data of the poem into something they and others could understand.

Conclusion

In *Authors of Pictures, Draughtsmen of Words*, in which Hubbard investigates how children use drawings and words to make meaning, she also cites adult authors (not just picture-book authors) who found drawing helpful in their works (see chapter 6). Writers like E. B. White, e. e. cummings, D. H. Lawrence, John Dos Passos, William Faulkner, S. J. Perelman, Gabriel García Márquez, Flannery O'Connor, and John Updike rise up to remind us not to relegate only to little kids the joy of making meaning through drawing.

Finally, referencing several teachers at the middle-school and high-school levels who are giving their students the freedom "to use visual as well as verbal solutions to their problems" (152), Hubbard concludes,

Drawing is not just for children who can't yet write fluently, and creating pictures is not just part of rehearsal for real writing. Images *at any age* are part of the serious business of making meaning—partners with words for communicating our inner designs. (157)

My experience again and again with drawing into meaning permits me to redouble her words. We must try to facilitate an environment where middle- and high-school students discover this powerful writing tool, for as Gabriele Rico reminds us, "Before there are words, there are images" (1983, 157).

New Jersey Writing Project in Texas
Spring, Texas 77389

Works Cited

Brautigan, Richard. 1979. "In a Cafe." *Postcard Poems: A Collection of Poetry for Sharing.* Ed. Paul B. Janeczko. New York: Bradbury. 46.

Bruner, Jerome S. 1971. *On Knowing: Essays for the Left Hand.* New York: Atheneum.

Cassirer, Ernst. 1946. *Language and Myth.* Trans. and preface by Susanne K. Langer. New York: Dover.

de Hamel, Joan. 1985. *Hemi's Pet.* Boston: Houghton.

Edwards, Betty. 1986. *Drawing on the Artist Within.* New York: Simon.

Elbow, Peter. 1973. *Writing Without Teachers.* New York: Oxford UP.

Emig, Janet. 1978. "Hand, Eye, Brain: Some 'Basics' in the Writing Process." *Research on Composing: Points of Departure.* Eds. Charles R. Cooper and Lee Odell. Urbana, IL: NCTE. 59-71.

Fulwiler, Toby, and Bruce Petersen. 1981. "Toward Irrational Heuristics: Freeing the Tacit Mode." *College English* 43.6 (Oct.): 621-629.

Hubbard, Ruth. 1989a. *Authors of Pictures, Draughtsmen of Words.* Portsmouth, NH: Heinemann.

_____. 1989b. "Inner Designs." *Language Arts* 66.2 (Feb.): 119-136.

Lamme, Linda. 1985. "From Scribbling to Writing." *American Baby* 47.8 (Aug.): 47-48, 50.

Rico, Gabriele Lusser. 1983. *Writing the Natural Way.* Los Angeles: Tarcher.

Skupa, Judith Ann. 1985. "An Analysis of the Relationship Between Drawing and Idea Production in Writing for Second Grade Children across Three Aims of Discourse." Diss. U. of Texas at Austin.

Torrey, Joanna. 1989. "Breaking the Code of Doodles." *Omni* 11.7 (Apr.): 65-69, 120-125.

Vygotsky, Lev S. 1978. *Mind in Society: The Development of Higher Psychological Processes.* Ed. Michael Cole et al. Cambridge: Harvard UP.

Winner, Ellen. 1986. "Where Pelicans Kiss Seals." *Psychology Today* 20.8 (Aug.): 24-26, 30-35.

Yanin, Valentin L. 1990. "The Archaeology of Novgorod." *Scientific American* 262.2 (Feb.): 84-91.

4

BRINGING ORDER OUT OF CHAOS
Teaching How to Shape Writing Using Genre

Ultimately every writer must follow the path that feels most comfortable. For most people who are learning to write, that path is nonfiction. It enables them to write about what they know or can observe and can find out. This is especially true of young people— they will write far more willingly about experiences that touch their own lives because that's what interests them. Motivation is at the heart of writing. If nonfiction is where you do your best writing, or your best teaching of writing, don't be buffaloed into the notion that it's an inferior species. The only important distinction is between good writing and bad writing. Good writing is good writing, whatever form it takes and whatever we call it.

—William Zinsser □

In Betty Edward's *Drawing on the Artist Within* there is an exercise that invites participants to draw lines that represent feelings (not pictures or symbols such as hearts or crosses—and no words). These lines become analogs for human emotions: anger, joy, depression, loneliness, love, and so forth. Her results indicate that although there is great variety, because no one's lines are exactly alike, there is a structural similarity, an almost visual vocabulary for like feelings. This similarity seems to point to a shared intuition, one that contributes to a collective understanding (Edward 66-95). In other words, given the same word, for example *bliss*, people draw like lines to express that feeling, and others looking at those lines "get" the same feeling.

Trying this with teachers, as they listened to poems and short stories, yielded similar results. They scratched stubby lines to approximate simple ideas; made twisted lines to parallel convoluted or complicated thought; ran jagged lines, often all over the page, to indicate something unpleasant; and used symmetrical or flowing lines to convey the beautiful, or the lyrical. Interesting, as line is such a simple a form, that it could be used to express meaning that others understand. What is most interesting, though, is that the meaning came first.

If this is the case with the simple line, consider form within the complexity of writing. There seem to be almost intrinsic forms writers use and readers understand. Prewriting often runs rampant with fragments, ramblings, turns, pauses, tentativeness—in short, with idiosyncratic messiness that makes it a "sloppy copy." But when writers begin to think of turning prewriting into a form fit for an audience, they begin making decisions about their purpose and how best to shape their meaning. Knowing the structure of different genres provides the basis, either consciously or subconsciously, for those decisions.

WHAT IS GENRE?

Genre, a word that comes from the French, is a category of literary composition. In literary criticism, it refers to a type of literature or literary form. In writing, genre refers to the form writers use as structure. As convenient but arbitrary models, genres offer forms for the human imagination and so serve students as literary models for their writing.

There are many genres and subgenres, and the criteria for the classifications are highly variable. Beginning with Plato and Aristotle, literature was ordered into three classes: poetic or lyric, epic or narrative, and drama. The most common genres come from ancient rhetoric: epic, tragedy, comedy, satire, and lyric. More recent arrivals are novel, essay, biography, and nonfiction.

M. H. Abrams offers these classifications:

Prose Genres: Biography, The Character, Essay, Exemplum; Fable; Fantastic Literature; Parable; Satire; Short Story.

Poetic Genres: Lyric, Ballad, Chivalric Romance; Emblem Poems; Epic, Epigram; Fable; Georgic; Fabliau; Lai; Light Verse; Occasional Poem; Pastoral.

Dramatic Genres: Chronicle Plays; Commedia dell'Arte, Comedy; Comedy of Humours; Drama of Sensibility; Epic Theater; Folk Drama; Heroic Drama; Masque; Melodrama; Miracle Plays, Morality Plays, and Interludes; Mummer's Play; Pantomime and Dumb-Show; Problem Play; Sentimental Comedy; Tragedy; Tragicomedy.

Novel: Fantastic Literature; Gothic Novel, Novel of Sensibility; Novelette; Utopias and Dystopias (213-218).

Although students may study many of the genres Abrams lists, their writing experiences are generally more limited. They tend to gravitate to the forms shown in table 4.1. These genres are examined later in this chapter.

GENRE AS FORM

Moving prewriting into genre is one way to organize meaning because readers have come to expect certain elements in certain genre. For example, little children know stories contain characters who become involved in some problem that is usually solved by story's end. Essays inform, and, unless the poem is of epic proportions, readers expect verse to be short, sometimes rhyming, and to appear on the page in a certain way. Therefore, any genre chosen emphasizes meaning, dramatizes meaning, or makes the meaning clearer for its audience.

Ken Macrorie, in *Telling Writing*, starts his chapter 16, "Creating Form," with:

> A recent textbook on writing says: Since learning to outline is one of the most important steps—perhaps the most important—in writing well, we want you to make at least four outlines. The man who wrote that must never have talked to a real writer. Eight out of ten writers say they never use outlines and the other two say they use them only in late stages of writing....
>
> In the first place, outlines freeze most writers. Professionals are looking for ways of breaking up the ice and poking around in new waters. They want writing and ideas to flow.
>
> In the second place—Wait a minute. The second place. By their form, outlines always imply there will be a second place. Maybe there won't be. Or should be.... The Outliners are full of stuff like that. They get a writer so interested in the form of the outline that he quits thinking of the writing he is outlining. (163-164)

Table 4.1

Genres Used Most by Student Writers

Fiction	Drama	Poetry	Nonfiction	Essay
Short story, novella	Scripts (film and television)	Narrative	Letter	Persuasive
Sudden fiction	Plays	Lyric	Autobiography	Narrative
Fables		Free verse	Biography	Definition
Myths, tales, and legends			Memoir	Problem/ solution
				Classification (comparison/ contrast)
				Informative (how-to)
				Descriptive
				Documented

Yet the writer and the reader do need some type of form. Form should not freeze; rather it should be the shape of things to come. Indeed, in writing the meaning determines the form.

Juxtapose Eugenio Montale's poem "The Eel" with "We Real Cool" by Gwendolyn Brooks. Montale uses the eel to symbolize the life cycle; Brooks uses the dialogue of pool players to convey their lives. "The Eel," written as a 30-line sentence, curls down the page with sleek words that play with consonance and assonance. The meaning of the poem demands that its form be like the eel— slick and sliding down the page. By contrast, "We Real Cool," written as eight three-word sentences in four two-line stanzas, whips the reader with abrupt words replete with alliteration and repetition. Brooks selects short words to punctuate the anger of the personae. The poem demands brevity so it can explode at the end, just as its meaning explodes to punctuate the desperate lives of the personae. Clearly each poet chose the best form to support meaning.

Meaning also dictates form in prose. Jack Matthews's short story "A Questionnaire for Rudolph Gordon" is a series of 100 questions that concludes, "Love always, Mom and Dad." These questions convey the meaning of the story. The reader mentally answers the questionnaire during the reading, thereby vicariously becoming Rudolph Gordon. Because Matthews uses a questionnaire form, the reader participates in the making of meaning, which is exactly what Matthews intends.

> After the first meeting with a freshman composition class, two young men stood arguing in the corner. As I walked by I asked, "What's the problem?"
> "Well, his senior English teacher told him every paragraph has five sentences and mine told me every paragraph has seven," stated one.
> "Which is it?" quipped the other.
> I had the overwhelming urge to say "Six!" and immortalize myself, but instead I explained that we would study the relationship of meaning to form and make our decisions accordingly.

This anecdote stands as a testimony to the absurdity of students thinking form *is* meaning. Clearly, the two young men had learned that form is primary, meaning is secondary. Write the assigned number of sentences and the grade is made. They missed that what is necessary to make such decisions is not a formula, but a clear sense of meaning, purpose, and audience, a working knowledge of various genres, and the right to choose. Donald Graves states, "Methods that prescribe form are suspect. Form should follow function" (1989, 57).

In prewriting, students find meaning; in writing, they find form. To do it the other way around is artificial. It is not form; it becomes formula. For example, when students have freedom in prewriting but are moved into writing with mandates of form, they become disenfranchised, give up ownership, and lose motivation. As a result students jump through hoops with little or no investment. They ask the form questions, "How long does this *have to* be?" "How many paragraphs *do you want*?" Those who own their writing, however, often argue in defense of their decisions on form and are reluctant to change simply for a grade. Their questions are generally meaning questions: "Do you understand what I mean here?" "How can I say this better?" "I think this would work better as a story than as an essay. Don't you?"

Doris Lessing says it this way: "I see every book as a problem that you have to solve. That is what dictates the form you use. It's not that you say 'I want to write a space fiction book.' You start from the other end, and what you have to say dictates the form of it" (93).

TEACHING GENRE AS FORM

Encourage students to risk and experiment and then to commit to writing with energy and meaning by exposing them to the choices that exist. Elementary students who have had their field of vision narrowed to the narrative are just as limited as secondary students who have had their field of vision narrowed to the essay. Instead, open students up to different genres and the right to choose among them.

Students who get their meaning down first and then work it into an appropriate form are using critical thinking skills. Making intelligent decisions about form involves having a repertoire of options and being exposed to print-rich environments with a multiplicity of genres that act as literary models. Further, rich discussion about those literary models invites speculation and commentary on the efficacy of form and structure—not merely that there *are* three witches in the opening of *Macbeth*, but how does that opener work? Not that Eric Carle designed holes for the pages of *The Very Hungry Caterpillar*, but do those holes contribute to Carle's meaning? Then students connect these models to their writing. They keep records of their reading and writing, and they taste often of different genres. If a student gets stuck in nonfiction, for instance, the teacher might nudge him or her toward poetry or fiction.

> There is an anecdote about Dorothy Parker, a celebrated journalist often noted for her wit. It seems that during the question-and-answer period after one of her speeches, a teacher in the audience asked whether she had any rules that would help students write.
>
> "Oh, yes," said Ms. Parker, "I have six."
> Everyone quickly rustled paper and poised pens in anticipation.
> "Read, read, read, and write, write, write," she said dramatically.

All too often students ask questions that demonstrate their misunderstanding about how meaning determines form.

"But what do you *want*?"
"How long does it have to be?"
"Just tell us what to do and we'll do it."

Answering her students with, "It depends on what *you* want," always seems dangerous to Becky Hicks, most recently a Northside ISD, San Antonio, teacher. Her students usually feel the same danger. They both know that choice stretches before them. This choice is like Wesley's fire swamp in *The Princess Bride*, zipping and zapping, threatening to suck down a whole class of novice writers and Becky, too. She asks herself these questions: How will I evaluate if students choose different genres? Will those who choose poems finish before those working on short stories? How can I teach to 30 different choices? In spite of her concerns, Becky encourages her students to take risks. Like Wesley and Buttercup, teachers and students who risk the fire discover that finding the best genre for their writing is a worthwhile adventure.

All writing teachers struggle with a variety of challenges. Each grade level has its own unique set. Yet often teachers learn from students. Watch elementary students, who will attempt almost anything without constraints. "They come to us that way," Edna Bubenik, Judson ISD, Texas, says when talking about her fifth-grade students' ability to take risks. "They have a story to tell, and given the permission to be free to write, they will tell it in one form or another."

Some secondary teachers sigh for this naturalness of the unspoiled. Many teachers deal daily with students who resist moving from the comfort of familiar modes of writing to the less familiar ones. Teachers may confront such resistance by inviting students to explore new forms, modes, and genres through awareness activities, literary explorations, and heuristic techniques. All of these techniques help develop a commitment to meaning, purpose, audience, and personal interest — influences that shape writing.

Awareness Techniques for Genre

Genre awareness activities may vary in scope, depth, and approach. Teachers adapt and adopt them for their grade levels. They do not omit examples of modes, genres, or shaping techniques as too sophisticated. They know through reading, writing, guidance, and encouragement that students on all levels can learn to respect the writer's craft while gaining enough confidence to experiment with various genres.

I fully intended to culminate this first-grade demonstration lesson on insects by inviting the students to write a story about spiders. But they were an eager, bright group, and despite the 20 teachers watching, I decided to take a risk.

"Boys and girls, I was going to ask you to write a story, but you are so smart, I'd like to try something different. Would you like that?" They assured me they would, and their excitement matched the challenge.

First we folded an eight-page book. Next we together made spiders from Oreo cookies and licorice. Then I said, "Now you know how to make spiders. Use your book to tell others how to make them."

Off they went writing how-to books by recalling how they made spiders. Jennifer wrote:

Monday   *Jennifer M.*

Arachnids are spiders. Tha do not have antennas. Tha have eight legs. Ther are 30,000 difrat spiders. Tha have two body parts. I no haw to mak a oreo spider. It is fun. I will tl you haw to mak it. You ned a oreo coke. Then you ned a likurusk stik. Then you ned a tuood uv frostng. Then you tac the oreo and you droc it in haf. The sib with the most creme. You tak ywr licuruswh stic thim onto the crem. Then you put the othr sib on top. then you get the tob with the frostng and gut two dots. Then you are thro. did you no thet chrechulus cud get ten ichus long.

The End

(Translation of this story is on page 106.)

[Arachnids are spiders. They do not have antennas. They have eight legs. There are 30,000 different spiders. They have two body parts. I know how to make an Oreo spider. It is fun. I will tell you how to make it. You need an Oreo cookie. Then you need a licorice stick. Then you need a tube of frosting. Then you take the Oreo and you break it in half. (Get) the side with the most cream. You take your licorice and stick them onto the cream. Then you put the other side on top. Then you get the tube with the frosting and put two dots (for eyes). Then you are through. Did you know that tarantulas could get ten inches long? The end.]

That at least some of them understood the difference between narrative and informative writing came as they juggled for their place in line. I overheard one girl say to a classmate, "Anybody can write a story, but we really are smart, aren't we?"

When raising awareness to genres, work with what students already know. Then move into areas that are new. The following is a list of awareness activities for students:

- List and share favorite stories, novels, poems, and so forth.

- List and share favorite modes of writing, such as narrative and descriptive. Record lists on laminated posterboard. As additional genres are discovered, add them to the list.

- Brainstorm genres used in writing.

- Bring in examples of various genres, such as short stories, novels, editorials, political columns, advertising copy, poems, and song lyrics. Discuss these.

Teachers can encourage students to experiment with various genres by practicing some or all of the following awareness activities for teachers:

- Introduce, define, and explain general terms, such as *shaping, form, mode,* and *genre.*

- Review reflexive and extensive writing.

- Model by writing in different genres.

- Encourage students to move from the genres they know to those less familiar.

- Reward risk takers.

The influence of the teacher in expanding students' awareness is invaluable.

Robert Cormier, author of The Chocolate Wars, I Am the Cheese, *and other fine young adult literature, said at the 1988 ALAN (Assembly on Literature for Adolescents) Workshop to NCTE, "I am a writer today because a teacher in seventh grade called me a writer. From that moment on, I was never anything else."*

Literary Exploration

In partnership with the genre awareness campaign is the continual extension of students' exploration of literature, as information, entertainment, through reading and writing. Many writing teachers are also reading teachers and literature teachers; and, as lovers of words, they experience the connections between writing and reading. Students, however, often compartmentalize subjects; therefore, for them, synthesis does not always happen.

Some teachers combat this problem by adopting a literature-based approach to the study of language. Such a strategy uses a major literary work as the focal point of all learning. Becky Hicks uses *Hamlet* as the center of study. She allows her students to choose journal topics, analogies, and multi-genre writing assignments as ways into their learning. She also conducts grammar and lexical mini-lessons that have connections to the ongoing readings and discussions of the play.

Other teachers work through a thematic strand of literature and employ a wide variety of genres within that strand. Edna Bubenik introduces her students to Lloyd Alexander's *Prydain Chronicles* by interspersing thematic drama throughout the study. They dramatize the themes in the novel. They may choose to write mini-plays as a part of their study. Edna helps the students find examples of other plays and develops what she calls "play sheets"—a page with blank speaker balloons down the page. With these sheets the students do not become bogged down in the formal logistics of writing a script. For these fifth-graders, form does not overwhelm meaning. They also may choose to write poems or stories that arise from the novel. Students will sometimes construct a biography for a favorite character. Once, several students collaborated on a sequel.

Other classes, like those of Anita Arnold at Jefferson High School, San Antonio ISD, become acquainted with wide-ranging literary selections through short daily readings. Students begin to appreciate varieties of forms and authors. Anita offers for some students one of their first exposures to contemporary poetry through collections such as Paul Janeczko's *Poetspeak* and *The Music of What Happens*. Poetry becomes accessible, and the B-flat personal narrative essay becomes the pungent, powerful narrative poem.

Anita also writes. Students in her classes know the power and excitement of genre. She does not weld herself to one mode of expression or one audience. Her poem "Eat Your Heart Out Barbara Courtland" was published in *The English Journal* (September 1992). Her article about athlete poets appeared in *Texas Coach* (July 1992). And her practice of taking the poem and the writing/language-experience model together with field trips to the Witte Museum and the San Antonio Botanical Gardens was printed in *English in Texas* (Winter 1991) as the article "Windows of Cultural Literacy."

Literary exploration incorporates the study of skill, genre, literature, spelling, reading, listening, speaking, and viewing with writing. If students truly explore, they truly make discoveries. Rather than force-feeding literacy, teachers need to create environments wherein students freely range over possibilities. That way students make the important connections between their writing and its form.

Heuristic Techniques

Heuristic techniques, discussed in chapters 2 and 3 specifically in relation to prewriting, also may be used as productive, systematic ways to move from prewriting into writing. The questions of classical invention as applied to a topic, for example, may be reapplied to the prewriting those original questions generated. Although independent thinkers often ask themselves questions as guides to give their thoughts form, students, who may or may not have achieved this level of independence sometimes require a heuristic model. Four heuristics are presented here: dialogue with self, the shaping conference, status of the class, and a taxonomy of questions.

Dialogue with Self. Increasing students' confidence in their ability to make decisions lies at the heart of dialogue with self. Begin by inviting students to write a dialogue with themselves about their prewriting. This often yields insights—if not immediately, sometimes later after a rereading or rethinking. Much like the prewriting activity of dialogue, students are given a first line that they write out of. Then they continue the dialogue by assuming at least two different perspectives. This technique is designed to lead the writer closer to form.

Me 1:   I'm reading my prewriting to see whether some form is hiding in the words.

Me 2:   It was easier when the teacher just told us what to write.

Me 1:   But she didn't, so get on with it.

Me 2:   OK. All my stuff seems to be about friends. It's like I'm on a friend kick.

Me 1:   Is all the prewriting saying the same thing?

Me 2:   All pretty much, except the one about Francey.

Me 1:   What's different about that piece?

Me 2:   Well, I was really angry she had to move away. I wrote a lot of stuff about kids' rights. I mean her parents decided to move so she had to move and leave all her friends.

Me 1:   Sounds like you'd like to convince her parents of something.

Me 2:   Yeah. I'd like to persuade them to move back.

Of course, all students' dialogue with self will not point so clearly to form as the above example. Sometimes, this technique does not help. Sometimes, though, it provides the needed focus, time, and direction to be beneficial.

The Shaping Conference. Because the shaping conference promotes discussion, even debate, it often helps students clarify meaning, purpose, audience—even interest. After the writer describes or reads the prewriting, peers share into how that prewriting came across. Did it foreshadow a passionate plea for change that begs to be a letter? Does it promise a solid, persuasive argument that needs the form of an essay? Is it an intensely emotional reaction that demands the condensed form of a poem? Sometimes in shaping conferences, especially with extremely disparate prewritings, group members may brainstorm a variety of forms to which the prewriting lends itself, as well as the pros and cons of each form. Ultimately, though, the writer makes the decision.

Status of the Class as a Heuristic. Atwell's status of the class (89), which she credits to Donald Graves, allows students to hear options and ideas discussed by other writers. This dialogic often spurs on the reluctant writer. The different responses proffered by others become a heuristic, a series of stepping stones, that the writer may think about and accept or reject.

The need for a class status arises out of "abandonment" of teacher-selected assignments and "whole-class deadlines." With classes of students working at their own pace independently, the teacher needs a way to graph what is being done and what needs to be done by both student and teacher. Atwell begins the status of the class on the second day of a writing workshop. She has a chart with her students' names written down the left-hand side. Then there are a series of boxes for the days of the week. She explains how she teaches status of the class to her students:

Each day, before you go your separate ways, I'll ask each of you to tell me very quickly what you're working on and where you are in your piece. This is called a status-of-the-class conference. It's my way of keeping track of who's doing what and how I can best help you do what you're trying to do.

Today, what will you be doing? You might be continuing draft one, the piece you started yesterday. Maybe you're starting draft two, a new version of this piece. Perhaps you're revising.... You might be having a conference with a friend or me.... Or you may have come up with a topic you like better and wish to abandon yesterday's piece and start a new first draft. Please take thirty seconds to look at what you wrote yesterday and decide what you'll be doing today. (89)

Atwell concludes this session by calling on each student, writing down on her chart what he or she intends to write about and what he or she intends to do during the day's writing workshop.

As teachers work through the class list, they have the opportunity to ask probing and heuristical questions to lead students in productive directions, to clarify misunderstandings or misconceptions, and to encourage. For example, the teacher may say:

"Mario, what are you going to do today?"
"I think I am going to start a new draft."
"What are you writing about?"
"The time my bike got run over in the driveway."
"Are you writing a story or a poem?"
"I don't know yet."
"What about a play?"
"No, I don't think so."
"Have you considered a memoir?"
"No, but maybe that is what I want."
"What will you have to do to determine what form you want?"
"Consider which works best."

And the teacher then moves on to the next student. Although this reads as though it takes up much time, the status of the class is meant to be a conference and does not have to be experienced by all students at the same time, nor does it need to be done every day. In those classes where reading and writing workshops happen simultaneously, the teacher can use status of the class not only as a heuristic but also for classroom management.

A Taxonomy of Questions. Sometimes, if the previous techniques fail to yield results, it helps to try a more direct approach. Students may work through the following questions in large groups, in pairs, with the teacher, or alone.

- What form does this writing sound like it wants to be or become (e.g., poem, play, mystery)?

- Whom is this for?

- What relationship do you want to have with your audience?

- How do you want your audience to feel? What do you want them to think?

- What do you want your audience to do after they read your piece?

- How might this look on the page?

- Can you change the genre but still keep the message?

Summary

Students may find that they come to genre from various points in the discovery process. Some use preliminary notes, only the very beginnings of prewriting, to choose a genre. Others may make the decision after a trial run of a draft. Still others may keep reworking the prewriting until the form presents itself.

The importance of discovering genre is the freedom to move from idea to poetry to travelogue to protest letter. In this freedom, most students find the best way to say what they have to say. The more experience a writer has selecting genre, the more critical the writer becomes. Through awareness and literary exploration the writer implements the characteristics of genre into writing. Genre gives form to writing.

FICTION

"Fiction is an imaginary but usually plausible and ultimately truthful prose narrative which dramatizes changes in human relationships. The author draws his [or her] materials from experience and observation of life, but he [or she] selects and shapes them to his [or her] purposes, which include entertainment and the illumination of human experience" (Altenbernd and Lewis 14).

However brief or lengthy a piece, whether it be an anecdote, vignette, short story, novella, or novel, it contains dramatic action that is concrete and specific, shows a purpose, manifests a relationship to life, and contains creative aspects. The length of the piece usually determines the level of complexity of those characteristics.

> *I always tell my students if they can recite "Little Miss Muffett" they know the essential elements of fiction. To put that to a test, I invite them to fold a paper in fourths. We draw a smiling Little Miss in the center of the first block, a frowning Little Miss in the center with a small spider in the right-hand corner of the second block, a shocked Little Miss side-by-side with a large spider in the third block, and a large spider in the center with a small Little Miss disappearing off the last block.*
>
> *We then identify the characters — protagonist and antagonist — the setting, action, problem, and solution. We label the beginning, middle, and end. We talk about who told the story.*
>
> *After this, it is easy for students to see how longer, more complex pieces have multiple characters, characters in conflict with themselves, subplots, and several problems and solutions. After they internalize this, they understand how authors break from these elements or change them to fit their meaning.*

Students like to write, read, and listen to fiction. Kindergartners revel in their early scribbles and drawings taking them into stories; second-graders exhaust readers or listeners with books that run chapter after chapter, detail after detail, in the sheer delight of the writing. Little ones eagerly gather around the teacher to hear a story read or told, and so do middle-school students.

> *Becky Corder, who teaches at Cleburne Junior High School, recently wrote about her seventh- and eighth-grade students:*
>
> *"Friday I read all four classes Sylvester and the Magic Pebble. Not sure how they would handle a children's book, my favorite remark came from a seventh-grade boy: 'Oh, boy, we haven't had story time in six years!' "*

"Even more surprising, the eighth-graders (boys especially) loved the reading time. All the rest of the day as I saw my students in the halls, they would hold out their hands — 'Here's my pebble.' I'm really curious about one boy who changed his whole pebble. He carefully picked out pieces of pebbles that he said fit into one so his story would tell about a magic pebble broken in pieces so the magic could spread."

Teachers such as Sylvia Bell, Sam Rayburn High School, Pasadena, Texas, and Helen Eiseman, Kerrville High School, Kerrville, Texas, report that even sophisticated seniors will sit around a storyteller with eyes wide during the telling.

Implementing the Writing of Fiction

Moving students into the writing of fiction is easy for several reasons: They are familiar with the genre, they like the genre, and they are able to tap their own experiences for the basic stuff of a story; it is the fundamental way people organize their reality. As Jerome Bruner explains in *Acts of Meaning*, "stories make 'reality' a mitigated reality. Children ... are predisposed naturally and by circumstance to start their narrative careers in that spirit. And we equip them with models and procedural tool kits for perfecting those skills. Without those skills we could never endure the conflicts and contradictions that social life generates" (97).

Encourage students to consider the following forms of fiction:

Sudden fiction	Fable	Fantasy
Short story	Myth	Science fiction
Novella	Legend	Adventure
Novel	Tall tale	Gothic (horror)

Because of the gamut of techniques and permutations fiction takes, students benefit from understanding the general characteristics of all fiction:

- anecdotal/narrative/plot items — the story drives the plot

- cause-and-effect pattern of events — the audience experiences the "action-reaction cycle" (Sedlacek 50)

- significant conflict — emotional or physical risk

- character development — the audience gains insights into motivations, personalities, and feelings; 3-dimensional versus 1-dimensional characters

- dialogue — authentic to the characters

- awareness of audience — tone and style that convey a genuine sense of readership

- emotional significance — for the characters, for the audience

- change — the character changes emotionally, physically, mentally

- literal, social, and universal implications — the stories work on one or all levels

- discovery by audience — insights discovered

- setting — emotional, physical, imaginary

(List continues on page 112.)

- description — of character(s), sets mood, sets tone

- point of view — first-, second-, or third-person or omniscient

- voice — author's understanding of characters and setting

PROBLEMS OF WRITING FICTION

Two major problems usually appear when students write fiction. The first problem — not dealing with possibility and plausibility — often leads students to think anything goes. Fiction may be possible or impossible, but it must be plausible. Aristotle says, "One should, on the one hand, choose events that are impossible but plausible in preference to ones that are possible but implausible; but on the other hand one's plots should not be made up of irrational incidents" (25, I.27). For example, the gods in myths reflect the human condition. If the story becomes too implausible, the reader scoffs. The reader can accept the plausibility that a mermaid disobeys her father and falls in love with a human in *The Little Mermaid*, because experience teaches that love is strong enough to cause someone to change. Although the reader may reject the possible existence of a mermaid, the reader accepts, perhaps as analogy, perhaps as symbolic, the tension between lovers who are different and whose love is strong enough to overpower a disbelieving parent and personified evil.

When students write fiction, they are not writing histories. They may still write from their own experiences in fictional ways, but they need to consider what is likely to happen versus what did happen. They go against Aristotle's advice in *Poetics* when they eschew the impossible but plausible in order to choose the possible but implausible, piling one irrational incident upon another. In short, students often strive for the unconvincing possibility rather than the likely impossibility. One way to clarify this for students is by viewing an Alfred Hitchcock film. Discuss how this master storyteller helps the audience identify with the characters, no matter how impossible the situation, because the story is always plausible. Hitchcock himself said, "Making a film means, first of all, to tell a story. That story can be an improbable one, but it should never be banal. It must be dramatic and human. What is drama, after all, but life with the dull bits cut out?" (Truffaut 103). Hitchcock provides a good place to start understanding possibility and plausibility.

The second problem with writing fiction is character. Characters are the central focus in fiction. Even if they are animals, they depict the changing human condition. Flat, one-dimensional characters lie lifelessly on the page. Round characters actively rise up from the pages. Students who strive for dramatically elaborated, three-dimensional characters develop "people" (human or otherwise) that the reader may identify with.

One way to help students develop characters is to ask them to list all the people they have come in contact with during the last 24 hours. Have them circle several of the more interesting persons, then create a dialogue with those persons, asking and answering questions until the characters come alive, take on a life of their own, make choices, and act in characteristic ways. Or, if the characters do something uncharacteristic, they respond characteristically.

SHORT STORY, NOVELLA/NOVEL

Specific fictional genres exhibit their own special attributes — the most significant are breadth and depth. The short story by definition is finite, with "tight plotting, close character development, and concise, effective expression" (Sedlacek 49). Because the short story has had a magical and wonderful evolution, examining contemporary short stories is imperative to teach this genre. Although modern short stories continue with the beginning, middle, and end structure, this is not necessarily true of all contemporary short stories. Writers such as Baxter, Max, and Oates take liberties with something so pat, arguing that the predictability fails to match contemporary life. The old standard of "once students master this form, then they can break the rules," may need rethinking. Does the mastery of aging, traditional characteristics ensure that students will be able to write for today's audiences? Certainly Dickinsonian descriptions engaged people who received weekly serials and had time to consider the significance of warts on noses and the way street lights reflected in the gutter water. In contrast, today's readers want immediacy. Today's writers may wish to withhold a beginning. Possibly there is no beginning or end to a story—there may be only a middle.

Teachers who teach genre balance the classic models with the contemporary. Thus, teachers who stay abreast of contemporary fiction know that the short story did not languish after Edgar Allan Poe—it simply changed. Unfortunately, many textbooks omit contemporary fiction because of copyright costs; many teachers omit contemporary fiction because they do not read it. With the present emphasis on multi-ethnic literature it will serve teachers and students to continue to search for and share a variety of short story authors.

> *Recently at a state-level textbook selection committee meeting, we heard the chair of the committee speak out against a text. The chair admitted, "I teach 12th-grade British Lit, and I've never heard of these people. They're unknowns."*
>
> *He was rejecting the books because he did not recognize the authors. He was referring to authors such as American Indian writers Elizabeth Cook-Lynn and Linda Hogan. Cook-Lynn is author of* Then Badger Said This, *and she has been published in* South Dakota Review, Prairie Schooner, *and* Sun Tracks. *Linda Hogan is author of* Calling Myself Home; Seeing Through the Sun; *and* Eclipse. *They are both included in the critically acclaimed collection* Spider Woman's Granddaughters: Traditional Tales and Contemporary Writing by Native American Women *edited by Paula Gunn Allen (Beacon Press, 1989). Nor had the chair of the committee selecting textbooks for high school students heard of Vivian Ling Hsu, author of* Born of the Same Roots: Stories of Modern Chinese Women. *The names Lao She, Wu Tsuhsiang, Hsiao Hung, Lo Hua-shen, Ping Hsin, Ling Shu-hus, T'ien T'ao, Teng Yu-mei, Ts'ao Ming, Ai Wu, and Hsi Jung did not fit into his construct of short story authors.*
>
> *Even contemporary African-American writers such as Doris Jean Austin, who writes for* The New York Times Book Review, The Amsterdam News, *and* Essence; *Toni Cade Bambara, author of* Gorilla, My Love, The Sea Birds Are Still Alive, *and* The Salt Eaters; *the Hugo and Nebula Award-winner Octavia Butler and her science fiction novels,* Dawn, Kindred, Adulthood Rites, Wild Seed; *Samuel R. Delany, a four-time Nebula Award winner; Rita Dove, the 1987 Pulitzer Prizewinner for her book of poems,* Thomas and Beulah; *and the 1978 Pulitzer Prizewinner for fiction, James Alan McPherson, were unknown to the committee chair.*
>
> *On the one hand, it is impossible to know all these writers; on the other hand, intolerance of ethnically diverse authors has led to a lack of recognition of these writers. As long as we select from those writers we all know—Wordsworth, Shelley, and Keats—how will students ever find the richness of differences and learn to accept these differences? Unfortunately, the chairman's argument was successful and the textbooks were not listed. The textbook companies present that day learned a valuable lesson: Don't invest in a program that has authors who are not readily recognized by those making adoption decisions.*

SUDDEN FICTION

One of the newest of the evolved forms of the short story is called sudden fiction. The exposition is short. The development is pared to necessity. The characters are complicated but are like fragments of a broken mirror. The author does not reveal everything. The uninformed reader usually and initially classifies the form as unelaborated, but, as in Oriental flower design, many knowing readers see less as better. Possibly it is just another way to write a story. *In media res* — "in the middle of things" — takes on a whole new meaning in sudden fiction. Transitions, like those in film and on television, are replaced with the jump cut.

Joyce Carol Oates describes sudden fiction:

> Very short fictions are nearly always experimental, exquisitely calibrated, reminiscent of Frost's definition of a poem — a structure of words that consumes itself as it unfolds, like ice melting on a stove. The form is sometimes mythical, sometimes merely anecdotal, but it ends with its final sentence, often with its final word. We who love prose fiction love these miniature tales both to read and to write because they are so finite; so highly compressed and highly charged. (Shapard and Thomas 246)

Author Barry Targan has this advice for writing sudden fiction:

> In writing, the short-short story rather than the more common short story comes closer to the classic *etude*, and for this reason is better suited to some of the initial needs of the creative writing student. Particularly, the main advantage is this: the writer can get a great deal of specific practice with various elements while staying within a true fiction form. He can pose specific technical problems of characterization, tone, mood, or whatever, and solve the problems in the terms of real stories. Using the short-short story, he avoids the artificiality of the set piece of assignment while at the same time protects himself from an uncertain commitment of energy and time entailed in the short story, for a short story is openended in the way a short-short story is not. That is the beauty of it. The shortshort story can no more get out of hand, go beyond its natural aim, than could Leonardo have drawn more on one sheet than size and design would allow. (Shapard and Thomas 247)

FABLES

The traditional fable with its stated moral, stereotypical animal characters, and brevity is a genre students can approach successfully. Students of all ages enjoy these oldest genres of literature — fables, myths, legends, and tall tales. These forms lend themselves equally to writing as well as reading. If the prewriting or trial draft offers an anecdote with a clear lesson or strong advice, the teacher may have the student consider working the text into this genre. Students may do this by:

- Reading examples of traditional fables (Aesop)

- Reading examples of contemporary fables (Katherine Paterson's *The Crane Wife* or Brian Jacques's *Redwall* or *Mossflower*)

- Selecting animals with personalities similar to the problem

- Writing out a moral

- Experimenting with the fable

As students progress in their development, James Thurber's fables offer fine examples of the modern fable. Although deceptively simple, the fable is not simplistic in its writing. When students have the opportunity to consider that the telling of their story can best be done through the genre of the fable, then they are well on their way to understanding the critical decisions writers make while employing their craft. They learn that deciding on genre is much like deciding on what to wear. The closet may be full, but the choice reflects what they want to project.

MYTHS

The myth and the related forms, the legend and the tall tale, have distinct characteristics. But all have the traits of adventure and exaggeration. The nature myth explains natural phenomena, the hero myth extols admirable virtues, and the epic examines religion, history, and culture. Few have used the myth to illuminate the workings of the mind as did Joseph Campbell. He wrote in *Creative Mythology*:

> In what I am calling "creative" mythology ... the individual has had an experience of his own—of order, horror, beauty, or even mere exhilaration—which he seeks to communicate through signs; and if his realization has been of a certain depth and import, his communication will have the value and force of living myth—for those, that is to say, who receive and respond to it of themselves, with recognition, uncorked. (3)

The other branches of this family lead students to the discovery of fairy tales, science fiction, and the Gothic (horror) thriller. The fairy tale is concerned with things that cannot really happen and is about people and creatures who do not exist, yet it has a logic within its reality. Whereas science fiction can have some of the same elements of the fairy tale, it is also a combination of the known and the unknown based on scientific theories. And the Gothic develops a gloomy or terrifying atmosphere with events that are uncanny, macabre, supernatural, or melodramatically violent—it sometimes explores the psychological state. As long as students have dreams and are not required to have a license to practice their imagination, these genres offer myriad opportunities. Teachers and parents should not be quick to dismiss such genres as frivolous and outdated or as detrimental to the young writer.

One way of moving students from their prewriting to myth is by helping them see the subjectivity of their experiences. Most students have been involved in an adventure or a frightening brush with danger. If students place these experiences in an exaggerated setting or add a colorful character, they are on their way to transforming experience into myth. Exaggeration allows the story to take on larger dimensions. Dealing with outside forces over which the writer has no control through the concept of the *deus ex machina* (a "god" lowered to the stage by some mechanism, who solves the problem) gives the writer the opportunity to end the myth with a renewed sense of confidence and control.

LEGENDS

Legends, too, spring from reality. They are myths with people, not supernatural beings, as protagonists. Legends, borrowing the episodic structure of the epic, add romantic elements and the possibilities of diversity. The sixth-grade girl who writes the cliché, "My dad is a knight in shining armor," has the beginnings of a medieval legend. The fifteen-year-old boy who looks on the beautiful, unattainable girl has the makings of a medieval romance. When prewriting hints at unsolvable situations, then dragon slayers cannot be far behind. Wise sisters who have troubled siblings invite "heroes" armed and ready for some personal battle.

The legend is so closely related to the folktale that studying the difference is tantamount to splitting hairs. One of the foremost contemporary folklorists, Jan Harold Brunvand, author of *The Vanishing Hitchhiker* and *The Choking Doberman*, records the differences this way as he writes about his collection:

It contained the results of some twenty years' study of many highly capti-
vating and plausible, but mainly fiction, oral narratives that are widely told as
true stories. We folklorists call them urban legends, although modern legends
might be a more accurate term.

The book set forth the history, variations, and possible meanings of some
popular belief tales found in contemporary storytelling, such as those about
hitchhikers who vanish from moving cars, alligators lurking in New York City
sewers, rats that get batter-fried along with the chicken in fast-food outlets, con-
vertibles filled with cement by jealous husbands, housewives caught in the nude
while doing laundry, hairdos infested with spiders, pets accidentally cooked in
microwave ovens, and so on....

Calling urban legends *folklore* requires an explanation. The usual definition
of verbal folklore is material that gets orally transmitted in different versions in
the traditions of various social groups. Proverbs, riddles, rhymes, jokes, anecdotes, and ballads are among the folk forms that circulate in oral and usually
anonymous variants, comprising the folklore of the people among whom they are
known. Urban legends, despite their contemporary sound, display the same
characteristics as older verbal folklore. They pass from person to person by word
of mouth, they are retained in group traditions, and they are inevitably found in
different versions through time and space. If an urban legend at first seems too
recent to have achieved the status of folklore, further study often reveals its plot
and themes to be decades or even centuries old. And even a new story partly
disseminated by the mass media soon becomes folklore if it passes into oral tradition and develops variations. (ix-x)

Urban tales are a part of the fabric of being storytellers. Allowing students to become researchers
of the oral tradition allows them to become writers and recorders of these stories.

TALL TALES

Tall tales emphasize humor, a strong sense of national identity, an outlandish exaggeration,
and unblemished imaginative heroes. "The characteristic of the tall tale that distinguishes it from
other humorous stories is its blatant exaggeration. Our older tall tales—with their swaggering
heroes who do the impossible with nonchalance.... They are such flagrant lies that the lyingest
yarn of all is the best one, provided it is told with a straight face and every similitude of truth"
(Arbuthnot and Sutherland 245). The imagination summons the tall tale. Everyday excuses are
ways into the tale. The lamer the excuse, the greater the opportunity to invent a wonderful tale.
Tardy excuses take on whole new dimensions as tall tales. Exaggeration becomes a byword for the
writer. The teller of the tall tale must show profound reasonableness, logic, and accuracy while
having everything take place in the middle of hilarious lunacy.

Three Quick Ways to Shape Fiction

STORY MAPS

The story map is a visual plotted out by students to better understand contemporary fiction.
The map of *Maniac Magee* is a good example of mapping a story (see fig. 4.1). Through it the student is able to deal with the flashbacks in a linear fashion. Writers such as Robin McKinley, in her
novels *The Blue Sword* and *The Hero and the Crown*, play with time. Readers are sometimes surprised to find that the second novel of the series is a prequel to the first. The story map made by a
student as a response to literature can help that student give shape to a story in the making.

Fig. 4.1. A *Maniac Magee* map. ꙮ

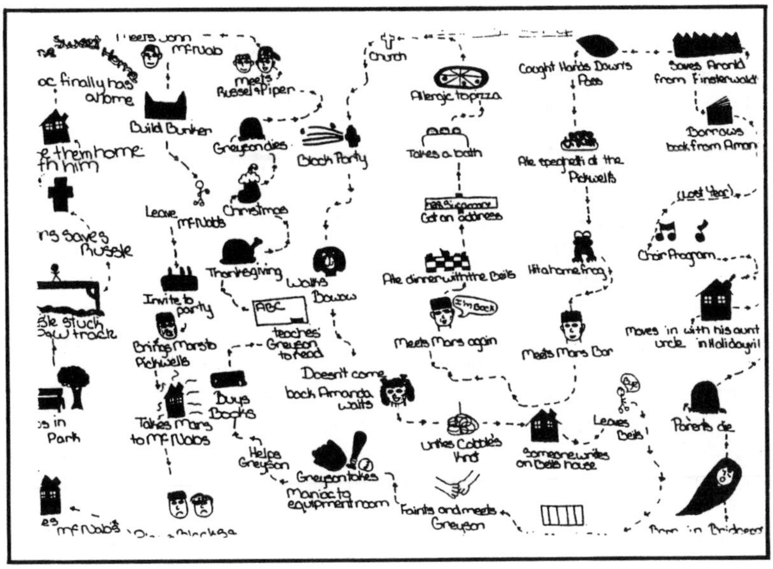

DIALOGUE

Dialogue allows the writer to catch the reader up on background. "The Sniper" has been on the rooftop for many hours when Liam O'Flaherty's story opens. Without the dialogue, the reader would have no idea why the sniper is on the roof. This is hardly new to fiction. Zeus and Athena discuss how Odysseus got himself in the mess he is in long before the reader meets the hero.

Dialogue also gives the reader an intimacy with the character. The voice of the grandfather in *Knots on a Counting Rope* stays true from the beginning — "I have told you many times, Boy. You know the story by heart ... listen carefully. This may be the last telling.... I promise you nothing, Boy. I love you. That is better than a promise" (2) — to the end — "Now Boy ... now that the story has been told again, I will tie another knot in the counting rope. When the rope is filled with knots, you will know the story by heart and can tell it to yourself.... I will not always be with you, Boy.... You will never be alone, Boy. My love, like the strength of blue horses, will always surround you" (Martin and Archambault 32).

In William Golding's *Lord of the Flies*, Piggy confronts Jack with the truth, asking, "What are we: Human? Or animals? Or savages?" The reply answers the questions and defines the character of Jack: "You shut up, you fat slug!" (82).

CHARACTER NAMING

Maxine Hong Kingston in a letter wrote: "I've noticed that most minority students write about stereotype Caucasian lovers. When you remind them to give their characters surnames, particularly of their own cultural background, many students will make a breakthrough that will amaze you" (Kingston 1). Fiction has moved away from Dick, Jane, and Spot. Characters such as Abuela in the children's book *Abuela*, by Arthur Dorros, or Elena Serafina Capalbo Chiradelli of Renée Manfredi's *Pushcart Prize XVI* short story, "Bocci," are infinitely more interesting. The more real the characters, the better the understanding and response from the reader.

Of course, whether the writer tells everything about the character is a matter of style and genre. But it is important that the writer know the character. Teachers such as Dawn Matthews McClendon, Northside ISD, San Antonio, have their students write histories for their main characters. Dawn has found that in writing these histories her students discover the characters' motivations.

The short story and its related forms are natural forms for the storyteller. Student writers can find their voice in this genre. As they master the showing and not telling (Macrorie), they truly capture the narrative.

DRAMA

Drama is a literary form first designed for theater and now extended to include film, television, and video. Students who thrive on the joys and tragedies of life, the wild swings of humor and pathos, find drama an exciting and challenging medium to explore. Although often only a few students have had the opportunity to personally see a professional stage production, film and television are natural extensions of students' lives. The visual learner adapts to the drama/script easily. These students often "see" what they write. They want the reader to "see" their story. Play/scriptwriting helps these students move into this genre.

The play has been a staple of English language arts teachers for years. Teachers have played records of dramas such as Dickens's *A Christmas Carol* or Shakespeare's *Hamlet*; they have divvied up the parts of Shaw's *Pygmalion* or Wilder's *Our Town*. But these teachers also know that nothing duplicates the full production of the script. The genre of drama is meant to be seen. Writers as well as actors, directors, and camera crews all share in production. Too often teachers encourage students to experience plays and scripts as a genre, but the students never get the opportunity to see them performed. "The play's the thing"—or so it should be.

The magazine *Scholastic Scope*, often used in English language arts classrooms, is probably the best source for contemporary stories presented in play form. Students of all levels and abilities enjoy reading these plays and find affirmation in this genre. These works provide excellent models for student-written drama.

Drama for the Very Young. Working with drama, film, and video does not have to be confined to secondary students. Elementary and early childhood students understand the natural workings of drama. Joyce Harlow, Summerfield Academy, Spring, Texas, works with dramatic play in her three-, four-, and five-year-old classes. They reenact classic tales. In her book *Story Play: Costumes, Cooking, Music, and More for Young Children*, Harlow shares the techniques and costumes she uses with her students. Together they read and discuss versions of a fairy tale. The children write their own version, illustrating and dictating as is developmentally correct. They act out their stories, and often someone videotapes the production. The students then write again, making shape books, flap books, even cookbooks. The drawing and writing become symbolic representations of their dialectics (logical discovery of truth). Together they watch their production and talk about it. The writing and the visual literacy emerge in ways that are often surprising.

For example, their symbolic reenactment becomes a manifestation of psychodrama. They not only reveal their understanding of the story they might reenact, such as *The Little Red Hen*, but they also reveal their understanding of social structures of parent and child while integrating the literature into their lives. They demonstrate attitudes and social behaviors. Joyce Harlow then confers with her students about their writing and praises their reenactments. The positive environment in which she works with her students deepens their literacy from surface environmental literacy to symbolic levels. Observing her students working is akin to watching what Suzanne K. Langer calls "symbolic transfer." They make metaphors; they make meaning. And using the visual genres allows for the meaning to happen in concrete, reinforcing ways. The students' multiple viewings of their stories and the stories of their schoolmates constantly gird up their emerging literacy.

The Collaborative Nature of Drama. Students cannot be totally independent and self-sufficient while working with drama. Not only does drama insist on collaboration but it is an excellent vehicle for exercising imaginative muscles and playing out riddles as students try to understand life. Out-of-reach adventure can be readily attainable because film can take place anywhere, anytime. The most ordinary problems and events take on new meaning. For example, in Charlie Chaplin's *The Gold Rush*, the famous "Dance of the Rolls" sequence has Chaplin daydreaming that the girl he loves from afar has come to his lonely cabin as his Christmas guest. Proudly he jabs forks into two bread rolls and goes into a dance. In this cunningly photographed sequence, it appears that Chaplin's huge head and the tiny roll "feet" are one body, and with a wonderful range of facial and pantomimic gestures, Chaplin does his "dance"—an episode that has to be seen rather than described to be fully appreciated for its grace and imagination in depicting a lonely man wishing for a dance.

Film and video allow for permanence and reviewing to experience again moments and ideas. To use D. W. Griffith's words, "Above all else I want to help you to see." Film and video allow for multiple viewings in ways different from drama. Drama creates new environments with each viewing.

Production requires students to work together. Students involved in these genres need to see and see again the presentations of their writings. The critical discoveries of what actors and directors can do with the writer's words are experiences unique to this genre. The one-act play, the documentary, the cartoon, the musical, the serial, and the news program all offer unique opportunities for students to see their words come alive, to work together, and to "see" writing for a different audience.

Implementing the Writing of Drama

THE LANGUAGE OF DRAMA

A certain amount of specific vocabulary used in theater and film needs to become a part of writing for dramatic genres. Students who want a fade, for example, need to write a fade into the script. To use these terms accurately, students need to read scripts and view films, television productions, and plays. Additionally they need to view these productions as writers, not as viewers. To help students view in this way, the teacher needs to be the voice overlay.

To do this the teacher needs to talk throughout the viewing of a film to identify what film technique is being used. Don Graves says in the beginning of *Writing: Teachers and Children at Work* that teachers need to know the twin crafts of teaching and writing (3). To teach drama genres, teachers need to know the art and craft of the visual arts. Figure 4.2 (see pages 120-21) is an RKO cutting continuity of Orson Welles's *Citizen Kane*. Ideally the teacher would provide the commentary during viewing of the film.

It is important to note that the entire segment delineated in figure 4.2 takes place in one minute and six seconds. Although certainly it is not the way to normally view a film, with the teacher explaining fades, cuts, and close-ups, it is the best way for students to learn how to view as a writer of film. This process of analysis will help students key into technique. This process, like any other, is difficult at first, but its magnificence becomes apparent with multiple experiences.

Why Writers Need to Analyze. Although Donald Graves observes that "analysis paralysis is the hallmark of too many American classrooms" (1989, 23), to have analytic skill is important to function in the world. Consider the Olympic Games. Students understand the sports coverage of the Olympics. They understand the analysis that the commentators give during events. In the 1988 Olympics, Olympic medalist Ester Williams was a consultant for the aquatic events. During one of the broadcasts of the women's high diving event, she made the comment, "I don't think she will get high marks for this dive—her ankles were too far apart on entry." To the untrained eye, it seemed that the diver quickly and gracefully cut through the air to enter the water rather effortlessly. But to Ester Williams and any others who viewed the dive not as a viewer but as a diver, they could see the parts of the dive to better evaluate the whole. Interestingly, during the 1992 Olympic Games, commentators remarked on how much better viewers became after watching earlier Olympics when commentators had talked through their analyses. Anyone who spent days in front of the screen became more discriminating in the analysis of the events. If students can learn to analyze sporting events, they can learn to analyze visual presentations, literature, and their own writing.

Once students have a working knowledge of the techniques of a certain genre, then they can better manipulate the constraints of the medium. Farrington, in "Words and Pictures by ... Writing for the Movies," points out, "For every one hundred words a novelist uses, a playwright may only need ten—and the screen writer needs about three" (4). Dialogue becomes important in screen genres, but motion plays just as vital a role. Even silence is a sound. Understanding the techniques allows for the words and the visual to merge with the action.

(Text continues on page 122.)

Fig. 4.2. Analysis of the opening segment of *Citizen Kane*.

Length Ft./Frame	Scene No.	

REEL I—SECTION 1A

19-5   1.   *Fade In-* [A punctuation device. The screen in black; gradually the image appears, brightening to full strength] TITLE #1—radio broadcasting

AN R.K.O. RADIO PICTURE

Fade Out

12-5   2.   *Fade In*—TITLE #2:

A MERCURY PRODUCTION
by Orson Welles

12-3   3.   TITLE #3:

CITIZEN
KANE

Fade Out

Night Sequence

37-   4.   *Fade In*—EXT. GATE CS- [Close shot] Music playing—sign reads: NO TRESPASSING. Camera pans up over sign and up wire fence

Lap Dissolve

[The superimposition of a fade out over a fade in.]

9-5   5.   *EXT. GATE CS*— camera pans up slowly over fence—music

Lap Dissolve

12-   6.   *EXT. HOUSE CS*— camera pans up slowly over ornate grillwork design on window

Lap Dissolve

12-   7.   *EXT. GATE MS* (Medium shot)—camera pans up over top of gate, showing letter "K"—Xanadu on mountain top in b.g. [background]

Lap Dissolve

13-2   8.   *EXT. XANADU LS* [Long shot]—castle above in b.g.—monkeys in cage at left

Lap Dissolve

12   9.   *EXT. WATER MS*—Camera shooting down—prows of two gondolas in f.g. [foreground], a wooden wharf in b.g.

Lap Dissolve

19   10.   *EXT. GROUND MLS* [Medium long shot]—camera shooting past moat to castle in b.g.—statue of animal in f.g.—drawbridge across moat suspended in mid-air.

Lap Dissolve

7-5   11.   *EXT. XANADU LS* [Long shot]—camera shooting up past sign at left on golf course in disrepair to castle above in b.g.

Lap Dissolve

Fig. 4.2 — *Continued*

Length Ft./Frame	Scene No.	
11-4	12.	*EXT. XANADU MLS* — camera shooting over water to building and castle in b.g.
		Lap Dissolve
9-	13.	*EXT. CASTLE MLS* — camera shooting up to light in window
		Lap Dissolve
15-6	14.	*EXT. CASTLE MLS* — camera shooting through window — bed inside b.g. — light lit — music heard — lights go out
		Lap Dissolve
12-	15.	*INT. ROOM MS* — light comes on softly in b.g., showing covered form on bed
		Lap Dissolve
9-3	16.	*INT. GLASS GLOBE* — snow falling
		Lap Dissolve
3-7	17.	*INT. GLASS GLOBE CU* [Close-up] — snow-covered house with snowmen surrounding it — camera moves back, showing Kane's hand holding globe
2-11	18.	*CLOSE-UP* of Kane's mouth — lips move
		KANE
		Rosebud!
5-11	19.	*INT. ROOM CU* — Kane's hand holding glass globe — drops it — music — it rolls to b.g. — down steps
1-10	20.	*INT. ROOM CU* — glass globe rolling down steps to f.g. — breaks
1-7	21.	*INT. ROOM MS* — distorted reflection through broken glass ball — door in b.g. opening — nurse comes in
10-1	22.	*INT. ROOM LS* — Reflection through broken glass ball — camera shooting through enormous bedroom to door in b.g. — nurse coming in — crosses to right, exits
21-3	23.	*INT. ROOM CS* — Kane's body partly on in f.g. — nurse partly on, bending over him — folds his arms on his chest — music — she pulls covers up, leaning over — camera pans up past Kane's face as she covers it up
		Fade Out
		Night Sequence
17-	24.	*Fade In* — *INT. ROOM MS* — shadow of body lying on bed — light shining dimly through window in b.g.
		Fade Out

[Note: The shots that are not fades or dissolves are cuts — one shot to another.] (Kael, Mankiewicz, Welles 309-10)

WRITING FOR TELEVISION

Television scripts are related to film scripts, but they have their own unique characteristics. The TV script has an even tighter format, and the limits of this genre adapt well to classroom writing and activities. With the advent of handheld video cameras, classroom productions of television scripts are easier to manage and much more accessible to all students. Besides the accessibility of the cameras and videotapes, television is a medium with which students are more familiar. The teacher's job becomes one of facilitating the physical/manipulative actions of video-taping and of helping the students adapt their many personal experiences of dramatic events. Students' prewriting has rich potential for the subgenre of sitcom, for instance, and teachers may help their students translate the human events into fictional characters and scripts.

Television Formats. Students can easily observe the structure and shape of writing for television. To analyze a program, start by having students note the number of minutes actually devoted to the story. Within a 30-minute segment, 7 minutes are usually devoted to commercials and 4 minutes for opening and closing credits. Television generally follows one of the formats shown in figure 4.3.

Fig. 4.3. Television formats.

Minutes	30-minute program	Minutes	60-minute program
3	Opening credits	2	Opening scene
5	Opening scene	3	Commercial break
3	Commercial break	14	Scene 2
8	Scene 2	2	Commercial break
3	Commercial break	8	Scene 3
6	Final scene	3	Commercial break
1	Final credits	14	Scene 4
1	Commercial break	2	Commercial break
		8	Final scene
		2	Final credits
		2	Commercial break

Once students get their ideas written for their scripts, then they can go about rearranging and structuring the dialogue and action to tailor the script to the format.

Using Television Scripts to Teach Persuasion. Not only is it easy for students to write using television as a model, they also may practice techniques of persuasion by writing and producing commercials. This way they hone writing skills, better their visual literacy, and have fun.

Literary-magazine-staff students at Westfield High School in Spring, Texas, wrote scripts to advertise the magazine. They wrote and produced a 15-minute video about the arts at Westfield. They included two commercials. The first was to encourage students to submit their writings to the magazine. With a spot rich in detail of where to submit, when to submit, and how it would be selected—all in a 60-second spot—they got their message across. They learned to tighten and to choose words carefully. Their final commercial was for the sale of the magazine. A 400 percent jump in sales from the previous year proved their success. This is the power of the media—and the power of good writing.

Techniques to Shape Drama

THE SETTING

The student whose prewriting presents a promising vignette with characters and conflict may begin by drawing a floor plan of the stage. This visualization reminds the writer that the setting becomes the set and that, like the short story, drama has its limits. Set design is influenced by tone, which in turn influences mood. Knowing the set helps shape the writing of the script.

DIALOGUE

On the stage, movement works in concert with speech. As the dialogue develops, students begin thinking about the actors' movements. Now the dimension of space affects the characters, and writers must think about what those limits say to the audience. Drawing or sketching this *stage business* while writing dialogue is especially helpful to visual learners. The sketches then become stage notes, a vital part of the genre.

Of greatest importance in a successful stage play is dialogue. The audience can only know what they see or what the characters tell them. So dialogue must supply information about setting, background, conflict—all the literary devices needed to move the story. Dialogue also must be natural and believable. The words out of the characters' mouths must sound like conversation, but must not be like talk. Talk is wordy and cumbersome in a play. Dialogue is tight and provides the essential information without sounding clipped.

Students attempting dialogue for a script need to be keen observers and careful listeners. Eavesdropping on conversations is one way to practice dialogue. Students need to heighten their listening skills, hone their ears to nuances of language, key into the different ways people communicate, and practice ways to capture that communication. When Orson Welles made *Citizen Kane*, audiences were somewhat taken aback by the overlapping sound; they were unaccustomed to it in film, yet it occurs naturally in life. Welles wanted dialogue to happen in the film the way it happens in life. In day-to-day experiences, speakers do not always wait for the other speaker to finish. Capturing the elusive nature of interruptions, nonverbal responses, and trailing off is difficult for the writer, but a good playwright writes a script that gives viewers the impression they are seeing and listening to real conversations, not fabricated ones.

PLOT

In all forms of drama, the writer places the characters in a conflict, creates complications, instigates crises, and then finds a way to resolve those crises. Jan Farrington, in the magazine *Writing!* tells budding writers her laws of drama: "1) put your characters 'up a tree'; 2) throw rocks at them; and 3) find a way to get them down" (6).

SCRIPT FORMAT

Professional scripts allow students to see the format of the genre, but note that shooting scripts are radically different from play scripts. Following a standard format makes for a smoother script. It also facilitates the production of the script when it is in the form that best matches the purpose of drama.

An excellent source of shooting scripts is the Classic Film Script series published by Simon and Schuster. They have the entire scripts of classics such as *Stagecoach, The Blue Angel,* and *Metropolis.* These scripts can then be used as a source of study and as models.

DRAMATIC TIMING

Students working in this genre soon learn the value of timing. A commercial in the wrong place is like a chapter ending in the wrong place. It is like a poem having a stanza break in the wrong place. So, not only do students need to be aware of good story elements, they also need to understand the narrative break. Plays, films, and television often follow two plot lines that intersect, whereas sitcoms normally are limited to a single thread. Students need to consider the following questions when writing for this genre:

- What seems to be more important — the characters or the plot?

- How important is predictability? Should there be foreshadowing?

- What about the complexity of plot? Will the viewer "get it"?

- How much attention to detail does the writer give?

- What can be said visually without words? Would music or sound effects help meaning?

A Practical Application of the Dramatic Genre

Generally, daily announcements in high schools are received one of two ways. Either the teachers act like wardens who demand and get total obedience during the announcements, or everyone disregards the announcements. The teachers grade papers. The students finish homework, talk to classmates, sleep — anything but pay attention.

In the midst of these two extremes is one high school whose daily announcements cause the school to come to a screeching halt. Killeen High School (KHS) is a typical large high school near Fort Hood Army Base. When it is time for the daily announcements, KHS students run to their homerooms because they do not want to miss them. A few years ago, KHS took advantage of the Channel One program. Every classroom has a monitor, and every morning the Channel One News and commercials are programmed in. Through these, students either sit in obedient attention, under duress, or they "blow it off." But, when the school news, "The KHS News," comes on, students tune in. Students in the "Radio and Television" classes write the commentary, and they anchor and produce the daily announcements. They emulate national news programs. They have exposés. They highlight winners. They get reactions to news from principals, students, parents, and community members. The school stops to view this show. Every kid looks for himself or herself. They joke when a friend is interviewed. They whoop when a team wins. They pay attention. Why? It is theirs. Once again, writing gives ownership.

POETRY

Nancy Willard writes in her essay "How Poetry Came into the World and Why God Doesn't Write It" (148) how she imagines herself as an insurance salesperson who is being visited by Adam and Eve. They have come in to file a claim because they "have lost everything through an act of God." As the agent, she wants Adam and Eve to specifically tell her what they have lost. They chronicle things such as eternal life, roses, free time, and both agree on the loss of poetry. As the agent in charge, Willard is excited by poetry because it is "the first thing you've mentioned that *can* be replaced."

Adam and Eve disagree with her. They tell her that poetry was invented in Eden and it came from a well. All one had to do was put an ear to the well and he or she heard a poem. Drink from the well, and you spoke a poem. "Poetry was so easy. No waiting, no revising, no dry spells."

Willard ends her essay by summing up the claim Adam and Eve wish to make. She asks, "You wish to declare a total loss?" They tell her no, because they did not lose everything. They explain that as the avenging angel was showing them to the gate, he berated them. Adam agrees that they were "dumb," but what he really hated to lose was the well. The angel told them they could keep the well; God did not want it. Adam wanted to know where the well is.

> "The well is inside you," replied the angel. "Much more convenient to carry it that way. Of course it's not going to be as easy to find as it was in the garden, when you could just lean over and take a drink. Sometimes you'll forget the words you're looking for, or you'll call and the wrong ones will answer. Sometimes they'll be a long time coming. But everything the well gave you it will give you again. Or if not to you, to your children. Or your great-great-great-great-grandchildren.... By the grace of dreams we may meet again, blown together by an emerald wind. And I hope you'll remember me with metaphors and make a lovely web of words about me. I hope you'll make some marvelous—what do you call it?"
>
> I [Adam] said the first word that came into my head: "Poetry." (Willard 148)

Willard's essay is worth reading. No summary can do it justice because it illuminates the power and beauty of poetry the way no one but Willard can. Her liquid images, her essences of truth, all touch and inspire. And she has revealed something about the nature of poetry: It is in all of us.

Students working with poetry are like a well. Water comes flowing forth or the well is clogged and dry. And then there is the difficulty of what students do with the poem after they find it. Teachers can help students recognize poetry within their own writing by continually sharing with their students contemporary and traditional poetry. Discussing what they like about these poems encourages students to think about why a particular poem works and how they as poets can shape their feelings and ideas into poems of their own. It helps them listen to the well inside.

When considering genre in poetry, there is no need to consider the genres as exclusive of each other. Writers continually push established genres to the limits. They continue to develop new genres. It is possible to find contemporary poems that have a story in a lyric poem that deals with emotions. Dialogue is being used with both lyric and narrative poems. For the neophyte poet, these two subgenres are good departing spots. As the writer matures, he or she must read extensively and study all types of poetry, but for the novice, the narrative and the lyric are comfortable places to start.

The Narrative Poem. The narrative poem is written in the poet's own voice. The poet has a story to tell the reader. Generally, the narrative poem is told chronologically and the persona of the poem is the poet. In some cases, the poet assumes another persona. Sometimes the poet tells about the persona of the poem. Narratives like "Sarah Cynthia Sylvia Stout Would Not Take the Garbage Out," by Shel Silverstein, and Ericka Mumford's "The White Rose: Sophie Scholl 1921-1943" are excellent examples of the poet telling about someone else. Sarah Cynthia Sylvia Stout should remind children of themselves or someone they know, while Mumford writes a historical account of a Nazi resistance fighter in Germany.

The Lyric Poem. The first place to start the lyric with students is with song. The ancient *lyric* was a poem accompanied by the lyre. Today we refer to the words of a song as the lyrics. Oral in its tradition, a lyric is intended to be read aloud now rather than sung. The musical elements still affect the lyric poem—patterns, rhymes, the sound of words. The lyric poem is generally more emotive—the sound of the words join with the feelings of the poem.

Barbara Drake (153) says a lyric is usually:

- personal or individualistic.

- emotional; concerned with feeling.

- musical; not necessarily metrical, but sound elements—such as rhythm and rhyme—are an integral part of sense. Consequently, paraphrasing and translating are difficult.

- organized by association rather than by chronology.

- compressed, so that figurative speech, allusion, and so forth suggest rather than state explicitly.

The Lyric as Narrative or the Narrative as Lyric. Consider the poem "The Animal That Drank Up Sound," by William Stafford, now available as a children's picture book illustrated by Debra Frasier. The poem has qualities of myth and fable. It tells a story of sorts. It is mysterious and compelling. It is rich with beautiful imagery. The words create a mood that almost blends into sounds. Is the poem lyric or narrative? Looking at the poem it becomes clear that the distinctions between lyric and narrative are not as important to contemporary writers.

Again, Barbara Drake:

> The point is not to discourage anyone from writing a modern narrative poem either long or short, dealing with the past or present. One should, however, be cautious of this tendency toward the artificial, inflated rhetoric of a period piece. Faced with the dominance of the lyric, it might be a challenge to experiment with narrative in poetry, and doubtless instructive to think of how your present poetry might be changed by developing its narrative or dramatic qualities. Other questions also arise: should your poetry imitate life? should lyric poetry become more musical, more abstract, more associative? is poetry an effective medium for social criticism or the exploration of aesthetics or psychology? Set yourself a problem of one of these areas and experiment with the idea of genre. (174)

Free Verse and Line Breaks. At the beginning of the twentieth century, poetry began to break away from the structure of rhythm and the predictability of rhyme. Ezra Pound and his followers wrote and theorized about this new form. They called it free verse. The purpose was to "compose in the sequence of the musical phrase, not in the sequence of a metronome" (Nims 273). Free verse also has been called "open form." Open verse allows the poet to discover the way the arrangement of the words should appear in the poem. Without a rhyme scheme or a basic meter dictating the form, the poem relies on other ways to engage the reader. Relying on intuition, and on visual and aural effects, the poet places the words in a natural position. In placing these words, the poet also considers the line breaks. Line breaks lend emphasis to the last word on the line and the first word of the next line. The meaning of the line usually dictates where the break occurs.

When working with students who want to write poetry, remember what Stephen Berg and Robert Mezey say: "The best poems of the last twenty years don't rhyme (usually) and don't move on feet of more or less equal duration (usually). That nondescription moves toward the only technical principle they all have in common" (ix).

Good Versus Bad Poetry. Teaching the genre of poetry is difficult. Equally difficult is helping students know what a good poem is. Poet X. J. Kennedy discusses good versus bad poetry in his book *Literature: An Introduction to Fiction, Poetry, and Drama.* He uses two poems on the same subject—death of defenseless animals. One example is William Stafford's "Traveling Through the Dark," and the other is Rod McKuen's "Animal Rights." When the two poems are juxtaposed, it is easy to see the difference. Stafford's poem rings rich with imagery and metaphoric language. McKuen's poem manipulates the audience's emotions with trite phrases and cute images. Stafford does not tell. He takes the reader through the experience of hitting a deer while traveling along a treacherous road. The poem never says the driver feels badly, but the reader knows it to be true. A good poet does not have to tell. The reader knows.

Chris Allen, a student at Cooper High School, Abilene ISD, Texas, worked hard at his writing. Committed to becoming a poet, he wrote and rewrote; he read and read. As a student, he showed the diligence of real writing. One day he entered the classroom and asked for a teacher conference. He read:

🏃 It has snowed again.
The world is crackling with ice.
I see death at every icicle.
There is the deer who tried to jump the fence last night.
Her leg caught and she hung there until she froze to death.
I see the death and think of my father in South America.
Children are being killed by stray bullets.
Stray bullets and freak snow storms
They both kill.

In the conference the teacher pointed out that Chris was trying to deal with two powerful images — the deer and the children. With suggestions, Chris realized that he had the possibilities for at least two poems here. His results were:

Another Freezing Season

🏃 Snowmen made of soil and unclean snow decompose
as children with red noses
watch in frustration
from behind smeared windows.
Maple trees crackle free
from their icy bondage
and jagged chinks of crystallized death
shatter on the wet pavement.
An icicle of blood
dissolves from the nose of a frozen deer,
its body hanging stiffly from a barbed wire fence,
too high for its legs to conquer.
Decay drifts from the breaths of cracked-filled sidewalks
as the sun lifts
the souls of a million different identities.
My eyes fill with tears
from the rising, moist air,
and blur the magnificent sight of
another winter's steam bath.
Pine trees no longer emit laughter or screams from
clumps of swirling wind, but instead
whisper mild breezes through their
needle-laden tongues.
My younger brother smuggles snow into our house
at an attempt to salvage the crippling scene.
I watch all this
while a blue truck speeds by
showering my lawn with gray, aging slush,
which slaps an image onto my chapped face and I sit quietly,
satisfied at the thought of another dying season.

The other image resulted in a concrete poem, shown in figure 4.4.

Fig. 4.4. Chris Allen's concrete poem. 👤

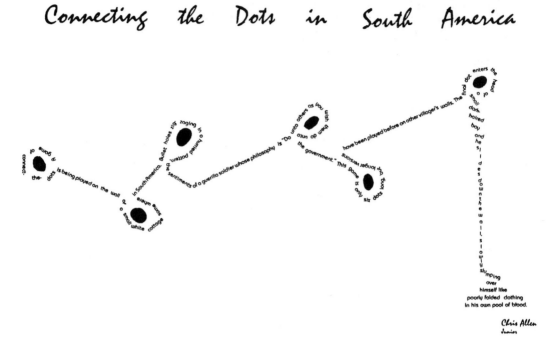

Chris wanted his form to match his meaning, so he felt the second image was best served by being concrete. Chris does not constrain himself to any particular form of poetry. He experiments. His finished products were selected to be included in the school literary magazine.

Implementing the Writing of Poetry

When third-grade teacher Jo Pyle, Northside ISD, San Antonio, sees a poem in the making during a conference or grouping, she uses it as a springboard for the class. Jo shares poetry she knows her students will love, especially Byrd Baylor's "I'm in Charge of Celebrations," "The Way to Start a Day," and "Everybody Needs a Rock." The class enjoys the poetry and discusses how Baylor writes it. Students then write. Jo says, "My budding poetry writers go even farther than I can suggest. They love experiencing new ideas and playing with form. They like to take their ideas and find the best way to poetically write them."

Cheryl Collins, North East ISD, San Antonio, and her fifth-grade students had read, studied, and researched dinosaurs and the Jurassic period. They were ready to write. And write they did, drafting together all their information with interest. Then came the best part. Cheryl pulled out Jack Prelutsky's *Tyrannosaurus Was a Beast*, a book of poems about dinosaurs. Cheryl read ten poems and asked her students to look and listen, to notice stanzas, lines per stanza, rhyme scheme, and repeated lines. They took notes on the variety of patterns and shapes in the poems and discovered that poems have countless arrangements. They also decided that free verse is free but also complicated. Cheryl then read the incredibly literate *Sleeping Dragons All Around* by Canadian Sheree Fitch (a children's poet largely undiscovered by U.S. audiences). Cheryl followed that book with *Where the Sidewalk Ends* by Shel Silverstein. Students were then asked to go through their prewriting and find ideas that could become poems. As they tried writing drafts of poems, their understanding of poetry increased.

One student Edna Bubenik remembers from a second-grade class refused to write anything. "I was seeing nothing," Edna said, "not even drawings." She continued:

> I searched through Judith Newman's work looking for ways to engage Tina. I tried prewriting techniques. I tried letting her become a part of groups working on an idea. Nothing seemed to click for her. Then one day, during one of these moments when I needed to fill in some time before P.E., I took Barbara Bergers' *Gwinna* off the shelf. [Edna says she reads orally to the class "every time we have five minutes to share."] I read the book. The class went to P.E. They came back. Several days went by. I noticed Tina re-reading this fantasy/fairy tale, and before I knew it she was writing poetry. She incorporated all the elements found in the book—the symbolism, the rich language. Tina really got the idea of poetry.

Tina and Edna, student and teacher, both learned one of the lessons of literacy: Writing literature is one response to literature. Together they connected with the written word. Together they celebrated the response to literature. Edna did not give up on Tina as a writer. She tried different techniques. She individualized when the need was warranted. Maybe Tina was just displaying Murray's "natural resistance to writing," or maybe she just had a deeper well from which to draw.

Techniques to Shape Poetry

MOVING THE PREWRITING TO POETIC FORM

Prewriting and trial drafts that sing with imagery and figurative language and affect the audience with an immediacy of power and emotion cry out for poetic form, not formula. Students discover their own patterns by freely experimenting, trying as many forms as they find interesting, and then changing the rules as meaning dictates. Free verse can find rhyme, lyric can turn narrative. Students often discover that in writing poetry there are no limits.

The student who panics with, "But I can't write a poem," should begin where he or she is most comfortable—the traditional prose trial draft. After drafting, they share in small groups, ask for help in noting striking phrases, images, or figures of speech. Then they mark these for special attention.

When the poet Richard Hugo visited Hardin-Simmons University in Abilene, Texas, just before his death, not only did he conduct a poetry reading, he also held a session about writing poetry. In this session he shared some suggestions:

- Make your first line interesting and immediate. Start in the middle of things. When the poem starts, things should have already happened.

- When rewriting, write the entire poem again.

- Don't erase. (It's gone then.) Cross out or circle. (You may want to reconsider.)

- If you want to change something—first try leaving the same words but play with the syntax.

- Use strong verbs. Don't overuse "to be" forms.

- Consider the aptness of *each* word.

- Use "love" only as a transitive verb (for at least 15 years).

(List continues on page 130.)

- Don't use more syllables or more words than you absolutely need.

- Use any word that you "own." Don't be afraid to possess words. If you love them enough to own them, you will be secure with them. If you don't love them enough to own them, you will have to be very clever to write a good poem.

- Beware of certain words that seem necessitated by grammar to make things clear but dilute the drama of your poem (e.g., meanwhile, while, as during, and, a, an, the, this, that).

- If you ask a question, don't answer it, or answer a question not asked, or defer. (If you can answer the question, to ask it is to waste time — and words.)

There will be a new list tomorrow. (Hugo)

THE SOUND OF POETRY

When reading their drafts aloud, students begin noting the natural groupings of words, or the sounds that words make when placed next to each other. These words can extend into lines of a poem. They can be rearranged, changed, or omitted to sound better in the mouth and to the ear. Twelfth-grade teacher Patricia S. Gray, Texas Military Institute, San Antonio, has her students take out all the articles/determiners from prose to help discover the poetic nature of words. After they have done this artificially, she has them put the words back in and work on making the line poetic, not vague. She has her students circle any word that is an abstraction. She then has her students write the concrete image or narrative of the abstraction.

Listening is a big part of the process in which Patricia's students discover their poems. The sound of the individual word and the rhythm of word to word come into play. If the sound of the line is off, her students usually discover they have too many words. As in the movie *Amadeus*, when the court musician says of Mozart's work, "There are too many notes," in poetry, the writer can have too many words. The line and poem become weighed down. However, caution students against their tendency to cut arbitrarily, because they often cut out the information needed to make the poem work.

IMAGERY

One way to lead students into writing strong imagery is by having them mark descriptive words and phrases that show instead of tell. The poet deals in sight, sound, touch, and smell, rather than telling about objects, ideas, or feelings. Imagery brings life to the poem.

Imagery supplies the breath to a poem and metaphors keep it breathing. Poet Levered Noes did not write the simile, "the road was like a ribbon of moonlight." Instead he used a metaphor, "the road was a ribbon of moonlight." The metaphor strengthens the line and moves it along. The writer and reader see the twists and turns of the moonlight on the road.

When students first attempt poetry they should remember these things:

- Keep the poem about concrete things, concrete happenings. Write what you know.

- Assume the persona of the poem. Become the main character of the poem.

- Do not tell everything. Give a snapshot of what the reader needs to see. What is obvious, what is wordy, what is extra needs to be cut from the poem.

- Take the reader through the experience. Let the reader vicariously participate in the poem.

- Do not forget to add conflict or tension. (Remember Sarah Cynthia Sylvia Stout is in conflict with taking the garbage out.) Even a lyrical poem has tension, such as "The Animal That Drank Up Sound."

ABSTRACTION IN POETRY

Ambiguity is good, abstraction is not, and concrete is better. Ambiguity invites intellectualizing; it allows the reader to have different interpretations. Abstractions spiral into infinity—no one knows what the poem is trying to say. Concrete images give body to the idea.

More than any other poetic techniques, ambiguity and concrete imagery fit the both/all characteristics of the process paradigm. Ambiguity invites the magnificent interconnections of the mind. Concrete imagery turns ideas into images. However, sometimes students become too ambiguous; they get caught up in their own abstraction. They know what they mean, but no one else can figure it out.

Tracy, a student at Westfield High School in Spring, Texas, wrote draft after draft of poems like

Butterfly

Fly, smooth, pretty
heart, love, fly
cocoon, love, pretty
butterfly, me, fly.

When she went to group, her peers asked what the poem was about. She told them she felt like the only way she could ever get out of her family situation of 14 brothers and sisters and unemployed parents was by becoming a butterfly. Her group gave her good advice. "Why don't you just write that? We didn't know what was going on. It's too abstract."

Tracy revised; the result was

Cocoon me

Mother's pregnant again.
For every year since I was two
She has had a child.
At sixteen, I want to be cocooned,
wrapped tight,
So one day I may come out
Wings bright.
I will butterfly
Away from the tight beds
of two kids on my right,
two on my left.
I will find the sky
and space to fly.

Tracy mastered a major concept in poetry. She replaced the abstractions with what caused the abstractions. Then everyone understood the poem.

NONFICTION

> Nonfiction is the place where much of the best writing of the day is being done. Yet many writers and teachers of writing continue to feel vaguely guilty if they prefer it to fiction—nonfiction is the slightly disreputable younger brother in the royal house of literature. No such guilt is necessary. While the keepers of the temple weren't looking, nonfiction crept in and occupied the throne. (Zinsser 57)

What is nonfiction? It is such a complicated genre that most experts are not exactly sure. William Knott, for example, devotes an entire chapter in his book *The Craft of Fiction*, distinguishing fiction from nonfiction, and M. H. Abrams in *A Glossary of Literary Terms* ignores it completely. Facts do not distinguish nonfiction from fiction. Neither does topic; both fiction and nonfiction include writing about science, technology, popular culture, women's issues, urban issues, economics, politics, travel, psychoanalysis, television, nature, baseball, or anthropology. Consider, then, this definition: Nonfiction is the writing of actual happenings, true events, and real people.

> *"He won't let me do anything! I can only talk on the phone for 15 minutes. I can't go to the mall. I can't have any friends over. And he won't let me ...," a student in Emily Flores's middle-school class reads. Emily, a teacher at Stevens Middle School in Northside ISD, San Antonio, asserts that these laments are not uncommon in middle-school students. She reports that on this occasion all the members of the writing group were girls and they all nodded their heads in affirmation.*
>
> *The writer asked, "So what can I do with this?"*
> *"Write a letter to your father."*
> *"Write a letter to Dear Abby."*
> *"Write an exposé about how hard it is to be a Hispanic teenager with an overprotective father."*
> *"What about writing a 'How to Cope with Parents' article for the school newspaper?"*
>
> *The students in Emily Flores's eighth-grade English class know that there is more than one way to inform, persuade, or express themselves and that by determining audience and purpose, the shape of the writing becomes more meaningful.*

Implementing the Teaching of Nonfiction

In the experience of many students and teachers, school writing is limited to the conventional essay, the literary analysis, the occasional book report, and the predictable research paper. This curriculum would limit the options in Emily's class. The student elected to write a letter to her father. If she were held to the third-person essay, she would not be able to address her audience or her father in the same way. With options for exploring genre, Emily's student was able to use her writing as a valuable tool to meet her personal and educational needs.

LETTERS

The letter is the expression of one person to another. In contemporary life, letter writing seems a lost art. Few individuals spend time or energy writing letters when the phone is so accessible. But phone calls from yesterday are hard to recall, whereas letters last far beyond lifetimes. Letters can be the writer's personal connection to an impersonal world.

As always, audience and purpose are major determiners. Informal letter writing to friends and family is equivalent to a long talk over the kitchen table. Past experiences are recalled and news is exchanged. Problems can be faced, and emotion, which the writer may not want to express face to face, can be revealed. Disagreements can be worked through when the brain has had time to overrule the tongue. Letters make life more interesting.

Letter-writing activities engage students in ways that cannot be duplicated. When studying past events, encourage students to write grandparents to ask them to recall the events as they remember them. Histories may be explored through such letters.

Letters that address public issues are no less engaging. These letters may be written to inform or persuade, protest or support. Students have strong opinions, and these opinions offer unique opportunities for letter writing.

For many students the letter as genre is a new experience. Teachers often emphasize writing for an audience, but writing *to* an audience who will actually read and respond is a powerful inducement to produce authentic writing. Elementary teachers traditionally encourage students to write to their favorite authors. Although there is certainly nothing wrong with writing to an author, some common sense should be followed. Staging a letter that all students copy and sending the whole batch in a large envelope probably will generate little response. Many children's authors tell of packages of letters requesting pictures, books, and autographs. Although these authors do not want to alienate their readers, they prefer letters that reflect genuine questions that arise from the reading such as, "Where do you get your ideas?" or "Do you know what you did for me in your last book?" These letters are real and magical things happen. Perhaps the most magical relationship between reader and author is between a fan and Brian Jacques. At NCTE's 1991 ALAN Workshop in Seattle, he said, "She has written from the very beginning of the Redwall series. She loves my characters. She tells me what she likes about them. I have written her to tell her that one of my characters in *Mossflower* will bear her name."

A Note About the Letter as Fiction: The Epistolary. The first English novel, *Pamela; or Virtue Rewarded*, published and written in 1740 by Samuel Richardson, is in epistolary form, which means the narrative is conveyed entirely by an exchange of letters. Probably no one uses the epistolary more imaginatively than Bram Stoker does in *Dracula*. The novel is the story of change told through letters, recordings, and news articles. Although letters are contained here as nonfiction, they should not be discounted as a form for fiction. Nor should any form be restricted. Christopher Nolan writes his autobiography as if it were the biography of Joseph Meehan in *Under the Eye of the Clock*. Nolan is frequently compared to James Joyce, William Butler Yeats, and Dylan Thomas; John Carey says about him, "Plain statements and straightforward reportage now intermix with the bravura passages, allowing Nolan new kinds of tonal contrast, a new capacity for extended narrative, and a new realism" (Nolan x).

AUTOBIOGRAPHY

The autobiography is the ultimate reflexive writing. James Olney says autobiography allows the memory to bring "back some things, neglecting other things ... seems to argue that selfhood is not continuous; for it brings up one self here and another self there, and they are not the same as one another" (25, 26).

Sometimes even teachers wonder, "Students writing autobiography? What could they have to say?" Students who find their own lives to be the primary focus of their writing need a chance to examine where they have been and where they hope to go. This genre may find a prominent place in the repertoires of such young authors.

Each year teachers and classmates hear funny and sad, frightening and happy stories about each other's lives. From time to time, these stories are especially arresting, and they have an impact on the lives of writers and readers. All students should write autobiography; their stories can affect others.

When Becky Hicks's sophomore students began to write about turning points in their lives, they had been writing since the beginning of the school year, more than six weeks, and this time, they knew they would share with their study groups. Everyone was getting to know each other in these four-member groups, so sharing was comfortable. No one knew that reading their autobiographies would change things forever.

Lucy was the third person in her group to read. "It was the second week of August and everyone had been having a wonderful time. The party was at the park and all the family was there. My dad and my uncle were getting ready to leave. My brother, Raul, decided to leave with them too. When he walked to the car, the shot rang out." As Lucy continued, her group became silent and still. Lucy's study group asked her to read during a whole-class share session, and everyone was riveted as Lucy's love and pain took over the room.

The death of Lucy's brother because of a gang became a defining event in her life. Her unyielding intolerance of the gang mystique and her persistent questioning of why that happened never faded during the year; therefore, gangs and gang members were not popular in first period. Autobiography did that.

Teachers can direct students to autobiographical selections at the appropriate level. Secondary choices might include *A Christmas Memory*, by Truman Capote, *West with the Night*, by Beryl Markham, *AKE*, by Wole Soyinka, and *Hunger of Memory*, by Richard Rodriguez. Autobiographical writings by Maya Angelou, Dylan Thomas, Anne Frank, and Helen Keller also interest students. Elementary suggestions could include *Homesick: My Own Story*, by Jean Fritz, and *ME, ME, ME, ME, ME: Not a Novel*, by M. E. Kerr. The following list provides suggestions for writing autobiography.

- Create a personal timeline—include whatever comes to mind—small events may prove significant.

- Create a story map of your life—draw the pictures and symbols to enrich the meaning.

- Search through old letters and notes, look for memorabilia—find the things that jog memories.

- Interview family members and friends about past events—consider the other point of view.

- Select the event that is significant and reveals the most—let the metonymy of that event reflect life.

- Consider starting points of memoir—sometimes it is best to start at the end, or after an event has occurred.

As students work through autobiographical writing, they arrive at intersections that allow them to continue on or change direction by rearranging or altering facts. The real test at the intersections is keeping the writing true but not necessarily accurate. Accuracy can be dull, drawn out, and boring, whereas the truth liberates and holds interest. For example, if the writer tells about a broken leg caused by not heeding Mother's repeated advice, then the writer may reconstruct the events so Mother gives a final warning rather than leave the warning wedged in between other episodes. What is important is not the accuracy of when the warning was given, but that the warning was given. Writers of nonfiction make these decisions of truth and accuracy to empower the truth. Often in revision the writer sees that revising the accuracy while maintaining the truth heightens the dramatic effect.

Students in Becky Ebner Hoag's ninth-grade classes at Clark High School, Northside ISD, San Antonio, work through their autobiographies by first sharing childhood toys, photographs, and the reading/writing connection responses to *Ira Sleeps Over*. The results are always rich with meaning. Becky says, "With the right stimuli, and the right models, students approach autobiography with sincerity and a need to write substantially. Their experiences are filtered through and sifted until they have the right details in the right order to reveal who they are."

BIOGRAPHY

Students who are curious about their own lives are often curious about the lives of others. Those who attend every concert of a favorite rock star, constantly quote a special relative, follow a politician, or know all the statistics about an athlete are ready to research and write biography.

Students of Kathey Rothen, a teacher in Northside ISD, San Antonio, discuss and study heroes as a major thematic strand. They begin their study close to home. She directs them to develop surveys that reflect the opinions of family and friends about someone they consider heroic. After students have conducted interviews and tallied the surveys, they examine the collected data. Then they compile questions to reveal details hinted at but not clear. Finally they return to their sources for more information.

Next the students create annotated scrapbooks of their heroes. Some make collages, others make photo albums. Together, they study classic and contemporary models of heroes. The students search and discover, collecting information that can serve as comparisons to their heroes. With more information than they can use, students realize it is easier to write a biography.

As they begin writing, Kathey encourages them to do personal interviews to collect actual quotes. Then she helps her students analyze and characterize during writing conferences, teaching the value of the quotation and documentation. The final realization her students make that affects writing biographies is audience, a realization Kathey shares because "I learned it from my own writing." Students and teacher share, group, and confer as they shape their biographies. The following list provides suggestions for writing biography.

- Read biographies as writers and analyze how they are written.

- Limit biographies to a certain period or certain event.

- Place periods and events within a broader historical context.

- Interview people who know the subject.

- Read the writings or view the accomplishments of the subject.

- Interview the subject and use his or her own words.

- Strive for a true picture of the subject.

Although most student-authored biographies are short character portraits, not lengthy works, the biography gives students experience in authentic research and encourages inquiry. Frequently, when students begin to evaluate others' lives, they learn about their own.

MEMOIR

Related to the biography is memoir. Memoir is the eyewitness account of the writer's participation in the events and characters around him or her. A strong sense of objectivity coupled with the ability to analyze and interpret make this an interesting genre for student writers.

"My Time in Third Grade" was used by one student to review his educational and social growth. Teachers use this prompt as a way to guide students into memoir. One creative student created a brochure titled, "What I Should Have Done as a Freshman." Jay Henderson, a student at Westfield High School in Spring, Texas, based his memoir upon his brother's first year at MIT. His memoir was so powerful that it was published by the MIT alumni magazine.

Memoir is an excellent genre to use while teaching social studies. Memoir places the writer within a historical context. Richard Beach says memoir "recounts experiences which portray another person whom the writer knew in the past" (1). He delineates further:

Memoir differs from portrait (writing about someone in the present) in that students usually have more direct access to the subject of a portrait: they can interview the subject of a portrait, while they must depend more on their memories in writing about someone in the past. As with phase autobiography, memoir writing is most successful when it focuses on specific events or incidents representing characteristic behaviors. (5)

Techniques to Shape Nonfiction

THE INTERVIEW

Students need to practice conducting interviews before they ever actually conduct one. Heuristics like the reporter's formula and classical invention for the modern student can be departure points to develop questions for the interview. Key aspects of interviewing include:

- Ask open-ended questions.

- Think before responding to the interviewee.

- Get the interviewee talking.

- Be honest in the questions asked—this isn't an exposé.

- Admit ignorance—if the interviewee refers to something unknown to the interviewer, show curiosity.

- Do not be afraid to cut out parts of the interview.

- Do not try to record every word in an interview. Only record those statements that will make good quotes.

ELEMENTS OF THE ESSAY

Dennis, a sophomore in a large suburban school district, was writing about George Bernard Shaw. Dennis found that he had something in common with Shaw—a caustic sense of humor. Upon the suggestion of his teacher, he had read some of Shaw's classic works and a biography. It then seemed natural that he write about Shaw. Dennis wrote, "Shaw was also known as a Saist." When the teacher read the paper he questioned Dennis about his meaning. Dennis replied, "You know, Shaw wrote *s a*'s."

S. A's. or Saist—students in schools know what an essay is. They may not be able to spell *essay*, nor do they necessarily consider themselves essayists, but traditionally, the essay has been the standard for school writing for the past 100 years. Often the reason given for assigning the essay is, "You'll have to write essays in college." Colleges vary so much—from institution to institution and department to department—that preparing students for college by teaching them only the essay is like bailing out a sinking boat using a colander.

Some teachers further divide the essay into subgenres: the persuasive essay, the how-to essay, the narrative essay, the definition essay, the comparison/contrast essay, the informative essay, and the documented essay. Each essay has its own idiosyncratic characteristics and guidelines. Although in their purest state there is nothing wrong with any of these essays, the problem occurs when teachers "teach" the essay. When weekly assignments of "write the persuasive essay to turn in on Friday" are given, form starts to dictate what the writer has to say. Teachers and students instead should explore contemporary essays and find real reasons to write real essays for real audiences.

A more deductive approach to writing essays might be saner and more profitable for student writers. When teachers help students find what they have to say, they allow the writer to make the decision on how best to say it. Then real writing occurs. The characteristics of essays are shown in table 4.2 (see page 138).

In their isolated state, the essay forms are rather boring and trite. Writers with a voice and style would never confine themselves to such strict confines of form. Instead, an essay might persuade while at the same time it describes. Another essay might inform and define by way of a personal narrative. These essays exist everywhere in fine publications. Essayists such as Joan Didion are not bound to a form; instead they use their style, wit, and voice to say what they need to say. Unfortunately, all too often students do not have the freedom to write in their style, wit, and voice — which they do have.

ORGANIZATIONAL PATTERNS

Kenneth A. Bruffee in *A Short Course in Writing* gives detailed forms for the writing done by students. He says, "The purpose of this book is to provide a new model for learning the principles of discursive writing." The writing exercises allow for "freedom of subject matter and opinion, but limits their form of presentation" and are worth some consideration.

When the forms are taught as a natural outgrowth of what the writer has to say, rather than as an imposed form, then deeper understanding of organization occurs. The forms are given here to explore, not to prescribe. The anecdote at the conclusion of this section reveals one way this exploration can happen. Figure 4.5 gives graphic presentation of the forms.

Fig. 4.5. Bruffee's organizational patterns for the essay (Bruffee 28-85). From Kenneth A. Bruffee's *A Short Course in Writing*.

TWO REASONS

Introduction
Proposition

First reason developed
Explanation or defense

Second reason developed

NESTORIAN ORDER

Introduction
Proposition

Second best reason developed
Minor reasons

Major reason developed

STRAWMAN AND ONE REASON

Introduction
Proposition

Main opposing argument
Refute the opposition

Major positive reason developed

CONCESSION

Introduction
Proposition

Important opposing argument

Concession
Positive argument developed

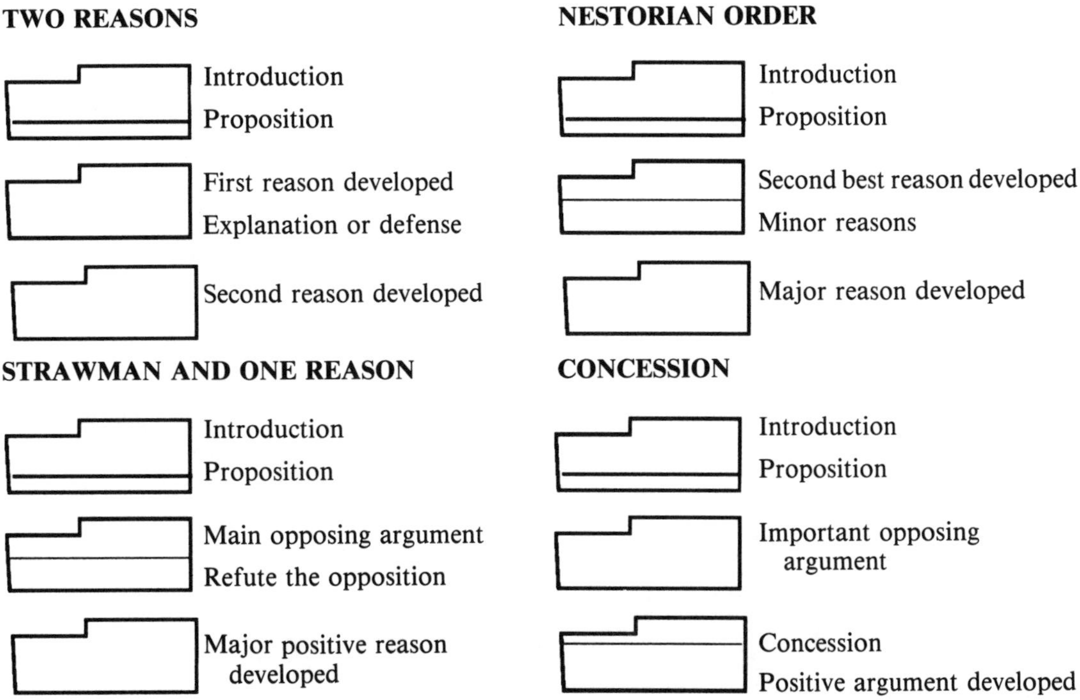

(Text continues on page 139.)

Table 4.2

Characteristics of Essays

Type	Purpose	Major Characteristics
Persuasive	to persuade	uses facts and opinions uses emotional arguments
How-to	to give steps or procedures	linear steps from beginning to end sequence is important
Narrative	to tell a story	personal in nature has a beginning, middle, and end uses flashbacks
Definition	to define an issue or problem	has a clear bias has facts to support definition offers no solution
Problem/solution	to consider a problem and offer a solution	clearly states the problem considers causes of the problems offers at least one solution to the problem
Comparison/contrast	to compare similarities and consider differences	follows a pattern of comparison, such as 1) first describing similarities in terms of elements of A compared to elements of B and then describing differences in terms of elements in B contrasted to elements in A. OR 2) first describing all similarities in terms of A and B, then describing all differences in terms of A and B. OR 3) taking a topical approach, describing similarities and differences of A and B in relation to each topic.
Informative	to inform	clearly gives information
Descriptive	to describe an object or thing	uses space, time, or order sequences
Documented	to accomplish any purpose	uses quotations, facts, statistics from documented sources to support ideas

Two Reasons. Two reasons is a typical pattern to organize ideas in a straightforward manner. This pattern seems to be a favorite of testing agencies and traditionalist.

Nestorian Order. A favorite organizational pattern of ministers is the Nestorian order. When we examine the minister's purpose, it becomes clear why this pattern is favored. The minister starts with a punch and ends with a bang. The minister wants to leave the listener with an idea that lasts throughout the week. Students might also consider the essay exam and its constraints. The constraints of the testing situation demand that the meaning be clear and concise. The meaning then can best be presented using a Nestorian pattern. The teacher grading the answer is left with a strong impression instead of the rambling on of ideas or, worse yet, a falling short of the mark.

Strawman and One Reason. In examining the strawman pattern, students can find examples in daily life that mirror the pattern. For example, the lawyer uses the Strawman approach because the argument needs to be knocked down. The lawyer must discredit the opposing view to win the case.

Concession. When considering concession, the rhetoric of politicians comes to mind. They may need to recognize the opposing viewpoint, but that doesn't mean they can or will do anything with this opposing view other than recognize it. They concede that it exists. But this is the purpose of concession. The writer uses this organizational pattern when the opposing view cannot be refuted, cannot be knocked down as in the strawman pattern. To ignore the opposing view lessens the perspective of the writer; the writer has to acknowledge the opposing viewpoint to make his or her view viable.

> *A favorite example of concession occurred in a town meeting in the panhandle of Texas. A state senator was explaining why the federal government was going to build a nuclear waste dump in the community. He explained how the Army Corps of Engineers would dig down below the aquifer to the salt caverns below. He recognized that there was danger to the water source; in fact, he conceded that he wouldn't want it in his back yard. But the dump had to go somewhere. And because they were poor farmers, and because this would bring in money for the community, and because an aquifer has never been the site of a major EPA cleanup, it would be best for the dump to go there.*

AN EXAMPLE OF SHAPING THE ESSAY

> *Jodi came to my office and pronounced, "You can't teach below-level, disadvantaged students how to organize—they could never use Bruffee's patterns."*
>
> *Accepting the gauntlet she had thrown down, I replied, "Yes, you can."*
>
> *I asked Jodi what her goals were for her unit of study. She replied that she wanted them to be able to use organizational patterns as Bruffee described them in* A Short Course in Writing. *I volunteered to teach her students. She further said that they were going to write an essay about* Of Mice and Men *and that she wanted to see the patterns used. We arranged that each day I would watch Jodi one period, and she would watch me the next. This is a reflection of what happened.*

Monday

Jodi made the writing assignment topic "The Moral Dilemma in Of Mice and Men." Asking for a thesis statement from the students, she received blank stares. She asked questions about what they could write about. Two students commented. She vetoed. She went to the board and wrote: "George did the correct thing by taking Lenny's life." She informed them this was the thesis statement. Giving them a handout of Bruffee's organizational patterns—two reasons, strawman, concession, and Nestorian order—she explained each pattern, assigning students to prewrite a paper for tomorrow.

As the students came into class I gave them large sheets of butcher paper and divided them into two groups. Explaining the rules of brainstorming, I asked them to brainstorm all the things they could write about from the book. Hesitantly, they started. With markers they made lists on the butcher paper. We discussed both groups' lists. They hung the lists on the wall.

I asked the students which items were the most interesting to them and we starred those. We then prioritized the starred statements in order of the highest interest. We wrote those on clean butcher paper strips and hung them up.

Tuesday

Students were instructed to write their rough drafts from their prewriting. The students spent the entire period writing on the drafts. Few had any prewriting done. Some slept, some talked.

Each student was given a small strip of butcher paper. I asked them if they had a personal favorite from yesterday's final list. Most did. Those who did not, said they could pick one. They wrote this statement on their butcher paper. Then the students were asked to consider whether there was an opposing viewpoint of the statement they had on their sheets. Some students found the opposing ideas faster than others. Because some were having trouble we completed this orally—every student with the help of the class wrote down an opposing statement. The students had previously done the prewriting technique of webbing, so I asked them to complete a web on their butcher paper. After they had written, they were asked to star the three or four items they liked the best, and then they had more they could write about.

Wednesday

Students were instructed to revise their papers. They were given a revision "check sheet" that covered items such as spelling, subject-verb agreement, and fragments. They spent the period working on their papers. Most recopied yesterday's draft over more neatly.

Students were given six 5-by-8-inch index cards—two yellow, two blue, and two green. They were asked to label the yellow cards Pro, the blue cards Con, and the green cards Props. Using Bruffee's guidelines for propositions, we wrote propositions on the green cards.

We discussed these statements. Then the students were instructed to place the Pro and Con cards on opposing sides of their desktops. Next they were instructed to use their ideas from the butcher paper to find support for the proposition statements. This was difficult. They asked lots of questions. They were encouraged to orally try out different supports. The class became a trial-and-error discussion of what constitutes supporting arguments. By the end of the period everyone had at least two supports for each proposition they had considered.

Thursday

Students were told to write their final draft to turn in the next day.

Students were given copies of the book and were shown how quotes could be pulled from the text to support the ideas written down on the cards. At this point, more cards were passed out. We discovered that we had written more than one support per card. We discussed the value of having one support per card. The students decided it was easier that way. I decided that if they had been given better directions we would not have had to use up valuable instruction time redoing what we had done. When I said this to the students, they agreed. But they added they liked figuring out a better way of doing it. I decided students make the best teachers. After each card had one support argument and at least one quote to support the argument, I modeled how the writer expounds, explains, and elaborates the idea and quote. We made a list of the types of things I did in the modeling: repetition, facts from the book, personal anecdotes, examples, instances and more details, and comparison/contrast. We spent the rest of the period writing out the elaboration for each card.

Friday

Students handed in papers and worked on a vocabulary handout.

Examination of the papers showed that all of them were organized using the two-reasons-in-defense pattern. None of the papers incorporated quotes from the book to support any idea.

Using the cards as manipulatives, each student rearranged the cards as I wrote Bruffee's organizational patterns (two reasons, which we expanded to three and four reasons; strawman; concession; and Nestorian) on the board. They realized that with some configurations they did not need all of their cards — with other arrangements, they used *them all. Students were then asked to identify which pattern best fit what they had to say and make a commitment to an organizational pattern. They rearranged their cards. When they decided on a pattern we rubber-banded the cards together and labeled the top with the pattern being used. I concluded class with a mini-lesson on transitions.*

Monday

The class began a new unit of study.

We examined essays to identify where we needed transitions between ideas as a review of Friday's mini-lesson. The students were asked to write transitions to connect the cards. Students suggested that the transitions needed to be written on white cards and taped together. This took the rest of the period.

Tuesday

Students were instructed to write drafts and were given rules for conferring. Few students took advantage of the conference. They spent the period transferring the prewriting from the cards to notebook paper.

Wednesday

Students had almost finished their drafts and were feeling very pleased with their papers. We discussed whom we were writing the paper for—the teacher and for ourselves. The students decided that the audience wouldn't change the way they wrote this paper. I conducted a mini-lesson on ratiocination (see chapter 7, pages 227-230). Students started to confer. Rest of class period was spent with students ratiocinating their papers and conferring.

Thursday

I conducted a mini-lesson on introductions, sharing examples of the typical intro, the action intro, the dialogue intro, and the reaction intro. Students wrote an intro for their papers and, using the grouping technique of "Say Back" (chapter 5, page 157), they grouped on these intros. By the conclusion of class, every student had an intro she or he liked.

Friday

Students were asked what they needed to do to complete their paper. Most felt they were close to completion. Most felt they could be finished by Monday. I explained the concept of clocking (chapter 9, pages 282-283). They decided they could be ready on Monday to clock.

Monday

I went through the clocking technique with the students. Students were given time to make the corrections based upon the clocking. I conducted a debriefing on patterns they used. No one used the two reasons pattern.

Because objectivity might have been a problem on the evaluation, Jodi requested that the papers be evaluated by an impartial party. A teacher from another high school in the district evaluated the papers. She did not know which paper was from which class. The papers that used the two reasons pattern were one to two grades lower when compared to the papers that used the Nestorian, strawman, and concession organizational patterns. The implications seem clear. First, meaning does dictate form. The students decided how to organize their papers based on what was the best way to structure what they had to say. Second, it is not enough to tell students how to organize; teachers need to show how to organize. Third, students can use more sophisticated organizational patterns when they see in concrete ways how these patterns work. They cannot abstract organization. Possibly the most important lesson, though, was that teaching is not telling, and it is not assigning—it is experiencing.

SUMMARY

Genre offers choices to students. For every choice considered in this chapter there are a gamut of others. When writing teachers implement the freedom of choice, the freedom of genre, then meaning takes on a force that moves the writing. Genre is not a mold that plaster is poured into, it is the clay that needs kneading, shaping, and firing. It is the clay that may be a dish, a bowl, or a sculpture. Genre is meant to free students from the mundane and inane, neurotic activities of writing for purposes and modes that shackle thought. Independence as a learner, as a person, cannot be achieved if genre is dictated to the writer.

Tess Gallagher writes in her introduction to Raymond Carver's *A New Path to the Waterfall*:

> Ray had so collapsed the distance between his language and thought that the resulting transparency of method allowed distinctions between genres to dissolve without violence or a feeling of trespass.... Ray used his poetry to flush the tiger from hiding. Further, he did not look on his writing life as the offering of products to a readership, and he was purposefully disobedient when pressures were put on him to write stories because that's where his reputation was centered and that's where the largest reward in terms of publication and audience lay. He didn't care. When he received the Mildred and Harold Strauss Living Award, given only to prose writers, he immediately sat down and wrote two books of poetry. He was not "building a career"; he was living a vocation and this meant that his writing, whether poetry or prose, was tied to inner mandates that insisted more and more on an increasingly unmediated apprehension of his subjects, and poetry was the form that best allowed this.

Student writers have their inner mandates, and they need the form that best allows for the expression of these mandates. Teachers of writing can use form as a way to allow for expression.

WORKS CITED

Abrams, M. H. *A Glossary of Literary Terms*. New York: Holt, Rinehart & Winston, 1981.

Alexander, Lloyd. *Prydain Chronicles*. New York: Henry Holt, 1978.

Allen, Paula Gunn, ed. *Spider Woman's Granddaughters: Traditional Tales and Contemporary Writing by Native American Women*. New York: Beacon Press, 1989.

Altenbernd, Lynn, and Leslie L. Lewis. *A Handbook for the Study of Fiction*. New York: Macmillan, 1966.

Arbuthnot, May Hill, and Zena Sutherland. *Children and Books*. Glenview, IL: Scott, Foresman, 1972.

Aristotle. *Poetics*. Translated by Gerald R. Else. Ann Arbor: The University of Michigan Press, 1978.

Arnold, Anita. "Athlete Poets." *Texas Coach* (July 1992).

_____. "Eat Your Heart Out Barbara Courtland." *English Journal* (September 1992).

_____. "Windows of Cultural Literacy." *English in Texas* (Winter 1991).

Atwell, Nancie. *In the Middle: Writing, Reading, and Learning with Adolescents*. Portsmouth, NH: Boynton/Cook, 1987.

Austin, Doris Jean. *After the Garden*. New York: New American Library, 1988.

Bambara, Toni Cade. *Gorilla, My Love*. New York: Random House, 1981.

_____. *The Salt Eaters*. New York: Random House, 1981.

_____. *The Sea Birds Are Still Alive*. New York: Random House, 1977.

Baylor, Byrd. *Everybody Needs a Rock*. New York: Macmillan, 1986.

_____. *I'm in Charge of Celebrations*. New York: Macmillan, 1986.

_____. *The Way to Start a Day*. New York: Macmillan, 1978.

Beach, Richard. *Writing about Ourselves and Others*. ERIC, 1977.

Berger, Barbara. *Gwinna*. New York: Putnam, 1990.

Brooks, Gwendolyn. "We Real Cool." In *Western Wind*, edited by John Frederick Nims. New York: Random House, 1983.

Bruffee, Kenneth A. *A Short Course in Writing*. Cambridge, MA: Winthrop, 1972.

Bruner, Jerome. *Acts of Meaning*. Cambridge, MA: Harvard University Press, 1990.

Brunvand, Jan Harold. *The Choking Doberman and Other "New" Urban Legends*. New York: W. W. Norton, 1984.

Butler, Octavia E. *Adulthood Rites*. New York: Warner Books, 1989.

_____. *Dawn*. New York: Warner Books, 1987.

_____. *Kindred*. New York: Warner Books, 1988.

_____. *Wild Seed*. New York: Warner Books, 1988.

Campbell, Joseph. *The Masks of God*. Vol. 4: *Creative Mythology*. New York: Viking, 1968.

Capote, Truman. *A Christmas Memory*. New York: Random House, 1966.

Carver, Raymond. *A New Path to the Waterfall*. Introduction by Tess Gallagher. New York: Atlantic Monthly Press, 1989.

Classic Film Scripts. New York: Simon & Schuster.

Cook-Lynn, Elizabeth. *Then Badger Said This*. Fairfield, WA: Ye Galleon, 1983.

Delany, Samuel R. *The Bridge of Lost Desire*. New York: St. Martin's Press, 1989.

_____. *Dhalgren*. New York: Bantam Books, 1983.

_____. *Stars in My Pocket Like Grains of Sand*. New York: Bantam Books, 1984.

_____. *The Straits of Messing*. New York: Serconia Press, 1988.

Dorros, Arthur. *Abuela*. New York: E. P. Dutton, 1991.

Dove, Rita. *Grace Notes*. New York: W. W. Norton, 1989.

_____. *Thomas and Beulah*. Pittsburgh, PA: Carnegie Mellon Press, 1985.

Drake, Barbara. *Writing Poetry.* New York: Harcourt Brace Jovanovich, 1983.

Edward, Betty. *Drawing on the Artist Within.* New York: Simon & Schuster, 1986.

Farrington, Jan. "Words and Pictures by ... Writing for the Movies." *Writing!* (April 1984): 3-12.

Fitch, Sheree. *Sleeping Dragons All Around.* Toronto: Doubleday Canada Limited, 1989.

Fritz, Jean. *Homesick.* New York: Putnam, 1986.

Golding, William. *Lord of the Flies.* New York: Harcourt Brace Jovanovich, 1969.

Graves, Donald. *Investigate Nonfiction.* Portsmouth, NH: Heinemann Educational Books, 1989.

_____. *Writing: Teachers and Children at Work.* Exeter, NH: Heinemann Educational Books, 1983.

Harlow, Joyce. *Story Play: Costumes, Cooking, Music, and More for Young Children.* Englewood, CO: Teacher Ideas Press, 1992.

Hogan, Linda. *Calling Myself Home.* Greenfield Center, NY: Greenfield Review Press, 1978.

_____. *Eclipse.* Native American Series. Berkeley, CA: University of California, 1983.

_____. *Seeing Through the Sun.* Amherst, MA: University of Massachusetts Press, 1985.

Hsu, Vivian Ling, ed. *Born of the Same Roots: Stories of Modern Chinese Women.* Bloomington, IN: Indiana University Press, 1981.

Hugo, Richard. From notes of lecture at Hardin-Simmons University on writing poetry, 1982.

Jacques, Brian. *Mossflower.* New York: Putnam, 1988.

_____. *Redwall.* New York: Putnam, 1987.

Janeczko, Paul. *The Music of What Happens: Poems That Tell Stories.* New York: Orchard Press, 1988.

_____. *Poetspeak: In Their Work, About Their Work.* New York: Bradbury Press, 1983.

Kael, Pauline, Herman J. Mankiewicz, and Orson Welles. *The Citizen Kane Book.* New York: Bantam Books, 1971.

Kennedy, X. J. *Literature: An Introduction to Fiction, Poetry and Drama.* New York: Scott, Foresman, 1987.

Kerr, M. E. *ME, ME, ME, ME, ME: Not a Novel.* New York: New American Library, 1983.

Kingston, Maxine Hong. Letter to author, 16 October 1980.

Knott, William C. *The Craft of Fiction.* Reston, VA: Reston Publishing, 1973.

Lessing, Doris. "The Art of Fiction CII." *Paris Review* 106 (Spring 1988).

McKinley, Robin. *The Blue Sword*. New York: Greenwillow Books, 1982.

_____. *The Hero and the Crown*. New York: Greenwillow Books, 1984.

McPherson, James A. *Elbow Room: Short Stories*. New York: Charles Scribner's Sons, 1987.

_____. *Hue & Cry*. New York: Fawcett, 1979.

Macrorie, Ken. *Telling Writing*. New York: Hayden, 1970.

Manfredi, Renée. "Bocci." *The Pushcart Prize XVI*, edited by Bill Henderson. New York: Simon & Schuster, 1981.

Markham, Beryl. *West with the Night*. Berkeley, CA: North Point Press, 1983.

Martin, Bill, Jr., and John Archambault. *Knots on a Counting Rope*. New York: Henry Holt, 1987.

Matthews, Jack. "A Questionnaire for Rudolph Gordon." In *Sudden Fiction: American Short-Short Stories*, edited by Robert Shapard and James Thomas. Salt Lake City, UT: Gibbs M. Smith, 1986.

Montale, Eugenio. "The Eel." In *Western Wind*, edited by John Frederick Nims. New York: Random House, 1983.

Mumford, Ericka. "The White Rose: Sophie Scholl 1921-1943." In *The Music of What Happens*, edited by Paul Janeczko. New York: Orchard Press, 1988.

Newman, Judith. *The Craft of Children's Writing*. Portsmouth, NH: Heinemann Educational Books, 1985.

Nims, John Frederick. *Western Wind*. New York: Random House, 1983.

Nolan, Christopher. *Under the Eye of the Clock*. New York: St. Martin's Press, 1987.

O'Flaherty, Liam. "The Sniper." In *The Martyr*, by O'Flaherty. London: Jonathan Cape, A. D. Peters, 1933.

Olney, James. *Metaphor of Self: The Meaning of Autobiography*. Princeton, NJ: Princeton University Press, 1972.

Prelutsky, Jack. *Tyrannosaurus Was a Beast*. New York: Greenwillow Books, 1988.

Rodriguez, Richard. *Hunger of Memory*. New York: Bantam Books, 1982.

Scholastic Scope Magazine. Scholastic, Inc. 730 Broadway, New York, NY 10003-9538.

Sedlacek, Gary C. "Voices." *English Journal* (March 1987).

Shapard, Robert, and James Thomas, eds. *Sudden Fiction: American Short-Short Stories*. Salt Lake City, UT: Gibbs M. Smith, 1986.

Silverstein, Shel. "Sarah Cynthia Sylvia Stout Would Not Take the Garbage Out." In *Where the Sidewalk Ends*. New York: Harper & Row, 1974.

Soyinka, Wole. *AKE: The Years of Childhood*. New York: Random House, 1983.

Spinelli, Jerry. *Maniac Magee*. Boston: Little, Brown, 1990.

Stafford, William. *The Animal That Drank Up Sound*. New York: Harcourt Brace Jovanovich, 1992.

Sumiko, Yagawa. *The Crane Wife*. Translated by Katherine Paterson. New York: Morrow Junior Books, 1987.

Thurber, James. *Many Moons*. New York: Harcourt Brace Jovanovich, 1973.

Truffault, François. *Hitchcock*. New York: Simon & Schuster, 1983.

Waber, Bernard. *Ira Sleeps Over*. New York: Houghton Mifflin, 1972.

Willard, Nancy. *A Nancy Willard Reader: Selected Poetry and Prose*. Hanover, VT: Middlebury College Press, 1991.

Zinsser, William. *On Writing Well*. New York: Harper & Row, 1988.

5

COLLABORATIVE LEARNING
Strategies for the Writing Group, Writing Conference, and Writing Debriefing

> What the child can do in cooperation today
> he can do alone tomorrow.
>
> — Lev Semonovich Vygotsky☐

Once, after students had completed a group technique, Marsha, a freckle-faced, red-headed adolescent, said, "You know, we can't do this solitary work alone." I was impressed with the profundity of her words. Writing is solitary work, but at some point in this solitary sojourn we want and need the input of others.

Research corroborates dire statistics on the status of today's young people. A look at just a few of these figures raises serious challenges for educators. For example, it has been estimated that by the time students reach the age of 16, they will have been exposed to six hours of "electronic miracles" for each hour spent with parents (Caine and Caine 17). Approximately 50-68 percent of children live in single-parent homes (Brophy, et al. 58-63). Gangs and drug use are increasing. "Many students' faltering academic skills—at every socioeconomic level—reflect subtle but significant changes in their physical foundations for learning" (Healy 45). These statistics suggest that many students need significant opportunities for interaction and a sense of belonging. With these challenges facing educators, it seems that collaboration—in this case, collaboration within the writing process—offers one way for students to experience collective goal setting and meaningful cooperation.

Although the present demands collaboration, projections into the future also call for collaborative skills. As Robert B. Reich states in his report *Education and the Next Economy*: "It is not enough to produce a cadre of young people with specialized skills. If our enterprises are to be the scenes of collective entrepreneurship—as they must be—experts must have the ability to broadly share their skills and transform them into organizational achievement; and others must be prepared to learn from them" (24). Reich focuses his report on what education can and should do to contribute to the emerging economy. He clearly makes the point that the more students learn about collaborating, the better they are prepared to enter into the new global economy.

Because writers paradoxically require both solitary and collaborative time—time spent writing alone juxtaposed with time spent receiving responses from others—students who write also should learn and practice collaborative strategies. These strategies extend students' learning and eventually become intrinsic to their writing processes. Therefore, the ease with which these strategies are implemented during writing instruction often determines the degree of students' immediate success. Repeating collaborative strategies often and at appropriate times promotes the integration of these strategies into each student's writing process. The three major ways to teach and practice collaboration in the writing classroom are the writing group, the writing conference, and the writing debriefing.

WRITING GROUPS

Trust and Immediacy

Trust is the foundation of the writing group. Trust is so important to the writing process that without it writing groups take on an unauthentic, even phony, feeling. There is a sense that everyone is simply going through the motions. Therefore, when teachers set about the business of setting up groups, they should truly grasp the power of people interacting. They should facilitate the process of writing groups in such a way that learning will occur. They should trust students, and usually through continual and successful grouping, students learn to return that trust. Successful writing groups provide ways for students to begin to trust others, themselves, and writing.

Immediacy builds upon this trust. Writing is immediate because the words on the paper call for response. In the classroom, this call provides students with first-hand practice in giving and receiving feedback, following the procedures of the group technique, attending and listening, tolerating ambiguity, responding genuinely, learning how to question, increasing their sensitivity to others, and decreasing game playing and manipulation. Further, students learn to focus on their writing and the writing of others in meaningful ways.

Satellite Skills

Writing groups not only enhance writing and reading skills (especially reading aloud, with expression); they also help students develop satellite skills such as flexibility, decision making, higher-level thinking, interaction, tolerance, discovery, listening, and leadership. These skills are fostered in simultaneous, overlapping ways. Writing in different modes and for different purposes, for instance, calls for flexibility not only in writing but also in sharing that writing with groups of various size. Sometimes the writing calls for pairing with just one other student; other times the writing requires feedback from a larger group. Also, deciding on the group's purpose prompts students to consider appropriate responses. For example, deciding whether an idea is worth writing about necessitates a different response than does deciding on the vitality of a lead.

Further, group cohesiveness happens when there are positive feedback and an absence of ridicule, both developed through an understanding of the sensibilities of others and reinforced through modeled verbal and nonverbal interaction. Thus, when teachers use their own writing to invite responses, students learn what comments can help, encourage, and extend writing. Conversely, they learn what might thwart further writing or sharing. This, in turn, helps students become tolerant of others as they work on using language to build up, not put down, the writing of their peers.

Creating an environment where discovery can occur means constantly furnishing a secure place where students may comfortably work together to analyze writing, risk new styles, find fitting genres, experiment with workable structures, and practice solving linguistic and metalinguistic problems. Ultimately, these authors make the final decisions about their writing, but they learn that by listening to others they can make more informed choices. This decision making, in turn, ensures ownership and calls upon higher-level thinking skills. In short, through group work, students learn to receive input from others while taking responsibility for their own decisions. Often this interaction leads to a deeper understanding coupled with better decisions not only about the writing but also about the decision-making process itself.

Writing groups help some students develop or refine leadership skills because the group becomes a learning community. If writing groups are well integrated into the English language arts classroom, most students find them a place to belong and a place where their contributions are valued. Because writing is a complex of processes, sharing with others and hearing the writing of others heightens students' awareness about writing. Students often begin to realize that they may excel in one area of writing, such as imagery, but have problems with something else, such as choosing apt metaphors. They also may discover that their weakness is another's strength. As they begin working with these strengths and weaknesses, they often learn self-respect and respect for others. Therein lies one of the energies of the writing group.

Finally, writing groups can be fun. Sharing a funny anecdote, hearing a gripping story, or musing over a powerfully written poem can be fun in two ways: (1) delight in language, in discovery, and in the learning process itself and (2) fruition in closure, in completion, in making the writing whole through others. However, fun in writing groups should not be confused with rollicking laughter, boisterous behavior, or acting up. Rather, fun in writing groups more closely matches what William Glasser suggests when he asserts that human beings have five basic needs: survival, love, power, freedom, and fun. These needs are built into our genetic structures (Glasser 43). Writing groups, then, furnish the fun of involvement and investment that gives rise to true emotion in the classroom. Caine and Caine cite several studies that indicate the interconnectedness of emotion and learning, concluding that "the enthusiastic involvement of students is essential to most learning" (57). Through writing groups, students engage in a process that prepares them in positive, substantive ways for a future that will demand responsibility and collaboration, decision making, meeting challenges, posing and solving problems, serious study, and a sense of humor.

Writing Group Strategies

The group strategies suggested here have been developed and used by writing teachers affiliated with the New Jersey Writing Project in Texas (NJWPT) for more than a decade. Pointing, telling, showing, and summarizing are strategies adapted from Peter Elbow's book *Writing Without Teachers* (85-92). Highlighting is a visual group strategy adapted from June Gould's *The Writer in All of Us* (115). Large-group share is a variation of Lucy McCormick Calkins's share meetings, which in addition to process share comes from Calkins's *Lessons from a Child: On the Teaching and Learning of Writing* (111). Analytic talk first appeared in *English Journal* (Carroll 101). Double dyads is an adaptation of "peer revision," an unpublished group strategy developed by Russ Barrett, an NJWPT trainer. The notion of reading twice, which is incorporated into most of the following group strategies, is based on the observation that listeners first experience a piece and then analyze it. Reading twice is not wasted instructional time; rather it is time spent developing finer listening skills and deepening sensitive responses.

POINTING

Explanation. Pointing invites group members to suggest what they find effective in a piece of writing. It is best used early in the group experience or early in the writing process because it is the most nonthreatening technique.

Implementation

1. Divide students into groups of four or five.

2. Writers read the whole piece, pause, and then read it again.

3. Listeners listen. Upon the second reading, listeners jot down words, phrases, images — anything that penetrates their skulls.

4. After each reading, listeners *point out* what they liked.

5. Nothing negative is allowed. Writers may not begin, "This is terrible, but...." Listeners may not even mumble, "That's the worst thing I've ever heard." All are charged to seek out what works in the piece.

Remarks. Through pointing, students become acquainted with each other and with the technique of grouping. They learn how groups function, develop spoken and unspoken norms of behavior, receive positive responses from peers, uncover the best in the writing, and discover that the group is a nonthreatening place.

TELLING

Explanation. Telling enables listeners to become aware of every possible reaction they have to the writing. It sets up an environment that works much like a full battery of physical tests so that something important is not overlooked. Telling is the MRI of techniques.

Implementation

1. Divide students into groups of five or six.

2. Writers read the whole piece, pause, and then read it again.

3. Listeners listen. Upon the second reading, listeners pretend they are hooked up to a variety of instruments that record everything physical: blood pressure, pulse, EKG, EEG, CAT scans, bone scans, and proprioceptions (these mechanisms occur in the subcutaneous tissues of the body and give "body images" or self-awareness, such as goose bumps, hair standing on end, blushes, sweaty palms, chills, or sudden tearing).

4. After each reading, listeners *tell* what their "instruments" have recorded.

5. Nothing negative is allowed because honest physical reactions are simply "recorded."

Remarks. As with pointing, all responses during telling are positive. Thus, telling is another strategy suitable for those inexperienced in grouping or participants beginning to group. Knowing the reactions of others (or even that there were reactions) to a piece of writing can be very helpful to the writer. The telling strategy meshes thinking and physical feeling.

SHOWING

Explanation. Showing provides a way for listeners to share perceptions that are tacit, which means they are locked in the mind. Tacit knowing is sometimes unlocked through the use of metaphor. Responding to another's writing this way often unblocks reluctant responders because students see this strategy as inviting a response that cannot be wrong.

Implementation

1. Divide students into groups of four.

2. Writers read the whole piece, pause, and then read it again.

3. Listeners listen. Upon the second reading, listeners jot down metaphors that match the writing: voices, weather, motion or locomotion, clothing, topography, colors, shapes, animals, fruits, vegetables, musical instruments, or songs. Some listeners may doodle or draw as they listen.

4. After the reading, listeners share their metaphors or drawings and talk about their responses.

Remarks. According to Michael Polanyi, tacit knowing is an inarticulate intelligence by which we know things in a purely personal manner (64). Putting that knowledge into precise words or accurate descriptions is sometimes impossible. By using metaphor (or simile), listeners come closer to what they know and are able to share, albeit indirectly.

> Student A: *Your writing reminds me of an eggplant.*
>
> Student B: *I hate eggplant. Does that mean you hate my writing?*
>
> Student A: *No, I thought it smooth and, well, there was something regal about it — you know, deep purple reminds me of royalty.*
>
> Student B: *Yeah. Now I get it.*

> Mary: *When you read I saw an old, faded pair of jeans.*
>
> Jesse: *Cliché, huh?*
>
> Mary: *No, I meant it had a comfortable feel about it.*

SUMMARIZING

Explanation. Summarizing invites listeners to synthesize what they have heard in four ways. Further, it prevents parroting. Its purpose is to let the writer know what stood out, what stuck in the listener's consciousness.

Implementation

1. Divide students into groups of five.

2. Writers read the whole piece, pause, and then read it again.

3. Listeners listen. Upon the second reading, listeners:
   a. focus on what they think is the main idea
   b. write the main idea as single sentence
   c. choose one word to express the main idea
   d. think of a synonym to express the main idea

4. Listeners share their summaries.

Remarks. Because it provides immediate application, this technique would be appropriate to use in conjunction with mini-lessons on main idea, paraphrasing, summing up, synopsizing, or research.

PLUS AND MINUS

Explanation. Plus and minus is a tabulated version of thumbs up, thumbs down. It is meant to be used on rough drafts simply to give the author an indication of first reactions to specifics in the writing.

Implementation

1. Divide students into groups of ten. Assign each student in a group a number from one to ten.

2. Distribute one chart (see fig. 5.1) to each group member.

3. A writer reads his or her paper through once.

4. One by one, the writer reads each of the criteria in the first column.

5. Group members signal thumbs up or thumbs down for each criteria.

6. The writer places a (+) if a group member gives a thumbs up or a (−) if a group member gives a thumbs down. The signs go in the column that corresponds with each student's number.

7. After the group has finished their charts, writers study their charts to consider appropriate revisions.

Remarks. Because plus and minus is almost a game format, students find it agreeable. Second, students like the idea of receiving so much feedback, especially because they can tabulate it and then use the tabulations to make decisions about their writing.

HIGHLIGHTING

Explanation. Highlighting provides verbal and visual feedback. Much like pointing, it enables the writer to *see* what listeners find outstanding.

Implementation

1. Divide students into groups of four or five. Remind students to bring a highlighter or colored marker to group.

2. Writers read the whole piece, pause, and then read it again.

3. Listeners listen. Upon the second reading, listeners write down the images they like.

4. After the reading, listeners repeat back these images.

5. Writers highlight these images on their papers.

Remarks. June Gould contends that "meaning resides in images, and highlighting reinforces image making" (115). Because modeling helps students make important connections, often after hearing each other's images, students seem to include more imagery in their subsequent writing. Also, highlighting may be adapted to other elements in the writing, such as dialogue, metaphor, and characterization.

LARGE-GROUP SHARE

Explanation. Large-group share is a time, usually early in the process, when the entire class meets. Its purpose is to provide a forum for students to test their ideas, to see whether others think their ideas are worth the commitment of continued writing (i.e., taking the piece through the process).

Fig. 5.1. Plus and minus chart.

Criteria	\multicolumn{10}{c}{GROUP MEMBERS}

Criteria	1	2	3	4	5	6	7	8	9	10
Title catches the reader's attention										
First two sentences hook the reader										
Purpose is clear										
Uses phrases that work										
Appeals to reader's interest										
Vocabulary is appropriate to audience										
Reels the reader in										
Believable characters										
Not confusing										
Ending works										
Grammar OK										
Language is fresh										
Overall evaluation										

Implementation

1. Gather students together in a tight group.

2. Invite volunteers to share their idea, purpose, audience, and where they intend to publish.

3. Class members respond informally.

Remarks. Large-group share is particularly effective at the onset of extensive writing, when audience is a paramount consideration. Following is an excerpt from a large-group share with twelfth-graders.

Student A: *I'm looking at* The Black Collegian. *I'm trying to get an interview with our mayor. I want to talk to him about his career. Since he is African-American, I think this magazine might be interested in his views if I can get them down well enough.* Writer's Market *says they take stuff on careers.*

Student B: *Do they take freelancers?*

Student A: *You bet, and they pay!*

Student C: *Did you know there's another magazine interested in that topic?*

Student B: *No. Which one?*

Student C: Career Focus.

Student D: *I think I'm going for the athlete.* Texas Coach *is always looking for articles, and I want to do something about how important trainers are to a football team.*

Student E: *I'm writing an editorial for the local paper.*

Student D: *On what?*

PROCESS SHARE

Explanation. Process share helps students focus on how their paper came to be and what it still needs. Recognizing their own writing process and hearing others describe theirs helps students relax and go with their processes rather than fight them. This reduces frustration.

Implementation

1. Divide students into groups of seven.

2. Writers talk about where they are in the process or share what they have written thus far. Together students informally probe their processes using the following questions as a guide:

    a. What problems have you encountered?

    b. How did you go about solving them?

    c. Have you made any changes? What were they? What prompted them?

    d. What are you planning to do next?

    e. What help do you need from this group?

3. After this, the whole class meets to discuss what students learned.

Remarks. This strategy is most beneficial at the beginning of a paper that entails research. It helps students understand that writing research is also a process, and it asks for the responses of others.

SAY BACK

Explanation. Say back is one of the most constructive strategies because it begins with positive comments and concludes with helpful suggestions. This strategy works best about midway through the process, when students think they have included everything in their writing or know they have some rough spots but are unsure how to clarify them.

Implementation

1. Divide students into groups of four or five.

2. Writers read the whole piece, pause, and then read it again.

3. Listeners listen. Upon the second reading, they jot down two things:

    a. what they liked

    b. what they want to know more about

4. Listeners say these back to the writer.

Remarks. The beauty of this strategy is its adaptability. Workable with any grade level, say back fosters extending the writing and elaborating upon it in a positive way.

ANALYTIC TALK

Explanation. The purpose of analytic talk is for writers to share their topic in such a way that they receive specific responses, which they may use to hone parts of their writing. This strategy works best when the writing has been through several drafts and is ready for final polishing.

Implementation

1. Divide students into groups of five.

2. Writers read, pause, and then read it again.

3. Listeners listen. Upon the second reading, they take notes—a word or phrase—to help them remember anything they may wish to comment upon.

4. After the reading, the group comments, suggests, advises, and discusses using the following questions as a guide:

    a. Did I like the opening sentence(s)?

    b. Was the opening clear and interesting?

c. Would I continue reading if I read the opener in a magazine?

d. Was there a lazy or phony question such as, "Have you ever been in love?"

e. After hearing the beginning, am I sure what the writing is about?

f. Did I ever get lost during the reading? If so, where?

g. Did I ever get confused during the reading? If so, where?

h. Was I left hanging at the end? If so, was it intentional and effective, or was it caused by lack of information?

Remarks. These questions may be modified, but generally they work well because they focus on specific parts of the paper, such as leads, theses, and conclusions without using terms students find threatening. Analytic talk provides "congenial motivation," to borrow a term from the poet William Stafford.

OLYMPIC SCORING

Explanation. Olympic scoring approximates the evaluation system used at the Olympic Games. Students work with one element of writing (in this case, character development) by grouping on that element with two different partners. Each writer then compares the values received in each of the ten areas and makes decisions for further work on the paper.

Implementation

1. Writers reread their papers and fill out a scoring sheet (see fig. 5.2) for themselves.

2. Divide class into groups of two.

3. Partners exchange drafts one and two.

4. Distribute one copy of the scoring sheet for each student.

5. Partners complete the scoring sheet for each other. They assign points 1 to 10 (1 is lowest, 10 is highest) to each area just as a judge would assign points to an Olympic participant.

6. Students repeat steps 3-5 with a new partner.

7. Students study all three scoring sheets and revise accordingly.

Remarks. This strategy may be adapted to any or all elements within a particular genre. It works best when used in conjunction with mini-lessons. For example, if the mini-lessons have centered on writing about characters, developing characters, rounding out flat characters, and so forth, then Olympic scoring on character provides the logical check of the application of those lessons.

Another level of collaboration can be achieved with this strategy by teaching mini-lessons on the appropriate elements within the genre and then encouraging groups of students to develop Olympic scoring sheets for those elements. Students may use the sheet in figure 5.2 as a model.

(Text continues on page 160.)

Fig. 5.2. Olympic scoring sheet.

Writer's name _____   Partner's name _____

Draft One	Score	Draft Two	Score
1. Characters' appeal		1. Characters' appeal	
2. Quality of characters' names		2. Quality of characters' names	
3. Authenticity of characters		3. Authenticity of characters	
4. Characters sound real		4. Characters sound real	
5. Characters look real		5. Characters look real	
6. Characters are consistent		6. Characters are consistent	
7. Characters are not stereotypical		7. Characters are not stereotypical	
8. Quality of dialogue		8. Quality of dialogue	
9. Story has beginning, middle, end		9. Story has beginning, middle, end	
10. Overall quality		10. Overall quality	
Total		Total	

From *Acts of Teaching*, copyright 1993 Teacher Ideas Press, P.O. Box 6633, Englewood, CO 80155-6633

DOUBLE DYADS

Explanation. Double dyads are kin to proofreading. Used immediately before the final copy is to be handed in, it allows peers to become editors. Further, this strategy facilitates input from two persons within a given structure, so it is effective with students not yet accustomed to grouping or with somewhat unruly students.

Implementation

1. Divide students into groups of two.

2. Distribute two "Preparing for Publication Sheets" to each student (see fig. 5.3).

3. Partners exchange papers.

4. Each student silently and carefully reads the paper and marks the sheet accordingly.

5. After marking the sheet, partners discuss the papers.

6. Students repeat the process with a new partner.

7. Writers evaluate their papers after taking feedback into consideration.

Remarks. Double dyads work best with the documented essay, although the "Preparing for Publication Sheet" may be adapted to other writing.

(Text continues on page 162.)

Fig. 5.3. Preparing for publication sheet.

Writer _____

Reviewer _____

Read the essay and rate the writing honestly in the following categories.	Super— outstanding	Really good	Just OK	Not so hot— could be better	Really needs help
How well does the introduction catch your attention?					
How well does the writer give you a clear objective of where the paper is heading and what the writer wants to say?					
Does the paper flow?					
Does the writer prove what he or she intended to prove?					
Does the writer document borrowed materials correctly?					
Does the writer wrap up the paper nicely with a sense of finality?					
Does the writer do a good job of convincing you of what he or she believes?					

What is the strongest part of the paper?

What is the weakest part of the paper?

Discuss the paper with your partner.

"The Sensuous Metaphor"

JOYCE ARMSTRONG CARROLL

Commentary

The symbolic transformation that Langer utilizes is simultaneously complex and simple. Borrowing from the abstract and the concrete, Langer develops the idea. Although not readily utilized, Langer's ideas are worth the discovery.

Any exploration a student makes into the workings of his or her mind will produce profound effects. Putting these explorations into words and images creates meaning for the writer or the reader.

Outside of Kress, Texas, along Highway 87, is a grain elevator with large black letters spelling out the word CONE painted on the curved sides. Each letter fills the entire curvature of the elevator. It looks something like this:

From the front, the grain elevator looks very much like any other grain elevator. It is the side glance that reveals the elevator in a symbolic way. Traveling from the south to the north, there is a point where the optical

Play the word game with *sensuous* and people name starlets in designer jeans, X-rated flicks, exotic perfumes, or erotic song lyrics. (With such associations, any mention of *metaphor* seems unlikely.) And be honest, if you ever expected *sensuous* in this column, you didn't expect to find it describing so respectable a figure of speech as the metaphor.

"She's trying to be clever," you might be muttering. "Is nothing sacred?"

I didn't invent the term. Borrowing *sensuous metaphor* from philosopher Susanne K. Langer, I'm using it here to invite a different look at metaphorical abstraction—a look which I hope will raise realizations about language processes, writing processes, and the mental activities involved in both.

The outward expressions of language—words, gestures, drawings, paintings, music, dance—since they are observable, somewhat orderly (suggesting an interplay of logical patterns), and give some semblance of rationality, encourage systematic investigation leading to intriguing speculations concerning the mind's functions. But the inward expressions—memories, fantasies, reflections, dreams, feelings, sensations—since they are unobservable, often chaotic (suggesting a multiplicity of complex interrelationships), and sometimes happen simultaneously, defy systematic investigation and perhaps cause us to miss equally intriguing speculations. By examining the sensuous metaphor, we may be able to perceive these less analytical aspects of language with more understanding. An analogy: When we look indirectly at a star, we more clearly discern its brilliance: if we cast a sidelong glance at language, we may better see its depth.

Ordinarily we regard metaphor as a figure of speech or a rhetorical device, but the *sensuous* metaphor appears as a curious symbolic projection which dips into sensory realms, cuts across sensory boundaries, and reunites sensations in synthetic ways to convey felt experiences, inward expressions. It is as if a feeling, so energy charged, cannot be expressed through conventional ways, so the mind ranges among maximum intensities picking and choosing, not to match meanings with feelings, but to approximate them.

We find many examples. W. S. Merwin describes "the darkness that flows from the sirens." Expressing sounds as *darkness* seems an attempt to approximate the mental state sirens generate. Joseph Conrad crosses into another art when he calls *Nostromo* his *largest canvas*, as do musicians who speak of *colors* and artists of *tonality*. Children freely arrest the sensuous metaphor. In *From Two to Five*, Chukovsky recounts:

> This child was drawing flowers; around them she drew several dots:
>
> "What are those? Flies?"
>
> "No! They are the fragrance of the flowers."

This child uses forms—dots—to express the formlessness of fragrance, something she clearly experiences.

But the sensuous metaphor suggests more than apt comparisons and synesthesia. Its significance transcends sense overlapping and lexical borrowing, not only by residing in poetic lines such as Kumin's "of a man who wore *hard colors* recklessly," (italics mine) or in everyday expressions like "feeling blue," but also by revealing important information.

First, the sensuous metaphor indicates the mind's ability to shift word meanings. These mental shifts uncover unusual, idiosyncratic sensory associations. For example, Faulkner in *As I Lay Dying* tucks a one-line chapter, "Vardaman," between two longer chapters. The one line, "My mother is a fish," at first strikes us as an incoherent interloper. Faulkner does not explain Vardaman's sensory association. We only know it exists. We accept it, returning later to figure its meaning, as we know even in the shift—ours and the author's—there is meaning.

Second, the very existence of the sensuous metaphor implies that the mind often works abstractly and creatively in real although ambiguous and inseparable ways. Maxine Hong Kingston's *The Woman Warrior* helps us see that sensoria may be more a matter of lamination than compartmentalization:

illusion creates the face of a clock at about four o'clock, that looks much like this

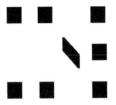

Travelers unaccustomed to looking at things with a sideways glance miss this wonderful illusion. So it is, too, with thinking, or perception. Those unaccustomed to looking at things differently miss much.

The poet Sandra McPherson at a recent National Council of Teachers of English convention described the language of her daughter. She refers to her as a poet because of her marvelous sense of metaphoric language. One consideration might be that children have this natural metaphorical language educated out of them at school.

Once students are introduced to sensuous metaphors, the more easily they find them and the more easily they create them.

Night after night my mother would talk-story until we fell asleep. I couldn't tell where the stories left off and the dreams began.... After I grew up, I heard the chant of Fa Mu Lan.... Instantly I remembered that as a child I had followed my mother about the house, the two of us singing.... I had forgotten this chant that was once mine, given me by my mother, who may not have known its power to remind.... The call would come from a bird that flew over our roof. In the brush drawings it looks like the ideograph for *human*.

In this excerpt we find layers of talk-stories, dreams, chants, memories, songs, drawings—all culminating in an extended sensuous metaphor, the chapter "White Tigers."

Kingston does this again in "The Ghostmate," a chapter in her book China Men *(New York: Alfred A. Knopf, 1980).*

Third, the sensuous metaphor discloses felt experiences correlating uniquely and individually with disparate sensations. For example, while Langer admits color associations with vowel sounds, Sir Isaac Newton associated colors with musical notes, and I know one person who associates colors with personalities. Although we all may not experience these associations, we all see, feel, and express uniquely, often through the sensuous metaphor.

Consider, too, the many books and articles that relate colors to style, mood, beauty, and feeling good.

Fourth, and most elusive, are the connections made with a concept, its opposite, and everything in between. For instance, the mind comprehends the archaic *wann*, meaning dark, and connects it with a feeling—probably as an outgrowth of nature, the forest perhaps. The mind then moves along a continuum, merges with the modern *wan*, which grew out of the old word but now means colorless. As expected, this yields a corresponding change in feeling. Hence, we uncover the conceptual roots for oxymora like Yeats's "terrible beauty" or "horrible splendor." Langer explains these paradoxes as intensity changes "from too faint to satisfy, to too intense to bear" (*Mind: An Essay on Human Feeling*, Vol. I, p. 197), a mental provision for the resolution of tensions, a balancing act performed by the mind.

In Aristotle's rhetorical tactic Classical Invention (see chapter 3), are provisions for the writer to consider a topic from varied and opposite points of view. When writing is implemented as a process, heuristics become a way of thinking and/or examining what the writer wants to write.

Children naturally use these types of metaphors. When children are allowed to explore the writing world, this language is nurtured and continues to grow. Children who are given worksheets and fill-in-the-blank questions find there is no room in that kind of writing for metaphors; thus they stop using them.

And tensions are inherent in language. Subjective reality must be symbolically transformed to be objectively recognized as an expression of experience. In other words, if we experience a poem, and if we want to convey that experience to another, we must write, draw, paint, dance, play, talk, or act it out in some recognizable manner that at once approximates what we experienced while approximating the experiences of our audience. That's not easy. As we know, our approximations often fall short. Frustration sets in; yet, if the desire to transform is intense enough, we rely on the sensuous metaphor.

Since writing is one form symbolic transformation can take, attempts to get close to the writing experience through metaphorical abstraction appear reasonable. So I "tested" the sensuous metaphor via the writing process.

Without mentioning the term, I invited three groups to complete "My writing process is ..." or "is like...." I gave no further directions. Responding were 11 prospective English teachers enrolled in a course in the teaching of writing and 31 English teachers participating in summer writing institutes. While 9.7 percent simply made statements such as "I write like I talk," or "My writing process is L-Modal," 89.9 percent employed the sensuous metaphor. They drew from psychical phenomena:

> ... a Buddhist's achievement of Nirvana.

> ... offering you my soul in hieroglyphics—decipher it and you decipher me.

They used physical comparisons:

> ... wanting to ride a horse I've trained myself.

> ... breathing—it is necessary to my existence.

One turned to the Bible, another to rhythms in rock 'n' roll. Some found meaning through nature:

> ... a thunderstorm. First the dark clouds of depression gather, and it is as if night descended. My best writing stems from depression, from feeling I have no hope left.

> ... a tornado. The prewriting and writing come quickly, but the rewriting is time-consuming and tedious like the reconstruction.

Janet Emig was fond of having her graduate students formulate their individual theories of writing through dance, architecture, geometry, mathematical equation, music, art, and words. The metaphor became paramount in the formulations of these students. Most would attest to the mental gymnastics they experienced while working through these assignments.

It has become a standard question in a debriefing session during the writing institute to ask, "What is your writing process like?"

In one writing institute in Northside ISD, San Antonio, Texas, a teacher/writer, Mabel, wrote about The Mare That Went to College. *The piece was ultimately published in a horse fanciers' magazine. It was natural for her to use the horse metaphor.*

These metaphors are reflections of the writer writing what he or she knows best. The weather that people live with each day is bound to figure into their writing.

... a rainstorm — a cathartic experience that leaves me physically tired and sopping wet.

The writing process, like other creative processes, is holistic, complex, and alive.

Others likened their process to building houses, making jelly, designing a dress, or taking trips. A few, more playful, compared composing to games:

> ... a pinball machine. The initial shot bounces hard and high, hitting many bumpers and going in all directions. I almost lose the ball, I hit it with the thumps and I am renewed. Ooops! I've lost it.

> ... playing pick-up-stix. You mess up three to get one good.

Brain research supports Langer's notions. Strong emotions are tied to the limbic system and thus linked to memory. The stronger the emotion, the stronger the memory.

Langer claims that *light, heat, movement, faintness, dullness, pain* and *threat* words lend themselves most to metaphor. Although no one used *heat* or *dullness*, of the participants engaged in this activity, 4.8 percent used *light*, 12 percent *faintness*, 9.7 percent *pain*, 14.6 percent *threat*, and 48.7 percent *movement* — a corroboration of her claim.

Interestingly, faintness translated into tentativeness:

> ... a small child learning to walk.

> ... the initial attempts of a young erratic spider spinning a web but not yet able to remove itself to a spot where it can know what the final product is going to be.

Pain proved vivid:

> ... bill paying and my writing process cluster.

> ... a struggle — a struggle to put my feelings on paper — a struggle to find the perfect word — a struggle from beginning to end, but one worth enduring over and over again.

> ... an Odyssey into a maelstrom.

Tish Frederick combined pain *and* movement as she explored a gamut of feelings:

Tish's metaphor came to her as a surprise. She didn't expect it. In fact, she reported that she didn't find meat packing especially rewarding, but the metaphor worked for what she had to say.

> ... a meat packing plant. Of all the animals in the world only certain ones are selected for butchering. Just so, only certain, selected stimuli undergo the writing

process. Butchering takes place between the thought and the page—so stimulus looks the same after that! Once the thoughts are out, like slabs of beef, I saw them apart: shoulder, ribs, rump. Excess bone and fat fall prey to a swift stroke, leaving only red meat. Of this I look for top quality steak. I waver, finally admitting some only suited for hamburger. Packaging begins.

Threat rose replete, with ancient as well as modern fears and even some light-hearted risk taking:

> ... The Cyclopean eye of prewriting bars the door to repose. Bloodshot and menacing it lies in my alphabet soup bowl more disturbing than a fly.

> ... a traffic jam. It lacks momentum and fosters frustration.

> ... planting a garden with Crazy Seeds, then waiting for the first sign of growth to break through the ground, anxious to see what strange fruit will emerge.

Besides providing a look at language, writing, and cognitive processes, the sensuous metaphor encourages exploration, fixes learning, and generates good writing. Take, as a final example, Vicki Yoder's "Cocoon":

> I don't meditate on cocoons much, nor do I sit and contemplate my writing process, but they are similar. Brushing back the leaves of everyday occurrences, I discover an idea—a cocoon—and my process creaks into gear. Encased in the cocoon my process lies dormant. Though not visible on the outside, inside something is changing, growing, moving. Sometimes a cocoon is knocked away at this stage and the inner mystery is never revealed. But the cocoon that remains intact reacts. Nibble by nibble the cocoon's paper-like casing is eaten away by pen—a dark, wet mystery! Slowly revealing itself, the insect is still weak, trembling, rather ugly, and tired from the stage before. Now any eyes can view my work. Because of my weaknesses, some insects are not strong enough to continue, they die at this stage. But most live, and I then observe what was born. Some of my

In writing these descriptions of their writing processes, respondents themselves use powerful language, vivid images, and precise diction.

Not only do metaphors allow for self-expression in unique ways, they also apparently open new and often untapped intellectual horizons via simple symbols. Through the sensuous metaphor deeper mysteries, sometimes closed off to us, are often uncovered.

healthy butterflies with surprising beauty, grace, and color. Other cocoons have bred brown, blind moths whose best place is the attic, cellar, or closet. Thus my writing process is finished—until I discover another cocoon.

The metaphor allows the writer to touch images, feelings, and ideas that would have been inaccessible initially. In turn, the metaphor allows the writer to touch the reader with metaphor. The writer communicates; the reader knows.

I doubt if Vicki or any of the other respondents could have expressed their writing process so precisely, individually, intensely, or directly without access to the sensuous metaphor.

In closing, a point of information: Columns following this one *will not* address the *sultry synecdoche, passionate personifications*, or *amorous allusions*. However, know that this editor will always make an effort to include all manner of lusty language.

REFERENCES

Chukovsky, Kornei. *From Two to Five.* Translated and edited by Miriam Morton. Berkeley: University of California Press, 1963.

Langer, Susanne K. *Mind: An Essay on Human Feeling.* Vol. I. Baltimore, MD: The Johns Hopkins University Press, 1967.

Classroom Management Strategies for Writing Groups

CONDUCTING WRITING GROUPS

When initiating writing groups, it is important for teachers to think of themselves as facilitators who structure the classroom so each group feels successful. Keeping three things in mind helps groups work smoothly and with purpose: (1) remain nondefensive, (2) act from a knowledge base, and (3) implement writing groups in increments.

Remain Nondefensive. Nondefensive teachers, equipped with reasonable expectations and explicit goals, set up writing groups by introducing specific strategies. They observe how the groups function using those strategies. Closely noting what occurs in each group enables the teacher to modify, adapt, continue, or disregard a strategy—always with future writing groups in mind. Nondefensive teachers expect some floundering as the groups find their rhythm and do not take the group behavior personally. They may sit near a group that seems raucous, they may nudge a group that appears idle, or they may interact with a lively group, but they refuse to take on the group. Later, during the debriefing, students may consider and reconsider the actions of the group. Debriefing often turns what may have been an unproductive session into a productive one.

"What happened in your groups today?" asked the teacher.

"Not much," quipped one young man.

"Let's talk about that," invited the teacher.

Act from a Knowledge Base. Teachers who write with students teach from a knowledge base. When they perceive a need for certain behaviors in writing groups, such as eye contact, close listening, respectful comments, or insightful questions, they set a standard by modeling and by using their own writing. Because they write, they are able to anticipate concerns, so they design mini-lessons based on those concerns as well as on the concerns they observe while students write, what students say in conferences and during debriefing, and what emerges during writing groups.

> *Kelley Smith's kindergartners sat on the floor in clusters. Each group was engrossed in categorizing animals and birds by fur and feathers. In the midst of one group endeavor, Carl began talking about the time he took his dog to the vet. Suddenly, as if on cue, all his classmates pointed the index finger of their right hands perpendicular to the open palm of their left hands. Kelley whispered to them, "Good. You remembered our signal for stick to the point." The boy stopped his rambling story and the group returned to categorizing.*

Implement Writing Groups in Increments. Those who want to initiate collaboration but who are inexperienced with group strategies should implement group work in increments. It is helpful to begin with a nonthreatening strategy, such as pointing, and with small, easy-to-structure groups, such as partners. As teachers and students become facile with groups, they move into the complicated strategies and larger or more flexible groups.

Sometimes past experiences with groups (or lack thereof) militate against using them, especially in middle and high school. On the one hand, some teachers may not have received training in group strategies and are understandably reluctant to risk losing control because of class dynamics. If they do take the risk, the results sometimes may be less than satisfying. This may lead teachers to the conclusion that groups do not work, and the teachers never try groups again. This is a disservice to students who require practice in collaboration.

On the other hand, students who have not collaborated since the primary grades often regard groups as "baby stuff" or time to fool around. These students are misinformed, which is all the more reason that teachers must deeply believe in the value of collaboration and learn its techniques. The best defense is to introduce writing groups slowly and in increments. But to group on mandate, to group because others do it, or to group because it is the trend will most certainly lead to problems.

INTRODUCING WRITING GROUPS: THE MINI-LESSON

Explanation. A clear sense of purpose and an organized system for initiating groups sets the tone. When teachers project security about groups, students feel secure. To achieve this mutual understanding and security, a mini-lesson works best.

Implementation. Before initiating writing groups, conduct a mini-lesson on this activity. It answers questions, anticipates problems, and provides a forum for learning.

1. Sit on a low chair in an open area in the classroom.

2. Invite the students to gather around, either on chairs drawn up close or on the carpet.

3. Together talk about group experiences they remember. Discuss why they think they worked in groups, their feelings about groups, the purposes of groups, and so forth.

4. Introduce the group technique to be used, model it with several students, and ask the remaining students to act as observers. Discuss the technique.

5. Divide the students into groups, reiterate where they may sit in the room (or outside if that is permissible), and designate the amount of time they will have. Caution them to keep time constraints in mind so all group members have time to share.

Remarks. Teachers who begin writing groups this way discover invaluable information that helps their direction with writing groups. For example, if the class has consistently grouped in various classes and seems comfortable with the strategy, little else is necessary except to validate that and move into groups. If the class has not grouped for several years or has only grouped in one class, or if the students generally convey negativity or even hostility about groups, it is important to talk through those feelings, do more preparation with the class, and move slowly into writing groups.

> The fourth-graders surrounding me for large-group discussion were active, bright, and sophisticated. But they all talked at once. No matter what I tried to subdue them, it didn't work. They did not listen to me or to each other. I reasoned that small groups would surely be a problem if that behavior continued.
>
> "I am sorry, but you must return to your seats. You are not ready to learn now," I said.
>
> The talking immediately ceased. They moved reluctantly to their regular seats. "I want you to think about what just happened. Tomorrow we will talk about it."
>
> The next day I gathered them around me again. "Let's talk about what happened when we came to large group yesterday." Almost in chorus, they began to apologize. "I'm sorry, too," I said, "because we lost valuable time. But today we must uncover what happened. Why did our large group not work?"
>
> Eventually, the students told me two important things: They had not grouped since first grade, and, perhaps most important, they told me, "You listened." Building on those responses, we together set about

establishing fourth-grade guidelines for grouping: respect for one another, listening for what we can learn from each group experience, not talking when someone else talks, and so forth.

Because the students worked on these guidelines in groups, they had already taken a giant step in collaboration.

STRATEGIES FOR DIVIDING STUDENTS INTO WRITING GROUPS

Number Groups. The easiest and most efficient way to divide a class into groups is to count off. Divide the number for each group by the number in the class and count off to that number. For example, for a group of 4 in a class of 28, divide 4 into 28. Then the class counts off to seven. All the "ones" form a group, all the "twos," all the "threes," and so forth. This strategy may be used repeatedly. To vary the participants in a group, simply begin the count with a different student each time.

Birthday Groups. A fun way to group is by birthday months. Ask all students who have birthdays in January to raise their hands. They become a group. Follow the same procedure for February, March, and so on. If there are too many in one month, split the group. If there are too few, combine two or even three months. An ancillary effect of this strategy is that students discover who else in the class shares their birthday month. The discovery of this commonality aids bonding among students.

Color Groups. Students pick colors from a box. They find that color somewhere in the room. There they group with others who picked the same color. This strategy allows chance to intervene and often produces wonderful interactions.

Genre Groups. Often it is productive to group by genre. For example, all those working on narratives form one group, all those writing letters form another group, all those working on persuasive essays form a third group, and so on. Generally, writers working in the same genre have similar problems. Through collaboration, students often find solutions to these problems.

Organic Groups: As students become comfortable with grouping, as trust and respect grow, and as they become aware of each other's strengths, it is effective to encourage groups to form organically. Students choose others with whom they would like to group. This strategy sends a direct message of trust and mutual respect to students. It also provides one more way for students to make decisions.

Small Groups. Certain categories of papers or writing for specific purposes sometimes call for small, tight groups. The dyad, a group of two, intensifies the group experience. This may be extended to the double dyad, which allows each one of the two members of the original dyad to regroup with a new partner. The double dyads permit each person to receive feedback from two other people in a structured way.

Triads or groups of three often work well if there is a need to connect ability levels. One student weak in some area, such as coherence or conclusions, may be teamed with two students strong in these areas. Conversely, the former student may be strong in an area in which the latter two show weaknesses.

WRITING CONFERENCES

Writing conferences, which are woven throughout the writing process, provide a time for teacher and student to discuss a piece of writing. Conferring demands active listening on the part of both conferees. If, as Judith Sanders suggests, some 93 percent of what we communicate is nonverbal, teachers trained in the techniques of the writing conference attend equally to the nonverbal and verbal language taking place. They know that tones, expressions, and gestures emerge as significant subtexts of meaning and can be as important as the words spoken.

When arranging the room for the conference, it is extremely important to set out the areas where talk is permitted and where it is not permitted. There should be no talk in the writing area. In the conference area all should talk in "one-inch voices." This also applies to middle- and high-school students, who may choose to call conference talk whispers or stage whispers. A cluster of chairs may be placed in the conference area for small peer-group conferences. One effective way to visually set apart these quiet areas is by making a demarcation line. Masking tape works nicely. One side is the quiet area; on the other side is the buzz of active learning.

Nancie Atwell states: "The point of a writing conference isn't to get kids to revise.... The nature of talk in my writing workshop depends on what a writer needs or what I need as a teacher of writers" (88). In chapter 5 of her book *In the Middle*, Atwell presents information on status-of-the-class conferences, content conferences, and conferring with self, as well as guidelines for and examples of how to confer. Because teachers often find writing conferences difficult, Atwell's chapter is well worth reading.

Introducing Writing Conferences: The Mini-Lesson

Explanation. Because meeting with the teacher might intimidate some students, it is a good idea to conduct a mini-lesson on student-teacher conferences.

Implementation

1. Gather the students around you in a comfortable area of the room.

2. Talk about talk, why we do it, and what purpose it serves.

3. Discuss how important it is for both student and teacher to understand why talk is needed during a conference. Explain that for a conference to be most productive, students should be able to analyze their writing and generate several questions about that writing. These questions "kick off" the conference.

4. Invite students to brainstorm questions that might be appropriate to ask when they come to the conference.

5. Model several writing conferences, such as the individual conference, the conference on wheels, and the group conference (see explanations of each below). Have students role play.

Remarks. Once students experience a successful writing conference, they usually like the individual attention it provides. They usually appreciate the fact that the teacher is with them during this part of the process, ready to help, advise, and encourage.

After several sessions with a class of tenth-graders, I asked them to look at their writing in small groups and generate questions they might ask in a conference about that writing. They generated the following list:

Is it OK to combine all my prewriting into one piece?

How can I stop repeating myself?

How will I know which piece will be worth publishing?

I don't use any dialogue; what do I do?

How do I decide what genre is best?

How can I get closure?

How do you feel when I read it to you?

Help me out of this dead-end.

Is my piece too trite or too personal for others?

How do I know when I'm dragging it out? What's the difference between fillers, elaboration, and depth?

Am I clear about audience?

How do I delete?

What about a certain grammar, punctuation, or usage rule?

Is it too long? Too short?

Did I indent in the right places?

Did I use enough imagery?

Is this word spelled correctly?

My characters won't come alive. Help!

I need help on my title. Is it dull?

How do I get this part to hang together?

Show me how to rewrite this paragraph.

I think I switch tenses. Do I?

We shared these on the board. We talked about them and then wrote them in our writing folders. Although this list is by no means exhaustive, it does serve as a model and keeps the student who comes to conference from asking, "Is this good?" Also, many of these questions would make meaningful mini-lessons.

Writing Conference Strategies

INDIVIDUAL WRITING CONFERENCES

Explanation. Individual conferences take place between one student and the teacher. They usually occur at specific times after prewriting.

Implementation

1. The teacher sits in a predetermined area alongside an empty, inviting chair.

2. The conference area should be a bit away from the writing area so the conference does not disturb those writing.

3. Students sign up on a nearby board or chart if they wish a conference.

4. As students complete the conference, they erase or cross out their names and tap the next person on the list. This procedure eliminates students queuing up and keeps talk to a minimum.

5. Students return to their places and work on their writing.

Remarks. Although individual conferences allow for intensity and individualization, they are time-consuming. In some cases the teacher must almost dismiss the conferee. However, in other cases, no matter how nonthreatening the environment, some students remain reluctant to approach the teacher.

One variation for the individual conference is the bullpen. Place another chair close to the chair of the conferee. The student next in line for a conference sits in that chair and is able to listen in on the conference. Sometimes the second student has his or her questions answered and does not require an individual conference. Although this arrangement often helps the time factor, it does limit the privacy of the conferee.

> *Marjorie Woodruff individually confers with her pre-kindergarten class. After Marjorie read a story about a party, she explained they would have a class Valentine's Day party, but they needed to send out invitations. After much modeling on writing invitations, Marjorie distributed paper, donned a plastic visor, drew a large square in the corner of the chalkboard, wrote in five numbers, and moved toward an area where two kindergarten chairs were placed side by side. As she did, students went to the board and made marks beside the numbers.*
>
> *Suddenly one of the four-year-olds tugged at her skirt. "I want a conference," he lisped.*
>
> *Marjorie stopped, turned to the square on the board, and studied the marks. "I don't see your name on the board, Juan," she said.*
>
> *Juan also studied the marks. Finally he replied, "It's not there."*
>
> *"You know the rules, Juan. You must write your name on the board and wait your turn."*
>
> *With that Marjorie walked to the awaiting chairs and soon became engrossed in the writing of the first child on the list.*
>
> *Juan proceeded to the board, where he made a series of squiggles next to the number 5.*
>
> *Not only did Marjorie reinforce a function of writing and her belief that the students could and would write, but she also demonstrated excellent classroom management.*

THE WRITING CONFERENCE ON WHEELS

Explanation. The most efficient writing conference is the one where the teacher moves to the student. Because the teacher starts the conference, the teacher may end it.

Implementation

1. The teacher sits in a chair on wheels and simply rolls from student to student.

2. If a student needs immediate help, some agreed-upon signal may be used, such as raising a hand or putting the writing folder to the left of the desk or table.

3. Students not conferring may remain comfortably where they are.

Remarks. The rhythm of movement keeps the conference from bogging down. There is an element of surprise. The teacher may meet with more students and may divide the time according to student needs. If a student is obviously deeply engaged in writing, the teacher may skip that student and return another time.

SMALL-GROUP CONFERENCES

Explanation. One way to facilitate the writing conference is for the teacher to meet with small groups of students who have similar questions or concerns.

Implementation

1. Begin by asking students how many want to confer.

2. Ask students to identify what they want to discuss during the conference.

3. Invite several who have similar problems or questions to confer together.

4. Those students, in turn, read their bothersome sections so that teacher and peers may interact and respond.

5. If the question or concern has been answered to the satisfaction of the student who raised the concern or other participating students, they may choose either to stay or to return to their writing.

Remarks. Small-group conferences work much like writing groups, except the teacher acts as group leader and major responder. The teacher invites students to raise the questions, and then teacher *and* group respond.

LARGE-GROUP CONFERENCES

Explanation. During large-group conferences, students meet as a class or in groups of 10 or more.

Implementation

1. One student volunteers to share while the other students informally respond.

2. All work together to make the paper better. They offer suggestions and constructive criticism, and they ask questions.

Remarks. Large-group conferences work well in classes that are experienced in collaborative learning and have achieved levels of trust with peers.

WRITING DEBRIEFINGS

Writing debriefings are designated, interactive talk times. A few minutes, three to ten, set aside at the close of a lesson or a class period, provide invaluable opportunities for students to share thoughts about what they learned, how they learned, and what they think about that learning. Debriefings balance the *what* with the *how* of learning. They are metacognitive: thinking about thinking.

Debriefings differ uniquely from what are erroneously called class discussions, during which students state or restate specific information to a logical line of questions. Rather, debriefings permit students to sort out their helter-skelter thoughts, to reflect, to make connections, and to share those connections aloud in a public forum. Students' thinking moves not necessarily inductively or deductively, but abductively. Abductive reasoning is what C. S. Peirce calls thinking that crosses a range of possibilities (Fulwiler 16). It is crablike. Thought-provoking statements or questions raised during debriefings foster abductive reasoning because they enable students to develop analogies, draw inferences, hypothesize, test assumptions, define presuppositions, pose questions, and take risks—in short, think out loud.

Oral quizzes, also often misnamed "discussions," are not to be confused with debriefings. During an oral quiz, the teacher generates a set of questions (usually requiring simple recall answers) to test knowledge. The mode works somewhat like a two-lane roadway: The teacher asks the questions; students answer. An oral quiz on Act I, scenes i and ii, of *Macbeth* might sound something like this: How many witches are in the opening scene? What does *graymalkin* mean? Who is Duncan? What is Malcolm's relationship to Duncan? and so on. Although this may serve the teacher's objective on occasion, this activity often degenerates into a flat, one-dimensional exchange with the teacher filling in long gaps of uncomfortable silences and the students making little or no commitment.

Likewise, a true discussion also must be distinguished from a debriefing. In discussion, the teacher sets a purpose but allows for more spontaneity, most often with occasional open-ended questions such as, "Why did Shakespeare open *Macbeth* with three witches?" Clearly, there is a desire to stimulate thinking and invite extensions, but the teacher still intends to lead students to the correct response. Between the question and the answer there may be conversation or conjecture, but more often than not, after the opening question or two, flags go up as the students realize they are being led to the exact answer. This is not to say that class discussions are unproductive or meaningless or that in some classes a question or concern will not spark the group, but much of the time everyone is clear that the discussion is geared to the teacher's agenda, so there is a falling off of student engagement, and answers become perfunctory.

Because the purpose of debriefing is not set by the teacher and it is always meant to allow students to discover nuances in their own learning, the teacher becomes a facilitator. To enhance diversity, to allow the multiplicity of voices to resonate, the facilitator begins with a global statement or an "iffy" question and then follows the lead of those being debriefed.

> *In a recent debriefing on* Macbeth, *when asked, "How do you think it would change the play if Shakespeare had not included the three witches?" students immediately knew there was no absolutely correct answer. They knew they were being invited to think, probe, listen to the answers of others, and entertain possibilities. As the students responded, the facilitator listened carefully (students began interacting with each other), making further statements or asking additional questions that arose authentically and appropriately from those responses.*
>
> *"We would not have gotten that Halloween opener."*
> *"They set everything up."*

> *"I wasn't expecting witches in a play by Shakespeare."*
> *"I was. Didn't they believe in witches then?"*
> *"Weird."*
> *"So what is it about the weird that captures people's interest?"* asked the facilitator. The students began comparing the witches with the bizarre in today's novels, television programming, and films. After a time, the facilitator said, "Talk to me, then, about what playwrights need to know when they write." They did.
>
> As a further example of debriefing, this time after writing groups, the facilitator began, "How are things happening as you write?"
> *"I'm getting excited because my writing is coming together."*
> *"It was easier today than yesterday. I think it was my attitude, my mood."*
> *"I found myself rehearsing—thinking about it."*
> *"Yeah, I dreamed about it. It's like it's physical or subconscious thinking."*
> *"What have you learned about your writing?"* the facilitator continued.
> *"I can't always rewrite."*
> *"I need quiet."*
> *"I often want to overhaul it, take a new direction. It's frustrating sometimes."*
> *"I started a new piece and wrote four pages nonstop, but the other day I couldn't write a thing. You can't force the process."*
> *"There was so much. I was overwhelmed. I had to put it away. It brought up too many memories I can't deal with right now."*
> *"How about the rest of you, are emotions surfacing as you write?"* the facilitator picked up on that thread, and the debriefing continued.

Debriefing resembles Faulkner's "method" of developing a character: "Once he stands up on his feet and begins to move, all I do is to trot along behind him with a paper and pencil trying to keep up long enough to put down what he says and does, that he is taking charge of it. I have very little to do except the policeman in the back of the head which insists on unity and coherence and emphasis in telling it. But the characters themselves, they do what they do, not me" (quoted in Fant and Ashley 111). The teacher begins the debriefing and then trots along behind the students' responses. Some guidelines for debriefing are provided in the following list.

1. Create an introductory global statement or thought-provoking ("iffy") question.

2. Allow plenty of wait time. Metacognition requires an unpressured, relaxed atmosphere.

3. Listen carefully to responses.

4. Do not cross arms or legs. Body language should invite openness.

5. When students begin interacting, move away from them. That movement encourages them to continue interacting with each other.

6. If someone monopolizes the debriefing, move to that person, make direct eye contact, and then at his or her first pause, turn to look at another person.

7. Watch for indicators that someone wants to speak, such as pursed lips, blinking eyes, or leaning forward.

8. Build commentary or further questions on responses. Do not lead the debriefing to what you want students to say.

9. Do not come to the debriefing with a set of questions or an agenda.

10. Trust the students' responses to lead you farther and deeper.

APPLICATION

1. Describe how you would divide a class of 27 ninth-graders for the analytic talk strategy. Give your rationale.

2. Your students have just completed a writing group. There are several minutes remaining before the bell. Write a global statement or thought-provoking question you might use to begin debriefing them. Share.

WORKS CITED

Atwell, Nancie. *In the Middle: Writing, Reading, and Learning with Adolescents.* Portsmouth, NH: Heinemann Educational Books, 1987.

Brophy, Beth; Maureen Walsh; Art Levine; Andrew Gabor; Betsy Bauer; and Lisa Moore. "Children Under Stress." In *U.S. News and World Report* (27 October 1986): 58-63.

Caine, Renate Nummela, and Geoffrey Caine. *Making Connections: Teaching and the Human Brain.* Alexandria, VA: Association for Supervision and Curriculum Development, 1991.

Calkins, Lucy McCormick. *Lessons from a Child: On the Teaching and Learning of Writing.* Portsmouth, NH: Heinemann Educational Books, 1983.

Carroll, Joyce Armstrong. "Talking Through the Writing Process." *English Journal* (November 1981): 100-102.

Elbow, Peter. *Writing Without Teachers.* New York: Oxford University Press, 1973.

Fant, Joseph L., and Robert Ashley. *Faulkner at West Point.* New York: Vintage, 1969.

Fulwiler, Toby, ed. *The Journal Book.* Portsmouth, NH: Heinemann Educational Books, 1987.

Glasser, William. *The Quality School.* New York: Harper & Row, 1990.

Gould, June. *The Writer in All of Us.* New York: E. P. Dutton, 1989.

Healy, Jane M. *Endangered Minds: Why Our Children Don't Think.* New York: Simon & Schuster, 1990.

Polanyi, Michael. *Personal Knowledge: Toward a Post-Critical Philosophy.* Chicago: University of Chicago Press, 1958.

Reich, Robert B. *Education and the Next Economy.* Washington, DC: National Education Association, 1988.

Rico, Gabriele Lusser. *Writing the Natural Way.* Los Angeles: J. P. Tarcher, 1983.

Sanders, Judith. "Teaching the Metaphoric Lesson." Paper presented at the annual convention of the Texas Joint Council of Teachers of English (TJCTE), Houston, Texas, February 1985.

Vygotsky, Lev Semonovich. *Thought and Language.* Translated by Eugenia Hanfmann and Gertrude Vakar. Cambridge, MA: The MIT Press, 1962.

"Enhancing Understanding Through Debriefing"

JAMES RATH

(From *Educational Leadership* 45, no. 2 [October 1987]. Reprinted with permission of the author and the Association for Supervision and Curriculum Development. Copyright © 1987 by the Association for Supervision and Curriculum Development. All rights reserved.)

Students in a tenth-grade class read an article in the class newspaper that discusses the probability that life exists on other planets. After asking a series of who, what, and where questions, the teacher shifts the discussion to another item in the newspaper.

Taking turns reading aloud, students in an honors English class hear recounted the agony of Oedipus making his horrifying discovery. The teacher asks several questions about the facts of the matter, and soon discussion of tomorrow's quiz dominates the interaction.

What meanings did the students in the above vignettes gain from their readings? What if there *were* life on another planet? What implications do students see for such an eventuality? What does the concept "incest" mean to the students?

In all subject areas, from the highly charged plays of Sophocles to new discoveries in science, students accommodate to their own conceptual systems the things they are told, what they hear, and what they perceive (Abelson, 1981). These accommodations form the essence of meaning. As Novak and Gowin (1984) point out, meaningful learning enables the student "to tie things together and connect part to part to whole." It is "meaning" in this sense that allows the student "to exercise the powers of inference, self-understanding, and thoughtful action" (110).

The student's process of accommodating new information to his or her own conceptual system, however, is fraught with pitfalls. A student may distort new learning to make it fit previously learned material. In this case, the accommodation may, in the long run, hinder future learning. Or the student may not see how the new content relates to *any* previous learning and may treat it as discrete material to be learned by rote, tested, and forgotten.

Commentary

Focusing on the what *instead of the* how *of knowing reduces the learning to plot and retelling.*

The answers to these questions are possibly one reason that students perform so poorly in large assessment projects. Without engagement why would students remember classroom instruction?

Certainly Piaget's work on accommodation and assimilation are support for using debriefing in the classroom. The brain activity generated by the two activities keeps students engaged.

Debriefing does not encourage specific answers to specific questions. Thus, it moves students away from the correct answer syndrome and encourages risk taking.

On the other hand, a student may see how the new learning relates to previous learning and resolves questions he or she has harbored for some time.

To ensure that students will accommodate new learning in positive ways, teachers can use debriefing.

Debriefing Strategies

Teachers will want to practice their listening abilities as they engage in debriefing activities. A good debriefer listens carefully to accommodate questions for their students.

I am sensitive about using a borrowed term to describe techniques teachers have used for years to advance the understanding of their students (Pearson and Smith, 1985), but in this case, "debriefing" seems especially apt and particularly graphic. A term originally used to describe the process of working with spies or astronauts after completing a mission, it is based on the belief that persons involved in such complex operations or experiences cannot remember all there is to tell, that they have impressions that are difficult to verbalize, and that they may forget or distort what they have seen or heard unless their accounts are thoroughly reviewed and shared. In schools, debriefing is a process of helping students reflect on their learning experiences, attach personal meanings to them, and deepen their understandings. Consider the following examples.

Not only does debriefing act as a wonderful way to verbalize, but it also acts as a reminder for the students. They know what they have done on a given day. They have verbalized it and it seems to stay with them longer.

After a field trip to a farm, the teacher asks students to draw a picture of the most important thing they saw on the visit. The pictures are collected and displayed before the class. The various representations are grouped, discussed and shared.

At the end of a unit on the Civil War, the teacher involves students in a culminating experience, that of preparing a simulated "60 Minutes" documentary on the war, designed to draw together and to integrate what the students have learned during the six-week period.

After carrying out a scientific experiment, students are asked to prepare laboratory reports to identify their assumptions, their findings, and their conclusions from the experiment.

These activities enable students to share what they learned through an experience, to summarize what the experience meant to them, and to provide the teacher with the opportunity to review what students did not understand well.

These activities also give a more accurate basis for the teacher to use in evaluating the student.

Debriefing: A More Precise View

Debriefing is not the same as summarizing. Summarizing is often a task performed by others, frequently the teacher, that gives the gist of what happened or what was covered. It might serve as a debriefing process for the person giving the summary. But listening to a summary does not give a student the opportunity to make sense of what has been taught or experienced, to operate on experience by organizing it, to emphasize some elements and not others, or to relate the experience to other events or ideas.

Each individual participates uniquely in the debriefing. One person cannot tell what has or has not been learned by someone else.

Preparing for a test is probably not a debriefing process either, since cramming is often a process that students do on the teacher's terms — working to understand the course as the instructor sees it. While insights and new meanings might well be a product of a cram session, it is not a likely outcome — especially if the test is an objective, short-answer examination. If the exam, on the other hand, asks students to share their own understandings, to identify the strengths or weaknesses in some narrative, or to reorganize what has been learned into a comprehensive whole, then debriefing is more likely to occur.

Preparing for a test is preparing for a test. It is not debriefing. Actually, it resembles prebriefing because it usually attempts to cover what will be on a test, not what has been learned.

Debriefing gives students relatively free rein to organize, compare, classify, evaluate, summarize, or analyze an experience. The product of the debriefing process is an articulated sense of "meaning." It is through this process of constructing personal meanings that students reveal their misunderstandings, oversimplifications, and personal theories.

This process will more likely get at what the students know, rather than what the teacher knows via student regurgitation.

Teachers can use several activities to help students attach meanings to learning experiences.

Writing logs/diaries can document students' reactions to events and are particularly useful if the entries interpret what has happened.

The writing not only fosters persistence of memory, but it also acts as a mode of learning.

Writing a precis, a concise abridgment, asks students to identify the gist of an experience, reading, or observation. It requires students to prioritize their own impressions and

This type of imaging is not what censors would have us believe. It is a form of considering possible outcomes.

What better way for students to become critical? The application for evaluations that must be made in everyday life will then have a new significance.

See Joyce Armstrong Carroll's article "Drawing into Meaning," pages 96-100.

Rico's Writing the Natural Way *is a wonderful source for* clustering, *her term for concept mapping.*

become more articulate about the meanings they have attributed to experiences.

Naming themes asks students to think of the personal lesson that was learned, message that was conveyed, or thrust of a reading passage or experience. Again, the task here is not to be too literal, but to abstract meaning from an experience. The question, "What does it (the assignment, topic, experience) remind you of?" encourages students to find themes or gists.

Imagining requires students to imagine "what if," to pretend, to create alternative endings, to surmise about alternatives. Each such effort, however, should be disciplined at least in part by the student's own interpretations of the experience.

Evaluating asks students to rate or rank an experience. Students can be invited to share or define the bases of their evaluations.

Role-playing gives students an opportunity to act out their understandings of processes, or a literary character's personality, or new problematic situations. Again, not just *any* behavior of the student is on target. Students need to try to use their interpretations of the elements of the experience.

Drawing is a nonverbal assignment that can help students identify major themes or issues. Since writing narratives can narrow the scope of shared meanings, the assignment to draw a picture often helps students identify salient meanings derived from experience.

Comparing requires students to relate reading a book or a poem or taking a field trip to another similar experience. This encourages them to identify features of each that they consider relevant.

Concept mapping is another nonverbal approach. It asks students to visualize and draw the relationships between concepts with a series of links or chains.

Outcomes of Debriefing

The recent work in cognitive psychology and cooperative learning supports the claim that debriefing enhances learning. Yager, Johnson, and Johnson (1985) assert that recent meta-analyses demonstrate that intermittent summarizing or recalling increase students' ability to remember what they have learned. They further claim that "cognitive rehearsal"—the process that occurs when students talk about what they have learned—is "one of the most promising of the mediating variables" examined to account for the success of cooperative learning (61).

By teaching students strategies to help them recall and reconstruct what they have learned, teachers can instruct not only for facts, but for understanding.

The how of knowing takes on greater importance in this type of learning than the what of knowing. Consider the information explosion: Already it is difficult to know the major items and latest research of a specific field. As information continues to expand, it will become impossible to know everything, but will be mandatory to know how to retrieve information.

REFERENCES

Abelson, R. P. "Psychological Status of the Script Concept." *American Psychologist* 36, 7 (1981): 715-729.

Novak, J. D., and D. B. Gowin. *Learning How to Learn*. New York: Cambridge University Press, 1984.

Pearson, M., and D. Smith. "Debriefing Experienced-based Learning." In *Reflection: Turning Experience into Learning*, edited by D. Boud, R. Keogh, and I. Walker. New York: Nichols Publishing Company, 1985.

Yager, S., D. W. Johnson, and R. T. Johnson. "Oral Discussion, Group-to-Individual Transfer, and Achievement in Cooperative Learning Groups." *Journal of Educational Psychology* 77, 1 (1985): 60-66.

6

GRAMMAR WITHIN THE WRITING PROCESS
Teaching How to Correct Writing

> The grammar has a rule absurd
> Which I would call an outworn myth:
> A preposition is a word
> You mustn't end a sentence with!
>
> — Berton Braley □

Teachers who understand how students learn teach grammar within the writing process. They create an environment in which students write daily, without threat and with purpose. Most often this environment results in writing students care about. Because this writing means something to them, because they own it, students are open to ways to make that writing better. They are ready to learn the grammar necessary to clarify their meaning. They are ready to correct, revise, and reformulate their writing. When students do this, two important things happen: (1) They learn grammar in a context and (2) they mark up and write on their papers. The approach is not to learn grammar for the sake of grammar, but to internalize it so it becomes a lifelong skill they may securely call upon when speaking and writing.

Grammar—the rules governing parts of speech, mechanics, punctuation, syntax, and structure of a language—is metalinguistic. It is language about language, and it is abstract. Think about the word *noun*. No one can see, taste, touch, smell, or hear *noun* because *noun* is a designation, an abstract term that names persons, places, things, qualities, and actions. But a noun is *not* the persons, places, things, qualities, or actions it names.

Even when students designate something as seemingly simple as *noun*, they must understand how a particular word works in a particular context. Consider the simple sentence *The white house has been painted*. Few would miss *house* as a common noun. However, if capital letters were added, *The White House has been painted*, the new context makes *House* part of a proper noun. With a syntactic change, *The Whites house their dog with the local vet when they travel*, the word *house* is no longer a noun but a verb.

Truly teaching grammar, not assigning and checking workbook exercises, requires an understanding of five basics:

- How language works contextually;

- How the brain works best to process information;

- That grammar study calls upon higher thinking skills, not rote memory;

- That teachers of grammar should themselves write; and

- That grammar must be taught first concretely.

Teaching grammar demands strategies that make the abstract concrete so students are able to correct their own writing not for correction's sake but for meaning's sake.

When students realize two things—that thinking is the basis for analyzing writing and that there are concrete, visual ways to tackle writing—they are able to start down the path of correcting, revising, and reformulating their writing. When engaged in this analysis, students use their ability to abstract, which is located in the left prefrontal lobe of their brain. Interestingly, this part of the brain is the last to develop, usually after puberty (Sanders). Based on this brain research, it is no surprise that expecting students to understand grammar abstractly, before that understanding has been worked with often and concretely, creates frustration on the part of the students. Sometimes this frustration translates into low self-esteem associated with learning grammar, which translates into, "I can't learn this stuff no matter how hard I try." Sometimes when grammar is taught abstractly with little application, students, who predictably find it difficult, decide they hate grammar. Either way, students adopt an attitude that is debilitating to writing and to language development. Expecting students to correct their writing based on rules and abstract terminology indicates a lack of knowledge about the way learners learn and the way writers write.

Frank Smith says it this way: "We all know there is a difference between being able to produce language grammatically and being able to talk about its grammar. Most of us can speak or write conventionally without being able to specify the rules. Even the ability to write grammatically does not guarantee that we will understand what a grammarian is talking about" (190).

Therefore, what is necessary for students to truly understand the grammar of their writing is for teachers to teach grammar within the writing process, within a context, and at developmentally appropriate times. Teachers help students most when they help students get their meaning down and then help them reenter their writing to correct, revise, and reformulate it.

A BRIEF HISTORY OF GRAMMAR

Studying Grammar in the Past

To the Greeks and Romans, grammar encompassed the theory of good speech, the study of classical poets, and the methodical study of the elements of language. In the Hellenistic schools, "grammar and composition were reserved for the secondary school at the earliest" (Marrou 218), whereas in Roman schools "children went on to the *grammaticus* when they got to the age of eleven or twelve" (Marrou 359). This is a fitting age, it seems, in light of contemporary brain and cognitive research, as at least one aspect of Latin grammar meant the abstract analysis of letters, syllables, words, parts of speech, and meticulous distinctions and classifications. For instance, nouns at that time were still not separate from adjectives. They were studied according to the six accidents of quality, degree of comparison, gender, number, figure, and case. As knowledge of pedagogy deepened, grammar slowly evolved into actual practice on systemic structure, mechanics, and syntax of the language (Marrou 371-372).

By the Middle Ages correctness of language became an end in itself. Little note was taken of common usage or differences. This stress on correctness caused a shift away from the discovery of principles to the transmission of rules. Thus, grammar shifted from strategy to formula.

Between the years 1500 and 1700 fewer than 5 million people in the world spoke English. But as England gained supremacy in the world, the English standardized their native tongue in order to legitimize it. During the Renaissance, scholars like Richard Mulcaster wrote rules to codify the vernacular. Most often these English scholars used Latin rules as their models. Applying the rules of one language to another explains why even to the present time there are dicta such as, "Never split an infinitive." Interestingly, in Latin, the infinitive cannot be split because it is one word. However, in English the infinitive is formed with two words: the preposition *to* plus the verb. Obviously these two words may be "split" as heard in the famous *Star Trek* phrase "to boldly go."

Sometimes this desire to standardize and legitimize language led to what John R. Trimble calls "literary prudishness" (84). Trimble describes how this may have occurred:

> These people arrived at their literary prudishness through a variety of routes: some through a puristic concern for the language which gradually rigidified into morbid scrupulosity; some through ignorance reinforced by others' ignorance; some through a hunger for the security of dogma and absolutes; and some, it would seem, merely through the appeals of snobbery and elitism. (84)

The point is that English is not absolute; it is alive and changing with times and purpose. Historically, words wax and wane. For example, rarely does anyone refer to a secretary as an *amanuensis*—it is not the popular word for that job. Expressions, once fresh, have become cliché or misleading. Using the phrase *like two peas in a pod* with the space-age generation fails to create the desired image. Students more likely conjure a space pod, not a pea pod. And technology alters conventions in more practical ways as well. The colon after the salutation in a business letter, although not formally dropped in standard English usage, is often omitted because the computer sees it as unnecessary. Because paper is no longer at a premium, white space often replaces the conventional marks once used to distinguish space, change, or emphasis. In short, English invites natural growth and constant refining to achieve precise communication.

It seems prudent to heed the advice of I. A. Richards: "My suggestion is that it is not enough to learn a language (or several languages), as a man [or woman] may inherit a business, but that we must learn, too, how it works" (317). People best learn how a language works by using it, grappling with it, writing it, reading it, listening to it, speaking it, being surrounded by multiple levels of it, and having fun with it. Not only do people learn language best in such rich contexts, but they come to a deeper appreciation of its power. Conversely, people rarely learn a language through isolated fragments, mindless worksheets, boring workbooks, meaningless exercises, or mind-dulling drills.

Studying Grammar Today

If teachers are to avoid mindless, isolated grammar drills, they need a new approach to teaching grammar. Reflecting how linguistic and social context affects meaning, grammar may be taught three ways: by teaching students how to correct, revise, and reformulate their writing. Correcting focuses on what Janet Emig calls "mechanical errors and stylistic infelicities" (43). Revising centers on the sentence as a unit of discourse and is discussed in chapter 7. Reformulating invites work with larger pieces of the writing—the paragraph. This is covered in chapter 8.

Correcting concentrates on punctuation, capitalization, minor agreement problems, and spelling. Correcting, in this sense, means ridding the writing of those niggling distractions, the little things that get in a reader's way of understanding. For example, neglecting to capitalize a proper name may momentarily bewilder a reader. Disregarding commas altogether or putting them anywhere often confuses meaning. Adopting the bizarre habit of writing *sp* over a word to absolve oneself from checking the spelling sends the signal that the writer is sloppy or careless. Although these mistakes may creep in during prewriting or early drafting, when the writer is seeking ideas and not mechanical precision, they should be corrected before the writing goes public. Hence, to correct is *not* to make deep changes in a paper, but rather to reenter the paper on behalf of the reader. And that is exactly why writers should not concern themselves with correcting too early in the process (or, in the most traditional sense, doing exercises on these matters six weeks before the process even begins). Premature attention to minutiae often short-circuits the process by interfering with fluency. Writers write. They get their thoughts down. They go with the flow. *Then* they go back, reenter, and make the writing better.

There are two major things to remember when teaching students to correct: (1) Begin concretely, and then move from the concrete to the abstract, and (2) create an environment in which students correct their own writing.

Three students met with grammar questions for a small-group conference with me. The first two raised simple questions easily answered. That left Donna. "Is the tense right here?" she asked, pointing to a sentence that read "My grandmother had died."

"I don't know," I answered.

"You don't know?" she repeated, as if she heard me incorrectly.

"I don't know."

"You don't know?" she stated incredulously.

"I don't know." At this point I wondered how long this would go on.

Finally, Donna, now standing arms akimbo, blurted, "Why not?"

I went to the board and wrote had died. *I circled* had. *"This is a signal word. In the English language it tells the reader that the action of the accompanying verb took place further back in time than the past action in the narrative. Since I don't know when your grandmother died in relation to the rest of the story, I can't help you out on the tense."*

"Is that why I memorized has, have, had?*" she muttered as she went to her seat.*

I met with another group. When the bell rang, Donna came bounding up all smiles, "It's had. *Thanks. I wanted that to be right because I'm going to read this to my family at Thanksgiving."*

PUNCTUATION

Punctuation indicates to the reader what groups of words belong together and often how the groups are related. Punctuation also shows what the voice does in speech. Although usually thought of as concrete marks, punctuation really is an abstract code. In and of itself, punctuation carries no meaning; it enhances meaning. For example, !!!,,,...?/?//"...{} \\\\';;;:(...) says nothing. When most students look at a comma, for instance, they see a detached mark, something abstract. They often puzzle over it. They know on the one hand it belongs in writing, but on the other hand they are rarely certain exactly where to use it or for what purpose. Comments such as, "I don't know where this comma goes" reflect their puzzlement. Teachers may help make these abstract marks more concrete by encouraging students to do two things: (1) Look at the marks with new eyes—as tools that aid meaning, and (2) use the grammar book as a reference, not as a book of codified rules to be memorized.

Because punctuation conveys emphases, pauses, stops, tones, changes in pattern and speaker, omissions, and possession, using these marks correctly eases reading. Working with punctuation in writing, not on worksheets, helps students learn how to use correct punctuation in a context. Frank Smith says, "Far more than spelling, punctuation requires the practice of writing and the confirmation of feedback" (188).

Problems with Punctuation

There are three basic punctuation problems: (1) Punctuation rules are *not* absolute, (2) punctuation is complex, and (3) punctuation depends upon the writer's style and intended meaning. Take, for example, this simple group of words: *Tom Smith called Sarah Lou is here.* There is no one absolute way to punctuate these words. The complexity of punctuation becomes apparent when we examine how three different students punctuated this group of words.

One used punctuation to indicate that Sarah Lou is announcing Tom Smith's arrival:

"Tom Smith," called Sarah Lou, "is here."

Another punctuated the same group of words to show that a person named Sarah is telling both Tom and Smith that Lou has arrived:

"Tom, Smith," called Sarah, "Lou is here."

Yet another punctuated the words to convey a dramatic purpose:

Tom: Smith called.
Sarah: Lou is here.

In truth, this group of words may be punctuated more than 70 different ways. By using every punctuation mark, from the exotic virgule, the less-popular bracket, the often-misunderstood ellipsis, and the flamboyant dash; to mundane parentheses, hyphens, apostrophes, commas, quotation marks, colons, and semi-colons; to the necessary terminals — periods and exclamation and question marks — varieties of meaning emerge. This proves interesting to students, if they are challenged to punctuate this group of words as many ways as they can. The teacher can build on their interest by using their variations to point out the complexity of punctuation and how punctuation alters meaning.

To further demonstrate the complexity of punctuation, use the same group of words, but make the comma, parentheses, and the dash concrete. For example, suggest a comparison between the comma and the small, thin disk, which can be slid into the sentence to cause a pause.

Tom Smith, called Sarah Lou, is here.

Or compare parentheses to the curved hand placed by the mouth, ready to capture a whisper or an aside.

Tom Smith (called Sarah Lou) is here.

For the dash, which is usually made by striking two hyphens on the typewriter or computer, a flashing neon light works. Picture a flashing neon sign in an out-of-the-way spot, and then picture one along a thoroughfare in Las Vegas. The former sign stands out; it is noticeable. The latter may go unnoticed because so many signs blur together until none is noticed. Thinking of the dash in this visual way often helps students use it sparingly.

Making Punctuation Concrete

AN EXAMPLE WITH QUOTATION MARKS

Explanation. Quotation marks are used to set off direct speech and information cited from other sources. Although students rarely have difficulty using quotation marks when excerpting from another source, they do have trouble using them in their own writing. The difficulty arises when they try to distinguish between direct and indirect statements. Read the two sentences below to better understand why students have trouble distinguishing between them, and therefore why they mispunctuate them.

My dad told me to go to the store.

My dad told me, "Go to the store."

Three things are necessary for students to understand the subtle difference between these two sentences: (1) They must grasp why it is rhetorically effective to use dialogue in writing, (2) they must comprehend why it is necessary to signal the reader that dialogue is occurring, and (3) they must know the tools to accurately send that signal.

Implementation

1. Focus the lesson by asking students to read the direct dialogue from a story. Turn this activity into a dramatic production.

2. Reword the story using only indirect dialogue. Discuss the differences. Pull other examples from literature to discuss.

3. Use a piece of writing (preferably the teacher's writing) on the overhead projector to model. Together look for places where indirect dialogue may be replaced with the direct words of a speaker. Then discuss what tools are needed to make this direct discourse clear for the reader.

4. Make quotation marks concrete by directing a discussion with students. Start by asking:

    "What moves when I talk?"
    "Your mouth."
    "What part of my mouth?"
    "Your lips."
    "So when I speak, you can see that I am talking. But when someone reads your writing, they cannot see when the characters speak. They may think the author is simply telling about what a character said. So someone came up with a wonderful way to signal the difference for the reader. These two marks look like two lips. If you think of quotation marks as lips, it is easy to remember to use quotation marks when someone begins to speak and when they are finished speaking. Then the reader sees and hears the direct words of the character."

5. Students reenter their writing and correct it for quotation marks. Then the teacher moves on to the attendant punctuation marks used with quotation marks: the comma to introduce the quotation and the terminal marks.

Remarks. Because quotation marks resemble lips and serve a like function, this concrete analogy reminds students to use quotation marks while at the same time clarifying the intent of the writer for the reader. In the case cited above, Dad would not say, "To go to the store." Those would not be his direct words. Students catch that subtlety when they visualize the words emanating from lips rather than thinking of the marks as one more rule to learn. Eventually this concrete connection becomes internalized.

TWO EXAMPLES WITH COMMAS

Explanation. Commas mark slight separations, short pauses, and relationships between and among grammatical units. Jim W. Corder and John J. Ruszkiewicz contend, "About two-thirds of all punctuation marks used are commas" (199). But it is the comma, one of the weakest punctuation marks yet one indispensable for determining meaning, that bedevils students.

Confounded by what to do and not to do with this mark, students usually deal with comma decisions in two ways. Some simply use the "salt and pepper" method; they know commas belong in writing, so they sprinkle them in so that the paper "looks good." Other students close their eyes, put their papers in the hands of fate, and insert a comma wherever their pointing index fingers fall. It is as if they consider learning the number of comma rules (more than 10 rules, most with one or more exceptions) a kind of cosmic overload so overwhelming they are left to sheer serendipity.

Implementation—Concreteness. Making the comma concrete enhances students' comprehension. While not foolproof nor totally inclusive, implementing this approach moves students into some degree of security accompanied with some depth of control.

1. Define three or four most-used reasons for the comma.

2. Provide a visual to make each reason concrete. See the sample comma chart in figure 6.1.

Fig. 6.1. Four ways to use a comma.

1. Insert a comma between two independent clauses (sentences) that are joined with a coordinating conjunction.

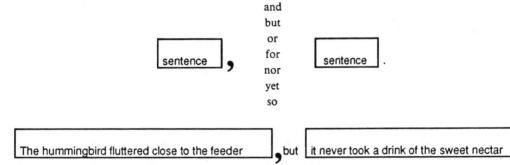

Students offer examples from their writing.

2. Use a comma after a long introduction at the start of a sentence.

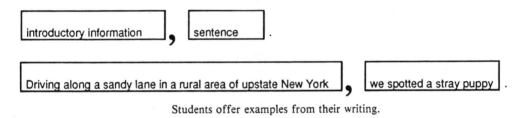

Students offer examples from their writing.

3. Use two commas to set off "grammatically unnecessary" information from the rest of the sentence.

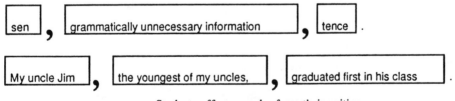

Students offer examples from their writing.

4. Use a comma after each item in a series.

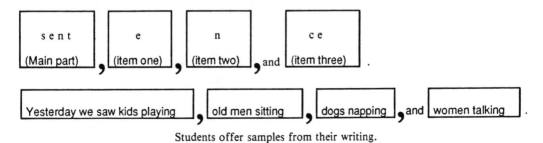

Students offer samples from their writing.

3. Give the model sentence by way of example.

4. Invite students to reenter their writing to find an example for each reason on the chart. Write several of these on the board and discuss.

5. Students then reenter their papers to reevaluate their use of commas by comparing each of their sentences to the visual models and example sentences. When they come upon an exception, they consult their grammar books. Hence, both the teaching of the comma and the subsequent correcting take place in a real context.

Implementation — Relevance. Making the comma relevant is another way to help students see its importance in their writing.

1. Share an example, such as this story of the million-dollar comma.

> The United States government lost a fortune because of a comma. A tariff passed in 1872 contained a list of duty-free items that read, "Fruit plants, tropical and semitropical." A clerk accidentally altered the line, "Fruit, plants tropical and semitropical." Those importing contended that the passage, with its misplaced comma, exempted all tropical and semitropical plants from duty fees. They won.

2. Students find other examples of commas causing confusion, or they create ways commas might cause problems. They may choose examples from sports, law, concert groups, money, business, school rules, or any aspect of everyday life. Share and discuss.

Remarks. Moving from the concrete to the abstract is as difficult for students as moving from the abstract to the concrete is for teachers. Once a concept has become abstract, thinking of ways to make it concrete becomes challenging, but worth the effort. Herbert Ginsburg and Sylvia Opper, scholars of the work of Jean Piaget, suggest that the prime implication from Piaget for educators is that "children learn best from concrete activities" (221). Further, they state that "when the teacher tries to bypass this process by imparting knowledge in a verbal manner, the result is often superficial learning" (Ginsburg and Opper 221).

Students need plenty of models and plenty of practice to see that "all these tiny scratches give us breadth and heft and depth. A world that has only periods is a world without inflections. It is a world without shade. It has a music without sharps and flats. It is a martial music. It has a jack-boot rhythm. Words cannot bend and curve.... Punctuation, then, is a matter of care. Care for words, yes, but also, and more important, for what the words imply" (Iyer 80).

CAPITALIZATION

Writing, using an agreed-upon system of symbols to convey thoughts and feelings, was for centuries considered a gift from the gods. As far as scholars can determine, "the process began in ancient Mesopotamia ... around the 3rd millennium B.C." (Jean 12). But using capital letters did not evolve until sometime around the fifth century B.C., when the Greek alphabet used uppercase straight letters for inscriptions in stone or metal, more rounded lowercase letters for writing on papyrus, wax tablets, hide, or later parchment (Gaur 119-121). Because the rounded lowercase letters were easier to write, they were used for the body of books and documents. The more difficult uppercase letters were reserved for beginning new thoughts, headings, and formal work — to signify something important. Rules did not control that choice, efficiency did.

Problems with Capitalization

Most rhetoricians agree that although convention dictates the use of capitals, conventions change. For example, tradition held that the first word in each line of poetry should be capitalized. Contemporary poetry does not follow this convention. If writers today follow the traditional convention, their poetry strikes the eye as archaic. The classic advice on capitals is expressed at the beginning of the chapter on capitalization in *The Little, Brown Handbook*. "Writers generally agree on when to use capitals, but the conventions are constantly changing. Consult a dictionary if you have any doubt whether a particular word should be capitalized" (Fowler 320).

The major rationale for the use of capitals is specificity. They are used to mark beginnings of new thoughts, signal titles and headings, indicate *I* and *O* when they stand alone, and designate proper nouns and adjectives. Therein lies the rub, as often what students consider specific, for example, "their" baseball game, is not. In addition, classifying general (common) and specific (proper) is difficult for younger students. This problem is often exacerbated by the "dumbing down" of textbooks. Sophisticated, precise words are often replaced with unsophisticated ones; terms are oversimplified, often to the detriment of meaning; examples and illustrations are often silly and unchallenging. In this context, textbook publishers often use common nouns as proper ones. They merely capitalize the species, for example, cat. Students who are visual learners or those who remain unclear about the use of capital letters, find this confusing. On the one hand, they are told *cat* is a common name that may be applied to any animal in that genus: tigers, lions, panthers. On the other hand, they read a story where the main character, a feline, is specifically addressed as *Cat* by the other animals in the story.

> *Recently while working with administrators from a large urban school district, I shared Heather Mitchell's "The Meanis Sub." We used her writing to talk about the abuse of worksheets, among other things. The next day, one of the principals who had been at the workshop sent me a first-grade workbook page on time sequence. There were three sentences on the page in random order. The students were to number them according to the time sequence in the story.*
>
> *One sentence read: Spider moves to where Dog lives. Another read: Sara does not see Spider.*
>
> *Clearly Dog and Spider are used on this worksheet as the proper names of two characters. Little wonder when I shared this workbook page with teachers, especially those in middle and high school, several exclaimed, "I'm beginning to understand why kids are confused about what to capitalize!"*
>
> *Another teacher in the group asked, "Why did the author make the animal's class its name? Now kids have something to unlearn."*

Making Capitalization Concrete: Five Examples

Explanation. To someone learning a written symbolic code, as with a young child learning to write English, signals within that code often appear complicated. After all, children are delighted with the simple making of marks. To a five- or six-year-old, a letter is a letter is a letter (to paraphrase Gertrude Stein), and to make one or several on a blank page is a feat, one worthy of celebration. Actually grasping the concept of a letter, then a group of letters as words, is quite a cognitive endeavor. When that endeavor is coupled with the addition of uppercase and lowercase letter distinctions and rules that govern their use, the concept often moves from complicated to confusing. To reduce the confusion and heighten the learning, it is helpful to teach capitalization as concretely as possible. Following are five ways to accomplish that.

Implementation — Naming. One of the best ways to make capitals concrete is through naming. Since students understand that they have a name, it is the logical place to begin.

1. Divide students into two groups. Each member in one group writes a name tag that indicates the general category to which that student belongs: boy or girl. These words are written in lowercase letters. Each member of the other group writes a name tag with his or her specific proper name. These names each begin with a capital.

2. Call on students according to their name tags. Talk about the problems that arise from being too general. Who should answer from a group of girls if "girl" is called, for instance. (This might be a good place to discuss how people feel when they are addressed this way.)

3. Help students understand why specific designations are needed and why capital letters are used to show these designations. Follow this line of thinking by extending naming to buildings, books, days, months, and other general and specific persons, things, or events within their students' experience.

4. Conclude by challenging the students to create lists of general and specific things, people, and events in and around the school and the community.

5. Share and discuss. Once again the teaching must take place within a context.

Implementation — Capital Searches. Working with books is another concrete way to teach capital letters.

1. Divide students into groups. Assign a time limit for book exploration.

2. Each group generates a list of words from the books that start with capital letters, excepting the first word in sentences.

3. Post these lists.

4. Follow with a class analysis of the words. This analysis forms the basis for generalizations about capital letters.

5. Together write these generalizations. Then compare those of the class with those in textbooks and handbooks. Discuss.

Implementation — Capital Narratives. One form of making an abstract concept concrete is through hyperbole. Often students best learn a concept by exaggeration. Because students perceive telling stories as fun, combining the two helps students learn.

1. Divide students into dyads, groups of two.

2. Each pair generates a story packed with titles and proper names, which they write in lowercase letters. The story should make sense and contain all the elements of a narrative.

3. After the writing, dyads combine to form groups of four.

4. They exchange stories and identify the capital letters in each other's stories.

5. Conclude with a discussion about the function of capital letters.

Implementation — Derivation Digs. Encouraging older students to collect derivatives often makes the abstract concrete.

1.   Students research words such as *sandwich* or *wisteria*. The former describes the eating habits of an earl from the geographical region of Sandwich, England; the latter describes a plant that bears beautiful bunches of lavender flowers named after Caspar Wistar, an American anatomist.

2.   After the initial research, students form groups. Each group creates a list of words with interesting derivations from proper names or places.

3.   Groups exchange lists and continue their research.

4.   Share findings.

Implementation — Sentence Checks. Some students need visuals to help them remember. This is especially true for young children.

1.   Provide each student with a red crayon.

2.   Students use the red crayon to signal capital letters at the beginning of sentences in their own writing. They circle the first letter of the first word of each sentence.

3.   Then they read until they reach a terminal mark. They circle in red the first letter in the word following that mark. They continue this procedure throughout their writing. If they only have one terminal mark in the entire piece of writing, they need to ratiocinate for sentences (see chapter 7).

Remarks. Capital letters are relatively recent arrivals in the history of written language. Young children use them much the way they were used historically — to point out something or someone important or to draw attention to something. Consider the four-year-old who writes MOMMY or the second-grade student who titles his book THE SPOKEY HOUS and writes chapter 1 in capital letters — GOBLEN. Once again, students gain control over the convention of the capital letter when they write and read often and when they are surrounded by a print-rich environment. Teachers use that rich language to teach the convention. Then students use what they learn about the convention to correct their own writing.

AGREEMENT

Agreement of subject and verb means that singular nouns and pronouns take singular verbs, and plural nouns and pronouns take plural verbs. When that happens, subjects *agree*, or fit with, the verbs. Agreement of pronoun and antecedent means that the pronoun is the same form as its antecedent — that is, it matches it in gender, number, and case.

Discussing agreement between subjects and verbs and pronouns and antecedents is a perfect example of metalinguistic abstraction — language about language. Abstract terms like *agreement, subjects, verbs, pronouns, antecedents* become confused with terms like *number, person, gender*. Even the word *take* assumes some heightened meaning. While grammarians revel in this terminology, students writhe in it. Teachers who teach agreement within the context of the students' writing find the students' comprehension deepens and they are able to correct their writing accordingly.

Problems with Agreement Between
Subject and Verb

There are three major difficulties with teaching subject-verb agreement:

1. The inability to distinguish between nouns and verbs. If students do understand that distinction, then the second problem often surfaces.

2. The singular verb looks plural. If students have learned that adding an *s* makes a noun plural — *flower/flowers, boy/boys* — then they have difficulty understanding why adding an *s* to a verb makes it singular — *make/makes, speak/speaks*.

3. Difficulty in identifying the subjects of sentences. This especially causes confusion when words intervene between the subject and the verb. Because students have not internalized the abstract concept of subject, they tend to make the verb agree with the closest noun or pronoun. If a prepositional phrase that sounds plural comes between a single subject and its verb, students most likely will choose a plural verb. Consider the sentence:

    The book about animals and birds provides many interesting facts.

    Students who see *animals* and *birds* as nouns and therefore automatically as subjects may write: The book about animals and birds provide many interesting facts. The problem is not agreement; the problem is comprehending the subject of a sentence.

Making Subject-Verb Agreement Concrete:
The Triptych

Explanation. The triptych comes from ancient, hinged, three-leaved tablets and three-paneled tapestries. Because people had no means for hanging one enormous picture, they would divide it into three sections so that each section could be hung individually. By mounting them close together on a wall, the picture could be viewed as a whole.

Implementation

1. Students draw a real or fantasy animal profile across a sheet of paper that has been divided into three parts: head in first section; body in second section; tail in third section (see fig. 6.2). They make sure the neck and tail fit the designated space so when one student's triptych is bound with others, there is consistency of graphic and sentence parts.

2. In the first section, the area below the drawing of the head, the students write a noun phrase, subject, or the name of their animal (depending upon grade level). They write a verb or verb phrase in the second section. They write a prepositional phrase in the third section.

3. Stack several triptychs. Staple together across the top.

4. Use a paper cutter to cut along the vertical lines, from the bottom of the sheet to the edge of the tape.

5. Students flip the sections to create new animals and different sentences.

6. Talk about what happens if a student used a plural verb with a single noun.

Fig. 6.2. Subject-verb agreement triptych outline.

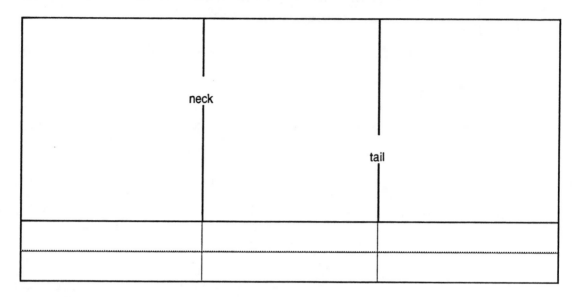

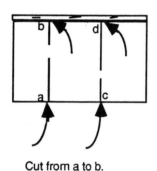

Staple and tape at top. Leave
1/2" strip at top uncut.

Cut from a to b.
Cut from c to d.

Remarks. Using the triptych not only provides a concrete way to apply subject-verb agreement, it reinforces the application in three ways: through writing, through silent and oral reading, and through aural learning. While drawing lines from subject to predicate or vice versa, a common practice in many grammar handbooks, may help students see connections, the triptych provides a way to practice agreement while making the concept concrete.

Problems with Agreement Between
Pronouns and Antecedents

The major difficulty with teaching pronoun-antecedent agreement is the meaning of the metalinguistic term *antecedent*. This concept could be simplified by explaining that when pronouns take the place of a noun they should match the noun they are replacing. Jack/he; tree/it; videos/they. Forgo introducing the abstract terms *antecedent, gender, number*, and *case* until the term has been learned concretely.

Making Pronoun-Antecedent Agreement Concrete: The Match Game

Explanation. One way to help students think of pronoun-antecedent agreement is by providing practice in matching pronouns.

Implementation

1. Divide students into two teams. Each team generates a list of nouns. For example:

Team 1 Nouns	Team 2 Nouns
Mary	crowd
family	members
boss	academy
Mr. Smith	campus
committee	group

2. The teams exchange lists. For each noun, each team writes a pronoun that might replace it. For example:

Team 1 Nouns	Team 2 Pronouns	Team 2 Nouns	Team 1 Pronouns
Mary	she	crowd	it
family	it	members	they
boss	he/she	academy	it
Mr. Smith	he	campus	it
committee	it	group	it

3. Share results. Discuss.

Remarks. Any other agreement problems, such as those based on exceptions, should be solved by consulting a good handbook. Expecting students to hold all the rules of grammar, usage, and spelling, along with exceptions in their heads, is tantamount to expecting them to learn all the synonyms in a thesaurus or all the definitions in a dictionary. Grammar handbooks should be regarded as references, and students should be taught to use them as such.

SPELLING

I went to the board and wrote ghoti. *"What does this spell?" I asked a group of administrators who had expressed deep concern over parental complaints about the teaching of spelling in their schools.*

Several volunteered, "ghetto," "ghostly," "gouty," "goatee."

"No, no, no, no," I responded in turn. "It spells fish."

To their dumbfounded expressions, I explained: gh *as in* enough; o *as in* women; *and* ti *as in* ambition. "Fish," *I proclaimed triumphantly.*

Then I continued, "There are thirteen spellings for sh: shoe, sugar, issue, mansion, mission, nation, suspicion, ocean, conscious, chaperon, schist, fuchsia, and pshaw. Now let's talk about spelling."*

These administrators represent many who, on the one hand, express genuine concern over what they regard as a deterioration of skills such as spelling, but who, on the other hand, suffer from the 10 myths J. Richard Gentry enumerates and then debunks in his book *Spel ... Is a Four-Letter Word*:

1. Spelling is serious business. Everyone must learn to spell.

2. People who can't spell are ignorant.

3. Spelling is supposed to be difficult.

4. Spelling errors should not be tolerated.

5. Good teachers reduce marks for poor spelling.

6. Good spellers memorize a lot of information.

7. Good spellers master a lot of rules.

8. To become good spellers, kids have to do hundreds of spelling-book exercises and drills.

9. The most important thing about spelling is making 100 percent on spelling tests.

10. Spelling is right or wrong. Good teachers always correct spelling. (8)

Problems with Spelling

In truth, the English spelling system is complex and inconsistent. Because of the influence of so many other languages, many English words reflect the spelling of another language: *sleigh* from the Dutch, *bayou* from the French, *stampede* from the Spanish, for instance. In addition, the English alphabet is about 14 letters short of all the letters it needs for the sounds it uses. That is why letters are doubled to create a new sound, *au, th*, and so forth. Then there is the troublesome habit of varying spelling according to the sound's position as in *judge* not *juj* simply because English words do not end in the letter *j*. Another problem surfaces with arbitrary rules unconnected to pronunciation, for example *basically*, which is pronounced *basicly*.

The spelling of homonyms also causes problems. Homonyms may keep meaning straight, but they prove confusing for the speller, especially the beginning speller. Consider young writers coming to words such as: *reign, rain, air, heir*, and so forth. Then there are silent letters, such as the *u* in *guide*, the *e* in *save*, and the *p* in *pneumonia*, to name just a few (Wilde 14-16). While all this makes for interesting reading, it may prove discouraging for students still trying to gain control of the act of writing itself, to make meaning, to reason through the complexity of clarifying that meaning, to observe the conventions of language and of writing, and finally to deal with standardized spelling.

The truth is, while no one expects everyone to know how to spell every word, educated people are expected to have a repertoire of words they are able to spell correctly. First-graders have their first-grade spelling; fourth-graders their fourth-grade spelling, and so forth.

> *Recently, as a way to focus a lesson on developmental writing and invented spelling with teachers, I administered a spelling "test." Among the words given were* kinesis, pneumatic, mnemonic, inveigle, ukulele, maieutic, and hemorrhage. *Clearly these were not words teachers use daily, so it was not unusual for everyone to have misspelled at least one of the words. After the "test" we discussed how we go about spelling a word we do not know. We applied our answers to what we know about how students go about spelling a word.*

As far back as 1837 Sir Isaac Pitman worked for spelling reform. He believed all language should be written phonetically, just like his shorthand system. In 1940 the British Simplified Spelling Society lobbied for simplified spelling. George Bernard Shaw bequeathed much of his fortune to the cause of more rational spelling. Yet aside from minor changes, such as *colour* to *color* and *theatre* to *theater*, "new generations of school children are still grappling with a spelling system that dates back to William Caxton" (McCrum, Cran, and MacNeil 47).

Strategy for Reassuring Parents or Caregivers

Explanation. Because concern about spelling exists and because a person's intelligence and ability are often measured by the way that person spells, it is imperative to be realistic about spelling and the teaching of spelling. Dismissing it entirely or obsessing over it are dangerous extremes. Teachers who understand the dynamics of spelling within the larger writing process use sensible strategies to foster spelling skills.

Implementation—Send Letters to Parents or Caregivers. At the outset of the school year, send home a letter that explains how spelling will be taught. This greatly reduces repeated individual conferences on the topic or misunderstandings about why spelling is being integrated with language arts and other subjects. In these letters, primary teachers generally explain how children learn to spell, provide several examples of development from scribbles through transitional spelling, promise to provide updates, and assure parents and caregivers that spelling will be learned through rich writing and reading activities. In addition, these teachers assure parents that a five-year-old's spelling of *was* as "woze" or "wus" is developmental and will not remain with the child throughout his or her life. These teachers avoid the term *invented spelling*. While that term is used and understood in academe, it carries the connotation of "anything goes" to the average person; this creates unnecessary concern. Instead of *invented spelling*, these teachers use terms like *kinder spelling*, or *first-grade spelling* when referring to words students use but do not yet own, words that are still in the developmental stage, such as "wr" for *were*.

> It was January. A dynamic principal invited me to do a demonstration lesson for her first-grade teachers. It seems they were wedded to the basal and to spelling books. The students hated to write.
>
> I gathered the students around me in the front of the room while the teachers sat in the back. I read Cynthia Rylant's The Relatives Came. Afterward we laughed and talked about what happens when our relatives visit. The stories were so good, I suggested we write them down before they got away from us. The students, fresh from the eagerness of it all, returned to their seats and got right to work. I walked around encouraging, prompting, nudging, hunkering down to read words and sentences on their way to becoming stories.
>
> As I rounded the back of the room, one of the teachers whispered, "Are you going to take spelling?"
>
> "No. I was aiming for fluency during this lesson."
>
> "Show us spelling," another stated.
>
> So after a bit more time, I interrupted the students. They wanted to continue writing, so I promised they could, but first they would learn something wonderful.
>
> "Everyone take out one crayon," I instructed. They giggled in excitement.
>
> "You all know I am an adult. When I write I use adult spelling. You are first-graders. When you write you sometimes use first-grade spelling. These are words you know but you don't know how to spell them the

way adults spell them." They understood. "Use your crayon to circle one of those first-grade spelled words." All but one student circled what we would consider a misspelled word. Then I invited someone to come to the board to write their word. All hands went up. I chose Alicia who wrote "littl." I asked Alicia to say her word and praised her for finding it. Then I asked Alicia to call on a friend who may know the way adults spell that word. She called on Ray, who came to the board and added an e. We all applauded. Then I told the students to read their stories. If they used the word little, they were to check their first-grade spelling against the adult spelling on the board. Next we deposited little into our class word bank (started through the reading). Ray wrote "sed," and so we proceeded through several words.

When our time was up, the students were genuinely disappointed. They wanted more. And I wondered when that kind of joyful literacy ever occurred during the teaching of lists of spelling words taken from spelling books generated in some other place and time.

During the debriefing with the teachers, we discussed that model lesson as one possible spelling strategy, which they agreed was developmentally appropriate for primary grades and could be adapted for upper grades.

Upper elementary teachers focus their letters to parents or caregivers on how students will learn to spell within the writing and reading processes through class word lists and other strategies. They explain how students will take the responsibility of designating their own spelling "demons" by keeping word lists. They clarify how teacher and students together will explore spelling patterns and rules that work, and how they will use spelling as part of proofreading and editing skills. These teachers may give an example or two of spelling rules that work, such as doubling the final consonant before adding *-ed* or *-ing* if a word ends in a single vowel and single consonant.

Middle school and high school teachers let parents and caregivers know that spelling is still considered an important skill. Because students are older and more independent, and because teachers at this level want to promote skills that students will be able to apply all their lives, the teachers emphasize the value of proofreading: the ability to spot misspellings, strategies for figuring out how to spell words, and using such devices as spell check, hand-held computer spellers, and dictionaries (including those that list words phonetically, such as *Webster's New World Misspeller's Dictionary* [Guralnik], *The Bad Speller's Dictionary* [Krevisky and Linfield], or *Webster's Bad Speller's Dictionary* [Wileman and Wileman]).

Making Spelling Concrete: Seven Examples

After working three weeks with a class of inner-city sixth-grade students on the narrative, we were ready to write our stories into our books. We had used only the best quality paper. We had invited the librarian in to show us the proper way to write the library cards and pockets we were affixing to the last page. We wanted our books to be as fine as those we had read during our study. It was then I did a mini-lesson on proofreading for spelling. The students knew they would have real audiences for their books, and they wanted them to be good. Never were the dictionaries used more.

Implementation – Teach Four Spelling Rules. As long ago as 1932, Leonard B. Wheat found that only four spelling rules are consistent enough to teach: doubling consonants, changing *y* to *i*, dropping the final *e* before suffixes, and writing *i* before *e* except after *c*.

1. Students memorize these four rules.

2. Divide students into four groups. Each group takes a different rule and finds examples of that rule in their writing and literature.

3. Students reenter their writing to check and correct the spelling of words by applying these four rules.

4. Share. Discuss.

Implementation – Develop Mnemonic Devices. When students learn several mnemonic devices to remember spellings, then they can design some for their own spelling demons.

1. Teach two examples of mnemonic devices:

   remember *dessert* has two letters *s*, like the dessert *s*trawberry *s*hortcake;

   remember *there* is a place because it has *here* in it; *their* is a person because it has *heir* in it; *they're* is a contraction because it has an apostrophe.

2. Students choose several words from their individual spelling lists. They create a mnemonic device for each word.

3. Share.

NOTE: Vary this idea by adding a visual dimension. Some students remember a word if they create a drawing for it.

Implementation – Model Dictionary Use. Teachers who write with their students also use the dictionary in front of the students. It is important for students to realize that it is both acceptable and intelligent to consult a dictionary when unsure of a spelling.

1. Write with the students.

2. When proofreading, model dictionary use.

Implementation – Integrate Phonics. Some English words retain a predictable relationship between sound and letter.

1. Teach sounding out words as one spelling strategy.

2. Take a word that has a predictable relationship between the word's letters and its sound. Model how to sound the word out. The word *bag* is a good example.

3. For words such as *phone*, teach students one of the other spelling strategies. It is just as important for students to learn that all words in English cannot be phonetically spelled as it is for them to have a strategy for those that can be phonetically spelled.

Implementation – Teach Spelling Patterns. Sandra Wilde lists 16 spelling patterns in her book *You Kan Red This!* The patterns are arbitrary, historical, homophones, letter-name, letter-string, meaning related, orthographic, permutations, phonetic, preconsonantal nasals, predictable, real words, silent letters, suffixes, syllabic, and variants. Some patterns she discusses in some detail, with many pages of explanation and many examples; others she treats briefly. Teachers who know all of the patterns are better able to use one or more of them with most students. It also might be helpful to share patterns (and the book) with concerned parents so they, too, may appreciate the complexity of spelling.

Implementation—Develop Positive Attitudes. Overemphasis on spelling early in the writing process often short-circuits the writing as students become overly concerned with correctness too soon in the process.

1. Allow students to make mistakes, abbreviate, and use invented or phonetic spellings in their sloppy copies, when the ideas are flowing.

2. Then, in the manner of published authors, as students move into final drafts, teach spelling strategies and proofreading skills so students may correct their spelling.

3. Finally, students edit their final copy. Not only is this process realistic, it also helps writers put in perspective what is important at what point in their writing. Correcting spelling becomes a matter of timing.

Implementation—Write and Read Often. Most people extend their vocabulary and learn spelling by reading. That way a word is embedded in a meaningful context and is connected to something, which makes remembering it easier. Second-grade students often astound adults with the correct names *and* spellings for various dinosaurs. They are able to do that because they want to be precise. They know that the exact names for various dinosaurs help designate the differences among these enormous animals. First-grade students correctly spell with ease the names of the Ninja Turtles—Michelangelo, Leonardo, and the others—when they write them into their stories. These are the same students who, when given the word *percolate* from a commercial spelling list, stumble and never get it. The former words are important and relevant; the latter word is archaic.

Remarks. When the writing is meaningful, authors want it to be correct. This harries the teacher who tries to spell every word for every child who asks, "Teacher, is this right?" Developing systematic strategies for attacking unknown words helps foster independence and heighten spelling consciousness. A good plan is this progression:

1. Try to sound out the word.
2. Experiment with other spelling strategies.
3. Consult the dictionary.
4. Confer with a peer.
5. Confer with the teacher.

If all this seems overwhelming, think about Elisabeth McPherson's conclusion to "Spelling, Revisited": "And cheer yourself up with an ironic reversal. Not too long ago, it was fashionable to say that persnickety school ma'ams were passionately devoted to spelling and ordinary people didn't care much about it. Now the public, or some of it, is wailing about illiteracy, while good language arts teachers are using a better definition of literacy: the ability to read with pleasure and understanding, and the ability to write something real. Spelling enters into those abilities, but it isn't the most important part."

APPLICATION

1. Choose any punctuation mark. Study its uses. Create a lesson for a chosen grade level in which you concretely teach it so that students may apply it to their own writing through the process of correcting.

2. Develop or research another spelling strategy. Create a way for students to apply this strategy to their own writing.

WORKS CITED

Braley, Berton. "No Rule to Be Afraid Of." Stanza I. In *Familiar Quotations*, by John Bartlett, centennial ed. Boston: Little, Brown, 1955.

Corder, Jim W., and John J. Ruszkiewicz. *Handbook of Current English*. Glenview, IL: Scott, Foresman, 1985.

Emig, Janet. *The Composing Process of Twelfth Graders*. Urbana, IL: National Council of Teachers of English, 1971.

Fowler, H. Ramsey. *The Little, Brown Handbook*. Boston: Little, Brown, 1980.

Gaur, Albertine. *A History of Writing*. New York: Cross River Press, 1992.

Gentry, Richard R. *Spel ... Is a Four-Letter Word*. Portsmouth, NH: Heinemann Educational Books, 1987.

Ginsburg, Herbert, and Sylvia Opper. *Piaget's Theory of Intellectual Development: An Introduction*. Englewood Cliffs, NJ: Prentice-Hall, 1969.

Guralnik, David B. *Webster's New World Misspeller's Dictionary*. New York: Simon & Schuster, 1983.

Iyer, Pico. "In Praise of the Humble Comma." *Time*, 13 June 1988, 80.

Jean, Georges. *Writing: The Story of Alphabets and Scripts*. New York: Harry N. Abrams, 1992.

Krevisky, Joseph, and Jordan L. Linfield. *The Bad Speller's Dictionary*. New York: Random House, 1963.

McCrum, Robert, William Cran, and Robert MacNeil. *The Story of English*. New York: Viking Penguin, 1986.

McPherson, Elisabeth. "Spelling, Revisited." *Slate Starter Sheet*. Urbana, IL: National Council of Teachers of English, January 1984.

Marrou, H. I. *A History of Education in Antiquity*. New York: Mentor, 1964.

Richards, I. A. *Practical Criticism*. New York: Harcourt, Brace & World, 1929.

Rylant, Cynthia. *The Relatives Came*. New York: Bradbury Press, 1985.

Sanders, Judith. "Teaching the Metaphoric Lesson." Paper presented at the annual convention of the Texas Joint Council of Teachers of English (TJCTE), Houston, Texas, February 1985.

Smith, Frank. *Writing and the Writer.* New York: Holt, Rinehart & Winston, 1982.

Trimble, John R. *Writing with Style.* Englewood Cliffs, NJ: Prentice-Hall, 1975.

Wilde, Sandra. *You Kan Red This! Spelling and Punctuation for Whole Language Classrooms, K-6.* Portsmouth, NH: Heinemann Educational Books, 1992.

Wileman, Bud, and Robin Wileman, eds. *Webster's Bad Spellers' Dictionary.* New York: Barnes & Noble, 1985.

"Grammar, Grammars, and the Teaching of Grammar"

PATRICK HARTWELL

(From *College English*, February 1985. Copyright 1985 by the
National Council of Teachers of English. Reprinted with permission.)

For me the grammar issue was settled at least twenty years ago with the conclusion offered by Richard Braddock, Richard Lloyd-Jones, and Lowell Schoer in 1963.

> In view of the widespread agreement of research studies based upon many types of students and teachers, the conclusion can be stated in strong and unqualified terms: the teaching of formal grammar has a negligible or, because it usually displaces some instruction and practice in composition, even a harmful effect on improvement in writing.[1]

Indeed, I would agree with Janet Emig that the grammar issue is a prime example of "magical thinking": the assumption that students will learn only what we teach and only because we teach.[2]

But the grammar issue, as we will see, is a complicated one. And, perhaps surprisingly, it remains controversial, with the regular appearance of papers defending the teaching of formal grammar or attacking it.[3] Thus Janice Neuleib, writing on "The Relation of Formal Grammar to Composition" in *College Composition and Communication* (23 [1977], 247-250), is tempted "to sputter on paper" at reading the quotation above (p. 248), and Martha Kolln, writing in the same journal three years later ("Closing the Books on Alchemy," *CCC*, 32 [1981], 139-151), labels people like me "alchemists" for our perverse beliefs. Neuleib reviews five experimental studies, most of them concluding that formal grammar instruction has no effect on the quality of students' writing nor on their ability to avoid error. Yet she renders in effect a Scots verdict of "Not proven" and calls for more research on the issue. Similarly, Kolln reviews six experimental studies that arrive at similar conclusions, only one of them overlapping with the studies cited by Neuleib. She calls for more careful definition of the word *grammar*—her definition being "the internalized system that native speakers of a language share" (p. 140)—and she concludes with a stirring call to place grammar instruction at the center of the composition curriculum: "our goal should be to help students understand the system they know unconsciously as native speakers, to teach them the necessary categories and labels that will enable them to think about and talk about their language" (p. 150). Certainly our textbooks and our pedagogies—though they vary widely in what they see as "necessary categories and labels"—continue to emphasize mastery of formal grammar, and popular discussions of a presumed literacy crisis are almost unamimous in their call for a renewed emphasis on the teaching of formal grammar, seen as basic for success in writing.[4]

An Instructive Example

It is worth noting at the outset that both sides in this dispute—the grammarians and the anti-grammarians—articulate the issue in the same positivistic terms: what does experimental research tell us about the value of teaching formal grammar? But seventy-five years of experimental research has for all practical purposes told us nothing. The two sides are unable to agree on how to interpret such research. Studies are interpreted in terms of one's prior assumptions about the value of teaching grammar: their results seem not to change those assumptions. Thus the basis of the discussion, a basis shared by Kolln and Neuleib and by Braddock and his colleagues—"what does educational research tell us?"—seems designed to perpetuate, not to resolve, the issue. A single example will be instructive. In 1976 and then at greater length in 1979, W. B. Elley, I. H. Barham, H. Lamb, and M. Wyllie reported on a three-year experiment in New Zealand, comparing the relative effectiveness at the high school level of instruction in transformational grammar, instruction in traditional grammar, and no grammar instruction.[5] They concluded that the formal study of grammar, whether transformational or traditional, improved neither writing quality nor control over surface correctness.

> After two years, no differences were detected in writing performance or language competence; after three years small differences appeared in some minor conventions favoring the TG [transformational grammar] group, but these were more than offset by the less positive attitudes they showed towards their English studies. (p. 18)

Anthony Petroskey, in a review of research ("Grammar Instruction: What We Know," *English Journal*, 66, No. 9 [1977], 86-88), agreed with this conclusion, finding the study to be carefully designed, "representative of the best kind of educational research" (p. 86), its validity "unquestionable" (p. 88). Yet Janice Neuleib in her essay found the same conclusions to be "startling" and questioned whether the findings could be generalized beyond the target population, New Zealand high school students. Martha Kolln, when her attention is drawn to the study ("Reply to Ron Shook," *CCC*, 32 [1981], 139-151), thinks the whole experiment "suspicious." And John Mellon has been willing to use the study to defend the teaching of grammar; the study of Elley and his colleagues, he has argued, shows that teaching grammar does no harm.[6]

It would seem unlikely, therefore, that further experimental research, in and of itself, will resolve the grammar issue. Any experimental design can be nit-picked, any experimental population can be criticized, and any experimental conclusion can be questioned or, more often, ignored. In fact, it may well be that the grammar question is not open to resolution by experimental research, that, as Noam Chomsky has argued in *Reflections on Language* (New York: Pantheon, 1975), criticizing the trivialization of human learning by behavioral psychologists, the issue is simply misdefined.

> There will be "good experiments" only in domains that lie outside the organism's cognitive capacity. For example, there will be no "good experiments" in the study of human learning.

> This discipline ... will, of necessity, avoid those domains in which an organism is specially designed to acquire rich cognitive structures that enter into its life in an intimate fashion. The discipline will be of virtually no intellectual interest, it seems to me, since it is restricting itself in principle to those questions that are guaranteed to tell us little about the nature of organisms. (p. 36)

Asking the Right Questions

As a result, though I will look briefly at the tradition of experimental research, my primary goal in this essay is to articulate the grammar issue in different and, I would hope, more productive terms. Specifically, I want to ask four questions:

1. Why is the grammar issue so important? Why has it been the dominant focus of composition research for the last seventy-five years?

2. What definitions of the word *grammar* are needed to articulate the grammar issue intelligibly?

3. What do findings in cognate disciplines suggest about the value of formal grammar instruction?

4. What is our theory of language, and what does it predict about the value of formal grammar instruction? (This question — "what does our theory of language predict?" — seems a much more powerful question than "what does educational research tell us?")

In exploring these questions I will attempt to be fully explicit about issues, terms, and assumptions. I hope that both proponents and opponents of formal grammar instruction would agree that these are useful as shared points of reference: care in definition, full examination of the evidence, reference to relevant work in cognate disciplines, and explicit analysis of the theoretical bases of the issue.

But even with that gesture of harmony it will be difficult to articulate the issue in a balanced way, one that will be acceptable to both sides. After all, we are dealing with a professional dispute in which one side accuses the other of "magical thinking," and in turn that side responds by charging the other as "alchemists." Thus we might suspect that the grammar issue is itself embedded in larger models of the transmission of literacy, part of quite different assumptions about the teaching of composition.

Those of us who dismiss the teaching of formal grammar have a model of composition instruction that makes the grammar issue "uninteresting" in a scientific sense. Our model predicts a rich and complex interaction of learner and environment in mastering literacy, an interaction that has little to do with sequences of skills instruction as such. Those who defend the teaching of grammar tend to have a model of composition instruction that is rigidly skills-centered and rigidly sequential: the formal teaching of grammar, as the first step in that sequence, is the cornerstone or linchpin. Grammar teaching is thus supremely interesting, naturally a dominant focus for educational research. The controversy over the value of grammar instruction, then, is inseparable from two other issues: the issues of sequence in the teaching of composition and of the role of the composition teacher. Consider, for example, the force of these two issues in Janice Neuleib's conclusion: after calling for yet more experimental research on the value of teaching grammar, she ends with an absolute (and unsupported) claim about sequences and teacher roles in composition.

> We do know, however, that some things must be taught at different levels. Insistence on adherence to usage norms by composition teachers does improve usage. Students can learn to organize their papers if teachers do not accept papers that are disorganized. Perhaps composition teachers can teach those two abilities before they begin the more difficult tasks of developing syntactic sophistication and a winning style. ("The Relation of Formal Grammar to Composition," p. 250)

(One might want to ask, in passing, whether "usage norms" exist in the monolithic fashion the phrase suggests and whether refusing to accept disorganized papers is our best available pedagogy for teaching arrangement.)[7]

But I want to focus on the notion of sequence that makes the grammar issue so important: first grammar, then usage, then some absolute model of organization, all controlled by the teacher at the center of the learning process, with other matters, those of rhetorical weight—"syntactic sophistication and a winning style"—pushed off to the future. It is not surprising that we call each other names: those of us who question the value of teaching grammar are in fact shaking the whole elaborate edifice of traditional composition instruction.

The Five Meanings of "Grammar"

Given its centrality to a well-established way of teaching composition, I need to go about the business of defining grammar rather carefully, particularly in view of Kolln's criticism of the lack of care in earlier discussions. Therefore I will build upon a seminal discussion of the word *grammar* offered a generation ago, in 1954, by W. Nelson Francis, often excerpted as "The Three Meanings of Grammar."[8] It is worth reprinting at length, if only to re-establish it as a reference point for future discussions.

> The first thing we mean by "grammar" is "the set of formal patterns in which the words of a language are arranged in order to convey larger meanings." It is not necessary that we be able to discuss these patterns self-consciously in order to be able to use them. In fact, all speakers of a language above the age of five or six know how to use its complex forms of organization with considerable skill; in this sense of the word—call it "Grammar 1"—they are thoroughly familiar with its grammar.
>
> The second meaning of "grammar" —call it "Grammar 2"—is the branch of linguistic science which is concerned with the description, analysis, and formulization of formal language patterns." Just as gravity was in full operation before

Newton's apple fell, so grammar in the first sense was in full operation before anyone formulated the first rule that began the history of grammar as a study.

The third sense in which people use the word "grammar" is "linguistic etiquette." This we may call "Grammar 3." The word in this sense is often coupled with a derogatory adjective: we say that the expression "he ain't here" is "bad grammar." ...

As has already been suggested, much confusion arises from mixing these meanings. One hears a good deal of criticism of teachers of English couched in such terms as "they don't teach grammar any more." Criticism of this sort is based on the wholly unproven assumption that teaching Grammar 2 will improve the student's proficiency in Grammar 1 or improve his manners in Grammar 3. Actually, the form of Grammar 2 which is usually taught is a very inaccurate and misleading analysis of the facts of Grammar 1; and it therefore is of highly questionable value in improving a person's ability to handle the structural patterns of his language. (pp. 300-301)

Francis' Grammar 3 is, of course, not grammar at all, but usage. One would like to assume that Joseph Williams' recent discussion of usage ("The Phenomenology of Error," *CCC*, 32 [1981], 152-168), along with his references, has placed those shibboleths in a proper perspective. But I doubt it, and I suspect that popular discussions of the grammar issue will be as flawed by the intrusion of usage issues as past discussions have been. At any rate I will make only passing reference to Grammar 3—usage—naively assuming that this issue has been discussed elsewhere and that my readers are familiar with those discussions.

We need also to make further discriminations about Francis' Grammar 2, given that the purpose of his 1954 article was to substitute for one form of Grammar 2, that "inaccurate and misleading" form "which is usually taught," another form, that of American structuralist grammar. Here we can make use of a still earlier discussion, one going back to the days when *PMLA* was willing to publish articles on rhetoric and linguistics, to a 1927 article by Charles Carpenter Fries,

"The Rules of the Common School Grammars" (42 [1927], 221-237). Fries there distinguished between the scientific tradition of language study (to which we will now delimit Francis' Grammar 2, scientific grammar) and the separate tradition of "the common school grammars," developed unscientifically, largely based on two inadequate principles— appeals to "logical principles," like "two negatives make a positive," and analogy to Latin grammar; thus, Charlton Laird's characterization, "the grammar of Latin, ingeniously warped to suggest English" (*Language in America* [New York: World, 1970], p. 294). There is, of course, a direct link between the "common school grammars" that Fries criticized in 1927 and the grammar-based texts of today, and thus it seems wise, as Karl W. Dykema suggests ("Where Our Grammar Came From," *CE*, 22 [1961], 455-465), to separate Grammar 2, "scientific grammar," from Grammar 4, "school grammar," the latter meaning, quite literally, "the grammars used in the schools."

Further, since Martha Kolln points to the adaptation of Christensen's sentence rhetoric in a recent sentence-combining text as an example of the proper emphasis on "grammar" ("Closing the Books on Alchemy," p. 140), it is worth separating out, as still another meaning of *grammar*, Grammar 5, "stylistic grammar," defined as "grammatical terms used in the interest of teaching prose style." And, since stylistic grammars abound, with widely variant terms and emphases, we might appropriately speak parenthetically of specific forms of Grammar 5—Grammar 5 (Lanham); Grammar 5 (Strunk and White); Grammar 5 (Williams, *Style*); even Grammar 5 (Christensen, as adapted by Daiker, Kerek, and Morenberg).[9]

The Grammar in Our Heads

With these definitions in mind, let us return to Francis' Grammar 1, admirably defined by Kolln as "the internalized system of rules that speakers of a language share" ("Closing the Books on Alchemy," p. 140), or, to put it more simply, the grammar in our heads. Three features of Grammar 1 need to be stressed: first, its special status as an "internalized system of rules," as tacit and unconscious knowledge; second, the abstract, even counterintuitive, nature of these rules, insofar as we are able to approximate them indirectly as Grammar 2 statements; and third, the way in which the form of one's Grammar 1 seems profoundly affected by the acquisition of literacy. This sort of review is designed to firm up our theory of language, so that we can ask what it predicts about the value of teaching formal grammar.

A simple thought experiment will isolate the special status of Grammar 1 knowledge. I have asked members of a number of different groups—from sixth graders to college freshmen to high-school teachers—to give me the rule for ordering adjectives of nationality, age, and number in English. The response is always the same: "We don't know the rule." Yet when I ask these groups to perform an active language task, they show productive control over the rule they have denied knowing. I ask them to arrange the following words in a natural order:

French   the   young   girls   four

I have never seen a native speaker of English who did not immediately produce the natural order, "the four young French girls." The rule is that in English the order of adjectives is first, number, second, age, and third, nationality. Native speakers can create analogous phrases using the rule—"the seventy-three aged Scandinavian lechers"; and the drive for meaning is so great that they will create contexts to make sense out of violations of the rule, as in foregrounding for emphasis: "I want to talk to the French four young girls." (I immediately envision a large room, perhaps a banquet hall, filled with tables at which are seated groups of four young girls, each group of a different nationality.) So Grammar 1 is eminently usable knowledge—the way we make our life through language—but it is not accessible knowledge; in a profound sense, we do not know that we have it. Thus neurolinguist Z. N. Pylyshyn speaks of Grammar 1 as "autonomous," separate from common-sense reasoning, and as "cognitively impenetrable," not available for direct examination.[10] In philosophy and linguistics, the distinction is made between formal, conscious, "knowing about" knowledge (like Grammar 2 knowledge) and tacit, unconscious, "knowing how" knowledge (like Grammar 1 knowledge). The importance of this distinction for the teaching

of composition—it provides a powerful theoretical justification for mistrusting the ability of Grammar 2 (or Grammar 4) knowledge to affect Grammar 1 performance—was pointed out in this journal by Martin Steinmann, Jr., in 1966 ("Rhetorical Research," *CE*, 27 [1966], 278-285).

Further, the more we learn about Grammar 1—and most linguists would agree that we know surprisingly little about it—the more abstract and implicit it seems. This abstractness can be illustrated with an experiment, devised by Lise Menn and reported by Morris Halle,[11] about our rule for forming plurals in speech. It is obvious that we do indeed have a "rule" for forming plurals, for we do not memorize the plural of each noun separately. You will demonstrate productive control over that rule by forming the spoken plurals of the nonsense words below:

thole   flitch   plast

Halle offers two ways of formalizing a Grammar 2 equivalent of this Grammar 1 ability. One form of the rule is the following, stated in terms of speech sounds:

a. If the noun ends in /s z š ž č ǰ/, add /ɪz/'

b. otherwise, if the noun ends in /p t k f Ø/, add /s/;

c. otherwise, add /z/.

This rule comes close to what we literate adults consider to be an adequate rule for plurals in writing, like the rules, for example, taken from a recent "common school grammar," Eric Gould's *Reading into Writing: A Rhetoric, Reader, and Handbook* (Boston: Houghton Mifflin, 1983):

> *Plurals* can be tricky. If you are unsure of a plural, then check it in the dictionary.
>
> The general rules are
> Add *s* to the singular: *girls, tables*
> Add *es* to nouns ending in *ch, sh, x* or *s*: *churches, boxes, wishes*
> Add *es* to nouns ending in *y* and preceded by a vowel once you have changed *y* to *i*: *monies, companies.* (p. 666)

(But note the persistent inadequacy of such Grammar 4 rules: here, as I read it, the rule is inadequate to explain the plurals of *ray* and *tray*, even to explain the collective noun *monies*, not a plural at all, formed from the mass noun *money* and offered as an example.) A second form of the rule would make use of much more abstract entities, sound features:

a. If the noun ends with a sound that is [coronal, strident], add /Iz/;

b. otherwise, if the noun ends with a sound that is [non-voiced], add /s/;

c. otherwise, add /z/.

(The notion of "sound features" is itself rather abstract, perhaps new to readers not trained in linguistics. But such readers should be able to recognize that the spoken plurals of *lip* and *duck*, the sound [s], differ from the spoken plurals of *sea* and *gnu*, the sound [z], only in that the sounds of the latter are "voiced" — one's vocal cords vibrate — while the sounds of the former are "non-voiced.")

To test the psychologically operative rule, the Grammar 1 rule, native speakers of English were asked to form the plural of the last name of the composer Johann Sebastian *Bach*, a sound [x], unique in American (though not in Scottish) English. If speakers follow the first rule above, using word endings, they would reject a) and b), then apply c), producing the plural as /baxz/, with word-final /z/. (If writers were to follow the rule of the common school grammar, they would produce the written plural *Baches*, apparently, given the form of the rule, on analogy with *churches*.) If speakers follow the second rule, they would have to analyze the sound [x] as [non-labial, non-coronal, dorsal, non-voiced, and non-strident], producing the plural as /baxs/, with word-final /s/. Native speakers of American English overwhelmingly produce the plural as /baxs/. They use knowledge that Halle characterizes as "unlearned and untaught" (p. 140).

Now such a conclusion is counterintuitive — certainly it departs maximally from Grammar 4 rules for forming plurals. It seems that native speakers of English behave as if they have productive control, as Grammar 1 knowledge, of abstract sound features (= coronal, = strident, and so on) which are

available as conscious, Grammar 2 knowledge only to trained linguists — and, indeed, formally available only within the last hundred years or so. ("Behave as if," in that last sentence, is a necessary hedge, to underscore the difficulty of "knowing about" Grammar 1.)

Moreover, as the example of plural rules suggests, the form of the Grammar 1 in the heads of literate adults seems profoundly affected by the acquisition of literacy. Obviously, literate adults have access to different morphological codes: the abstract print *-s* underlying the predictable /s/ and /z/ plurals, the abstract print *-ed* underlying the spoken past tense markers /t/, as in "walked," /əd/, as in "surrounded," /d/, as in "sacred," and the symbol /Ø/ for no surface realization, as in the relaxed standard pronunciation of "I walked to the store." Literate adults also have access to distinctions preserved only in the code of print (for example, the distinction between "a good sailer" and "a good sailor" that Mark Aranoff points out in "An English Spelling Convention," *Linguistic Inquiry*, 9 [1978], 299-303). More significantly, Irene Moscowitz speculates that the ability of third graders to form abstract nouns on analogy with pairs like *divine::divinity* and *serene::serenity*, where the spoken vowel changes but the spelling preserves meaning, is a factor of knowing how to read. Carol Chomsky finds a three-stage developmental sequence in the grammatical performance of seven-year-olds, related to measures of kind and variety of reading; and Rita S. Brause finds a nine-stage developmental sequence in the ability to understand semantic ambiguity, extending from fourth graders to graduate students.[12] John Mills and Gordon Hemsley find that level of education, and presumably level of literacy, influence judgments of grammaticality, concluding that literacy changes the deep structure of one's internal grammar; Jean Whyte finds that oral language functions develop differently in readers and nonreaders; José Morais, Jésus Alegria, and Paul Bertelson find that illiterate adults are unable to add or delete sounds at the beginning of nonsense words, suggesting that awareness of speech as a series of phones is provided by learning to read an alphabetic code. Two experiments — one conducted by Charles A. Ferguson, the other by Mary E. Hamilton and David Barton — find that adults' ability to recognize segmentation in speech is related to degree of literacy, not to amount of schooling or general ability.[13]

It is worth noting that none of these investigators would suggest that the developmental sequences they have uncovered be isolated and taught as discrete skills. They are natural concomitants of literacy, and then seem best characterized not as isolated rules but as developing schemata, broad strategies for approaching written language.

Grammar 2

We can, of course, attempt to approximate the rules or schemata of Grammar 1 by writing fully explicit descriptions that model the competence of a native speaker. Such rules, like the rules for pluralizing nouns or ordering adjectives discussed above, are the goal of the science of linguistics, that is, Grammar 2. There are a number of scientific grammars—an older structuralist model and several versions within a generative-transformational paradigm, not to mention isolated schools like tagmemic grammar, Montague grammar, and the like. In fact, we cannot think of Grammar 2 as a stable entity, for its form changes with each new issue of each linguistics journal, as new "rules of grammar" are proposed and debated. Thus Grammar 2, though of great theoretical interest to the composition teacher, is of little practical use in the classroom, as Constance Weaver has pointed out (*Grammar for Teachers* [Urbana, Ill.: NCTE, 1979], pp. 3-6). Indeed Grammar 2 is a scientific model of Grammar 1, not a description of it, so that questions of psychological reality, while important, are less important than other, more theoretical factors, such as the elegance of formulation or the global power of rules. We might, for example, wish to replace the rule for ordering adjectives of age, number, and nationality cited above with a more general rule—what linguists call a "fuzzy" rule—that adjectives in English are ordered by their abstract quality of "nouniness": adjectives that are very much like nouns, like *French* or *Scandinavian*, come physically closer to nouns than do adjectives that are less "nouny," like *four* or *aged*. But our motivation for accepting the broader rule would be its global power, not its psychological reality.[14]

I try to consider a hostile reader, one committed to the teaching of grammar, and I try to think of ways to hammer in the central point of this distinction, that the rules of Grammar 2 are simply unconnected to productive control over Grammar 1. I can argue from authority: Noam Chomsky has touched on this point whenever he has concerned himself with the implications of linguistics for language teaching, and years ago transformationalist Mark Lester stated unequivocally, "there simply appears to be no correlation between a writer's study of language and his ability to write."[15] I can cite analogies offered by others: Francis Christensen's analogy in an essay originally published in 1962 that formal grammar study would be "to invite a centipede to attend to the sequence of his legs in motion,"[16] or James Britton's analogy, offered informally after a conference presentation, that grammar study would be like forcing starving people to master the use of a knife and fork before allowing them to eat. I can offer analogies of my own, contemplating the wisdom of asking a pool player to master the physics of momentum before taking up a cue or of making a prospective driver get a degree in automotive engineering before engaging the clutch. I consider a hypothetical argument, that if Grammar 2 knowledge affected Grammar 1 performance, then linguists would be our best writers. (I can certify that they are, on the whole, not.) Such a position, after all, is only in accord with other domains of science: the formula for catching a fly ball in baseball ("Playing It by Ear," *Scientific American*, 248, No. 4 [1983], 76) is of such complexity that it is beyond my understanding—and, I would suspect, that of many workaday centerfielders. But perhaps I can best hammer in this claim—that Grammar 2 knowledge has no effect on Grammar 1 performance—by offering a demonstration.

The diagram on the next page is an attempt by Thomas N. Huckin and Leslie A. Olsen (*English for Science and Technology* [New York: McGraw-Hill, 1983]) to offer, for students of English as a second language, a fully explicit formulation of what is, for native speakers, a trivial rule of the language—the choice of definite article, indefinite article, or no definite article. There are obvious limits to such a formulation, for article choice in English is less a matter of rule than of idiom ("I went to college" versus "I

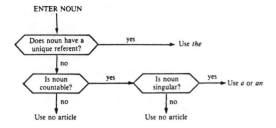

went to a university" versus British "I went to university"), real-world knowledge (using indefinite "I went into a house" instantiates definite "I look at the ceiling," and indefinite "I visited a university" instantiates definite "I talked with the professors"), and stylistic choice (the last sentence above might alternatively end with "the choice of the definite article, the indefinite article, or no article"). Huckin and Olsen invite non-native speakers to use the rule consciously to justify article choice in technical prose, such as the passage below from P. F. Brandwein (*Matter: An Earth Science* [New York: Harcourt Brace Jovanovich, 1975]). I invite you to spend a couple of minutes doing the same thing, with the understanding that this exercise is a test case: you are using a very explicit rule to justify a fairly straightforward issue of grammatical choice.

> Imagine a cannon on top of _____ highest mountain on earth. It is firing _____ cannonballs horizontally. _____ first cannonball fired follows its path. As _____ cannonball moves, _____ gravity pulls it down, and it soon hits _____ ground. Now _____ velocity with which each succeeding cannonball is fired is increased. Thus, _____ cannonball goes farther each time. Cannonball 2 goes farther than _____ cannonball 1 although each is being pulled by _____ gravity toward the earth all _____ time. _____ last cannonball is fired with such tremendous velocity that it goes completely around _____ earth. It returns to _____ mountaintop and continues around the earth again and again. _____ cannonball's inertia causes it to continue in motion indefinitely in _____ orbit around earth. In such a situation, we

could consider _____ cannonball to be _____ artificial satellite, just like _____ weather satellites launched by _____ U.S. Weather Service. (p. 209)

Most native speakers of English who have attempted this exercise report a great deal of frustration, a curious sense of working against, rather than with, the rule. The rule, however valuable it may be for non-native speakers, is, for the most part, simply unusable for native speakers of the language.

Cognate Areas of Research

We can corroborate this demonstration by turning to research in two cognate areas, studies of the induction of rules of artificial languages and studies of the role of formal rules in second language acquisition. Psychologists have studied the ability of subjects to learn artificial languages, usually constructed of nonsense syllables or letter strings. Such languages can be described by phrase structure rules:

$$S \Rightarrow VX$$
$$X \Rightarrow MX$$

More clearly, they can be presented as flow diagrams, as below:

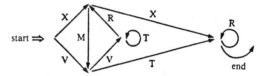

This diagram produces "sentences" like the following:

> VVTRXRR. XMVTTRX. XXRR.
> XMVRMT. VVTTRMT. XMTRRR.

The following "sentences" would be "ungrammatical" in this language:

> *VMXTT.   *RTXVVT.   *TRVXXVVM.

Arthur S. Reber, in a classic 1967 experiment, demonstrated that mere exposure to grammatical sentences produced tacit learning: subjects who copied several grammatical sentences performed far above chance in judging the grammaticality of other letter strings. Further experiments have shown that providing subjects with formal rules—giving them the flow diagram above, for example—remarkably degrades performance; subjects given the "rules of the language" do much less well in acquiring the rules than do subjects not given the rules. Indeed, even telling subjects that they are to induce the rules of an artificial language degrades performance. Such laboratory experiments are admittedly contrived, but they confirm predictions that our theory of language would make about the value of formal rules in language learning.[17]

The thrust of recent research in second language learning similarly works to constrain the value of formal grammar rules. The most explicit statement of the value of formal rules is that of Stephen D. Krashen's monitor model.[18] Krashen divided second language mastery into *acquisition*—tacit, informal mastery, akin to first language acquisition—and formal learning—conscious application of Grammar 2 rules, which he calls "monitoring" output. In another essay Krashen uses his model to predict a highly individual use of the monitor and a highly constrained role for formal rules:

> Some adults (and very few children) are able to use conscious rules to increase the grammatical accuracy of their output, and even for these people, very strict conditions need to be met before the conscious grammar can be applied.[19]

In *Principles and Practice in Second Language Acquisition* (New York: Pergamon, 1982) Krashen outlines these conditions by means of a series of concentric circles, beginning with a large circle denoting the rules of English and a smaller circle denoting the subset of those rules described by formal linguists (adding that most linguists would protest that the size of this circle is much too large):

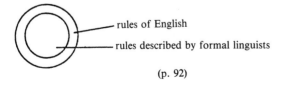

rules of English

rules described by formal linguists

(p. 92)

Krashen then adds smaller circles, as shown below—a subset of the rules described by formal linguists that would be known to applied linguists, a subset of those rules that would be available to the best teachers, and then a subset of those rules that teachers might choose to present to second language learners:

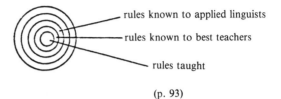

rules known to applied linguists

rules known to best teachers

rules taught

(p. 93)

Of course, as Krashen notes, not all the rules taught will be learned, and not all those learned will be available, as what he calls "mental baggage" (p. 94), for conscious use.

An experiment by Ellen Bialystock, asking English speakers learning French to judge the grammaticality of taped sentences, complicates this issue, for reaction time data suggest that learners first make an intuitive judgment of grammaticality, using implicit or Grammar 1 knowledge, and only then search for formal explanations, using explicit or Grammar 2 knowledge.[20] This distinction would suggest that Grammar 2 knowledge is of use to second language learners only after the principle has already been mastered as tacit Grammar 1 knowledge. In the terms of Krashen's model, learning never becomes acquisition (*Principles*, p. 86).

An ingenious experiment by Herbert W. Seliger complicates the issue yet further ("On the Nature and Function of Language Rules in Language Learning," *TESOL Quarterly*, 13 [1979], 359-369). Seliger asked native and non-native speakers of English to orally identify pictures of objects (e.g., "an apple," "a pear," "a book," "an umbrella"), noting whether they used the correct form of the indefinite articles *a* and *an*. He found no correlation between the ability to state the rule and the ability to apply it correctly, either with native or non-native speakers. Indeed, three of four adult non-native speakers in his sample produced a correct form of the rule, but they did not apply it in speaking. A strong conclusion from this experiment would be that formal rules of grammar seem to have no value whatsoever. Seliger, however, suggests a more paradoxical interpretation. Rules are of no use, he agrees, but some people think they are, and for these people, assuming that they have internalized the rules, even inadequate rules are of heuristic value, for they allow them to access the internal rules they actually use.

The Incantations of the "Common School Grammars"

Such a paradox may explain the fascination we have as teachers with "rules of grammar" of the Grammar 4 variety, the "rules" of the "common school grammars." Again and again such rules are inadequate to the facts of written language; you will recall that we have known this since Francis' 1927 study. R. Scott Baldwin and James M. Coady, studying how readers respond to punctuation signals ("Psycholinguistic Approaches to a Theory of Punctuation," *Journal of Reading Behavior*, 10 [1978], 363-383), conclude that conventional rules of punctuation are "a complete sham" (p. 375). My own favorite is the Grammar 4 rule for showing possession, always expressed in terms of adding -'s or -s' to nouns, while our internal grammar, if you think about it, adds possession to noun phrases, albeit under severe stylistic constraints: "the horses of the Queen of England" are "the Queen of England's horses" and "the feathers of the duck over there" are "the duck over there's feathers." Suzette Haden Elgin refers to the "rules" of Grammar 4 as "incantations" (*Never Mind the Trees*, p. 9; see footnote 3).

It may simply be that as hyperliterate adults we are conscious of "using rules" when we are in fact doing something else, something far more complex, accessing tacit heuristics honed by print literacy itself. We can clarify this notion by reaching for an acronym coined by technical writers to explain the readability of complex prose — COIK: "clear only if known." The rules of Grammar 4 — no, we can at this point be more honest — the incantations of Grammar 4 are COIK. If you know how to signal possession in the code of print, then the advice to add -'s to nouns makes perfect sense, just as the collective noun *monies* is a fine example of changing -*y* to -*i* and adding -*es* to form the plural. But if you have not grasped, tacitly, the abstract representation of possession in print, such incantations can only be opaque.

Worse yet, the advice given in "the common school grammars" is unconnected with anything remotely resembling literate adult behavior. Consider, as an example, the rule for not writing a sentence fragment as the rule is described in the best-selling college grammar text, John C. Hodges and Mary S. Whitten's *Harbrace College Handbook*, 9th ed. (New York: Harcourt Brace Jovanovich, 1982). In order to get to the advice, "as a rule, do not write a sentence fragment" (p. 25), the student must master the following learning tasks:

> Recognizing verbs.
>
> Recognizing subjects and verbs.
>
> Recognizing all parts of speech. (*Harbrace* lists eight.)
>
> Recognizing phrases and subordinate clauses. (*Harbrace* lists six types of phrases, and it offers incomplete lists of eight relative pronouns and eighteen subordinating conjunctions.)
>
> Recognizing main clauses and types of sentences.

These learning tasks completed, the student is given the rule above, offered a page of exceptions, and then given the following advice (or is it an incantation?):

> Before handing in a composition ... proofread each word group written as a sentence. Test each one for completeness. First, be sure that it has at least one subject and one predicate. Next, be sure that the word group is not a dependent clause beginning with a subordinating conjunction or a relative clause. (p. 27)

The school grammar approach defines a sentence fragment as a conceptual error — as not having conscious knowledge of the school grammar definition of *sentence*. It demands heavy emphasis on rote memory, and it asks students to behave in ways patently removed from the behaviors of mature writers. (I have never in my life tested a sentence for completeness, and I am a better writer — and probably a better person — as a consequence.) It may be, of course, that some developing writers, at some points in their development, may benefit from such advice — or, more to the point, may think that they benefit — but, as Thomas Friedman points out in "Teaching Error, Nurturing Confusion" (*CE*, 45 [1983], 390-399), our theory of language tells us that such advice is, at the best, COIK. As the Maine joke has it, about a tourist asking directions from a farmer, "you can't get there from here."

Redefining Error

In the specific case of sentence fragments, Mina P. Shaughnessy (*Errors and Expectations* [New York: Oxford University Press, 1977]) argues that such errors are not conceptual failures at all, but performance errors — mistakes in punctuation. Muriel Harris' error counts support this view ("Mending the Fragmented Free Modifier," *CCC*, 32 [1981], 175-182). Case studies show example after example of errors that occur *because of* instruction — one thinks, for example, of David Bartholmae's student explaining that he added an *-s* to *children* "because it's a plural" ("The Study of Error," *CCC*, 31 [1980], 262). Surveys, such as that by Muriel Harris ("Contradictory Perceptions of the Rules of Writing," *CCC*, 30 [1979], 218-220), and our own observations suggest that students consistently misunderstand such Grammar 4 explanations (COIK, you will recall). For example, from Patrick Hartwell and Robert H. Bentley and from Mike Rose, we have two separate anecdotal accounts of students, cited for punctuating a *because*-clause as a sentence, who have decided to avoid using *because*. More generally, Collette A. Daiute's analysis of errors made by college students shows that errors tend to appear at clause boundaries, suggesting short-term memory load and not conceptual deficiency as a cause of error.[21]

Thus, if we think seriously about error and its relationship to the worship of formal grammar study, we need to attempt some massive dislocation of our traditional thinking, to shuck off our hyperliterate perception of the value of formal rules, and to regain the confidence in the tacit power of unconscious knowledge that our theory of language gives us. Most students, reading their writing aloud, will correct in essence all errors of spelling, grammar, and, by intonation, punctuation, but usually without noticing that what they read departs from what they wrote.[22] And Richard H. Haswell ("Minimal

Marking," *CE*, 45 [1983], 600-604) notes that his students correct 61.1% of their errors when they are identified with a simple mark in the margin rather than by error type. Such findings suggest that we need to redefine error, to see it not as a cognitive or linguistic problem, a problem of not knowing a "rule of grammar" (whatever that may mean), but rather, following the insight of Robert J. Bracewell ("Writing as a Cognitive Activity," *Visible Language*, 14 [1980], 400-422), as a problem of metacognition and metalinguistic awareness, a matter of accessing knowledges that, to be of any use, learners must have already internalized by means of exposure to the code. (Usage issues — Grammar 3 — probably represent a different order of problem. Both Joseph Emonds and Jeffrey Jochnowitz establish that the usage issues we worry most about are linguistically unnatural, departures from the grammar in our heads.)[23]

The notion of metalinguistic awareness seems crucial. The sentence below, created by Douglas R. Hofstadter ("Metamagical Themas," *Scientific American*, 235, No. 1 [1981], 22-32), is offered to clarify that notion; you are invited to examine it for a moment or two before continuing.

> Their is four errors in this sentence. Can you find them?

Three errors announce themselves plainly enough, the misspellings of *there* and *sentence* and the use of *is* instead of *are*. (And, just to illustrate the perils of hyperliteracy, let it be noted that, through three years of drafts, I referred to the choice of *is* and *are* as a matter of "subject-verb agreement.") The fourth error resists detection, until one assesses the truth value of the sentence itself — the fourth error is that there are not four errors, only three. Such a sentence (Hofstadter calls it a "self-referencing sentence") asks you to look at it in two ways, simultaneously as statement and as linguistic artifact — in other words, to exercise metalinguistic awareness.

A broad range of cross-cultural studies suggest that metalinguistic awareness is a defining feature of print literacy. Thus Sylvia Scribner and Michael Cole, working with the triliterate Vai of Liberia (variously literate in English, through schooling; in Arabic, for religious purposes; and in an indigenous Vai script, used for personal affairs), find that metalinguistic awareness, broadly conceived, is the only cognitive skill underlying each of the three literacies. The one statistically significant skill shared by literate Vai was the recognition of word boundaries. Moreover, literate Vai tended to answer "yes" when asked (in Vai), "Can you call the sun the moon and the moon the sun?" while illiterate Vai tended to have grave doubts about such metalinguistic play. And in the United States Henry and Lila R. Gleitman report quite different responses by clerical workers and Ph.D. candidates asked to interpret nonsense compounds like "house-bird glass"; clerical workers focused on meaning and plausibility (for example, "a house-bird made of glass"), while Ph.D. candidates focused on syntax (for example, "a very small drinking cup for canaries" or "a glass that protects house-birds").[24] More general research findings suggest a clear relationship between measures of metalinguistic awareness and measures of literacy level.[25] William Labov, speculating on literacy acquisition in inner-city ghettoes, contrasts "stimulus-bound" and "language-bound" individuals, suggesting that the latter seem to master literacy more easily.[26] The analysis here suggests that the causal relationship works the other way, that it is the mastery of written language that increases one's awareness of language as language.

This analysis has two implications. First, it makes the question of socially nonstandard dialects, always implicit in discussions of teaching formal grammar, into a non-issue.[27] Native speakers of English, regardless of dialect, show tacit mastery of the conventions of Standard English, and that mastery seems to transfer into abstract orthographic knowledge through interaction with print.[28] Developing writers show the same patterning of errors, regardless of dialect.[29] Studies of reading and of writing suggest that surface features of spoken dialect are simply irrelevant to mastering print literacy.[30] Print is a complex cultural code—or better yet, a system of codes—and my bet is that, regardless of instruction, one masters those codes from the top down, from pragmatic questions of voice, tone, audience, register, and rhetorical strategy, not from the bottom up, from grammar to usage to fixed forms of organization.

Second, this analysis forces us to posit multiple literacies, used for multiple purposes, rather than a single static literacy, engraved in "rules of grammar." These multiple literacies are evident in cross-cultural studies.[31] They are equally evident when we inquire into the uses of literacy in American communities.[32] Further, given that students, at all levels, show widely variant interactions with print literacy, there would seem to be little to do with grammar—with Grammar 2 or with Grammar 4—that we could isolate as a basis for formal instruction.[33]

Grammar 5: Stylistic Grammar

Similarly, when we turn to Grammar 5, "grammatical terms used in the interest of teaching prose style," so central to Martha Kolln's argument for teaching formal grammar, we find that the grammar issue is simply beside the point. There are two fully-articulated positions about "stylistic grammar," which I will label "romantic" and "classic," following Richard Lloyd-Jones and Richard E. Young.[34] The romantic position is that stylistic grammars, though perhaps useful for teachers, have little place in the teaching of composition, for students must struggle with and through language toward meaning. This position rests on a theory of language ultimately philosophical rather than linguistic (witness, for example, the contempt for linguists in Ann Berthoff's *The Making of Meaning: Metaphors, Models, and Maxims for Writing Teachers* [Montclair, N.J.: Boynton/Cook, 1981]); it is articulated as a theory of style by Donald A. Murray and, on somewhat different grounds (that stylistic grammars encourage overuse of the monitor), by Ian Pringle. The classic position, on the other hand, is that we can find ways to offer developing writers helpful suggestions about prose style, suggestions such as Francis Christensen's emphasis on the cumulative sentence, developed by observing the practice of skilled writers, and Joseph Williams' advice about predication, developed by psycholinguistic studies of comprehension.[35] James A. Berlin's recent survey of composition theory (*CE*, 45 [1982], 765-777) probably understates the gulf between these two positions and the radically different conceptions of language that underlie them, but it does establish that they share an overriding assumption in common: that one learns to control the language of print by manipulating language in meaningful contexts, not by learning about language in isolation, as by the study of formal grammar. Thus even classic theorists, who choose to present a vocabulary of style to students, do so only as a vehicle for encouraging productive control of communicative structures.

We might put the matter in the following terms. Writers need to develop skills at two levels. One, broadly rhetorical, involves communication in meaningful contexts (the strategies, registers, and procedures of discourse across a range of modes, audiences, contexts, and purposes). The other, broadly metalinguistic rather than linguistic, involves active manipulation of language with conscious attention to surface form. This second level may be developed tacitly, as a natural adjunct to developing rhetorical competencies—I take this to be the position of romantic theorists. It may be developed formally, by manipulating language for stylistic effect, and such manipulation may involve, for pedagogical continuity, a vocabulary of style. But it is primarily developed by any kind of language activity that enhances the awareness of language as language.[36] David T. Hakes, summarizing the research on metalinguistic awareness, notes how far we are from understanding this process:

> the optimal conditions for becoming metalinguistically competent involve growing up in a literate environment with adult models who are themselves metalinguistically competent and who foster the growth of that competence in a variety of ways as yet little understood. ("The Development of Metalinguistic Abilities," p. 205; see footnote 25)

Such a model places language, at all levels, at the center of the curriculum, but not as "necessary categories and labels" (Kolln, "Closing the Books on Alchemy," p. 150), but as literal stuff, verbal clay, to be molded and probed, shaped and reshaped, and, above all, enjoyed.

The Tradition of Experimental Research

Thus, when we turn back to experimental research on the value of formal grammar instruction, we do so with firm predictions given us by our theory of language. Our theory would predict the formal grammar instruction, whether instruction in scientific grammar or instruction in "the common school grammar," would have little to do with control over surface correctness nor with quality of writing. It would predict that any form of active involvement with language would be preferable to instruction in rules or definitions (or incantations). In essence, this is what the research tells us. In 1893, the Committee of Ten (*Report of the Committee of Ten on Secondary School Studies* [Washington, D.C.: U.S. Government Printing Office, 1893]) put grammar at the center of the English curriculum, and its report established the rigidly sequential mode of instruction common for the last century. But the committee explicitly noted that grammar instruction did not aid correctness, arguing instead that it improved the ability to think logically (an argument developed from the role of the "grammarian" in the classical rhetorical tradition, essentially a teacher of literature—see, for example, the etymology of *grammar* in the *Oxford English Dictionary*).

But Franklin S. Hoyt, in a 1906 experiment, found no relationship between the study of grammar and the ability to think logically; his research led him to conclude what I am constrained to argue more than seventy-five years later, that there is no "relationship between a knowledge of technical grammar and the ability to use English and to interpret language" ("The Place of Grammar in the Elementary Curriculum," *Teachers College Record*, 7 [1906], 483-484). Later studies, through the 1920s, focused on the relationship of knowledge of grammar and ability to recognize error; experiments reported by James Boraas in 1917 and by William Asker in 1923 are typical of those that reported no correlation. In the 1930s, with the development of the functional grammar movement, it was common to compare the study of formal grammar with one form or another of active manipulation of language; experiments by I. O. Ash in 1935 and Ellen Frogner in 1939 are typical of studies showing the superiority of active involvement with language.[37] In a 1959 article, "Grammar in Language Teaching" (*Elementary English*, 36 [1959], 412-421), John J. DeBoer noted the consistency of these findings.

> The impressive fact is ... that in all these studies, carried out in places and at times far removed from each other, often by highly experienced and disinterested investigators, the results have been consistently negative so far as the value of grammar in the improvement of language expression is concerned. (p. 417)

In 1960 Ingrid M. Strom, reviewing more than fifty experimental studies, came to a similarly strong and unqualified conclusion:

> direct methods of instruction, focusing on writing activities and the structuring of ideas, are more efficient in teaching sentence structure, usage, punctuation, and other related factors than are such methods as nomenclature drill, diagramming, and rote memorization of grammatical rules.[38]

In 1963 two research reviews appeared, one by Braddock, Lloyd-Jones, and Schorer, cited at the beginning of this paper, and one by Henry C. Meckel, whose conclusions, though more guarded, are in essential agreement.[39] In 1969 J. Stephen Sherwin devoted one-fourth of his *Four Problems in Teaching English: A Critique of Research* (Scranton, Penn.: International Textbook, 1969) to the grammar issue, concluding that "instruction in formal grammar is an ineffective way to help students achieve proficiency in writing" (p. 135). Some early experiments in sentence combining, such as those by Donald R. Bateman and Frank J. Zidonnis and by John C. Mellon, showed improvement in measures of syntactic complexity with instruction in transformational grammar keyed to sentence combining practice. But a later study by Frank O'Hare achieved the same gains with no grammar instruction, suggesting to Sandra L. Stotsky and to Richard Van de Veghe that

active manipulation of language, not the grammar unit, explained the earlier results.[40] More recent summaries of research—by Elizabeth I. Haynes, Hillary Taylor Holbrook, and Marcia Farr Whiteman—support similar conclusions. Indirect evidence for this position is provided by surveys reported by Betty Bamberg in 1978 and 1981, showing that time spent in grammar instruction in high school is the least important factor, of eight factors examined, in separating regular from remedial writers at the college level.[41]

More generally, Patrick Scott and Bruce Castner, in "Reference Sources for Composition Research: A Practical Survey" (*CE*, 45 [1983], 756-768), note that much current research is not informed by an awareness of the past. Put simply, we are constrained to reinvent the wheel. My concern here has been with a far more serious problem: that too often the wheel we reinvent is square.

It is, after all, a question of power. Janet Emig, developing a consensus from composition research, and Aaron S. Carton and Lawrence V. Castiglione, developing the implications of language theory for education, come to the same conclusion: that the thrust of current research and theory is to take power from the teacher and to give that power to the learner.[42] At no point in the English curriculum is the question of power more blatantly posed than in the issue of formal grammar instruction. It is time that we, as teachers, formulate theories of language and literacy and let those theories guide our teaching, and it is time that we, as researchers, move on to more interesting areas of inquiry.

Notes

1. *Research in Written Composition* (Urbana, Ill.: National Council of Teachers of English, 1963), pp. 37-38.

2. "Non-magical Thinking: Presenting Writing Developmentally in Schools," in *Writing Process, Development and Communication*, Vol. II of *Writing: The Nature, Development and Teaching of Written Communication*, ed. Charles H. Fredericksen and Joseph F. Dominic (Hillsdale, N.J.: Lawrence Erlbaum, 1980), pp. 21-30.

3. For arguments in favor of formal grammar teaching, see Patrick F. Basset, "Grammar—Can We Afford Not to Teach It?" *NASSP Bulletin*, 64, No. 10 (1980), 55-63; Mary Epes, et al., "The

COMP-LAB Project: Assessing the Effectiveness of a Laboratory-Centered Basic Writing Course on the College Level" (Jamaica, N.Y.: York College, CUNY, 1979) ERIC 194 908; June B. Evans, "The Analogous Ounce: The Analgesic for Relief," *English Journal*, 70, No. 2 (1981), 38-39; Sydney Greenbaum, "What Is Grammar and Why Teach It?" (a paper presented at the meeting of the National Council of Teachers of English, Boston, Nov. 1982) ERIC 222 917; Marjorie Smelstor, *A Guide to the Role of Grammar in Teaching Writing* (Madison: University of Wisconsin School of Education, 1978) ERIC 176 323; and A. M. Tibbetts, *Working Papers: A Teacher's Observations on Composition* (Glenview, Ill.: Scott, Foresman, 1982).

For attacks on formal grammar teaching, see Harvey A. Daniels, *Famous Last Words: The American Language Crisis Reconsidered* (Carbondale: Southern Illinois University Press, 1983); Suzette Haden Elgin, *Never Mind the Trees: What the English Teacher Really Needs to Know about Linguistics* (Berkeley: University of California College of Education, Bay Area Writing Project Occasional Paper No. 2, 1980) ERIC 198 536; Mike Rose, "Remedial Writing Courses: A Critique and a Proposal," *College English*, 45 (1983), 109-128; and Ron Shook, "Response to Martha Kolln," *College Composition and Communication*, 34 (1983), 491-495.

4. See, for example, Clifton Fadiman and James Howard, *Empty Pages: A Search for Writing Competence in School and Society* (Belmont, Cal.: Fearon Pitman, 1979); Edwin Newman, *A Civil Tongue* (Indianapolis, Ind.: Bobbs-Merrill, 1976); and *Strictly Speaking* (New York: Warner Books, 1974); John Simons, *Paradigm: Lost* (New York: Clarkson N. Potter, 1980); A. M. Tibbets and Charlene Tibbets, *What's Happening to American English?* (New York: Scribner's, 1978); and "Why Johnny Can't Write," *Newsweek*, 3 Dec. 1975, pp. 58-63.

5. "The Role of Grammar in a Secondary School English Curriculum," *Research in the Teaching of English*, 10 (1976), 5-21; *The Role of Grammar in a Secondary School Curriculum* (Wellington: New Zealand Council of Teachers of English, 1979).

6. "A Taxonomy of Compositional Competencies," in *Perspectives on Literacy*, ed. Richard Beach and P. David Pearson (Minneapolis: University of Minnesota College of Education, 1979), pp. 247-272.

7. On usage norms, see Edward Finegan, *Attitudes toward English Usage: The History of a War of Words* (New York: Teachers College Press, 1980),

and Jim Quinn, *American Tongue in Cheek: A Populist Guide to Language* (New York: Pantheon, 1980); on arrangement, see Patrick Hartwell, "Teaching Arrangement: A Pedagogy," *CE*, 40 (1979), 348-554.

8. "Revolution in Grammar," *Quarterly Journal of Speech*, 40 (1954), 299-312.

9. Richard A. Lanham, *Revising Prose* (New York: Scribner's, 1979); William Strunk and E. B. White, *The Elements of Style*, 3rd ed. (New York: Macmillan, 1979); Joseph Williams, *Style: Ten Lessons in Clarity and Grace* (Glenview, Ill.: Scott, Foresman, 1981); Christensen, "A Generative Rhetoric of the Sentence," *CCC*, 14 (1963), 155-161; Donald A. Daiker, Andrew Kerek, and Max Morenberg, *The Writer's Options: Combining to Composing*, 2nd ed. (New York: Harper & Row, 1982).

10. "A Psychological Approach," in *Psychobiology of Language*, ed. M. Studdert-Kennedy (Cambridge, Mass.: MIT Press, 1983), pp. 16-19. See also Noam Chomsky, "Language and Unconscious Knowledge," in *Psychoanalysis and Language: Psychiatry and the Humanities*, Vol. III, ed. Joseph H. Smith (New Haven, Conn.: Yale University Press, 1978), pp. 3-44.

11. Morris Halle, "Knowledge Unlearned and Untaught: What Speakers Know about the Sounds of Their Language," in *Linguistic Theory and Psychological Reality*, ed. Halle, Joan Bresnan, and George A. Miller (Cambridge, Mass.: MIT Press, 1978), pp. 135-140.

12. Moscowitz, "On the Status of Vowel Shift in English," in *Cognitive Development and the Acquisition of Language*, ed. T. E. Moore (New York: Academic Press, 1973), pp. 223-260; Chomsky, "Stages in Language Development and Reading Exposure," *Harvard Educational Review*, 42 (1972), 1-33; and Brause, "Developmental Aspects of the Ability to Understand Semantic Ambiguity, with Implications for Teachers," *RTE*, 11 (1977), 39-48.

13. Mills and Hemsley, "The Effect of Levels of Education on Judgments of Grammatical Acceptability," *Language and Speech*, 19 (1976), 324-342; Whyte, "Levels of Language Competence and Reading Ability: An Exploratory Investigation," *Journal of Research in Reading*, 5 (1982), 123-132; Morais, et al., "Does Awareness of Speech as a Series of Phones Arise Spontaneously?" *Cognition*, 7 (1979), 323-331; Ferguson, *Cognitive Effects of Literacy: Linguistic Awareness in Adult*

Literacy: Linguistic Awareness in Adult Non-readers (Washington, D.C.: National Institute of Education Final Report, 1981) ERIC 222 857; Hamilton and Barton, "A Word Is a Word: Meta-linguistic Skills in Adults of Varying Literacy Levels" (Stanford, Cal.: Stanford University Department of Linguistics, 1980) ERIC 222 859.

14. On the question of the psychological reality of Grammar 2 descriptions, see Maria Black and Shulamith Chiat, "Psycholinguistics without 'Psychological Reality'," *Linguistics*, 19 (1981), 37-61; Joan Bresnan, ed., *The Mental Representation of Grammatical Relations* (Cambridge, Mass.: MIT Press, 1982); and Michael H. Long, "Inside the 'Black Box': Methodological Issues in Classroom Research on Language Learning," *Language Learning*, 30 (1980), 1-42.

15. Chomsky, "The Current Scene in Linguistics," *College English*, 27 (1966), 587-595; and "Linguistic Theory," in *Language Teaching: Broader Contexts*, ed. Robert C. Meade, Jr. (New York: Modern Language Association, 1966), pp. 43-49; Mark Lester, "The Value of Transformational Grammar in Teaching Composition," *CCC*, 16 (1967), 228.

16. Christensen, "Between Two Worlds," in *Notes toward a New Rhetoric: Nine Essays for Teachers*, rev. ed., ed. Bonniejean Christensen (New York: Harper & Row, 1978), pp. 1-22.

17. Reber, "Implicit Learning of Artificial Grammars," *Journal of Verbal Learning and Verbal Behavior*, 6 (1967), 855-863; "Implicit Learning of Synthetic Languages: The Role of Instructional Set," *Journal of Experimental Psychology: Human Learning and Memory*, 2 (1976), 889-894; and Reber, Saul M. Kassin, Selma Lewis, and Gary Cantor, "On the Relationship Between Implicit and Explicit Modes in the Learning of a Complex Rule Structure," *Journal of Experimental Psychology: Human Learning and Memory*, 6 (1980), 492-502.

18. "Individual Variation in the Use of the Monitor," in *Principles of Second Language Learning*, ed. W. Richie (New York: Academic Press, 1978), pp. 175-185.

19. "Applications of Psycholinguistic Research to the Classroom," in *Practical Applications of Research in Foreign Language Teaching*, ed. D. J. James (Lincolnwood, Ill.: National Textbook, 1983), p. 61.

20. "Some Evidence for the Integrity and Interaction of Two Knowledge Sources," in *New Dimensions in Second Language Acquisition Research*, ed. Roger W. Andersen (Rowley, Mass.: Newbury House, 1981), pp. 62-74.

21. Hartwell and Bentley, *Some Suggestions for Using Open to Language* (New York: Oxford University Prerss, 1982), p. 73; Rose, *Writer's Block: The Cognitive Dimension* (Carbondale: Southern Illinois University Press, 1983), p. 99; Daiute, "Psycholinguistic Foundations of the Writing Process," *RTE*, 15 (1981), 5-22.

22. See Bartholmae, "The Study of Error"; Patrick Hartwell, "The Writing Center and the Paradoxes of Written-Down Speech," in *Writing Centers: Theory and Administration*, ed. Gary Olson (Urbana, Ill.: NCTE, 1984), pp. 48-61; and Sondra Perl, "A Look at Basic Writers in the Process of Composing," in *Basic Writing: A Collection of Essays for Teachers, Researchers, and Administrators* (Urbana, Ill.: NCTE, 1980), pp. 13-32.

23. Emonds, *Adjacency in Grammar: The Theory of Language-Particular Rules* (New York: Academic, 1983); and Jochnowitz, "Everybody Likes Pizza, Doesn't He or She?" *American Speech*, 57 (1982), 198-203.

24. Scribner and Cole, *Psychology of Literacy* (Cambridge, Mass.: Harvard University Press, 1981); Gleitman and Gleitman, "Language Use and Language Judgment," in *Individual Differences in Language Ability and Language Behavior*, ed. Charles J. Fillmore, Daniel Kemper, and William S.-Y. Wang (New York: Academic Press, 1979), pp. 103-126.

25. There are several recent reviews of this developing body of research in psychology and child development: Irene Athey, "Language Development: Factors Related to Reading Development," *Journal of Educational Research*, 76 (1983), 197-203; James Flood and Paula Menyuk, "Metalinguistic Development and Reading/Writing Achievement," *Claremont Reading Conference Yearbook*, 46 (1982), 122-132; and the following four essays: David T. Hakes, "The Development of Metalinguistic Abilities: What Develops?," pp. 162-210; Stan A. Kuczaj, II, and Brooke Harbaugh, "What Children Think about the Speaking Capabilities of Other Persons and Things," pp. 211-227; Karen Saywitz and Louise Cherry Wilkinson, "Age-Related Differences in Metalinguistic Awareness," pp. 229-250; and Harriet Salatas Waters and Virginia S. Tinsley, "The Development of Verbal Self-Regulation: Relationships between Language, Cognition, and Behavior," pp. 251-277; all in *Language, Thought, and Culture*, Vol. II of *Language Development*, ed. Stan Kuczaj, Jr. (Hillsdale, N.J.: Lawrence Erlbaum, 1982). See also Joanne R. Nurss, "Research in Review: Linguistic Awareness and Learning to Read," *Young Children*, 35, No. 3 (1980), 57-66.

26. "Competing Value Systems in Inner City Schools," in *Children In and Out of School: Ethnography and Education*, ed. Perry Gilmore and Allar A. Giatthorn (Washington, D.C.: Center for Applied Linguistics, 1982), pp. 148-171; and "Locating the Frontier between Social and Psychological Factors in Linguistic Structure," in *Individual Differences in Language Ability and Language Behavior*, ed. Fillmore, Kemper, and Wang, pp. 327-340.

27. See, for example, Thomas Farrell, "IQ and Standard English," *CCC*, 34 (1983), 470-484; and the responses by Karen L. Greenberg and Patrick Hartwell, *CCC*, in press.

28. Jane W. Torrey, "Teaching Standard English to Speakers of Other Dialects," in *Applications of Linguistics: Selected Papers of the Second International Conference of Applied Linguistics*, ed. G. E. Perren and J. L. M. Trim (Cambridge, Mass.: Cambridge University Press, 1971), pp. 423-428; James W. Beers and Edmund H. Henderson, "A Study of the Developing Orthographic Concepts among First Graders," *RTE*, 11 (1977), 133-148.

29. See the error counts of Samuel A. Kirschner and G. Howard Poteet, "Non-Standard English Usage in the Writing of Black, White, and Hispanic Remedial English Students in an Urban Community College," *RTE*, 7 (1973), 351-355; and Marilyn Sternglass, "Close Similarities in Dialect Features of Black and White College Students in Remedial Composition Classes," *TESOL Quarterly*, 8 (1974), 271-283.

30. For reading, see the massive study by Kenneth S. Goodman and Yetta M. Goodman, *Reading of American Children Whose Language Is a Stable Rural Dialect of English or a Language Other Than English* (Washington, D.C.: National Institute of Education Final Report, 1978) ERIC 175 754; and the overview by Rudine Sims, "Dialect and Reading: Toward Redefining the Issues," in *Reader Meets Author/Bridging the Gap: A Psycholinguistic and Sociolinguistic Approach*, ed. Judith A. Langer and M. Tricia Smith-Burke (Newark, Del.: International Reading Association, 1982), pp. 222-232. For writing, see Patrick Hartwell, "Dialect Interference in Writing: A Critical View," *RTE*, 14 (1980), 101-118; and the anthology edited by Barry M. Kroll and Roberta J. Vann, *Exploring Speaking-Writing Relationships: Connections and Contrasts* (Urbana, Ill.: NCTE, 1981).

31. See, for example, Eric A. Havelock, *The Literary Revolution in Greece and Its Cultural Consequences* (Princeton, N.J.: Princeton University Press, 1982); Lesley Milroy on literacy in Dublin, *Language and Social Networks* (Oxford: Basil Blackwell, 1980); Ron Scollon and Suzanne B. K. Scollon on literacy in central Alaska, *Interethnic Communication: An Athabascan Case* (Austin, Tex.: Southwest Educational Development Laboratory Working Papers in Sociolinguistics, No. 59, 1979) ERIC 175 276; and Scribner and Cole on literacy in Liberia, *Psychology of Literacy* (see footnote 24).

32. See, for example, the anthology edited by Deborah Tannen, *Spoken and Written Language: Exploring Orality and Literacy* (Norwood, N.J.: Ablex, 1982); and Shirley Brice Heath's continuing work: "Protean Shapes in Literacy Events: Ever-Shifting Oral and Literate Traditions," in *Spoken and Written Language*, pp. 91-117; *Ways with Words: Language, Life and Work in Communities and Classrooms* (New York: Cambridge University Press, 1983); and "What No Bedtime Story Means," *Language in Society*, 11 (1982), 49-76.

33. For studies at the elementary level, see Dell H. Hymes, et al., eds., *Ethnographic Monitoring of Children's Acquisition of Reading/Language Arts Skills In and Out of the Classroom* (Washington, D.C.: National Institute of Education Final Report, 1981) ERIC 208 096. For studies at the secondary level, see James L. Collins and Michael M. Williamson, "Spoken Language and Semantic Abbreviation in Writing," *RTE*, 15 (1981), 23-36. And for studies at the college level, see Patrick Hartwell and Gene LoPresti, "Sentence Combining as Kid-Watching," in *Sentence Combining: Toward a Rhetorical Perspective*, ed. Donald A. Daiker, Andrew Kerek, and Max Morenberg (Carbondale: Southern Illinois University Press, in press).

34. Lloyd-Jones, "Romantic Revels—I Am Not You," *CCC*, 23 (1972), 251-271; and Young, "Concepts of Art and the Teaching of Writing," in *The Rhetorical Tradition and Modern Writing*, ed. James J. Murphy (New York: Modern Language Association, 1982), pp. 130-141.

35. For the romantic position, see Ann E. Berthoff, "Tolstoy, Vygotsky, and the Making of Meaning," *CCC*, 29 (1978), 249-255; Kenneth Dowst, "The Epistemic Approach," in *Eight Approaches to Teaching Composition*, ed. Timothy Donovan and Ben G. McClellan (Urbana, Ill.: NCTE, 1980), pp. 65-85; Peter Elbow, "The Challenge for Sentence Combining,"; and Donald Murray, "Following Language toward Meaning," both in *Sentence Combining: Toward a Rhetorical Perspective* (in press; see footnote 33); and Ian Pringle, "Why Teach Style? A Review-Essay," *CCC*, 34 (1983), 91-98.

For the classic position, see Christensen's "A Generative Rhetoric of the Sentence"; and Joseph Williams' "Defining Complexity," *CE*, 41 (1979), 595-609; and his *Style: Ten Lessons in Clarity and Grace* (see footnote 9).

36. Courtney B. Cazden and David K. Dickinson, "Language and Education: Standardization versus Cultural Pluralism," in *Language in the USA*, ed. Charles A. Ferguson and Shirley Brice Heath (New York: Cambridge University Press, 1931), pp. 446-468; and Carol Chomsky, "Developing Facility with Language Structure," in *Discovering Language with Children*, ed. Gay Su Pinnell (Urbana, Ill.: NCTE, 1980), pp. 56-59.

37. Boraas, "Format English Grammar and the Practical Mastery of English," Diss. University of Illinois, 1917; Asker, "Does Knowledge of Grammar Function?" *School and Society*, 17 (27 January 1923), 109-111; Ash, "An Experimental Evaluation of the Stylistic Approach in Teaching Composition in the Junior High School," *Journal of Experimental Education*, 4 (1935), 54-62; and Frogner, "A Study of the Relative Efficacy of a Grammatical and a Thought Approach to the Improvement of Sentence Structure in Grades Nine and Eleven," *School Review*, 47 (1939), 663-675.

38. "Research on Grammar and Usage and Its Implications for Teaching Writing," *Bulletin of the School of Education*, Indiana University, 36 (1960), pp. 13-14.

39. Meckel, "Research on Teaching Composition and Literature," in *Handbook of Research on Teaching*, ed. N. L. Gage (Chicago: Rand McNally, 1963), pp. 966-1006.

40. Bateman and Zidonis, *The Effect of a Study of Transformational Grammar on the Writing of Ninth and Tenth Graders* (Urbana, Ill.: NCTE, 1966); Mellon, *Transformational Sentence Combining: A Method for Enhancing the Development of Fluency in English Composition* (Urbana, Ill.:

NCTE, 1969); O'Hare, *Sentence-Combining: Improving Student Writing without Formal Grammar Instruction* (Urbana, Ill.: NCTE, 1971); Stotsky, "Sentence-Combining as a Curricular Activity: Its Effect on Written Language Development," *RTE*, 9 (1975), 30-72; and Van de Veghe, "Research in Written Composition: Fifteen Years of Investigation," ERIC 157 095.

41. Haynes, "Using Research in Preparing to Teach Writing," *English Journal*, 69, No. 1 (1978), 82-88; Holbrook, "ERIC/RCS Report: Whither (Wither) Grammar," *Language Arts*, 60 (1983), 259-263; Whiteman, "What we Can Learn from Writing Research," *Theory into Practice*, 19 (1980), 150-156; Bamberg, "Composition in the Secondary English Curriculum: Some Current Trends and Directions for the Eighties," *RTE*, 15 (1981), 257-266; and "Composition Instruction Does Make a Difference: A Comparison of the High School Preparation of College Freshmen in Regular and Remedial English Classes," *RTE*, 12 (1978), 47-59.

42. Emig, "Inquiry Paradigms and Writing," *CCC*, 33 (1982), 64-75; Carton and Castiglione, "Educational Linguistics: Defining the Domain," in *Psycholinguistic Research: Implications and Applications*, ed. Doris Aaronson and Robert W. Rieber (Hillsdale, N.J.: Lawrence Erlbaum, 1979), pp. 497-520.

Patrick Hartwell, Professor of English at Indiana University of Pennsylvania, is the co-author, with Robert H. Bentley, of *Open to Language: A New College Rhetoric* (Oxford University Press, 1982).

Professor Hartwell wishes to thank Wayne Edkin, Camden (New York) Public Schools; Michael Marier, Brigham Young University-Hawaii; and Ron Shook, Utah State University, for discussing these issues with him, and particularly to thank his colleague Dan J. Tannacito for references and discussion.

7

GRAMMAR THROUGH REVISION
Teaching Sentence Sense

To have something to say is a question of sleepless nights and
worry and endless ratiocination of a subject—of endless trying
to dig out the essential truth, the essential justice.
As a first premise you have to develop a conscience.

—F. Scott Fitzgerald□

Revising is deeper and more complex than correcting. When correcting, writers concentrate on the distractions that may affect the reader; when revising, writers concentrate on their intended meaning. When revising, writers reenter their writing to examine what they have written. They ask themselves if they have clearly expressed what they wanted to say. The answer determines the extent of subsequent manipulation of sentences and parts of sentences to best express their ideas. Clearly, when writers revise they quite literally have to make sense.

Because the act of revision is demanding, students should have had plenty of opportunity to write, to become fluent, to feel confident about putting words on paper. This confidence is essential. Feeling secure about writing provides the foundation for "re-visioning" or "seeing again." Without that security, students, who realize writing is an extension of themselves, shun anything that makes them look inadequate. If the proper groundwork has not been laid, or if revising demeans them in any way, they resort to mere recopying and miss the satisfaction that complements revising writing that matters to them.

Because everyone agrees that sentences are the basic constructed units of writing, revision calls upon students to spot problems of clarity and coherence in their sentences. Once students learn that sentences may be made complete by grammatical form and meaning (*She likes ice cream.*), or by context (*Not he!*), they have at their disposal the means to revise their writing in standard and unique ways.

In what seems to be a paradoxical statement, Frank Smith says, "It is often assumed that children need to understand metalinguistic terms like *noun, verb, sentence* (and *read* and *write*) in order to learn to read and write when in fact the opposite applies. One can learn to read and write without knowing the meaning of such terms; in fact, one cannot completely understand the terms without having first learned to read and write" (14-15). Likewise, students may revise their sentences without labeling every metalinguistic term in those sentences (*subject, predicate, noun, verb*). Yet, through the very act of revising their writing, they are better able to develop sentence sense. Usually accompanying this developing sentence sense is an understanding of not only the grammar of sentences but the power and meaning that sentences unleash when wrought by an informed writer. This understanding, in turn, enables students to revise with confidence.

REVISION IN THE PRODUCT PARADIGM

Typically, product-paradigm teachers taught grammar in isolation during a six-week grading period. Then they assigned a paper, most often due at the conclusion of the next six-week period. Students were expected to apply the previously learned grammar to the writing of that paper. Generally, there was no group work or conference time. And, while directives on deadline, format, length, and even topic were given, little direct instruction occurred on how to undertake the writing.

Sometime after the papers were handed in, teachers marked them up. Their red marks usually hovered over, around, or alongside punctuation, spelling, agreement, capitalization, sentence fragments, run-on sentences, and awkward phrasings, perhaps because these are easiest to grade, perhaps because teachers had little training in the teaching of writing. So obsessed did some teachers become with conformity to rules, they often bypassed what students attempted to say. So obsessed did students become with conforming to rules, they often bypassed any attempt at artistic expression, style, voice, or experimentation with true communication, to self or others.

Some teachers told students they could "revise" their papers for a higher grade. That meant rewriting them according to the marks made by the teacher, not rethinking the marks. Revising became a matter of getting those "stylistic infelicities" correct, not a matter of conveying meaning. In this school context, most often only teachers reentered the writing. Students, who often felt little ownership at the outset or during the writing, finally forfeited any sense of ownership when it was returned marked up with the thoughts, phrases, even the style of someone else. Few even bothered to "revise" for a higher grade. Those students who attempted to follow the rules gave what Howard Gardner calls "rote, ritualistic, or conventional performances. Such performances occur when students simply respond, in the desired symbol system, by spewing back the particular facts, concepts, or problem sets they have been taught" (9). Gardner explains that while this approach did not preclude comprehension, it did not guarantee it, either.

In this paradigm students began to think that longer, more syntactically mature sentences were "wrong" because most often in the weaving of meaning they created a run-on, erred with a comma splice, misplaced a modifier, dangled a participle, or produced an agreement slip. They began to belie the interconnections in their own minds by writing short, choppy sentences that invited redundancy but were safe. Mandated "never begin a sentence with *and* or *but*," students sometimes lost the one glue they had for coherence. With that loss went meaning. Papers read like some disjointed jigsaw puzzle. Often the linking sentence remained lodged in their minds and never appeared on their papers. Sometimes the writing did not even make sense to the writer. This eventually led to short, anorexic, or bland discourse or pages of sloppy thought – both proclaimed missed meaning. Both eventually led to negative feelings about writing.

Coordination became a decision about whether or not to put a comma before the coordinating conjunction – not about whether or not the intended relationship, clued by a coordinating conjunction, was evenly balanced. Subordination translated into merely memorizing subordinating conjunctions, not a deep understanding of subordination as a means of indicating the relative importance of persons, events, things, or ideas. Parallelisms presented still more difficulties. Neophyte writers avoided them because of their need for sophisticated punctuation. Not willing to risk a *C* grade because of a comma error, they lost the opportunity to play with the rhythm and repetition of language; they lost a way of making writing smoother; they lost a device for preventing unnecessary shifts in person, number, tense, and mood; and they lost the gratification of written self-expression.

Consider the frustration of both students and teachers – after weeks of drill on subjects and predicates, after weeks of doing exercises straight from grammar books – looking at papers teeming with mistakes. When students were allowed to write after weeks of stilted grammar exercises, they became confused by realistic syntax. More complicated structures, such as compound subjects and predicates, inverted word order, or subjects followed by *as well as* (for example, *The president as well as the secretary calls the class together*), did not always match the endless sentences they had diagrammed. Without application, all those wooden worksheets simply convinced students that grammar was something beyond them, something they could never master.

"I'm no good at grammar," they would intone, while teachers wailed, "They still don't know what a sentence is. How will they ever learn to revise?"

REVISION IN THE PROCESS PARADIGM

Most of this has changed. There are four solid reasons why revising is taught differently in the process paradigm. First, because contemporary scholars in composition and rhetoric make a distinction between grammar as an academic subject and grammar as a tool for writing improvement. (See Patrick Hartwell's article, "Grammar, Grammars, and the Teaching of Grammar" in chapter 6.) As an academic subject, grammar is a discipline unto itself. It is detailed, rigorous, and worthy of study. As a tool for improving writing, grammar serves a different purpose (Noguchi 17). Grammar as a tool in writing is endemic to revising—it is sentence sense.

Second, research studies, such as those by the team Richard Braddock, Richard Lloyd-Jones, and Lowell Schoer and by George Hillocks, criticize formal grammar instruction in schools. Hillocks contends:

> The study of traditional school grammar (i.e., the definition of parts of speech, the parsing of sentences, etc.) has no effect on raising the quality of student writing. Every other focus of instruction examined in this review is stronger. Taught in certain ways, grammar and mechanics instruction has a deleterious effect on student writing. In some studies, a heavy emphasis on mechanics and usage (e.g., marking every error) resulted in significant losses in overall quality. School boards, administrators, and teachers who impose the systematic study of traditional school grammar on their students over lengthy periods of time in the name of teaching writing do them a gross disservice which should not be tolerated by anyone concerned with the effective teaching of good writing. (1963, 248-249)

Third, research from cognitive developmentalists suggests that teaching what is developmentally appropriate for students better advances that learning. Just as there are natural stages in physical development, just as there are natural stages in the development of speech, so, too, there are natural stages in the acquisition of language skills. Compare children stumbling as they learn to walk, children mispronouncing or misusing words as they learn new vocabulary, to students making mistakes in writing. The child who falls when first walking is not berated; the child is encouraged to get up and try again. The child who misspeaks is not humiliated; the word is spoken correctly, and the child is encouraged to try again. So, too, when a student writes. Errors need not be red-inked and punished with a low grade. Discussing the writing, highlighting the good points, modeling how to revise it, and encouraging students to try again helps students grow into written expression. "Students who have not yet reached a level of formal operational thought or a level of ego development where they can step outside themselves should not be forced into grammar exercises that can have no meaning for them" (Sanborn 77). Teaching the grammar that students need to write effectively, and using language widely and constantly through revising, enhances both their writing and their understanding of grammar and how language works.

Fourth, new information about the way the human mind works indicates that learning grammar is an incredibly complicated process. Antonio R. Damasio and Hanna Damasio, medical doctors who have been studying the neural basis of language for two decades, believe language is processed by the brain through three interacting sets of structures. One is a large collection of neural systems that represents anything that a person does, feels, or thinks. Another is a smaller number of neural systems that assembles word forms and generates sentences. The third mediates between those two. Further, Damasio and Damasio point out that the idea of mediation is also held by psycholinguists Willem J. M. Levelt and Merrill F. Garret (89-90). This oversimplification serves only to illustrate that teaching grammar is both physical and psycholinguistic. Also consider that the brain holds as many neurons as there are stars in the Milky Way, with the potential of making 1 million-billion connections (Nash 81), and the notion of equating the memorization of rules with learning grammar seems primitive. By contrast, the practice of teaching grammar within the writing process through revision parallels the brain's natural processes of making meaningful connections.

Contrary to those who believe otherwise, grammar, especially grammar through revision, remains important in the process paradigm. As Constance Weaver says in *Grammar for Teachers*, "Students *do* need to develop a good intuitive sense of grammar, but they can do this best through *indirect* rather than direct instruction. Instead of formally teaching them grammar, we need to give them plenty of structured and unstructured opportunities to deal with language directly" (5). The question, therefore, is not if grammar should be taught, but when and how grammar should be taught. In short, teaching grammar in the process paradigm is a matter of timing (Carroll 51). "Ideally, this grammar [as a tool for writing] will be integrated with writing instruction and presented as quickly as possible so that students can use it during the revision or proofreading states of writing" (Noguchi 18). Informed teachers understand that for students to truly understand grammar, they must learn it and apply it within the writing process. These teachers do not teach grammar in isolation, rather they incorporate it after students have generated writing and want to revise it for an audience. As Joseph Doenges, Superintendent of the Boerne ISD Schools, says, "What difference does it make if writing skills are taught in specific grammar lessons or as a composing process? The difference is significant in terms of impact on numbers of students." He goes on to explain that while the more academically gifted students will become effective writers no matter how they are taught, writing as a process turns almost everyone into a writer. He concludes, "Just as everyone should be able to read in order to be described as literate, so should everyone be able to write in order to be described as educated" (3).

RATIOCINATION AS REVISION

Definition of Ratiocination. Ratiocination is a systematic revision strategy (see pages 240-245). It invites students, through a process of coding and decoding clues, to manipulate sentences, consider syntax and diction, activate verbs, vary sentence beginnings, avoid weak repetition, refresh clichés, and in general develop and clarify their thinking and writing.

When teachers teach ratiocination, they

1. share visual codes for clues students may use to reenter their writing;

2. provide a schema for decoding these clues;

3. model by using the students' sentences as examples; and

4. teach grammar within the writing process.

(Reprinted with special permission of King Features Syndicate.)

When students use ratiocination, they

1. see a way to reenter their writing;

2. learn concrete alternatives to convey their meaning;

3. acquire models to reference as they revise;

4. use higher-level thinking skills; and

5. mark up their own writing.

Rationale for Ratiocination

Using ratiocination as a revising strategy fits what Howard Gardner calls "performances of disciplinary (or genuine) understanding. Such performances occur when students are able to take information and skills they have learned in school or other settings and apply them flexibly and appropriately in a new and at least somewhat unanticipated situation" (9).

With ratiocination, students take "the information and skills" of grammar, and they, not the teachers, do the reentering. Their writings continually present "other settings." And when students mark their own papers by coding the clues, then thinking through the decoding of those clues to make their meaning clearer, they are applying that information "in a new and at least somewhat unanticipated situation."

Ratiocination does what Wayne Booth suggests in "Rhetoric, Mere Rhetoric, and Reality": "instead [of spending a month or so preparing to pass competency exams and saving the rest of our time for genuine education] that we go about it the other way 'round, that if we think hard enough about our own notions of the basics, and then teach with full devotion according to those notions, we will find the competencies following quite naturally" (15).

Further, ratiocination as revision enables the teaching of grammar within the writing process, thereby reinforcing findings that appeared as early as 1936. At that time the Curriculum Commission of the National Council of Teachers of English (NCTE) recommended "all teaching of grammar separate from the manipulation of sentences be discontinued ... since every scientific attempt to prove that knowledge of grammar is useful has failed" (Monroe 392). In other words, if students do not apply the grammar they learn, there is some question as to the degree of their learning.

A Sample Lesson Using Ratiocination: Sentence Variety and Parts of Speech

Explanation. Using ratiocination supports instruction within a context, one of the problems noted over twenty years ago by the team Braddock, Lloyd-Jones, and Schoer. "The teaching of formal grammar has a negligible or, because it usually displaces some instruction and practice in composition, even a harmful effect on improvement in writing" (38). For instance, students, who begin almost every sentence with *and* or *and then* because they are attempting to keep all their thoughts together, are not well served by the dictum, "Never begin a sentence with *and*." Taking something away from students without replacing it with something better usually results in frustration, or in this case, incoherence. Better to provide other ways to begin a sentence; and along the way teach or reteach parts of speech and sentence variety.

Implementation

1. Students fold a sheet of paper in quarters lengthwise. On that slim strip they list the first word of each sentence from their papers.

2. Invite several students to share their lists. As they do, write their lists on the board.

3. Explain the purpose of these lists. They provide writers with visual ways to reenter their writing to add sentence variety.

4. Read excerpts to show how, by varying sentence beginnings, writers create a certain rhythm and make their writing enjoyable.

5. On the board, circle one word in each list: a repeated article; *it; and, and then*, or *then*; or a repetitive noun or pronoun.

6. Invite the students whose work you are using as examples to accept the challenge to change the circled word, rearrange the sentence, or combine sentences.

7. All other students challenge themselves by choosing a word on their lists to circle.

8. On the overhead projector, display a chart similar to the one in figure 7.1 or one adapted for the grade level. In the figure, the parts of speech are in a context and should be analyzed within that context.

9. Review the functions of the parts of speech; then discuss the effectiveness of using different openers.

10. Together revise a sentence from the teacher's writing as a model.

11. Students independently revise the sentences with the word they circled.

12. Students who have a list on the board share their "before" and "after" sentences. Discuss.

> *"OK Ben, you circled* And. *Read your before and after sentences."*
> *"And we went for a hamburger after the game. We went for a hamburger after the game."*
> *"Great. What did you do to make that change?"*
> *"Dropped the And."*
> *"How did you come up with that, Ben?"*
> *"I just looked around the and, and discovered I didn't need it."*
> *"What a good idea. Sometimes doing something so simple helps our writing — just taking a look around the problem. Now the sentence begins with what part of speech?"*
> *"Pronoun."*
> *"So when you work on your own sentences, see if a pronoun might be what you need. You might want to follow Ben's idea. Look around. Now let's talk about Luci's sentence."*

13. Ask several students who do not have lists on the board but challenged themselves to share their "before" and "after" sentences.

14. Suggest that students use these peer models and the chart as they continue through their writing.

15. While they revise, walk around and monitor. Some students may require individual help.

Fig. 7.1. Sample overhead for use in studying sentence variety.

Variations of Sentence Beginnings

NOUN	Mary is an intelligent girl and pretty, too.
PRONOUN	He participated in the race.
ARTICLE	The champion received the gold trophy.
GERUND	Traveling can be inspirational, educational, and fun.
INFINITIVE	To succeed in life is her ambition.
ADVERB	Slowly and carefully, he walked through the forest.
PARTICIPLE	Having expressed his view, he left for class.
ADVERB CLAUSE	While Juan fished, Jesse worked.
EXPLETIVE	There are only six days until summer vacation.
PREPOSITIONAL PHRASE	Over the bridge the cars passed rapidly.
NOUN CLAUSE	That Mother will recover from her fall, is our wish.
ADJECTIVE	Yellow and white daisies covered the windowsill.

Remarks. When students use ratiocination with their own writing, mindless repetitive exercises that seem purposeless are eliminated. Consequently, ratiocination is one way to answer Bullock's assertion in *A Language for Life*:

> It has not been established by research that systematic attention to skill and technique has no beneficial effect on the handling of language. What has been shown is that the teaching of traditional analytic grammar does not appear to improve performance in writing. This is not to suggest that there is no place for any kind of exercises at any time and in any form.... What *is* questionable is the practice of setting exercises for the whole class, irrespective of need, and assuming that this will improve every pupil's ability to handle English.... Most [exercises] give the child no useful insight into language and many actually mislead him. (171)

Working with sentences from students' writing intensifies the interest of the class and says loudly that the teacher wants to offer help *before* the paper is handed in to be graded. Grappling with a student's sentence on the board as a class creates bonds and undergirds the purpose for learning—to more effectively communicate reflexively or extensively.

When students identify and then circle "to be" verbs to eliminate the passive or to replace them with more precise verbs, they are involved in the basics of grammar, choice, thinking, and revision. They are constantly asking themselves, "Is this the best possible way to say this?" When students underline sentences in alternating colors to avoid monotony and add zip to their writing, they are getting at what is basic to powerful writing. When they vary sentence order to eliminate the consistent and boring subject-verb-complement order of the declarative sentence, they understand the rhetoric of emphasis. When students label sentences "stringy" and realize they have lost the reader along the string, they demonstrate the importance of knowing their audience. When students rework a knotted, convoluted sentence that confuses rather than convinces, they show a knowledge of purpose in writing. When students watch wordiness, they indicate a grasp of the need for directness and accuracy of expression. In short, when students employ ratiocination to their writing they are doing what skilled writers do all the time. They are revising.

Philosopher and educator Alfred North Whitehead, in *The Aims of Education and Other Essays*, appeals to "practical teachers" (5) to beware of " 'inert ideas'—ideas that are merely received into the mind without being utilized, or tested, or thrown into fresh combinations" (1). Using ratiocination as revision enables students to grapple with what they are trying to say. Conversely, working with worksheets, workbooks, or the grammar book without offering students the chance to use, test, or try these concepts in their own writing, renders those exercises inert. They remain on the page as mindless and boring; students see little connection between those exercises and their own writing.

SENTENCE SENSE

Three noticeable problems disturb sentence sense: fragments, comma splices, and run-on sentences. Sometimes these occur because of a lack of sentence sense, but most often they occur because of poor proofreading skills or sloppy editing.

Fragments. A fragment is defined as an incomplete sentence that is punctuated as a sentence. A fragment is a piece of something, a splinter. If a splinter gets under the skin, it irritates. It does not belong there. So, too, with a splinter or fragment of writing; it gets under the reader's skin and irritates, usually because it does not make sense or because the reader has to work harder at understanding the meaning.

There are four reasons why fragments happen. First, the writer does not understand what a sentence is. Often this is the first assumption when reading a fragment in a student's writing, but that assumption invites reconsideration. Unless most of the writing contains fragments, more than likely the student has sentence sense but is trying something rhetorical or needs help with punctuation.

Second, the writer has a subordinate idea but does not know how to punctuate it. Most often introductory modifiers and concluding modifiers cause this difficulty. For example:

Although he was the most qualified for the job. He didn't get hired.

The line at the voting booth was a mile long. Which caused some people to leave.

Teaching students how to link ideas and punctuate that link helps this problem. Sometimes asking the student to rephrase the idea makes a difference.

Third, the writer wants to emphasize rhetorically some word, clause, or phrase. This is an acceptable use of fragments. Fragments are most commonly used as answers to questions or as exclamations, but they also may be used for emphasis. John Barth, the novelist, began his essay "Writing: Can It Be Taught?" with, "Can it be learned? Sure" (1). Later in the essay he writes, "Not necessarily by a hotshot writer, either, though not impossibly by one" (37). Of course this line makes sense in context, but it also works as a fragment. Because it makes an unusual read, the reader pauses, thinks a minute. The point is, fragments are used for rhetorical effect. Therefore, it is prudent to find out what the budding writer means before deciding a fragment requires drill on subjects and predicates or before attempts at style or effect are smothered.

Finally, the writer has answered questions, usually on worksheets, that invite the "because" clause, for example, "I like chocolate. Because it's sweet." There are three solutions to this problem. First, do not use worksheets that invite brief answers that become internalized as correct and show up later as irritating splinters. Second, create a literate, print-rich environment where students are exposed to much reading and writing and have opportunity to talk about the way writers write. Third, work with sentence combining (see pages 232-234).

Comma Splices. Comma splices, sometimes called comma faults, occur when two main clauses (grammatical sentences) are joined by a comma. They pervade students' writing. For example, it is not unusual to see sentences such as: "I love my two dogs, they love me." The best way to take care of comma splices is by using the sample comma chart in figure 6.1 (see page 190).

Run-on Sentences. Run-on sentences, or fused sentences, are two sentences run together with no punctuation. For example: "I love my two dogs they love me." This problem is more often caused by sloppiness or a disregard for the writing than by the inability to see two simple sentences in the construction. The sample comma chart (fig. 6.1) may help students overcome this problem.

Baffled by students in freshman comp who persisted in comma faults and run-on sentences, I decided to try an off-beat solution. My thinking was that the traditional approaches didn't seem to take. Here these students were, after at least 12 years of school, popping commas between main clauses. Surely they could recognize a main clause as a simple sentence. So I devised a plan.

I located a heavy wooden chair, the kind teachers used years ago, and I lugged it to class well before the students arrived. I bought some rope, the heavy-duty type suitable for tow-truck use. Then I pocketed a thumb-tack. I was ready.

"I've got a problem," I confided to the class. "I want to use this chair to introduce theater of the absurd to my seniors, but I need to hang it from the ceiling." Accustomed to my sometimes unorthodox approaches to lessons, they thought that seemed cool. "But it's awfully heavy. Wouldn't you agree?" And I called on the biggest fellow in the class to pick it up.

In true macho style, he lifted the chair with one hand but patronized me by agreeing that to me it would probably seem heavy.

"I thought I'd use this rope to suspend it," I continued. "Where do you think I should hang it?" As I had hoped, they thought I should use the beam. The material on the ceiling itself didn't look too sturdy.

So I tied the rope to the back of the chair, lifting it slightly in the direction of the beam. Then I took out the thumb-tack. At first, perhaps to be polite, they just looked at the tack and me. Then they burst into laughter, "You can't use that!" They chorused.

"Why not?" I asked, keeping to my plan.

"It's not strong enough. It won't hold."

I walked to the board and wrote, "I ran up the stairs, I entered my office."

"You do it all the time," I said. "You join two strong sentences with a weak punctuation mark."

That object lesson was a hit. Did it totally obliterate comma splices and run-on sentences? Not entirely, but they definitely diminished. Sometimes a nonstandard play wins the game!

SENTENCE COMBINING

Sentence combining—pioneered by Kellogg W. Hunt and John Mellon, extended by Frank O'Hare and popularized by William Strong and William L. Stull—is a practical and effective way to help students strengthen their writing skills and practice stylistic choices. The idea is to enable students to create more syntactically mature sentences through oral and written practice. That is, the words in the sentences (the syntax) are put together better. They no longer read as short, choppy bits. They contain "(1) the increasing modification of nouns by large clusters of adjectives, relative clauses, and reduced relative clauses; (2) the increasing use of nominalizations other than nouns and pronouns for subjects and objects (clauses and infinitival and gerundive construction, all increasingly unique); and (3) the embedding of sentences to an increasing depth" (Moffett 162-163). Combined sentences have within them embedded or conjoined ideas. These sentences are generally longer, more complex, more syntactically versatile, and constructed with more maturity. (See chapter 14, page 459.)

By its very nature, sentence combining invites elaboration through the expansion and combination of simple sentences. For example, a student might write the following series of simple sentences, each with the predictable sentence structure: subject, verb, complement.

> I went to the football game. I saw the cheerleaders. They were dressed in blue and white. I saw the coaches. They looked worried. This was a tough game. Mojo had a reputation. They always won.

After practicing some sentence combining, that student might manipulate those sentences into several alternatives, each more syntactically mature than the original.

Problems with Sentence Combining

Earlier in this chapter, sentence combining was offered as one way students could solve problems of sentence variety. When ratiocinating, students often combine several sentences when meaning calls for it or it seems appropriate to do so. All too often, however, isolated, repeated exercises on combining sentences are merely a slightly more sophisticated version of doing worksheets. Students do not grapple with meaning; they fool around with syntax. In time, this becomes boring and meaningless.

> *As I walked down the hall, I passed Mrs. B. toting the overhead projector into the classroom. Further down the hall, two students stood by their lockers. I couldn't help overhearing their conversation.*
> *"Did you see Mrs. B.?" one asked. "She's got the overhead."*
> *"That means another day of sentence combining," the other groaned.*

Of course, anything can be overdone. The point is, while sentence combining exercises may provide practice in gaining fluency in syntax, as with every other skill, students should immediately make application in their writing.

Balance of instruction is all. Juxtaposing the obviously more sophisticated manner of expressing ideas effectively (i.e., a range of ideas presented through a hierarchy or subordination) with a brief statement makes the point that length is not the aim in writing, clarity is. Sometimes sentences need levels of embedding to match the complexity of the thought. Consider Merlin's plea to Stilicho in Mary Stewart's *The Last Enchantment*, "It was grim business, and it took a long time, not least because, when he would have left me to go for help, I begged him, in terms of which I am now ashamed, not to leave me" (444). Other times fewer words say more. They become syntactical exclamation points. Consider the impact of the shortest sentence in the New Testament: "Jesus wept."

Making Sentence Combining Concrete: Seven Examples

Explanation. There are several ways to teach sentence combining: large group, small group, pairs, and individually. The combinations may be oral or written. No matter which approach is taken, make the point repeatedly that there are many ways to combine sentences; one way is not inherently better than another. Sometimes one combination is preferred as a matter of style; sometimes a combination just works better or sounds better in a given context. At first, avoid focusing too much on terminology (i.e., identifying parts of speech or sentence patterns). Rather, make the experience interesting and fun.

Implementation—Introduction. Write several short sentences on the board or overhead and, with the class, combine them in several different ways. (Strong and Stull offer many exercises and are good sources for sentences.) This sets a positive tone, suggests everyone can participate, and models how sentence combining is done.

Implementation—Students' Writing. Ask students to read aloud several short sentences from their writing. Write these on the board or overhead and, working with the class, combine them. This affords immediate application, and it lets students know the purpose of sentence combining.

Implementation—Class Clusters. Prepare a transparency of several clusters of sentences. Mask off those not under consideration. Invite different students to orally combine each cluster. Talk about the number of different ways a group of sentences may be combined. As students become comfortable with this activity, begin challenging them. "Who can begin this cluster with a noun? Would anybody venture beginning it with a participle or gerund (or, for the younger students, with an *ing* word)? I can think of still another way to say this. Can anyone else?" This strategy is particularly good for the aural learner. Certain unfamiliar sentence patterns begin to "sound right."

Write some of the suggested combinations on another transparency or on the board. This makes the combined sentences visual, thereby helping the visual learner.

Implementation—Independent Clusters. Divide students into groups. Each group works with a series of clusters related to a single topic. For example, Strong's topics range from hamburgers to health care. A scribe in each group writes out the suggested combinations, which the group later shares with the class or hands in. The group stars the combination it thinks is best or most effective. The group presents rationales for its decision. These collaborative sessions enhance learning, are less threatening than large-group work, and are enjoyable.

This strategy may be used with pairs of students or with students working individually.

Implementation—Gateway to Other Topics. Use sentence combining as a way into grammar, spelling, and organization. Begin using parts of speech as you receive suggested combinations. Insist on accuracy in spelling. Discuss the logic of coordinations, subordinations, transitions, and levels of supporting information.

Implementation—Literature. Use sentence combining with literature. Both Strong and Stull offer such clusters. As students become facile with sentence combining, they often enjoy comparing their combinations to the original.

Implementation—Rhetoric. Use sentence combining to discuss the rhetoric of the combined sentences.

NOTE: While most texts refer to the sentences to be combined as "kernel sentences" and the process as "transformations," the more general terms are used here to avoid any confusion with transformational grammar.

Remarks. In his 1986 study, William Strong, author of several books on sentence combining, presents comprehensive documentation on the theory and research of sentence combining. Following is a truncation of his concluding assumptions:

1. Sentence combining is not real writing. It is a skill-building adjunct to a language/ composition program.

2. Sentence combining is not a model of the composing process. Most sentence combining pertains to revision and editing, not invention or drafting.

3. Sentence combining exercises may be cued, which target transformations, or open, which teach stylistic decision making.

4. Sentence combining is one approach to improve syntactic fluency.

5. Sentence combining instruction assumes that mistakes are natural and provide feedback that enables learning.

6. Sentence combining should move from oral rehearsal to written transcription.

7. Sentence combining can be used to teach virtually any language/composition concept inductively.

8. Sentence combining requires that teachers model editing and decision making skills with students.

9. Sentence combining is mainly a synthetic process, not an analytic one.

10. Sentence combining works best when done two or three times a week for short periods and when transfer is made to real writing. (22)

PROFESSIONAL AND STUDENT WRITERS REVISE

Most writers agree that revising is a significant aspect of the writing process. In *Writers at Work*, the first in the series of the Paris Review interviews, Frank O'Connor answered the question "Do you rewrite?" with "Endlessly, endlessly, endlessly. And keep on rewriting" (Cowley 168). This series of books captures not only the words of respected authors but also excerpts of their works in progress, including pages of the author's actual writing that show revision processes.

> *Second-grade writers are no different. They, too, have a sense of the need for endless revision. For example, Latoya Fennell, a second-grade student who loves to write about sharks, told me she worked on her two-page shark story for "one whole week. I wrote it about twenty thousand times," she said proudly. I looked over one of those drafts. Latoya had color coded every then. In one part, five thens glowed from her draft:*
>
> > ⚓ Then *we went back to the beach and picked up seashells.* Then *I went into the beach water.* Then *these black fish started swimming.* Then *I stepped up and the fish swam away.* Then *I screamed and ran back to shore.*

Curious about how Latoya revised this section, I found her book hanging on the wall and flipped through it until I found that same section. It read:

> ⚔ *We went back to the beach and picked up seashells. Then I went into the beach water and these black fish started swimming around my leg. I stepped up and the fish swam away, then I screamed and ran back to shore.*

After marking up her own paper, Latoya was able to focus in on the then *words. She obviously considered some alternatives and made some decisions. She dropped the first* then, *kept the second, and eliminated the third by combining two sentences. And, as she combined them, she must have remembered that important detail "around my leg." She dropped the next* then, *finally using the last one as meaning* consequently. *I told Latoya she was truly a writer.*

Latoya's revision process is similar to James Thurber's. When an interviewer asked James Thurber, "Is the act of writing easy for you?" he replied, "For me it's mostly a question of rewriting.... A story I've been working on—'The Train on Track Six,' it's called—was rewritten 15 complete times. There must have been close to 240,000 words in all the manuscripts put together, and I must have spent 2,000 hours working on it. Yet the finished version can't be more than 20,000 words" (88).

When queried, "Do you do much rewriting?" Thornton Wilder chose to quote a poet. "I forget which of the great sonneteers said: 'One line in the fourteen comes from the ceiling; the others have to be adjusted around it.' Well, likewise there are passages in every novel whose first writing is pretty much the last. But it's the joint and cement between those spontaneous passages that take a great deal of rewriting" (105). William Faulkner admits that he wrote *The Sound and the Fury* five separate times (130).

May Sarton describes her process thus, "The revision process is fascinating to me. Some of my poems have gone through 60 or more drafts by the time I'm satisfied. I think it's very important for poets to have others read their work, get all the criticism they can as well as be extremely self-critical" (Strickland 157). As for revising a novel, Sarton says, "Some of this shaping is done when one has roughed out the whole thing and can revise for the dynamics of each scene in relation to the dynamics of the whole. I find myself cutting ruthlessly to keep the rising curve clean" (Strickland 157). In either case, poetry or the novel, Sarton knows that the process of revising is organic to the balance of the final outcome.

When students get hooked on ratiocination, they share Sarton's fascination. They begin to realize their own power. This is especially true of middle school or junior high school students. With so much in their lives beyond their control—their growth, their awkwardness, even their privileges—they revel in revision that is presented as a form of power.

> *Paul Gonzales wrote about a Hispanic boy named Bamboo. At first Paul has the boy crying in the face of danger from a gang. "On that Tuesday was the saddest day of Bamboo's life." In later drafts, however, Paul flexes his muscles, feels the power of writing, and takes control of Bamboo's fate, concluding his story, "On that Tuesday, Bamboo showed all the other boys his secret all right. He had been studying karate. And after that they didn't bother him no more."*
> *Paul's teacher remarked on how hard Paul had worked on that story. "I think once he thought about how he was like Bamboo, how the big boys often picked on him, he got caught up in it."*

In a personal glimpse, Anaïs Nin describes Henry Miller's process as talking through the revising. She tells how she "read the pages as he unwound them from the typewriter," then how they "talked endlessly about his work, always in the same manner, Henry flowing, gushing, spilling, spreading, scattering, and I weaving together tenaciously" (Blythe 258).

Pulitzer Prize-winning journalist for the *Boston Herald*, contributing editor of *Time*, and professor of English at the University of New Hampshire, Donald M. Murray claims, "All good writing is rewriting.... Rearrange the sentence order so that you have strong sentences at the end of each paragraph and of the theme.... Re-writing helps you say what you mean. As you re-write, and *only* as you re-write, do you begin to become a writer" (Murray 230).

> *Sylvia Van, a twelfth-grade student at Clements High School, Fort Bend ISD, Texas, rearranged sentences in her "A Filial Obligation" at least three times, finally coming up with this:*

> ⚡ *Mankind has never treated Mother Nature well. From the beginning of time we have cut down forests and helped ourselves to generous portions of Mother Nature's supply of wildlife. We have burned fields and woods, polluted streams and lakes, and we still show no signs of correcting our bratty behavior.*

> *It's the word* bratty *that works, and when Sylvia landed that word in that phrase, she knew the truth of Donald Murray's words, "good writing is re-writing."*

Just as professional writers realize the importance of revising, so do student writers. Students who have teachers who write; students who see the revisions of professional writers in books like *Writers at Work*; students who have the opportunity to hear professional writers; students who have commitment to writing, who are engaged in the process, who feel ownership over their writing: These students know writing is the most rigorous intellectual activity in which a person can engage—taking an idea, something ephemeral, and embodying it on the page so that others may understand it. These students ratiocinate. They think about their meaning; they consider their structure. They make decisions. They revise.

> *Kelley Smith entered her kindergarten classroom with a bag from McDonald's. The 5-year-olds eyed her and the bag with interest. They had been Ms. Smith's students for almost a year now. They were used to her unusual but effective ways to teach; they broke into smiles and questions. "What's in the bag?" "Are we gonna eat hamburgers today?"*

> *"You know, Friends, how much Ms. Smith likes a hamburger." They nodded. "Well, yesterday I stopped for one to take home. When I opened it, this is what I saw." She unwrapped the hamburger so everyone could see a believable looking burger made from materials and felt. She opened the bun to reveal a lonely-looking piece of dark brown felt. The students groaned. At this, Ms. Smith said, "Dry. Whoever made my hamburger forgot to put on all the things to juice it up. I just got a plain piece of meat. I like my hamburgers juicy. What do you like on your hamburgers?"*

> *The students volunteered everything from cheese to jalapeno peppers. As they mentioned an item, Ms. Smith produced it from the bag and added it to the burger. When they had exhausted all the possibilities, she closed the bun. The burger did indeed look juicier. "That's what we need to do with our writing," she said. "Sometimes it is dry and we need to juice it up."*

> *She turned to a chart story the children had written. "Let's see how we can juice up the story we wrote yesterday."*

Soon the children were offering adjectives, even clauses and phrases, although they didn't call them that. In their minds, they were just busy adding juice to a dry story.

"Where's the meat in this sentence?" Ms. Smith asked as she pointed to Rosie walked to the store. *"What's most important?"*

They thought Rosie and the store were important. Ms. Smith coded those two words with bright red circles. "How can we juice Rosie and the store up?" she nudged.

After lots of fun and laughter, the students came up with: Rosie the funny hen walked to the pizza place.

"Do you think we should tell what she got there?"

They thought they should, and so they added, "and bought a pepperoni pizza with extra onions."

"Do you think we should tell what Rosie was doing before?"

They thought they better do that, so they added, "After the haystack."

"What about the fox? Should we leave him out of this?"

They thought they better not, so they added another sentence. "She didn't give the fox any."

"Let's read our juicier writing together," Ms. Smith suggested.

They read, "After the haystack, Rosie the funny hen walked to the pizza place and bought a pepperoni pizza with extra onions. She didn't give the fox any."

"Which one do you like better?" Ms. Smith asked.

"The juicier one," they chorused.

"Why is that?"

" 'Cause it's got more things." This made Ms. Smith smile. So effective were the results of this hamburger revision, I shared the idea with other teachers. Recently a high school teacher called. "I tried the hamburger with my tenth-graders," she said. "They loved it. It has made a difference in their attitude toward revising. Now they just call it 'juicing' and do it more than they ever did revising."

APPLICATION

Choose one of your drafts. Color code all the "to be" verbs. Count the number and challenge yourself to rid your paper of half of them using the decoding alternatives on page 241. Get with a partner and compare your revisions with the originals. Draw conclusions.

WORKS CITED

Barth, John. "Writing: Can It Be Taught?" *The New York Times Book Review*, 16 June 1985, sec. 7, 36-37.

Blythe, Ronald, ed. *The Pleasures of Diaries: Four Centuries of Private Writing*. New York: Pantheon Books, 1989.

Booth, Wayne. "Rhetoric, Mere Rhetoric, and Reality: Or, My Basics Are More Basic Than Your Basics." In *The English Curriculum Under Fire*, edited by George Hillocks, Jr. Urbana, IL: National Council of Teachers of English, 1982.

Braddock, Richard, Richard Lloyd-Jones, and Lowell Schoer. *Research in Written Composition*. Urbana, IL: National Council of Teachers of English, 1963.

Bullock, Sir A. *A Language for Life*. London: Her Majesty's Stationery Office, 1975.

Carroll, Joyce Armstrong. "Grappling with Grammar: A Matter of Timing." *Florida English Journal* 23 (Spring 1987): 51-56.

Cowley, Malcolm, ed. "William Faulkner." In *Writers at Work*. The *Paris Review* Interviews, First Series. New York: Penguin Books, 1958.

_____. "James Thurber." In *Writers at Work*. The *Paris Review* Interviews, First Series. New York: Penguin Books, 1958.

_____. "Thornton Wilder." In *Writers at Work*. The *Paris Review* Interviews, First Series. New York: Penguin Books, 1958.

Damasio, Antonio R., and Hanna Damasio. "Brain and Language." *Scientific American* (September 1992): 89-95.

Doenges, Joseph. "Superintendent's Report: Shifting the Emphasis in the BISD Writing Program." *Hill Country Recorder* (November 4, 1992): 3.

Gardner, Howard. *The Unschooled Mind: How Children Think and How Schools Should Teach*. New York: Basic Books, 1991.

Hillocks, George Jr. *Research on Written Composition: New Directions for Teaching*. Urbana, IL: National Council of Teachers of English, 1986.

Hillocks, George Jr., ed. *The English Curriculum Under Fire*. Urbana, IL: National Council of Teachers of English, 1982.

Hunt, Kellogg W. *Grammatical Structures Written at Three Grade Levels*. Champaign, IL: National Council of Teachers of English, 1965.

Mellon, John C. *Transformational Sentence-Combining: A Method for Enhancing the Development of Syntactic Fluency in English Composition*. Champaign, IL: National Council of Teachers of English, 1969.

Moffett, James. *Teaching the Universe of Discourse*. Boston: Houghton Mifflin, 1968.

Monroe, Walter S., ed. *Encyclopedia of Educational Research*, rev. ed. New York: Macmillan, 1950.

Murray, Donald M. *A Writer Teaches Writing: A Practical Method of Teaching Composition*. New York: Houghton Mifflin, 1968.

Nash, J. Madeleine. "The Frontier Within." *Time*, Vol. 140, no. 27 (Special Issue, Fall 1992), 81-82.

Noguchi, Rei R. *Grammar and the Teaching of Writing*. Urbana, IL: National Council of Teachers of English, 1991.

O'Hare, Frank. *The Effect of Sentence-Combining Practice Not Dependent on Formal Knowledge of Grammar on Student Writing*. Urbana, IL: National Council of Teachers of English, 1973.

Sanborn, Jean. "Grammar: Good Wine Before Its Time." *English Journal* (March 1986): 72-79.

Smith, Frank. *Writing and the Writer*. New York: Holt, Rinehart & Winston, 1982.

Stewart, Mary. *The Last Enchantment*. New York: William Morrow, 1979.

Strickland, Bill, ed. *On Being a Writer*. Cincinnati, OH: Writer's Digest Books, 1989.

Strong, William. *Creative Approaches to Sentence Combining*. Urbana, IL: ERIC, 1986.

_____. *Sentence Combining*. New York: Random House, 1983.

Stull, William L. *Combining & Creating*. New York: Holt, Rinehart & Winston, 1983.

Weaver, Constance. *Grammar for Teachers: Perspectives and Definitions*. Urbana, IL: National Council of Teachers of English, 1979.

Whitehead, Alfred North. *The Aims of Education and Other Essays*. New York: Free Press, 1968.

"Ratiocination and Revision, or Clues in the Written Draft"

JOYCE ARMSTRONG CARROLL

(From *English Journal*, November 1982. Copyright 1982 by the National Council of Teachers of English. Reprinted with permission.)

Commentary

Carroll chronicles a childhood in which words and wonder were a natural part of growing-up. Unfortunately, today's society seems to militate against childhoods in which imagination and rich reading experiences abound. Day care, Little League, T-ball, computer camp, latch-key survival, TV, and poverty, pull at children's lives. Book dealers at the Red Balloon Bookstore in San Antonio, Texas, say that 10 percent of the American public purchase 90 percent of the books. In an informal survey of the parents of 150 seniors at Cooper High School in Abilene, Texas, 47 of the parents reported not having a single book in their homes. Thirty-two of the homes had one book — a dictionary. It is highly unlikely that these students had childhoods that were rich with literary experiences.

Knowing how to revise requires years and years of experience in writing. Emergent writers do not readily revise. Neophyte writers struggle with revision. And the experienced writer can still find it difficult.

My fascination with clues began with a Captain Marvel decoder ring. After drinking jars of Ovaltine, I collected enough labels to send for that prize. When it arrived, the clues read by the radio announcer at program's end no longer formed incomprehensible cryptograms. Eagerly I copied them; anxiously I turned the ring's painted silvery dial to decode them. Figuring every word became an adventure — every message a solved mystery.

Progressing from radio to reading, I collected Carolyn Keene's books like those Ovaltine labels. Nancy Drew, her chum Helen Corning, and I were amateur detectives. No clue escaped us. Soon, my literary tastes refining, Sherlock Holmes and Dr. Watson replaced Nancy and Helen, then Agatha Christie's Hercule Poirot became my hero — I had been well prepared for secret packets and revolutionary *coups d'état*. But fascination flowered while following C. August Dupine, Edgar Allan Poe's smart (and I knew handsome) sleuth, especially when I discovered the sophisticated word for this process of logically reasoning out clues — *ratiocination*.

Although no Holmes, Poirot, or Dupin, in one *eureka!* moment I realized how I apply this ratiocinative process, how like a detective I become while revising. Relentlessly I go back through my writing searching for clues in the language, decoding them in order to make the writing better. For example, in an early draft, my opening sentence read: My fascination with clues *may* have started with a.... When I reentered the writing, *may* and *have* provided clues for decoding. *May* expresses contingency; *have* indicates the perfect tense. Since I wanted certainty in the past, both proved inaccurate — the sentence had to be revised.

Students, however, do not share this relentlessness; they cower during revision as if terrorized, failing to realize that a piece of writing, like a story, is essentially over at the beginning, the crime already committed when the author introduces the clues. Usually, the structure of the story revolves around the detective figuring out those clues to discover the culprit and bring the story to a satisfactory close. So, too, with a written draft in need of revision. It's an unsolved mystery. Most everything is essentially there, but the writer must reenter the writing as a detective, checking the significance of linguistic clues to bring the piece to a satisfactory close.

Students, most neophyte writers, most unskilled detectives of language, are unable to reenter their writing without clues, are unable to do revision as Frank Smith describes it in *Writing and the Writer*: "review the draft of the text from their own point of view to discover what the text contains" (127). Therefore students avoid revision: they abhor it and, if pressed, usually do a shoddy job of it. Directions, fine as they may be for the practiced writer (*lower the noun/verb ratio* or *transform passive constructions into active ones* in Linda Flower's *Problem-Solving Strategies for Writing* [New York: Harcourt Brace Jovanovich, 1981, 177-179]), strike students as vague or meaningless since they give no clues pointing where to begin.

If clues hold the secret to revision, then teachers must show students how to code the clues which will enable them to reenter their papers the way practiced writers do. Further, by following those coded clues and by using the process of logical reasoning to decode them, students figure out words and meanings to solve the mystery of their written drafts and bring their papers to a satisfactory close.

The Procedure

Instruct students to bring colored markers, pens, pencils, or crayons—colored coders—or keep a box of these in class. After students have shaped their prewritings (clearly labeled at the top) into their rough drafts (also clearly labeled), introduce "Clue Day."

Present the clues (see "Coding the Clues," page 242) that you want students to code for this paper. For example, if you want students to work on the first clue, you might list all the "to be" verbs on the board, telling students, "Each time you come across one of these verbs, circle it clearly with one color." For the next clue, they would use another color. Depending upon the length of the papers, and the number of clues, this coding process could easily take the rest of the period. What emerges are drafts clearly filled with visually coded clues.

The teacher who approaches teaching revision by pronouncement, has the same effect on a student's writing as a politician at a national convention. Proclaiming a candidate as a "man or woman of the people" doesn't make it so. Telling isn't teaching. The uninformed, untrained teacher announces, "today you will revise your paper." Then the teacher wonders why the students did not revise. Revision must be taught in order for it to be incorporated into writing.

One good way to teach this technique makes use of a chart that shows the relationship of the code to the clue and the decoding tips. On the chalkboard the teacher can write:

Code	Clue	Decode
⬭ (circle)	"to be" verbs is are was were be being been	• do not change • change to a livelier verb • indicate passive voice • indicates a knotted, weak sentence. • do not change if the "to be" verb is in a quote • consider leaving it in dialogue—characters speak this way

A word about using the chalkboard versus the overhead: The chalkboard invites interaction and simultaneous discovery. Presentation on the chalkboard keeps the pacing of the presentation at a comfortable rate for students.

Ratiocination guarantees that students will use:

- *higher-order thinking skills,*

- *revision skills in a context, and*

- *concrete signals to reenter their own writing.*

With ratiocination, teachers find they use some codes, clues, and decodes every piece of discourse. In time, student writers internalize some clues.

As with most good techniques, however, ratiocination can be abused. One well-meaning teacher may insist that her students use all 10 codes, clues, and decodes on each paper they write, and the result: cognitive overload and illegible drafts. This overteaching can be detrimental and discouraging.

Next, explain how decoding their clues involves logical thinking (ratiocination— although you may not wish to introduce the term at this time) as well as decision making, since there are many options and alternatives available when working with language (see "The Decoding" below). After this explanation, students reenter their trial rough drafts, decoding their clues, making decisions, and rewriting onto what will become their rough drafts. As students engage in decoding, the teacher may move about the room offering individual help.

When students polish their rough drafts into their final papers, they hand in all their drafts, fastened together in descending order with the final paper on top. This order makes assessment easier, while the coding and the decoding make it more thorough, more specific, and quicker. Grading should be keyed directly to the concepts covered in the clues and to the quality of writing after decoding those clues.

For the first paper, I'd recommend presenting the first two clues; for the second paper, review them; then add one or two more depending upon the level and writing abilities of the students. For slow students, one clue per paper is sufficient. I have sequenced these clues in a workable order so that by the end of the semester, through this process of accumulation, all ten clues will become part of the student's repertoire. A word of caution: do not rush this giving of clues because the ratiocination which each clue generates is a highly complex and intricate transformational process.

Coding the Clues

1.   Circle all "to be" verbs.
2.   Make a wavy line under repeated words.
3.   Underline each sentence.
4.   Bracket each sentence beginning.
5.   Draw an arrow from subject to predicate in each sentence.
6.   Place a box around cliches.
7.   Mark words that might be imprecise with a check.
8.   X out the word very.
9.   Draw two vertical lines next to anything underdeveloped.
10. Put *it* in a triangle.

The Decoding

1. When decoding a circle, students determine if the "to be" verb should be untouched because changing it would diminish the composition or if it should be replaced because changing it to a livelier verb would enhance the composition. Sometimes a "to be" verb signals a passive construction which might entail either revising its order to subject-verb complement or leaving it to focus on the complement. Other times a "to be" verb suggests a weak sentence which should be omitted or drastically revised.

   One teacher told us that "to be" verbs is the only code she uses with her students. Through it she is able to teach everything from word choice and grammatical concepts to syntax and style.

2. When approaching a wavy line, students consider if the repetition is necessary and should remain to make the meaning emphatic, to show continuity between sentences or paragraphs, to retain parallel form, or to make the sentence function, as is the case with words such as *a, an, the.* If the repetition is unnecessary, it should be eliminated or changed because it reveals careless word choice or confuses by using homonymic words.

3. Underlining invites students to study their sentences. For example, if they are about the same length, shortening or lengthening a few adds variety and provides visual relief. If choppy (each sentence contains a minimal number of words or a simple idea divided into two or more sentences), combining sentences produces a smoother effect. If stringy (ideas are strung together with coordinating conjunctions as if all elements are equal), cutting down on conjunctions and subordinating ideas solves the problem.

   We have learned from other teachers that this works best when the students underline the sentences in alternating colors.

4. Bracketing heightens awareness of the tendency to start each sentence with a noun or pronoun subject, thereby lowering the overall impact of the writing. Students decode by experimenting with a variety of beginnings—modifiers, phrases, clauses.

   See pages 227-229.

5. While most arrows will point to subject/predicate agreement, some will uncover dialect problems: *I do, you do, he do, she do, it do.* Using a current handbook *and* the student's writing, individualize

instruction on this problem. Students should compare examples in handbooks with what they have written, since many rules and exceptions govern these situations.

This is a good time to work collaboratively.

6. Students might miss boxing in all their trite expressions. Because they are so common, students use them without thinking. When they do catch a cliché, they decode the clue by asking how they could more freshly express the hackneyed.

7. Word precision problems arise when students fail to distinguish nuances of meaning. Decoding a check demands cross-reference work with both thesaurus and dictionary.

Teachers have extended this to include alot (as one word), really, good, and other overused words.

8. *Very* in my class is considered a four-letter word and as such gets X-ed. But students should understand the rationale behind the X [mark] so they may intelligently decode it. As an adverb, *very* acts as an intensifier for the word it precedes. There's nothing wrong with that, although students often grab *very* instead of mentally wrestling with precise word choice. To avoid this corroding of precision, students determine if they have used *very* as an adjective or if they have used it as an adverb. If adjectival, it remains; if adverbial, it tips off imprecision. Students untangle this clue by omitting *very* and choosing an exact word for its modificand.

One way to help students develop is by using charts (see table 8.1, pages 253-256) and the SEE strategy (page 257).

9. By the time students reach this clue, they should have had ample work on development by detail, narration, example, illustration, and fact. Coding with two vertical lines encourages close reading to be sure all points have been developed; decoding reminds that more writing is needed.

This may be extended to all personal pronouns.

10. *It,* clearly a pronoun meant to refer to an idea previously expressed, is often used by students to refer to an idea still in their heads. (How many times have we received compositions beginning with *it?*) The triangle warns students to examine the referent. If the referent is

clear, *it* remains; if unclear or nonexistent, *it* must be replaced with something specific or the sentence must be reworked.

The Objectives

These clues and decodings

1. enable teachers to integrate lexical, syntactical, rhetorical, and grammatical concepts with composition instruction *during* the writing process;

2. encourage students to test these concepts immediately in a context that matters to them;

3. provide students with visual ways for reentry into their writing in order to make it better;

4. help students take the responsibility for their own writing;

5. permit students to revise *during* their process, thereby improving their papers *before* they are handed in for a grade;

6. aid teachers' work evaluating those papers and lightening their paper load.

After all this detective work, our class may close as a Carolyn Keene mystery closes. Students discussing this venture will wonder if they'll ever have another so thrilling. Assure them they will, perhaps calling the next paper "Secrets of Sentence Beginnings" or "Hidden Word Meanings." And be sure to explain that this, their first paper in a series, should serve as a pleasant reminder of their first solved mystery. Just fiction? Maybe. But maybe not.

Primary teachers may adapt ratiocination to their students' appropriate developmental level. For example: Code: Red dot. Clue: Stop! Every place you stop when you read ... Decode: Put a period (.), an asking mark (?), or an excitement mark (!).

Ratiocination is one technique, one strategy, one concrete way teachers have to integrate the teaching of grammar with the teaching of writing during revision. Too many writing projects, too many classrooms, too many writing courses spend too much time on prewriting, and not enough time on revision. Ratiocination is the single most effective way 475 teachers surveyed have found to teach revision.

8

GRAMMAR THROUGH REFORMULATION
Teaching the Paragraph

Paragraphs are not composed; they are discovered.
To compose is to create; to indent is to interpret.
—Paul Rodgers□

The third act of reentry into a piece of writing is reformulation. The deepest of the correcting-revising-reformulating triad, reformulating invites writers to work with large blocks of their writing. Because paragraphs represent distinct divisions of a composition, working with them requires different strategies and a different depth of purpose than does correcting "stylistic infelicities" or revising through sentence manipulation. When writers reformulate, they consider each paragraph in relation to other paragraphs, to the entire piece, and to the author's meaning. Writers often rewrite paragraphs, combine paragraphs, break apart paragraphs that are too lengthy, add support to paragraphs, write in transitional paragraphs, or move existing paragraphs around. Sometimes when reformulating, writers feel as though they are working a jigsaw puzzle because they put parts aside for further consideration, remove parts that do not fit, rearrange parts for better clarity, or scrap the whole thing to begin again.

Scholars such as Corder and Ruszkiewicz maintain, "There are no absolute rules about paragraphing and no general models of ideal paragraphs.... The fact is that the effectiveness of any paragraph depends on how well it serves its readers, not how closely it adheres to abstract models and concepts" (443). Still, the practice of teaching a paragraph through patterns or formulae remains far too prevalent. Even more prevalent is the assignment, "Write a paragraph," as if a paragraph were all, as if a paragraph were enough. This often sends an incorrect message to students, suggesting that a paragraph *is* the ultimate goal. Add that message to a formulaic approach to teaching writing, and the result is that meaning is once again slighted in favor of number of sentences, number of similes, or other determiners that can be counted up easily for a grade or a score.

Nevertheless, a paragraph is not a willy-nilly group of sentences. Paragraphs are coherent, that is, they represent a chain of thought. Most are unified, that is, each part works together to convey a purpose. When teaching properly and in context, teachers keep one eye on the real world of writing, not on predetermined formulae.

A BRIEF HISTORY
OF THE PARAGRAPH

There are many stories about the beginning of the paragraph, its history, and how indenting happened to occur. Some of these stories have reached the level of legend. It all began, some say, with the illuminated manuscripts of monks. Because illumination served a cosmetic purpose and made reading easier, it became the natural guide for paragraphing.

Oscar Ogg in *The 26 Letters* recounts a legend that explains one origin of illumination. This legend comes from the extraordinary *Book of Kells*, which contains the Gospels in Latin from the seventh century. Supposedly, Saint Patrick brought semiuncials, small and decorative but readable letters, to Ireland. Irish scribes eventually became famous for their mastery of semiuncials and the beauty of their manuscripts. Two such scribes, the monks Columba and Finnian, engaged in friendly competition in producing beautifully lettered books.

As the story goes, Columba vowed to secretly copy an original Psalter worked on by Finnian and to make it more beautiful in order to present it to his friend. Nightly he labored to copy the original by candlelight. One night, in what Columba considered to be a miracle, a beam of light shone through the ceiling onto a portion of the page, thereby illuminating several letters and seeming to bless them. Because of the light, Columba was able to decorate the letters with more precision. In time this highly decorated and illuminated text became most sought after (156-160).

Another story describes a bored monk who was copying seemingly endless words across page after page of manuscript. One day he looked out the window of his cell and his gaze lingered over the sight of birds, trees, vines, plants, and the sun glowing over the landscape. So overcome was he with the beauty of the scene that when he returned to his work he painted the scene in and around the first letter on each page. His work was so much in demand by the nobility that others copied his style. Eventually, illuminations graced more and more capital letters in manuscripts.

A third story holds that one of the monks who worked as a scribe came upon the idea of illuminating his manuscript as he knelt in the monastery chapel before the votive candles. Then it was fashionable to arrange the candles in figures that imitated nature (a bird, a flower, the circle of the sun), in letter shapes that suggested some sacred name, or in the shape of holy words. This monk simply transferred that concept of illumination to the letters in the manuscripts he was transcribing. Eventually these decorations became so intricate and complex that they mirrored not only nature or religion but all aspects of medieval Europe.

Wherever the truth lies among these stories, illumination provided an aesthetic quality to a manuscript page. It freed and rested the eye of writer and reader from the relentless letters that marched from page end to page end. It is little wonder these manuscripts were prized.

In time, Charlemagne charged an English scholar named Alcuin to revise and rewrite all church literature. In training his scribes, Alcuin modified writing, systematized punctuation, and divided writing into sentences and paragraphs (Ogg 166-174).

The advent of movable metal type more accurately illustrates how illumination served as the foundation of indention and the beginning of paragraphing. The metal letters used in printing could not capture the beauty of the illuminated letters found in the hand-transcribed books. Yet with the popularity of illuminated books, printers wanted to continue this decorative touch. In order to integrate illumination with printed books, they devised a mark that is used even today. It looks somewhat like a backward *P* with an extra parallel vertical line. Printers used that symbol to mark the place of the original illumination. In truth, the word *paragraph* (*para* — beside, *graph* — mark) means *mark beside*. This symbol signaled printers to leave the marked section free of letters (see fig. 8.1, page 248) so that illuminators could reenter the page in order to handcraft, design, and color initial letters in those spaces (see fig. 8.2, page 249). With the law of supply and demand and more versatility with type, manual lettering and art was replaced with a more ornate metal type capital letter, which in time became less and less ornate. Finally, when an ordinary capital letter was used, it was simply moved in from the margin, contemporary testimony to medieval illumination. Thus indention indicated the beginning of a paragraph (Ogg 204-208).

(Text continues on page 250.)

Fig. 8.1. The opening page of book 2 of Pliny's
Naturalis Historia, **unilluminated.**

C. Plynii Secundi naturalis historie Liber . II .

Vndus & hoc qd alio nose celum appellari libut:cuius arcuflexu
teguntur cuncta : numen esse credi par est . eternu . immensu . neq;
genitum . neq; interiturum ung. huius extera indagare . nec interest
hominum : nec capit humane coniectura menus:sacer est . eternus.
immensus. Totus in toto : immo uero ipse totum.infinitus ac finito
similis. omnium rerum certus: & similis incerto . Extra intra cuncta
complexus in se . idemq; rerum nature opus. & reru ipsa natura.
Furor est mensuram eius animo quosdam agitasse . atq; prodere ausos. Alios rursus
occasione hinc sumpta aut his data innumerabiles tradidisse mundos. ut totidem reru
naturas credi oporteret . aut si una omnes incubarent: totidem tamen soles:totidemq;
lunas & cetera etia in uno & immensa & innumerabilia sidera : qsi non eade questioe
semper in termino cogitationis occursura desiderio finis alicuius. Aut si hec infinitas
nature omnis artificia possit assignari:non illud idem in uno facilius sit intelligi.tanto
preferim opere. Furor est profecto furor:egredi ex eo.& tag interna eius cucta
plane iam sint nota:ita scrutari extera.quasi uero mensuram ulliusrei possit agere.q
sui nesciat.aut mens hominis uidere:quem mundus ipse non capiat. Formam eius
in speciem orbis absoluti globatam esse : nomen in primis & consensus in eo mortaliu
orbem appellantium:sed & argumenta rerum docent. Non solum quia talis figura
omnibus sui partibus uergit in sese:ac sibi ipsa tolleranda est seq; includit & continet:
nullaru egens compaginum:nec finem aut initium ullis sui partibus sentiens: nec quia
ad motum quo subinde uerti debeat: ut mox apparebit:talis aptissima est :sed ocu/
lorum quoq; probatione q conuexus mediusq; quacunq; cernatur.cum id accidere in
alia non possit figura. Hanc ergo formam eius eterno & irrequeto ambitu inenar/
rabili celeritate . xxiiii . horarum spatio arcuag; solis exortus & occasus haud dubium
reliquere. An sit immensus: & ideo sensu auris excedens tante molis rotate uertigie
assidua sonitus non equidem facile dixerim. non hercule magis q arcuactorum simul
tinnitus sideru : suosq; uoluentiu orbes:an dulcis quide & incredibili suauitate cocentus.
nobis q intus agimur iuxta diebus noctibusq; tacitus labit mudus. Esse innumeras
et effigies animaliu rerumq; cunctarum impressas:nec ut in uolucrum notamus ouis
lenitate continua lubricu corpus qd clarissimi autores dixere tenes: argumetis idicat:
quoniam inde decidus rerum omniu seminibus:innumere in mari preapue ac plerisq;
confusis monstrifice gignantur effigies. Preterea uisus probatioe . alibi plaustra.alibi
ursi.tauri alibi.alibi littere figura.candidiore medio super uerticem arculo. Eqde
& consensu gentium moueor . na que Cosmon Greci nomine ornamen appellauerut.
eum & nos a perfecta absolutaq; elegantia mundu. Celu quidem haud dubie celati
argumento diximus:ut interpretatur.M.Varro. Adiuuat rerum ordo: descripto
arculo qui Signifer uocatur :in. xii. animalium effigies & per illas solis cursu cogrues
tot seculis ratio. Nec de elementis uideo dubitari:quotuor esse ea. Igneu summo.
inde tot stellarum illos collucentium oculos. Proximum spiritus:quem greci nostriq;
eodem uocabulo aera appellant.uitalem hunc ac per cuncta rerum meabilem.totoq;
confertu.cuius ui suspensam cu quarto aquaru elemento librari medio spatii tellure.
Ita mutuo complexu diuersitatis effia nexum.& leuia poderibus inhiberi quo minus
euolent.contraq; grauia:ne ruant:suspendi leuibus in sublime tendentibus.sic pari in
diuersa nisu in sua queq; subsistere irrequieto mudi ipsius costricta circuitu.quo semp

Fig. 8.2. The same page, illuminated.

Historically, then, it seems paragraphing was done intuitively, when there was a need for a break or so readers could follow the written thought. It was Alexander Bain, a Scottish logician, not a teacher of rhetoric, who in 1866 indurated the paragraph as "simply a sentence writ large." (See Arthur A. Stern's "When Is a Paragraph?" pages 270-278.) Bain took rules from classical rhetoric and applied them to writing, and teachers still teach as if his century-old theory holds—always begin a paragraph with a topic sentence.

Both Stern and William Irmscher, in his book *Teaching Expository Writing*, cite the research of Richard Braddock. Braddock found that publications such as *The Atlantic, Harper's, The Reporter, The New Yorker*, and *The Saturday Review* use paragraphs beginning with topic sentences only about 13 percent of the time. Irmscher's replication of Braddock's study concludes, "percentages vary greatly among individual writers; an overall average, however, is more likely to be closer to 40 percent or 50 percent than 13 percent" (98). Irmscher like Braddock found that, "part of the problem is determining exactly what a topic sentence is" (98). But as Stern contends, "Today's paragraph is not a logical unit and we should stop telling our students it is" (111).

If scholars have difficulty determining absolutely what constitutes a paragraph and a topic sentence, and if writers use topical paragraphs only approximately 50 percent of the time, then teachers who use their own writing and realistic models for teaching paragraphing come closer to helping students do what professional writers do—that is, use the paragraph to meaningfully shape their own prose. If students are encouraged to find form in their meaning, if students learn to give that meaning shape, then, even if they often fall short, they are on the road to becoming self-sufficient writers.

The question has been, "But how do I teach the paragraph if I don't use a formula?" Obviously, teaching and grading by formula may be easier, but as research suggests, it is not totally honest. Formula paragraphs and five-paragraph themes exist nowhere but in archaic classrooms. Further, teaching formula paragraphs does not develop strong, independent writers. Eventually, students will have to pay the piper. But it is important not to confuse formula with strategy. Formula presents a set form. It gives a recipe: "There must be X number of sentences in each paragraph. The first sentence must be the topic sentence. It does thus and so. The second sentence does thus and so. The third sentence must contain a comparison. The fourth sentence..." ad nauseam. A strategy presents a plan or a blueprint with which the writer can work. A formula tends to be rigid, either/or, product paradigm. A strategy allows for permutations, adaptations. It is flexible, both/all, process paradigm. Better to teach strategies within the context of real writing. Better to use models from literature and real writing to analyze paragraphs. Better to help students examine their writing in relation to intended meaning. When teachers teach paragraphing that way, they foster authenticity, security, and independence.

PARAGRAPH TYPES

There are three types of paragraphs: topical, functional, and paragraph blocs. Students are traditionally taught only the *topical* paragraph, one with a stated topic sentence, usually written at the onset of the paragraph. Students learn that this topic sentence states the main idea of the paragraph and the remainder of the paragraph develops that idea. While this is sometimes true, there is also the *functional* paragraph, which usually serves some rhetorical purpose, such as transition or emphasis, and the *paragraph bloc*, a term coined by William Irmscher to define "a segment of discourse longer than the paragraph that operates as a single unit" (101). When teaching writing, teachers who do not provide these other paragraph types for students to use withhold valuable tools from them. Consider, as one example, the intellectual turmoil a student experiences when told to indent direct dialogue after being drilled in topical paragraphs. Teaching all three paragraph types provides students with a repertoire of tools for reformulating, for shaping their meaning in the most powerful way.

The Topical Paragraph

Definition. The topical paragraph is a group of sentences that contains a key sentence to which the other sentences are related. This key sentence is most often called the topic sentence, although some refer to it as the thesis statement. The latter term is pure abstraction for most students. (First they would have to conceptualize *thesis*, then they would have to thoroughly understand a thesis as an essay that embodies original research. Finally, defining original research becomes problematic. Clearly the term *topic sentence* seems more practical, although for contemporary students, *key sentence* probably works best.) The topic sentence may appear anywhere in the paragraph. If the writer wants to write out of the topic sentence, it will open the paragraph. If the writer wants to write toward the topic sentence, it will be at the conclusion of the paragraph. Sometimes writers want to write around the topic sentence. In that case, it will be somewhere in the middle of the paragraph. Occasionally a writer may want a frame; then the topic sentence may begin and end the paragraph. The point is there is no absolute rule on placement. Teaching the topical paragraph honestly — as one strategy students may use effectively and appropriately in their writing — furnishes them with a practical way to first formulate and later reformulate their writing. The topical paragraph enables students to test their ideas, their logic, their sequencing, their specifics.

Problems. To take a sample paragraph, separate it into a topic sentence with X number of supporting sentences, and then to expect students to exactly replicate that paragraph no matter what their meaning, is to teach paragraphing formulaically. Teachers who teach paragraphing this way either do not write or they slavishly hold to some outdated or simplistic grammar book, one that belies the complex nature of this generative process.

> *A nontraditional college student visited my office one afternoon. She was exasperated. "What's wrong?" I asked.*
>
> *"I have to do this paper for another class. The professor wants every paragraph to begin with a topic sentence with five to seven sentences in each paragraph, and he wants five paragraphs. Why do they do that? I read lots of paragraphs that aren't like that."*
>
> *Sharing her frustration, I responded with another question, "What if you only need four paragraphs?"*
>
> *"I guess I'll just split one in two."*

That attitude neither advances students' writing nor does it foster respect for academic credibility. The woman knew better. She knew she was "doing the formula" for the grade, but she was also well aware that it was both unrealistic as an assignment and unrealistic in comparison with writing in the world.

Another problem with teaching the topical paragraph formulaically is that often teachers who do not write teach as if students were able to grab main ideas from the air, or as if these students sat like mythical Zeuses with main ideas rising full-blown out of their heads. "First get a main idea," echoes from classrooms at every level. This dictum leads students to erroneously dismiss prewriting with all its attendant behaviors (doodling, thinking, day-dreaming, reading) as a legitimate way to discover or uncover main ideas. They strive to get anything down, hoping it will work. Normally writing does not work that way (although some rare writing comes by grace). As writers write they uncover meaning, and in the meaning there is form. To try to force meaning into a predetermined form is to negate the entire process of thinking into writing or using writing as a mode of thinking. "Composing is not as simple as outlining and fleshing out the sub-topics with prose or simply adding up parts to make a whole" (Irmscher 99). Rather, it is first answering the question E. M. Forster asks, "How do I know what I think until I see what I say?"

TEACHING THE TOPICAL PARAGRAPH

If 40-50 percent of written paragraphs are topical, certainly teachers should teach topical paragraphs as one way for writers to organize their information. But writing precedes shaping; it uncovers ideas. Therefore, when teachers employ strategies to cultivate the habit of writing into meaning, they teach students to write first, then shape that meaning. Like the words of Paul Rodgers, students compose first, then they interpret.

Students:

- Prewrite using freewriting or looping, for example.

- Get down their thoughts.

- Follow associations.

- Make connections between ideas.

- Reread what they have written in an effort to uncover something that tugs at them, something that wants to become their topic.

- Hone this "tug" into a sentence, which becomes their key sentence.

- Weave that sentence into the beginning, middle, or end of their paragraph. More sophisticated writers may grapple with the notion of implying their topic. The concept here is to write first, reformulate second.

Teachers:

- Display a chart that lists various types of elaboration, a definition, example, and explanation for each type, and a possible model of each (see table 8.1). Teaching from this chart will help students learn ways to support or elaborate their topics. Many students are unclear about the use of facts; statistics; examples, illustrations or instances; details; anecdotes; descriptions; explanations; and comparisons and contrasts as strategies for elaboration. These are best covered in a series of mini-lessons.

- Model ways students may develop their topic sentence. Use an overhead and your own writing to talk students through the act of developing first your topic sentence, then theirs. Follow one of the models in table 8.1 to provide a concrete example that students may emulate. The directives, "Develop!" or "Support your topic sentence!" without instruction on how to do that serves only to baffle or frustrate neophyte writers.

- Allow plenty of time for reformulation.

(Text continues on page 257.)

Table 8.1

Strategies for Elaborating or Supporting a Topic

Types of Elaboration	Definition, Example, and Explanation	Model
Facts	*Definition* A fact is something that has been objectively verified, something real or actual. *Example* You are students in (name) school. *Explanation* That they are students in a school is a fact that can be verified through school records. Finding facts, writing the facts down, and how they may be verified helps students internalize the concept.	• Freewrite on a relevant topic, such as school spirit. • Develop the topic into a topic sentence, such as *We show school spirit at football games.* • Brainstorm facts that elaborate or support the topic sentence. *After every touchdown, the student body does the wave. We stand when the band plays the alma mater. We jump and cheer for our team when the players run onto the field. We wear school colors and spirit ribbons to the homecoming game. We buy spirit ribbons. We hold pep rallies before games. Classes are dismissed 10 minutes early on Fridays so students can attend football games.*
Statistics	A statistic is a fact, exact or estimated, usually stated in numbers. There are 2,105 students in X High School. This is a statistic because it is an exact number. Students can create statistics about their classroom or their school. They may figure the number of students absent for a day, a week, or a month and organize the figures as statistical information. Based on the data gathered about the class, students may estimate absenteeism in the school or in the district. Doing this generally makes students feel comfortable with statistics.	• Take one of the brainstormed facts above and back it up with numbers. For example, count the number of students who actually wear spirit ribbons and school colors to the homecoming game. • Demonstrate how this number could be woven into the discourse. *We wear spirit ribbons and school colors to the homecoming game. Last year the pep squad sold 1,610 spirit ribbons to students. That means over three-fourths of the school showed their support of the team by buying a spirit ribbon for homecoming.*

Table 8.1 *(continued)*

Types of Elaboration	Definition, Example, and Explanation	Model
Examples, Illustrations, or Instances	An example, illustration, or instance is a specific thing, person, or event that illuminates a general thing, person, or event. When one student describes his or her writing process, it serves to clarify the concept of the writing process for others.	• Show students how, in their writing, one student with school spirit might serve as an example for most students in the school. *Take John Doe, for example. He not only buys a spirit ribbon for homecoming, but he buys season tickets so he may attend every game. He sits in the bleachers near the pep squad and shouts the loudest of all. Last year he was hoarse from all the cheering.* *"I can't be on the field because of my bad leg, but I can be there in spirit," he says. "I can be part of the cheering squad."*
Details	Details are specifics that clarify what is written. They are parts of a whole. Sometimes students confuse details with examples. The difference is that details are even smaller parts than examples. When providing details, writers look at all the significant particulars and show the relationship among these particulars to the whole. Distribute index cards. Using a pencil, each student punches a small hole in the card, then looks through the hole. The hole magnifies the details, the small things. Students may write or talk about what they see.	• Return to the topic of spirit ribbons to show students how giving the particulars aids to the sense of school spirit. *John's spirit ribbon, which he wears on his bomber jacket, sparkles with green and silver glitter. As he enters the stands, all see his green cushion, silk-screened with the school mascot and the cheer "Go, Cougars, go!" His wool plaid blanket is mostly green, and his cap bears the school motto across its brim.*

Types of Elaboration	Definition, Example, and Explanation	Model
Anecdotes	An anecdote is a brief narrative. It is perhaps the most ancient of all ways to support information. Its pervasiveness and the ease with which it can be incorporated into writing sometimes makes it suspect. "You mean I can tell a story to make a point?" is not an uncommon remark. Yet brief vignettes, parables, and snippets of experience often best undergird a point. People identify with other people and their experiences; thus anecdotes pull readers in and cause them to nod their heads in agreement. Tell a story that makes a point. Ask students to think of a personal story or experience that makes a point. Informally share these anecdotes aloud.	• While not always needed or even effective, writing a story often makes a point most powerfully. Anecdotes provide students with another option for development. Elaborate the topic of school spirit using an anecdote about the exemplary John. *One day John arrived at the game early. Some kids came over from the opponent's side and began harassing him.* *"Look at the big guy sitting with his big spirit ribbon — too nerdy to get out on the field. Afraid of getting roughed up? Afraid of getting your clothes dirty, nerd?"* *With some effort, John stood up. When he did, his harassers could see his deformed leg.* *"No. But I show my loyalty the best way I can. Go back and show your team your loyalty. What you're doing now isn't school spirit; it's just dumb!"*
Descriptions	Not to be confused with details, descriptions paint pictures through visual and aural imagery. As the image intensifies the meaning is revealed. Choose something in the classroom to describe. Describe it aloud. Call on volunteers to guess what it is you are describing. Continue this activity, with students doing the describing.	• Ask students to pretend they are looking at the football stands through a zoom-lens camera. They are to zoom in on one area of the stands and provide a word picture of what they see. *The green and silver section of the stands undulated; it seethed with activity. From afar the green formed an enormous C for Cougar. The silver section outlined the letter. When the home team made a touchdown, each person jumped up, causing the green to bulge out as if it would burst while the silver outline glistened its glee.*

Table 8.1 *(continued)*

Types of Elaboration	Definition, Example, and Explanation	Model
Explanations	Explanation is a statement or definition with elaboration. Explanation permits layering of meaning: first making something comprehensible, then giving reasons, putting it in a context, analyzing it, exploring it, and finally adding any special insights or implications. Work with students on common statements like "Yesterday I was absent." Then encourage them to add reasons, give a context, and so forth.	• Help students understand that explanations create depth in writing. • Model that depth by inviting students to layer the topic sentence. *School spirit is the excitement and support students show toward school events. One such event is a football game. While the game actually takes place on Friday night, weeks and even months are spent in preparation for it. The cheerleaders practice; the pep squad practices; the band marches up and down the field in daily drills, making ready for their Friday night halftime show. Some school clubs make and sell spirit ribbons for students to buy to wear. The entire school buzzes in anticipation. All hope for a win.*
Comparisons and Contrasts	Comparisons show likenesses; contrasts show differences. To support an idea through comparison or contrast is to show how that idea matches something else or how it is different from something else. Take any object in the room and compare and contrast it to any other object in the room. Tell how each is alike or different. Let students choose objects and continue the activity.	• This is the time to introduce or review similes and metaphors as one way to compare, and to remind students that extended metaphors or allegories may be used. Also remind students that when comparing or contrasting, it is best to give the reason for the comparison or contrast. *The students in the stands look like a hive of bees. Most hover in the center, but streams of them in green and silver fly up and down the stairs. An occasional green bee buzzes onto the field, or a silver one flits to where the cheerleaders cluster. When the team runs onto the field, it is as if the hive had been jostled by some giant's hand. All the students seem to take wing, failing their arms in sweeping gestures.* *In contrast, the visiting team stands like zombies. They must know death is near.*

LAYERING IDEAS IN THE TOPICAL PARAGRAPH

When writers layer ideas, they promote comprehension and enrich the topic for the reader. Layering makes a piece strong. With layered ideas, the substance of a piece emerges part by part until its essence is revealed. When writing is not layered, it is weak. Without layers of meaning, writing is often a mere sketch of what could be. This sketchiness leads to misunderstanding.

Using the acronym *SEE* helps students better understand layering. The *S* stands for *statement*; the sentence that states the topic. The first *E* represents an *extension* of that statement, or a restatement; it links the statement to its elaboration. The last *E* stands for *elaboration*, an additional working out of the statement either by degree or by quality of development.

The metaphor of a lamp helps students visualize layering. The plug represents the *statement*. The cord represents the *extension*. The lamp represents the *elaboration*. When the plug is in the socket and the cord is attached to the lamp, the lamp can be turned on and there will be light. When a statement has been written, extended, and elaborated, readers are able to "see" the meaning.

Topical paragraphs lend themselves to layering because all the sentences in this type of paragraph are there to support the topic. One way to reinforce the notion of layering is to analyze a sample paragraph. The sample in figure 8.3 is the concluding paragraph of the epilogue in *The Story of English* by Robert McCrum, William Cran, and Robert MacNeil.

Fig. 8.3. An example of layering from *The Story of English* (McCrum, Cran, and MacNeil 351).

Excerpt from the epilogue of *The Story of English*	Analysis
Language has always been—as the phrase goes—the mirror to society. English today is no exception. In its world state, it reflects very accurately the crises and contradictions of which it is a part. In Britain, its first home, it has become standardized and centralized in the South, apparently cautious of change. The English of the United States (heard on television, films and radio through the world) has become the voice of the First World in finance, trade and technology. Within the United States, the huge socio-economic significance of the South and West—oil, beef, and the high-tech aerospace and computer industries—has given the voice and accents of the South-West a new and preponderant influence. In the British Commonwealth, the independent traditions of Australia, Canada and New Zealand have breathed a new life into the English that was exported from Britain two hundred years ago. In the Caribbean, it is the focus of an emergent nationalism. In Africa, it is a continent-wide form of communication. In South Africa, it is the medium of Black consciousness. In India and South-East Asia, it is associated with Third World aspirations, and, reflecting the confidence of these Asian countries, it is taking on its own distinctive Asian forms. In the words of Emerson, with whom we began [the introduction to the book], "Language is a city, to the building of which every human being brought a stone."	• First sentence is topical; it clearly states the main idea. • The second sentence limits the main idea to English. • Third sentence extends the main idea to the complexity of the world. • *Britain* signals the first support by identifying the source of English. • *United States* signals the second support by placing English into a technological, social, and economic context. • *Australia, Canada, and New Zealand* offer support through the new life they have given the language. • The *Caribbean* supports emerging English. • *Africa* uses English for communication while in *South Africa* it is a medium of Black consciousness. • *India and South-East Asia* represent areas of hope and confidence. • Countries and continents form layers of support for the topic sentence. • The paragraph links information in a systematic way and concludes with a restatement of the topic with a quotation.

Teaching Functional Paragraphs:
Five Examples

Definition. Functional paragraphs are those that serve a rhetorical purpose. They may be used to arouse or sustain interest, present a special effect, emphasize a point, show a shift from one speaker to another, or provide a transition. They may be one word, one sentence, or a series of sentences. Without functional paragraphs readers may become confused, lose interest, miss a segue, or fail to catch who is speaking in dialogue.

Explanation. One of the most effective ways to teach functional paragraphs is by using examples from classic and contemporary literature. This section offers a sampling of functional paragraphs used for the purposes listed above. These, or others that are appropriate for the grade level, may be used with students.

Implementation — General

1. Divide students into small groups.

2. Distribute a functional paragraph to each group. They read it and identify its function.

3. They find another example of this type of functional paragraph. Share and discuss.

4. Students look for functional paragraphs in their own writing. Share and discuss.

5. Students reenter their writing to reformulate, by adding functional paragraphs.

Arouse or Sustain Interest. Stephen W. Hawking, considered one of the great minds of physics during this century and author of *A Brief History of Time*, echoes questions asked since the beginning of time. His paragraph is clearly designed to arouse and sustain interest.

> We find ourselves in a bewildering world. We want to make sense of what we see around us and to ask: What is the nature of the universe? What is our place in it and where did it and we come from? Why is it the way it is? (171)

Special Effect. George Bernard Shaw achieves a sardonic effect in the concluding paragraph of a letter written to Hesketh Pearson when World War II was a mere two weeks old. His one-sentence ending functions totally for effect.

> What a comfort to know that if we kill 20 million or so of one another, we'll none of us be missed! (Weintraub 688)

Emphasis. Loren C. Eiseley, a respected naturalist and conservationist, inserts a five-word, one-sentence paragraph between two long paragraphs in his essay "The Brown Wasps." This paragraph serves as a syntactical exclamation point. Its emphasis resides in its brevity, its timing, and its isolation as a paragraph.

> I saw the river stop. (Decker 151)

Dialogue. When Gottfried von Strassburg, the genius of medieval romance, set up the exchange between King Mark and his chief huntsman in *Tristan and Isolt*, he relied on indention to carry the conversation forward with proper pacing and without distraction.

"Sir King," said the huntsman, "I will tell thee a marvel; I have but now found a fair adventure!"

"Say, what adventure?"

"I have found a Love Grotto!"

"Where and how didst thou find it?"

"Sire, here, in this wilderness."

"What? Here, in this wild woodland?"

"Yea, even here."

"Is there any living soul within?" (Loomis 214-215)

Transition. While the first paragraph in the prologue of James Clavell's *Shogun* sets the scene, and the third paragraph provides more elaboration, the second paragraph, slipped in between, is a one-sentence transitional paragraph used for the purpose of introducing the main character and a minor one.

> His name was John Blackthorne and he was alone on deck but for the bowsprit lookout—Salamon the mute—who huddled in the lee, searching the sea ahead. (9)

Remarks. Like Shaw, Hawking, Clavell, and the rest, students, even young students, understand the need for functional paragraphs.

> *A group of second-graders recently wrote letters at the end of the year. Although somewhat tentative about exactly how to paragraph, they managed to use several types of functional paragraphs.*
> *Lance began his writing with a childlike strategy clearly meant to arouse interest, "How are you? I am fine."*
> *David indented to emphasize, "I loved you coming to vezit us."*
> *Shannon began her letter with a paragraph giving all the details of their Author's Tea. She concluded with "rite now were learning about the ocean." Between those two paragraphs, she wrote a one-sentence paragraph that served to emphasize her meaning: "I still remember the lesson you gave us."*
> *And Cindy's "We went to see the Gate Berer Refe in the Omni" definitely qualifies as a special effect in a long letter all about what they did in school that year.*

These students' year-long work with reading and writing shows in their sense of what a reader might need. Taught by teachers who use writing (not exercises) as models, these students grasp the idea of a paragraph and what it can do for them.

Teaching Paragraph Blocs

Definition. The paragraph bloc is a handy label for those segments of writing where a topic sentence elongates itself into several paragraphs. These are most noticeable in social studies essays, in which the topic may be the causes of a war or the implications of a treaty. Each subsequent paragraph may embrace the topic by enumerating the causes or implications and then elaborating on each. "Thus, the paragraphing a writer chooses may be only one way—that writer's way—of partitioning the material" (Irmscher 101).

Again, the paragraph bloc has been used in all types of writing. Herman Melville in "The Apple-Tree Table" sets the protagonist in search of strange sounds he hears. There follows eighteen paragraphs, most of them one line, that deal with the sound and the search. When his wife speaks, she breaks the paragraph bloc.

Paragraph blocs fill books that deal with theory and research in specialized fields, primarily because they allow the writer to stretch topics through several paragraphs. They are most useful when delineating functions or dysfunctions, identifying levels, presenting characteristics, itemizing concepts, listing propositions, enumerating components, establishing rules, outlining frameworks, labeling resources, pinpointing processes, extending views, determining dimensions, making assumptions, ascertaining implications, advancing views, citing causes, addressing concerns, making recommendations, generating heuristics, planning strategies, constructing taxonomies, preparing purposes, distinguishing modes, recognizing conditions, gathering indicators, naming cycles, formulating designs, drafting prescriptions, and giving directions. Paragraph blocs are so prevalent, it is good to name them and teach them.

One of the most extreme examples of a paragraph bloc comes from Stephen Jay Gould's book *Bully for Brontosaurus*. Midway through the chapter titled "Glow, Big Glowworm," he describes the total life cycle (egg to egg) of a glowworm. *Carnivory is the focus of larval existence* is the main idea. Gould follows his topical paragraph with five paragraphs that operate as a single unit. Then he further extends this unit with an elaborate four-paragraph footnote, one that covers three-fourths of the page in much smaller print (261-263).

Invite students to reread their writing in an effort to identify paragraph blocs. If and when they do locate one, they circle it with a marker and share why their meaning works best as a bloc. The rhetoric of explanation is as important as the identification of the blocs. Often students will discover that the bloc does not serve them best. Then they may reformulate what they have written.

Teaching Paragraph Patterns: TRI and PS/QA

Definition. One way to help students understand the flexibility of paragraphing is to use the two paragraph patterns identified by Alton Becker in his article "A Tagmemic Approach to Paragraph Analysis." TRI is the first pattern; PS/QA is the second.

The acronym TRI stands for the traditional *Topic, Restatement, Illustration* pattern. When using this pattern, the writer states a topic, expands that topic, and uses examples to support that topic. After learning this traditional pattern, students working in groups may brainstorm permutations, for example, TIR, TII, ITR, and TRIT. After brainstorming, they may use these permutations to analyze their writing.

The acronym PS/QA stands for *Problem/Solution* and *Question/Answer*. These may, in fact, take up many sentences or may be shaped into paragraph blocs.

Explanation. After students have generated some prewriting and have made a commitment to take one piece of writing through the process, after they have worked with correcting and revising that writing, then they are ready to reformulate using paragraph patterns.

Implementation

1. Students reenter their writing.

2. They use the acronym to mark in the margins their topical paragraph patterns (TRI or PS/QA).

3. They label functional paragraphs by function.

4. They mark paragraph blocs with a { } brace.

5. They study the patterns and decide if any additions, deletions, or rearrangements are needed.

6. They reformulate accordingly.

Remarks. Using these paragraph patterns lends structure and security to students' reformulations. They may discover they have T and R but no I. Or they may have a string of Is that relate to nothing, because a T is nowhere to be found. They may have raised a question, restated it, but failed to answer it. Further, this approach to paragraphing invites choices, higher-level thinking, decision making, problem solving, and, perhaps most importantly, it reinforces ownership.

FROM START TO FINISH:
INTRODUCTIONS, COHERENCE, CONCLUSIONS

The Introduction and Teaching Leads

Definition. The major function of the introduction is to attract the reader's attention and literally lead the reader into the rest of the writing. The writer attempts to hook the reader with the first several sentences, then reel the reader in during the remaining introduction. With uncomplicated pieces of writing, the introduction may be one paragraph; with more complex pieces, it may form a bloc of two or even three paragraphs.

Poet Richard Hugo told his audience during a poetry reading in Abilene, Texas, that something should have already happened when the poem begins. Elizabeth Cowan and Gregory Cowan say, "You must hook the reader immediately. You probably have about two sentences, or twenty seconds, to do that" (173). And June Gould in *The Writer in All of Us* states, "Your lead not only has to hook the reader instantaneously but also has to be so powerful that it sets up a chain reaction until everything—even your ending—is a logical outgrowth of its promise and intention" (141).

Modeling with Literature. Reading several leads to students raises their consciousness to what draws readers into writing.

> *While teaching the narrative to inner-city sixth-grade students, I introduced the notion of the hook. "I'm going to read the first several sentences from novels and stories. If they hook you into wanting to read more, give a thumbs up sign; if not, give a thumbs down. If you are undecided, turn your thumbs sideways."*
>
> *As I progressed through several short stories and a collection of young adult novels, the students made their choices — but never unanimously. Then I read from Gary Soto's* Taking Sides. *"Tony," Lincoln Mendoza whispered into the telephone. "It's your buddy, Linc." I looked up to see everyone's arms raised high in the air, hands extended, all with thumbs up.*
>
> *When we talked about why the reaction was so universal, they offered, " 'Cause that's the way we talk," "Sounds like us," "I want to know why he whispered," and other comments that spelled identification. After that, it was easy to move the students into writing zippy hooks and leads for their narratives. I distributed half sheets of fluorescent-colored copy paper and told them to try several. "Make your hook electric," I invited, "then follow that electricity through the lead."*

Writers, both classic and contemporary, know the importance of the introduction. The following samples may be shared with students to illustrate the hook.

> To the red country and part of the gray country of Oklahoma, the last rains came gently, and they did not cut the scarred earth.
>
> *The Grapes of Wrath* (John Steinbeck)

> Jean: Miss Julie's mad again to-night: absolutely mad!
>
> *Miss Julie* (August Strindberg)

> Whenever my mother talks to me, she begins the conversation as if we were already in the middle of an argument.
>
> *The Kitchen God's Wife* (Amy Tan)

> Three weeks after Granny Blakeslee died, Grandpa came to our house for his early morning snort of whiskey, as usual, and said to me, "Will Tweedy? Go find yore mama, then run up to yore Aunt Loma's and tell her I said git on down here. I got something to say. And I ain't a-go'n say it but once't."
>
> *Cold Sassy Tree* (Olive Ann Burns)

> I sit on the bed at a crooked angle, one foot on the floor, my hip against the tent of Mom's legs, my elbows on the hospital table. My skirt is too short and keeps riding up my thighs.
>
> *A Yellow Raft in Blue Water* (Michael Dorris)

We are planning a party, a very special party, the women and I. My name is Miriam, and this is where I live. Hut 18, bed 22.

Let the Celebrations Begin!
(Margaret Wild and Julie Vivas)

And they lived happily after after.

Dicey's Song (Cynthia Voigt)

"Hold on, boy!" A harsh voice called to him from the dim light on Brattle Street. He held himself in and managed to sound calm when he asked, "What do you want of me?"

Anthony Burns: The Defeat and Triumph of a Fugitive Slave (Virginia Hamilton)

Modeling by Writing Leads

1. Choose a draft of your writing, one with an ordinary lead. Prepare an overhead transparency of that lead. Share it with the students.

2. Discuss the opener in your draft. Point out how ordinary it is, how it would not intrigue readers, how it is only one step away from "It was a dark and stormy night." Following is the one that was used with the sixth-grade students, discussed previously.

One day I was walking along the path in the woods on my way to Duck's Nest. I wasn't thinking much about anything until I got to the creek that serves as the mid-way point between home and my favorite swimming hole.

3. Together with students, rewrite that opener using a quotation, description, statement, dialogue, thoughts, or action.

Quotation

Ernest Hemingway once wrote, "The only thing that could spoil a day was people" and that's exactly what spoiled mine the day I walked the woods to Duck's Nest. I wasn't thinking ...

Description

The trees and bushes, looking like they had been smudged with giant emerald crayons, formed an aisle along the warm, loamy path to Duck's Nest. I wasn't thinking ...

Making a Statement

The woods on the way to Duck's Nest seemed safe enough. I wasn't thinking ...

Dialogue

"Hello," I called to the trees that lined the path to Duck's Nest, "Hello, birch. Hello, cypress. Hello willow." I wasn't thinking ...

Thoughts

Since I had challenged myself to walk the entire way through the woods to Duck's Nest without a thought, I wasn't thinking ...

Action

Running along the path to Duck's Nest would get me to there faster, but today I just lallygagged in the woods. I wasn't thinking ...

Coherence

Definition. Coherence is the Velcro of writing. Without coherence, neither sentences nor paragraphs would make sense. They would be disjointed, disconnected – a jumbled mass of words. Just as something inserted between two pieces of Velcro keep it from cohering, an unrelated thought inserted between sentences or paragraphs muddles the writing.

Internal Coherence. Internal coherence is the glue that coheres one sentence to another in a given paragraph. It may be created by a repeated word or synonym, a sustained thought, a clause that harkens back to the previous sentence, parallel structure, a pronoun, chronology, or a coordinating or subordinating conjunction that indicates the relationship between one sentence and the next. In a well constructed paragraph, each sentence coheres or sticks to the one before it in some way.

Young writers or inexperienced writers often choose the connecting word or words *and* or *and then* to cohere sentences. They might write something like:

> I went to the store. And I bought some candy. And I bought some soda pop. And I paid the lady. And I came home.

That paragraph is coherent; each sentence coheres to the previous one. Sometimes, however, teachers, striving for sentence variety, say, "Never begin a sentence with *and*." (For a full explanation of why *and* and *but* are perfectly proper ways to begin a sentence, see John R. Trimble's *Writing with Style*, chapter 9.) When teachers make that statement without providing other alternatives for coherence, students often lose the one glue they owned. Without that glue, students lose the connections, and their paragraphs take on a surreal quality. It is somewhat like affixing paper. Using white paste works. Young children use it. If someone took their jar of white paste away without replacing it with alternatives, such as rubber cement, glue, staples, tape, or a way to fold the paper, children's one way to cohere would be lost and the papers would fall apart. Thus, strategies, no matter how unsophisticated or repetitive, should never be taken away from writers unless alternative strategies are taught.

> *A teacher who is also a mother brought me something her 7-year-old son had written at home. She told me after he wrote his name, Dustin, at the top of the page, he continued*

> > *Once i saw a canoe and*
> > *there was pepl in it and they*
> > *were going down stream.*

> *At that point he looked up at her and said, "And they got to some Indian tents." Then he mumbled, "Can't use it. Can't."*
> *"Can't use what, Dustin?" his mother asked.*
> *"And. Can't use it there."*

Again he bent over his work:

> *They went in the tent and got*
> *something to eat.*

As written, the piece is incoherent because the cohesive sentence—*And they got to some Indian tents*—remains in Dustin's head. Interestingly, because he carefully followed the rules and had no replacement for *and*, he merely left a space for it (see fig. 8.4).

Fig. 8.4. Dustin's writing. 🕴

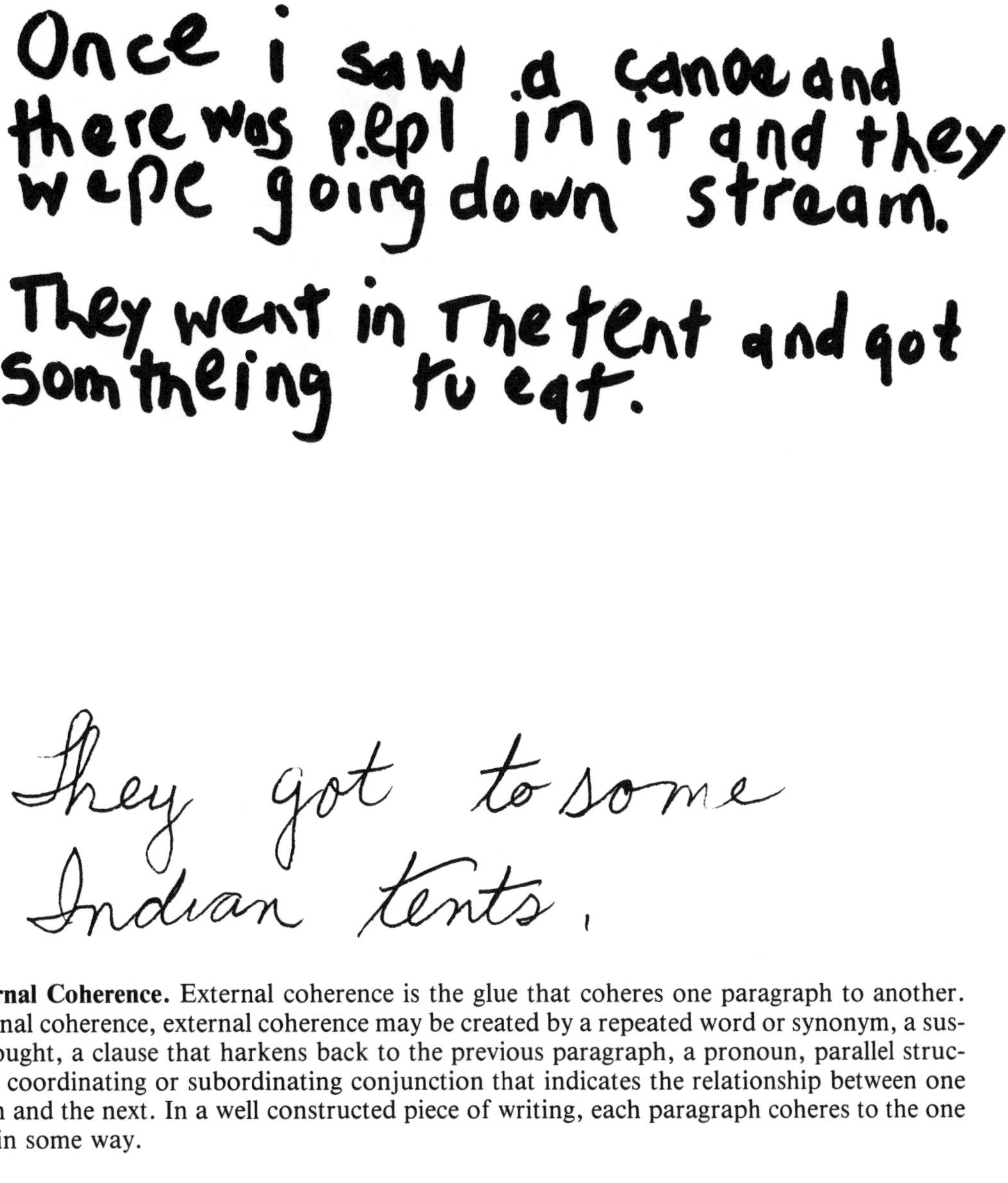

External Coherence. External coherence is the glue that coheres one paragraph to another. Like internal coherence, external coherence may be created by a repeated word or synonym, a sustained thought, a clause that harkens back to the previous paragraph, a pronoun, parallel structure, or a coordinating or subordinating conjunction that indicates the relationship between one paragraph and the next. In a well constructed piece of writing, each paragraph coheres to the one before it in some way.

CONCLUSION

William Zinsser says in *On Writing Well*, "Knowing when to end an article is far more important than most writers realize. In fact, you should give as much thought to choosing your last sentence as you did to your first" (77). That advice applies equally well to other genre.

Often, studying beginning and ending sentences verifies Zinsser's point. Quotations, dialogue, statements, descriptions, thoughts, and action may just as appropriately conclude a piece as open it. To teach conclusions, follow the same procedure used for leads. Sometimes matching introductions and conclusions proves interesting. Following are the concluding lines to the openers used to illustrate leads.

She looked up and across the barn, and her lips came together and smiled mysteriously.

The Grapes of Wrath (John Steinbeck)

Jean: ... It's horrible! But there's no other possible end to it! — Go!

Miss Julie (August Strindberg)

But see how fast the smoke rises — oh, even faster when we laugh, lifting our hopes, higher and higher.

The Kitchen God's Wife (Amy Tan)

I still have a piece of that root, put away in a box with my journal, my can of tobacco tags, the newspaper write-up when I got run over by the train, a photograph of me and Miss Love and Grandpa in the Pierce, my Ag College diploma from the University — and the buckeye that Lightfoot gave me.

Cold Sassy Tree (Olive Ann Burns)

As a man with cut hair, he did not identify the rhythm of three strands, the whispers of coming and going, of twisting and typing and blending, of catching and of letting go, of braiding.

A Yellow Raft in Blue Water (Michael Dorris)

The women and I wink at one another and pass old Jacoba another helping of chicken soup — and so the celebrations begin!

Let the Celebrations Begin!
(Margaret Wild and Julie Vivas)

So Gram began the story.

Dicey's Song (Cynthia Voigt)

He hated human slavery. But through it all, he never lost his faith in people and his belief in God. He cherished freedom to the last.

Anthony Burns: The Defeat and Triumph of a
Fugitive Slave (Virginia Hamilton)

None of these endings lets the reader down. Each holds a sense of finality or what Zinsser calls "the unexpected last detail" (80). The point is that the old maxim: "Tell what you're going to tell; tell it; tell what you told" is no longer viable. This redundant form no longer fits today's fast-paced, instant-replay, nanosecond world.

Other Genres. Students may conduct their own investigation of leads and endings. They may consider them in other genres. While studying essays, students may select leads and endings for discussion. David Quammen's "Strawberries Under Ice," chosen for *The Best American Essays 1989*, offers an intriguing frame.

Lead:	Antarctica is a gently domed continent squashed flat, like a dent in the roof of a Chevy, by the weight of its ice.
Conclusion:	I believe, with Leontiev, in salvation by ice (quoted in Wolff 212-224).

Or, if working with biography, autobiography, or memoir, students may compare the opening and closing lines of Eudora Welty's memoir, *One Writer's Beginnings* to those of Annie Dillard in *The Writing Life*.

Welty's lead:	In our house on North Congress Street in Jackson, Mississippi, where I was born, the oldest of three children, in 1900, we grew up to the striking of clocks.
Dillard's lead:	When you write, you lay out a line of words.
Welty's conclusion:	As you have seen, I am a writer who came of a sheltered life. A sheltered life can be a daring life as well. For all serious daring starts from within.
Dillard's conclusion:	Teihard de Chardin wrote, "To see this is to be made free."

Studying the writing of others as an avenue to one's own connects the two in powerful ways for students. They begin reading as writers and writing as readers. They see, for example, that hooks are used in all genres, that endings are not synonymous with abandonment. Perhaps most importantly, they see by looking closely at parts of writing what all writing aspires to be: "clear, vigorous, honest, alive, sensuous, appropriate, unsentimental, rhymic, without pretension, fresh, metaphorical, evocative in sound, economical, authoritative, surprising, memorable and light" (Macrorie 22).

APPLICATION

Take a draft of any prose piece. Reenter the piece in order to analyze its paragraph structure. In or near the margin label each paragraph according to TRIPSQA, functions, and use the brace { } to identify paragraph blocs (see page 260).

After this analysis, meet in small groups to discuss the implications of your findings to the teaching of paragraphs.

WORKS CITED

Becker, Alton L. "A Tagmemic Approach to Paragraph Analysis." *CCC* 15 (October): 136-140.

Burns, Olive Ann. *Cold Sassy Tree*. New York: Dell, 1984.

Clavell, James. *Shogun*. New York: Dell, 1975.

Corder, Jim W., and John J. Ruszkiewicz. *Handbook of Current English*. Glenview, IL: Scott, Foresman, 1985.

Cowan, Gregory, and Elizabeth Cowan. *Writing*. New York: John Wiley, 1980.

Decker, Randall E. *Patterns of Exposition 8*. Boston: Little, Brown, 1980.

Dillard, Annie. *The Writing Life*. New York: Harper & Row, 1989.

Dorris, Michael. *A Yellow Raft in Blue Water*. New York: Warner Books, 1988.

Gould, June. *The Writer in All of Us*. New York: E. P. Dutton, 1989.

Gould, Stephen Jay. *Bully for Brontosaurus: Reflections in Natural History*. New York: W. W. Norton, 1991.

Hamilton, Virginia. *Anthony Burns: The Defeat and Triumph of a Fugitive Slave*. New York: Alfred A. Knopf, 1988.

Hawking, Stephen W. *A Brief History of Time*. New York: Bantam Books, 1988.

Irmscher, William F. *Teaching Expository Writing*. New York: Holt, Rinehart & Winston, 1979.

Loomis, Roger Sherman, and Laura Hibbard Loomis, eds. *Medieval Romances*. New York: Modern Library, 1957.

Macrorie, Ken. *Telling Writing*. New York: Hayden Books, 1970.

McCrum, Robert, William Cran, and Robert MacNeil. *The Story of English*. New York: Viking, 1986.

Melville, Herman. *Great Short World of Herman Melville*. New York: Harper & Row, 1966.

Ogg, Oscar. *The 26 Letters*. New York: Thomas Y. Crowell, 1961.

Quammen, David. "Strawberries Under Ice." In *The Best American Essays 1989*, edited by Geoffrey Wolff. Pp. 212-224. New York: Ticknor & Fields, 1989.

Rodgers, Paul. *The Sentence and the Paragraph*. Champaign, IL: National Council of Teachers of English, n.d.

Soto, Gary. *Taking Sides*. New York: Harcourt Brace Jovanovich, 1991.

Steinbeck, John. *The Grapes of Wrath*. New York: Bantam Books, 1969.

Strindberg, August. *Miss Julie*. In *Eight Great Tragedies*, edited by Sylvan Barnet, Morton Berman, and William Burton. New York: Mentor, 1957.

Tan, Amy. *The Kitchen God's Wife*. New York: G. P. Putnam's, 1991.

Trimble, John R. *Writing with Style.* Englewood Cliffs, NJ: Prentice-Hall, 1975.

Voigt, Cynthia. *Dicey's Song.* New York: Fawcett Juniper, 1982.

Weintraub, Stanley, ed. *The Portable Bernard Shaw.* New York: Penguin Books, 1983.

Welty, Eudora. *One Writer's Beginnings.* Cambridge, MA: Harvard University Press, 1984.

Wild, Margaret, and Julie Vivas. *Let the Celebrations Begin!* New York: Orchard Books, 1991.

Zinsser, William. *On Writing Well.* New York: Harper & Row, 1988.

"When Is a Paragraph?"

ARTHUR A. STERN

(From *College Composition and Communication*, October 1976.
Copyright 1976 by the National Council of Teachers of English.
Reprinted with permission.)

Commentary

This experiment is worth conducting not only with teachers, but also with students. A favorite section we like to use is affectionately referred to as "Queen Victoria." It can be found in Teaching Expository Writing *by William F. Irmscher (New York: Holt, Rinehart & Winston, 1979) or* The Sentence and the Paragraph *by Alton Beckner (Champaign, IL: National Council of Teachers of English, n.d., 35). The piece, written by Lytton Strachey, is about the English Constitution. Stachey wrote the piece as one paragraph.*

The English Constitution—that indescribable entity—is a living thing, growing with the growth of men, and assuming ever-varying forms in accordance with the subtle and complex laws of human character. It is the child of wisdom and chance. The wise men of 1688 molded it into the shape we know, but the chance that George I could not speak English gave it one of its essential peculiarities—the system of a Cabinet independent of the Crown and subordinate to the Prime Minister. The wisdom of Lord Grey saved it from petrification and set it upon the path of democracy. Then chance intervened once more. A female sovereign happened to marry an able and pertinacious man, and it seemed likely that an element which had been quiescent within it for years—the element of irresponsible administrative power—was about to become its predominant characteristic and change completely the direction of its growth. But what chance gave, chance took away. The Consort perished in his prime, and the English Constitution, dropping the dead limb with hardly a tremor, continued its mysterious life as if he had never been.

For the past few years, for reasons that will soon become apparent, I have asked students in one of my courses to take part in a small, informal experiment. Each student receives a duplicated copy of the same 500-word expository passage. The passage, I explain, has been transcribed verbatim from Cleanth Brooks and Robert Penn Warren's *Fundamentals of Good Writing* (New York: Harcourt, Brace & Co., 1950), pp. 290-291, departing from the original in only one respect: the original passage was divided into two or more paragraphs; the copy contains no paragraph indentations. Their task is simply to decide into how many paragraphs they think it should be divided and to note the precise point (or points) at which they would make their divisions.

The exercise usually takes fifteen minutes or so, and we spend another ten or fifteen analyzing the results, which are invariably intriguing. We discover that some students have divided the passage into two paragraphs, others into three, still others into four or five. What is more, nearly all of these possible divisions seem justifiable—they "feel right." Most surprising of all is the fact that only five students out of the more than 100 who have tried the experiment have paragraphed the passage precisely as Brooks and Warren originally did.

These results are hardly earthshaking, I realize. They prove, if they prove anything, only that different students have different intuitions about paragraphing and that many of these intuitions turn out to be equally acceptable, equally "correct." But perhaps a few facts I have so far neglected to mention will make this discovery less trivial than it may at first appear.

First of all, the students who took part in the exercise were not college freshmen; they were teachers of English. Secondly, most of them were committed to the theory, promulgated by many handbooks, that the paragraph is a purely "logical" unit of discourse. They believed, that is to say, that a paragraph is a group of sentences developing one central idea. They believed that good paragraphs always (or usually) contain identifiable topic sentences which always (or usually) occur toward the beginning of the paragraphs. They believed that a well-developed paragraph is "a composition in miniature." They believed, accordingly, that good English teachers should concentrate on teaching their students to write good paragraphs, because good paragraphs are really good essays writ small.

My purpose in having them try my little experiment was to induce them to question the adequacy of the theory they had accepted. If, as the handbooks declare, a paragraph represents a "distinct unit of thought," why is it that we can't recognize a unit of thought when we see one? If every paragraph contains an identifiable topic sentence, then why don't all of us identify the same topic sentence? If good paragraphs are really compositions in miniature, why do some of us, given a passage not marked off into paragraphs, find in it two mini-compositions, while others find three or four or five? Aren't compositions—even miniature ones—supposed to have clear beginnings, middles, and conclusions?

Too many of us, I suspect, have based our teaching of the paragraph on a theory whose origins we do not know and whose validity we have not tested. Like the poet's neighbor in Frost's "Mending Wall," we go on repeating our fathers' sayings without ever going behind them.

Behind the logical (or "organic") theory of the paragraph lies a history replete with facts that cast doubt upon its authenticity. That history, as Paul C. Rodgers, Jr. has told us, begins a little more than a hundred years ago with Alexander Bain, a Scottish logician.[1] The fact that Bain was a logician, not a teacher of rhetoric, is itself of first importance; for he conceived the paragraph as a deductive system, a collection of sentences animated by unity of purpose, a purpose announced in an opening topic statement and developed through a logically ordered sequence of statements that "iterate or illustrate the same idea."[2]

What is more, Bain appears to have constructed his deductive model by a purely deductive procedure. Making no empirical analysis of actual paragraphs, he simply

Watching teachers and students mark where they would paragraph the selection gives the same types of results that Stern chronicles. So often teachers and students paragraph and have little metacognitive reasons behind this paragraphing. Most paragraph intuitively.

When writing a paragraph, teachers in Stern's classes and other writing institutes do not follow the rule that they teach their students. Their response is, "But students must first learn how to do it by the rules before they can break them." Rather than re-examining the rule, their approach is to promulgate the rule.

There exists the possibility that answers to questions such as Stern's could vary between cultures and experiences. A unit of thought in a culture that values brevity will be radically different from the thought in a culture that values indirect and implied meaning. A case in point: growing up in the Panhandle of Texas, language experience in our family was different from the language experience in a family from the Northeast. A typical childhood exchange would have included certain avoidance of the real issue. In fact, so often, we talked around the problem, without ever directly assaulting the situation.

In contrast to the language of my paternal family was the language of my maternal grandfather. Born and raised in Scotland, he was a man of few words. He, like Bain, dismissed anything not logical. Both grandparents raised animals for food consumption, and as a child, I thought feeding the animals was a treat. Often I would adopt and anthropomorphize a chick or a bunny. When it was time for grandmother to wring the neck of the pullet, she would say something like, "I have to get dinner" or "You like my fried chicken, don't you?" On the other hand, my grandfather would say, "Don't get attached. I will have to kill the rabbit for food."

The point is that life and language affect the way we perceive structure and function. When communicating with my grandmother, I could be more lyrical. With my grandfather,

I made my point and accepted his reply knowing there would be no lengthy discussions.

Soon, Rodgers's observation will read, "for placing twenty-first century paragraph rhetoric...."

See page 250.

Teaching these "types" would extend students' awareness of the complexity of topical paragraphs.

transferred to his collection of sentences the classical rules governing the individual sentence—rules, now discredited, which defined the sentence as a group of words containing a subject and predicate and expressing a "complete and independent thought." Bain's paragraph, notes Rodgers, "is simply a sentence writ large,"[3] that is, an extension by analogy of logic-based grammar.

Others—John Genung, Barrett Wendell, and George R. Carpenter among them—subsequently refined Bain's theory without questioning its assumptions, reducing Bain's original six principles of paragraph construction to the now familiar triad of Unity, Coherence, and Emphasis, and tacking on the added notion that the paragraph is the discourse in miniature. Bain's influence is thus responsible, Rodgers observes, "for placing twentieth-century paragraph rhetoric in a deductive cage, from which it has yet to extricate itself."[4]

The work of extrication has been quietly going forward, however. The most recent empirical testing of Bain's theory, and the most damaging to it, was undertaken by Richard Braddock in 1974.[5] Braddock's study, completed shortly before his untimely death, took specific aim at two of Bain's assertions: that all expository paragraphs have topic sentences and that topic sentences usually occur at the beginnings of paragraphs. Braddock's method of research and his findings call into question not only Bain's century-old paragraph theory but also, as I shall try to show, the procedures and generalizations of such "new" rhetoricians as Francis Christensen and Alton L. Becker.

Braddock began by making a random selection of essays published in *The Atlantic, Harper's, The Reporter, The New Yorker,* and *The Saturday Review.* Almost immediately, he ran into trouble, finding it extremely difficult to define the very item he was looking for—the topic sentence. "After several frustrating attempts to underline the appropriate T-unit where it occurred," Braddock reported, "I realized that the notion of what a topic sentence is, is not at all clear."[6] In an effort to define this central term, he developed an entire catalogue of "types" of topic sentence: the *simple* topic (the kind the handbooks say all paragraphs should contain); the *delayed-completion* (a topic stated in two T-units, not necessarily adjacent); the *assembled* (not actually a sentence at all, but a composite, gummed together from fragments of several sentences running through the paragraph); and the *inferred* (a "topic sentence" nowhere explicitly stated by the writer, but construed by the reader).

But even after thus extending—one might say stretching—the definition of "topic sentence," Braddock found that a considerable proportion of the paragraphs in his sample contained no topic sentence of any type. In some instances, a single topic sentence governed a sequence running to several paragraphs; in others, the indentations seemed "quite arbitrary." All told, fewer than half the paragraphs contained a simple topic sentence; even when topic sentences of the delayed-completion type were included, the total came to little more than half (55%). How many paragraphs *began* with topic sentences? Fewer than one out of seven (13%) in all the paragraphs Braddock analyzed.

These findings, Braddock noted with quiet understatement, "did not support the claims of textbook writers about the frequency and location of topic sentences in professional writing."[7] Although scientific and technical writing might present a different case, with respect to contemporary professional exposition the textbooks' claims were "just not true."[8]

Braddock's study thus effectively disposes of the hand-me-down Bainalities of the textbooks. But it does more than that: as I have already suggested, Braddock's empirical method and his findings cast some doubt upon certain conclusions reached by Francis Christensen and A. L. Becker, and upon the evidence those conclusions are based on.

In his "Generative Rhetoric of the Paragraph," Professor Christensen proposes, as did Alexander Bain, "that the paragraph has, or may have, a structure as definable and traceable as that of the sentence and that it can be analyzed in the same way."[9] From this premise he moves rather swiftly to conclusions hardly distinguishable from Bain's:

1. The paragraph may be defined as a sequence of structurally related sentences.

2. The top sentence of the sequence is the topic sentence.

This is what Irmscher calls the paragraph bloc.

This seems to be a chicken-or-egg syndrome. Textbooks propagate a notion of the topic sentence "because teachers demand it." Teachers teach it "because that's the way it is in textbooks." And so it goes.

banality—*ordinary and uninteresting.*
Bainality—*overgeneralized or incorrect.*

3. The topic sentence is nearly always the first sentence of the sequence.[10]

Although he subsequently allows for exceptions (some paragraphs have no topic sentence; some paragraphing is "illogical"), there is no mistaking that Christensen's second and third "rules" are essentially those which Braddock found to be false. Unlike Braddock, Christensen seems to believe that the term *topic sentence* is self-explanatory, requiring no precise definition. In support of his claims, Christensen cites the "many scores of paragraphs I have analyzed for this study."[11] He does not tell us how these paragraphs were selected or from what sources; he tells us only that in the paragraphs he analyzed "the topic sentence occurs almost invariably at the beginning."[12] Had he detailed his procedures as he did in his study of sentence openers,[13] we would have reason to be more confident of his conclusions. But he doesn't. The evidence underlying his statements about the paragraph is soft and rather vague.

A. L. Becker's "Tagmemic Approach to Paragraph Analysis," viewed in the light of Braddock's study, seems similarly flawed. Like Christensen, Becker applies to the paragraph the instruments of sentence-analysis, with the purpose of "extending grammatical theories now used in analyzing and describing sentence structure ... to the description of paragraphs."[14] He cautions at the outset that he intends to examine the paragraph from only one of three possible perspectives—the "particle" perspective—and that his description will necessarily be somewhat distorted because it suppresses the "wave" and "field" aspects of paragraph structure. But this disclaimer hardly prepares us for his subsequent assertion that there are "two major patterns of paragraphing in expository writing,"[15] and only two: the TRI (Topic-Restriction-Illustration) pattern and the PS (Problem-Solution) pattern. Becker continues:

> Although there are more kinds of expository paragraphs than these two, I would say that the majority of them fall into one of these two major types. Many expository paragraphs which at first appear to be neither TRI or [sic] PS can be interpreted as variations of these patterns.... There are also minor paragraph forms (usually transitional paragraphs or simple

---

Sometimes teachers assign writing in ways that assume collective, universal knowledge of such terms as topic sentence. This often breeds misunderstanding.

If considered from the perspective of the old paradigm A = 1, 2, 3, TRIPSQA suggests a cause and effect that is logical, linear, rigid, and absolute.

If considered from the perspective of the new paradigm that subsumes the particle, wave, and field theory of quantum physics, TRIPSQA suggests something quite different. According to Gary Zukav in The Dancing Wu Li Masters *(Bantam 1984), quantum theory does not state that something can be wavelike and particlelike simultaneously, rather it depends upon the field (200-201).*

Applying particle, wave, and field quantum theory to TRIPSQA implies that paragraphing can be static and dynamic, depending upon its context.

Use TRIPSQA to ratiocinate a paragraph (see "Application," page 267), rather than as a way to write up to a paragraph.

lists)—and, finally, there are "bad" paragraphs, like poorly constructed, confusing sentences.[16]

Again, one is left in doubt as to the evidence on which these generalizations rest. Surely, in preparing his study, Professor Becker cannot have read *all* expository paragraphs; how, then, can he justify a claim concerning a "majority" of them? What were his sampling procedures? Were "bad" paragraphs included in his total count, or were they summarily rejected as unworthy of consideration? To these and other questions he provides no answers. We know only that his findings conflict sharply with Braddock's, and that, in Becker's case as in Christensen's, we find, somewhat disguised by modern terminology, the century-old claim that a "good" paragraph begins with a topic sentence and develops the idea stated by the topic sentence.

If we are ever to rid ourselves of Bain's lingering legacy we must, it seems clear, abandon his exclusively sentence-based, "particle" approach to paragraph description, an approach that treats the paragraph as if it were an isolated, self-contained unit, and imposes upon it a rigid set of logical and quasi-grammatical rules. We must adopt an approach that describes not only the internal structure of a paragraph but also its external connections with adjoining paragraphs and its function in the discourse as a whole. What we need, Paul Rodgers proposes, is "a flexible, open-ended *discourse-centered* rhetoric of the paragraph":

> All we can usefully say of *all* paragraphs at present [Rodgers explains] is that their authors have marked them off for special consideration as *stadia of discourse*, in preference to other stadia, other patterns, in the same material. Paragraph structure is part and parcel of the discourse as a whole; a given stadium becomes a paragraph not by virtue of its structure but because the writer elects to indent, his indentation functioning, as does all punctuation, as a gloss upon the overall literary process under way at that point.[17]

Paragraphing, Rodgers here suggests, is governed by rhetorical choice rather than by logical or grammatical rule. Like the structure

William Irmscher had his students replicate Braddock's research. They found much the same. Braddock is so well respected as a researcher that the National Council of Teachers of English awards outstanding research in his name each year. The Braddock Award is coveted and worthy of his legacy.

It has been 16 years since Stern called for an adoption of an approach to paragraphing that describes the internal and external functions of a paragraph, and still texts have not changed.

Rhetorical choice, of course, fosters higher-level thinking skills.

"Someday it will be possible to teach paragraphing by rule and formula, though I frankly doubt it." Powerful words from Stern. The rules are not there to support the continuation of teaching paragraphing as if there were such rules. No wonder students feel cheated when they find out they were taught and graded on something that was not even true.

One powerful activity to use with students is a comparison of paragraphs from a work of Charles Dickens to those of most contemporary writers.

of a sentence or that of a fully-developed essay, the structure of a paragraph arises out of an *ethos* and a *pathos* as well as out of a *logos*—out of the writer's personality and his perception of his reader as well as out of his perception of the structure of his subject-matter. The logic and "grammar" of a given paragraph are conditioned—sometimes powerfully—by what may be termed the psycho-logic and socio-logic of a particular rhetorical occasion.

As every experienced writer knows, paragraphing helps establish a tone or "voice." (Editors know this, too. That is why they frequently re-paragraph a writer's prose to bring it into conformity with their publication's image.) Short paragraphs appear to move more swiftly than long ones; short paragraphs lighten up the appearance of a page, whereas long ones, containing the identical information, give the page a heavier, more scholarly look. Just as he adjusts his sentences and his diction, the writer may adjust his paragraphs, deliberately or intuitively, to achieve a variety of rhetorical effects—formality or informality, abruptness or suavity, emphasis or subjunction.

Paragraphing practices are also governed by changes in fashion and social convention. Today's paragraphs are considerably shorter than those of fifty or a hundred years ago. "In books of the last century," Paul Roberts reminds us, "a paragraph often ran through several pages, but the modern reader wants to come up for air oftener. He is alarmed by a solid mass of writing and comforted when it is broken up into chunks."[18] In consequence of this change in literary fashion, nineteenth-century rules of "logical" paragraphing, dubious in their own day, are outmoded now. What might once have appeared as a single paragraph is today routinely broken up into smaller units which, taken together, comprise what William Irmscher has labeled a "paragraph bloc."[19] Indeed, when Richard Braddock observed that one topic sentence frequently governed an entire sequence of paragraphs, he was suggesting that contemporary professional writers use blocs rather than single paragraphs as logical units much of the time.

In sum, today's paragraph is not a logical unit and we should stop telling our students it is. It does not necessarily begin with a topic sentence; it does not necessarily "handle and exhaust a distinct topic," as the textbooks say it must do. It is not a composition-in-miniature, either—it is not an independent, self-contained whole, but a functioning part of discourse; its boundaries are not sealed but open to the surrounding text; it links as often as it divides. Shaped by the writer's individual style and by the reader's expectations as well as by the logic of the subject-matter, the paragraph is a flexible, expressive rhetorical instrument.

Perhaps some day it will be possible to teach paragraphing by rule and formula, though I frankly doubt it. In any case, the rules and formulas that govern the paragraphing practices of professional writers have yet to be discovered. Let us, therefore, focus our students' attention on what they have to say—on the arguments they want to present, the points they want to make—and not on the number of indentations they should use in saying it. Let us make them think about the topics they plan to discuss rather than about the "correct" location of their topic sentences. Let us, in other words, make our teaching discourse-centered. If the whole does indeed determine the parts, their paragraphs should improve as their essays mold them into form.

We must also stop telling students to begin a paragraph with such statements as, "I'm going to tell you a story about..." or "This is about...."

Stern, and many scholars like him, keep saying the same thing over and over—we must teach, in context, all that is to be learned. Students will learn how to paragraph if paragraphing is taught within the writing process.

Teachers College
Columbia University

NOTES

1. Paul C. Rodgers, Jr., "Alexander Bain and the Rise of the Organic Paragraph," *Quarterly Journal of Speech*, 51 (December, 1965), 399-408.

2. Alexander Bain, *English Composition and Rhetoric* (London: Longmans, Green, 1866), cited by Rodgers, p. 404.

3. Rodgers, "Alexander Bain," p. 406.

4. Ibid., p. 408.

5. Richard Braddock, "The Frequency and Placement of Topic Sentences in Expository Prose," *Research in the Teaching of English*, 8 (Winter, 1974), 287-302.

6. Ibid., p. 291.

7. Ibid., p. 301.

8. Ibid., p. 298.

9.   *Notes Toward a New Thetoric* (New York: Harper & Row, 1967), p. 54.

10.   Ibid., pp. 57-58.

11.   Ibid., p. 58.

12.   Ibid.

13.   Ibid., pp. 39-51.

14.   A. L. Becker, "A Tagmemic Approach to Paragraph Analysis," in Francis Christensen *et al., The Sentence and the Paragraph* (Champaign, Ill.: National Council of Teachers of English, 1966), p. 33.

15.   Ibid., p. 34.

16.   Ibid., p. 36.

17.   Paul C. Rodgers, Jr., "A Discourse-Centered Rhetoric of the Paragraph," in Francis Christensen *et al., The Sentence and the Paragraph* (Champaign, Ill.: National Council of Teachers of English, 1966), p. 42.

18.   Paul Roberts, *Understanding English* (New York: Harper & Row, 1958), p. 423.

19.   William F. Irmscher, *The Holt Guide to English* (New York: Holt, Rinehart and Winston, Inc., 1972), p. 86.

9

FINISHING THE PIECE
Proofreading, Editing, and
Publishing

It is no good imagining that one is going to be a writer—be it of romance,
history, biography, stream-of-consciousness novel, or whatever—
unless one can deal with this inherent loneliness and the self-discipline
that has to go with it. Your finished product comes from the inside
of your own head, and no person but you has the ability
to set it down and so, set it free.

—Rosamunde Pilcher □

Writers write with an audience in mind. If their writing is personal, such as notes jotted in a journal or diary, their process stops there. There is no need to worry about a fragment or incoherence; there is no need to flesh out an image or make sure the spelling is correct. If, however, writers intend their writing to be shared with others, the processes of proofreading, editing, and ultimately publishing take on an importance tantamount to a school's drama production, a sporting event, a band concert, or an edition of the school's newspaper. Going public means making sure that the writing is clear for the reader, eliminating distracting errors, and choosing the best format.

Just as professional writers reject some of their writing early in the process, choosing for publication only what is worth what Faulkner calls "the agony and the sweat," of taking the piece through the various processes leading to publication, so, too, not every piece of a student's writing goes through the entire process from prewriting through publishing. Only after choosing to commit to one piece does a student work through the process schema to publishing.

WRITING PROCESS SCHEMATA

Figure 9.1 (see page 280) shows three models of the writing process. The first model highlights the process's recursive nature; the second emphasizes its dynamic nature; and the third conveys the sense of juggling many simultaneous tasks. No one model can show the path a writer must take from prewriting through publication. There are times when the writer feels forces moving in and out of the writing; the writer must be prepared for this. The writing process is complex and cannot be simply diagrammed.

Fig. 9.1. The complex of writing processes.

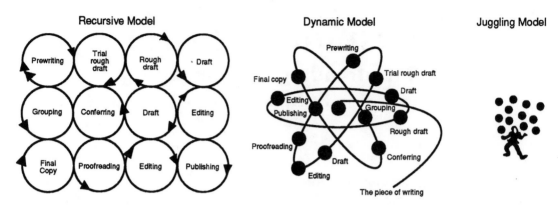

The degree of implementing the process schema for publishing depends upon grade level, the purpose of the writing, and, of course, the recursive nature of writing itself. The following list summarizes the various processes in the overall process schema.

- Prewriting: whatever list, loop, freewrite, or other exercise gave birth to the idea or focused the idea.

- Trial rough draft: the first attempt at giving that prewriting form.

- Rough draft: honing the form, usually through a genre.

- Drafts: reworking the writing by correcting, revising, and reformulating.

- Groups: an immediate audience for the piece, a way to get needed feedback.

- Conferring: a way to hear the writing through another's ears, to see it through another's eyes, to seek advice on specifics, or to get another opinion about the writing. Conferences may be with peers or the teacher.

- Drafts: reworkings generated by feedback from groups and conferences.

- Editing: checking clarity, coherence, and development; the writer reads the writing as an editor would.

- Final copy: the final rework of the writing.

- Proofreading: the last read of the final copy for the purpose of catching any minor errors.

- Editing: correcting any errors caught by proofreading.

- Publishing: taking the writing public.

Figure 9.2 shows the process schemata for various grade levels.

Process Schema for Primary Grades. Prekindergarten and kindergarten students need only to prewrite (draw, scribble) and share what they have written. To be sure, these pieces merit display in and about the classroom, and may even be affixed together as class books or individual books, but the purpose of writing at this level is to achieve fluency; to have fun with sounds, letters, and words; and to gain confidence.

(Text continues on page 282.)

Fig. 9.2. Process schemata for various grade levels.

Prekindergarten and Kindergarten

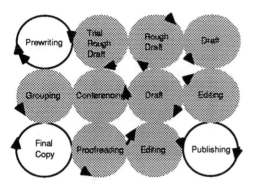

First and Second Grades

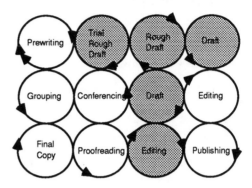

Third, Fourth, and Fifth Grades

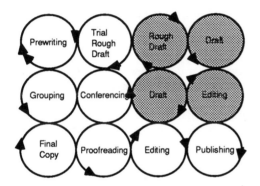

Sixth, Seventh, and Eighth Grades

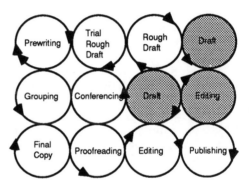

Ninth Through Twelfth Grades

First- and second-grade students may prewrite and then practice their handwriting and appropriate skills as they prepare their prewriting for publication, perhaps in book format. After the prewriting, these students may engage in a group activity, such as Say Back (see page 157) to receive some comments on their pieces from their peers, or they may talk about their writing with the teacher before they write their final copy. Minimal proofreading or editing may take place. Writing a final copy legitimizes writing legibility and certain skills, such as capital letters and periods, since publishing helps young writers understand the reader's need to know things like when sentences begin and end.

Process Schema for Intermediate Grades. Third-, fourth-, and fifth-grade students may prewrite; work the prewriting into a trial rough draft, which they color code and ratiocinate; and complete the process with a final copy. The trial rough draft enables the teaching of grammar within the process and provides a time and place for students to do some revising and reformulating. The trial rough draft is often what the students share in group or in conference with the teacher. After that, the students write the final copy, then proofread and edit that copy. These young writers are old enough to prepare and submit their writing for publication. Children's publications are discussed later in this chapter.

Process Schema for Middle Grades. Sixth-, seventh-, and eighth-grade students may prewrite; do a trial rough draft, which they color code and ratiocinate; and extend that trial rough draft into a rough draft, which permits some depth with revision and reformulation. After they take their rough drafts to group or conference, they write their final copy and proofread and edit that copy. This is followed with some sharing or some form of publishing.

Process Schema for High School. Ninth- through twelfth-grade students may prewrite; do a trial rough draft, which they color code and ratiocinate; extend that trial rough draft into a rough draft for more depth of revision and reformulation; then further extend that rough draft into as many drafts as it takes for even deeper revising and reformulating before they write the final copy. At some point during the drafting, students may group and conference. Students proofread, edit, and publish their final copies.

CLOCKING FOR PROOFREADING

Clocking is the proofreading/editing technique that finds its roots in a brief article "Peer Proofreading" by Irene Payan (124-125). During clocking, students sit facing each other in two concentric circles. This arrangement approximates the face of a clock. The teacher calls out details to be checked. Students in the inner circle remain seated; the other students move one place to the right after each detail is checked. In this way different students proofread each other's work.

To prepare for clocking, students first create packets of their writing.

1. Students gather all their writing and arrange it in descending order—final copy on the top, prewriting on the bottom.

2. They label a sheet of paper "The Proofreading Page" and number from 1 to the number the teacher designates. (Each number represents a different detail to be checked.)

3. Across the top of The Proofreading Page they write, "This paper belongs to _____," filling in their name.

4. They place the proofreading page on top of the final copy.

5. They take a seat in one of the circles.

Clocking then begins.

1. Students exchange papers with the persons opposite them.

2. They write their names next to the number of the detail about to be checked. They are the editors for that detail.

3. Depending on what has been taught, the grade level, and the students' proofreading skill, the teacher calls out a detail to be checked. For example, the teacher may invite them to check the spelling of *its* (the pronoun) and *it's* (the contraction).

4. Students rapidly skim the paper. When they find the detail they are to examine, they check its correctness in the context of the sentence. If there are no errors, they indicate that in some way (a smiley face, a positive comment). If there is an error, *they do not correct it*; rather, they indicate the page and line so the writer may reconsider it.

5. This continues through all details to be proofread.

At the conclusion of clocking, all students receive their papers and the proofreading sheet.

1. Students read their proofreading sheet.

2. They decide if any corrections need to be made by rethinking what has been pointed out. For example, they may look up words in the dictionary, check their grammar books, discuss a correction with a particular editor, or ask the opinion of the teacher.

3. If the writer decides an editor has found a valid error, the writer has the opportunity to correct it.

4. If the writer disagrees with an editor, the writer may leave it.

5. When students have had sufficient time to look over their proofreading sheets and have edited them, they *must* sign off on the proofreading sheet and turn it in with all the papers of the process.

Not only does clocking teach students the worthwhile habits of proofreading and editing, it sharpens their awareness of details and places upon them the responsibility of an acceptable final copy. The clocking technique enables the teacher to once again present instruction in a context in which the learning is important, is real. As each detail is checked, the teacher may present it as a micro-lesson. Also, peer proofreading is enhanced by the act of each editor identifying himself or herself. If students are allowed time to edit after the proofreading, a tactic they see as improving their grade, and if they are encouraged to take the time to make necessary corrections, they will soon value the peer who helps them make their papers and their grades better. Thus, the teacher's paper load is lightened because the students *do* catch many of those peevish errors that teachers feel obligated to correct.

On occasion teachers have been observed preparing editing sheets ahead of time. While this might allow for smoother transitions and a more rapid progression through the experience, consider why it might be best for students to make their own editing sheets. First, because writing is a mode of learning, when students write the skill being "clocked" on their paper, they have one more opportunity to internalize, or reinforce prior concepts. Second, student-prepared material has the "feel" of discovery; thus, students have a higher degree of engagement. Third, students consider one concept or detail at a time, so they focus more intently on it rather than trying to do everything at once—or nothing at all.

There was no doubt Dawn was destined to become an editor. She caught errors that often bypassed even the closest reader in the class. And she was conscientious. During one particular class, she spent maximum time on a new classmate's paper that was riddled by comma problems.

When I received that final paper, I noticed so many comma errors, I looked back over the proofreading sheet. Clearly the errors had been noted but were ignored. I was taken aback by the student's disregard of Dawn's help.

"Please see me after class," I wrote on her analytic scale. Something was amiss and I wanted to investigate.

When the student stopped by after class, I showed her Dawn's suggestions. "Did you choose not to consider these?" I asked.

"Oh," she replied, looking totally dumbstruck, "Is that why we did all that stuff? I thought if I did that I was cheating!"

The moral of the story, as the saying goes, is to make certain that students are clear about the purpose of clocking. The notion of having this opportunity—one more time—to perfect their pieces is often foreign to them. They may need to be reassured; it is a legitimate part of the process.

VARIATIONS OF SELF-PUBLISHING

Patience will have to be the rule of thumb for the teacher and students who practice self-publication. Self-publication is noisy, messy, chaotic, and exciting. Possibly these descriptors apply to most learning, but unfortunately, they often do not. The school culture that identifies quality learning with silent seatwork will be unnerved by the classroom that engages in self-publishing. Self-publishing does not mean that the teacher has no control or should abandon control; rather, self-publishing means that students will be active and engaged in a process that demands collaboration, communication, synthesis, and exploration.

As with genre, writers cannot determine prior to the writing what type of publishing their work will require. The genre, the meaning, and the purpose of the writing influence the writer's decisions on where and how to publish.

Publication can take place many different ways. For some students, writing the final copy on colored paper with colored ink is enough. Others want to see their byline in the school newspaper. Some embrace the class anthology. Some students will publish this piece in the school's literary magazine. Some will create a piece of extraordinary power.

Verbal Sharing

Teachers can encourage their students to read their works aloud by establishing a time and place to do so and by establishing ground rules for audience behavior. Teachers who create a safe atmosphere for sharing find students eager to read their own works—and listen to others.

AUTHOR'S CHAIR

Some publishing may simply be via an author's chair or a read-around. The author's chair is a special chair in the room that is only used for the sharing of one's writing. The more special the chair, the more special the sharing. Helen Parks at Mission Valley Elementary in Victoria, Texas; Rosemary Denk at Smithfield Elementary, Birdville ISD, in Fort Worth, Texas; and Jill Reason at Armand Bayou Elementary, Clear Creek ISD, in Houston, Texas, are three excellent teachers who make use of the author's chair. On most days, at least two to three students have something they have written that they want to share in the author's chair. The students wait expectantly for the time to share and are respectful of each other as the author shares.

These teachers structure their classrooms and schedules so there is a place and time for authors to share. The students meet on a rug or carpet squares. They come with their writing. An author is invited to share. He or she goes to the author's chair and reads. If there is artwork to share the author invites a friend to assist. Students sit respectfully listening and applauding the writing. After the author shares, she or he selects the next author to share. Initially students may be hesitant or shy, but after time and positive experiences, they all want to share. Teachers find they often have more readers than time can allot.

READ-AROUND

Patricia Schroyer at Clements High School, Fort Bend ISD, in Sugarland, Texas, and Alana Morris at Lewisville High School in Lewisville, Texas, both make the read-around a special culminating experience for their student writers. On selected days through the year, usually after final copies have been completed, students come to the read-around, and everyone shares. Students move their chairs to form a large circle or they sit on the floor. One student begins the reading. When that student finishes, the next student reads, and so on, moving around the circle until everyone has read. The students listen and respond nonverbally with nods, smiles, or applause. While some teachers find it difficult for secondary students to read aloud their writing, Pat and Alana find the opposite—their students want to share. While these two techniques are successful, most teachers find book-making an efficient and successful way to initiate self-publishing.

Literary Magazine

The school literary magazine is an excellent vehicle for student publication. Readers and contributors can share in its display as a place for student writing, art, and photography. Consider the foreword and cover art (fig. 9.3, page 286) of the *Pegasus*, a student publication of Westfield High School in Spring, Texas.

The foreword reads:

> With the world changing as much as it is, it is difficult to be timely, especially when attempting to comment on the state of the world. The USSR is suffering from an implosion; she is at once pulling towards her insides and tearing at the old grey head of communism. The Soviet Union has finally realized that walls, physical or mental, hinder growth and thought.
>
> This realization has led to the destruction of the Berlin Wall and the opening of the Brandenburg Gate. These happenings are symbolic of the changes the people are experiencing and they act as representations of the future. The new-found freedom of the Wall coming down marks the opening of minds, the creativity of wills, the refusal to permit things to stay as they always have been.
>
> With the Walls removed, people will attain a renewed vigor for the creative and imaginative. Never again will Walls stop them from thought or meditation not endorsed by a higher power.
>
> The Wall is down, crumbled and broken, and people are opening the unstoppable forces of the imagination and the mind. These people have gone *Beyond the Wall*." (i)

As mentioned previously, the writing in student literary magazines can display extraordinary power, as in one young writer's first published piece reprinted in figure 9.4 (see page 287).

The cover of *Pegasus* reinforces the students' theme.

Fig. 9.3. Cover of student literary magazine, *Pegasus*.
(Westfield High School, Spring, Texas)

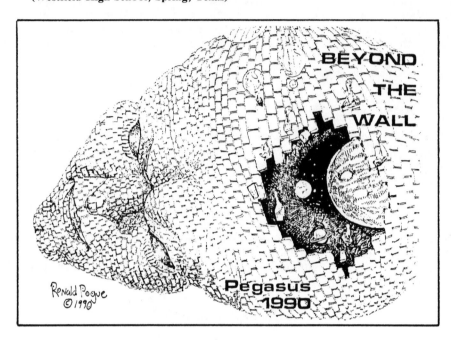

(Text continues on page 288.)

Fig. 9.4. A young writer's first published piece.

PEGASUS
BEYOND THE WALL

Living Through the Holocaust

Writing about my childhood in a communist Cambodia under the bloody and vicious reign of the Khmer Rouge brings back a flood of unpleasant and painful memories. It was a time when life and work fused into one single inseparable entity, until the exhausted mind refused to function and simple survival reflexes took over. From then on, existence was a routine compliance to the rules and regulations established by the leader.

My childhood was a time of destruction in Cambodia. The country under the leadership of Sihanouk was at was with its rebellious people, most of whom were simple uneducated peasants lured by the promises of "Liberty, Equality, and Fraternity." The civil war which ravaged the country ended in the Khmer Rouge's victory. Vividly, I remembered April 25, 1975 when the clock struck seven, and I awoke with confused cries ringing in my ears. Looking out through the opened window, I recalled my hurried scrambling with my clothes on seeing the roof of a nearby theater licked by flame. Outside, distraught mobs pushed and shoved each other trying to get ahead; soldiers in black uniforms with long red kerchief tied around their waists were yelling into the speaker: "Get out quick! Americans are bombing! Head into the country!" I remembered my mother holding my hand so tight that it hurt as we pushed through the panicked throngs and my grandmother's repeated warnings for us to stay close together.

We fought our way forward, leaving our home and most of our belongings behind us. Near the city limit, an incident occurred which left me and most of the crowd silent and subdued throughout our exodus. Several bodies piling on top of the others lied at odd angles, staining the ground around them a dark red. Near the scene, a beautiful and majestic house stood: its porch was full of dark uniformed soldiers with brilliant red kerchief around their waists, gleaming rifles on their shoulders, and a double strings of shiny bullets across their chest. I remembered those black figures standing on the porch with the sun glinting on the barrels of their rifles and prisms of light dancing on their armored chest. Amongst those stern figures, a slight youth in unrelieved black sat on a swing, humming under his breath as he lovingly polished his rifle with a red kerchief. As I watched fascinated, a gentle breeze wafted by caressing the youth's hair. Abandoning his task, the boy looked up and tilting his head toward the sky drank in the cool air. Soon the breeze was gone, and the boy resumed his position and continued with his work.

The pile of corpses, the bloody ground, the black clothed youth with a rifle in his hand, and even my mother's pale lace registered dimly but had no reality for me. Strangely, it was the swing that somehow brought me out of my inertia. Dizziness overwhelmed me. Suddenly, my head throbbed, my stomach tied itself in knots, and my legs trembled. I tried to speak but my throat seemed swollen and my tongue stuck to the roof of my mouth, and no words came out. I tugged at my mother's sleeve; she looked down at me, then handed me the water bottle, telling me to drink slowly and rest for a moment. As I stood there staring at the swing, I felt a hand behind my back propelling me forward and heard my grandmother's voice in my ear telling me not to stare at the soldiers. When we caught up with my father, I was allowed to ride on his shoulders, and soon we had left the city behind us.

Looking back to the time of my childhood, I remembered not so much terror as tiredness. Yet terror was everywhere. In the evening, afraid to be alone and be accused of having individualistic tendency, neighbors gathered around in groups and, anxious to appear enthusiastic about their "freedom, equality, and fraternity", spent the little time they had away from work extolling the government and the leader. At night, husbands and wives avoided each other's company, fearing and distrusting one another for each had been enthusiastic at the meeting where they had seen husbands and wives reporting one another to the authority. But terror was highest during the three-day holiday when all works were suspended, and the children were allowed to leave school and visit their parents. This was a dangerous time for everyone, for these children had been meticulously indoctrinated by the village leaders, and their sharp eyes were quick to detect treasons in thoughts and in actions against the teaching of the Leader. However, terror had little part in my childhood. I recalled sudden screams and gunshots that pierced the silence of the night; but I felt no fear at these unearthly sounds, only resentment that they had interrupted my sleep. Working fourteen hours a day had deprived me of all feeling except that of tiredness. I recalled feeling so exhausted that I was unable to eat and fell asleep with the food in my mouth. Then again, there were times when I could not sleep because I was too wearied and hungry.

Death has a lot to recommend when life means living under the Khmer Rouge's regime. Looking back now, I wonder that people should cling so tenaciously to life when hope for a better future was nonexistent. I was too young then to know of suicide. Yet even if I had been old enough, I doubt that I would have committed suicide. Not because of religious tenets against killing oneself, for having experienced the holocaust, religion has lost its meaning for me. No, the reason is much simpler. To consciously choose death requires drastic thoughts and emotion such as despair, boredom, apathy, or even religious fervor; all of which require energy. I had not enough energy even to generate these thoughts and feelings, let alone the will power needed to overcome the human's survival instinct which also requires tremendous energy. But life has been kind to me: I have survived the holocaust. I have done nothing to deserve life, but I have been granted life, just as those others who have not done anything to deserve death, have had life taken away from them. I am luckier than those others, just as there are others luckier than I who had not lived through the holocaust. Enough! The past is dead if not yet buried. I am alive today; the sum of all my past has gone and tomorrow may or may not come. Ω

The author of this writing has asked to remain anonymous. It is not the policy of the *Pegasus* to print work unless the author wants to be recognized. But policy is being abandoned for this single instance. The writing reflects the horror of a regime that still oppresses innocent people, people that could be affected if the author were known. We have retained the original language for authenticity. — The Editors

Making Books

Before making books in the classroom, teachers should practice making their own books. Once the teacher has gone through the process, then she or he can anticipate where students need assistance and where they need to be left alone. No two classes, nor for that matter no two students, will duplicate the way they make books. Experience readies the teacher. (See examples of various types of self-published books in fig. 9.5, pages 295-297.)

Generally, the following guidelines prepare the teacher and the students for bookmaking:

1. Have materials available in a publishing center or corner of the room.

2. Instruct students about the materials and label them.

3. Prepare guides for making various types of books. Illustrated instructions for making 11 kinds of books follow. These can be photocopied, cut apart, affixed to oak tag, and laminated for extended use.

4. Teach responsibility in the care and maintenance of the publishing center.

5. Have a place to display the books.

ACCORDION BOOK

1. Fold an 8½-by-11-inch sheet of paper in half, short end to short end.

2. Fold back flaps to center fold.

There will be a cover and seven pages of text and artwork. Works well with circle stories or pattern books.

EXTENDED ACCORDION BOOKS

Begin with an 8½-by-11-inch sheet of paper.

1. Cut strips 3 inches wide and 11 inches long. You will get two strips from each sheet of paper. Throw away the scraps.

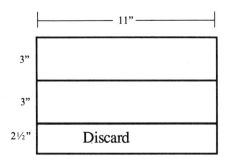

2. Fold the strips to form 3-by-3-inch squares. This leaves an extra 2-inch piece at the end.

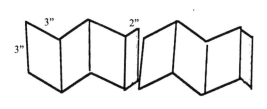

3. Repeat steps 1 and 2 to create the number of pages desired.

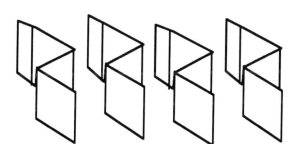

4. To assemble the pages, glue together as shown.

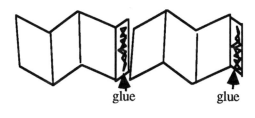

5. The basic book is finished.

6. Make hard covers for front and back. To make the covers, cut a 4-inch square from oak tag or some other sturdy stock. Cut a 5-inch square from decorative cover paper. Glue the cover paper to the oak tag, trim as shown. Fold back the edges and glue in place.

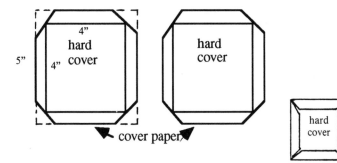

(Instructions for completing cover for Extended Accordion Books continue on page 290.)

Extended Accordion Books *(continued)*

7. Glue the first and last pages to the inside
    of the front and back covers.

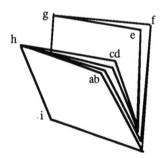

NOTE: If students write their stories onto the pages before the covers are attached, be sure they
leave the first and last pages blank or they will be lost when the covers are attached.

EIGHT-PAGE BOOK

1. Fold an 8½-by-11-inch sheet of paper in   2. Fold again, short end to short end.
    half, short end to short end, and crease.

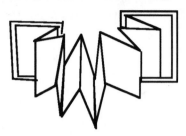   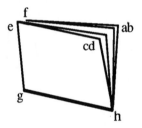

3. Fold again, short end to short end.   4. Open up the page to reveal the 8 sections.

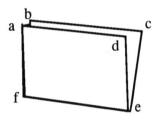   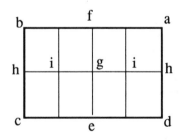

(Instructions for Eight-Page Book continue on page 291.)

5. Make the original fold again, short end to short end. Cut from center point (g) to the mid point (i) along the crease.

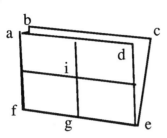

6. Open back up and fold long side to long side. Push left and right ends to center.

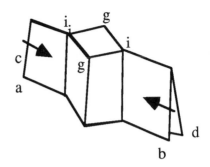

7. Fold flat along all creases to form the eight-page book.

There will be six pages for writing and artwork, and a front and back cover.

DIORAMA BOOK

1. Make the eight-page book through step 6.

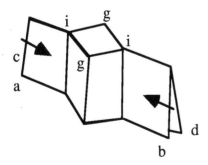

2. Cut flaps out of interior box as shown.

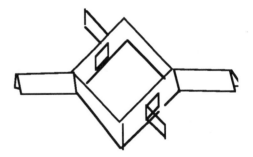

3. Decorate the inside of the box with a scene that illustrates the writing.

ENVELOPE BOOK

1. Staple together as many envelopes as needed along the left side.

2. Illustrate the envelopes.

3. Write the text on cards or paper and place them inside the envelopes.

NOTE: Two excellent examples of envelope books and the epistolary are *The Jolly Postman, or Other People's Letters* by Janet Ahlberg and Allan Ahlberg and *Griffin & Sabine: An Extraordinary Correspondence* by Nick Bantock. Using these books as models, students on all grade levels have produced books with such titles as *The Bard, or Correspondence Among Shakespeare's Characters, Charlotte and Wilbur: Letters from the Farm,* and *Scout and Boon.* These books are not only highly imaginative, they also serve as responses to literature.

POP-UP BOOK

1. Fold page in half and cut through the double page in two places. Do not cut more than half way down.

2. Fold down top panel. Crease.

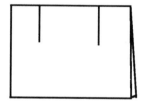

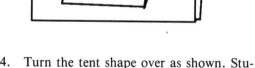

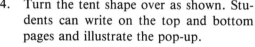

3. Make a tent shape and push the cut flap in between the outer pages.

4. Turn the tent shape over as shown. Students can write on the top and bottom pages and illustrate the pop-up.

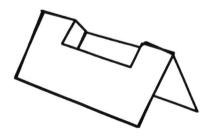

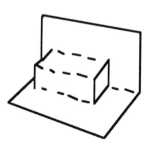

BAGGY BOOK

1. Staple up to ten resealable, gallon-sized plastic bags together along the bottom.

2. Cover the stapled area with plastic tape.

3. Cut sheets of paper to fit in the bags. Write and illustrate on paper—front and back. Place the sheets inside the baggies.

4. Store baggy books in decorated paper-towel tubes. The tubes can be stored together in a box.

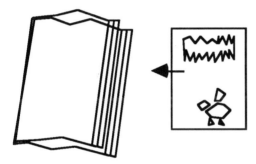

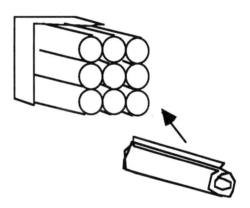

SADDLE-STITCHED BOOK

1. Stack several sheets of paper. Fold the stack in half. Open it out and draw a line down the crease in the top sheet of paper. Using a ruler, draw a dot every half inch along the crease.

2. Get a wooden block or piece of very hard plastic that measures 9½ by 12 inches. This is the tabletop protector. Place a towel on the tabletop and place the tabletop protector on top of the towel. (The towel will help stop the protector from sliding.)

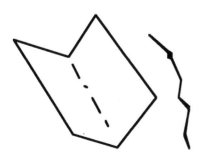

(Instructions for Saddle-Stitched Book continue on page 294.)

Saddle-Stitched Book *(continued)*

3. Place the stack of papers on the tabletop protector. Be sure the stack is neat and no ends are hanging off the tabletop protector.

4. Have one student hold the stack in place.

5. Have a second student use a rubber mallet and nail to make a small hole at each dot along the crease.

6. Using a darning needle and dental floss, sew the pages together.

FITTED BOOK

1. Fold a sheet of paper in half, short end to short end. Cut a long sliver off the fold, leaving 1 inch on each end.

2. Fold another sheet, short end to short end. Cut a 1-inch notch out of each end of these. Do this, one sheet at a time, to as many sheets as needed.

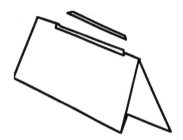

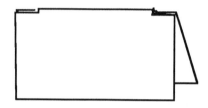

3. Take the sheet from step 1 (the sheet with the long sliver cut out). Open it and lay it flat on the table.

4. Take the sheets from step 2. Open them flat, one on top of the other, to make a stack *next to* the sheet from step 1.

5. Slide the stack of sheets from step 2 through the sliver in the sheet from step 1. Stop when the notches are lined up with the sliver. You can slide the stack of sheets through the sliver all at once, or you can slide in one sheet at a time. To make it easier to slide the sheets through the sliver, you can lightly fold the stack long end to long end, then open the sheets up when they are in place.

6. Tidy up the pages so all the edges are even. Fold at the creases to make the book.

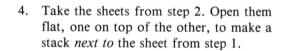

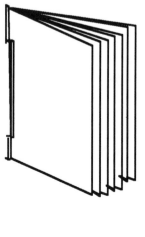

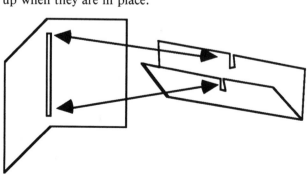

RING BOOK

1. Use a three-hole punch to punch holes down the left-hand side of pages.

2. Place rings in the holes.

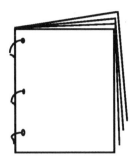

A NOTE ABOUT SHAPE BOOKS

Students have been writing shape books for years. Generally the teacher uses a black line master or a stencil and the students cut out the shapes. They all look the same and they all read pretty much the same. These books harken back to the reference in chapter 2 of "perfectly bland papers." One second grader responded to a pre-prepared, apple-shaped page of sixteen lines, "Do real people make these?" There is nothing inherently wrong with the shape book; the problem is the implication that children cannot produce their own shapes or thoughts, or that students must master the prepackaged form before inventing their own.

Art educators have long fought the mass production of copy-cat art. Expression and creativity become impotent in an atmosphere of precut, premade, prethought work. What students produce from their own imaginations is far more meaningful to them.

The guidelines for shape books are simple: let the author and illustrator select the shape. Allow the shapes to reveal what the writing has to say. When students write about pumpkins, let them make their own shapes for their own pumpkins. When students write about Chaucer, let them investigate shapes appropriate for the Middle Ages. When students publish poems about nature, let them experiment with natural shapes.

(Text continues on page 298.)

Fig. 9.5. Examples of self-published books.

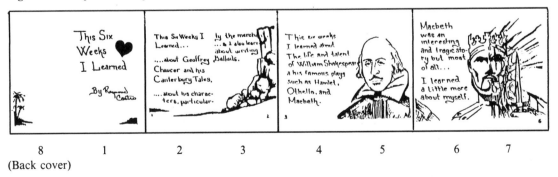

8   1   2   3   4   5   6   7

(Back cover)

Twelfth-grader Raymond Castro's eight-page book, *This Six Weeks I Learned*. (Edison High School, San Antonio ISD)

(Fig. 9.5 continues on page 296.)

Fig. 9.5 *(continued)*

Ninth-grader Omar Leos's eight-page book *SAISD vs. Coleman.* (Edison High School, San Antonio ISD)

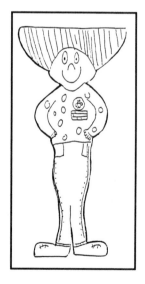
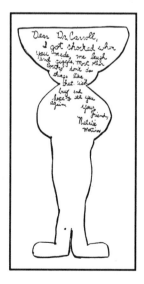

First-grader Natalie Martinez's shape book, *Dear Dr. Carroll.* (Oak Hill Terrace Elementary, Northside ISD, San Antonio)

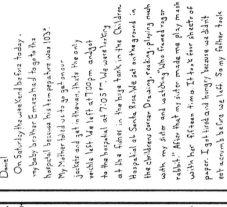

Emazo and the Hospital

By Daniel Molina

RED CROSS

Lucia Luna, Teacher

Translation

Dolores, my sister, Ihas a that made me play mash with her fifteen times, Ernest my foster brother Ihas a that were glasses and turns around and never knows where he is going. Me Daniel, and of corse, my father to Mc Donalds. Dolores, Ernst and I got a happy meal and my father bought a Mc rib. Dolores and Ernst got a Dr. Pepper and I shared a Byrd. We went back to the hospital parking lot and ate. Then we got out of the stuffy van. At that time it was 9:00pm I could not belive my eyes it only seemed like 7:00pm because the sun was partly up and it was still light. When we got inside my mother was still waiting to see the slow doctor in the waiting room. All the adults were watching Young guns, when all of a sudden

TO My fourth grade teacher for my baby brother Emazo and my sister Dolores, Ernest, Edward, Teresa, my mother and of corse Dr. Mc Vertain.

the hospital t.v. broke. So all the parents watched the looney tune cartoons. All the parents were turning red like Beets with hair, eyes, noses, and worst of all mouths! The children weren't at all happ they were bord to death like a lumpon a log because all they could see were backs of adults. At last they called my mother and Emazo in to the room. I went too! She carried him into the room and put him on the stretcher. My brother tryed to grab all the Equepment. My mother toled me to go to the waiting room and ask my father what time it was. My father said 1:15 am. So I tolled my mother and she tolled me to go back to the waiting room. So I waited 2 whole hours and at 3:00pm My mother came out of the Examadion room. I felt sleepy. We left.

Daniel
On Saturday, the weekend before today, my baby brother Emazo had to go to the hospital because his temperature was 103°. My Mother toled us to go get our jackets and get in the van, that's the only vechile left. We left at 7:05pm and got to the hospital at 7:05pm. We were looking at the fishes in the huge tank in the Children Hospital at Santa Rosa. We sat on the ground in the childrens corner Drawing, reading, playing mash with my sister and watching "Who framed roger rabbit." After that my sister made me play mash with her fifteen times. It took four sheets of paper. I got tired and hungry because we didn't eat a crumb before we left. So my father took

In the van. I asked my mother why we waited so long and she said "because there was only one Doctor. I never asked my mother what was wrong with E damzo because at that time I fall asleep and I slept like a baby.

Fourth-grader Daniel Molina's baggy book, *Emazo and the Hospital.* (San Antonio ISD)

The Publishing Center

Self-publishing requires a cache of supplies. There is no need for this to create considerable expense. Often, when students are left to their own devices, with a minimum of supplies and freedom to explore, they find, make, or improvise the supplies they need or require. Following is a list of general supplies:

- X-acto® knives—very sharp, not recommended for use without adult supervision

- cutting mats—good cutting mats, available from art suppliers, are expensive but indestructible

- metal rulers—these keep their shape and can not be cut into

- adhesives—Elmer's® glue is still the best and safest; glue sticks are also easy to use

- needles—large darning needles available from fabric stores work well

- cover board—everything from cardboard and posterboard to oak tag

- paper—8½-by-11-inch or 11-by-17-inch paper of any quality and color

- chicken rings—plastic rings available at craft stores for binding

- string—dental floss works best for saddle stitching

- tape—3M's plastic tape cannot be beaten for quality and durability.

DESKTOP PUBLISHING

The printing press allowed everyone to become a reader. The computer allows everyone to be a publisher. Desktop publishing, virtually unthinkable 20 years ago, offers new and exciting possibilities for the classroom. Programs such as *PageMaker®* and *Quark XPress®* allow students to practice pasteup and copyediting, and create professional-looking publications. Figure 9.6 shows three publishing formats offered in *PageMaker®*. Note that format 1 uses a 4-column layout in a variety of configurations, format 2 uses a straight 3-column format, and format 3 uses a 3-column format with double-wide columns on pages 1 and 3.

Fig. 9.6. Model formats offered in *PageMaker®* desktop publishing software.

Format 1

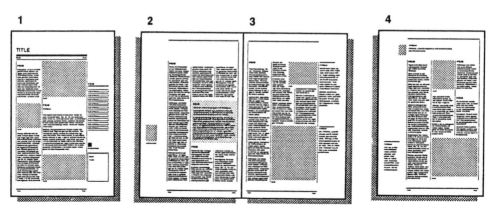

Format 2

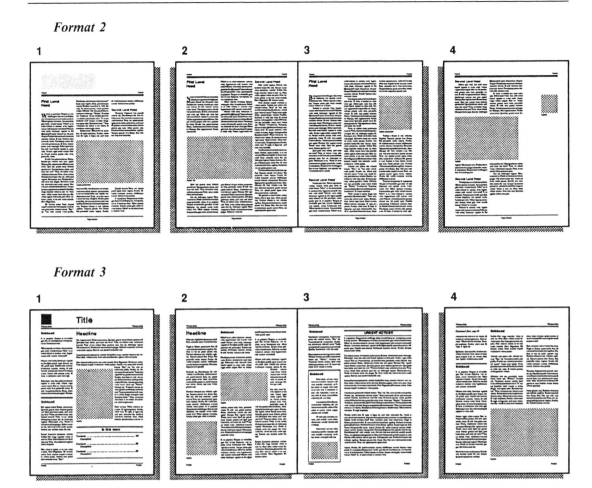

Format 3

MAKING SELF-PUBLISHED BOOKS AVAILABLE

The natural place to display the students' books is the classroom. But displays need not be limited to single experiences. Librarian Barbara Jansen of Live Oak Elementary in Round Rock, Texas, has constant, rotating peer-authored book displays. These books include both fiction and nonfiction. The librarian places check-out cards with individual call numbers in every book. Students who wish to read someone's book simply check it out. (The students at Live Oak have never lost one of the peer-authored books.) And at the end of the year, the librarian conducts a Reader's Choice awards campaign where any student who has read *all* the student books for a certain grade level can vote for his or her favorite. The librarian places a gold seal bearing the embossed school emblem on the cover of the winners' books. When the students learn that their principal, Marla Mcghee, checks out every book, they see that their writing has value in a larger world. This is true self-publishing.

Professional and Commercial Publication

Another way for writers to engage in publishing is by preparing their manuscripts for publication in commercial magazines, journals, and books. Writing for publication in this manner is the ultimate extensive writing. Teachers often do not see themselves as writers. But if classroom teachers do not write and publish, how will they share the richness of discovery? And how will they model publication for their students? Teachers are experts in areas other than academe. For example, Melisse Lee, Abilene, Texas, writes about genealogy; Mary Warren, San Antonio, Texas, writes about herbs; Anita Olmstead, Pasadena, Texas, writes about antiques and collectibles; and Sylvia Bell, Pasadena, Texas, writes about yearbooks. Teachers of language arts know more than just the practice and theory of teaching English. So do students. Students can and need to write for publication.

But wait. Before getting all wound up in the glamor of publishing, heed what William Stafford says about writing for publication, "By following after money, publication, and recognition, you might risk what happened to the John Cheever character who in like manner 'damaged, you might say, the ear's innermost chamber where we hear the heavy noise of the dragon's tail moving over the dead leaves' " (5). His advice is to follow the writer's compass, by "allowing in your own life the freedom to pay attention to your feelings while finding your way through language" (4). Good advice for both teachers and students who write. The writer must first have something to say.

Then comes the challenge. Finding a place to get the "stuff" published. Stephen King advises writers to know the markets. "Only a dimwit would send a story about giant vampire bats surrounding a high school to *McCall's*. Only a dimwit would send a tender story about a mother and daughter making up their differences on Christmas Eve to *Playboy* ... but people do it all the time" (19). Nothing strikes an editor as inane as the inappropriate manuscript.

Reading what writers say about publishing may confuse the writer who wishes to publish. Some say, "Write first for yourself; then find a place to send it." Other say, "Write what sells." Others, such as Madeleine L'Engle say, "Whom does the writer write for? It is only a partial truth to say that I write for myself, out of my own need, asking, whether I realize it or not, the questions I am asking in my own life. A truer answer is that I write for the book" (27).

Writing for publication can be a writer's most rewarding experience. Gloria Foster, Conroe ISD, Conroe, Texas, had her first article published in *Learning* about the gray child, the one that disappears in class. Gloria was elated when she received the notice of acceptance. When the magazine came out, and the cover featured a child painted gray standing in a crowded classroom, Gloria carried the magazine around with her for days. Finally her daughter said, "Mother, get over it." Gloria finally did get over the initial elation, but she has never gotten over seeing her name in print for the first time. Barbara Wurthmann, another teacher in Conroe, Texas, had a similar experience with her article, "First Grade Reflections," when it was published in *English in Texas*. Barbara's confidence as a writer and a teacher increased because of this publication. When the piece was read at the school-board meeting and she received recognition as a teacher who writes, Barbara understood the power of words in a new way.

The experiences of teachers mirror those of students.

> *Danielle and Erin, students at Westfield High School in Spring, Texas, had decided to work together on an exposé of prejudicial attitudes and practices of department-store sales clerks. They had observed on one of their shopping excursions that some people had difficulty getting waited on by some clerks. They set up an experiment. Danielle dressed up and went to one of Houston's most famous shopping malls. She entered each store, and Erin timed the responses of the sales clerks. They recorded their experiences and took notes. Danielle had no trouble getting assistance. Before going back to the mall the next Saturday, Danielle and Erin stopped at the Salvation Army and purchased clothing for Erin from the discarded apparel. Erin did not comb her hair, wore no make up, and generally appeared quite sloppy. They then*

proceeded to the mall. This time Erin entered the shops, and Danielle timed the responses. Of the 126 stores Erin entered, she was asked to leave 25. The average time that it took the sales clerks to ask Erin if she needed assistance was 7 minutes compared to Danielle's 48 seconds.

Erin noted that the clerks were rude, spoke to her in a pejorative tone. Erin, who was slated to be the valedictorian of a large high school, was angry. At one exclusive woman's name-brand, leather-goods store, she at the counter for 20 minutes. Growing restless after 10 minutes, she began asking the clerks for assistance. The clerks ignored her. Finally, the store security guard came and asked if he could help her.

Proud of their research, they were eager to write up their findings. The result was a 15-page account of two girls going shopping — one who appeared privileged in every way, the other whose only flaw was a lack of a privileged appearance.

Not satisfied by writing the paper alone, they wanted a wider audience. They prepared their paper as a manuscript and sent it to the management of the mall. Three days later they had a call from the assistant manager. A week later they met with the assistant and the manager. Two weeks later they were presented copies of their writing at the store manager's monthly luncheon. Letters of apology and copies of store clerk policies, which clearly noted that discrimination based on status, race, or creed would not be tolerated clearly sent the message that Danielle and Erin had found an audience.

Writers cannot get published if they do not send out their manuscripts. Obvious enough, but, unfortunately, some writers put a great deal into a piece of writing only to give up at this point. Now is not the time to become faint-hearted. Nor is it the time to play what Peter Elbow calls the "doubting game." The adage applies here: "If you think you can, you can; if you think you can't, you can't." Teachers who send out for publication get published. Teachers who have classrooms where publication is encouraged, nurtured, and taught have students who get published. Some of the publications are stunning and prestigious, some are local and ordinary — both are rewarding.

BASIC VOCABULARY OF PUBLISHING

If a writer wants to join the ranks of the professional, he or she must learn the jargon. Following is a brief glossary. For a more comprehensive guide to the vocabulary of publishing, see a current edition of *Writer's Market*.

Advance. Money the publisher pays prior to publication. The advance is against the royalty, that is, the total amount to be paid for the piece of writing.

Byline. The author's name, which usually appears below or beside the title of an article. The term *byline* is not used for books.

Chapbook. Small booklet of stories and poems, usually paperback.

Contributor's copies. Copies of the issue of the magazine in which an author's work appears, sent to the author. For academic publications, this is generally the only payment the writer receives.

Copyright. The protection that an author has to keep someone from stealing the work. It is not necessary to register the work with the Copyright Office. The moment the author writes the work it is automatically protected. Registering is usually done after publication or infringement. Publishers generally purchase all rights or some rights when they purchase a manuscript.

Cover letter. A brief letter that accompanies the manuscript. The cover letter contains only the title of the manuscript and assurance that it is not being submitted simultaneously to another publisher.

Kill fee. Fee paid for manuscript that was accepted but not used. For example, several Cold War spy novels were "killed" after the Berlin Wall came down.

Payment on acceptance. As soon as the editor accepts the manuscript for publication, payment is made.

Payment on publication. Payment is not made until the manuscript is printed—several months to a year or more after acceptance.

Query. A letter to the editor to arouse or see if there is interest in what the writer is writing. A query letter contains a brief summary of the article, written in the style and tone that will be used in the article, length of the article, and the author's credentials.

Release. A guarantee that the manuscript is original and unpublished.

Royalty. An amount paid to an author, usually for books. The royalty is generally a percentage— 10-15 percent—of the cover price of the book.

Self-publishing. The author retains all proceeds from sales, because the author pays for all the production, manufacturing, and marketing of the piece. Also called vanity publishing.

Simultaneous submission. Sending a manuscript to two or more editors at the same time. Most publishers do not accept simultaneous submissions. If the writer does simultaneously submit a manuscript, the writer should inform the editor in the cover letter.

Unsolicited manuscript. Any manuscript the editor did not request. Some magazines, such as *Reader's Digest* and *The New Yorker*, do not accept unsolicited manuscripts.

PREPARING THE MANUSCRIPT

All manuscripts should be double-spaced. The exception is very young children writers. Magazines that publish emergent writers often want to see the original work; in that case, a typed transcription should accompany the manuscript. No writer is too young to find an audience; the magazine *Stone Soup* publishes the writing and artwork of young children.

Generally the manuscript being mailed out should contain a cover letter; manuscript, including title page; self-addressed, stamped envelope for return of the manuscript, and the mailing envelope. The cover letter must be a standard business letter. All of the conventions should be observed.

1. *Heading*: first three lines of letter
   a. writer's street address and apartment number (if any)
   b. writer's city, state, and ZIP code
   c. date on which the letter is written

2. *Date*

3. *Inside Address*: addressee
   a. name of editor
   b. title (editor, editor in chief, features editor, etc.)
   c. magazine name (underlined)
   d. street address or P.O. box number
   e. city, state, and ZIP code

4. *Salutation*: formal and followed by a colon
   a. use Mr., Ms., or Dr., and the person's full name

5. *Body*: begins two spaces below the salutation
   a. paragraph as any writing

6. *Closing*: formal and followed by a comma
   a. *Yours truly* and *Sincerely yours* are the most formal
   b. writer's signature
   c. writer's name typed

The manuscript should always have a title page. It should contain the title of the manuscript; author's name, home address, and home phone number as well as the author's work address and work phone number. Be sure to include the area code on phone numbers. Pagination of the manuscript starts with the first page of the writing. The page number should appear in the upper right corner of each page following a one- or two-word head that identifies the manuscript. This identifier may be a short form of the article title or the author's last name. When manuscripts are peer-reviewed or juried (readers for the magazine read the piece and advise the editor on publishing), the author's name should appear only on the title page. In the manuscript, the identifier is the short form of the article's title: "The American Scholar/1." When manuscripts are not peer-reviewed or juried, the author's name should appear on each page as well as the title page, "Dickens/1."

The title page and the manuscript pages are held together with paper clips. Editors generally do not like staples — they make it too hard to turn the pages without folding the manuscript. When placing the paper clip onto the manuscript, most writers like to first place a small slip of paper where the clip will go. This keeps the paper clip from marring the pages, or leaving rust marks.

If more than one copy of the manuscript is requested, most editors will accept one original plus photocopies. They even allow for a few hand-corrected typos. Writers who use the older dot-matrix printers should be warned that most editors find the print too difficult to read and may reject a manuscript solely on this basis. Newer dot-matrix printers with a letter-quality mode are usually acceptable. Advice for all writers preparing a manuscript, whether on computer or the trusty old typewriter: Buy a new ribbon and do not use onion-skin paper. Do not give the editor any excuse to reject the work — a new ribbon and good paper are worth the investment.

THE SASE

The SASE, or self-addressed, stamped envelope, is necessary in publishing. Since not every manuscript finds publication, the writer must observe the conventions and enclose a return envelope with the manuscript being submitted—even if the writer does not want the manuscript back. When preparing the SASE, put the writer's name and address as both addressee and as the return address on the envelope. This way there is little chance the manuscript will be lost in the mail.

Acceptances and rejections may appear illogical or unjust. For example, an editor of a professional journal recently rejected a very fine piece because he had just published a similar piece. Normally, he would have published the second piece but its topic was too similar to the piece he had just published. In this case, the published piece was inferior to the rejected one. On the other hand, editors are known to accept articles because they "fit" or they fill out an issue—reasons that strike some writers as illogical or serendipitous. The writer cannot be discouraged by the rejections; he or she must not take rejections personally.

Most editors prefer the use of large 9-by-12-inch envelopes for manuscripts. Why? When manuscripts are folded to fit in smaller envelopes, they are more difficult for the editor to manage. The writer does not want something like management of the manuscript to be the reason for rejection. Also when preparing the envelope, the writer generally does not affix the return postage on the envelope. Instead, place the postage in a piece of folded paper just large enough to cover the stamps. Then clip the postage in the slip to the return envelope. If the editor accepts the manuscript, the SASE will not be needed. This keeps postage from being wasted. While it is not necessary, it is a courtesy.

PLACES TO PUBLISH

For Teachers. The best place to start is the teacher's professional library. Most teachers belong to their subject matter's professional organization. Language arts teachers may belong to the International Reading Association (IRA) or the National Council of Teachers of English (NCTE). Both organizations have local affiliates. The national organizations have many journals for various audiences. IRA has *The Reading Teacher* for pedagogical articles, *Reading Research Quarterly* for research, a tabloid called *Reading Today*, and others. NCTE has, among others, *Language Arts* for pedagogy and research on the elementary level, *English Journal* for pedagogy on the middle- and high school levels, and *College English, College Composition and Communication, English Education*, and *Research in the Teaching of English*, for research. Most affiliates have local publications.

For the teacher who wants to explore other audiences, the public library is a good place to start. Read the magazines before sending out for publication, and match what has been written to the best audience. Once a magazine has been found, the resource *Writer's Market*, published annually, is the best source of information about most magazines. The directory lists basic publishing information on markets, fees, manuscript requirements, and so forth.

For Students. The same advice for teachers applies for students. An excellent source for student writers is *Children's Writer's and Illustrator's Market*. This directory focuses exclusively on children's and young adult publications. It is published by Writer's Digest Books. Following is a list of selected magazines for student writers.

Alive
Box 179
St. Louis, MO 63188

Cricket
Cricket League
Box 100
La Salle, IL 61301

Highlights for Children
803 Church Street
Honesdale, PA 18431

Sesame Street Magazine
1 Lincoln Plaza
New York, NY 10023

Child Life
P.O. Box 567B
Indianapolis, IN 46206

Ebony, Jr.
820 South Michigan Avenue
Chicago, IL 61301

Jack and Jill
P.O. Box 567B
Indianapolis, IN 46206

Seventeen
850 Third Street
New York, NY 10022

Children's Digest
P.O. Box 567B
Indianapolis, IN 46206

The Electric Co.
1 Lincoln Plaza
New York, NY 10023

Scholastic Scope
50 West 44th Street
New York, NY 10036

Stone Soup
Box 83
Santa Cruz, CA 95063

CONCLUSION

John Ciardi, the poet, writes, "At a recent writer's conference I sat in on a last-day session billed as 'Getting Published.' Getting published was, clearly, everyone's enthusiasm. The hope of getting published will certainly do as one reason for writing. It need not be the only, nor even the best, reason for writing. Yet that hope is always there" (376). Ciardi is right. Hope is always there. Yet he goes on to say,

> Emily Dickinson found reasons for writing that were at least remote from publication. Yet even she had it in mind. She seems to have known that what she wrote was ahead of its time, but she also seemed to know that its time would come ... she spent her last ten years writing her "letters to the future." The letters, to be sure, were addressed to specific friends; yet they were equally addressed *through* her friends to her future readers.... Emily spent ten years writing her poems (1,776 of them), and then ten more years stating the terms for their reception. (376)

To lead students to think that everything they write is worthy of publication is unfair. Surely teachers will allow publishing to take on broader meanings. The student will see, feel, hear, and think about these broader meanings. To move publishing from just print, or final copy, to the self-satisfaction of the completeness of expression is the best "publishing." How does the teacher do this? Each in his or her own way. By finding the satisfaction in his or her own writing. By sending out and receiving rejections. By sending out and seeing the printed copy. By sitting in a chair and watching the faces of the listeners. By having hope.

APPLICATION

Choose one piece of writing you have taken from prewriting to publication. Research a magazine or journal to which you might submit your piece. Write a cover letter and prepare the self-addressed stamped envelope and mailing envelope.

WORKS CITED

Ahlberg, Janet, and Allan Ahlberg. *The Jolly Postman, or Other People's Letters*. London: William Heinemann, 1986.

Bantock, Nick. *Griffin & Sabine: An Extraordinary Correspondence*. San Francisco: Chronicle Books, 1991.

Ciardi, John. "Everyone Wants to Be Published, But...." In *The Writer's Handbook*, edited by Sylvia K. Burack. Boston: The Writer, 1989.

Foster, Gloria. "The Gray Child." *Learning Magazine* (January 1993).

King, Stephen. "Everything You Need to Know About Writing Successfully—In Ten Minutes." In *The Writer's Handbook*, edited by Sylvia K. Burack. Boston: The Writer, 1989.

L'Engle, Madeleine. "Don't Think: Write!" In *The Writer's Handbook*, edited by Sylvia K. Burack. Boston: The Writer, 1989.

1993 Writer's Market. New York: Writer's Digest Books, 1993.

PageMaker®. Version 3.2. Seattle, WA: Aldus Corp.

Payan, Irene. "Peer Proofreading." In *How to Handle the Paper Load*, edited by Gene Stanford. Urbana, IL: National Council of Teachers of English, 1979-80.

Quark XPress®. Version 5.0. Denver, CO: Quark, Inc.

Stafford, William. "The Writer's Compass." In *The Writer's Handbook*, edited by Sylvia K. Burack. Boston: The Writer, 1989.

Wurthmann, Barbara J. "First Grade Reflections." *English in Texas* 15, no. 4: 17-18.

10

LEARNING HOW TO LEARN
Cognitive Developmental Theory

When adult members of the Kpelle, an African tribe, were asked to sort, they did so functionally rather than hierarchically. Thus *fish* might be sorted with *eat*. Even when urged to reconsider their sorting procedure, the Kpelle continued to sort in this seemingly intellectually primitive way. Typically, cross-cultural psychologists might cite this sorting pattern as yet another example of how the people of another culture, in this case, the Kpelle, are less intelligent than their North American counterparts. But the psychologists who conducted this study were persistent in their examination. In desperation, they finally asked the Kpelle to sort the way they thought a stupid person would. The Kpelle then had no trouble sorting hierarchically. It became obvious that they lacked not the intelligence to sort hierarchically but the Western notion of intelligence that would have led them to sort this way. They initially sorted in what they believed to be the intelligent way. And, indeed, if you think about apples, for example, you're just as likely to think of eating them as of their being a kind of fruit.

—Robert J. Sternberg□

The importance of cognitive developmental theory for teachers of writing is based on the premise that by closely observing students one can understand their cognitive structures. Because cognitive developmentalists generally chart learning through actively developing mental structures or stages that build upon each other, teachers who watch what students do before, during, and after they write, in addition to studying the writing itself, will better comprehend the composing processes and capabilities of their students.

Cognition, defined here as the process of knowing inextricably tied to learning, is most often realized through the observable actions and language that students use to construct meaning as they interact with the world. Writing is such an observable action. Writing captures language and renders it perceptible. Writing, as Emig reminds us, is both a mode and a manifestation of cognition. It is a way to learn and a way to learn how to learn.

Jean Piaget, Lev Semenovich Vygotsky, Benjamin S. Bloom, and Jerome S. Bruner are four major cognitive developmentalists who have worked on the diverse processes of cognition and language and the interactive or hierarchical structure of those processes. Their theories are particularly relevant to the teaching of writing as studying them causes a recasting of traditional methods.

Traditional teachers, those trained in the product paradigm, often base instruction on the assumption that students of the same age learn the same way, often through lecture, worksheets, textbooks that keep all students on the same page, or other instructional strategies that fix lessons regardless of the needs of the learner. These teachers control all learning and perceive students' talk or too much activity as disruptive behaviors.

In contrast, teachers who understand learning as a process look to the cognitive developmentalists for support for an active environment, one in which students are exposed to print-rich, language-rich experiences, one in which they interact in meaningful ways with that environment. The cognitive developmentalists' research supports manipulation, not only for younger children, but for anyone coming to a new concept. While they contend that some degree of novelty piques interest in learning, they also hold that connecting new concepts to the familiar is an important way to guarantee learning. Teachers following the cognitive developmentalists individualize their teaching.

While there, certainly, is controversy over some of Piaget's theories, studying and applying cognitive developmental research to the teaching of writing supplies teachers with a theoretical foundation that functions in concert with the developing abilities of students. Ultimately, teaching to these abilities fosters intelligent strategies and confidence in self and in writing.

JEAN PIAGET

Jean Piaget, Swiss biologist, philosopher, psychologist, and genetic epistomologist, has so greatly influenced cognitive developmental theory that Howard Gardner credits him as "the single dominant thinker in his field" (28). It seems little wonder that someone who, by the age of eleven, had categorized all the mollusks in the natural history museum of Neuchatel, would go on to taxonomize thought. His early work with Lev and Pie in 1923 first recorded responses to a trilogy of questions: How does the child think? How does the child speak? What are the characteristics of the child's judgment and the child's reasoning? (1969, 11) Since those initial questions, Piaget wrote copiously on the nature, structure, and functions of intelligence.

Piaget's Invariant Operations of Intellectual Development

Piaget contends that there are two invariant operations (ways of getting something from the world into the mind so it can be used later) of mental development: organization and adaptation. Organization is the tendency of an organism to integrate structures into coherent systems—it systematizes. Adaptation is the tendency of an organism to adjust to its environment—it fits in. Adaptation occurs because of the complementary processes of assimilation and accommodation. Assimilation incorporates new experiences into the cognitive structure or framework. Accommodation modifies and enriches those new experiences. When assimilation and accommodation are in balance there is equilibrium. When they are not in balance, there is disequilibrium, which is manifested in discomfort or inner conflict.

Piaget posits four factors that influence cognitive development during any stage: maturation, experience, social transmission, and equilibration. Simply put, maturation refers to physical structures; experience refers to contact with objects; social transmission describes interactions with others; and equilibration coordinates the other three, none of which is sufficient by itself for mental growth. Piaget believes that these factors repeat in a spiral to construct knowledge.

Piaget's Stages of Intellectual Development

Piaget's concept stages or periods of intellectual development — sensorimotor, preoperational, concrete operational, and formal operational — have become classic divisions in cognitive theory. Full explanations of each of these stages may be found in Piaget's work (representative works are referenced at the end of this chapter), and in any number of secondary sources. Here the stages are briefly reveiwed in terms of their relevance to thought and language and with implications subsequently drawn to teaching writing.

THE SENSORIMOTOR STAGE (0-2 YEARS) AND THE IMPLICATIONS FOR TEACHING WRITING

Sensorimotor is a term used to describe motor activities or movements caused by sensory stimuli. During this stage children explore their world. As they handle, manipulate, and watch, they repeat actions and patterns, and recognize, imitate, and even invent simple solutions. Rudimentary symbolic play begins.

This period lays the foundation for thinking and eventually for writing. Two brief examples: A child observes that kicking makes things move. This observation later evolves into a sense of cause and effect. A child follows a moving object from right to left. This ability to follow something, at first with the eyes, eventually leads to the ability to sequence.

With increased information about the brain becoming part of educators' knowledge, this stage takes on new significance. The brain's plasticity and the powerful role that enriched environments play in developing the density of its dendritic branches and those environments' ultimate effect on the neural transmissions themselves, suggest that what happens during this early developmental stage may make a lasting difference for individual learners.

Consider the delight young children express upon hearing pattern books read aloud again and again. Couple that image with the delight they show when making marks on empty pages. The ability to hear patterns and to enjoy them has its roots in the sensorimotor stage. Likewise with the ability to make marks, which is an outgrowth of imitation. Even so simple a deed as giving very young children clay to manipulate establishes a message — things can be moved, changed, and transformed. These concepts endure and may reemerge in the acts of moving words, sentences, or paragraphs, or in being a risk taker.

> A television advertisement shows, in part, a baby sitting on the floor with a box of facial tissues. One by one the baby takes the tissues from the box. Suddenly there are no more, so the baby turns the box upside down. Every time I see that ad, two thoughts flit through my mind. The first is hardly stunning: The baby is imitating someone who has taken tissues from the box. The second is more academic: What wonderful patterning for future problem solving, hypothesizing, experimenting, asking questions.

Rudimentary symbolic play — carrying a doll or hugging a pet — is the young child's way of acting out his or her world through concrete role representations. Thumping the table or clapping may be natural imitations of a rattle or gesture. Playing peek-a-boo initiates what later turns into holding a mental image of someone or something — the genesis of abstract thought. In time, these beginnings become part of more elaborated symbolic play: "I'll be the mommy and you be the daddy." By school age these elemental plays surface as stories with characters, voice, tone, action, and a sense of language's rhythm. They show up first in telling scribbles; they grow into drawings; finally they become written stories, poems, and plays.

Apparently, this stage resurfaces throughout life. It is not unusual to see middle school students scribbling, high school students drawing all over their book covers, or adults doodling.

> *May was closing in. With only a few more classes remaining before the pomp and circumstance of college graduation, my seniors had a bad case of "senioritis." They had their lives planned. Most had job offers, although some were still looking. Many were accepted to graduate schools. A few intended to travel or visit relatives. Several were about to marry. Christi was in that group, and she could think of nothing else. Class after class she needed to be nudged from repeatedly writing her about-to-be-new name on page after page of yellow-lined paper. She never tired of writing or reading it.*

Even at the sensorimotor level, Piaget contends, children take an active role in adapting and organizing experiences. As the child grows these actions are repeated and expanded.

THE PREOPERATIONAL STAGE (2-7 YEARS) AND THE IMPLICATIONS FOR TEACHING WRITING

This is the stage of representational and prelogical thought. Throughout this stage children learn that something is like something else in certain ways. Because they are not miniature adults, they perceive the world through developing cognitive structures, which in turn give rise to colorful, fresh language. Because they are processing external concrete realities, they image that way. One 3-year-old told her mother, "I am the pattern and Becky [the babysitter] is the material." Children at this stage employ what Piaget calls transduction, a childlike reasoning that "moves from particular to particular" (1969, 233). They speak easily in similes: "That dog is like a car with legs." They create metaphors. Vardaman, a youngster in Faulkner's *As I Lay Dying*, simply states, "My mother is a fish" (79). He metaphorically connects the dead fish his sister Dewey Dell fixes for supper with his mother's dying. This transductive thinking eventually develops into deduction—thinking that moves logically from the general to the particular—and induction—thinking that moves logically from the particular to the general. This logical thought, however, does not begin to make its appearance until about the age of eleven or twelve (1976, 181).

During the latter part of this stage, operations begin. To Piaget, operations are mental actions that have their roots in the physical actions of the previous period. They also are general actions that take place within a group or organization. Because external actions are still in the process of becoming internalized, children in this stage often base their classifications only on the attributes they see.

> *Two little boys were at the pool. As they splashed in the water, one of the boys spotted two teenage girls entering the pool area. "Look," he said pointing to the girl in the one-piece bathing suit, "she's adopted."*
> *"How do you know?" asked his friend.*
> *"She doesn't have a belly button."*

Although children make awesome leaps in cognition during this stage, Piaget identifies as cognitive limits irreversibility (sometimes called the concept of reversibility), centration, and egocentrism. Irreversibility is the young child's inability to think of an object the way it was before it changed. Children are also unable to undo a physical action.

Centration refers to the child's inability to think simultaneously about changes that take place in two dimensions or subgroups. In other words, children can understand one set of changes but not a second set of changes. The example Piaget gives is the classification of flowers. When a child classified flowers into two groups—primulas and other flowers—there was no problem. Then the child divided the primulas into yellow and others. At this point the child had difficulty understanding that the yellow primulas were a smaller part of all the primulas and that the primulas were a smaller part of all the flowers (Ginsburg and Opper 125-126).

Egocentrism is the child's inability to see another's point of view. Children are stuck in their own perception, which affects their thinking.

To put this stage in perspective, think of a kindergarten, first-grade, or second-grade child. Teachers of young children and parents will confirm the remarkable things children say at this age. The poet Sandra McPherson would tell her 3-year-old daughter every time she said something extraordinary, "Let's write down what you just said. You spoke a poem." Children are able to speak so creatively and adults react with such delight because at this stage specific words do not mean the same thing to children as they do to adults; the child's mental structures are qualitatively different. Words carry different meanings and images when the brain and cognition are young. Perhaps that is why children laugh uproariously at the literal antics of Amelia Bedelia or at books that engage in language play, such as *The King Who Rained* or *A Chocolate Moose for Dinner*.

The point is clear — students learn what they see. Using abstractions or expecting students to understand something in the abstract is futile. They do not understand because they cannot; they are not yet ready.

This is the time to revel in novelty. Almost everything is new to children in this stage. And just as infants observe, then touch, children during this time should continue to explore, discover, and glimpse the wealth of possibilities around them. Teachers should create joyfully literate classrooms where children have fun with language and learning language. There should be many books, materials, pictures, and objects of various textures, configurations, shapes, and size. Children's natural use of figurative language should be encouraged, for it represents the seeds of the study of figurative language that will enrich literature and find its way into writing.

> *Recently while reading a book about pumpkins to a group of urban second-grade students, I used the term "envelopes of seeds." I looked up to a sea of blank faces. Of course, how would these city kids know envelopes of seeds? I envisioned what they probably were envisioning — bunches of seeds shaped like envelopes. I thought how we sometimes underestimate the learner and forget where they are developmentally. I vowed to take some envelopes of seeds with me to show the kids the next time I read that book.*

Teachers who interrupt primary students in the middle of reading their writing have experienced firsthand Piaget's theory of irreversibility. When students recommence, they always begin again at the beginning. Or, if they have added anything to what they have written, they will not just read the addition, they will start all over again. It is difficult, perhaps impossible, for these children to conceptualize that they have already shared part of the story. Because they cannot go back over their action, they begin again. It also works that way with writing. Once young writers begin a story, they write until the story is told. The concept of revision in the abstract holds no meaning for them. Revision, unless it is concrete and immediate, such as Kelley Smith's idea of juicing up a hamburger (see pages 236-237), is not a cognitively appropriate activity based on Piaget's theory of irreversibility.

Sometimes teachers become exasperated when students forget a capital letter or a terminal punctuation mark. They should take comfort in Piaget's theory of centration. Asking students to write, capitalize, and punctuate asks students to hold more than one thing in their minds at the same time. Think of how often caregivers of children this age say, "Do one thing at a time." When students are getting their meaning down, they are unable to think of other things. At this stage, let them get the meaning down. If they on occasion remember other things, consider that a sign of cognitive growth. Later, when they can mentally juggle more variables, they will consistently remember other things. Interestingly, prewriting at any level frees the mind of this hierarchical juggling and the simultaneity of meaning and mechanics.

Almost everyone is familiar with Piaget's theory of egocentric thought. Observing young children makes that plain enough. For example, after students share what they have written with others, say in the Author's Chair, they listen to peer comments such as, "I like the way you described the dinosaur," but it is unlikely those comments make any impact until students develop out of the egocentric stage. That is not to say this practice should be discontinued; it promotes listening skills, collaboration, and helps their growth toward sociocentric behavior. Rather, it is important to realize that at this stage, children hear that feedback egocentrically. Perhaps the most telling example of egocentrism in young children comes from Lucy Calkins. She writes, "The youngsters [two first-graders] pulled chairs close together, then each girl took hold of her story and, in unison, they read their stories to each other. Neither child listened and neither child was listened to, but both girls seemed pleased with their conference" (61).

These limitations do not preclude learning. Knowing them simply invites understanding. Sowing the seeds for revision, for multiple levels of simultaneous thinking, and for developing response groups and working in collaboration remain important activities on this preoperational level.

THE CONCRETE OPERATIONAL STAGE (7-11 YEARS) AND THE IMPLICATIONS FOR TEACHING WRITING

This is the stage of concrete logical thought. This period leads children toward the ability to conceptualize in the abstract. However, unless they have sufficient concrete experiences, their later development will be stunted. Piaget insists that children must pass through one stage before entering the next, holding that each stage is both a culmination of the preceding one and a preparation for the one to follow. Nothing is gained by pushing children too early into a stage for which they are not ready.

Piaget repeatedly emphasizes the need for plenty of concrete activities for children at this stage, believing that they must act and interact in order to understand. While they are restricted to concrete things, there are developing new mental capabilities, such as mentally reversing an action, holding more variables in their minds as they think through a problem, and reconciling contradictions. At this stage, they are becoming less egocentric. What is perhaps most significant for teachers is that sometimes responses are the result of generalizing observable attributes, not manifestations of the ability to abstract. It is not unusual, for example, for students at this stage to call any -ing word a gerund by noting the attribute of -ing. That an -ing word may be a participle confuses the students because they cannot abstract the difference; they do not understand the concept. All of which seems to militate against teaching any concept out of a context and before the learner is able cognitively to learn it.

At this stage, children are generally unable to think purely in the abstract, yet, according to at least one researcher, "a great number of texts written for middle schoolers are inappropriately abstract" (Cheatham 15). They are intellectually fettered to actual objects, actual events, actual people. Obviously, then, the first implication for writing is that students write—not do worksheets. Students should write daily. They should be given real reasons to write, such as to pen pals, in learning logs, as the basis for interactions with each other and the teacher. They should practice writing in different genres. They should see writing everywhere. It should be intrinsic to the classroom environment—on walls, from ceilings, in folders, on tables—everywhere. Reading and books should pervade the environment.

Second, there should be plenty of opportunity for peer-response groups and teacher conferences. This helps students move from egocentrism. Modeling by the teacher helps students handle analytic aspects of writing and begin moving to more formal thought. For example, if teachers demonstrate how they combine sentences in their writing, students have a concrete model to follow. This modeling should be followed throughout the entire writing process. The teacher should model and provide concrete experiences during prewriting; during the move to writing; while correcting, revising and reformulating; and while proofreading and editing. Specific strategies are described in chapters 5 through 9.

English/language arts skills should be taught concretely and should be taught within the writing process, not six or sixteen weeks before any writing happens. While strategies that employ logical reasoning should be introduced, concrete connections should be made among those strategies and writing and life experiences, and between writing and reading. This helps students develop out of transduction. Writing and reading should be integrated into other subjects in the curriculum so students see reasons for writing in other disciplines.

Every effort should be made to use tables, not desks, because students need space to spread out to be able to concretely consider all their writing. There should be flexibility yet structure in the classroom. There should be places designated for specific activities, such as private reading space (no matter how small, kids love small places because the sensory stimuli are intensified and because this allows for more social interaction), areas where writing can happen undisturbed, conference areas, and so forth. Most importantly, students should have blocks of time, large blocks of time, to engage in writing and reading.

The writing folder and writing portfolio are essential at this stage. Students (as well as teachers, parents, administrators, and other interested persons) are able to assess the work done, work in progress, and their achievement.

THE FORMAL OPERATIONAL STAGE (11-15 YEARS) AND THE IMPLICATIONS FOR TEACHING WRITING

The main difference between this stage and all the preceding ones is that youngsters in this stage can think beyond present tasks and form theories. They are able to deal with proportions, probabilities, correlations, permutations, and aggregations. They can hold several abstract factors in their minds while considering others.

While Piaget suggests that at this point in cognitive development students are capable of abstract thinking, several studies suggest that this is not the case. Conrad F. Toepfer contends that overchallenging youngsters to meet unrealistic expectations for higher level thinking during the 12-14 age plateau may cause almost irreversible problems. He calls for a reexamination of the assumption held by middle-school and high-school teachers that a majority of learners can function at abstract thinking levels.

Toepfer cites studies by Herman Epstein, a prominent biophysicist, which raise serious questions about formal operational thinking in middle and high school. Toepfer attributes this jump too soon into abstraction as the cause of what he calls the "turned-off syndrome" (4). Students who experience low achievement may be victims of too great an emphasis upon formal operations before the students are ready. While the percents vary, albeit not appreciably, Epstein's work has been corroborated by other studies (Shayer and Arlin; Sayre and Ball; Martorano). These data suggest a reexamination of curricula. In brief, Epstein's research shows:

1. Nationally, no more than 1 percent of 10-year-olds, 5 percent of 11-year-olds, and 12 percent of 12-year-olds can even initiate formal operations.

2. Statistics on youngsters who have initiated or can perform mature formal operations show that only 20 percent of 13-year-olds and 24 percent of 14-year-olds can learn with some degree of formality. Clearly, 80 percent of 13-year-olds and 76 percent of 14-year-olds still cannot think and learn at the formal operational level.

3. Between the ages of 14 and 18, the increase in percentage of learners having the capacity for formal operational thinking rises to the point where 15 percent of 18-year-olds display initiated formal operations capabilities and 19 percent have mature formal operation skills. Thus, only 34 percent can do some kind of formal operations processing, even at age 18.

4. It is estimated that 38-40 percent of American adults can think at the formal operations level. This means about 60 percent cannot.

5. Most disturbing is that in the final period of great brain growth, 14-16 years, learners did not, for the most part, reverse any prior poor achievement. (Toepfer 3-5)

In his early research Piaget thought formal operations began in early adolescence. Later writings, however, reflect a rethinking. "Piaget thought later that his sample in Switzerland perhaps showed earlier development than other populations" (14).

The overarching implication of Piaget's theories on the teaching of writing is that writing should be taught as a recursive process, with skills, collaboration, and modeling integral parts of that process.

LEV SEMENOVICH VYGOTSKY

Lev Semenovich Vygotsky was an innovative Russian cognitive developmentalist whose investigations and research in the fields of developmental psychology and education were cut short because of his untimely death of tuberculosis at the age of 38. Jerome Bruner describes his work as "quantitatively meager but brilliant" (1971, 8). Briefly, Vygotsky believed that the mind cannot be understood in isolation from the cultural and human contributions that interact as processes during its development. Vygotsky was incredibly ahead of his time. He insisted that psychological functions are brain-based, and he advocated combining experimental cognitive psychology with neurology and physiology. In short, he believed in the biology of the mind. Most recently Gerald M. Edelman, a Nobel Laureate, echoes Vygotsky. "Cognitive science is an interdisciplinary effort drawing on psychology, computer science and artificial intelligence, aspects of neurobiology and linguistics, and philosophy" (13).

While the theories of Vygotsky and Piaget generally correspond, Vygotsky differed with Piaget on four counts: (1) Piaget in his early work maintains that a child's egocentric speech eventually subsides; Vygotsky believes it evolves into inner speech, a "thinking for oneself," or shorthand thinking. (2) Piaget's "view of human development centers upon the capacity of our species to achieve sophisticated knowledge about numbers — or Number" (Gardner 29). For Vygotsky, the use of "word" is an integral part and guiding function in forming a concept. (3) Piaget believes that thought stimulates language; Vygotsky believes that language influences thought. "A word is a microcosm of human consciousness" (1962, 153). (4) Piaget argues that intelligence moves from inside out; Vygotsky argues it moves from outside in.

Vygotsky's Stages of
Intellectual Development

Vygotsky continually focuses on the process involved in the formation of a concept, holding that word and thought are related in a continual ebb and flow. The process of concept development that follows is both an abridgment and a synthesis of chapter 5, "An Experimental Study of Concept Formation," of Vygotsky's *Thought and Language*. (One additional point: Vygotsky cautions that concept formation in the experimental setting differs from the process in real life, where the phases mix.)

UNORGANIZED HEAPS

This is the first step toward concept formation. Here the child takes objects and piles them together. This phase subsumes three distinct stages: (1) trial and error, in which the child groups objects at random and adds other objects by guess; (2) line of vision, in which the child groups objects together that are seen together, that is in the same spatial area; and (3) rearrangement, in which the child newly combines objects only to create different unorganized heaps. In the rearranging, it is not that the child sees bonds or connections, rather the rearrangement happens because of some chance impression that causes the child to simply put something in a different place. Vygotsky uses Blonski's term to describe this trait — "incoherent coherence" (60).

THINKING IN COMPLEXES

During this phase, the child begins to see connections among objects by subjective impressions and by actual bonds and is able to discern the difference between the two. There are five basic complexes: (1) Associations are based on anything the child notices as the same among the sample objects. The child may add one block because it is the same color but another because of size. Associations are generally based on similarities. (2) Collections are groups of which all items have one characteristic that differs from the sample, so the child sees differences. Often collections are assembled because of their function. (3) Chains are dynamic links with meaning carried from one link to the next. Vygotsky considers the chain complex the purest form of thinking at this point in the formation of a concept because the concrete grouping is connected among single elements, nothing more. (4) Diffuse complexes are indefinite limitless ways of connecting things. Basically, the child adds objects to a group because one thing reminds him of something else, for example, child who picks out trapezoids as well as triangles because the trapezoids remind him of triangles. This complex is fluid. (5) Pseudo-concepts resemble genuine concepts but are not. Pseudo-concepts are the bridge between complexes and concepts. It is important to note that these concepts appear to be genuine concepts but they are not, because the thinking process behind them differs. Vygotsky says:

> In the experimental setting, the child produces a pseudo-concept every time he surrounds a sample with objects that could just as well have been assembled on the basis of an abstract concept. For instance, when the sample is a yellow triangle and the child picks out all the triangles in the experimental material, he could have been guided by the general idea or concept of a triangle. Experimental analysis shows, however, that in reality the child is guided by the concrete, visible likeness and has formed only an associative complex limited to a certain kind of perceptual bond. Although the results are identical, the process by which they are reached is not at all the same as in conceptual thinking (1962, 66).

> *Teacher and students worked hard on adverbs. They had completed many fill-in-the-blank worksheets; they had completed the blackline masters that accompanied the grammar book; they were ready for the final test. On the test, students were to identify the adverb in each sentence. Later, the teacher showed me the results. Most students missed the demonstrative adjectives, none identified almost, and although all caught adverbs ending in -wise, the -ly ending was clearly a pseudo-concept for the students who identified butterfly as an adverb. The students who received 85 percent on the test believed they knew adverbs. Equally, the teacher believed that those who scored 85 percent understood adverbs. Both, it seems, demonstrate pseudo-concepts — the students for thinking they knew a term although they were guided only by an attribute (-wise or -ly) and the teacher for thinking they had formed a concept.*

Pseudo-concepts serve as the connections between two levels of thinking—thinking in complexes and thinking in concepts. Therefore, pseudo-conceptual thinking is concrete, *not* abstract, thinking.

GENUINE CONCEPTS AND THE IMPLICATIONS FOR TEACHING WRITING

When the level of advanced genuine conceptual thinking has been reached, individuals are able to abstract and single out elements and view those elements apart from the original concrete experience (analyze), sometimes in a new way (synthesis). Because thinking in complexes precedes synthesizing *and* analyzing, analysis and synthesis must be combined in genuine concept formation. Further, the concept emerges only when the abstracted elements are synthesized anew.

To summarize: Vygotsky's theory of concept development applies to any level at which the assimilation of new information is undertaken. It applies equally to young children first learning to read and to high-school students tackling algebra. It applies to learning a grammatical concept or the way a motor works. And it is a process.

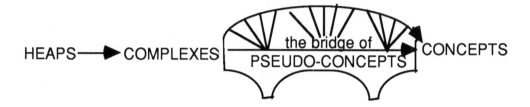

The first and overarching implication is that Vygotsky's process of concept development parallels the writing process. Rightly so, if writing is thinking on paper. Consider the possibility of heaps as analogous to the chaos of prewriting. Writers often experience trial and error, trying one idea, rejecting it, trying another, recycling thoughts, arranging and rearranging them. Also, writers write what they know, what exists, so to speak, in their "line of vision." During thinking in complexes, the writer moves into some form—judging the similarity and differences of genres—finally reaching the genuine article, the finished piece.

Second, written language requires a high level of abstraction. "In learning to write, the child must disengage himself from the sensory aspect of speech and replace words by images of words.... Our studies show that it is the abstract quality of written language that is the main stumbling block, not the underdevelopment of small muscles or any other mechanical obstacles" (1962, 98-99). The implication is clear: surround students with concrete examples of writing; engage them in language play; provide print-rich environments; and, above all else, give them many opportunities to engage in the act of writing.

Third, writing to or for someone absent is new to a child. "Our studies show that he has little motivation to learn writing when we begin to teach it. He feels no need for it and has only a vague idea of its usefulness" (1962, 99). Therefore, having an audience—the principal, a caregiver, a friend, the teacher—makes writing real. After being read to and reading books, writing their own books becomes both a purpose and a motivation. And this does not pertain only to young children. Middle school and high school students are often disengaged from writing because they see no purpose or are poorly motivated.

Fourth, writing is analytical. When speaking, words flow, perhaps from a need for information or to convey information. People speak. They may think about what they are going to say, but they rarely ponder over exact syntax. They have questions that must be asked or they have demands for answers. Requests arise naturally from situations. On the other hand, writing requires deliberation, analyzing the phrase, choosing the precise word. The syntax of inner speech is opposite the syntax of written speech, with oral speech in the middle. In that design, writing requires "deliberate structuring of the web of meaning" (1962, 100).

Fifth, the study of grammar is important in mental development, but it should be taught within writing so that the student becomes "aware of what he is doing and learns to use his skills consciously" (1962, 101).

Vygotsky's Theory of the
Zone of Proximal Development
and Its Implications for Teaching Writing

The zone of proximal development is "the distance between the actual developmental level as determined by independent problem solving and the level of potential development as determined through problem solving under adult guidance or in collaboration with more capable peers" (1978, 86). Restated, it is the space between cognitive actuality and latency. By so clearly defining this phase of development, Vygotsky has illuminated a niggling problem in teaching. So often teachers observe students who work well during and after peer consultations or teacher conferences but seem incapable of working out a problem independently. Teachers worry that these students are not working hard enough, are becoming too dependent, or are getting off too easily. Because of these anxieties, they are tempted to derail the process by skipping group work. But these teachers should be heartened by Vygotsky's suggestion that some functions used by students are not yet matured enough for independent work. He calls them the "buds" rather than the "fruits" of development. He offers the zone of proximal development as a tool to understand and to take into account those functions that are still in the process of development.

The zone of proximal development clearly supports collaborative learning. Group work, cohort groups, conferences, clusters, teams, peer tutoring, modeling with immediate application, and guided practice are collaborative activities that are served well by using the zone of proximal development as an educational tool.

An example: Mary confers with Miss A. During the conference, Mary lucidly describes a problem she cannot solve in her writing. Miss A. asks a series of questions, which Mary answers. This exchange helps Mary, so she leaves the conference area, returns to the writing area, and sets about "getting her writing right." But this baffles Miss A. Mary is bright. She can diagnose problems in her paper, but she seems incapable of walking herself through those problems to solutions. Miss A. comments, "Mary drives me crazy. She can't seem to make any decisions about her writing without checking with me first."

Explanation: Mary comes to the teacher at her actual developmental level. Her teacher works with Mary at her potential developmental level. What exists in between these two levels is Mary's zone of proximal development. When Mary hits another problem beyond her actual developmental level, the process will be repeated. Because of the changing nature of problems and levels of development, this process is dynamic, that is, it is always changing with the function and the development of the child.

Vygotsky believes collaboration is key. His now-famous line supports his belief, "What the child can do in cooperation today he can do alone tomorrow" (1962, 104).

BENJAMIN S. BLOOM

Benjamin S. Bloom, an American cognitive developmentalist, is perhaps best known for the *Taxonomy of Educational Objectives: The Classification of Educational Goals*, which was published in 1956. Under his general editorship, this taxonomy provided a new and different tool for curriculum analysis and course planning. Earlier he, together with L. J. Border, studied the problem-solving processes of college students. They found that the major difference between more able and less able problem solvers was the degree to which the students were active or passive in how they processed the problems. The students who spent extra time on a problem, developed steps for solving the problem, and looked for new ways to approach the problem did better than did those who gave up if the solution did not immediately present itself. Coming from this perspective, Bloom differs from Piaget and Vygotsky. His taxonomy adds another dimension to cognition—the pedagogical dimension of student behavior coupled with goals. For example, by using Bloom's taxonomy, the intuitive teacher who formerly asked, "What should I teach today?" may become the teacher researcher who systematically assesses how students respond in relation to the goals of the lesson. More specifically, a teacher may intend to teach map making but may have a hazy objective. With Bloom's taxonomy, that teacher may begin by focusing on the knowledge level in an effort to determine what the students already know about cartography.

Bloom's Taxonomy of Educational Objectives: The Cognitive Domain

Bloom's taxonomy of educational objectives is a hierarchical classification of the goals of an educational plan. It is arranged from the simple to the complex and implies both the behavior intended and the content or goal of that behavior. The taxonomy of cognition or thought, which in this case affects written and oral language, deals with the development of intellectual abilities and skills. Further, it provides a way to advance students from lower to higher levels of thinking. Bloom's taxonomy may be adapted to curriculum or to lessons. For example, if one teacher states, "I want my students to really *understand* nouns," and another teacher says, "I want my students to *internalize* nouns," and a third teacher declares, "I want my students to *comprehend* nouns," are all three saying the same thing? More importantly, how specifically will their students demonstrate "understanding," "internalizing," and "comprehending"? Bloom's taxonomy attempts to give educators a set of standard classifications that facilitates defining such terms more precisely. Thus, if these teachers applied the taxonomy, they might rephrase their statements so that both the behavior and the goal would be explicit, "Students will be able to explain in their own words why they chose the common and proper nouns they used in the introduction of their 'How to Carve a Pumpkin' papers to illustrate their understanding of nouns."

The Six Classes of Bloom's Cognitive Taxonomy as Related to Writing

Just as biology taxonomizes plants and animals according to their natural relationships, so Bloom and his group of educators and research specialists attempted to order levels of thinking in a way consistent with cognitive theories so that the order would reveal relationships among the levels (17). In Bloom's hierarchy, the objectives and behaviors of one class most likely build on the objectives and behaviors of the preceding classes. Bloom's taxonomy contains six classes: knowledge, comprehension, application, analysis, synthesis, and evaluation. Each of these classes may be appled in specific ways to activities involving writing as a process.

KNOWLEDGE

Knowledge involves the psychological processes of remembering. Sometimes this class is called "memory" or "the memory level." Students are expected to:

- recall specific information, e.g., name the author of specific books;
- define terminology, e.g., "What is a noun?";
- repeat facts, e.g., "Sentences begin with capital letters";
- follow processes, e.g., fold an eight-page book;
- employ conventions, e.g., using the correct form in a documented essay;
- repeat sequences, e.g., use sequence words like *first, second, then, next, last*;
- recognize classifications, e.g., take prewriting into a genre;
- follow methods by doing the pointing technique during a group activity;
- observe rules, e.g., not talking in the designated writing spaces; and
- identify structures, e.g., state the elements in a story.

When teaching to the knowledge level, teachers direct, tell, show, examine, read, a⸍ They expect students to memorize, recall, and know the subject matter. Students demon⸍ knowledge by quoting, repeating, recording, reciting, defining, listing, naming, or statin⸍ bits of information. This level involves little more than retrieving information.

One sample writing activity on this level is for students to take strips of cash register tape and construct a timeline of the events in a narrative they have written. By recalling this information and setting it out visually, students may move to higher levels of thought in predicting what they still need in their stories, analyzing if they have an event out of chronological order, and so forth.

COMPREHENSION

Comprehension refers to that level of cognition where information is understood without consulting other material for further explanation or clarification. Students are expected to:

- translate information, e.g., by paraphrasing for a peer what they heard in the writing;

- interpret, such as summarizing the meaning of a peer's writing in a word or sentence;

- extrapolate, by predicting what needs to be done next in their writing.

When teaching for comprehension, teachers demonstrate, question, suggest comparisons or contrasts, and listen. They expect students to associate, compare, contrast, differentiate, discuss, estimate, and predict. Students demonstrate their comprehension by changing the form of the ideas without changing the meaning. Comprehension represents the lowest level of understanding.

One sample writing activity on this level is for students to illustrate their writing. Doing this enables students to interpret their writing pictorially while translating from one symbolic form to another.

APPLICATION

Application means that whatever has been learned in one situation can be used in another situation or in the same situation with new elements. If students understand metaphor on this cognitive level, for example, they will be able to not only identify metaphor in a specific poem under study (knowledge level), tell what it means in their own words (comprehension level), but also find metaphor in other poems or write their own metaphors (application level). This is what is called the transfer of learning. That means students have to not only know and comprehend what is being taught but be able to restructure it cognitively in order to use it elsewhere.

When teaching for application, teachers show, facilitate, observe, critique, challenge and motivate, especially since one of the major reasons for lack of application is lack of motivation. Teachers expect students to relate, solve, apply, calculate, illustrate, use, and make connections. Students demonstrate their ability to make application when they use what they have learned. The effectiveness of education depends upon students' ability to make applications.

A sample writing activity on this level is to write a how-to book on some process learned in class. For example, the first-graders who first made arachnids out of Oreo cookies, then wrote how-to books, were applying the process in a new situation—a book.

ANALYSIS

Analysis involves breaking down the information into its constituent parts to better under- stand the relationship of these parts to the whole. For example, when the Challenger disaster oc- curred, everyone watching it on television and in person saw the explosion. Later, viewing au- diences saw replays of that explosion as it was filmed with different cameras. Still later, as experts wrestled with possible causes, audiences were shown various close-ups and different angles of the shuttle and its flight. Ultimately, the spurt from an O-ring, one almost infinitesimal part of the spacecraft was analyzed and determined to be the cause of the tragedy. Thus, by analyzing the parts, the whole experience was explained. On this level, students are expected to:

- analyze elements, e.g., be able to differentiate fact from opinion in a persuasive piece;

- analyze relationships, e.g., identify a thesis (implicit or explicitly stated) and the information that supports that thesis;

- analyze organizational principles, to be able to see the organizational structure in a peer's writing, e.g., analytic talk (page 157).

When teaching for analysis, teachers probe, guide, observe, and act as a resource. They expect students to order, relate, separate, dichotomize, dissect, split up, sever, group, and classify. Students demonstrate their ability to analyze by being able to explain the various parts of what they are studying, by relating the different parts of a subject in relation to the whole, and by categorizing relationships according to facts, ideas, or other commonalties. Analysis is a more advanced level of thinking than that of comprehension and application.

The prewriting strategy of blueprinting (page 72) is one writing activity that invites analysis. This activity is particularly effective, especially for the visual learner, because it originates with sketches or drawings so the relationships may be seen.

SYNTHESIS

Synthesis calls for the putting together of constituent parts into new forms. This involves working with pieces, parts, elements, sections, portions, segments, and so forth and rearranging and recombining them in uniquely different ways. This is the class of cognition that most clearly encourages creative behavior. When synthesizing, students:

- produce something unique, e.g., a reflexive piece of writing—an experience recreated in words and set out in a new format—in some chosen genre;

- develop a plan of work or a proposal for a plan, e.g., an extensive piece of writing in which they offer a creative proposal or write out something they intend to do or make;

- develop a set of abstract relations either to classify or explain something, e.g., creating a language code for a certain subject or writing a contemporary slang dictionary.

When teaching for synthesis, teachers reflect, extend, analyze, evaluate, and open up the process. They expect students to rearrange, recombine, construct, create, design, develop, formulate, integrate, produce, and propose. Students demonstrate their ability to synthesize by being creative, doing things in new and different ways, thinking innovatively, displaying ingenious plans, and producing original ideas. In one sense, all writing is synthesis.

A writing activity that invites synthesis is to divide students into four groups. Each group must come up with a "new" idea. One group writes a biography for their idea. Another group creates an advertisement for their idea. The third group conveys their idea through music. The fourth group presents their idea through some type of artwork.

EVALUATION

Evaluation is making quantitative and qualitative judgments on information, materials, and ideas. These judgments must be made against an appropriate criteria or standard. Jumping from merely being able to repeat or retell something—"Shakespeare's play *Romeo and Juliet* is about star-crossed lovers" to a judgment — "That play's stupid" is called a snap judgment. In true evaluation, the person judging ranges through all the cognitive levels — getting to know it, expressing it in different words, applying it to life, taking it apart, putting it together in new and different ways — before evaluating it. To do this, students should be able to make judgments

- by internal standards, e.g., whether the writing is apt, clear, and lively;

- by external standards, e.g., comparing a piece of writing to a literary model.

When teachers want students to evaluate, they accept and harmonize. They expect students to appraise, assess, critique, grade, judge, measure, rank, rate, recommend, and test. Students demonstrate their ability to evaluate by making a judgment and providing supports for that judgment. Evaluation not only concludes the taxonomy of cognitive behaviors but links it to the affective domain, where values, likes, and dislikes are identified.

Students who participate in the group activity of producing an analytic scale (see chapter 14, page 464) are involved in every level of cognitive thought, and they culminate that thinking by prioritizing what was taught and what was learned. Briefly, in creating an analytic scale, students identify concepts taught, use their own words to convey those concepts, discuss how the concepts were used in their writing, break the concepts into parts, put them together in a new way through a class brainstorming session, and then rank them in order of importance.

Related Books Based on Bloom's Taxonomy

Classroom Questions: What Kinds? by Norris M. Sanders closely follows Bloom's categories of thinking. Examples, uses, and theory are presented in an-easy-to-follow format. This slim volume would prove equally helpful for the new teacher who feels uncomfortable with questioning techniques or for the experienced teacher who wants to polish up on questioning skills or who desires to challenge students by raising their level of thinking.

Sanders cautions, "It is wrong to assume that a question inevitably leads to a single category of thinking or that all students are necessarily using the same mental process to arrive at an answer" (8-9). Therefore, he identifies three factors that affect questions: the nature of the question; the student's knowledge of the subject; and the instruction that preceded the question (8). He expresses concern about overemphasis on "what," "where," and "when" questions and lack of emphasis on "why" and "how" questions. He reminds teachers that a question should be classified at its highest level, since the lower levels of cognition are present in the higher levels of questions.

He advises teachers to present subject matter from a variety of sources, contending that textbooks are "the biggest deterrent to thinking in the classroom" (158). He holds that the authors of the texts are the ones who have done all the thinking.

Suppose the Wolf Were an Octopus? A Guide to Creative Questioning for Primary Grade Literature, by Joyce Paster Foley and Michael T. Bagley, is also based on Bloom's taxonomy. It demonstrates procedures for building various levels of questions, provides examples through literature, and presents several questioning strategies. The authors share two hypotheses: "Teachers who show an appreciation for questioning, who establish a climate where diverse questions are valued, who consistently ask high quality questions will develop students who demonstrate greater involvement in the questioning process" (2); Teachers who use higher level questions on a consistent basis will increase their students' higher level thinking skills in terms of frequency, depth, appropriateness and complexity" (3).

Although specifically geared to the teacher of young children, this book with its many models from classic children's literature serves a model for teachers of all levels. Following is a sample of one question for each cognitive level. The questions pertain to Beatrice Schenk de Regniers's version of *Little Red Riding Hood*.

Knowledge: Who saved Little Red Riding Hood and her grandmother?

Comprehension: Why did Little Red Riding Hood's mother worry about a trip through the woods?

Application: Try to imagine what you would do if you were to meet a wolf on the way to your grandmother's house.

Analysis: In what ways could the wolf have resembled the grandmother? How was he different?

Synthesis: Suppose that Little Red Riding Hood met a rabbit instead of a wolf. Make up a new story telling what might happen.

Evaluation: Select the character that you think is most clever. Give reasons. (31-32)

These questions or questions like them may be discussed and then their answers written out, or each question may serve as a prompt for a larger writing. The knowledge question could be expanded to an informative piece; the comprehension question could result in persuasion; the application question begs imaginative writing, perhaps a poem or a script; the analysis questions are clearly compare and contrast; synthesis actually invites a narrative; and evaluation could become an essay with support. By turning questions into prompts, teachers of writing ensure writing and thinking on higher levels.

Bloom's Taxonomy and Implications for Teaching Writing

To prepare students for a world of unknowns is to prepare students to think. Using Bloom's taxonomy provides educators with a helpful tool to raise the level of thinking for all students on any grade level. It also offers a base for curriculum restructuring, especially in the area of writing. Rebuilding a curriculum not of generalizations such as "Students should learn to think clearly" but with concrete writing situations and prompts based on Bloom's taxonomy helps that restructuring happen in specific ways. Also, basing written examination and test questions on Bloom's taxonomy ensures a movement from the recitation of simple facts to the higher levels of creating and evaluating.

> After completing a writing lesson with eleventh-grade students on perception as a focus to introduce the Salem witch trials of 1692, I asked what they had learned. They responded with information about Cotton Mather, the New England Puritans, and the 19 persons who were hanged. They remembered Giles Corey, no doubt because he alone had been pressed to death. And so they recounted details, made assumptions, and shared connections.
> Then I asked, "What could I have done to make this lesson better?" These loquacious adolescents were struck dumb. They stared at me wide-eyed. Obviously it never occurred to them to share in the appraisal of a lesson. Then we talked about why doing that might be a learning experience for them and helpful to me.

If writing is a mode of thinking and of learning as Janet Emig suggests, then using Bloom's taxonomy assumes even greater significance for the teacher of writing. On the one hand, it offers categories that foster writing at all developmental levels; on the other hand, it presents a classification system for analyzing writing produced by students in any classroom. When a student, for example, writes a poem as a response to a piece of literature, much the way William Carlos Williams did for the Icarus and Daedalus myth, knowing Bloom's taxonomy will help the teacher see the response as one of synthesis, a high-level cognitive response. When a student's prewriting shows arrows and asterisks connecting names and thoughts during prewriting for a reflexive piece, the teacher who knows Bloom's taxonomy sees those arrows and asterisks as rudimentary analysis. And the student who consistently writes plot summaries or writes only in one genre can be targeted by the informed teacher as someone stuck in the comprehension level of cognition. These students need instruction and challenge to develop patterns for higher level thinking.

> *I remember a course I took on William Faulkner for my master's degree. The professor, a scholarly gentleman and a Faulkner expert, conducted the class through inquiry only. One day he called on a fellow to answer, "Why do you think Quentin [in* The Sound and the Fury*] committed suicide?" The fellow began with what amounted to a plot summary of the book. Dr. Graham listened patiently for a time, but then interrupted with a rephrasing of the same question. Again the fellow began retelling the plot. Slightly exasperated, Dr. Graham asked the question a third time. This time he prefaced it by saying, "Now be clear about this, I'm not asking for a paraphrase of the story. That's not what I'm asking. Can you answer this question, do you have any thoughts about why Quentin killed himself?"*
> *The fellow fidgeted and finally mumbled. "I can't answer that."*

If writing is indeed thinking on paper, then students should write for a variety of purposes, in many modes, and for different audiences. Through writing, students develop logical skills, clarify thought, and engage in the act of doing. Blending Bloom's taxonomy with the teaching of writing encourages students to use writing as a place to ask questions or raise concerns, which, in turn helps students acquire skill in asking and answering questions. There is a delightful children's book called *Agatha's Feather Bed* by Carmen Agra Deedy that perhaps best encapsulates the power of cognitive thought. Agatha always tells her customers, especially children:

> Everything comes from something,
> Nothing comes from nothing.
> Just like paper comes from trees,
> And glass comes from sand,
> An answer comes from a question.
> All you have to do is ask. (9)

JEROME SEYMOUR BRUNER

Jerome Seymour Bruner was born in New York City in 1915. Educated at Duke and Harvard Universities, he served with distinction in various capacities in the American Psychological Association, as a consultant on psychological problems to the departments of state, navy, and defense, as a member of the Institute for Advanced Study at Princeton, and as a Guggenheim Fellow at Cambridge. He has guest lectured at the University of London, the University of Chicago, and the Federation Suisse de Psychologie. At Harvard, he was Professor of Psychology and Director of the Center for Cognitive Studies. He has been awarded the American Psychological Association Distinguished Scientific Contribution Award and the international Balzan Prize for his lifelong contribution to human psychology. Presently, he is Research Professor of Psychology at New York University and author of many books.

Generally, the interests of this American cognitive developmentalist have centered on learning and perception. His wartime experience led him deeply into the analysis of propaganda and public opinion, which led him further into exploration into the nature of processes underlying opinion formation, such as perception, thoughts, learning, and language. Ultimately he concentrated his research on the study of development in children and the nature of the educational process. His latest book, *Acts of Meaning*, in addition to tracing the cognitive revolution from its beginnings to the present, brilliantly investigates what he calls "folk psychology," the narrative, and the role of meaning-making as a mediator between mind and culture.

Three of Bruner's major contributions have special relevance for the purposes of this chapter and raise implications for the teaching of writing. These are his views on the process of education, the process of knowing, and the process of discovery.

The Process of Education

In broad terms, Jerome Bruner believes that education enriches life. Learning is not simply the amassing of skills for skills' sake, rather education develops skills that are immediately useful and develops attitudes and principles applicable to situations throughout life. Having learned how to write stories as children, for example, adults are better equipped to transfer that learning into writing letters, memos, proposals, and so forth. Further, if the experience of learning to write was pleasant, encouraging, and rewarding, then people are more likely to continue self-sponsored writing in their adult lives. It may emerge in journals, diaries, letters to the editor, articles, or it may reappear through reading as a love of the writing of others.

More specifically, Bruner contends that "any subject can be taught effectively in some intellectually honest form to any child at any stage of development" (1963, 33), a contention that lies at the very heart of teaching writing as a process. There is no doubt that some children will learn to write, become skilled at its craft, and enjoy the process of writing, but equally there is no doubt that some children will not learn to write, remain capable of only very rudimentary marks or incoherent phrases, and will avoid it at all costs. These students are not well served in the future. Writing as a process enables teachers to, in an "intellectually honest form," meet the individual needs of any child.

To be able to do that, teachers need to understand three general notions: intellectual development in children; the act of learning; the spiral curriculum.

INTELLECTUAL DEVELOPMENT IN CHILDREN

Bruner, like Piaget, maintains that there are stages of intellectual development and that at each stage the child views the world uniquely. Bruner discusses three such stages. During the first stage, which Bruner considers a mesh of sensorimotor and preoperational (basically preschool), children are active. They principally manipulate their world. When they move to learning symbols, they use them in generalized ways with no separation between inner self, i.e., feelings or motives, and outer reality. A child in this stage could easily be the son in Nancy Willard's poem "Questions My Son Asked Me, Answers I Never Gave Him," a child whose internal and external world are viewed as one. He asks questions such as "Who tied my naval? Did God tie it?" and "If I drop my tooth in the telephone will it go through the wires and bite someone's ear?" (3)

During the second stage, children move into operations, which means that they can understand by hands-on activities, and they can represent things and relations in their minds. Things become internalized. The important thing to remember about this stage, however, is that children are only able to give structure to what is immediately present. Bruner says, "This is not to say that children operating concretely are not able to anticipate things that are not present. Rather, it is that they do not command the operations for conjuring up systematically the full range of alternative possibilities that could exist at a given time" (37).

The third stage is characterized by intellectual operations. "It is at this point that the child is able to give formal or axiomatic expression to the concrete ideas that before guided his problem-solving but could not be described or formally understood" (37-38).

Bruner encourages educators to find challenging opportunities for children at every level, while cautioning that formal explanations before the child is ready are futile. For Bruner, the process of education is enhanced by a deep understanding of the mind so that its power and sensibilities may be fully developed.

THE ACT OF LEARNING

For Bruner, learning is an act, a thing done. It is also a process that subsumes within it three simultaneous processes: acquisition, transformation, and evaluation. Acquisition refers to new information that sometimes demands a refinement of what was previously known. Transformation is the wielding of knowledge to fit new situations. It is knowing and going beyond that knowing. Evaluation serves to check and balance those transformations.

Think of the act of learning, for the moment, as a lesson in any typical classroom. The teacher begins the lesson usually with some artifact, challenge, or connection to prior knowledge to arouse interest or to motivate. The new information is introduced. The teacher models the new knowledge by using it in some way. And here Bruner is adamant, "The teacher is not only a communicator but a model. Somebody who does not see anything beautiful or powerful about mathematics is not likely to ignite others with a sense of the intrinsic excitement of the subject. A teacher who will not or cannot give play to his own intuitiveness is not likely to be effective in encouraging intuition in his students. To be so insecure that he dares not be caught in a mistake does not make a teacher a likely model of daring. If the teacher will not risk a shaky hypothesis, why should the student?" (1963, 90) Next, the students manipulate the information in some way, perhaps applying it to something they have done or discussing it in relation to what they know. All this time they are working to fit the new information into what they know; all this time they are in the act of learning. Finally, the lesson ends with some type of check on the learning.

Now think of the act of learning in the continuum of life. If people are open to learning, then life provides daily acts of learning, moments of learning, learning that takes years, learning that is somewhat transformed, learning opportunities that are never acquired. When writing is taught with the objective of making students lifelong writers and readers, for example, students have the *process* of education, the *act* of learning opened for them. The students, in turn, become open to the process and act of learning. This is evidenced by an open-mindedness, which Bruner defines. "I take open-mindedness to be a willingness to construe knowledge and values from multiple perspectives without loss of commitment to one's own values. Open-mindedness is the keystone of what we call a democratic culture" (1990, 30).

Bruner uses the phrase *the spiral curriculum* to return to his belief that any subject can be taught to any child in some honest form. He advises respecting the ways children think and teaching to those ways. If curricula are built upon the stages of development and address the issue of continuity, the curricula will not deteriorate into shapeless masses but spiral upward to include all subjects and all students.

The Process of Knowing

Bruner maintains that the process of knowing occurs in three modes: enactive, iconic, and symbolic. These three forms are at once representations of reality and ways to represent experience.

ENACTIVE KNOWING

In enactive or motoric knowing, students learn by doing. Here the hand predominates. This type of knowing is used to describe certain actions appropriate for achieving certain results. It also describes actions that manifest the mastery of those results. For example, if a student recombines sentences until they "feel" right, that student knows the combination works through the manipulation of the words.

ICONIC KNOWING

In iconic or ikonic knowing, students learn by depicting an image. Here the eye predominates. This type of knowing uses images, pictures, or graphics to represent what is known, and it describes images that are created to demonstrate knowing. For example, a student may describe an image of the ocean from memory. That the student is able to recreate the image suggests the knowing.

SYMBOLIC KNOWING

In symbolic or representational knowing, students learn by a restatement in words. Here the brain predominates. This type of knowing includes knowledge gained through symbolic systems, such as a number system or a language system, which are transformed into meaning by the mind. Using a symbolic system in a logical way, such as putting letters together to form words and words to form sentences, stands as proof that symbolic system is known. For example, taking a totally new or creative idea from the mind and transforming it onto paper is a type of symbolic knowing.

In the essay "Tolstoy, Vygotsky, and the Making of Meaning," Ann E. Berthoff echoes Bruner: "As soon as the form-finding and form-creating powers of mind are engaged, purposes are given shape; intentions are realized; meanings are created" (46). Teachers of writing galvanize those powers when they engage students in writing. As Janet Emig says, "If we are sighted, we make use of all three modes at once since the writing hand (motoric) produces the piece (iconic) that is a verbal symbolization (representational)" (65). Emig applies this thought to the teaching of writing by suggesting that there should perhaps be greater emphasis on writing as the making of an icon, such as self-made books. Ann Ruggles Gere, in her introduction to *Roots in the Sawdust* maintains that writing as a focused activity using hand, eye, and brain, coupled with its linearity of word following word, "leads to more coherent and sustained thought than thinking or speaking. The physical limitations imposed on writers make writing a slow process (slow relative to thinking or talking), and this slowness seems to free some parts of the brain for the discoveries so common among writers" (4).

The Process of Discovery

Discovery in the Newtonian sense is rare, argues Bruner. For most, discovery is "in its essence a matter of rearranging or transforming evidence in such a way that one is enabled to go beyond the evidence so reassembled to new insights" (1971, 82-83). To place discovery in perspective, Bruner defines two types of teaching: expository and hypothetical. In the former, the teacher is the presenter and the student the "bench-bound listener" (1971, 83); in the latter, the teacher and student cooperate in the learning process. Therein lies the possibility for discovery. Bruner identifies four benefits for learning by discovery: intellectual potency, intrinsic and extrinsic motives, heuristics of discovery, and conservation of memory.

INTELLECTUAL POTENCY

Bruner's studies lead him to contend that students who expect to find something in their environment or in a task show an observable increase in cognitive activity, connect information in a more organized way, and persist longer at the task than do students who did not expect to find something. This translates into an emphasis on discovery, active learning, and high expectations for both teacher and student.

INTRINSIC AND EXTRINSIC MOTIVES

Bruner posits that extrinsic rewards tend to limit even overachievers to conform to what is expected or to try to please in order to get the reward. He believes that learning about something is less effective for cognitive development than learning as a process of discovery. "The degree to which the desire for competence comes to control behavior, to that degree the role of reinforcement or 'outside rewards' wanes in shaping behavior" (1971, 92). In other words, the more students discover, the greater their ability to discover, and vice versa.

HEURISTICS OF DISCOVERY

Bruner encourages practice for discovery: practice at trying to figure things out and practice in the heuristics of inquiry. He states, "Of only one thing am I convinced: I have never seen anybody improve in the art and technique of inquiry by any means other than engaging in inquiry" (1971, 94). So, too, with writing. One learns to write by writing.

CONSERVATION OF MEMORY

Basically, Bruner's research shows that if students construct their own cognitive processes, what he calls "mediators" for remembering information, rather than using none at all or one given to them by someone else, they make that information more accessible for retrieval. The point is students will discover a mediator that works for them based on interest and their cognitive structures. According to Bruner, if given pairs of words to remember, students who are given no mediator for remembering them will do poorly. Those given a mediator, such as "think of the two words in a story" do better at remembering them. But the students who are given the notion of a mediator or a way to remember, but who are allowed to come up with their own mediator, remember up to 95 percent of word pairs.

APPLICATION

Vygotsky designed 22 wooden blocks to use for his concept formation tests. There were 5 different colors, 6 different shapes, 2 heights, and 2 sizes. *Lag* was written on the back of the tall large blocks; *bik* on the flat large ones; *mur* on the tall small ones; and *cev* on the flat small ones, irrespective of color. (A full explanation of Vygotsky's test may be found in *Thought and Language,* pages 56-57). Administer your test to a group of children or adults and write your conclusions.

Make a set of these blocks (bath blocks work well). Then devise a test that could be given to a group in order to check their concept formation level.

WORKS CITED

Berthoff, Ann E. "Tolstoy, Vygotsky, and the Making of Meaning." In *Composition and Its Teaching*, edited by Richard C. Gebhardt. Findlay, OH: Ohio Council of Teachers of English Language Arts, 1979.

Bloom, Benjamin S., Max D. Engelhart, Edward J. Furst, Walker H. Hill, and David R. Krathwohl, eds. *Taxonomy of Educational Objectives: The Classification of Educational Goals*. New York: David McKay, 1956.

Bruner, Jerome S. *Acts of Meaning*. Cambridge: Harvard University Press, 1990.

———. *On Knowing: Essays for the Left Hand*. New York: Atheneum, 1971.

———. *The Process of Education*. New York: Vintage Books, 1963.

Calkins, Lucy McCormick. *The Art of Teaching Writing*. Portsmouth, NH: Heinemann Educational Books, 1986.

Cheatham, Judy. "Piaget, Writing Instruction and the Middle School." *Middle School Journal* (March 1989): 14-17.

Deedy, Carmen Agra. *Agatha's Feather Bed: Not Just Another Wild Goose Story*. Atlanta: Peachtree, 1991.

De Regniers, Beatrice Schenk. *Little Red Riding Hood*. New York: Macmillan, 1972.

Edelman, Gerald M. *Bright Air, Brilliant Fire: On the Matter of the Mind*. New York: Basic Books, 1992.

Emig, Janet. "Hand, Eye, Brain: Some 'Basics' in the Writing Process." In *Research on Composing: Points of Departure*, edited by Charles R. Cooper and Lee Odell. Urbana, IL: National Council of Teachers of English, 1978.

Faulkner, William. *As I Lay Dying*. New York: Vintage Books, 1957.

Foley, Joyce Paster, and Michael T. Bagley. *Suppose the Wolf Were an Octopus? A Guide to Creative Questioning for Primary Grade Literature*. New York: Trillium Press, 1984.

Gardner, Howard. *The Unschooled Mind: How Children Think and How Schools Should Teach*. New York: Basic Books, 1991.

Gere, Anne Ruggles, ed. *Roots in the Sawdust: Writing to Learn Across the Disciplines*. Urbana, IL: National Council of Teachers of English, 1985.

Ginsburg, Herbert, and Sylvia Opper, eds. *Piaget's Theory of Intellectual Development: An Introduction*. Englewood Cliffs, NJ: Prentice-Hall, 1969.

Gwynne, Fred. *A Chocolate Moose for Dinner*. New York: Simon & Schuster, 1976.

———. *The King Who Rained*. New York: Simon & Schuster, 1988.

Martorano, S. "A Development Analysis of Performance on Piaget's Formal Operations Tasks." *Developmental Psychology* 13 (1977): 666-672.

Parish, Peggy. *Amelia Bedelia*. New York: Harper & Row, 1963.

Piaget, Jean. *Judgment and Reasoning in the Child*. Totowa, NJ: Littlefield, Adams, 1976.

_____. *The Language and Thought of the Child*. New York: World Book, 1969.

_____. *The Origins of Intelligence in Children*. New York: W. W. Norton, 1963.

Pilcher, Rosamunde. "The Road to Romance." In *The Writer's Handbook*, edited by Sylvia K. Burack. Boston: The Writer, 1989.

Sanders, Norris M. *Classroom Questions: What Kinds?* New York: Harper & Row, 1966.

Sayre, S., and D. W. Ball. "Piagetian Cognitive Development and Achievement in Science." *Journal of Research in Science Teaching* 12 (1975): 165-174.

Shayer, M., and P. Arlin. "The Transescent Mind: Teachers Can Begin to Make a Difference." *Transescence* 10 (1982): 27-34.

Sternberg, Robert. *The Triarchic Mind*. New York: Viking Penguin, 1988.

Toepfer, Conrad F., Jr. "Brain Growth Periodization: Implications for Middle Grades Education." *Schools in the Middle* (April 1981): 1-6.

Vygotsky, L. S. *Mind in Society*. Edited by Michael Cole, Vera John-Steiner, Sylvia Scribner, and Ellen Souberman. Cambridge: Harvard University Press, 1978.

_____. *Thought and Language*. Edited and translated by Eugenia Hanfmann and Gertrude Vakar. Cambridge: MIT Press, 1962.

"Writing as a Mode of Learning"

JANET EMIG

(From *College Composition and Communication*, May 1977.
Copyright 1977 by the National Council of Teachers of English.
Reprinted with permission.)

Commentary

Teachers of other content areas will need to understand the effect of Emig's straightforward thesis. No longer can they ignore the importance of writing. Writing in the content areas can serve these teachers well. Not only will their students benefit from the writing experience, but they will have evidence of the students' learning.

Since Emig wrote her article in 1977, too little change has occurred in the teaching of English. Too many classrooms are still exclusively reading and listening — lecturing is still the method of instruction in most high schools. During one week of spring 1992, we examined a large high school. One hundred ten out of 123 English classes per day were devoted to lecture four out of five days per week. The social studies department did not fare any better — 90 classes per day out of 91 were devoted to lecture five of the five days. The only time the lecture method was not in use was during testing. The schedule in 98 out of 105 math classes was divided equally between lecture and seat work (working problems every day) except when tests were given. The one teacher in the math department that used collaborative learning and group presentation was labeled a rebel.

Nor did we find a medium-size college English department a paragon of change. Out of the 36 sections of Freshman Writing, 30 were taught by the lecture method with writing assigned, not taught. Of the 92

Writing represents a unique mode of learning — not merely valuable, not merely special, but unique. That will be my contention in this paper. The thesis is straightforward. Writing serves learning uniquely because writing as process-and-product possesses a cluster of attributes that correspond uniquely to certain powerful learning strategies.

Although the notion is clearly debatable, it is scarcely a private belief. Some of the most distinguished contemporary psychologists have at least implied such a role for writing as heuristic. Lev Vygotsky, A. R. Luria, and Jerome Bruner, for example, have all pointed out that higher cognitive functions, such as analysis and synthesis, seem to develop most fully only with the support system of verbal language — particularly, it seems, of written language.[1] Some of their arguments and evidence will be incorporated here.

Here I have a prior purpose: to describe as tellingly as possible *how* writing uniquely corresponds to certain powerful learning strategies. Making such a case for the uniqueness of writing should logically and theoretically involve establishing many contrasts, distinctions between (1) writing and all other verbal languaging processes — listening, reading, and especially talking; (2) writing and all other forms of composing, such as composing a painting, a symphony, a dance, a film, a building; and (3) composing in words and composing in the two other major graphic symbol systems of mathematical equations and scientific formulae. For the purposes of this paper, the task is simpler, since most students are not permitted by most curricula to discover the values of composing, say, in dance, or even in film; and most students are not sophisticated enough to create, to originate formulations, using the highly abstruse symbol system of equations and formulae. Verbal language represents the most *available* medium for composing; in fact, the significance of sheer availability in its selection as a mode for learning can probably not be overstressed. But the uniqueness of writing among the verbal languaging processes does need to be established and supported if only because so many curricula and courses in English still consist almost exclusively of reading and listening.

Writing as a Unique Languaging Process

Traditionally, the four languaging processes of listening, talking, reading, and writing are paired in either of two ways. The more informative seems to be the division many linguists make between first-order and second-order processes, with talking and listening characterized as first-order processes; reading and writing, as second-order. First-order processes are acquired without formal or systematic instruction; the second-order processes of reading and writing tend to be learned initially only with the aid of formal and systematic instruction.

The less useful distinction is that between listening and reading as receptive functions and talking and writing as productive functions. Critics of these terms like Louise Rosenblatt rightfully point out that the connotation of passivity too often accompanies the notion of receptivity when reading, like listening, is a vital, construing act.

An additional distinction, so simple it may have been previously overlooked, resides in two criteria: the matters of origination and of graphic recording. Writing is originating and creating a unique verbal construct that is graphically recorded. Reading is creating or re-creating *but not* originating a verbal construct that is graphically recorded. Listening is creating or re-creating but not originating a verbal construct that is *not* graphically recorded. Talking is creating *and* originating a verbal construct that is *not* graphically recorded (except for the circuitous routing of a transcribed tape). Note that a distinction is being made between creating and originating, separable processes.

For talking, the nearest languaging process, additional distinctions should probably be made. (What follows is not a denigration of talk as a valuable mode of learning.)

classes devoted to literature study, all but the 3 classes on film were taught by the lecture method. The one course devoted to teacher education was process oriented and student centered.

Sometimes distinctions are made that are neat and tidy but, upon closer inspection, become blurred.

Consider children who mark up walls and "write" in their food.

Actually, watching television comes closer to passivity than does reading.

It proves interesting to graph these four processes according to one's own experiences. Then share and compare them to the experiences of others.

In addition, a school filled only with the principal's voice, or a district filled only with the superintendent's voice, is anathema to learning.

This very issue—that writing is not written talk—coupled with the desire to model, causes the dilemma in preschool, pre-kindergarten, kindergarten, and even first grade concerning the value of taking dictation, that is, writing the talk of children. More research may be needed in this area.

In "Non-Magical Thinking: Presenting Writing Developmentally in Schools" Emig hypothesizes on a revision of her statements here. She writes, "But what if, as evidence from many disciplines now suggests, writing is developmentally a natural process? What if it is just as natural ... to write books and to read them as it is natural to die or be born?"

A silent classroom or one filled only with the teacher's voice is anathema to learning. For evidence of the cognitive value of talk, one can look to some of the persuasive monographs coming from the London Schools Council project on writing: *From Information to Understanding* by Nancy Martin or *From Talking to Writing* by Peter Medway.[2] We also know that for some of us, talking is a valuable, even necessary, form of pre-writing. In his curriculum, James Moffett makes the value of such talk quite explicit.

But to say that talking is a valuable form of pre-writing is not to say that writing is talk recorded, an inaccuracy appearing in far too many composition texts. Rather, a number of contemporary trans-disciplinary sources suggest that talking and writing may emanate from different organic sources and represent quite different, possibly distinct, language functions. In *Thought and Language*, Vygotsky notes that "written speech is a separate linguistic function, differing from oral speech in both structure and mode of functioning."[3] The sociolinguist Dell Hymes, in a valuable issue of *Daedalus*, "Language as a Human Problem," makes a comparable point: "That speech and writing are not simply interchangeable, and have developed historically in ways at least partly autonomous, is obvious."[4] At the first session of the Buffalo Conference on Researching Composition (4-5 October 1975), the first point of unanimity among the participant-speakers with interests in developmental psychology, media, dreams and aphasia was that talking and writing were markedly different functions.[5] Some of us who work rather steadily with writing research agree. We also believe that there are hazards, conceptually and pedagogically, in creating too complete an analogy between talking and writing, in blurring the very real differences between the two.

What are these differences?

(1) Writing is learned behavior; talking is natural, even irrepressible, behavior.

(2) Writing then is an artificial process; talking is not.

(3) Writing is a technological device—not the wheel, but early enough to qualify as

primary technology; talking is organic, natural, earlier.

(4) Most writing is slower than most talking.

(5) Writing is stark, barren, even naked as a medium; talking is rich, luxuriant, inherently redundant.

(6) Talk leans on the environment; writing must provide its own context.

(7) With writing, the audience is usually absent; with talking, the listener is usually present.

(8) Writing usually results in a visible graphic product; talking usually does not.

(9) Perhaps because there is a product involved, writing tends to be a more responsible and committed act than talking.

(10) It can even be said that throughout history, an aura, an ambience, a mystique has usually encircled the written word; the spoken word has for the most part proved ephemeral and treated mundanely (ignore, please, our recent national history).

(11) Because writing is often our representation of the world made visible, embodying both process and product, writing is more readily a form and source of learning than talking.

Unique Correspondences between Learning and Writing

What then are some *unique* correspondences between learning and writing? To begin with some definitions: Learning can be defined in many ways, according to one's predilections and training, with all statements about learning of course hypothetical. Definitions range from the chemo-physiological ("Learning is changed patterns of protein synthesis in relevant portions of the cortex")[6] to transactive views drawn from both philosophy and psychology (John Dewey, Jean

Natural for this context must be quickly defined: As humans we seem to have a genetic predisposition to write as well as to speak; and, if we meet an enabling environment, one that possesses certain characteristics and presents us with certain opportunities, we will learn."[1]

Vygotsky in "A Prehistory of Written Language" writes, "The gesture is the initial visual sign that contains the child's future writing as an acorn contains a future oak. Gestures, it has been correctly said, are writing in air, and written signs frequently are simply gestures that have been fixed."[2]

Writing allows us to see the mind at work. No other symbolizing system is so complete. If students cannot write clearly, then they have not thought clearly. If their writing is unorganized, then their thinking is random and nonsequential. They have not harnessed their own thoughts, and writing shows this.

---

1. Janet Emig, *The Web of Meaning*, ed. Dixie Goswami and Maureen Butler (Upper Montclair, NJ: Boynton/Cook, 1983), 136.

2. L. S. Vygotsky, *Mind in Society*, ed. Michael Cole, Vera John-Steiner, Sylvia Scribner, and Ellen Souberman (Cambridge, MA: Harvard University Press, 1978), 107.

It may be helpful to write out two definitions, one for writing and one for learning. Doing this may be revealing.

NJWPT trainers read from a suggested reading list and synthesize their reading into summaries. They always remark how this part of their training benefits them. For most, it becomes exactly what Emig describes as involving "the fullest possible functioning of the brain."

Piaget) that learning is the re-organization or confirmation of a cognitive scheme in light of an experience.[7] What the speculations seem to share is consensus about certain features and strategies that characterize successful learning. These include the importance of the classic attributes of re-inforcement and feedback. In most hypotheses, successful learning is also connective and selective. Additionally, it makes use of propositions, hypotheses, and other elegant summarizers. Finally, it is active, engaged, personal—more specifically, self-rhythmed—in nature.

Jerome Bruner, like Jean Piaget, through a comparable set of categories, posits three major ways in which we represent and deal with actuality: (1) enactive—we learn "by doing"; (2) iconic—we learn "by depiction in an image"; and (3) representational or symbolic—we learn "by restatement in words."[8] To overstate the matter, in enactive learning, the hand predominates; in iconic, the eye; and in symbolic, the brain.

What is striking about writing as a process is that, by its very nature, all three ways of dealing with actuality are simultaneously or almost simultaneously deployed. That is, the symbolic transformation of experience through the specific symbol system of verbal language is shaped into an icon (the graphic product) by the enactive hand. If the most efficacious learning occurs when learning is re-inforced, then writing through its inherent re-inforcing cycle involving hand, eye, and brain marks a uniquely powerful multi-representational mode for learning.

Writing is also integrative in perhaps the most basic possible sense: the organic, the functional. Writing involves the fullest possible functioning of the brain, which entails the active participation in the process of both the left and the right hemispheres. Writing is markedly bispheral, although in some popular accounts, writing is inaccurately presented as a chiefly left-hemisphere activity, perhaps because the linear written product is somehow regarded as analogue for the process that created it; and the left hemisphere seems to process material linearly.

The right hemisphere, however, seems to make at least three, perhaps four, major contributions to the writing process—probably to the creative process generically. First, several researchers, such as Geschwind and Snyder of Harvard and Zaidal of Cal Tech, through markedly different experiments, have very tentatively suggested that the right hemisphere is the sphere, even the *seat*, of emotions.[9] Second—or perhaps as an illustration of the first—Howard Gardner, in his important study of the brain-damaged, notes that our sense of emotional appropriateness in discourse may reside in the right sphere:

> Emotional appropriateness, in sum— being related not only to *what* is said, but to how it is said and to what is *not* said, as well—is crucially dependent on right hemisphere intactness.[10]

Third, the right hemisphere seems to be the source of intuition, of sudden gestalts, of flashes of images, of abstractions occurring as visual or spatial wholes, as the initiating metaphors in the creative process. A familiar example: William Faulkner noted in his *Paris Review* interview that *The Sound and the Fury* began as the image of a little girl's muddy drawers as she sat in a tree watching her grandmother's funeral.[11]

Also, a unique form of feedback, as well as reinforcement, exists with writing, because information from the *process* is immediately and visibly available as that portion of the *product* already written. The importance for learning of a product in a familiar and available medium for immediate, literal (that is, visual) re-scanning and review cannot perhaps be overstated. In his remarkable study of purportedly blind sculptors, Géza Révész found that without sight, persons cannot move beyond a literal transcription of elements into any manner of symbolic transformation—by definition, the central requirement for reformulation and re-interpretation, i.e., revision, that most aptly named process.[12]

As noted in the second paragraph, Vygotsky and Luria, like Bruner, have written importantly about the connections between learning and writing. In his essay "The Psychobiology of Psychology," Bruner lists as one of six axioms regarding learning: "We are connective."[13] Another correspondence then between learning and writing: in *Thought and Language*, Vygotsky notes that writing makes a unique demand in that the writer must engage in "deliberate semantics"—in Vygotsky's elegant phrase, "deliberate structuring of the web of meaning."[14] Such structuring is required because, for Vygotsky, writing

After working with the concepts and strategies that make up this book, after reading and rereading the theories of the scholars and the pedagogies of the teachers presented here, we agree that the process of writing this book became a unique and penetrating learning experience.

centrally represents an expansion of inner speech, that mode whereby we talk to ourselves, which is "maximally compact" and "almost entirely predicative"; written speech is a mode which is "maximally detailed" and which requires explicitly supplied subjects and topics. The medium then of written verbal language requires the establishment of systematic connections and relationships. Clear writing by definition is that writing which signals without ambiguity the nature of conceptual relationships, whether they be coordinate, subordinate, superordinate, causal, or something other.

We are reminded of Jasper Neel's words that when students engage in the traditional classes of expository writing "they can avoid writing altogether by providing shells with no interior: spelling, punctuation, sentences, paragraphs, structure, and coherence that are nothing but spelling, punctuation, sentences, paragraphs, structure and coherence."[3] What they produce is not writing, but antiwriting. This type of writing does not show the mind at work, it shows writing conventions at work.

Successful learning is also engaged, committed, personal learning. Indeed, impersonal learning may be an anomalous concept, like the very notion of objectivism itself. As Michael Polanyi states simply at the beginning of *Personal Knowledge*: "the ideal of strict objectivism is absurd." (How many courses and curricula in English, science, and all else does that one sentence reduce to rubble?) Indeed, the theme of *Personal Knowledge* is that

> into every act of knowing there enters a passionate contribution of the person knowing what is being known, ... this coefficient is no mere imperfection but a vital component of his knowledge.[15]

In *Zen and the Art of Motorcycle Maintenance*, Robert Pirsig states a comparable theme:

> The Quality which creates the world emerges as *a relationship* between man and his experience. He is a *participant* in the creation of all things.[16]

Finally, the psychologist George Kelly has as the central notion in his subtle and compelling theory of personal constructs man as a scientist steadily and actively engaged in making and re-making his hypotheses about the nature of the universe.[17]

We are acquiring as well some empirical confirmation about the importance of engagement in, as well as self-selection of, a subject for the student learning to write and writing to learn. The recent Sanders and Littlefield study, reported in *Research in the Teaching of English*, is persuasive evidence on

---

3. Jasper Neel, *Plato, Derrida, Writing* (Carbondale, IL: Southern Illinois University Press, 1988), 165.

this point, as well as being a model for a certain type of research.[18]

As Luria implies in the quotation above, writing is self-rhythmed. One writes best as one learns best, at one's own pace. Or to connect the two processes, writing can sponsor learning because it can match its pace. Support for the importance of self-pacing to learning can be found in Benjamin Bloom's important study "Time and Learning."[19] Evidence for the significance of self-pacing to writing can be found in the reason Jean-Paul Sartre gave last summer for not using the tape-recorder when he announced that blindness in his second eye had forced him to give up writing:

> I think there is an enormous difference between speaking and writing. One rereads what one rewrites. But one can read slowly or quickly: in other words, you do not know how long you will have to take deliberating over a sentence.... If I listen to a tape recorder, the listening speed is determined by the speed at which the tape turns and not by my own needs. Therefore I will always be either lagging behind or running ahead of the machine.[20]

Writing is connective as a process in a more subtle and perhaps more significant way, as Luria points out in what may be the most powerful paragraph of rationale ever supplied for writing as heuristic:

> Written speech is bound up with the inhibition of immediate synpractical connections. It assumes a much slower, repeated mediating process of analysis and synthesis, which makes it possible not only to develop the required thought, but even to revert to its earlier stages, thus transforming the sequential chain of connections in a simultaneous, self-reviewing structure. Written speech thus represents a new and powerful instrument of thought.[21]

But first to explicate: writing inhibits "immediate synpractical connections." Luria defines *synpraxis* as "concrete-active" situations in which language does not exist independently but as a "fragment" of an ongoing

Perhaps each of us should create a huge banner that reads ONE WRITES BEST AS ONE LEARNS BEST, AT ONE'S OWN PACE. This banner might be hung in classrooms everywhere.

If there is any truth to the theory that there is intelligence in every molecule of the body, Luria's "fragment" theory assumes vast implications.

Again we find Emig further defining her stance. In "Non-Magical Thinking: Presenting Writing Developmentally in Schools" she writes,

What are the possible implications of these research findings for the presentation of writing in schools?

1. *Although writing is natural, it is activated by enabling environments.*
2. *These environments have the following characteristics: they are safe, structured, private, unobtrusive, and literate.*
3. *Adults in these environments have two especial roles: they are fellow practitioners, and they are providers of possible content, experiences and feedback.*
4. *Children need frequent opportunities to practice writing, many of these playful.*

None of these conditions is met in our current schools; indeed, to honor them would require nothing less than a paradigm shift in the ways we present not only writing but also other major cognitive processes as well.[4]

What are teachers and schools waiting for before they change? What research do these teachers and schools have to support their adherence to the aging paradigm?

---

4.   Emig, 139.

action "outside of which it is incomprehensible."[22] In *Language and Learning*, James Britton defines it succinctly as "speech-cum-action."[23] Writing, unlike talking, restrains dependence upon the actual situation. Writing as a mode is inherently more self-reliant than speaking. Moreover, as Bruner states in explicating Vygotsky, "Writing virtually forces a remoteness of reference on the language user."[24]

Luria notes what has already been noted above: that writing, typically, is a "much slower" process than talking. But then he points out the relation of this slower pace to learning: this slower pace allows for—indeed, encourages—the shuttling among past, present, and future. Writing, in other words, connects the three major tenses of our experience to make meaning. And the two major modes by which these three aspects are united are the processes of analysis and synthesis: analysis, the breaking of entities into their constituent parts; and synthesis, combining or fusing these, often into fresh arrangements or amalgams.

Finally, writing is epigenetic, with the complex evolutionary development of thought steadily and graphically visible and available throughout as a record of the journey, from jottings and notes to full discursive formulations.

For a summary of the correspondences stressed here between certain learning strategies and certain attributes of writing see Figure 1.

This essay represents a first effort to make a certain kind of case for writing—specifically, to show its unique value for learning. It is at once over-elaborate and under specific. Too much of the formulation is in the off-putting jargon of the learning theorist, when my own predilection would have been to emulate George Kelly and to avoid terms like *re-inforcement* and *feedback* since their use implies that I live inside a certain paradigm about learning I don't truly inhabit. Yet I hope that the essay will start a crucial line of inquiry; for unless the losses to learners of not writing are compellingly described and substantiated by experimental and speculative research, writing itself as a central academic process may not long endure.

Figure 1

*Unique Cluster of Correspondences between
Certain Learning Strategies and Certain
Attributes of Writing*

Selected Characteristics of Successful Learning Strategies	Selected Attributes of Writing, Process and Product
(1) Profits from multi-representational and integrative re-inforcement	(1) Represents process uniquely multi-representational and integrative
(2) Seeks self-provided feedback:	(2) Represents powerful instance of self-provided feedback:
(a) immediate	(a) provides product uniquely available for *immediate* feedback (review and re-evaluation)
(b) long-term	(b) provides record of evolution of thought since writing is epigenetic as process-and-product
(3) Is connective:	(3) Provides connections:
(a) makes generative conceptual groupings, synthetic and analytic	(a) establishes explicit and systematic conceptual groupings through lexical, syntactic, and rhetorical devices
(b) proceeds from propositions, hypotheses, and other elegant summarizers	(b) represents most available means (verbal language) for economic recording of abstract formulations
(4) Is active, engaged, personal—notably, self-rhythmed	(4) Is active, engaged, personal—notably, self-rhythmed

*Rutgers—The State University
New Brunswick, NJ*

Notes

1. Lev S. Vygotsky, *Thought and Language*, trans. Eugenia Hanfmann and Gertrude Vakar (Cambridge: The M.I.T. Press, 1962); A. R. Luria and F. Ia. Yudovich, *Speech and the Development of Mental Processes in the Child*, ed. Joan Simon (Baltimore: Penguin, 1971); Jerome S. Bruner, *The Relevance of Education* (New York: W. W. Norton and Co., 1971).

2. Nancy Martin, *From Information to Understanding* (London: Schools Council Project Writing Across the Curriculum, 11-13, 1973); Peter Medway, *From Talking to Writing* (London: Schools Council Project Writing Across the Curriculum, 11-13, 1973).

3. Vygotsky, p. 98.

4. Dell Hymes, "On the Origins and Foundations of Inequality Among Speakers," *Daedalus*, 102 (Summer, 1973), 69.

5. Participant-speakers were Loren Barrett, University of Michigan; Gerald O'Grady, SUNY/Buffalo; Hollis Frampton, SUNY/Buffalo; and Janet Emig, Rutgers.

6. George Steiner, *After Babel: Aspects of Language and Translation* (New York: Oxford University Press, 1975), p. 287.

7. John Dewey, *Experience and Education* (New York: Macmillan, 1938); Jean Piaget, *Biology and Knowledge: An Essay on the Relations between Organic Regulations and Cognitive Processes* (Chicago: University of Chicago Press, 1971).

8. Bruner, pp. 7-8.

9. Boyce Rensberger, "Language Ability Found in Right Side of Brain," *New York Times*, 1 August 1975, p. 14.

10. Howard Gardner, *The Shattered Mind: The Person After Brain Damage* (New York: Alfred A. Knopf, 1975), p. 372.

11. William Faulkner, *Writers at Work: The Paris Review Interviews*, ed. Malcolm Cowley (New York: The Viking Press, 1959), p. 130.

12. Géza Révész, *Pscyhology and Art of the Blind*, trans. H. A. Wolff (London: Longmans-Green, 1950).

13. Bruner, p. 126.

14. Vygotsky, p. 100.

15. Michael Polanyi, *Personal Knowledge: Toward a Post-Critical Philosophy* (Chicago: University of Chicago Press, 1958), p. viii.

16. Robert Pirsig, *Zen and the Art of Motorcycle Maintenance* (New York: William Morrow and Co., Inc., 1974), p. 212.

17. George Kelly, *A Theory of Personality: The Psychology of Personal Constructs* (New York: W. W. Norton and Co., 1963).

18. Sara E. Sanders and John H. Littlefield, "Perhaps Test Essays Can Reflect Significant Improvement in Freshman Composition: Report on a Successful Attempt," *RTE*, 9 (Fall 1975), 145-153.

19. Benjamin Bloom, "Time and Learning," *American Psychologist*, 29 (September 1974), 682-688.

20. Jean-Paul Sartre, "Sartre at Seventy: An Interview," with Michel Contat, *New York Review of Books*, 7 August 1975.

21. Luria, p. 118.

22. Luria, p. 50.

23. James Britton, *Language and Learning* (Baltimore: Penguin, 1971), pp. 10-11.

24. Bruner, p. 47.

11

IN THE BEGINNING
Studying Developmental Writing
and Invented Spelling

From this perspective [recent early-language research],
language learning is seen as a process of sense making.
Aspects of this process include making meaning, sharing meaning,
extending meaning, evaluating meaning, savoring meaning,
and generating new meaning.

— Jerome C. Harste□

What if writing were natural? What if children came to it as they come to other languages? What if teachers looked at writing as does semiologist Christian Metz, who "groups natural language with signifying systems as diverse as those of myth, dress, food, cinema, kinship, politeness, painting, poetry, and cartography" (Guzzetti 177)? What if students were biologically predisposed to write? What if writing were another way to interpret or infer? What if writing were a constant constructing and reconstructing of thought, not just the adding of letters to letters or words to words? What if writing were considered implosive, that is, bursting inward on the learner; as well as explosive, that is, exploding outward to the reader? What if writing grew out of an ability to make sense of things? What if teachers thought about these questions? Would writing be taught differently?

Not too many years ago most educators held that speaking and listening were primary activities because, in most normal circumstances, they simply happened. Reading and writing were considered secondary activities because they appeared to require systematic teaching. A child at the beach making marks in the sand or a child scribbling did not constitute an act of writing in these educators' minds. However, the research of nativist theorists, such as Eric Lenneberg and David McNeill, and the cognitive theorists, such as Jean Piaget, Lev Vygotsky, and Jerome Bruner, coupled with burgeoning brain research, such as the work of Gerald M. Edelman, suggests that there are innate structures in humankind that enable children to process linguistic information in uniquely human ways. That is, if writing is a code that stands for something else, then symbolic play, for example, may be as developmentally important to writing as babbling is to speech or crawling is to walking. After all, babbling is a way of making sound, just as speech is a way of making sound. Crawling is movement, just as walking is movement. Just so, symbolic play is a way of constructing meaning, just as writing is a way of constructing meaning. The difference rests in sophistication of degree, of extent, and of developmental significance. Each is a natural part of an incredibly complicated growth and learning process. More broadly, writing may be thought of as the manifestation of a process of comprehension that places the reality of the writer within a culture. In and through this transformation called writing, the writer engages in a process of comprehension. Even so, as developmental psychologist Margaret Donaldson reminds, " 'Understanding' is a very complex notion.... The 'correct' interpretation of a word on one occasion is no guarantee of full understanding on another" (72-73).

Further, years of research by scholars the caliber of Durkin, Clay, Lamme, Bissex, Dyson, and others who have long studied the features of writing in young children, undergird statements drafted by organizations such as the National Council of Teachers of English, the Association for Childhood Education International, the International Reading Association, and the National Association for the Education of Young Children. Each has generated position papers or published articles that support the developmentally appropriate teaching of writing. They advocate experience-centered environments; they promote activities like scribbles, drawings, and invented spellings; they advise teachers to "encourage risk-taking in first attempts at reading and writing, and accept what appear to be errors as part of children's natural patterns of growth and development" (Early Childhood 6).

The artificial teaching of writing with its concomitant teaching of isolated letters and isolated skills is being replaced with more integrated, sometimes incremental, sometimes holistic, approaches to writing. Those who believe that children cannot write until they have mastered the alphabet are being superseded by those who build upon the living language of their students. They regard writing as "a particular system of symbols and signs whose mastery heralds a critical turning point in the entire cultural development of the child" (Vygotsky 106), so they fill their rooms with words, labeling everything. They expose students to books, stacking them on tables, piling them in baskets, and covering every available shelf with them. They frequently read to and often talk with their students. They encourage students to read and talk to each other. They write and invite their students to write. And they allow plenty of time for writing. They know students can read without writing, but they cannot write without reading—that the two are inextricable. They create writing and reading centers; they confer; they meet and work in groups. And they announce to everyone the importance of writing by displaying it everywhere. Even scribbles, drawings, and awkward letters made randomly on a page proclaim from ceilings, bulletin boards, walls, and doors the excitement of writing, the excitement of making meaning. In short, the environment becomes an eloquent social context and a joyfully literate climate, both conducive to growth.

> A principal called me. She expressed dismay at her third-graders' results on the state-mandated writing test. She observed her primary teachers and determined they were not teaching writing. She called me to provide in-service training for the teachers.
>
> The school, located in one of the nicest suburbs of the city, was new, big, and beautiful. The classrooms were most spacious, almost double rooms. There was plenty of room for any activity. Entering the first-grade classroom I noticed laminated, store-bought pictures, posters, and letters displayed. A huge paper tree, obviously made by the teacher, squatted in a corner. Its branches, bereft of anything made or written by a child, curled up to the ceiling. The room was showy but without substance. I saw one storybook on the teacher's desk—none were apparent anywhere else in the room. Then I spotted cubbies and cubbies filled with worksheets, all categorized—reading, mathematics, science.
>
> What made this experience so indelible for me was the fact that I arrived at this school immediately after visiting an urban school in a poor neighborhood. That school was old, with stuffy, overcrowded classrooms. In that first-grade classroom, its one window, high on the wall, provided neither ventilation nor light. Those first-graders sat in oversized chairs at oversized desks, obviously leftovers from some higher grade. They literally had to kneel on their chairs to write at their desks. But the atmosphere in that room was electric. The children were eager and responsive. They shared their writing and discussed it in groups. The teacher facilitated. Writing and books were everywhere. I did not see one worksheet. I remembered Slade, whose brain tumor made learning difficult, proudly reading, "Poochie died. I got a cat. Boots is my cat" (see fig. 11.1).

Fig. 11.1. Slade's writing. 🕴

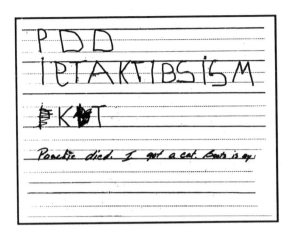

I asked him for a copy. Not to be outdone, Lindsy ran to me with her writing. Lindsy, who had been retained, wrote the note reproduced in figure 11.2 to another first-grader about the need for proper bathroom manners.

🕴 *frum Lindsy win you go to the bathroom pritee plees flus toolit and donte waste stuf in the bathroom and plees doo not potee on the sid of toolit.*

[From Lindsy — When you go to the bathroom pretty please flush the toilet and don't waste stuff in the bathroom. And please do not potty on the side of the toilet] (fig. 11.2).

Fig. 11.2. Lindsy's writing.

>*Perhaps because of those memories, I turned to the principal who was serving as my host at the suburban school and asked, "Where are the children in this room?"*
>
>*Misunderstanding me, she nodded in the direction of 15 well-dressed, incredibly well behaved students, who were patiently sitting cross-legged on the floor.*
>
>*"What I mean is, I don't see their work anywhere. The room seems sterile. There is no life," I whispered.*
>
>*"That's why you're here," she whispered back.*
>
>*The writing those 15 privileged students produced that day made me heartsick. Before and after Bernard Most's* The Cow That Went Oink, *they interacted monosyllabically, with little verve, but politely. Then, when asked to write a story "about some animal you know," these children, who by all accounts should have been fluent, confident writers, drew only a small box on their papers to surround an even smaller animal. A word or two accompanied the picture. I can still see the terror in one child's eye as she asked if she had spelled* kat *correctly.*
>
>*Examining the children's writing, I could see what they had produced. They had all made worksheets—a word, a box, a drawing, a line from the box to the drawing. They modeled what they knew—worksheets.*

The difference between these two experiences has little to do with buildings, rooms, space, or socioeconomic levels but a great deal to do with the knowledge base of the teachers. Decorating a room is decidedly different from co-creating one. When teachers and students come together in meaningful ways, the classroom becomes an extension of that meaning. The classroom becomes theirs together—not the teacher's alone. It at once reflects the making of meaning that has occurred there and serves to inspire the making of additional meaning. In a co-created classroom, students feel ownership. They feel comfortable. They are not disenfranchised from a context that can foster their development, nor are they simply marshaled through a series of rote activities. Just as children expand their oral language through the environs of their cultural context, so, too, they expand their written language according to the environs of their academic culture. The more that culture opens children's minds, the more it undergirds writing with sound theory and pedagogy; the more teachers understand the processes that advance the natural development of children in writing, the less the culture delimits that growth.

As Margaret Donaldson states, "A child's ability to learn language is indeed something at which we may wonder. But his language-learning skills are not isolated from the rest of his mental growth.... It now looks as though he first makes sense of situations (and perhaps especially those involving human intention) and then uses *this* kind of understanding to help him to make sense of what is said to him" (56).

ARENAS IN WRITING AND SPELLING DEVELOPMENT

To pull away from writing as a motor skill or mere copying and to move to writing as what Vygotsky calls "a system of signs" (106) involves knowledge of a complex of processes that are oxymora: they are chaotically structured and complexly simple. This chapter traces these processes through seven arenas of recursive and overlapping writing and spelling development: rhythms, gestures, initial visual signs, symbolic play, symbolic drawing, transitional writing and spelling, and standard writing and spelling.

I have chosen the term arena *to indicate a sphere of activity. The word* stage *doesn't work for me because it suggests development that is linear or lock-step. The term* characteristic *doesn't work for me, either, because while it denotes a distinguishing quality, it often connotes that which is typical. Children's writing is more often atypical because their language arenas are more closely tied to all the other learning going on. After years of observing and collecting children's writing, I find so often a child will produce an astonishing piece in one context but become almost mute in another. Kindergartners will write pages of discourse, for example, way beyond stages labeled as phonemic or letter-name spelling as demonstrated in Crystal's writing in figure 11.3.*

Fig. 11.3. Crystal's writing.

🏃 *the moon and the sun wer chasn meandi felt dize Lika tornado thn i fel nto a Big Big Ho and it waz soft n the Ho and i sa a shine str on the Pelos*

[The moon and the sun were chasing me and I felt dizzy like a tornado. Then I fell into a big, big hole. And it was soft in the hole. And I saw a shiny star on the pillow] (fig. 11.3).

True, aspects of development may be typical and may be distinguished from other aspects, but the intent here is to use a term that is most inclusive and widely applicable. Sometimes students in middle school and high school display writing that much younger children normally generate. They may draw, doodle, or even employ the recurring principle of repetition as they think into meaning. In other words, writing arenas overlap because ways of generating meaning overlap. As I suggest in my article "Drawing into Meaning," (see chapter 3, pages 96-100) the dimensions of literacy cross grade levels.

Rhythms

I had been invited to keynote at a local National Association for the Education of Young Children conference on the topic of developmental writing. After the introduction but before the talk, I asked to have the house lights dimmed. I switched on the large monitor hooked up to a VCR that held a sonogram tape. An image of a fetus dramatically appeared as if carved by some antediluvian hydrographical system in a subterranean cavern. Then it moved. Everyone saw the baby slowly, silently sway among the black and white shadows. The audience sat spellbound.

"This, ladies and gentlemen, is where writing begins," I said.

Rhythm marks life. From the gentle swaying felt *in utero* to the diastolic expansion and systolic contraction of the heart, people are held by it. From the rising moon to the setting sun, people are reinforced by it. From sowing to spinning, people are connected by it. People work in rhythm, sing in rhythm, pray in rhythm. Rhythm soothes and fascinates. It is the drumbeat of lives, marking time. And when a rhythm goes awry, people feel disconnected, fragmented, disturbed. Rhythm mesmerizes or tranquilizes; it deafens or bores; it excites or quiets; but whatever the reaction, rhythm is imprinted on the human consciousness.

Two physicians, Fernand Lamaze, author of *Painless Childbirth*, and Frederick Leboyer, author of *Birth Without Violence*, understand the significance of these imprints. Creating a metaphor that arises from the sea, Leboyer calls birth "a tidal wave of sensation surpassing anything we can imagine" (15). To ensure positive imprints, Lamaze and Leboyer believe that massaging the baby throughout the birthing process continues the womb's rhythms. Leboyer poetically explains that "the hands holding [the child] should speak in the language of the womb" (60). He believes this action gentles the neonate's entry into the world and produces happier, untraumatized babies. As if to prove his point, Leboyer includes pictures in his book of babies smiling, not crying, at birth.

Children, whether birthed by rhythm or not, begin life with some pattern of recurrence. As they mature, they continue like "dwellers by the sea [who] cannot fail to be impressed by the sight of its ceaseless ebb and flow, and are apt, on the principles of that rude philosophy of sympathy and resemblance ..., to trade a subtle relation, a secret harmony, between its tides and the life of man, of animals, and of plants" (Frazer 39). Therefore, it seems likely that those fundamental rhythms and those rhythms that run from the synaptic responses in the brain down the arm onto the paper, share an affinity.

Kornei Chukovsky, the most beloved author of children's books in Russia, tells how children cherish rhythm and use it to learn language. He says children think of words in pairs as if every word has a twin. Having learned one word, the child looks for another that is related—or makes one up, e.g., curly/stringly. He claims, "Children who have just begun to talk in phrases make use of rhyme to ease the task of pronouncing two words in a row. It is easier for the very young child to say 'night-night' than 'good night,' 'bye-bye' than 'good-bye' " (63). That makes sense. Little wonder that Chukovsky calls children linguistic geniuses.

Is it such a stretch, then, to speculate that writing and its flip side, reading, may find roots in rhythm and rhyme? If children enjoy saying word twins, is it not logical that they would be attracted to them in stories and poems? Is it not logical that they would write them? Karen Kutiper, professor at Southwest Texas State University and NJWPT trainer, in her study of the poetry preferences of seventh- , eighth- , and ninth-graders, discovered that "rhythm was an influencing factor in student selection of preferred poetry" (83). She culled the comments of several students, all of whom verified their connection with rhythm. "It ["We Real Cool," Gwendolyn Brooks] has real rhythm and sort of sing-songy" (grade 8). "It ["Railroad Reverie," David McCord] had a catchy rhythm" (grade 8). "I like it ["We Real Cool"] because of the rhythm" (grade 7). "I like the poem ["The Dance of the Thirteen Skeletons," Jack Prelutsky] because I like the rhythm" (grade 7). "I think the poem ["Mother Doesn't Want a Dog," Judith Viorst] is OK because it has rhythm and pattern" (grade 9). "It ["Stopping By a [sic] Woods," Robert Frost] has a good and steady rhythm" (grade 9) (83). Kutiper also found that "A seemingly universal preference for rhyme was probably the most significant factor in the low ratings of haiku and free or blank verse" (124). In fact, "Of the 25 most popular poems, all but 'Brothers' [Bruce Guernsey] had rhyme. The 25 least popular poems consisted of 23 poems that had no rhyme and two that had such inconsistent rhyme as to be hardly recognizable" (84).

Take, as further proof, how young children respond to Margaret Wise Brown's *Goodnight Moon*. Of course they identify with bunny, who prolongs bedtime by repeating "good night" to everything in the "great green room." Of course they are expanding their vocabulary through delightful repetition. But there is also the compelling rhythm created by Brown's rhyme. Children never tire of hearing it read and often chorus the lines. They take this classic and "read" it, even before preschool. Then they write it into their books. To speculate more specifically, perhaps that is what Maria Teresa Rivera did when she was a young child. Perhaps she fooled around with rhythm and rhyme; then, in fourth grade, she was able to write a line that rings with alliterative rhythm, a line that contains a stunning comparison of the moon to a burning black apple. So stunning is the line that the poem in which it appears was chosen by Kenneth Koch for his book *Wishes, Lies, and Dreams* (94). And could this speculation, this hypothetical conjuring, lead to poets such as Marge Piercy? What is her writing history? How did her writing metamorphose? As a child, did she imagine the moon's face? Did she mouth moon words? Might her poems "How the Full Moon Wakes You" and "The Hunger Moon" (148-149) have come from those rhythms?

Perhaps those suppositions are not too far afield. Eudora Welty tells of growing up to the whistling back and forth of her parents and the striking of clocks. She describes the dancing gyroscope and the box kite that tugged in her hands, and she tells of being read to, in a rocker "which ticked in rhythm as we rocked, as though we had a cricket accompanying the story" (5). The point is: language, its power and its force, is rooted in rhythm. Young children know that. So do professional authors.

While visiting friends who had recently become parents, we were treated to a trip to the nursery as Londi was being prepared for bed. As luck would have it, she became a bit restive and would not settle down no matter what they both tried. Finally, Londi's dad picked up a stuffed lamb and began turning the key in its back. I expected a lullaby or at least some rendition of "Mary Had a Little Lamb." Instead, I heard a soft, rhythmic, whooshing sound. To erase what must have been perceived as a perplexed look, our friends explained, "This, they say, is like the sound heard in utero. It always puts Londi to sleep." Almost immediately Londi's breathing indicated she had drifted into a deep slumber. My immediate comment was, "How great. I need to get one of those."

The coda to the story is that merchandisers have discovered the lulling rhythm of the womb, the heartbeat, the sea. For a reasonable sum anyone may purchase devices that create this "white sound" to promote sleeping. Rhythm is basic.

Gestures

Vygotsky maintains that gestures "contain the child's future writing as an acorn contains a future oak" (107). Gestures convey meaning. People recognize the meaning of a pointed finger, crossed arms, or a head shake. They understand a nod, thumbs up, or a clenched fist. These gestures are signs. Almost archetypal, they convey a universal language. Such is the power of gestures. Transforming gestures into writing is a matter of changing signs, changing modes.

Two researchers, William S. Condon and Louis W. Sander, from the Boston University School of Medicine, carried out highly sophisticated research on 16 neonates at Boston City Hospital and Boston Hospital for Women. Their purpose was to investigate the linguistic-kinetic interactive process between neonates and adults; that is, they studied the correspondence between adult speech and infant movement. Using a Bell & Howell modified 16-mm Time/Motion Analyzer, they were able to conduct a microanalysis of the movement of any part of the body, frame by frame or across frames. Their equipment also enabled a frame-by-frame analysis of speech. For example, they could examine an arm motion "event" for x number of frames while simultaneously hearing and seeing the speech through an oscilloscopic display.

Their study reveals "a complex interactional 'system' in which the organization of the neonate's motor behavior is seen to be entrained by and synchronized with the organized speech behavior of adults in his environment" (461). To rephrase, the neonates gestured to the rhythm of the adult speech. This occurred as early as the first day of life. Further, the correspondence occurred whether the adult speaking was actually present or was taped, whether the stimulus was American English or Chinese, whether the neonates were supine or held. Interestingly, however, "Disconnected vowel sounds failed to show the degree of correspondence which was associated with natural rhythmic speech" (461).

This research on language acquisition has implications for the development of writing because the acquisition of language in one form often illuminates the acquisition of language in another form—in this case, writing. The work of Condon and Sander seems to suggest that language acquisition is organismic not, atomistic. Learning language seems to be a living, integrated human event, not something reduced to mastering tiny bits of information. Consider this: "If the infant, from the beginning, moves in precise, shared rhythm with the organization of the speech structure of his culture, then he participates developmentally through complex, sociobiological entrainment processes in millions of repetitions of linguistic forms long before he will later use them in speaking and communicating" (461-462). It seems logical, then, to continue that shared-organization structure when teaching writing. Just as Lamaze and Leboyer continue the rhythm of the womb during birth, the teacher of writing might continue to build on this expressive bond. It seems evident that long before children speak, the form and structure of the culture, its rhythm, syntax, paralinguistic nuances, and body-motion styles may have already been absorbed. This bond between gesture and speech reinforces the continuation of participatory interaction within shared constructs, not "isolated entities sending discrete messages" (462). That translates into the need for an active learning environment where listening, speaking, writing, reading, and viewing are actively integrated with culture, not the opposite—a silent, often mindless environment. This applies to all students in all cultures, which includes those enrolled in ESL classes and bilingual classes.

To conclude, gestures, as an outgrowth of rhythm, command a rightful arena in the development of writing. As Vygotsky says, "Gestures are writing in air and written signs are simply gestures that have been fixed" (107).

Initial Visual Signs

Initial visual signs are extensions of gestures and as such are extensions of self. Random graphics—lines and scribbles—are the child's first way of saying, "I am." For example, a line scribbled on a paper or a sidewalk is nothing more than the fixed extension of the index finger. Hold a pencil in the normal position as if to write to see how it extends the index finger. Vygotsky says that at first young children do not draw or write in the conventional sense of those words; rather, they indicate. They talk as they run their hands over the paper; they make what looks like random marks to indicate what they are saying.

> One holiday a former student paid a visit with three children in tow. The baby slept the entire time; the 6-year-old would most assuredly grow up to be an electrical engineer since he demonstrated such fascination with the electrical outlets; but the 3-year-old is destined to become a writer. Taking the inside of a dress box and some crayons she spent the afternoon "indicating" the stories she talked. (See fig. 11.4.) She covered the entire area of the box with random scribbles that apparently stood in her mind for a recent trip to the park.

Fig. 11.4. A preschooler's indication of her visit to a park. 🏃

RANDOM SCRIBBLES

At first, children are not even aware they are making marks (see fig. 11.5). Children most often use their index fingers to mark in sand, smear circles on frosted windows, or track paths in their food. It is not uncommon for a young child to take a crayon and run with it along a wall, look back at the mark, and giggle. Likewise, upon finding a tube of lipstick, a young child may hold it to a wall while hopping up and down. The results delight the child, although they may exasperate the caregiver. The randomness of the marks suggest that just seeing the marks appear is enough to satisfy the child.

Fig. 11.5. Katie's scribbles. 🏃

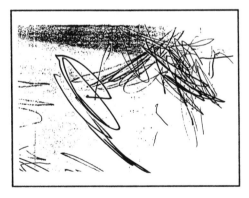

Crockett Johnson's book *Harold and the Purple Crayon* shows how a child might perceive the discovery of visual signs. Harold holds a purple crayon after making scribbles all over the page. Then he decides to go for a walk. From that point on, Harold creates the reality he wants—the moon, a path, an apple tree, and so on—just by drawing lines. The reader participates in Harold's discovery—knowing at some point random scribbles give way to meaningful marks.

INSTRUCTIONAL STRATEGIES FOR RANDOM SCRIBBLES

Encourage children to make more marks but in specific places. Ask them to repeat a random pattern by naming it. For example, "That's a wonderful long line. Can you make it again?" Always respond to what the child has done as writing, for example, "I like what you wrote." *Do not* say something like, "I can't tell what that is," "You can't write," or "That's not writing."

Symbolic Play

Symbolic play, sometimes called dramatic play, is a key arena in the development of writing and spelling. Vygotsky believes that "symbolic representation in play is essentially a particular form of speech at an earlier stage, one which leads directly to written language" (111). This is perhaps the most crucial arena, for it is the time when many aspects of language come together as having meaning for children. Margaret Donaldson calls this "the grasp of meaning" (32-33). When children try to make sense out of things, out of what people do and say, and out of events, they often do so through symbolic play. Here children play games with objects that stand for reality. They put pieces of colored felt together to make a sandwich. They sit in tubs of colored dry rice and pretend they are swimming. They wear a T-shirt with a tail and make believe they are a wolf. Subsumed in this arena are controlled scribbles, named scribbles, approximations, and alphabet writing and spelling.

CONTROLLED SCRIBBLES

Controlled scribbles are marks that exhibit some deliberation. For example, the page may be filled with lines or circles or a combination of both. As children develop, they gain more control over their motor actions. Instead of making an apparently wild display of marks hodgepodge on a page, children begin to deliberately make shapes and lines. Bent over their work like nuclear scientists, brows furrowed in intense concentration, they will make shapes endlessly or get caught up in a movement, as 3-year-old Bill did as he moved his crayon repeatedly up and down (see fig. 11.6). Marie Clay calls this tendency "the recurring principle" (20). Later, in another arena, this principle continues as children repeat letters, drawings, even groups of words or sentences. When self-initiated, not teacher mandated, this act of repetition often helps students experience a sense of accomplishment.

Fig. 11.6. Bill's repetitive marks.

INSTRUCTIONAL STRATEGIES FOR CONTROLLED SCRIBBLES

Children like the challenge of making a line longer or a repeating circle in another place. Guiding children by asking for an extension of a line or a duplication of a shape helps them refine motor skills and gain control over their writing. They also should be encouraged to experiment with many different colored markers and crayons. Always ask, "Tell me about what you have written." Do not encourage the child to "stay in the lines."

NAMED SCRIBBLES

When children move into this arena, they talk-write. There is intention and it is usually expressed during the writing. Given a rabbit from a coloring book to color, 3-year-old Kristen turned it over, dismissing the premade one and opting to make one of her own. She chose purple, green, and red markers. As she "wrote" (fig. 11.7), she said aloud, "This is my bunny. Here are ears. He eats lotsa carrot. He can hop. Hop, bunny." Also at this stage children begin to differentiate between manuscript and cursive writing.

Fig. 11.7. Kristen's written bunny. 🕈

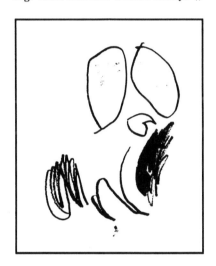

INSTRUCTIONAL STRATEGIES FOR NAMED SCRIBBLES

Label everything in the room so the children see print everywhere. Create opportunities to display their names. Provide real reasons to write: books, letters, labels. Take dictation after you ask, "Tell me what you have written."

APPROXIMATIONS AND PREPHONEMIC SPELLING

Approximations are marks that somewhat resemble letters. They often appear all over the page. At first they occur by accident, simply because the marks children make look like a letter form. Sometimes they are reminiscent of hieroglyphs. Prephonemic spelling begins about this time. *Prephonemic* is the term used to describe letters made by children without regard to connecting those letters to sounds. Just as children indicate with their awkward, clumsy scribbles that they lack graphic discrimination, so too they evidence an indiscriminate use of letters.

Approximations and *prephonemic spelling* are closely related. The former term is generally used when referring to children's writing; the latter term is generally used when referring to children's spelling. Sometimes, however, the terms are used interchangeably. To distinguish between the two, approximations often simply happen in the course of the child's scribbles; yet after they happen the child may recognize the letter, although not always. Other times approximations occur as an outgrowth of an attempt to form a letter or letters. In prephonemic spelling, children often know they are making or attempting to make letters, but they do not know that a sound corresponds to the letters. In other words, when children are prephonemic, letters, any letters, are significant. For example, Toya made letters that look like *G* or *C*, but she read "This is a balloon" (see fig. 11.8). Therefore, Toya is approximating letters. But when children try to form letters that are important to them, for example, ones they see in their name or in writing displayed in their environment, their approximations become prephonemic as are Aaron's in figure 11.9. It is apparent that Aaron is in prephonemic spelling as his letters obviously are meant to imitate a title of sorts. Therefore, for Aaron, they are meaning-bearing symbols, probably influenced by the titles he sees on television or in books, but they are not yet connected to sounds. The work of Toya and Aaron illustrate why it is so important for teachers of writing to encourage students to talk about their writing and listen closely to what they say. These indicators of growth are often subtle and can be easily overlooked, over-interpreted, or under-interpreted without the intervention of the child as writer.

Fig. 11.8. Toya's approximations. 🖎

Fig. 11.9. Aaron's prephonemic letters. 🖎

INSTRUCTIONAL STRATEGIES FOR APPROXIMATIONS AND PREPHONEMIC SPELLING

Modeling becomes paramount. Children should see not only labels around the room but should see the teacher produce those labels. It is important that children see and hear the connection between thought and writing, so teachers should habitually say aloud the thoughts that engender their own writing. It is not a matter of reading aloud what was written (while that is good pedagogy) but of speaking from the mind. In other words, saying what prompted the writing. For example, say, "Yesterday I went shopping. Maybe I could write about that today. Let me write down something—'I like to go shopping'—and go from there." Continue to take dictation, but provide plenty of opportunity for children to share their writing.

ALPHABET WRITING AND SPELLING

Children form strings of letters almost as if once they start on a letter they are unable to stop. Often, letters are made upside-down and backward, but generally they still are not associated with sounds. In this stage, children try to copy writing from adults or from print.

INSTRUCTIONAL STRATEGIES FOR ALPHABET WRITING AND SPELLING

Model writing and continue to talk and write. Persist at dictation, as the child's writing still cannot be read. Provide many opportunities for children to write. Point out real examples of writing, for example, cereal boxes, magazines, letters, and advertisements, that help children discover letter and sound correspondences and help them realize the importance of writing in the world.

Symbolic Drawing

The arena of symbolic drawing superimposes itself, in part, upon the arena of symbolic play as another dimension of literacy. As children move from random marks on a page to mark-meaning, they begin to understand those marks as objects (not yet understood as symbols or representations) that can convey their meaning to others. For example, when 5½-year-old Cory drew a peacock feather, he named it and colored its front in bright blue and yellow hues. Then he turned the paper over, named it again, and drew it again. This time he depicted the back of the feather as a plain brown oval (see fig. 11.10).

Fig. 11.10. Cory's peacock feather: two views.

(front)

(back)

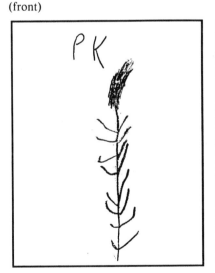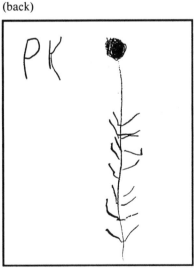

Clearly, Cory saw the similarity between his drawing and the feather in his mother's vase, but just as clearly he regarded his drawing as a similar object, not a representation—hence, the attention to detail on both sides. Vygotsky verifies how children relate to drawings as if they were objects with this example from his research: "When a drawing shows a boy with his back to the observer, the child will turn the sheet over to try to see the face. Even among five-year-olds we always observed that, in response to the question, 'Where is his face and nose?' children would turn the drawing over, and only then would answer, 'It's not there, it's not drawn' " (113).

Eventually children discover that "one can draw not only things but also speech" (Vygotsky 115).

> In an article entitled "Writing as a Natural Moment in Development: Barbara and the Terrible Whatzit," I recount making a discovery. I was in first-grade—our school did not yet have preschool or kindergarten.
>
> "I vividly remember my first day of school. We were given paper and invited to write. I made lines—straight lines, long and short straight lines, even an occasional crooked line—all over my paper. When there was no more room, I waved my paper at the teacher. She walked over, looked intently at my work, smiled, and said, 'Joyce, what a wonderful page of ones!' Then she pasted a gold star at the very top.
>
> "I ran all the way home with that paper. Breathlessly I entered the kitchen, shaking my paper at Mom. She looked at it, then said, 'A gold star—I'm proud of you.'
>
> "I wanted to explain my breathlessness, my excitement, but couldn't. I didn't know the word 'metacognition,' but I did know what I knew. The gold star didn't cause the excitement—the writing did. I knew in that natural moment that I could write and that someone could read what I had written. I knew in that natural moment the connection between making symbols and knowing symbols" (114).

For children, drawing is a natural way to make meaning. Usually their drawings fall into two categories: pictographs and ideographs. About this time prephonemic spelling begins to change into consonant writing and phonemic spelling, when children begin to discover letter-sound correspondences.

PICTOGRAPHS

Pictographs are pictures, signs, or symbols that capture what children *know*, not what they see. When a child constructs a pictograph it is tantamount to a teacher teaching or a writer writing. Just as teachers cannot teach what they do not know, just as writers cannot write what they do not know, children cannot draw what they do not know. Two examples come from 5-year-old Mary. Her daddy was mowing the lawn. After watching him for a time, Mary went inside and created a pictograph. When asked about the lines coming out of his feet, Mary simply replied, "Daddy is barefoot." Mary could not see her daddy as she drew her pictograph, but she knew he had fingers and had toes.

Mary drew a second pictograph of her grandmother, who appears happy but neckless (see fig. 11.11). When asked about her "writing," Mary was straightforward, "That's how grandma looks when I run to her."

Fig. 11.11. Mary's pictographs of Daddy and Grandma. 🕴

Of course, I thought upon hearing Mary's explanation. Grandma hunkers down for the hug, big smile of anticipation on her face. Mary runs to her outstretched arms and later remembers the smile, the arms, and the legs. The body, which telescoped itself to accommodate Mary, is nowhere to be seen on Mary's pictograph because in the context of the hug Mary didn't know it — for her at that moment, it wasn't there. As Ruth Hubbard warns, "In interpreting the behaviors and motives of children, adults are liable to approach the task from their own world views and conceptions; they are often quite adultcentric*" (13). Apparently we, as adults, sometimes interpret what children mean from our own assumptions. We need to ask children more often to tell us about their "writing" — not ask, "What is it?"*

IDEOGRAPHS

Ideographs broadly refer to written or graphic symbols that represent an idea or depict some relationship.

During a writing institute, a teacher brought me the work of her 4-year-old son (fig. 11.12, page 356). "What do you think this is?" she asked, referring to his drawing.

I suggested, "Why don't you ask him to tell you about his writing?"

The next day she returned with the following explanation. "It's a map. The circle on the far left is where he started."

"I messed up here, so I started again," he told her. "This is where we live," he said as he ran his hand around a loosely triangular form. "Up here," he said, pointing to a small circle to the left inside the triangle, "is our house. This is the road to Gina's" [the babysitter], he continued as he traced the line down under a loop and up to a second almost-circle. "This is Gina's."

Fig. 11.12. An ideograph of a 4-year-old's hometown.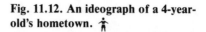

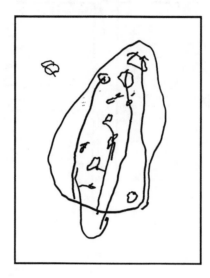

"Did he tell you about this third, larger shape?" I asked, pointing to one on the right.

"He told me that was our church."

Truly this captured the entire world of that youngster. Every weekday before and after school hours, he travels to and from the babysitter's house. On Wednesday evenings and twice on Sundays he goes with the family to church. This ideograph completely captures Cisco, Texas, for this child.

Often, children combine both writing and drawing to depict relationships. An ideograph done by another 4-year-old, Brian Ellis, the son of Linda Ellis, an NJWPT trainer, illustrates that point (see fig. 11.13). Brian told his mother, "This is me." Then he read "4 B H" as, "for Brian Ellis," indicating a rudimentary knowledge of phonemic spelling but not as yet quite getting all the letter-sound correspondences.

Fig. 11.13. Brian's ideograph.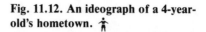

"What are these?" his mom asked, pointing to the two marks in one ear.

"Earlashes," Brian replied. "You know eyelashes? Well, Daddy has earlashes." Even though Brian depicted himself, he took something he knew, his hirsute father, and projected that characteristic onto himself.

Again, it is important to note how very important it is to ask children about their symbolic drawing; it is equally important to note that these arenas cut across chronological age. Sometimes a 5-year-old consistently constructs pictographs while a 4-year-old attempts ideographs. These arenas are not strictly hierarchical but, like all of writing, are recursive.

That fact is proven by 3½-year-old Amy. She was at first deeply involved playing house with an old box. She had her doll propped on a chair opposite the box, and her brother's toy boat on the floor. "Outside house," she said as she pushed the boat further away. After playing for about 10 minutes, she retrieved some paper, a red marker, and a pink marker. She settled down on the floor in the middle of her play area. First she drew the box at the top of the page. "House," she said. She held the paper out in front of her as if taking inventory; then she made the marks inside the box. She picked up the pink marker and mumbled something indistinguishable about the house as she scribbled the marks to the right of the house. Next she turned the paper upside down and drew the face with the red marker at the bottom of the page. Immediately, she returned the paper to its original position. In pink, she drew the other little face. Then she talk-wrote to the top and right of the small pink face "This is Amy's face. This is Amy's feet." (In a purely egocentric act, she named her doll after herself.) Beyond that pink writing she drew "beautiful boat" in red. Finally she made some red letters. The first few overlap the upside-down face. At the risk of over-interpreting, one looks like the letter *D*. The *A* and *M* appear to be deliberate letters of her name or her doll's. What follows seem to be approximations. "Done," she pronounced. (See fig. 11.14.)

Fig. 11.14. Amy's ideograph of her play time.

What is significant about this writing event is that Amy moves fluidly from her symbolic play arena, where she clearly enacted a real event, to the arena of symbolic drawing, which was coupled with named scribbles and approximations. Her attempt to write her name may have been coincidental imitation or a degree of phonemic spelling.

Finally, some ideographs approach folk art forms. Derek Wayne Trigo, a 6½-year-old, sat down to produce a wordless ideograph (fig. 11.15, page 358). After completing it, Derek verbally identified each character by its specific name: Tyrannosaurus Rex, saber-toothed tiger, Pteranodon, Archaeopteryx, and, of course, cavemen. Derek had already learned that writing is a way to extend memory.

Fig. 11.15. Derek's ideograph.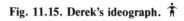

CONSONANT WRITING AND PHONEMIC SPELLING

Consonant writing, phonemic spelling, or, as it is sometimes called, letter-name spelling, refers to an early stage of spelling where every letter stands for a sound, no extra letters are used, and often only the initial consonant is used to stand for a word. Children in this arena are becoming conscious that different letters have different sounds. They try to make the two fit. Interestingly, Cory's symbolic drawings (fig. 11.10) also contain consonant writing. He wrote the letter *P* to stand for *pea*, and he wrote the letter *K* to stand for *cock*. He read the word *peacock*.

INSTRUCTIONAL STRATEGIES FOR PICTOGRAPHS, IDEOGRAPHS, CONSONANT WRITING, AND PHONEMIC SPELLING

Take dictation as children talk through their symbolic drawings. As letters appear, and as teacher and writer can read them, stop taking dictation. Create author's chairs so the children have a place to formally read and share their writing. Continue to model and provide many functions for writing.

Transitional Writing and Spelling

Transitional writing and *spelling* are terms used to define an arena of passage. This is the time when children move in dynamic, implosive, and explosive ways from rudimentary writing to the standard writing of their culture. They no longer draw things; they draw words. Their brains are growing. Jane M. Healy, an educational psychologist, details just how those nerve cells, or neurons, expand. She explains that the dendrites, which receive messages and develop synaptic connections, become heavier and grow new branches; the glial cells, the supporting cells, increase in number; the axons, or output parts of the neurons, develop coats of myelin. "By the time the child is two years old [the brain's] weight will triple, and by age seven its 1,250 grams will represent 90% of adult weight" (Healy 66). Couple that information with neuroscientist Gerald M. Edelman's contention that language is *not* independent of cognition. He presents compelling data by George Lakoff suggesting that "individual humans construct cognitive models that reflect concepts concerned with the interactions between the body—brain and the environment" (246). It seems, perhaps at the risk of overstatement and underconceptualization, that the brain, cognition, body, and culture are all part of how meaning is made; perhaps at no other time in the development of a child is meaning making more manifest than within this transitional arena.

The transition from simple idea transmission to a systematic, phonetic writing probably occurs naturally as it did historically—to aid memory. Albertine Gaur, in her comprehensive study of the history of writing, tells how the ordinary picture-writing of North American Indians, *kekewin*, differs from their specialized picture-writing, *kekinowin*, which was known only to their priests. They memorized *kekinowin* in order to use their spells and incantations exactly. *Kekewin* represents an idea, concept, or event—somewhat like a child's ideograph. *Kekinowin*, known to only a select few, contains pictures that represent a sentence or verse with only one possible spoken form for each picture (28). Similarly, perhaps, to the Indians' use of *kekinowin*, children, who live in ever-expanding worlds of ever-expanding knowledge, seem to sense their need for a system to keep track, more exactly, of what they know.

Equally interesting as testimony to the influence of environment upon writing are the "semitic scripts." These scripts are characterized by the use of consonants, almost as an abbreviation, with vowels playing a secondary part. Thus *B* may mean book or to read a book. Eventually, as this script was adopted by others, it developed into an alphabet and syllabic script forms (Gaur 88). What makes this particular script so interesting to teachers of writing is that the evolution of semitic scripts seem to parallel what happens as children write in this transitional arena: they tend to use the consonants more in their writing and, in time, they begin to incorporate more of the vowels. For example, young children might write the word *because* many different ways as they develop into standard writers. Often they write the word several different ways in one piece of discourse. Following are some variations of the word culled over an academic year from first-grade writers in Huntsville, I.S.D., Texas. First came *bks, bcs*; after that came, *bkus, bcoz, BCos, bcos, bcus*; next, *bcuse, becus, becos, becas, becoss*; then *becuse, becase, becose*; finally, *because*. Of course, not all the first-graders developed in exactly this order. Some regressed, moved forward, regressed, only to move forward with what seemed to be more security. Many jumped quickly from consonant spelling to standard spelling. At year's end, few remained in transition with this word. The point is, the transitional arena is just that—a time for the body, the brain, and cognition to gain physiological, neurological, and cultural balance.

KINDERGARTEN EXAMPLES

Alison. Alison used writing as a response to *Here Are My Hands* (Martin and Archambault) by chronicling the things she knows. (See fig. 11.16, page 360.) Not only does Alison generate meaning through the repetitive pattern she chose for her writing on her first page, she takes liberties with the pattern on her second page. Clearly Alison's writing belongs in the transitional arena. She uses standard spelling for some words, such as *things, you, eyes*; she omits the final silent *e* for some words, for example, *hav* and *nos*, which is very common even among so-called "good" spellers; she takes risks with some words that are precise but obviously not in her repertoire, for example, *ubowt, stumic*. But where she demonstrates most that she is transitional is with the words *toes* and *feet*. On the first page she stumbles around with *fyt*, crossing out part of what might have been the letter *Y*, yet on the second page she writes the word correctly. She may have received help, remembered how it was spelled, found the word in print, or sounded it out. No matter, writing words different ways in one piece of discourse is commonplace among transitional writers and spellers. Similarly, she writes *tows* on page one, but *tos* on the next page. She is still transitioning with that word, and considering that *tow* is pronounced like *toe*, her problem may be homonymic. She omits the *E* in *fingers* and the *U* in *mouth*; reverses the *A* in *ears*; and inserts an *E* between the *U* and *R* in *your*. Some of her words are invented spellings, e.g., *vary* for *very*, *yusfol* for *useful*, and *wac* or *woc* for *walk*. The most significant point to note in analyzing Alison's writing is not her inconsistencies but that there is much more right with her writing than there is wrong.

Fig. 11.16. Alison's transitional writing.

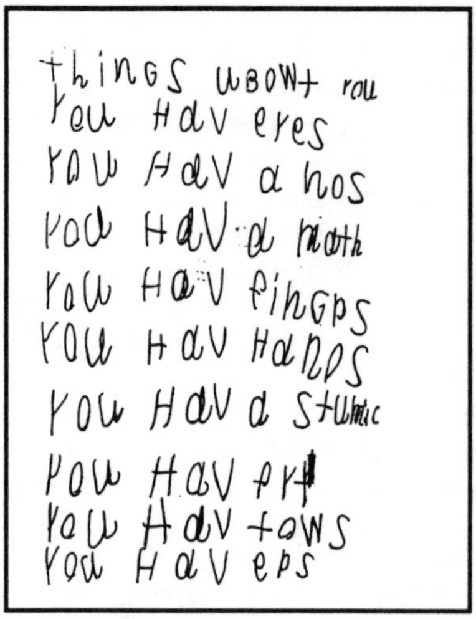

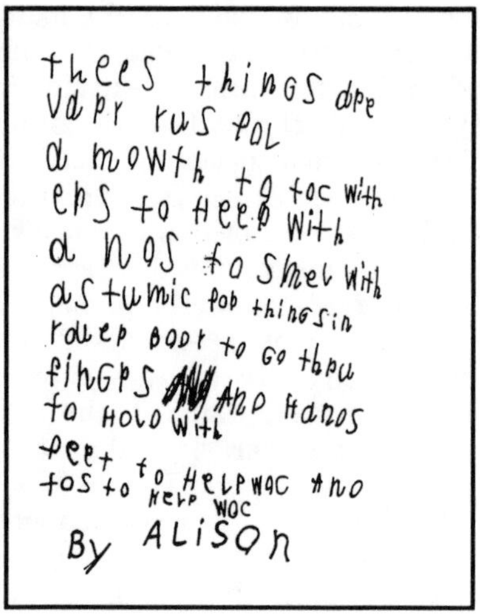

things ubowt you
You Hav eyes
You Hav a nos
You Hav a math
You Hav fingrs
You Hav Hands
You Hav a stumic
You Hav fyt
You Hav tows
You Hav ers

thees things are
vary yusfol
a mowth to toc with
ers to heer with
a nos to smel with
a stumic for things in
youer body to go thru
fingrs and hands
to hold with
feet to help woc and
tos to help woc
By Alison

[Things about you. You have eyes. You have a nose. You have a mouth. You have fingers. You have hands. You have a stomach. You have feet. You have toes. You have ears. (Then she goes on to explain these things.) These things are very useful. A mouth to talk with. Ears to hear with. A nose to smell with. A stomach for things in your body to go through. Fingers and hands to hold with. Feet to help walk and toes to help walk. By Alison.]

Jenny. Five-year-old Jenny's parents had just purchased a bi-level home. They laid out the perimeters to Jenny. The den was fair game. There she could munch, watch television, and visit with her friends. The living room, with its new ecru carpet, was off limits. Not too many days after they moved in, Jenny, grape juice in hand, tripped and spilled the juice on the new carpet. Daddy sent her to her room upstairs. Jenny cried for a while, but suddenly she stopped. Her mom became worried and tip-toed up the stairs. Just as she reached the top step, a piece of paper slid from under Jenny's door (see fig. 11.17).

Fig. 11.17. Jenny's apology.

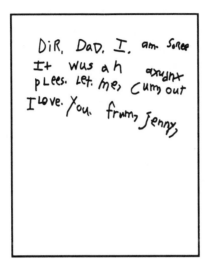

Dir. Dad. I. am. Soree It wus an axudnt plees. Let. me, cum out I Love You. frum, Jenny,

Apparently Jenny, who obviously knew the conventions of letter writing, decided to write a formal apology. First she extends her apology. Then she offers an explanation. Next she pleads. Finally, if all else fails, she proclaims her love. She closes and signs the letter to make it official. There are 19 words in this letter, 13 of them are spelled correctly. The remainder, a mere 6 words, are invented spellings. She must use words such as *soree* (sorry) and *axudnt* (accident) even though they are not in her writing repertoire, because no other words would do.

Seth. Seth, a precocious 5-year-old whose father works at NASA and whose grandfather is an inventor, also wrote a letter. This one is to his grandfather (see fig. 11.18, page 362). (The name and address in the top right corner has been blurred. The place where the picture was affixed has been indicated.)

Fig. 11.18. Seth's letter.

🧍 *Love Seth. Dear granDaddy I am intrested in a LaBoratory. All the stuff in the catalog is for oldr kides. Can you Design a LaBortory for Beginrs? I already have a microscope. I cut out pictures to show you what I like. I want to Be a mad-sientist. I want real potions that can change real things tell granMaMa Thank you for that piano Book. Love Seth*

First, it is worth noting that nothing is wrong with Seth's ego. He begins his letter as he ends it — with a request or a reminder or a command — to love him. Seth, like Jenny, knows letter form. Probably both these children see letters being written and received. In Seth's home, especially, letters from family are fussed over. There is no question that they are valued, and apparently Seth realizes their value as well, but he also knows they can serve a function — as a way to request things.

Second, Seth knows how to find information. The catalog he uses also provides him with the spelling of words such as laboratory, catalog, microscope. Notice the second time he used the word *laboratory* he omitted the *A*. Even though he demonstrates his precocity with words such as *already, love, change, stuff, cut, out, show, what, like,* and so forth, he proves he is still in the transitional arena with the invented spelling of *intrested, oldr, kides.*

Third, Seth's punctuation is quite remarkable. Rarely do kindergartners use a hyphen, yet he correctly uses it twice and the third time he almost gets it right. While he ignores commas, all his terminal punctuation is correct. There is also a sense of paragraphing.

Fourth, Seth writes with purpose and knows his audience. The entire letter is geared to the request. The thank you for the piano book at letter's end is placed last, apparently an afterthought. The voice in the sentence, "I want to be a mad scientist" coupled with "I want real potions that can change real things," indicates a sense of audience — surely a grandfather who also happens to invent things is just the right person to "design a laboratory for beginners."

Seth's writing (which he did without help) supports the ever-increasing corpus of empirical data that indicate children are often capable of more than is realized and sociocultural events affect the making of meaning.

FIRST-GRADE EXAMPLE

Roxanne Trann, who spoke no English when she came to the United States from Vietnam two years prior to the writing in figure 11.19, grew into the English language through the rich sociocultural context created in the classroom by veteran teacher Lu Ann Kubis, Spring ISD, Spring, Texas. Lu Ann integrates all the language arts, and her classroom is alive with her constant modeling and her students writing and sharing.

On the day Roxanne composed this piece, she wrote diligently during the entire writing time. Before grouping, Lu Ann conducted a mini-lesson on a simplified version of Say Back (see page 157). In group, Roxanne volunteered to read her piece.

Fig. 11.19. Roxanne's writing.

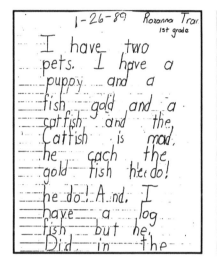 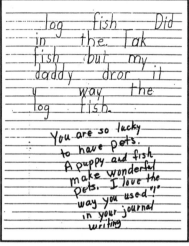

I have two pets. I have a puppy and a fish gold and a catfish and the Catfish is mad. he cach the gold fish he do! he do! And. I have a log fish but he Did in the log fish Did in the Tak fish but my daddy dror it y way the log fish.

[I have two pets. I have a puppy and a fish gold, and a catfish. And the Catfish is mad. He catch the gold fish. He do! He do! And I have a long fish, but he died in the long fish died in the tank fish. But my daddy threw it away, the long fish] (fig. 11.19).

When she finished, she looked up ready for the "what do you like best" part of Say Back. Almost in unison, her group said, "He do! He do!"

There are several noteworthy things about Roxanne's writing. First, her handwriting is impeccable. She painstakingly and deliberately forms each letter. She cares about her writing but is careful to write what she is sure she knows. Roxanne wrote this in her daily journal; the repetition in the next to the last sentence is most likely due to turning the page.

Second, the words that she spells inventively seem to be words with sounds that still sound foreign to her ear, for example, the *T* in *catch* or the *TH* in *threw*, which she pronounces *drew*. Interestingly, however, she spells and pronounces *the* correctly.

Third, she is still grappling with the adjective preceding the noun in English, because like Spanish, the adjectival form follows the noun form in Vietnamese. She sometimes gets the adjective placed correctly according to standard English grammar, but she sometimes places it as in the Vietnamese language. For instance, she writes *fish gold* and *tank fish*, yet she also writes *catfish* and *long fish*. The appropriate use of exclamation marks is impressive because, unlike so many other children who first discover them, Roxanne does not overuse them.

Finally, although the "he do! he do!" is indeed delightful, it shows that Roxanne still follows a verb pattern from her original language. Lu Ann avoids mentioning Roxanne's verb forms in her note at the end of the writing. Rather, she affirms Roxanne's pets and emphasizes what Roxanne did well—the use of the exclamation point. Lu Ann Kubis is interested first in the children becoming fluent. She works on skills when they take something from their journals to publication.

SECOND-GRADE EXAMPLE

The author of "My Granpope" (fig. 11.20) comes from West Texas. After a weekend in October on the ranch with his grandparents, he wrote this informative piece.

Fig. 11.20. A story drawn from life.

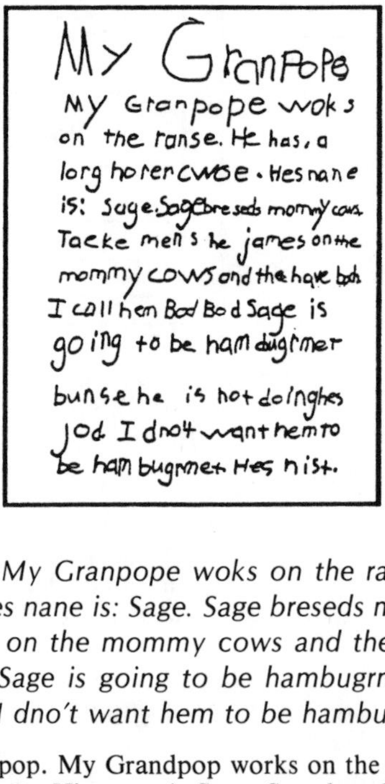

♀ My Granpope. My Granpope woks on the ranse. He has, a lorg horen cwoe. Hes nane is: Sage. Sage breseds mommy cows. Taeke mens he james on the mommy cows and thee have body. I call hem Bod Bod Sage is going to be hambugrmet bunse he is not doing hes jod. I dno't want hem to be hambugrmet. Hes nist.

[My Grandpop. My Grandpop works on the ranch. He has a long horn cow. His name is Sage. Sage breeds mommy cows. That means he jumps on the mommy cows and they have babies. I call him Bad. Bad Sage is going to be hamburger meat because he is not doing his job. I don't want him to be hamburger meat. He is nice] (fig. 11.20).

Perhaps better than any other piece in this chapter, this writing clearly shows the influence of culture. Discussing the ranch, bulls, cows, and breeding and its consequences are as natural in a ranching community as clients, accounts, and paying bills might be elsewhere. So this young man writes about the world he knows.

Clearly this writer is in the transitional arena. He may have overlearned the silent *E*. He tacks it onto *Granpope*; he writes it on *ranse*; and he puts it at the end of his invented spelling of *cwoe*.

He also makes some errors in word details. For example: *horen, breseds, dno't*. Marie Clay says these errors often occur "because the child is trying to write down his speech, using what he knows of letter-sound correspondence" (58). Sometimes he reverses the letters themselves, e.g., the obvious attempt to correct the *b* in *hamburger* and the *b* in *job*. These are the errors that signal the help he received during writing.

The young author displays a sense of story. He begins with a title and carries that title deftly into the defining first sentence. The piece is internally coherent. Each sentence coheres to the previous sentence with the first sentence cohering to the title. His message quality is enhanced by the use of punctuation: the period, the apostrophe, and, interestingly, the colon. He uses the specificity of *Sage*, naming the bull and telling exactly what will happen to Sage if he does not do his job. And, contrary to Piaget's theory of egocentrism, which holds that young children do not act altruistically, this author shows compassion for Sage's plight. Not incidentally, there is a growing corpus of data that demonstrate even children as young as 2 years of age exhibit decentered and therefore altruistic behavior (Hubbard 1989; Black 1981; Donaldson 1978).

THIRD-GRADE EXAMPLE

Janie Whitney wrote a book. That she was influenced by books in her environment is evidenced by the large *Pg.X* that heads her story and by the wide margins she allows on either side of the writing. But Janie also evidences that she has internalized the writings of her culture. From school and home, she weaves the fairy tale of castles, princesses, and princes; from community, she brings wagons, drivers, and bridges; from nature, she combines flowers, grass, sun, and the personification of spring; and from her religion, she integrates prayer, heaven, God, and faith (see fig. 11.21).

Fig. 11.21. Janie's book.

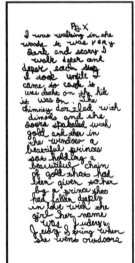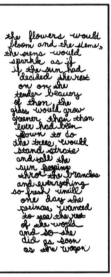

(Translation of this story is on page 366.)

✝ *I was walking in the woods it was very dark and scary I walk deper and deper each step I took untile I came to castle it was deakt on the hile it was on. The chimney dazzled with dimods and the doors spakaled with gold and ther in the window a beautiful princes sat holding a beautiful chain of gold that had been given to her by a prince that had fallen deeply in love with the girl her name was Judey, Judy Spring when she went outdoors the flowers would bloom and the stems, the stens would sparkle as if if the sun had decided the rest on on the tender beauty of then the grass would grow greener than then ever had been nown to do the trees would stand strate and tall the sun peeping throe the branches and every-thing so fresh untill one day the princes wanted to see the rest of the world and so she did as soon as the wagon drove away the trees droped down the flowers stope ther blooning and leaves stoped ther sparkeling and every thing was dry on the way the said let us pick the flowers on the side of the street after we get of the bridge I would have to tell you what happened nekse the driver torend to soon and ran off the birde people saw this and so she was buried on a pad on top of the the ground with a glass covering over her and one day a prince came and prayed for her grave god looked down form heaven and was so plesed with his faith that he renewed the girl and the worlld lived happrely ever after.*

[I was walking in the woods. It was very dark and scary. I walked deeper and deeper [with] every step I took until I came to [a] castle. It was dark on the hill it was on. The chimney dazzled with diamonds, and the doors sparkled with gold. And there in the window a beautiful princess sat holding a beautiful chain of gold that had been given to her by a prince that had fallen deeply in love with the girl. Her name was Judy, Judy Spring. When she went outdoors, the flowers would bloom and the stems, the stems would sparkle as if the sun had decided to rest on the tender beauty of them. The grass would grow greener than it ever had been known to be. The trees would stand straight and tall. The sun peeping through the branches and everything so fresh—until one day the princess wanted to see the rest of the world. And so she did. As soon as the wagon drove away, the trees drooped down. The flowers stopped their blooming, and leaves stopped their sparkling, and everything was dry. On the way, she said, "Let us pick the flowers on the side of the street after we get off the bridge." I would hate to tell you what happened next. The driver turned too soon and ran off the bridge. People saw this, and so she was buried on a pad on top of the ground with a glass covering over her. And one day a prince came and prayed over her grave. God looked down from heaven and was so pleased with his faith that he renewed the girl. And the world lived happily ever after.]

First, the sheer poetic beauty of this writing from a child who has walked on this earth eight years quite simply reinforces the capabilities students will demonstrate if given the time and the opportunity. Yet Janie was considered an average student in school and at home. True, she uses invented spellings for words that perhaps should be in her repertoire, e.g., *deper, deake, stens, throe*, but considering this was a draft, perhaps Janie was simply pulled along by the narrative. Perhaps she deliberately attempted to abbreviate *deeper* or *through* so she did not lose her train of thought. Clay calls this tendency the abbreviation principle (38). Also, the *M* in the word *stem* may have been formed as it is formed in manuscript writing.

Second, while her word choice is sophisticated, e.g., *dazzled, sparkled, peeping* it is her figurative language that is remarkable. She begins with the imagery of the dark and scary woods; she describes the castle vividly; she personifies the princess. While this draft lacks much punctuation—one period after *Judy* and one at the conclusion of the piece—the comma after the first use of "the stems" is written so boldly, it rises up almost to suggest Janie is reaching out to some new phase in her writing development.

Third, although she sometimes becomes a bit muddled by her words, e.g., "I walked deeper and deeper each step I took, until I came to a castle," she manages incredible virtuosity with the syntax of language and thought in lines such as, "When she went outdoors, the flowers would bloom and the stems, the stems would sparkle as if the sun had decided to rest on the tender beauty of them." Twice she repeats for rhetorical emphasis. Once with the name Judy and again with the phrase, "the stems, the stems."

Fourth, Janie has already developed a narrative style. She steps out of the story and directly addresses her audience, e.g., "I would hate to tell you what happened next." This technique is reminiscent of the storytelling style of Wanda Gág. In her translations of Grimm's fairy tales, Gág often switches her rhetorical stance so she may address the reader directly. In "Hansel and Gretel," she follows Hansel's comment "It *is* good enough to eat" with "And, if you can believe it, that's just what it was" (135). Later, when the Old One looks at the sleeping children and claims them as hers, Gág writes, "Now why should she do that? Well, I must tell you the real truth about the Old One" (136). In "Snow White and the Seven Dwarfs," after explaining that the wicked Queen mistook the boar's heart for Snow White's and ate it, she inserts, "I am sorry to say, with salt and great relish."

Finally, Janie shows that she is far from egocentric. She has decentered to such an extent that she is able to tie the story together with a global ending. The renewal of the princess renews the entire world. That world view is quite exceptional for a third-grader.

Despite Janie's obvious linguistic and narrative talent, however, she is still in the transitional arena. Her writing promises breakthroughs when she obtains better control over her spelling and punctuation. What appears in this youngster's draft at this point indicates style, voice, pacing, and rhythm.

Standard Writing and Spelling

Students in this arena write and spell using the standard conventions. Their language level indicates their knowledge of the alphabet, words, phrases, clauses, sentences, and paragraphs. Their writing contains proper punctuation and correct spelling. While errors may occasionally occur, it is clear that the student has a firm grasp of how to write and spell. Additionally, the writing is meaningful, clear, coherent, and appropriate.

CONCLUSION

One way to examine writing and spelling development is by longitudinal studies of several students. Another way is to collect one student's writing over a period of time. This chapter ends with the collected writings of Jason Sapp, a kindergartner who was not formally taught writing. His teacher taught the children their names and uppercase and lowercase letters. She exposed them to reading and writing and invited them daily to "choose something you have written today for your big books." Applying Piaget's theory of conservation to books, she provided each child with a big wallpaper book, which, because of its immense size, was considered extremely important. Because their writing went into this big important book, their writing must also be important, they seemed to reason as they carefully chose from their writing a daily entry that they affixed to each page in the book. The samples in figure 11.22 (see page 368) were culled from a year of Jason's work. There are nine examples, representing his writing in September, October, early November, late November, December, February, March (when Jason turned six), April, and May.

Fig. 11.22. Samples of Jason's writing over the course of a school year.

In September, Jason created an ideograph. He dictated to his teacher, "I went to go spend the night with my cousin." Aside from one boy looking like he is levitating, the picture clearly depicts bunk beds and the relationship of the two cousins. Clearly, he began writing in the arena of symbolic drawing.

By October, Jason had learned his name and uppercase and lowercase letters, which he practiced. Here he drew an interesting framed ideograph. Under it he strung the words "Me and my dad wr patent t hols" [Me and my dad were painting the house]. With these words, he began his trek through the levels of transitional writing and spelling. For the most part Jason used uppercase letters with no punctuation and no space between the words. *WR* is consonant writing and spelling, and despite growth into other arenas, Jason consistently stayed with *WR* for *were* during the entire year.

"On the walk," chosen in early November, reveals an ideograph with a revealing perspective— Jason wrote about his class going on a walk and pictured the class. What makes this ideograph unique is that Jason was capable of viewing the scene of which he was a part (he is fourth from the left) from another point of view. Jason also used a capital letter to begin his phrase and used the parenthesis to separate the words. Notice that the children are smiling. Indeed, most of Jason's people smile.

Later in November Jason created what K. Buhler, cited by Vygotsky, calls "x-ray drawings" (112). Two children play under the stairs. This is an example of a child writing what he knows, not what he sees. (This page is cut off a bit on the right because the big book would not lie flat on the photocopy machine.) It says, Me and my friend were playing house. Jason began putting hyphens in his writing to separate words.

Christmas presented a dilemma for Jason. He was told their Christmas tree was as tall as his dad, so Jason stretched his father to match the tree. He wrote "Me and my dad ur puting up ur Rresmts tree" [Me and my dad are putting up our Christmas tree]. To Jason *are* and *our* sound the same, so he is consistent, albeit incorrect, in spelling both words. It is an example of consistent inconsistency common in young writers. Prior to this writing, Jason asked his teacher, "Why doesn't my writing look like the writing in books?"

"Because you don't leave space between the words," she replied.

"Why didn't you tell me that?" asked Jason, arms akimbo. He strutted back to his table and began putting in spaces as he wrote.

Sentences, with capital letters and terminal punctuation, made their way into Jason's writing by February. Although he still relied on drawings, his compound sentence indicates that his writing was becoming more sophisticated: "My frend came ovr uestr day and we plyed stor wors" [My friend came over yesterday and we played star wars].

Notice the cognitive development apparent in March, evidenced by the extended compound sentence that Jason wrote. "iestrday Cory came to my haese and we went to the crece and we tru rocs in the wotr" [Yesterday Cory came to my house and we went to the creek and we threw rocks in the water]. Several words are inventively spelled, but Jason is clearly mastering connections between what he thinks and what he writes.

By April there seems to be no need for pictures. It is as if the more control Jason gains over his written language, the less he needs the other symbolizing system. Interestingly, this writing shows an extreme attempt at indenting. The sentence beginning with *And* is three-quarters of the way across the page, an example of how learners tend to exaggerate something new. Jason wrote, "Las nit I had a tee ball Game. And It was a ti 43 to 43 and It was une tel 7 o coc." This piece of writing is informative, clear, and detailed. He capitalized *Game* because it was important to him. He capitalized *It* because it references that important game. While he does not put the apostrophe in *o'clock*, he leaves space as if he knows something might go there.

In May, Jason showed a sense of paragraphs—this time block type. He used capital letters and punctuation. His cognitive ability to hold several ideas in his mind while writing those ideas in sequence is obvious. He took risks with his invented spelling. *Miniature* is not a word considered part of a kindergartner's written vocabulary, but it is the precise word. "uestrday I saw a play. and aftr that me and Dad went to play menecher gofe Satrday wil mom and uncl rone wr jujing and Sunday wil mom and grendmo wr having a drenc" [Yesterday I saw a play. And after that me and Dad went to play miniature golf. Saturday while Mom and Uncle Ronnie were judging and Sunday while Mom and Grandma were having a drink].

Janet Emig, in "Writing, Composition, and Rhetoric," cites the work of Sylvia Scribner and Michael Cole with the Vai tribe of northwest Liberia. The Vai use three languages: English for politics; Arabic for religion; and their own invented language for personal and tribal writing (see fig. 11.23). These researchers found cognitive consequences of the Vai's practice of writing in their own invented language. Emig points to the significance of those consequences. "Only if we acknowledge the true range of diversity in literacy practices in cultures other than our own can we make sensible, accurate, and nonparochial statements about the relations of language and learning and about unique values of given modes — say, exposition — for cognitive growth" (2026). It seems if cognitive growth was evidenced with the Vai, why would not reading and writing among children in their own language also have cognitive consequences? Although much more research, perhaps neverending research, is needed to more closely pinpoint the relationship of writing to cognition, much can be learned by watching closely as students write, by listening closely as students read their writing, and by talking frequently to students about their intended meaning.

Fig. 11.23. Vai writing systems.

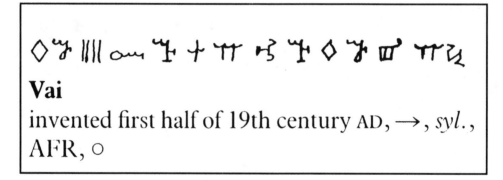

APPLICATION

Convey your understanding of the information in this chapter by responding to Jerome C. Harste's opening words in writing, by drawing, through discussion, or in some other way.

WORKS CITED

Black, Janet K. "Are Young Children Really Egocentric?" *Young Children* (September 1981): 51-55.

Brown, Margaret Wise. *Goodnight Moon*. New York: Harper & Row, 1947.

Carroll, Joyce Armstrong. "Writing as a Natural Moment in Development: *Barbara and the Terrible Whatzit*." *Language Arts* 70 (February 1993): 110-114.

Chukovsky, Kornei. *From Two to Five*. Translated by Miriam Morton. Berkeley: University of California Press, 1963.

Clay, Marie M. *What Did I Write?* Portsmouth, NH: Heinemann Educational Books, 1975.

Condon, William S., and Louis W. Sander. "Synchrony Demonstrated between Movements of the Neonate and Adult Speech." *Child Development* 45 (1974): 456-462.

Donaldson, Margaret. *Children's Minds*. New York: W. W. Norton, 1978.

Early Childhood and Literacy Development Committee. *Literacy Development and Prefirst Grade*. Newark, DE: International Reading Association, 1988.

Emig, Janet. "Writing, Composition, and Rhetoric." In *Encyclopedia of Educational Research*, 5th ed. Vol. 4, edited by Harold E. Mitzel. Pp. 2021-2036. New York: Free Press, 1982.

Frazer, James George. *The Golden Bough*. Abridged ed. Vol. 2. New York: Macmillan, 1972.

Gág, Wanda, trans. "Hansel and Gretel" and "Snow White and the Seven Dwarfs." In *Anthology of Children's Literature*, 4th ed., edited by Edna Johnson, et al. Pp. 133-150. Boston: Houghton Mifflin, 1970.

Gaur, Albertine. *A History of Writing*. New York: Cross River Press, 1992.

Guzzetti, Alfred. "Christian Metz and the Semiology of the Cinema." In *Film Theory and Criticism*, edited by Gerald Mast and Marshall Cohen. New York: Oxford University Press, 1985.

Harste, Jerome C. "Inquiry-Based Instruction." *Primary Voices K-5* (Fall 1992): 2-5.

Healy, Jane M. *Endangered Minds: Why Our Children Don't Think*. New York: Simon & Schuster, 1990.

Hubbard, Ruth. *Authors of Pictures, Draughtsmen of Words*. Portsmouth, NH: Heinemann Educational Books, 1989.

Johnson, Crockett. *Harold and the Purple Crayon*. New York: Scholastic, 1955.

Koch, Kenneth. *Wishes, Lies, and Dreams*. New York: Vintage Books, 1970.

Kutiper, Karen S. *A Survey of the Adolescent Poetry Preferences of Seventh, Eighth, and Ninth Graders*. Ed.D. diss., University of Houston, Texas, 1985.

Lamaze, Fernand. *Painless Childbirth*. New York: Contemporary Books, 1987.

Leboyer, Frederick. *Birth Without Violence*. New York: Alfred A. Knopf, 1974.

Martin, Bill Jr., and John Archambault. *Here Are My Hands*. New York: Henry Holt, 1985.

Most, Bernard. *The Cow That Went Oink*. New York: Harcourt Brace Jovanovich, 1990.

Piercy, Marge. *Mars and Her Children*. New York: Alfred A. Knopf, 1992.

Vygotsky, L. S. *Mind in Society*. Edited by Michael Cole, Vera John-Steiner, Sylvia Scribner, and Ellen Souberman. Cambridge: Harvard University Press, 1978.

Welty, Eudora. *One Writer's Beginnings*. Cambridge: Harvard University Press, 1984.

"Understanding and Supporting Children's Invented Spelling"

DONALD J. RICHGELS

(From *Illinois Reading Council Journal* 17, no. 1.)

Commentary

The term invented spelling *is often misunderstood by parents. Sometimes parents better understand terms such as* temporary spelling, developmental spelling, *or* first-grade spelling, second-grade *spelling, and so on because these terms suggest the nonpermanence of what they perceive as misspellings.*

Children know more words than they can spell according to standard spelling (just as many adults do). To limit their desire to communicate only in those words that they can spell conventionally is to limit their vocabulary and writing development. In essence, when parents, teachers, and students insist on using only the words they can spell correctly, they are dumbing down the language.

When you encourage children to write at an early age, their first spellings are very unlike your spellings. They may write only one letter for a whole word, usually a letter that stands for the first sound in a word (for example, N for nose). Later, they may write one letter for each sound in a word (for example, KRI for cry and BRD for bird). Still later, they may use patterns that they have noticed in other people's spellings, but put them in unexpected places (for example, THAY for they and ALLSO for also). The term invented spelling describes these early stages of spelling development. In all of this, children are moving toward spelling like you and I do. The final stage in this development is correct spelling or conventional spelling.

WHAT INVENTED SPELLING IS

Invented spelling *is* writing.

When children use invented spelling, they are using writing to communicate. They have many of the same purposes for writing that adults have. In the example below, 5-year-old Carrie used invented spelling to write a very important, personal message to her brother (I want to play with you, Ted. Why won't you let me? Love, Carrie).

Invented spelling *is* spelling!

Inventive spellers have discovered a system that is based on the same principles as conventional spelling (letters stand for sounds). What they do not yet know are the fine points of how their spelling system differs from the conventional spelling system that you and I use. Eventually, they will learn the conventional system, but they have already learned the most important thing — what spelling is all about.

Invented spelling *is* phonics in use.

Inventive spellers discover phonics on their own. They learn the names of the letters of the alphabet; they begin to pay attention to sounds in words and to sounds in the names of letters; and they put those two discoveries together (if "mmmm" is in the word milk and in the name of the letter M, then maybe the letter M can be used to write the [word] milk).

While it is exciting for students to make these discoveries, it is the role of the teacher to help them make these discoveries through reading and writing experiences that are rich. For example, using a book such as Charles G. Shaw's It Looked Like Spilt Milk *(New York: Harper & Row, 1947) would ensure the introduction of the M sound, just as Jill Bennett's* Teeny Tiny *(New York: G. P. Putnam's Sons, 1986) would ensure experiences with the letter T. When allowing for invented spelling during the teaching of reading and writing, teachers are teaching phonics. They are teaching phonics within a meaningful context in which the letters and sounds make sense.*

Invented spelling *is* a companion of early reading.

Children who write by paying attention to letters and sounds in their writing, also begin to pay attention to letters and sounds in other people's writing. For example, in the same week that Carrie wrote the message on this page, she was looking at *Life* magazine. She asked what L-I-F-E spelled. When a grown-up told her, she said, "I thought so, but why does it have an E at the end?" This shows that she had been applying her idea of phonics (that letters are in words because they stand for sounds in words) to her reading.

One problem with a totally phonetical approach to spelling is regional dialectics, for example, "doeg" for dog in the southwest or "dawg" for dog in the northeast.

WHAT INVENTED SPELLING ISN'T

Invented spelling *is not* the first writing most children do.

Pictographs and ideographs, or drawings that represent what children know and drawings that represent relationships, are also precursers to writing.

Invented spelling is never totally abandoned by writers. The best writers get their ideas down first, often inventing spellings, so as not to interfere with their fluency; then they reenter their writing and observe the conventions.

Although invented spelling appears before conventional spelling, there are many steps in writing development that occur before invented spelling. Earlier, for example, children may write with scribbles, with mock letters, and with real letters that they do not combine into words or do not associate with sounds in any systematic way. (Inventive spellers may also use these earlier strategies for some writing tasks, especially if the task is very demanding.) All of these writing strategies deserve our understanding and support.

Invented spelling *is not* laziness.

Evidence that invented spelling is not laziness or habit forming may be found in Alison's fyt/feet *and Heather's* meanis *in the title of her story to* meaist *in the body. The inconsistency points to trial and error, not habit. She is truly in transition. Clearly, though, if she can write* mean while, *the step to* meanest *is only a matter of time.*

Inventive spellers work diligently at their writing. They carefully analyze the words they want to write. They listen for individual sounds in words, usually in the correct sequence; they review the letters they know, looking for one that can represent the sound they have isolated; and then they write the letter. They then repeat these steps, moving on to other sounds in a word and to other words in their message.

Invented spelling *is not* habit forming.

Inventive spellers are not learning bad habits. They do not memorize their invented spellings. They do the diligent sound-by-sound analysis described above each time they write a word. Later, when they come to the point of using memories for how words look, they have plenty of conventional spelling models in books and in the other print all around them (in signs and on T-shirts and on TV screens, etc.).

Invented spelling *is not* every child's preferred way of writing.

Some children do not go through all the stages of invented spelling before becoming conventional spellers. Inventive spellers use what they hear in words and what they know about letter sounds. Some children are inclined right from the beginning to depend instead on how words look. Other children are perfectionists. They compare their first spellings to a conventional standard and refuse to spell differently. They want to be right. They may frequently ask for help with spelling. Sometimes these children can be encouraged to make invented spelling discoveries, to risk being unconventional. If they can learn to use sound and letter knowledge and to depend on themselves at least some of the time, then the risk taking will have been worthwhile.

HOW TO SUPPORT CHILDREN'S INVENTED SPELLING

Observe and reinforce.

Watch and listen to children when they read and write. Do they know the names of many letters of the alphabet? Do they comment about and ask about sounds in words that they see in books and elsewhere? If so, they may be ready for your reinforcing comments. For example, point out the first letter in the title of *Make Way for Ducklings*. Say, "That's an M. *Make* begins with M, 'mmmm', doesn't it?"

Teachers need to move neophyte spellers from dependence to independence by showing perfectionists when in the writing process to make corrections.

Treat early writers as you treat early speakers.

You would not criticize and correct a beginning talker who has invented a two-year-old's system for making sentences ("All gone dog" or "Daddy shoes"). Do not criticize and correct a beginning writer who has invented a spelling system different from yours.

More could be done to help the development of spelling by abolishing spelling tests and spelling as a subject on report cards. Students learn to spell by writing, not by weekly pretests and posttests.

Encourage children to try their own spellings.

If you know children know the names of most of the letters of the alphabet and you have heard them talk about sounds in words, then occasionally refuse to tell them how to spell a word. Say, "I think you can spell that word yourself. Pay attention to the sounds in *mosquito* and think about the letters you could use." Carrie spelled *mosquito bites* in the example on the first page after first asking how to spell it and then being encouraged in this way to spell it herself.

In addition to modeling and instead of pointing out misspellings, teachers can write responses that include the correctly spelled word.

Write with children.

Be a good example. When you are writing, children want to join in. Then you have opportunities to do the observing and give the support described here. Carrie did the drawing and writing on the first page while her father was writing a letter to a friend. She asked if she could write a letter too and he said, "Sure."

Choose your words carefully.

Use "I" language rather than "right-and-wrong" language. When a child writes SRE for *sorry*, say, "That's good spelling—I can read that!" rather than "That's good, but it is not right. It should be S-O-R-R-Y." Point out that you are aware of what the child's spelling shows about his or her stage of development. Say, "Good for you—I can see that you have figured out what letter goes with 'ssss' in *sorry*."

12

UNDERSTANDING THE NEUROPSYCHOLOGICAL PROCESSES
Brain Theory

> To me, the most exciting current theorizing has its roots
> in biology and concerns that most primal fount of information—
> the brain and its functions.
>
> —Janet Emig☐

With the present explosion of research on the brain—in estimates it is calculated that brain research doubles every five weeks—theories relating to consciousness, knowing, thinking, and language, as well as theories relating to paleoanthropology, differences between Eastern and Western brains, gender and the brain, the brain's anatomy, the developing brain, the aging brain, and brain disorders are literally erupting. James Watson, codiscoverer of the double helix that is DNA, calls the brain "the most complex thing we have yet discovered in our universe." He offers it as "the last and greatest biological frontier" (iii).

At this writing, brain experts from the United States, Japan, Canada, Great Britain, France, Germany, Sweden, Russia, and Australia are convening in San Antonio, Texas, as part of the Human BrainMap Project to pursue study and to share research about this inner frontier. Spearheaded by University of Texas Health Science Center professor Peter T. Fox, BrainMap is an international effort to create a global computer database of the latest scientific developments about the brain. Fox predicts that a standardized system of recording data "will make the quality of research much higher" and could lead to improved treatments for people with neurological problems and brain injuries (McAuliffe B-1). Therefore, even as this chapter is being written, new and exciting information is emerging that will date what is here and predict what is yet to come. This information will, of course, have an impact on education.

That the brain affects how learners learn and how teachers should teach is best understood by noting that neurobiology, the science of the brain, and cognitive psychology, the science of mind, have gradually blended together since the animal studies conducted on the brain during the 1950s and the work with grand mal epileptic patients during the 1960s by Roger Sperry, his collaborators, and students at the California Institute of Technology. Further, technologies such as electroencephalogram (the EEG, an early brain-monitoring device), CAT (computer-assisted tomography), PET (positron emission tomography), BEAM (brain electrical activity mapping), SPM (significance probability mapping), SQUID (a superconducting quantum interference device), MRI (magnetic resonance imaging), SPECT (single-photon emission computerized tomography), and NMR (a nuclear magnetic resonance diagnostic tool), enable specialized brain cartographers to quite directly read the brain. That is, they are able to determine through scans what parts of the brain are energized during a given activity. Several examples: These specialists do not see evidence of the old notion that "before you say a word, the brain must change a visual code into a sound code." They do, however, see dime-size clusters light up for nonwords that obey conventional English rules, like those found in "Jabberwocky," but do not light up for words that can have no legitimate English usage—*nlpfz*. They can identify grape-size areas that process proper but not common nouns. And they can watch pictures of what they call "women's mental acrobatics" compared to men's compartmentalizations when both men and women are given certain words (Begley et al. 69-70).

Consider how revelatory it would be to have the electrical activity of a student's brain monitored with a computer processing this activity during a writing experience. Teachers could watch moving images in color on an anatomical map of their students' brains. Consider how the colors would represent the level of engagement of different parts of the brain. Consider how much information that would render about writing, the student, levels of engagement, topics, teaching, environment, and so forth.

It seems logical, then, to conclude that when teachers of writing better understand brain theories, the brain's components and processes, and the information gained through technological probes, they will possess a depth of knowledge about how learners learn never before possessed in the history of education. As they apply this new information, their teaching will truly become brain compatible. As Leslie Hart writes in *How the Brain Works*, "Hope, I think, lies in a brain-based theory serving as a guide ... to create pilot schools, institutions that for the first time in ... history will not reflect folklore, ritual, and cut-and-try, but will be rationalized, coherent environments designed for the society we are in, not one that has disappeared" (215-216).

MAJOR STRUCTURES AND FUNCTIONS OF THE BRAIN AND THEIR IMPLICATIONS FOR TEACHING

There is an adage held by the psychologists, neurophysiologists, chemists, molecular biologists, cyberneticists, mathematicians, quantum physicists, educators, and others studying the brain: "The organ by which we know, we know the least about." Examining the average human brain does give pause. It weighs only about 3-4 pounds and is approximately the size of a small cantaloupe. Yet the brain houses a trillion cells, about 100 billion of them neurons, and it controls all activities from the mundane to the mystical, from the necessary to the aesthetic, from the reflexive to extensive, from the instinctive to the thoughtful. It is no wonder that "after thousands of scientists have studied it for centuries, the only word to describe it remains *amazing*" (Ornstein and Thompson 21).

Often educators who work with gifted and talented learners define giftedness in terms of the brain. "A high level of intelligence is viewed as advanced and accelerated brain function" (Clark 20). While they understand that the number of neurons cannot be increased, they also understand that the quality of those neurons can be increased, and they work with that understanding. For example, Clark contends that glial cells can be influenced by rich environments and, in turn, these glial cells accelerate synaptic activity. Increasing the speed of synaptic activity affects the process of learning. Further, Clark maintains that through changes in teaching methods and learning procedures, dendritic branching and neural interconnections can be enhanced—that there can be an actual change at the cellular level in children. "In this way gifted children become biologically different from average learners, not at birth, but as a result of using and developing the wondrous, complex structure with which they were born. At birth nearly everyone is programmed to be phenomenal" (Clark 25).

That everyone is programmed to be phenomenal is the basic thesis and philosophy of this book. Teaching writing with verve, knowledge, and as a process advances that philosophy. Giving children mindless worksheets and repetitive boring drills does not champion the phenomenal in students; it deadens it. Brain researcher after brain researcher maintain that to make the most of the brain is to give the brain rich experiences in a context that is meaningful and interesting. These rich experiences then enable the brain to make more of experiences.

Peter Russell, author of *The Brain Book*, contends that "A child is born with a natural insatiable curiosity to explore and find out more about the world.... Yet too often in trying to help children we hinder them. We don't give them problems to solve so much as answers to remember, and if this intense curiosity is not exploited, it may be wasted forever" (10). Russell cites examples to show how this thirst for knowledge can be kindled. He tells how a survivor of a Nazi concentration camp, Aaron Stern, exposed his daughter Edith to a rich environment from birth. Because of this environment, she skipped alternate years in elementary school, totally skipped secondary school, and taught higher mathematics at Michigan State University at the age of 15. Her IQ is 200.

Russell also tells of Maria Montessori's work with six Down's syndrome children whom she treated just like the other children in her school. "By the time they had finished, they were equal in intellectual abilities to 'normal' children in conventional schools" (12).

Russell uses 96 studies of Head Start children as examples of increased development of socially deprived children. These studies show increased IQ, increased mathematical and linguistic abilities, greater self-confidence, and a more highly developed social competence than children in control groups.

> In another study forty babies, all of whom had mothers with an IQ of 70 or less, were divided into two groups. One group received personal, highly intensive enrichment treatment on a daily basis. By the time they were four years old, they showed an IQ of 130—which is gifted by normal criteria. The other group, who had no special attention, had an IQ of 80 on the same tests. (12)

The point is this: If children can literally accelerate on the cellular level through enriched environments, personal attention, interaction, and diversity of experiences; if study after study in the United States, England, and Europe confirm this, why would not every child in every classroom receive this type of education. How can educators on any level justify teaching children in any other way?

To better understand the functions of the brain, the major parts are described below.

The Brain Stem. The brain stem, like the stalk of a mushroom, is located at the top of the spinal cord. It consists of the medulla, pons, and midbrain. It acts as a warning system, and it controls basic bodily functions associated with survival.

The Cerebellum. The cerebellum, sometimes called the little brain because it is inferior to the cerebrum, stores simple learned responses. It sits at the back of the brain stem, where it coordinates muscle movements and maintains posture.

The Limbic System. The limbic system, often called the old mammalian brain, is located in the center of the brain. It holds the master gland of the body, the pituitary gland, as well as the hypothalamus. Carl Sagan, in his Pulitzer prizewinning book *The Dragons of Eden* explains that the limbic system is "so called because it borders on the underlying brain. (Our arms and legs are called limbs because they are peripheral to the rest of the body)" (58). The limbic system functions in the emotional aspects of behavior that relate to survival. Because of this, it is sometimes referred to as the visceral or emotional brain. The limbic system is discussed further on pages 388-389.

The Cerebrum. Supported on the brain stem, surmounting the rest of the brain and forming the brain's bulk, is the cerebrum, sometimes called the cerebral cortex or neocortex. It is the largest portion of the brain and is composed of grey matter that is less than 3/8-inch thick. It has a crumpled, corrugated surface that forms *sulci*, or fissures—the downfolds—and *gyri* or convolutions—the upfolds. If spread out flat, it would roughly cover an area of a small desk top. The cerebrum is divided into two symmetrical cerebral hemispheres joined by its *corpus callosum*. These two cerebral hemispheres are further subdivided into four lobes: frontal, parietal, temporal, occipital. The frontal lobe decides and plans. The parietal lobe receives sensory information. The temporal lobe hears, perceives, and remembers. The occipital lobe sees. The cerebrum (discussed further on pages 389-390) is the part of the brain that makes us uniquely human; it is the brain that thinks (see fig. 12.1).

Fig. 12.1. The brain.

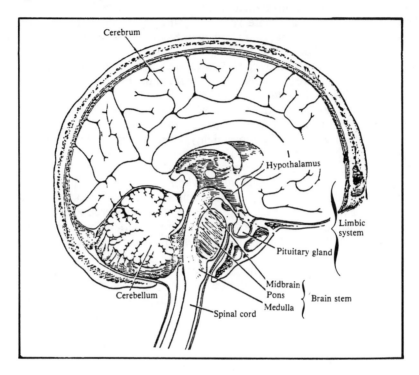

The Corpus Callosum. The two hemispheres of the brain are connected by a pencil-length, pencil-shaped bundle of approximately 300 million nerve fibers. The function of this major neural system connecting the two hemispheres is to allow cross-talk and collaboration between the two hemispheres.

The Nerve Cells. The nerve cells, or neurons, contained in the brain are numerous and diverse. Santiago Ramón y Cajal, called the father of modern brain science, described them as "the mysterious butterflies of the soul, the beating of whose wings may some day—who knows?—clarify the secret of mental life" (Fischbach 49). While neurons seem to group according to kind and seem to conduct information in similar ways, they differ in shape, structure, and function. This causes researchers to speculate about the possibility of each neuron being unique. To study each of the approximately 100 billion neurons and their possible interconnections boggles the mind, especially when considering that researchers at Cambridge University spent three years analyzing the mere 23 neurons of a simple worm.

In *Endangered Minds*, Jane M. Healy suggests the human hand is a convenient analogy to better understand the composition of a neuron (51-52). By holding up the hand with fingers extended, there is immediately visible an approximation of a neuron. The palm is like the cell body or soma, with its fatty part the nucleus. The extended fingers represent the dendrites, which comes from the Greek word *dendron* meaning "tree." Dendrites, in fact, resemble trees with twigs. The arm to the elbow stands for the axon, from the Greek *axis* or *axle*, which is encased and insulated in a myelin sheath. The elbow represents the synapse—the site of communication between neurons. It is important to remember that the synapse does not actually touch another neuron, as was once thought. Actually there is a minute space or cleft across which signals are sent.

Typically neurons communicate like this: a neuron receives information at its dendrites. The information is then processed in the cell body before being sent as electrical impulses called action potentials down the axon. The axon widens near a synapse into a number of tiny buttons, which contain mitochondrion, and into a number of synaptic vesicles, which contain chemical neurotransmitters ready to be released into the synaptic space. Chemical signals induce the release of the neurotransmitter molecules that diffuse across an infinitesimally small synaptic space and bind to the receptors in the new dendrite that have been activated. This is commonly called a synaptic connection, and learning, knowing, and remembering are generally attributed to it (see fig. 12.2).

Fig. 12.2. Synaptic connection.

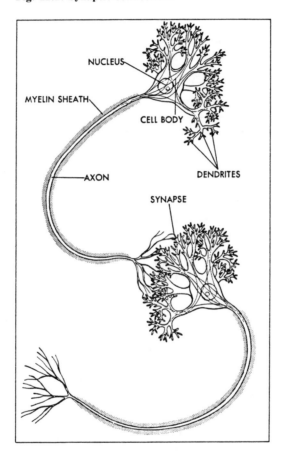

To add to the brain's complexity at this level, there is also a synapse that transmits signals through direct electrical coupling. "An electrical synapse is about 3 nanometers (nm), or billionths of a meter, wide, as compared with the 25-nm gap of a chemical synapse" (Ackerman 30). In short, there are chemical and electrical synapses.

The Neuroglial Cells. Neuroglial, or glial, cells in the brain probably outnumber nerve cells 10 to one. These cells do not have axons or dendrites but rather are packed between, around, and over the neurons. Not only do glials form the styrofoam peanuts or bubble wrap for the brain, they also nourish it and consume its waste. The only part of the neuron that glial cells do not cover is the synaptic space. The name glial comes from the Greek for glue, *glia*. Glial cells do not actually glue neurons together, rather they render a cellular support system.

HEMISPHERICITY THEORY AND
ITS IMPLICATIONS FOR TEACHING

Hemisphericity is the notion that "the two hemispheres are specialized for different modes of thought ... the idea that a given individual relies more on one mode or hemisphere than the other" (Springer and Deutsch 287-288). A cursory glance at even an elementary drawing of the brain readily reveals two hemispheres that foster conjecture about the function and relationship of these two "sides." Early Greek physicians, among the first to dissect the body, were also among the first to develop theories about the brain. Hippocrates (460-377 B.C.), for example, considered reason as well as sensations and motor activities existent in and dependent upon the brain. A. M. Lassek's *The Human Brain from Primitive to Modern* contains a brief summary of major brain theories and experiments dating from an ancient Egyptian medical test (2000 B.C.) to the early twentieth-century neurologist, Henry Head.

Twenty-some centuries after Hippocrates, in the 1940s, W. P. Van Wagenen cut the corpus callosum, the connecting nerve tissue between the two hemispheres of a patient with incurable epilepsy. A decade after that, Ronald Myers and Roger Sperry severed a cat's corpus callosum and the optic chiasm, the crossover optic nerves (Myers and Sperry). Ten years later, tests referred to collectively as the *commissurotomy* and performed on split-brain patients led Sperry to conclude that, "Everything we have seen so far indicates that surgery has left each of these people with two separate minds, that is, with two separate spheres of consciousness" (1973, 117).

Extensive and ingenious experiments conducted by Sperry and others at his laboratory, which earned Sperry the 1981 Nobel Prize in Physiology of Medicine, confirmed the contralaterality concept. Due to the fact that the entire central nervous system in humans is bisymmetric—one side the mirror image of the other—each hemisphere of the brain controls the opposite side of the body. That is, the left brain controls the right side of the body and vice versa. This crossover or contra-lateral effect applies to body movement and touch and in more complicated ways to vision and hearing. Thus, when stimuli is presented to only one hemisphere of the brain, it is said to be lateralized. By conducting tests on split-brain patients, researchers were able to identify how information was processed in each hemisphere. "The left hemisphere is specialized for language functions, but these specializations are a consequence of the left hemisphere's superior analytic skills, of which language is one manifestation. Similarly, the right hemisphere's superior visuo-spatial performance is derived from its synthetic, holistic manner of dealing with information" (Springer and Deutsch 54-55). Generally, the left hemisphere functions linearly, analytically, and logically. It is considered both verbal and dominant. The right hemisphere functions simultaneously, synthetically, and creatively. It is considered both spatial and intuitive.

Educational systems in Western cultures tend to emphasize and value faculties associated with the left hemisphere, that is, logical and linear approaches to teaching and learning. Pervasive in all cultures, however, are discriminations about left-handedness. *Webster's New World Thesaurus* (Laird) lists the following synonyms for left-handed: *clumsy, careless, gauche,* and suggests additional synonyms under *awkward.* The French word for left is *gauche*, which means inept; the Italian word for left is *mancino*, which also means deceitful. The Spanish *no ser zurdo* idiomatically means "to be very clever," but it literally means "not to be left-handed." Betty Edwards in *Drawing on the Right Side of the Brain* treats "The Bias of Language and Customs" but reminds the reader "those terms were all made up, when languages began, by some persons' left hemispheres—the left brain calling the right bad names!" (33-34).

Michael Corballis, of the University of Auckland, presents a different interpretation for this right-hand, left-brain bias. He suggests that right-handedness is unique to humans. "Perhaps this is why virtually all cultures hold the right to be sacred and the left profane, as though right handedness, like human beings themselves, is a gift of the Gods" (2).

Considering the possibility that the two hemispheres perceive reality uniquely seems to suggest that individuals prefer one cognitive style of teaching, learning, or administrating to another. For example, Eloise Scott Soler, in her doctoral study, found that of a total of 197 Texas male school superintendents and 22 female superintendents who took the Herrmann Brain Dominance Instrument (HBDI), 69.1 percent were left-brained. Keep this in mind when considering that educational institutions are traditionally sequential and lock-step. The superintendents in the Soler study definitely showed certain behaviors that preclude change; their responses were decidedly not holistic. Soler recommends retraining for these people (iv-v).

What has happened with the hemisphericity theory, the Soler and other serious studies notwithstanding, is that it has become oversimplified by some who see it as an easy way to generalize their own preferences and behaviors and the preferences and behaviors of others. They respond to the spate of commercially produced left-brain/right-brain psychographic tests, questionnaires, and surveys usually found in magazines to test their hemisphere preference. They use the results to justify behavior, "I can't do that. I'm right-brained." These people who misunderstand hemisphericity suffer from *"dichotomania*, a term coined to refer to the avalanche of popular literature fostered by the speculative notions" (Springer and Deutsch 287). They take the incredibly intricate and complex nature of the brain's interconnections — so numerous, if we are to use Gerald Edelman's example, it would take some 32 million years to count them (17) — and interpret them via a few questions and answers in a popular magazine.

It is important to note that while, historically, dichotomic divisions have been a convenient way to organize intellectual faculties (see table 12.1, page 384), two things must be remembered: (1) The original evidence about right and left brain ways of knowing and processing information was based on studies of brain-damaged or split-brain patients, not with neurologically normal people; (2) The normal brain is incredibly adaptable and is capable of almost instantaneous information transmission between the hemispheres. This complicates gross generalizations about lateralization.

While neuroscientists seem to agree that there is hemisphere specialization, they also hold that it is not always neatly separated, that experience and goals affect which brain hemisphere carries out an activity. Perhaps the distinction neurologist Richard M. Restak makes based on the research of John Mazziotta and other scientists at UCLA will help dispel the sometimes too-easy designation of left-brain/right-brain learners (or teachers) and will support brain-balanced education. "The PET scans confirmed that the hemisphere activation differed, suggesting something quite remarkable — that hemisphere specialization is dependent on the strategy employed by the listener" (250). Restak concludes, "People may not only be of a 'different mind' on issues, but they may also use different parts of their brains to do the same thing" (250). With that information, Restak suggests that "Division of the hemispheres into *symbolic-conceptual* (left hemisphere) versus *nonsymbolic directly perceived* (right hemisphere) avoids many oversimplifications" (250-251).

As Carl Sagan says, "There is no way to tell whether the patterns extracted by the right hemisphere are real or imagined without subjecting them to left-hemisphere scrutiny. On the other hand, mere critical thinking, without creative and intuitive insights, without the search for new patterns, is sterile and doomed. To solve complex problems in changing circumstances requires the activity of both cerebral hemispheres: the path to the future lies through the corpus callosum" (190-191).

The hemisphericity theory has become an oversimplification of localized brain function discoveries that date back to early researchers like Dryander (1537), who showed diverse parts of the brain (Ackerman); Paul Broca's discovery of the area of articulated speech in the nineteenth century; and the work in the 1940s, 1950s, and 1960s with split-brain patients. The data remain inconclusive, but not without implications, three of which are major.

First, the overarching implication of left- and right-brain theory is that the brain's two hemispheres interact through uniquely complicated and integrated processes. While researchers agree that the brain contains regions identifiable by function, they are finding that each hemisphere is not so autonomous as originally suspected and should not be so rigidly defined. Yet original left- and right-brain research in learning styles, reading styles, and administration styles broaden views on how better to reach all learners.

Writing teachers with a thorough knowledge of brain research realize that both sides of the brain communicate and are involved in most activities. Therefore, instruction should be holistic and brain-balanced. Students should be focused by purpose, yet should be given great latitude in topic, style, genre, and mode. If the purpose is narrative, for instance, a student may make up a story, recount a story, write a fable in a self-made book, write a historical tale as a narrative poem, and so forth. They may need green paper with lines or yellow paper without lines. They may prefer to write with markers, pen, or pencil. They may like sitting by the window, by themselves, or they may wish to sprawl on the floor. They may write best in a group. The point is how does the brain best process during any given activity, not what is the best way to keep students doing the same task in the same way at the same time. All brains simply do not work the same way.

Table 12.1

Cross-Disciplinary Dichotomies (Carroll 19)

Suggested by	Dichotomies	
Plato	Form	Ideas
Aristotle	Body	Soul
Abelard	Particular objects	Universal concepts
Aquinas	Reason	Faith
Pomponazzi	Objective truth	Religious truth
Francis Bacon	Mind	Instincts/emotions
Descartes	Matter	Spirit
Hume	Experience of ideas	Experiences of impressions
Kant	Reason	Judgment
Cassirer	Theoretical	Mythical
Langer	Discursive	Presentational
Polanyi	Explicit	Tacit
Revesz/Sapir	Imitative	Ontogenetic
Hippocrates	Reason	Sensation
Tiger	Science	Fancy
Jaynes	Language of men	Language of gods
Ornstein	Left hemisphere	Right hemisphere
Dickman	Action mode	Receptive mode
Gazzaniga	Verbal	Visuospatial
Bogen	Propositional	Appositional
I Ching	Ch'ien	K'un
Lee	Lineal code	Nonlineal code
Domhoff	Right is good	Left is bad
de Saussure	Speaking	Language synchrony diachrony
Bloomfield	Mechanistic	Mentalistic
Ogden & Richards	Symbolic	Emotive
Chomsky	Performance	Competence
Piaget	Organization	Adaptation
Bruner	Analytic	Intuitive
Vygotsky	Speech	Thought
Dewey	Other ways of thinking	Reflective thinking
Rosenblatt	Afferent	Aesthetic
Britton	Transactional	Poetic
Emig	Extensive	Reflexive

Another implication is offered by Caine and Caine by way of an example:

> A poem, a play, a great novel, or a great work of philosophy. They all involve a sense of the "wholeness" of things and a capacity to work with patterns, often in a timeless way. In other words, the "left brain" processes are enriched and supported by "right brain" processes. Similarly, great artists do not just set up an easel and paint; they may do a significant amount of preliminary design and analytical thinking. That is why we have so many sketches from, say, Picasso and da Vinci, before the final product was painted. (34)

For teachers of writing, this implication is most specific. Like Picasso, da Vinci, and others, students should enjoy plenty of practice sketching out their ideas through prewriting, then take the best of those "sketches" through a process into a final product. The old view that they have to learn "the right way" before they can break the rules simply does not work for every learner. Sometimes it is the learner that is broken.

The third implication for teachers of writing builds upon the observation "all knowledge is 'embedded' in other knowledge" (Caine and Caine 36), that is, parts and wholes interconnect. This observation suggests a different notion of how teaching should occur. The practice of teaching bits that grow into bigger bits—sounds before letters, letters before words, words before sentences, sentences before paragraphs, paragraphs before larger pieces of discourse—simply does not hold true in light of left- and right-brain research. As Margaret Donaldson says:

> The old idea was that the associations were built up in quite mechanical automatic ways. They were bonds between isolated elements. The person in whom these bonds developed was passive.... The associations came first. Insofar as there was "meaning" it was an outcome of the (conditioning) process by which the associations were established.
>
>   The newer account differs from this in the most fundamental way. The primary thing is now held to be the grasp of meaning—the ability to "make sense" of things.... It is the child's ability to interpret situations which makes it possible, through active processes of hypothesis-testing and inference, to arrive at a knowledge. (32-33)

The call here is to provide many opportunities to write with a sense of wholeness, a sense of meaning. Students should be invited to write poems, plays, stories, and essays about social studies; story problems, responses to problems, and games in mathematics; reports of experiments, research, and observations in science. Students should be invited to write whole pieces of discourse—not lines of letters out of context, lists of unrelated words, isolated sentences, or a single paragraph. Students should feel comfortable in both the reflexive and extensive modes. They should be encouraged to be both creative and logical; they should share their intuitions and defend their propositions. Working with writing within a context rich with the writings of others— books, stories, plays, poems, contexts in which writing really exists and where sounds, words, sentences, and paragraphs have meaning—helps students discover contextual meaning that is interesting and relevant. Vocabulary, style, and voice become one with literary merit and the grappling with one's own thoughts on paper, which helps students see how everything fits with everything else.

Integrated curricula, larger blocks of time for sustained teaching, thematic teaching, team teaching, grouping across grade levels, collaborative learning, and teaching writing as a process also rise out of this brain research. The point is not so much that Tisha is left-brained or Raul is right-brained, but that all learners are whole-brained with capacities that have not yet been tapped.

GENDER AND BRAIN DIFFERENCES
AND THE IMPLICATIONS FOR TEACHING

In their controversial book *Brain Sex*, Anne Moir and David Jessel create a useful analogy—photography—to explain the dual effects of hormones on the brain. They explain that while the brain is developing *in utero*, hormones control the layout of the neural networks, somewhat like a photographic negative. Then, during puberty, hormones cause the brain to switch on the network they had laid out, like chemicals developing a negative. The bulk of present evidence seems to indicate that sex hormones affect brain organization so early that girls and boys have differently wired brains (38-49). And, there is a growing corpus of research that seems to suggest that this wiring also affects cognitive abilities. In short, the brains of women and men are physically different and that difference may manifest itself in patterns of intellectual abilities—not to be mistaken for the overall levels of intelligence (IQ) (Kimura 119-125).

Citing a series of studies that grew out of problem-solving tests, Doreen Kimura, a professor of psychology at the University of Western Ontario in London, lists some differing patterns of intellectual abilities. Women tended to outperform men in perceptual speed, that is, matching items and finding displaced items; ideational and verbal fluency, such as generating certain lists by color or initial letter; precise manual tasks, for example, fine motor coordination; and mathematical calculations. Men tended to outperform women in certain spatial tasks, for example, mentally rotating or manipulating objects; target-directed motor skills, such as throwing darts at a dartboard; disembedding, that is, finding a simple shape in a more complex one; and mathematical reasoning (120-121).

As physical anthropologist Marie Christine de Lacoste of the Yale School of Medicine dissected human brains as part of her research while a doctoral candidate at Columbia University, she noticed that the corpus callosum was more extensive in women's brains than in men's brains. This so intrigued her that she went on to study areas of the brain. In an interview with Carol Johmann in 1983 she said, "All I've shown is that there is a difference in the number of connections between hemispheres" (Johmann 26). Her findings, and those of Marian Diamond and others, led to speculation about lateralization—in this case that women's brains are more diffuse or less specialized laterally than men's brains. The theory is if there are more connecting fibers between the two hemispheres, the hemispheres would communicate more fully. Indeed, de Lacoste found structural differences in fetuses as young as 6-7 months, suggesting that lateralization begins *in utero* and continues to puberty. Cautioning against sexist misunderstandings, de Lacoste explains, "We don't have two brains evolving separately, just one brain that reflects the differences in sex hormones and reproductive functions.... We're talking about differences in the way men and women screen information" (Johmann 113). A decade later, "Allen and Gorski found the same sex related size difference in the splenium" (Kimura 123), the rear portion of the corpus callosum.

Kimura is quick to point out, however, that sex differences in cognitive functions have yet to be conclusively related to callosal size, but agrees that researchers have long held that the male brain is more asymmetric than is the female brain. The assumption, then, is that "men's and women's brains are organized along different lines from very early in life. During development, sex hormones direct such differentiation" (Kimura 125). She adds hormones may affect cognitive patterns throughout life.

Additionally, it seems girls develop their left hemispheres first, whereas boys develop their right hemispheres first. Researchers are not certain if this is due to wiring or to environment. Between the ages of 6 and 9, girls are extremely verbal, whereas boys are mechanically and spatially curious. Sometime around the age of 9 or 10 the process reverses, and by the end of puberty the processes have leveled.

The way boys and girls screen information at any given age may be due to gender difference marked by lateralization—the female is more diffused, the male is more specialized. Also, since it seems boys have lateral consciousness whereas girls have bilateral consciousness, the way they process information or go about a task may be decidedly different. What this means is that when boys are given a task, they may tend to stay in one hemisphere until the task is accomplished. Girls may tend to skip back and forth across the corpus callosum using information from both hemispheres. Recognizing that gender may affect the way students go about the writing process may help teachers of writing. For example, girls may want to talk more about their topics before they put pen to paper; boys may doodle or even draw their topic. One way is not preferable—it is simply different.

TRIUNE BRAIN THEORY

Looking at the brain another way, there are "three formations that constitute a hierarchy of three brains in one, or what may be called for short a triune brain" (MacLean 309). These three formations, identified by Paul D. MacLean, Chief at the National Institute of Mental Health, are the R-complex, the limbic system, and the cerebrum.

The triune (three-in-one) brain offers interesting implications for teaching. Considering the brain from this tripartite theory "is significant for educators because it provides us with a different and useful way of looking at behavior, is compatible with relevant psychological and sociological theories, and provides some coherent direction for what it will take to generate change" (Caine and Caine 52). It is important to note that just as the two hemispheres interact horizontally, the three parts of the brain interact vertically. A tragic but powerful example of this vertical interconnection is the story of Phineas Gage. (The entire story may be found in Richard Restak's *The Brain*.) After a freak accident with a railroad tamping iron that penetrated his skull and frontal lobe, Gage, once a just and equable foreman, was rendered emotionally unstable. Yet he lived more than 12 years after the accident. Restak makes this point, "His injury and the effects it had on his personality provided the first clear indication of the delicate physical balance with the brain between thought and emotion" (151).

R-complex and
Its Implications for Teaching

The R-complex, which includes the brain stem, part of the midbrain area, and a primitive cortex, is the seat of instinctual behavior. By analogy, it holds as much information as a pocket dictionary. It takes care of physical needs, survival, and sexuality. This part of the brain engages in rudimentary signaling, imitation, routine displays, formation of social groups, mating, and ritualistic and deceptive behavior, characteristics that are primarily automatic and resistant to most change. The R-complex is the part of the brain that reacts to threat. When people downshift to the R-complex level because of what they perceive to be a threatening experience, they usually freeze, flee, or fight.

Many people experience writing anxiety or panic, and the thought or suggestion that writing will be done in class poses enough of a threat to cause some people to downshift. In classrooms where students have downshifted to their R-complexes because of some real or imaged threat associated with writing, they may display the "freeze" syndrome. When invited to write they will stoically sit in their places. It is almost as if they cannot take out paper or pencil; they are almost catatonic. If they do write, they write little or what is safe.

When students who display the downshifted behavior of "flight" are told they will write or share what they have written, they either cut the class or school altogether. If those are not viable options, they will flee interaction in the classroom by putting their heads down on their desks, or they will sit glassy-eyed, heads bobbing, as they fall into a reverie that transports them, at least mentally, elsewhere. They are the students who never have paper or pencil, who lose what they have written, or who only parrot back, copy, or produce minimally.

Finally there are the fighters. Their way to deal with the threat of writing is by hostile, recalcitrant behaviors. They may direct these behaviors toward the teacher, toward peers, or even toward themselves. They argue about why they have to write, about their grades; they hassle about their seat; they complain about classmates, the principal, the school, rules, regulations—all as reasons why they cannot write. They see the traditional writing topic as unrelated in any way to their world, so they use it as an opportunity to question or to clench their fists. These are the students who may write for a time, but then, in the ultimate demonstration of downshifting, wad up their papers and toss them in the trash.

If writing teachers heighten their sensitivity to the possibility that some students may have had negative experiences with writing or may have become convinced they could not write, which in turn triggers behavior that is both automatic and reactionary, that sensitivity helps them prevent or circumvent downshifting. Modifying classroom practices that might convey threat and building upon the instinctual R-complex often helps redirect these negative behaviors. For example, by inviting students to model, a teacher productively calls upon their instinct to imitate; incorporating a routine as part of the classroom management system enlarges upon the innate desire for ritual; using groups and cooperative projects capitalizes on the flocking instinct. Consistently monitoring teaching behaviors is the best defense against signaling a threatening situation. The main objective at this point is to move students into their cerebrums.

In departmentalized elementary schools, middle schools, and high schools, teachers must reckon with the halo effect of threat. When students leave one threatening classroom, the brain does not immediately upshift as they enter a nonthreatening one. Nor does the brain level of students always distinguish the difference. If school becomes perceived as threatening territory, then is it any wonder that hundreds of thousands of students every day find the inside of their room, the vacant lot of their neighborhood, gangs, drugs, or isolation preferable or more comforting than the place called school?

> Recently I conducted an awareness session for a group of administrators in a school district that had made a commitment to NJWPT. Several NJWPT trainers were also present at this session. At the first break, one of the trainers casually commented, "I can't believe my principal is here. She is terrified of writing. She even confided that she hoped you didn't make them write."
>
> The morning moved along with the sharing of informative and interactive sessions. The principal with the writing anxiety was enthusiastic, positive, and obviously proud of her teachers' efforts and their students' writing. As the morning waned, I said, "Now this afternoon I'll take you through a micro-mini experience with writing as it is taught as a process."
>
> That principal did not return after lunch. For her, the perceived threat of writing, perhaps coupled with the idea she may have had to share that writing, outweighed the risk of returning to the session.

Limbic System and Its Implications for Teaching

The second formation of the triune brain is the limbic system, which includes the limbic lobe, hippocampus, amygdaloid nucleus, hypothalamus, and the anterior nucleus of the thalamus. By analogy, it holds as much information as an encyclopedia set. The limbic system is basically involved in the experience and expression of the emotions. MacLean identifies the limbic brain as the emotional guide for self-preservation and the preservation of the species. As the limbic system and the neocortex interconnect, Caine and Caine cite several researchers who contend that "memory is impossible without emotion of some kind, that emotion energizes memory" (57).

Make no mistake, however, emotion as the energizer of memory does not translate into raucous laughter, copious crying, and outlandish behavior. Rather, emotion in the classroom is palpable through enthusiasm, intensity, involvement, self-satisfaction, enjoyment, fun, realizations of what did work, what did not work, commitment, engagement, ownership, purpose, and feeling good.

Because the limbic system mediates emotions, it handles life's pressures. For example, if a loved one dies, the brain handles the pressure of loss with feelings of sorrow and emptiness. This is often manifested by crying. If there are deadlines or time constraints, the brain handles that pressure with feelings of tension, impatience, or irritability. This is sometimes manifested by fiery displays of temper.

It is important to remember that pressure is synonymous with stress, but that not all stress is bad. There is good stress, called eustress and bad stress, called distress. The difference lies not in the stress itself but in the perception of the situation that produces the stress. It is like the maxim, "some see a glass half full; others see it half empty." If the situation kindles feelings of challenge, the person will experience eustress. If the situation kindles feelings of helplessness, the person will experience distress.

It seems both the body and brain respond to stress. Citing several studies, Caine and Caine explain that chronic stress and distress cause the body to produce a hormone called cortisol that affects the immune system and the short- and long-term memory systems. On the other hand, eustress, or noncontinuous challenges, add levels of adrenalin and noradrenalin in the body, which actually strengthens a person's ability to handle the stress (65-66).

There are two dominant implications for teachers of writing related to the limbic system. The first is the need for enthusiastic teaching; the second is ways to apply proper pressure.

First, both teachers and students need to be enthusiastically involved in their writing processes. If teachers write, honestly and zealously on occasion, with their students, if they share that writing, students are more likely to become involved. While educators have always known that enthusiastic teachers motivate their students to learn, having neurophysical data to support that knowledge makes anything less than enthusiastic teaching moot. If teachers harbor any real or imagined fears or concerns that give rise to feelings of inadequacy when it comes to writing, they should seek some training in the teaching of writing. Those teachers educated before the emphasis and research on writing as a process need updating on this philosophy in order to approach the teaching of writing with security and ardor. Students will not be fooled. The enthusiasm of the teacher carries over into feelings of genuine delight in self-sponsored writing and the writing of others. In this way writing becomes a celebration in the classroom. Evidences of that celebration fill the room: writing folders, an author's chair, books, and various displays of writing.

Pressure to write should elicit challenge, not fear or threat. With plenty of modeling, sharing, and taking writing through the process, eustress, not distress, will help students approach writing as an adventure and an opportunity to extend oneself, not as a demanded, prescribed undertaking that must be completed for someone else. Teasing out meaning from the mind onto a page is difficult even under the most inspiring circumstances; therefore, assigning writing under duress does little to foster writing, writing improvement, or growth. Rather, because of downshifting, it may cause writing debilitation.

Time exerts another pressure on writing. More will be learned about writing if short bursts of writing, such as trigger words and brief reader responses to literature, are juxtaposed with exercises in taking one paper through the entire process. These short interludes of writing between taking a paper through the process enable some writing to occur daily in a natural and brain/body compatible way. The concept of mini-lessons as a focus, followed by guided group practice, then individual application, ensures challenge, not coercion, and produces eustress, not distress. Ample warm-up time helps relax the brain and renders it more receptive. Daily writing can be short, fun, and varied. All writing does not need to be perfect, nor does all writing need to go through the entire process.

Cerebrum (Neocortex) and Its Implications for Teaching

Surmounting the rest of the brain and providing the surface of the cerebrum, is the third formation—the neocortex, which quite literally means new bark or rind. By analogy, it holds as much information as the entire New York Public Library. "The neocortex culminates in the human brain in which there develops a megapolis of nerve cells devoted to the production of symbolic language and the associated functions of reading, writing, and arithmetic. Mother of invention, and father of abstract thought, the new cortex promotes the preservation and procreation of ideas" (MacLean 332). The cerebrum is the seat of thinking.

Because the cerebrum thinks, it also responds to risk. When discussing high order thinking skills, the assumption is that the thinker is operating from the cerebrum or cerebral cortex, which is where the higher brain functions occur. The cerebrum simultaneously weighs chances, considers compromises, hazards guesses, deliberates, reflects, speculates, and hypothesizes. These higher order functions range from the unsophisticated—the child who challenges another to "I bet I can do this longer or further or better than you can" to the sophisticated—the scientist who hypothesizes a cure for cancer. Both take knowledge and project that knowledge into new areas or onto different situations.

The potentialities of any one human brain are so great, so unique, and heretofore so little realized, educators have a challenge before them. They face the brain—the brain as Edelman describes it, "the most complicated material object in the known universe—something unlike anything else in the universe." To make his point he explains that "there are about one million billion synaptic connections in the cortical sheet." He suggests an analogy to better understand the magnitude of that number: "Consider that a large match head's worth of your brain contains about a billion connections. Notice that I only mentioned counting connections. If we consider how connections might be variously combined, the number would be hyperastronomical—on the order of ten followed by millions of zeros. (There are about ten followed by eight zeros' worth of positively charged particles in the whole known universe!)" (17). That is quite a challenge.

In discussing the cerebrum, Edelman raises questions about such things as "silent synapses," (those synapses that show no detectable firing system), the uniqueness of brain maps (how individual maps vary according to the available input they receive), and the ability to categorize or recognize any number of novel objects after initially confronting only one or several similar objects. He builds upon Henry James's theory that the mind is a process, and upon modern scientific theory that considers matter as amassed processes. His thesis is that mind is a special kind of process that depends upon special arrangements of matter (6-28). He is speaking of the biology of the mind, the same biology that teachers work with daily.

While sounding perhaps too philosophical or scientific and not pedagogical enough, it is nonetheless imperative to point out that the information known about the cerebral cortex and its functions carries far-reaching implications for the teacher of writing, not the least of which is that writing must first and foremost occur within situations that have meaning. Knowing something or learning something does not seem to occur independent of all other cognition. Therefore, putting the magnificence of the brain in perspective, there is immediate correspondence to the both-all paradigm. Leading students to believe that there is only one way to write a paragraph, for example, the "box" paragraph, while relying on teachers of subsequent grade levels to teach other ways of writing paragraphs belies the brain's power to understand complexities. It is not a question of whether or not other types of paragraphing should be taught, it is a question of the appropriate method of teaching them.

Because the neocortex works best within a context, writing about social studies, for example, offers opportunities to learn skills and mechanics. Writing about a remembered holiday provides a vehicle for lessons on research and organization. Writing a lab report begs for organization and observation of detail. Writing a response to literature is a perfect time to discuss style, genre, and the observed and observable conventions. Writing in logs facilitates synthesis and evaluation. Writing letters holds out teachable moments for word choice, sense of audience, and intention. Concisely put, writing takes place in the global arena of learning. Like the neural network of the brain, writing may shoot off in certain directions, focus on subjectively interesting areas, and make silent, synaptic connections that remain tacit, only to explode later in some mysterious way into a very different piece of writing. Each mind is unique; each body is unique. As an extension of mind and body, each writer is unique. Perhaps more than anyone else in the educational system, teachers who teach and use writing in their disciplines and classrooms will do best in validating that uniqueness. Far more individualization needs to occur. Every student doing the same thing, the same way, at the same time ignores the brain's uniqueness and has the potential of boring the brain.

MEMORY

Perhaps the most exciting aspect of brain research is the potential for interpreting new data in a multitude of ways. As it relates to memory, this potential for multiple interpretations of new data has special implications for teachers. Traditionally, the students who best remembered the material received the highest marks. But now—when the *Statistical Abstract of the United States* carries staggering data, such as 41,223 new books were published last year, American consumers were offered 3,130 new food products, and the price of a 1-megabyte computer memory chip fell from $162.50 in 1985 to $6.33 in 1990—it is virtually impossible to remember everything. With the rapidly exploding, expanding, and changing nature of the information age, the emphasis has shifted from memorization as an exercise of the mind to the question of how does memory work? Theoretically, the better the understanding of memory, the better the understanding of learning.

Interpretations of Data on Memory

Following are brief discussions of major thought and interpretations of the research data on memory.

Eight Types of Memory. In the not-too-distant past, memory was divided several ways. One commonly studied set of categories, recounted by Russell, include episodic, memories of past episodes and events; factual, memory for facts; semantic, memory for meaning; sensory, memory for sensory input (e.g., people's faces, music, aromas); skills, memory of basic functions, such as how to throw a ball or get dressed; instinctive, genetic rememberings, such as how to breathe, sleep, or digest food; collective, the access to archetypal symbols; past-life, memories of events from before birth (82-83).

Genetic Memory and Memory Codes. Another interpretation of the data on memory, offered by Robert Ornstein and Richard F. Thompson, is that of genetic memory and memory codes. The former are literally millions of bits of information coded in the DNA of the cell; the latter is the cellular encoding of memory in the brain. Ornstein and Thompson define the fundamental difference between genetic memory and memory codes as unique to each individual. "Memories are stored among the neurons of the brain in some kind of relatively permanent form as physical traces, which we call memory traces. If only we knew the code, we could read the entire life time of experiences and knowledge from these traces in the brain. This is perhaps the greatest challenge in neuroscience—to understand how the brain stores memories" (133).

Declarative and Procedural Memory. A third interpretation divides memory into declarative and procedural. Declarative memory holds names of things, people, occurrences, and facts, whereas procedural memory enables people to learn and remember how to do things (Klivington 171).

Short- and Long-Term Memory. Short-term memory is memory in a person's immediate awareness, which is retained for brief periods of time, i.e., less than 24 hours. Long-term memory is the ability to store new information more than 24 hours or even permanently. Researchers contend that short-term memory and long-term memory reside in different parts of the brain. Also, observations of patients with head injuries like concussions, seems to indicate that there is a critical period needed to switch from short- to long-term memory.

Taxon and Locale Memory. Citing and synthesizing the research of John O'Keefe and Lynn Nadel, Caine and Caine advance taxon memory and locale memory as memory systems that help us to better understand natural memory versus memorization. They see taxon memory as an information-processing model that takes signals from the sensory register and moves them into short-term memory and, if rehearsed enough, stores them in long-term memory. In short, taxon is memorization. Caine and Caine list five characteristics of taxon memory: it takes practice and rehearsal, it responds to rewards and punishments, it is resistant to change, it is relatively isolated but sometimes interacts with other memories, and it can recall something without understanding it.

In the writing classroom, taxon memory holds to the rules and conventions that are practiced and rehearsed. Once they become habits, they are difficult to change. Students learn that certain topics receive better grades, just as they learn that certain usage receives better grades. If mechanics are learned in isolation and only on occasion are used in a context similar to the one in which they were practiced, it is often difficult for the learner to apply those mechanics in a new context.

Locale memory is defined as the process of constantly creating and testing spatial maps and mental or thematic maps that provide information about locations, life relationships, and ideologies. These maps are critical for establishing sophisticated transfer of knowledge, for example, seeing the patterns or stories in our lives. These "maps" describe interconnections through association. Locale memory has seven characteristics: (1) It is a virtually unlimited spatial memory system that is survival oriented. (2) It is dynamic, contextual, and relational in that it records ongoing life events and actions. (3) Its interconnections form almost instantaneously. (4) It constantly updates open-ended, flexible maps with comparisons made between past and present. (5) Its interconnections are stimulated by expectations, novelty, and curiosity. (6) It is heightened by sensory acuity. (7) Its maps may form instantly or take a long time to form (Caine and Caine 37-43).

Locale memory generally remembers learning that has taken place within a context. For example, the writers' space, comfort, and sensory perceptions work together to develop interconnected impressions of how writing occurs. Learners begin to develop a sense of how writing, mechanics, organization, meaning, and so forth work together to form an extension of what is known. Self-discovery and exploration from significant experience are key for locale memories.

Although the taxon memory is limited, it is needed by the locale memory. When writing, the locale memory places the knowledge of what is being written within a context and calls upon the taxon memory for the parts and rules (grammar, mechanics, punctuation, and so forth) so they may be practiced and directly rehearsed in the complexity of the writing process. In other words, writing as a process is the thematic map which needs and utilizes the memorization of taxon memory.

Working Memory. Patricia S. Goldman-Rakic, professor of neuroscience at the Yale University School of Medicine, defines working memory as "the combination of moment-to-moment awareness and instant retrieval of archived information" (111). Marcel Just and Patricia Carpenter of Carnegie Mellon University refer to the working memory as "the blackboard of the mind" (Goldman-Rakic 111). According to Goldman-Rakic, this memory enables humans to plan, predict, and sequence thoughts and ideas. Most evidence indicates that these operations occur in the prefrontal lobes of the cerebral cortex. Thus, working memory complements associative or long-term memory by activating, storing, and manipulating symbolic information for the short term. An example would be constructing one sentence about childhood in a story. To do this requires accessing the information about some childhood incident from the long-term memory and storing it in the working memory. While doing that, the working memory also retrieves other stored symbolic information, such as the parts of speech, conventions of a sentence, and lexical and syntactical information. The working memory then manipulates all that information into a meaningful sentence. This is done in addition to the bigger plan, also made possible by the working memory, to place that sentence in the larger context of a story.

Memory as a System Property. At this point in the recent scientific research on memory, Nobel Laureate Gerald Edelman offers a new and exciting theory that he calls "the principle of memory" (199). This theory is highly complex. The brevity of its presentation in this chapter belies that complexity, yet no chapter on the brain would be complete without some reference to the work of one of the world's foremost brain scientists, who argues that biology will unlock the mysteries of the mind.

Edelman begins with his definition of memory, which is "the ability to repeat a performance." He explains that performance is dependent upon "the structure of the system in which the memory is manifest"; therefore, he maintains that memory is "a system property" (102). What he means is that there are different memories in different systems of the body. For example, he holds that the memory in the DNA is different than neural memory. Identifying hereditary memory, which resides in DNA, immune responses in the lymphocyte, reflex (neural) learning, true learning following recategorization in complex brains, and the various forms of consciousness, he contends that memory is an essential property of these biologically adaptive systems, and, as such, involves an apparently open-ended set of connections between subjects (203-205). Further, Edelman believes these systems create a dynamic, continually changing memory, one that results in both categorization and recategorization. He states that, given its dynamic nature, "it is no surprise that different individuals have such different memories and that they use them in such different fashions" (104).

Because memory takes on the properties of whatever system or function it serves, and because each system is unique to each individual, Edelman believes memory underlies the mind and meaning. "By its nature, memory is procedural and involves continual motor activity and repeated rehearsal in different contexts. Because of the new associations arising in these contexts, because of changing inputs and stimuli, and because different combinations of neuronal groups can give rise to a similar output, a given categorical response in memory may be achieved in several ways" (102). What Edelman's theory means to teachers is that humans make meaning through and because of their very being and that minds create what is real for them through their culture and language. In addition, it means that categorization and recategorization should take place within contexts and that there is not one way to learn something. This theory of blending of biology and cognition, as Edelman himself suggests, remains to be tested. But he predicts, "If the future course of science is determined at all by its present reach, we may expect a remarkable synthesis in the next century" (208).

Implications for Teaching

The primary implication of research on memory is its complexity. This complexity militates against spending valuable instructional time on rote memorization for the sake of memorization. Memory and understanding are not synonymous. Placing skills in their rightful place, as parts of a greater whole, gives them new importance for the learner. They become reinforced because of other memories and other associations, in other words, to learn them, to remember them, makes sense. For example, asking students to memorize the rules of punctuation for use in isolated drills makes little sense to a learner, especially one relatively unsophisticated as to the conventions of writing and the reasons for these conventions. However, when a student reads a peer's paper without punctuation and tries to understand what the writer means, but cannot, that student begins to integrate the reason for punctuation in writing. Fragmented learning does not generally "take" the way more integrated learning does. The more meaningful the connections, not only with prior knowledge but also with emotion, the longer the memory. Emotion is the energizer of memory.

Because movement from the short-term into the long-term memory takes time, it is good to reteach concepts at intervals during the day, week, month, or over several months. Even information stored in the short-term memory should be called upon for tasks that have relevance. The notion of the semester review was a good one, not because it highlighted what would be on the test but because such review refreshes the memory.

Novelty and curiosity enhance memory. This implies the need for teachers to have an angle. Just as journalists strive to create or find angles to interest readers, teachers who get an angle on a lesson better interest their students. This interest contributes to high retention of the material covered. A focus or an anticipatory set for a lesson is a path for achieving this, but always be certain the focus integrates and has meaning for the lesson. When teachers teach from a script—be it a basal or an ancient lesson plan—students respond in kind. Compare this need for spontaneity with the teacher who introduces the myth of Icarus with Jane Yolen's *Wings* or with the teacher who wears an African kente while introducing narrative and telling a story. The students become hooked into learning and into the context, and the class takes on a sparkle.

People remember best when they organize and relate new material in subjective ways. In a student-centered environment, the learner manipulates the information. As Wittrock says, "The brain does not usually learn in the sense of accepting or recording information from teachers. The brain is not a passive consumer of information. Instead, it actively constructs its own interpretations of information and draws inference from it. The brain ignores some information and selectively attends to other information. One implication is that instruction should begin with careful observation of learners, their constructive processes and individual differences.... Instead of age, sex, and intelligence, the strategies of learners, such as analytic and holistic strategies, promise to lead more directly to theoretically interesting instructional procedures" (101).

DEVELOPMENT OF THE BRAIN

The growth and development of the brain is markedly different than the growth and development of any other organ in the human body. Carla Shatz, professor of neurobiology at the University of California, explains, "The neural connections elaborate themselves from an immature pattern of wiring that only grossly approximates the adult pattern. Although humans are born with almost all the neurons they will ever have, the mass of the brain at birth is only about one fourth that of the adult brain. The brain becomes bigger because neurons grow in size, and the number of axons and dendrites as well as the extent of their connections increases" (61). So, while the neuron potential is present in the brain at birth, as these neurons grow, they become more complexly interconnected.

In utero there are brain growth spurts. During these times there is rapid proliferation of nerve cells in the brain. For example, on the average the brain grows about 250,000 nerve cells per minute during a pregnancy. That means, for example, in 12- to 14-week-old embryos, nerve cells proliferate at the rate of about 15 million per hour (Ackerman 86-87).

After birth, somewhere between 18 and 24 months, no new neurons are added. For the most part the cells in the brain have migrated to distinct regions and have aggregated together, that is, arranged themselves with other like cells in what neuroscientists call "cytoarchitectonic" or "architecture of the cells" (Ackerman 95). Then cell bodies elongate, extend axons, form dendrites, and ready themselves for the work of creating synapses or connections with one another. There is also a pruning process that selectively eliminates some of the cells until a stabilized number of some 100 trillion or so remain (Ackerman 88).

Accordingly, during childhood and adolescence, the fatty insulating substance called myelin continues to coat the neural axons from lower to higher systems. This process does not end until long after puberty. Jane Healy contends that,

> before brain regions are myelinated, they do not operate efficiently. For this reason, trying to "make" children master academic skills for which they do not have the requisite maturation may result in mixed-up patterns of learning — reading, math, spelling, handwriting, etc. — may be accomplished by any of several systems. Naturally, we want children to plug each piece of learning into the best system for that particular job. If the right one isn't yet available or working smoothly, however, forcing may create a functional organization in which less adaptive, "lower" systems are trained to do the work. (67)

Because synapses may occur between the axon and dendrite, between axon and cell body, or, in the case of electrical synapses, between cell bodies directly, eventually synapses enable everything to connect to everything else, which makes the human brain a remarkable integrator of stimuli and information.

Neural Plasticity

For educators, one of the most significant research findings about the brain is its plasticity. The term *plasticity* refers to its ability to be shaped or changed through external stimuli. Research on rats, which is now considered classic, performed by psychologist Mark Rosenzweig at the University of California and neuroanatomist William Greenough of the University of Illinois, showed anatomical differences in rats kept in impoverished environments and those kept in enriched environments. Rosenzweig's experiments revealed that rats exposed to enriched environments showed changes in brain chemistry and increases in brain mass. What makes these data even more significant is the fact that these changes appeared in both young and mature animals. Greenough's rats, challenged by new tasks, actually developed new dendritic branches, which, of course, helps synaptic connections.

The rats in enriched environments had larger cages, more playmates, and many and varied toys that aroused curiosity and invited exploration. (Also, these toys were changed often.) "We now have evidence to illustrate the details of the anatomical changes that do occur with modification in the environment. This evidence addresses many of the questions that concerned the early sociologists and educators, including the effects of the environment on the young as well as the elderly, sex differences, and the effects of nutritional deprivation, isolation, or crowding. It is now clear that the brain is far from immutable" (Diamond 2).

Implications for Teaching

While rats certainly are not to be equated with human beings, researchers agree that the basic plasticity principle is "constant across such species as mice, gerbils, ground squirrels, dogs, cats, and primates (e.g., monkeys, Japanese macaques)" (Healy 72). If animals can benefit from an enriched environment, think how dismaying it is to hear this spoken of children, "They can't do it. They come from a poor environment." Those who say this have warped the research; they have blurred its import. The point for educators is not to lament prior environments over which they have no control; the point is not to abdicate responsibility because of some prior lack of enrichment. Rather the point, indeed the challenge, is to *provide* enriched environments for all children. That is the function of the brain—to create meaning. The data indicate that even those who are past puberty will benefit. According to Healy, "the process of myelination in human brains is not completed at least until most of us are in our twenties and may continue even longer" (67).

Donald Hebb, one of the leading scientists in the study of the brain mechanisms of learning, contends, "Every human being is creative all the time, thinking of new ways to make bread, new ways to serve breakfast, new ways to plant the garden. Creativity is not something that occurs only in the brain of outstanding individuals. It is a normal aspect of human brain function" (Restak 228-229). Learners should be encouraged to explore, to extend, to dig deep, to solve problems, to become question posers, to create.

As Healy states, "Any activity which engages a student's interest and imagination, which sparks the desire to seek out an answer, or ponder a question, or create a response, can be good potential brain food" (73).

Clearly, students should never sit idly waiting for the next worksheet; rather, they should be actively engaged in some aspect of learning all the time. Enrichment quite literally feeds the brain. Educators must enable learners to exercise their normal brain functions. Simply put, the brain needs food and it needs exercise.

There are tremendous differences in the rate of brain development of children. Like Robert Kraus's protagonist Leo in *Leo the Late Bloomer*, some children just blossom later than others. That is one of the mysteries of the brain. "There can be as much as a five-year difference in the early years. One consequence is that assessing children by reference to chronological age is often worse than useless. Each brain appears to have its own pace, which renders the 'failing' of a child in the first year of school entirely inappropriate" (Caine and Caine 30).

CONCLUSION

The data available on the brain are staggering. Most of what has been presented in this chapter is either basic information or views that enjoy a consensus among brain researchers. Having said that, it is equally important to note that considerable disagreement remains in many areas, for example, the connection between mind and brain, the brain and the process of aging, exceptional children and the brain, and even controversies about consciousness. These uncertainties, rather than being negatives in this area, should provide inspiration for all educators to continue study into this most complex and most mysterious organ in the universe.

Implications for teaching are varied and many. Perhaps no one has stated them as elegantly as Merlin C. Wittrock, professor of educational psychology at the University of California.

> In sum, the teacher, more than the subject matter, is given new importance and original challenging functions to perform with students. The basic implication for teaching is that teachers need to understand and to facilitate the constructive processes of the learner.
>
> The learner is also given a new, more important active role and responsibility in learning from instruction and teaching. To learn, one should attend to the information and concepts, and construct, elaborate, and extend cognitive representations of them. The teacher can facilitate these processes, but the learner is the only one who can perform them. (101-102)

> *Every scientist and researcher I have studied uses superlatives in describing the brain—the most astonishing, the last frontier, the greatest, the most magnificent—yet they use provisional diction when discussing its functions. See, for example, the following sentence: The brain is amazing, but the physical and chemical differences between brains may be unique. Just when researchers think they have a handle on understanding the brain, the mind or technology introduces new information that leads to questions.*
>
> *We also find the brains of other creatures intriguing. For decades, the brains of monkeys and cats have been used for study. Researchers intimate that since whales and dolphins have larger brains with more folds and perhaps more specializations, they may have superior intelligence. Peter Russell recounts experiments from John Lilly's The Mind of the Dolphin that demonstrate that dolphins speak in stereo and hold two or three conversations at once. In one experiment, dolphins put their noses out of the water to make humanlike sounds, as if they were trying to communicate with the experimenters—this before the experimenters had any ideas about the language of dolphins. Then dolphins were found teaching other dolphins to count to 10 in English more effectively than the experimenters could teach them. They also live in love and harmony—not competitively. "When John Lilly, one of the pioneers in dolphin research, realized that he was probably dealing with very advanced beings, he closed down his laboratories, feeling that his research could not be ethically justified." (21)*
>
> *All aspects of brain research represent a frontier. We still have so much to learn. Truly "the organ by which we know, we know the least about."*

APPLICATION

As brain research may double every five weeks, it is important to stay abreast of recent findings. Working in small teams, groups, with a partner, or individually, research recent publications associated with the brain. Choose one. Analyze its information in relation to the information in this chapter. Does it support, validate, extend, reject, refute, or elaborate on what is here? Be specific and be prepared to share.

WORKS CITED

Ackerman, Sandra. *Discovering the Brain*. Washington, DC: National Academy Press, 1992.

Begley, Sharon, Lynda Wright, Vernon Church, and Mary Hager. "Mapping the Brain." *Newsweek* (20 April 1992), 66-72.

Caine, Renate Nummela, and Geoffrey Caine. *Making Connections: Teaching and the Human Brain*. Alexandria, VA: Association for Supervision and Curriculum Development, 1991.

Carroll, Joyce Armstrong. "Reflections on Dichotomic Divisions." *Southwest Philosophical Studies* V (April 1981): 17-25.

Clark, Barbara. *Growing Up Gifted: Developing the Potential of Children at Home and at School*, 4th ed. New York: Macmillan, 1992.

Corballis, Michael C. "The Origins and Evolution of Human Laterality." In *Neuropsychology and Cognition,* Vol. 1, edited by R. N. Malateska and L. C. Hartlage. The Hague: Martinus Nijhoff, 1982.

Diamond, Marian. *Enriching Heredity: The Impact of the Environment on the Anatomy of the Brain*. New York: Free Press, 1988.

Donaldson, Margaret. *Children's Minds*. New York: W. W. Norton, 1978.

Edelman, Gerald M. *Bright Air, Brilliant Fire: On the Matter of the Mind*. New York: Basic Books, 1992.

Edwards, Betty. *Drawing on the Right Side of the Brain*. Los Angeles: J. P. Tarcher, 1979.

Emig, Janet. Personal conversation with authors, May 1979.

Fischbach, Gerald D. "Mind and Brain." *Scientific American*, special issue (September 1992): 48-57.

Goldman-Rakic, Patricia S. "Working Memory and the Mind." *Scientific American*, special issue (September 1992): 111-117.

Hart, Leslie A. *How the Brain Works*. New York: Basic Books, 1975.

Healy, Jane M. *Endangered Minds: Why Our Children Don't Think*. New York: Simon & Schuster, 1990.

Johmann, Carol. "Sex and the Split Brain." *Omni* 5 (August 1983): 26, 113.

Kimura, Doreen. "Sex Differences in the Brain." *Scientific American*, special issue (September 1992): 119-125.

Klivington, Kenneth. *The Science of Mind.* Cambridge, MA: MIT Press, 1989.

Kraus, Robert. *Leo the Late Bloomer.* New York: Simon & Schuster, 1971.

Laird, Charlton, ed. *Webster's New World Thesaurus.* New York: Simon & Schuster, 1985.

Lassek, A. M. *The Human Brain from Primitive to Modern.* Springfield, IL: Charles C. Thomas, 1957.

Lilly, John. *The Mind of the Dolphin.* New York: Avon Books, 1969.

MacLean, Paul D. "A Mind of Three Minds: Educating the Triune Brain." In *Education and the Brain: The Seventy-seventh Yearbook of the National Society for the Study of Education,* edited by Jeanne S. Chall and Allan F. Mirsky. Chicago: University of Chicago Press, 1978.

McAuliffe, Suzanne. "Researchers Compare Notes on Mapping the Brain." *San Antonio Light* 1 (December 1992): B-1.

Moir, Anne, and David Jessel. *Brain Sex: The Real Difference Between Men and Women.* New York: Dell, 1991.

Myers, Ronald E., and Roger W. Sperry. "Interocular Transfer of Visual Form Discrimination Habit in Cats After Section of the Optic Chiasma and Corpus Callosum." *Anatomical Record* 115 (1953): 351-352.

Ornstein, Robert E., ed. *The Nature of Human Consciousness: A Book of Readings.* San Francisco: W. H. Freeman, 1973.

Ornstein, Robert, and Richard F. Thompson. *The Amazing Brain.* Boston: Houghton Mifflin, 1984.

Restak, Richard M. *The Brain.* New York: Bantam Books, 1984.

Russell, Peter. *The Brain Book.* New York: E. P. Dutton, 1979.

Sagan, Carl. *The Dragons of Eden: Speculations on the Evolution of Human Intelligence.* New York: Ballantine Books, 1977.

Shatz, Carla J. "The Developing Brain." *Scientific American*, special issue (September 1992): 61-67.

Soler, Eloise Ida Scott. "Brain Hemisphere Characteristics and Leadership Style of Selected School Superintendents in Texas." Ph.D. diss., Texas A&M University, College Station, Texas.

Springer, Sally P., and Georg Deutsch. *Left Brain, Right Brain.* New York: W. H. Freeman, 1989.

Watson, James D. "Foreword." In *Discovering the Brain*, by Sandra Ackerman. Washington, DC: National Academy Press, 1992.

Wittrock, M. C. "Education and the Cognitive Processes of the Brain." In *Education and the Brain: The Seventy-seventh Yearbook of the National Society for the Study of Education*, edited by Jeanne S. Chall and Allan F. Mirsky. Chicago: University of Chicago Press, 1978.

Yolen, Jane. *Wings.* New York: Harcourt Brace Jovanovich, 1991.

"Balance the Basics: Let Them Write"

DONALD H. GRAVES

(Ford Foundation Report. Copyright © Ford Foundation, 1978).

People want to write. The desire to express is relentless. People want others to know what they hold to be truthful. They need the sense of authority that goes with authorship. They need to detach themselves from experience and examine it by writing. Then they need to share what they have discovered through writing.

Yet most of us are writing less and less. Americans are writing fewer personal letters, and the U.S. Postal Service estimates an even lower volume in the years ahead.[1] Studies undertaken for this report show that people of many occupations and all educational levels turn to writing only as a last resort.[2]

When we do write, we often write badly. The press continually reminds us that students can no longer punctuate, use proper grammar, spell correctly, or write legibly. But the crisis in writing goes well beyond these visible signs. People do not see themselves as writers because they believe they have nothing to say that is of value or interest to others. They feel incompetent at conveying information through writing. Real writing, they seem to think, is reserved for the professional.

For the rest of us, writing is perceived as a form of etiquette in which care is taken to arrange words on paper to avoid error rather than communicate with clarity and vigor. When writing, Americans too often feel like the man who has been invited to a party of distinguished guests. Being a person of modest station he attends with great reluctance and discomfort. He has but one aim — to be property attired, demonstrate correct manners, say as little as possible, and leave early.

This view of writing was taught to us in school. In the classroom learners are viewed as receivers, not senders. A far greater premium is placed on students' ability to read and listen than on their ability to speak and write. In fact, writing is seldom encouraged and sometimes not permitted, from grade one through the university. Yet when students cannot write, they are robbed not only of a valuable tool for expression but of an important means of developing thinking and reading power as well.

Commentary

Graves is straightforward. There is no sense skirting the issue or dressing it in different clothing: writing is a basic human need.

If writing is a need, why is it on the decline?

This crisis, Graves suggests, stems from attitude. So the next logical question is, where does that attitude come from?

Graves further suggests that these attitudes of reluctance and discomfort are learned behaviors.

Democracy demands literate citizens, and Graves offers hope. He contends, as we contend, that good writing instruction results in good writing by students.

Writing as an extension of academics must take precedent over athletics. Too many students think of sports as the ticket to the future. Until society and education address this issue, the crisis of writing, of learning, will continue.

Not only is writing a manifestation of intelligence, but writing contributes to intelligence. Brain studies of enriched environments support what Graves says here. Many of the teachers trained at the NJWPT have stories like Marcia's.

The imbalance between sending and receiving should be anathema in a democracy. A democracy relies heavily on each individual's sense of voice, authority, and ability to communicate desires and information.

There is hope, however. Barriers to good writing are not as high or insurmountable as they seem. Students who write poorly can improve quickly with skilled, personal attention that concentrates on what they know and can tell others. Good teaching *does* produce good writing. There *are* schools where writing and expression are valued.

This study reports on several such schools and identifies one broad, flexible, and effective approach to the teaching of writing. It also addresses two central questions underlying the crisis of writing in America:

Is it important to write? And, if so, why don't we write?

I. WHY WRITING IS IMPORTANT

Writing is most important not as etiquette, not even as a tool, but as a contribution to the development of a person, no matter what that person's background and talents.

Writing contributes to intelligence. The work of psycholinguists and cognitive psychologists shows that writing is a highly complex act that demands the analysis and synthesis of many levels of thinking. Marcia, an eighth-grade student, has written a composition about handguns, a subject of her own choosing. She first became interested in the problems raised by handguns when a shooting occurred in the family of a friend. She knew the family, had seen the gun on an earlier occasion, had felt the shock of the incident, and had experienced with neighbors the emotions that surfaced in its aftermath.

To begin writing her composition, Marcia listed key words and details surrounding the incident: the expressions on the faces of her friends, the statements of neighbors, the appearance of the gun itself. As she set down these impressions she recalled details that otherwise would have escaped her. The process of writing heightened a remembered experience. It developed a way of seeing.

Later, Marcia found further material to add to her initial draft. She gathered general information on handguns, their use in robberies, their suitability for protection or for sport. She reviewed data on accidental shootings. Taking all this information, she analyzed and synthesized it through the process of writing.

In successive drafts, Marcia shaped her material into a structure that gave more meaning to the details. A sense of order and rightness came from the new arrangement. Through organization, the mass of data was simplified. This simplicity, in turn, made it possible for Marcia to stand back from her material to see new details and meanings, such as the evident concern of the police, the effect of the shooting on the family, and her own feelings.

What Marcia would have expressed orally at the time of the shooting was different from what she later developed on the page. Reflection and discovery through several drafts led to depths of perception not possible to reach through immediate conversation. Marcia now can say with authority why she has always opposed the sale of handguns. Through the successful analysis and synthesis of fact and feeling she has strengthened her cognitive abilities.

In addition to contributing to intelligence, writing develops initiative. In reading, everything is provided; the print waits on the page for the learner's action. In writing, the learner must supply everything: the right relationship between sounds and letters, the order of the letters and their form on the page, the topic of the writing, information, questions, answers, order.

Writing develops courage. Writers leave the shelter of anonymity and offer to public scrutiny their interior language, feelings, and thoughts. As one writer phrased it, "A writer is a person with his skin off."

There lie both the appeal and the threat of writing. Any writer can be deeply hurt. At no point is the learner more vulnerable than in writing. When a child writes, "My sister was hit by a terck yesterday" and the teacher's response is a red-circled "terck" with no further comment, educational standards may have been upheld, but the child will think twice before entering the writing process again. Inane and apathetic writing is often the writer's only means of self-protection.

On the other hand, writing, more than any other subject, can be the means to personal breakthrough in learning.[1] "I was astounded," a student reports, "when the

Writing is a way for students and teachers to find order in their lives, a quality certainly needed outside of school.

To summarize, writing develops initiative and courage, contributes to reading and mathematics, and is active learning.

Again, in teaching, concern should be placed in the "how" of teaching, rather than in the content.

Recently, while working with a group of students in a prealgebra class, the teacher was amazed at one student's ability to use the predictions and estimations of mathematics to strengthen his writing. He discovered writing and math can be integrated. The teacher discovered he could express his ideas and understand the principles of estimation.

teacher read one of my paragraphs in class. Until then I had no idea I could write or have anything to say. I began to think I could do something right for a change." Another says, "Writing for the school newspaper turned me around. Other people started reading my stuff and saying, 'Did you really write that?'" This kind of discovery doesn't always happen in an English class. Another student observes, "I learned to write in a chemistry course in high school. The chemistry teacher was a stickler for accuracy and economy. Writing up lab reports was really disciplined writing. I began to see things differently."

Writing can contribute to reading from the first day a child enters school. Donald Durrell, a pioneer in the reading field and an authority for fifty years, strongly advocates the use of writing as a help to reading. "Writing is active; it involves the child; and doing is important," Durrell says. "Teachers make learning too passive. We have known for years the child's first urge is to write and not read and we haven't taken advantage of this fact. We have underestimated the power of the output languages like speaking and writing."[2]

Writing also contributes to reading because writing is the making of reading. When a child writes she has to know the sound-symbol relations inherent in reading. Auditory, visual, and kinesthetic systems are all at work when the child writes, and all contribute to greater skill in reading.

As children grow older, writing contributes strongly to reading comprehension. Students who do not write beyond the primary years lose an important tool for reading more difficult material.[3] Research has tied reading comprehension to the ability of students to combine sentences in writing. The ability to revise writing for greater power and economy is one of the higher forms of reading. Reading is even more active when a writer has to read and adjust his own ideas.

It is just beginning to be recognized that writing also contributes to learning in the field of mathematics. A great number of mathematics students consistently fail to solve problems at the point of reading. Seldom are these students in the position of writing problems, or creating the reading of mathematics. Until they work "on the other side," at the point of formulating examples, they will not fully understand the reading contained in mathematics.

II. WHY DON'T WE WRITE?

Five-year-old Paul writes. Children want to write before they want to read. They are more fascinated by their own marks than by the marks of others. Young children leave their messages on refrigerators, wallpaper, moist windowpanes, sidewalks, and even on paper.

Six-year-old Paul doesn't write. He has gone to school to learn to read. Now that he is in school, the message is, "Read and listen; writing and expression can wait." Paul may wait a lifetime. The odds are that he will never be truly encouraged to express himself in writing.

Paul will wait and wait to write because a higher premium is placed on his ability to receive messages than on his ability to send them. Individual expression, particularly personal messages in writing, will not be valued as highly as the accurate repetition of the ideas of others, expressed in *their* writing. Since Paul will write so little, by the time he graduates from high school he will think of himself as a poor writer and will have a lowered sense of self-esteem as a learner. He will have lost an important means of thinking and will not have developed his ability to read critically. Worse, as a citizen, employee, and parent, he will tend to leave the formulation and expression of complicated ideas to others. And the "others" will be an ever decreasing group.

The recent national attention given to the weaknesses of American elementary education has not improved Paul's prospects. All signs point to less writing, not more. The so-called return to basics vaults over writing to the skills of penmanship, vocabulary, spelling, and usage that are thought necessary to precede composition. So much time is devoted to blocking and tackling drills that there is often no time to play the real game, writing.

The emphasis on before-writing skills may have the matter backward. When children write early, their experiments with sounds and symbols produce spellings that may not be entirely accurate, but research shows that if these children continue to have ample opportunity to write they gradually

If teachers teach children as if they want to write, consider the implications.

There are too many students like Paul in today's schools.

We learn to write by writing—not by learning skills in isolation.

Once when working with a group of middle school teachers, one admitted he did not want his students to think. He said, "I can't control all of their thoughts." True. But is a nation of nonthinkers preferred?

increase in spelling power.[1] Moreover, it has been shown, the freedom to experiment with spelling (as with other aspects of writing) is important to the development of fluency and confidence.

Another reason that there will be less writing is that too often our schools show little concern for the individual development of the learners themselves or the important ideas they may have to share. Our distrust of children is most evident when we insist that they always be receivers rather than senders. If our approach to writing is to change, that change must be born of a confidence that what students have to say is worth saying. Writing is a matter of personal initiative. Teachers and parents must have confidence in that initiative or there will be little real writing.

The teaching of writing also suffers because reading dominates elementary education in America today. Nowhere else in the world does reading maintain such a hold on early learning. Although reading is valued in other countries, it is viewed more in the perspective of total communication.

Our anxiety about reading is a national neurosis. Where else in the world are children scrutinized for potential failure in a subject area in the first two months of school—or even before they enter school? And our worst worries are fulfilled. Children fail.

Concern about reading is today such a political, economic, and social force in American education that an imbalance in forms of communication is guaranteed from the start of a child's schooling. The momentum of this force is such that a public reexamination of early education is urgently needed. As we have seen, when writing is neglected, reading suffers. Neglect of a child's expression in writing limits the understanding the child gains from reading.

A review of public educational investment at all levels shows that for every dollar spent on teaching writing a hundred or more are spent on teaching reading. Of exemplary programs in language chosen for recognition by the U.S. Office of Education in 1976, forty-six were in reading, only seven included any writing objectives at all, and only one was designed for the specific development of writing abilities.[2]

Research on writing is decades behind that on reading. Research on all aspects of writing has produced only about as many studies as has research on the topic of reading readiness alone. A National Institute of Education analysis of research in basic skills does not even include writing in that category, mentioning only "reading and mathematical skills" as being required "for adequate functioning in society."[3]

Of research articles in education published in 1969, 5 per cent were on reading; articles on writing were included in a category labeled "other," which constituted less than 1 per cent.[4] The U.S. Office of Education has published numerous studies to show the effectiveness of compensatory reading programs. Not one study has been published on writing programs.

Teacher-certification requirements also assure a continuing imbalance between reading and writing. Most states require one course in teaching reading, many require two, and some are attempting to raise the requirement to three. A survey of superintendents of schools in a New England state asked, "What should be the minimum standards or criteria used when interviewing candidates for a vacant position in the elementary years?"[5] Seventy-eight per cent of the superintendents thought that teachers should have had a minimum of three courses in the teaching of reading. No comparable criterion relating to the teaching of writing was felt necessary.

Publishers' investments in new language series have followed the research dollars and the wishes of school systems. Their textbook lists directly reflect the one-sided emphasis on reading. More than 90 per cent of instruction in the classroom is governed by textbooks and workbooks.[6] But only 10 to 15 per cent of language-arts textbooks for children are devoted to writing. Most of the texts are dominated by exercises in grammar, punctuation, spelling, listening skills, and vocabulary development.

One textbook editor spoke for his profession when he said, "When writing is part of a reading series or when much writing is required, the materials won't sell. Teachers want more labor-saving devices, like easier scoring. If you have to respond to a lot of writing, there is more work involved. Some

In 1978 when Graves wrote this report, research on writing was decades behind reading, but that has changed. Now the problem is to get that research into the hands of teachers.

Typically, workbooks are bound worksheets. These hardly foster independent writing, which is needed for a democracy.

Once again, the problem with writing is not writing; it is NOT writing. This is further complicated when teachers assign writing

instead of teaching it, or when they teach writing only to satisfy the state-mandated test.

Charlatans, though, are making their way into this concern over writing abilities. One offers prepackaged writing prompts, guaranteeing higher test scores; another with computer expertise and no background in language arts sells "workshits" on a computer, promising higher scores; a third teaches that Emig, Graves, and Atwell are misinformed and that sentence combining is the only way to improve writing. All of these imposters miss the mark: we learn to write by writing.

publishers have tried, and they have been hurt by their ventures."[7]

Even a casual survey of elementary-school workbooks shows that pupils are customarily required to circle, underline, or draw a line to identify correct answers. Rarely are they asked to respond in full sentences. In secondary schools and universities, students are asked more and more only to fill in squares with pencils for computer analysis. Examination essays are disappearing.

Thus, although writing is frequently extolled, worried over, and cited as a public priority, it is seldom practiced in schools. Orders for lined paper, principally used for writing compositions, are going down.[8]

In a recent survey a large sample of seventeen-year-olds were asked how much writing they had done in all their courses in the previous six weeks. The results: 50 per cent had written only two or three pages, 12 per cent had written only one short paper, and 13 per cent had done no writing at all.[9] Thus only a quarter of the students had written anything more often than once every two weeks.

Even in school systems reputed to stress writing as a major concern, there is often little writing. A survey of three such systems discovered that children from the second through the sixth grade on the average wrote only three pieces over a three-month period.[10] Even less writing was asked for at the secondary level. Yet if writing is taken seriously, three months should produce at least seventy-five pages of drafts by students in the high-school years.

The current emphasis on testing and documenting pupil progress makes writing a stumbling block. Writing resists quantitative testing. A sixth-grade teacher says, "I know why writing isn't emphasized more; it can't be tested. We are so hung up on reporting measured gains to the community on nationally normed tests that we ignore teaching those areas where it can't be done. How do you say, 'Susie has improved six months in the quality of her writing'? We test them to death in reading and math and do some assessing on language conventions, but that's all."

The demand for other evaluation of writing is also a deterrent to the teaching of writing. Evaluation is hard work. Most English teachers who take home a hundred compositions to mark feel they must meticulously review each word, make comments, and wrestle with a grade. Such work is exhausting, and not many English teachers have as few as a hundred students. This work is different from that of colleagues who score multiple-choice tests or run down the answer column on the right-hand side of a mathematics paper. Many teachers, knowing its importance, would like to offer more writing, but just don't have the time to correct papers as thoroughly as they think necessary. Research data now show, however, that scrupulous accounting for all errors in a student paper is actually harmful to good writing development (a point returned to in the next section).

As we have seen, few adults write. Teachers are no exception; they do not write either. Teachers report that they do not write because they don't like writing, feel they are poor writers, do not have time to write because of teaching demands, or do not believe it necessary to practice writing in order to teach it.[11]

Seldom do people teach well what they do not practice themselves. It would be unheard of for teachers of music or art not to practice their craft. For some reason, the craft of writing is seen as an exception. What is not valued by teachers in their personal lives will not be introduced into the lives of children. It is therefore little wonder that writing is taught, if at all, as an afterthought, even when it is spoken of approvingly in public.

Most elementary-school teachers have not been prepared to teach writing. Even for teachers who want to get help, adequate courses in the teaching of writing are simply not available. A recent survey of education courses in 36 universities shows that 169 courses were offered in reading, 30 in children's literature, 21 in language arts, and only 2 in the teaching of writing.[12] Teachers do not teach a subject in which they feel unprepared, even when the subject is mandated by the school curriculum. Writing is such a subject.

The situation of teachers in secondary schools is no improvement. Those who were English majors in college are not trained for the teaching of writing. In colleges there is little formal attempt to teach writing beyond freshman English courses, although even in them the emphasis is on literature. There is little writing. Indeed, writing is given low priority in most English departments, and the

Trained teachers know many other ways to evaluate.

The cycle repeats itself. Teachers dislike writing probably because of the way it was or was not handled when they went to school. Unless this attitude has been shifted, therefore, they pass it along, albeit sometimes unintentionally.

Teachers on all levels simply must be deeply and thoroughly trained in the teaching of writing. This training may be through colleges and universities or through proven, substantive writing projects. One afternoon of in-service does not constitute training in writing. Teachers cannot teach what they do not know, even if, as Graves says, it is mandated by the curriculum.

Not only do students need to see teachers writing, they also need to hear a talk-write monologue as the thinking into writing happens. For example, teachers might stand at the overhead and talk-write for several minutes as one way to get students into the act of writing.

teaching of it is often relegated entirely to graduate students and junior faculty members. At one large state university, the contract offered teaching assistants recommends that student assignments in the English writing course be limited to 7,500 words per semester, or about two typewritten pages weekly.[13] With this kind of university background, it is not surprising that most high-school English teachers would much rather teach literature than have anything to do with writing. The writing achievements of high-school students reflect this attitude.

Writing models thus do not exist for most children, in school or out. Children may see adults read and certainly hear them speak, but rarely do they see adults write. And it is even less likely that they will actually observe how an adult composes. We know of the importance of models in reading and speaking. Although we have no good research data on how adult models affect children's writing, clear inferences can be drawn as warnings about the future of writing in America. Children begin to lose their natural urge to put their messages down in writing as soon as they begin to have a sense of audience, at eight or nine years of age. It is at this point that adults begin to have a strong influence as models. It is also the time when teachers' comments on children's papers begin to have an impact. This impact affects children for the rest of their lives.

Collages of haunting memories dominate the thinking of people from all walks of life as they recount learning experiences in writing: "There was something dark or sinister about it." "Be neat and tidy or you flunk." These are typical memories of children and housewives, businessmen and engineers, garage mechanics and laborers, teachers and politicians who were interviewed in the preparation of this report. For most people, the way in which they were taught has determined their view of writing and the degree to which they practice it.

Writing as punishment is one surefire way to make students hate writing.

Writing is a form of discipline, in the best sense of that word, and has been turned into a form of punishment. A castor-oil syndrome plagues writing from the first grade through the university: "It's good for you." Punishments in the form of compositions and mechanical writing exercises are still not uncommon in the classroom. "Write a hundred times, 'I will not chew gum in school.'" "Write a three-hundred-word composition on how you will try to improve your attitude." School discipline, grammar, and spelling are often mentioned together as a single package containing what is most needed in education today.

In speaking critically of his early school experiences, a businessman says, "There was no emphasis on content in writing—they worried about grammar and spelling but not about what was said." The same person, asked about what is needed in education today, replies, "Today there is too much emphasis on whether or not the kids have a good time. When I was in school we were physically punished. It was a form of discipline. That's the biggest difference today—no discipline and not as much teaching of mechanics."

Parents often reflect this view that the mechanics of writing are more important than its content. In one suburban community, it was found, parents regularly checked their children's papers to make sure that teachers had identified all errors.[14]

Teachers' impressions of what constitutes effective teaching of writing are similar to those of the general public. As we have seen, neither the teachers of college courses nor their advanced professional training have aided them in teaching writing in any other way. They therefore teach as they were taught.

And so the links in the chain are forged. Seven-year-old children were asked, "What do you think a good writer needs to do in order to write well?" Children who had a difficult time with writing responded, "To be neat, space letters, spell good, and know words." Children who were more advanced in writing added, "Have a good title and a good ending." Children were also asked, "How does your teacher decide which papers are the good ones?" The following criteria were commonly cited by children of all ability levels: "It has to be long, not be messy, and have no mistakes."[15] In both cases, the children's impressions of what good writing demanded were connected with their teachers' corrections on their papers. And clearly, teachers did not tend to call attention to the content of the papers. Not once did children speak of good writing as providing information of interest to others.

Writing as punishment is still being practiced. When we confronted a teacher with this, asking "Why?" she said, "The principal says it is the best punishment." The principal told us, "You don't have the right to question how I run my school." This is what we observed: a child wrote for an entire class period, 55 minutes, I will remember my book tomorrow. The child missed the entire lesson, the introduction to a three-week unit. It is time someone questioned this practice. Writing as punishment is not only anathema to learning, it is unethical. This practice should be outlawed in schools.

Teachers must change their attitudes about writing and the teaching of writing if students are to love it, willingly engage in it, and take ownership of their writing.

We persist in seeing writing as a method of moral development, not as an essential mode of communication. The eradication of error is more important than the encouragement of expression. Clearly underlying this attitude toward the teaching of writing is the belief that most people, and particularly students, have nothing of their own to say. And therefore, why should they write?

III. HOW WRITING CAN BE TAUGHT

A way of teaching writing called the process-conference approach is a proven, workable way to reverse the decline of writing in our schools.

Graves offers the process-conference as one way of teaching writing, but without training, teachers would have a hard time implementing this.

Teachers using this method help students by initiating brief individual conferences *during* the process of writing, rather than by assigning topics in advance of writing and making extensive corrections after the writing is finished. Emphasis is given to the student's reasons for writing a particular composition. The teacher works with the student through a series of drafts, giving guidance appropriate to the stage through which the writer is passing. By putting ideas on paper the student first discovers what he or she knows and then is guided through repeated drafts that amplify and clarify until the topic is fully expressed. A single completed paper may require six or more conferences of from one to five minutes each.

The process-conference approach in a seventh-grade classroom might follow a script such as the following one. Notice that the teacher doesn't even review a draft until the fourth conference.

Conference 1

Jerry: I want to write about sharks but I have a hard time getting started. I'm not much of a writer.

Teachers who have been trained in writing as a process and who are implementing conferences in their classrooms will find these exchanges reminiscent of those in their classrooms. Uncovering the students' interests, tapping those interests, and questioning, probing, nudging, suggesting, and extending are all functions of a good conference.

Ms. Putnam: Well, have you had any experiences with sharks, Jerry? How did you get interested in the subject?

Jerry: Yeah, me and my dad were trolling for stripers and all of a sudden this fin pops up just when I got a hit. That was it. No more fishing that day. Can they move! I got to talking with the guys down at the dock; they said we've got more than usual this year. Blue sharks they were.

Ms. Putnam: You have a good start with what you have just told me. Many people talk about sharks but few have actually seen them. What else do people at the dock have to say about sharks? Any old-timers who might have had run-ins with them? You say the sharks moved quickly. Well, how fast can sharks swim?

Ms. Putnam validates Jerry's experience. This is an important function of the conference.

Conference 2

Jerry: Hey, listen to this. Charley Robbins, the old lobsterman, saw a thirteen-foot blue, nudged his boat — didn't know whether he just got bumped or the shark intended to get him. Said he'd hit the bastard with a boat hook the next time he saw him.

Ms. Putnam: Well, do sharks attack or not? Have there ever been any shark attacks in this area? Do you think this is important information? Where can you find out?

Ms. Putnam listens. By listening hard she is able to ask meaningful and specific questions.

Conference 3

Jerry: I asked at the newspaper and they didn't know of any shark attacks over the last five years. So, I asked them who might know. They said I ought to call the Coast Guard station. They said, no attacks but lots of sightings; they were more worried about people doing stupid things in their boats with this shark craze that's around.

Ms. Putnam: What do you mean, doing stupid things?

Here Ms. Putnam urges Jerry to be specific.

Jerry: Well, now when a beach gets closed, people stop swimming, but these crazy kids go out in small boats to harpoon them. They could get killed. Sharks really don't harm people, but if you start poking them, who knows what will happen?

Ms. Putnam: Jerry, you certainly have good information about sharks. I suspect that very few people know what the Coast Guard is up against. And what do you think will happen if some eighteen-year-old has to prove he's a man?

Positive reinforcement is followed by another question.

Ms. Putnam helps Jerry see that rearranging can strengthen the piece for the reader.

Conference 4

Jerry: Well, here's the first shot. What do you think?

Ms. Putnam: You have a good start, Jerry. Look at these first four paragraphs. Tell me which one makes you feel as if you were there.

Jerry: This one here, the fourth one, where I tell about two kids who are out trying to harpoon a shark.

Ms. Putnam: Don't you think this is the one that will interest readers most? Start right off with it. Hit 'em hard. This is an actual incident.

Conference 5

Jerry: I've got so much stuff on sharks I don't know what to do with it all. All those interviews and these books.

At this point, Ms. Putnam shows Jerry how to synthesize material. She suggests five points of information as a manageable number.

Ms. Putnam: You can't use it all, can you? I want you to put down the five most important things you want to leave your audience with. Don't look at your notes; just write them down off the top of your head. You know so much you don't have to look any more.

Conference 6

Constantly, Ms. Putnam allows Jerry to make decisions about his own writing.

Jerry: Well, I took those five points. I feel better now. But look at all this stuff I haven't used.

Ms. Putnam: That's the way it is when you know a lot about a subject. Over here on the third page you get a little abstract about people's fear of sharks. Can you give some more examples? Did you get some in your interviews? What needs to be done before this becomes your final copy?

Jerry: Put in those examples of fear — I have plenty of those. I have plenty of weird spellings — guess I'd better check those out — never could punctuate very well.

Ms. Putnam: I think you have information here the newspaper or the Coast Guard might be interested in. Had you thought about that? Let me know what you want to do with this.

Most of Jerry's time was spent in gathering information from many sources to develop what he already knew. Without information a student has nothing to write about. This is why in three of the six conferences Jerry's teacher worked on developing information and strengthening the authority of the writer. Until students feel they have information to convey, it is difficult for them to care about writing or to feel they can speak directly and with authority. From the first wave of information a rough draft emerges. Succeeding drafts include more information, more precise language, and changes in organization.

Teachers who use the process-conference approach do not see a composition as something that can be "wrong." It can only be unfinished. The teacher leads the writer to discover new combinations of personal thought, to develop the sense of knowing and authority so valuable to any learner. Indeed, the main task of the teacher is to help students know what they know.

In a city school in upper New York state, children make readings for themselves and others. Each child maintains a folder in which writings are kept over a ten-day period. At the end of this period, the children are helped to evaluate their progress in writing. Sometimes a child and the teacher may agree that a very good piece of writing belongs in the class collection. Sometimes the children put their own writings into books that they construct themselves.[1]

Writing folders become sources of more extended writing.

When children are able to see their own writing used by others, their concepts of themselves as writers are heightened. When writing is not just a context between the child and the teacher but serves a broader audience, the teacher does not have to attend continually to correcting technical errors, but can concentrate on other matters essential to good writing.

As with older students, writing conferences are essential to the young child's growth as a writer. With younger children, perhaps 90 per cent of the conferences are only a minute in length, occurring throughout the day. A roving teacher in a second-grade classroom might teach like this: "And what are you writing now, Sandra? Oh, you're telling about prehistoric animals. Are there some words you will need for your word page? Some of those names are hard to spell. Now

A quick conference may be all a student needs.

When teachers take an interest in the child's writing, the child's learning, improvement naturally occurs.

this is interesting, Derek. Which sentence do you think tells best about what racing cars look like?" Throughout, the teacher's questions are related to the message first and to the mechanics and finer points second.

The same method of teaching can apply with equal effectiveness to other kinds of classroom work: "What do you like best about the picture you're painting, Martha? Perhaps we could find the best part with these cropping Ls. What do you think?"

This teacher in this classroom was not dealing with either the initiation of compositions or their final evaluation. Rather, she was participating at points within the process where help counted most. With Sandra she was trying to find out how far her pupil was thinking ahead in the writing process. She asked Derek himself to choose the line that had the best imagery, at the same time letting him know she cared about his interests in cars. Although Martha was not writing, the teacher's attention to her composing with water colors was another way of helping the learner develop critical powers basic to both writing and painting—of finding a way of seeing and a way of looking for the best parts in a whole.

In a rural school in Connecticut where writing conferences were the norm, I asked Rebecca, a second-grade child who was about to write, "What does a good writer need to do well in order to write well?" Rebecca replied, "Details. You have to have details. For example, if I walked down the street in the rain, I wouldn't say, 'I walked down the street and it was raining.' I would say, 'As I walked down the street in the rain, I sloshed through the puddles and the mud splattered to make black polka dots on my white socks.'"

In this instance Rebecca demonstrated one of the important contributions of writing: heightened experience. Writing is a kind of photography with words. We take mental pictures of scenes when we're out walking but don't really know what we have seen until we develop the words on the page through writing. Rebecca noticed what happened when she walked through puddles with white socks on. Having written down what she saw, she will notice even more details the next time she walks in the rain.

In our conversation, Rebecca went on to show me in a book how another writer had used words to give the reader more details.

Because of this child's confidence in her own writing voice, she could read the writing of others with a critical eye.

One of the common complaints of reading teachers is that children fail in the higher forms of comprehension: inferential and critical questions. It is difficult for many readers to separate their own thinking from that of the author, to stand far enough back from the material to see the author's point of view as distinct from their own. On the other hand, children who are used to writing for others achieve more easily the necessary objectivity for reading the work of others.

I wouldn't have expected to find process-conference teaching when I first looked in on a primary school in Scotland in which the rooms were formally arranged with neat rows of desks and chairs. However, teachers there were clearly well versed in the individual strengths of each child, even though there were thirty-five children to each room. It was obvious that high standards were set. I asked a child how he managed to write so well. His reply: "I am from Aberdeen, and this is the way we do it." Indeed, this spirit prevailed throughout the school. Children had a sense of voice and expressed themselves with confidence, both orally and in writing, as if it were their birthright.

Teachers in the Aberdeen school felt it was the children's responsibility to proofread their work. Few marks were seen on papers. A teacher would merely say, "But you're not finished yet, Matthew. You must be having an off day. Perhaps Margaret will look it over with you."

The process-conference approach flourishes in schools where administrators, teachers, and children trust one another. Such teaching cannot occur otherwise. Writing is affected by school climates. The stance of the school system as a whole shows quickly in the way writing is taught. A California teacher reported that her children were given four different tests for language skill. Four levels in the educational hierarchy—the federal granting agency, the state department of education, an independent community committee commissioned by the local board of education, and the school principal—all wished to know how her children compared with other children nationally. Although this program of testing took up valuable time, its other effects were greater: it created suspicion and fear that

Reading is the flip side of writing. When students think inferentially as they write, they find it easier to think inferentially as they read.

The nation, the state, school district administrators, teachers, and students are in this together. If administrators resort to mandating skills and drills, or if teachers refuse training, writing will not flourish. In the best of all possible worlds, administrators should also take training in teaching writing as a process. First, they would be doing their job as the instructional leader; second, they would have an internalized philosophy upon which to draw in order to assess writing progress in their school. NJWPT has had many principals, several assistant superintendents, and a few superintendents take the three-week training course.

Telling is not teaching. In the training of trainers for the NJWPT, teachers practice the art of retraining teachers. They know that telling teachers to change their teaching practices will not result in change. Instead, they show them a better way.

some children might lower the class scores, that other teachers' classes might do better, and that the test scores might be misused by administrators. Under these conditions the teachers inevitably became more concerned with the measurable surface elements of writing and less able to respond to the content of the writing of individual children. The teaching of writing was severely hampered.

School systems don't have to work this way. In a New Hampshire system, the teaching of writing turned around after the superintendent of schools enrolled, almost by accident, in a writing course given as an elective in an advanced program in school administration.

In the course, the teaching of writing was approached through the process of writing, not through reading about writing. As the superintendent gradually saw improvement in his own writing, he saw what might be possible for teachers and students in his own system. He made arrangements for a cooperative venture in writing instruction between his school system and the local university. The university would work with teachers on the process-conference approach, and the school system would aid in the development of new procedures for the assessment of writing.

Working in the schools, university faculty members sought to help teachers discover the power of their own writing. The writing process itself was studied, as well as the use of the process-conference approach with students. Thirty teachers from grades one through twelve took part in the training sessions. And the professors, the superintendent and other administrators, and the teachers all wrote and shared their writing.

Once the teachers began to understand the writing process and their own powers as writers, they could develop an effective approach to assessing student writing. Together, a teacher and a student would choose the student's four best papers for assessment. Thus students were assessed at their points of strength, as they wrote on topics of their own choosing in a variety of genres.

In a school whose teachers follow the process-conference approach in teaching children to write, a teacher might think, "Jennifer is ready for quotation marks in her writing now." In a school that teaches to meet predetermined test-oriented standards for correct writing, a teacher would be more likely to think, "Paul had better get going on quotation marks or he'll pull us down in the next city-wide achievement test."

Jennifer will meet quotation marks when dealing with the conversation of characters in the story she is writing. She will also look at models from literature: "See, this is how this author shows that people are talking. You put your marks here and here. There, now you can show that this is your knight talking." Jennifer masters the conventions of language in the process of conveying information.

Paul is more likely to struggle with quotation marks as an isolated phenomenon. He will punctuate sentences provided for him in a workbook. He will not see himself as a sender of information, a writer.

Paul wanted to write before he went to school. He is less eager to write now.

Paul should write because it will develop his self-concept as a learner and his pwoers as a thinker. Writing will strengthen his work in other subjects. If he writes throughout his school years, he will later make more effective contributions as a citizen, parent, and worker.

Writing is the basic stuff of education. It has been sorely neglected in our schools. We have substituted the passive reception of information for the active expression of facts, ideas, and feelings. We now need to right the balance between sending and receiving. We need to let them write.

The Jeffersonian purpose of education is to protect democracy. A democracy cannot be protected by a nation of nonwriters.

Writing is indeed basic to education.

Notes

1. "Americans are writing fewer personal letters..."
"First Class Mail Volume Forecasts by Categories of Use, 1972, 1978 and 1983," RMC Research Corporation. Final Report UR-221, December 21, 1973.

2. "Studies undertaken for this report show that people of many occupations..."
A series of 150 on-site personal interviews were conducted with persons from many occupations as well as professionals engaged in public and higher education. Questions related to individual reading and writing habits, views of education, and personal educational experiences were asked. Persons interviewed represented many levels of educational attainment from non-completion of high school to doctoral level and were from four different regions of the United States. Data for this portion of the study were cross-referenced by questions as well as used within the context of the entire interview itself. People were also interviewed in Scotland and England.

I. Why Writing Is Important

1. "On the other hand, writing, more than any other subject can be the means to personal breakthrough in learning."
Data for this were taken from the interview responses about educational background and experiences. Although people cited writing most often as the personal breakthrough in learning, another group cited it as a negative, punishing experience. There seemed to be little middle ground in referring to writing experiences.

2. "Donald Durrell, a pioneer in the reading field for fifty years advocates..."
Although Durrell has stated this same point in recent writings, this is a quotation from an interview with him.

3. "Research has tied reading comprehension..."
This kind of research is in its infancy, yet early data returns are more than promising. These studies, as well as the Stotsky article, are important beginnings in portraying the contribution of writing to reading.

Combs, Warren E. "The Influence of Sentence-Combining Practice on Reading Ability." Unpublished Doctoral Dissertation, University of Minnesota, 1975.

Obenshain, Anne. "Effectiveness of the Precise Essay Question in Programming the Sequential Development of Written Composition Skills and the Simultaneous Development of Critical Reading Skills." Master's Thesis, George Washington University, 1971.

Smith, William. "The Effect of Transformed Syntactic Structures on Reading." Paper presented at the International Reading Association Conference, May, 1970.

Stotsky, Sandra L. "Sentence Combining as a Curricular Activity: Its Effect on Written Language Development and Reading Comprehension," *Research in the Teaching of English*, 9 (Spring, 1975), 30-70.

II. Why Don't We Write?

1. "When children write early, their experiments..."

Chomsky, Carol. "Beginning Reading Through Invented Spelling," *Selected Papers from the 1973 New England Kindergarten Conference*, Cambridge, Massachusetts, Lesley College, 1973.

Chomsky, Carol. "Write First, Read Later," *Childhood Education*, 1971, 47 (No. 6), 296-299.

Paul, Rhea. "Invented Spelling in Kindergarten," *Young Children*, March, 1976 (No. 3), 195-200.

2. "Of exemplary programs in language..."

Educational Programs That Work, U.S. Office of Education (U.S. Government Printing Office: Washington, D.C.) 1976.

3. "Research on all aspects of writing..."

1976 DATABOOK — The Status of Education Research and Development in the United States, (The National Institute of Education: Washington, D.C.) 1976.

4. "Of research articles in education published in 1969..."

Persell, Carolyn. *The Quality of Research on Education*, (New York: Columbia University, Bureau of Applied Social Research) 1971.

5. "A survey of superintendents of schools in a New England state..."

A Survey of Current Instructional Practices in and Approaches to the Teaching of Reading/Language Arts in New Hampshire, (Division of Instruction: State Department of Education, Concord, NH) 1976.

6. "More than 90 per cent of instruction in the classroom..."

"National Survey and Assessment of Instruction," *Epigram*, 4 (April 15, 1976). (Published by Educational Products Information Exchange, New York City, New York).

7. "One textbook editor spoke for his profession..."

Interviews with both publishers and writers spoke of the risks of publishing. A number of publishers have gone back to publishing texts of ten or twenty years ago because of their stress on the basics, and the basics do not include *actual writing*.

8. "Orders for lined paper, principally used for writing compositions..."

Our surveys of school supply companies and the purchasing of paper by school districts show a decline in the use of lined paper. There is also an accelerated purchase of ditto paper, which is rarely used for writing.

9. "In a recent survey of a large sample of seventeen-year-olds..."

These data were cited by Rex Brown, Education Commission of the States, Denver, Colorado at the National Council of Teachers of English, Secondary School English Conference, Boston, Mass., April, 1976.

10. "A survey of three such systems discovered..."

As part of this study three systems in rural, suburban, and urban communities in three different states were examined. All three were *making efforts* to improve student writing.

11. "Teachers report that they do not write..."

Teachers from grade one through the university were interviewed. Individual writing was a universal problem.

12. "A recent survey of education courses in 36 universities..."

Our own survey of the catalog offerings in departments of education in 36 universities. Most of the universities were state schools engaged in teacher preparation. In the 1960s the United States made an effort, through the National Defense Education Act, to better prepare teachers to teach writing. Since that time, however, the effort has languished.

13. "At one large state university, the contracts offered teaching assistants..."

This was a contract recently agreed upon at a Big Ten university in freshman composition.

14. "In one suburban community, it was found, parents regularly checked children's papers..."

This was a common concern of teachers surveyed in a suburban school system near Boston, Massachusetts.

15. "Seven-year-old children were asked, 'What do you think a good writer needs...'"

Graves, Donald H. "Children's Writing: Research Directions and Hypotheses Based Upon an Examination of the Writing Processes of Seven-Year-Old Children." Unpublished doctoral dissertation, SUNY at Buffalo, 1973.

III.   How Writing Can Be Taught

"In a city school in upper New York state..."

The examples that follow in this section were from schools in four regions of the U.S. These schools were visited to provide contrast and perspective on the status of writing in the U.S. As mentioned earlier, schools were also visited in England and Scotland.

13

RESEARCH
The Truth About Inquiry

For many decades high schools and colleges have fostered
the "research paper," which has become an exercise
in badly done bibliography, often an introduction to the art of
plagiarism, and a triumph for meaninglessness —
for both writer and reader.

—Ken Macrorie□

No one has all the answers to all the questions. Most have hunches; some have indications; others have proofs. Sometimes while searching for answers more questions evolve. Often when writers need answers they go to the library. They ask questions of experts. They investigate. They read. They collect from the least likely places. They observe. Ultimately they immerse themselves in inquiry.

Why then does the inquiry process seem so foreign to the research process done in most schools? To answer this question, teachers must first examine the way research is still being done.

In the elementary classroom, a topic is assigned to the student. Usually this topic is related to science or social studies. For example, Mr. Blank assigns Marie to write a report about Italy. Marie goes to the library. She finds the "*I*" volume of the *World Book Encyclopedia*. She takes it to a library desk, because reference materials may not leave the Learning Resource Room. She finds Italy wedged between entries on Itaipu and Ithaca. She copies down information like: "Chief manufactures include iron and steel, refined petroleum, chemicals, textiles, motor vehicles, and machinery." Marie continues her report with "North and Central Italy saw the rise of separate city-states; these, despite constant internecine warfare, built huge commercial empires, dominated European finance, and produced the great cultural flowering known as the Renaissance." Marie writes pages about Italy—most of which she does not understand. Most of the things she plagiarizes, she has no context for understanding. She includes information on Vatican City, the Etruscans, the Roman Empire, the Lombards, the Papal states, Risorgimento, the Triple Alliance, and finishes it off with a word about the Red Brigade.

Marie turns in her report. She gets high marks. As she should—fine writers and researchers spent years writing what she has turned in for a grade. Both Marie and her teacher think they have been successful. They celebrate Marie's report by having a food day. Marie brings pizza. Her friend Joey brings Swiss cheese—he wrote a report on Switzerland. Her other friend Tamarah brings in a bag of corn chips for Mexico.

And so goes report writing in classrooms where research is seen as finding out what someone else knows, not what students can discover and know themselves.

In middle school the scenario goes something like, "Write a report on euthanasia." Again students scurry to the library. Some go to the encyclopedias; others go to the subject card catalogue. Those with the encyclopedias copy down what the book has recorded. If their books have two pages of typeface, the students rewrite it into six pages of report. If the encyclopedia has a paragraph, the student writes a one-page report. Sometimes when the teacher is pressed for time, the assignment is, "Write a one-page report on euthanasia." Some students, panicking over the magnitude of the topic, search for the smallest entry. Others write a page and simply stop—mid-sentence, mid-paragraph, mid-point. They write their page.

Meanwhile, the students at the subject card file scramble for the "E" drawer. If the subject catalogue has a single entry for euthanasia, the students go for the book on the shelf. Depending upon the library's holdings, there might be one book or there might be several. These students then look for the chapter, subhead, section on euthanasia. They copy down what is written. If the subject catalogue has no entries on the topic, then the students give up or go with their friends who are using the encyclopedia. Sometimes students even reject the book listed in the subject catalogue if the title of the book does not explicitly use the word "euthanasia." These "researchers" tend to be highly literal and do not see research as creative.

Occasionally, there is a student whose parent takes him or her to the local public library or even a college or university library. If a research librarian helps the youngster, he or she has more information than they know how to assimilate. They resort to copying again. On rare occasions, a parent writes the report—this report may be largely plagiarized, but it is harder to detect, because the parent picks and chooses from various sources.

Then there are the students who opt for a failing grade. They refuse to do the report. These may be the most honest students, for they know before they even begin that they cannot do this assignment. Invariably there is the student who will write the highly original report about "Youth in Asia."

The teacher will grade these reports. Sometimes a student will receive a disciplinary notice for copying another student's work. The student who has been "copied from" is grateful that the teacher does not discover where he or she got the information. Usually, all the students who have like reports fail the assignment. If Mr. Blank is highly creative, the block of students will get one grade—say, a 90 divided equally among the conspirators. All too often, however, the students get good marks for writing a "good report."

To circumvent plagiarizing, the teacher resorts to placing the book selection on reserve for student use. These and only these are the texts to be used. On reflection, Mr. Blank has been known to make statements such as, "These students don't know how to do research."

By the time students reach high school, the research paper has become a highly refined neurotic exercise. Tom Romano says of the literature-based writing done in high schools, "Such repeated, narrow engagement in composition, I believe, prevents students from developing open, flexible attitudes about writing. It inhibits their ability to use writing as a learning tool, and it promotes habits of mind and perceptions of how writing is done that may cripple their growth as writers" (131).

Typically the high school research paper comes in two varieties—the literary research paper or the current-topic research paper. The literary paper is usually teacher-driven. The teacher selects topics for the students. When challenged about students choosing their own topics, this teacher types up a list of topics, cuts them into strips, and allows the students to select their topics through a drawing. The more creative teachers conduct auctions of topics that range from literary persons, for example, Donne, Yeats, Shelley, to theme approaches, for example, the water imagery of Donne's metaphysical poetry or the collected works of D. H. Lawrence. These teachers believe they are preparing their students for college and see themselves as protectors of the literary canon.

The current-topic research paper is a more sophisticated version of the report writing done in the middle grades. Rules engulf this process. Requirements, such as 50 notecards for an A or 5 books and 10 magazine articles used as sources, are tenets the students must master.

On all levels the teachers' mantra is, "We're preparing them for next year."

These papers swamp the curriculum—six or nine weeks of class time. Three weeks of this time are spent in the library—libraries that cannot even support the research being required. And what do the students do? Some make valiant and even genuine attempts at accomplishing the research. Most papers, though, lack ownership and voice. If these classrooms were financial institutions, they would go bankrupt from the "high" cost of this assignment. Classroom time and learning are too valuable to whittle away while "doing" the research paper.

Saner voices must prevail amid this research mania. Rational examinations reveal that all students should be involved in real research for appropriate reasons. Effective teachers incorporate the use of research and library skills in a multitude of ways. This chapter examines some of those ways.

REPORT WRITING

Young children can and should write reports. Their first engagement with report writing should come in the form of all-about books. They can write all they know about what they have become experts in or on. For example, Troy Hull, a first-grader, writes about dinosaurs.

> 🏃 *the is up the hill.*
> *the dinosar aet met.*
> *the dinosar is a brontusaris.*
> *the brontusaris kild a bad dinosar.*
> *he kild a trontusarirex at the kav*
> *he ess plans at his kav on his*
> *prpde and under the sun shin.*

> [The dinosaur is up the hill. The dinosaur eats meat. The dino-
> saur is a Brontosaurus. The Brontosaurus killed a bad dino-
> saur. He killed a Tyrannosaurus Rex at the cave. He has plants
> at his cave on his property and under the sunshine.]

Troy has studied dinosaurs in his class. He has read picture and story books about them. He does not need to copy what someone else writes, because he is developing his own knowledge of the dinosaur.

Teachers should not be too quick to dismiss the interest of the child researcher. Jean Piaget had classified all of the known mollusks in the natural history museum of Neuchatel by the age of 11. Children know a great deal about things that are important to them. They can talk for extended periods of time about topics the teacher might not think children would normally be interested in.

> *My fourth-grade teacher, Mrs. Crosby, was the oddest person I had
> ever seen. She was shorter than any of us and outweighed us by 300
> pounds. She did not walk — she lumbered from side to side. The summer
> before we started fourth grade, Mrs. Crosby went to Egypt. For the first
> three days of class she showed us her slides. There were 56 trays of
> them. My friends and I spent hours on the evening of the second day
> discussing how she ever got on the camel. Her slides took us to a world
> we had never known. Most of our parents had never traveled past the
> border of our home state. A few of us had fathers who had served in
> World War II or Korea. But they did not talk much about those experi-
> ences. As a class we were enthralled.*
>
> *Memory fades the details of how we started our research on Egypt
> that year, but memory does not dim the effects of our research. We
> built a replica of the Nile River down the counter of the room. We had
> barges and papyrus ships. We reproduced the Valley of the Kings,
> temples, and the Sphinx. Our play, "Dr. Livingston, I Presume," was a
> sold-out performance. We made a mummy, built a sarcophagus, carved
> death masks, learned to write hieroglyphics. Egyptology filled our year.
> Everything we read, listened to, or watched in math, science, social
> studies, art, music, and language arts centered around one of the
> world's oldest developed civilizations. Not once did we copy a report
> from a book. Instead, we became experts in given fields of study. At 10,
> my love affair with everything that was foreign to a small town in the*

panhandle of Texas began. When the Tutankhamen exhibit opened in the National Museum in Washington, D.C., I knew well Howard Carter's words when asked if he could see anything, "Yes, wonderful things...."

If practices like those of Mrs. Crosby's and Troy's teacher are indicative of how research should be taught, then what will students and teachers need to do to listen to the saner voices? The first step might be understanding the research processes involved for the level being taught.

THREE LEVELS OF RESEARCH LOOPS

Research Loop for Young Writers

The child, with guidance from the teacher, selects an area to research. Key to this process is the focus and organization that the act of selection requires. As the child dismisses and prioritizes, direction from the teacher should allow the child to explore and take risks. When Troy writes about dinosaurs, his research area, he shows that he has a working knowledge of the prehistoric beasts. When he narrows his topic to the Brontosaurus, he limits what he reports on. While his fact about Brontosaurus being a meat eater is incorrect, he does know that plants are key to survival and that dinosaurs were territorial.

Troy's process followed exactly the research loop illustrated in figure 13.1. He selected his topic and then focused it. He read several books and watched a video in an effort to analyze the information. In groups he talked to his classmates about the Brontosaurus. His interview, while not reflected in his writing, consisted of a dialogue with an all-important third-grader he had met in the library when he had gone to get a book on dinosaurs. The third-grader shared his favorite dinosaur book with Troy.

Fig. 13.1. Beginning-level research loop.

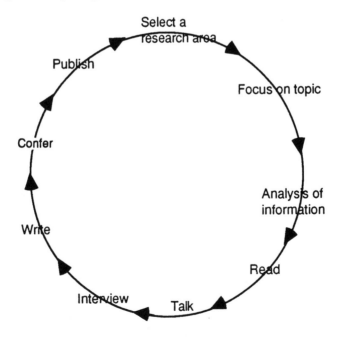

When Troy started to write, he dismissed many things he could have said. His drafts showed evidence of selecting information that stuck to his topic. When he conferenced with his teacher, he added the *trontusarirex* after his teacher asked him what kind of dinosaur Brontosaurus killed.

He typed his piece on the computer and shared it with students in a read around. His research completed for the time being, he went on to write about other dinosaurs he had learned about while researching the Brontosaurus.

Children as Experts

For children, inquiry is natural. Daily living brings discovery. The goal for children beginning research-based writing is not to have them master some form or genre, but to nurture their affection for discovery. Children want to know more about things; however, they do not always want to know about the things the teacher decides is important. They prefer to select what they want to discover. Their needs are interpersonal and representational—interpersonal in the sense that they codiscover as classmates discover, and representational in the sense that they want tangible proof for what they have learned. When students are allowed to choose their own topics for research, the teacher needs only to teach the skills of research.

Often, teachers worry needlessly over a child's occupation and preoccupation with a given topic. The child becomes consumed with writing, learning, experiencing, playing everything related to the area of obsession. This is possibly nothing more than becoming an expert on the topic.

Instead of discouraging such inquiry, the teacher should direct the study. Children taught at a young age to trust their own learning make better researchers. Personal knowledge translates into formal knowledge. What a child discovers today can be studied tomorrow.

Julie Fannin, a third-grader, shares her original and important research, "How I Got My Name," with an impressive eye and ear for detail. She has learned the lessons of accuracy. She quotes her sources. She shows instead of tells. As she takes the reader through the experience, she informs and settles for all time how and why she got her name (see fig. 13.2).

Fig. 13.2. Julie's research on her name.

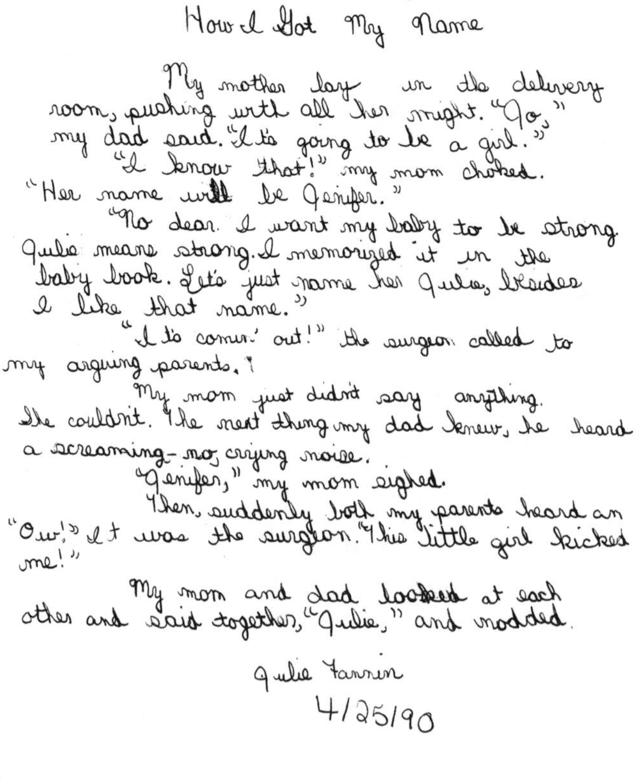

How I Got My Name

My mother lay in the delivery room, pushing with all her might. "Go," my dad said. "It's going to be a girl."
"I know that!" my mom choked. "Her name will be Jenifer."
"No dear. I want my baby to be strong. Julie means strong. I memorized it in the baby book. Let's just name her Julie, besides I like that name."
"It is comin' out!" the surgeon called to my arguing parents.
My mom just didn't say anything. She couldn't. The next thing my dad knew, he heard a screaming—no, crying noise.
"Jenifer," my mom sighed.
Then, suddenly both my parents heard an "Ow!" It was the surgeon. "This little girl kicked me!"
My mom and dad looked at each other and said together, "Julie," and nodded.

Julie Fannin
4/25/90

What could be more important to a child—exploring her name or copying information about ecology or the internal-combustion engine? How much easier it will be to engage Julie in understanding genealogy after she researches her name. She may enjoy discovering what experts in the field say. Julie's curiosity may be piqued by watching videos about names and family histories. Allowing Julie to become acquainted with her topic and discovering its richness will get Julie as involved in genealogy (as an extension of her research) as she was involved with her name. Often in teaching it is not what a teacher does, but how a teacher does it.

Nor does the child have to report the research in dry, dull prose. Bruner, in *Acts of Meaning*, reminds teachers of the power of the narrative.

> Narrative requires ... four crucial grammatical constituents if it is to be effectively carried out. It requires, first, a means for emphasizing human action or *agentivity*—action directed toward goals controlled by agents. It requires, secondly, that a sequential order be established and maintained—that events and states be *linearized* in a standard way. Narrative, thirdly, also requires a sensitivity to what is canonical and what violates canonicality approximating a narrator's perspective: it cannot, in the jargon of narratology, be *voiceless*. (77)

If teachers want to engage young students into the ownership of research, then the research should be narrative in nature and structure and voice.

Leonor Dombroski, Pond Springs Elementary, Round Rock ISD, shares two pieces of research written by Audrey and Leah, first-graders:

🛉 *The Mice, by Audrey.*

Over the weekend our mice had babys and there were twelve babys. My teacher said that Leah and I could have a baby mouse but Leah has first choise. The mice are pink and thier ears and eyes are closed when they are born. They sort of look like very very small pigs. They are very cute and they were born on Saturday. We are going to keep a journal about the mice and write a little every day.

🛉 *The Mice.*

After about 2 weeks of waiting the baby mice were born! They were born late Friday night. I called Mrs. Dombroski Saterday to ask it Dewey had her babys. She said yes she also said she moved the dady into the other kage incase he ate any babys. & she said I could come Sunday to see the baby mice. Some times I wunder how little pink harless baby mice will become beutiful mice like thair Mom and Dad. Thair were at least 12 or more. We are going to keep ajrnal on them. by Leah.

Both researchers are becoming experts on baby mice. Already they know to establish time and place in research. They are careful in the descriptions. Audrey understands that a metaphor of what the babies look like will better inform the reader. Leah makes the superior insight into scientific experimental research, projecting that if the daddy eats the babies there will be nothing left—there will be no more data. They both know that they can record the observations of their research in journals to keep track of what they discover.

Research Loop for Middle School Learners

The middle school student, like the elementary student, has a wealth of knowledge and a diversity of interests upon which to draw. Part of the difficulty working with research at this age level is that these students think they do not know enough. Because they are moving from an egocentric perception of their world to a more adult perception, they realize that they may not be the center of the universe and therefore may not have enough of a handle on a topic to be considered an expert. While this perception is certainly debatable and erroneous, it nevertheless exists.

Middle school students have trouble focusing on a topic. This can be seen in their approach to daily living. They experiment with clothing styles, hair styles, attitudes, and peer groups. Getting them to settle into an area to research is difficult, but not impossible. Instead of concentrating a large amount of time and effort on one big research project, these students profit with smaller projects. Projects more manageable and less intimidating work best.

Carroll, in "TV and Term Papers," outlines one approach teachers may use to turn research into more creative assignments by following the model of television news shows like "60 Minutes" (85). Carroll suggests assimilating into the teaching of the research paper what students assimilate when watching TV news shows that demonstrate research, documentation, investigation, exploration, and inquiry. Carroll's article clearly shows that by shifting the focus from the genre to the methods of research, students may explore within limitations.

When considering the intermediate level of the research loop (see fig. 13.3), teachers can draw on any of the prewriting techniques covered in this book. In fact, the writing process does not necessarily change because research is being used. The key for the middle school student is selecting the research area. The intermediate level of the research loop builds upon the same processes as the beginning level, but asks students to consider primary sources and interviews. The publishing aspect of this level can also be broadened to include other ways of going public with research. Again, the idea of using a news program format intensifies the motivation for most students. For students unable to use or acquire a video camera, live performances can be equally motivational. Of course, assignments like science fair projects allow research skills to be integrated with other disciplines.

Fig. 13.3. Intermediate-level research loop.

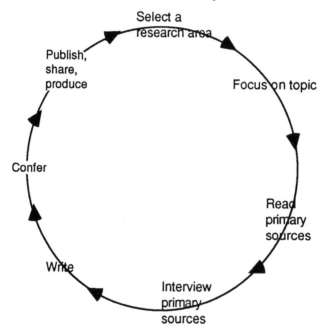

RESEARCH AREAS FOR THE MIDDLE SCHOOL

Regardless of the socioeconomic characteristics of students or their educational background, all students have interests. Working with a group of eighth-grade, inner-city students revealed that their interests differed from students' interests in rural areas. One inner-city student expressed dismay when the teacher announced they would be studying and researching the medieval period. The teacher asked him what he was interested in. "Weapons," he answered. Undaunted, the teacher responded, "Then you're going to love the weaponry of this period. Why don't you see what you can find out about cat-o'-nine-tails and the catapult?"

As the class made its way through a study of Arthurian legends and a selection of *The Canterbury Tales*, the students delved into topics such as alchemy, dungeons, and dragon lore. Students read Cynthia Voight's *On Fortune's Wheel* and studied herbology and illumination. The young man who at first scoffed produced a series of drawings depicting ancient weapons and their uses. Not only did he search out information, he also spoke with local collectors of weapons. The principal of the school was surprised when this student arranged for a local retired general to speak to the class about his collection.

What on the surface had the earmark of gang activity and antisocial behavior was productively rechanneled by the teacher. She guided the student into research that directly placed the student in contact with one of the most conservative members of the community—the general. Instead of looking at the differences between the student and the general, the teacher exploited their similarities. Was this student saved from the ravages of gang neighborhoods and a fascination with the bizarre? No. But neither was the student alienated from research, discovery, or inquiry. Neither was the student turned away from a learning process and a place called school. In fact, the retired general made quite an impact on the young man, and the young man was allowed to help with the display of the general's weapons collection at a local museum.

MOVING THE RESEARCH INTO A PRODUCT

The major consideration at the middle school level is not whether the student masters the conventions of writing research as much as it is understanding the process of research and the skills required to conduct research. Middle school is not the place to snare students into the documentation trap. Yet, these writers need to understand when the importance of differentiating between an idea or words that are their own and ideas or words that are borrowed. One way to help students understand is to use an analogy based on the convention of "borrowing" in mathematics. Borrowing from the "tens" column for the "ones" column has consequences. The borrowing must be noted or something is lost. Sometimes, when the borrowing is done incorrectly, there is too much— mathematically. Students have been working with this concept since the second grade and should be able to transfer it to research. Information not their own is borrowed and needs to be accounted for by giving credit. The concept itself is relatively simple. Worrying students over footnotes and correct bibliographical form may repel students rather than attract them to research.

Once they internalize the "rightness" of giving credit, middle school students must grapple with the appropriateness of giving credit. The writing teacher should expect students to give credence to the validity of others. When students write and incorporate the ideas and words of others, they are developing the skills that will allow them to become better researchers. Carroll, in "Plagiarism: The Unfun Game," recommends the "personnoting page." This page is "the place where students can acknowledge everyone who helped with their papers in any way—teachers, friends, family, librarians, authors, lyricists, lecturers, and editors (even Webster and Roget)" (93). Her practical idea cultivates the student researcher.

CULTIVATING RESEARCHERS

A researcher is not made in a day. Researchers are nurtured and guided through the processes of inquiry. Never should research be an isolated exercise done in one paper on one occasion during the year. Research is a state of mind. Again, saner voices must influence the curricula of middle schools. When students use research once a year for one paper, the skills necessary to understand and utilize research as a lifelong skill will not develop. Teachers intuitively and educationally know this to be true. They know that research is not something done in May. They, too, have been the victims of too many courses where the end product is a research paper. They remember what and how they went about doing this research. They remember when it was real research and when it was false. Teachers who record what they do in their classrooms—what they diagnose, treat, and cure, what they watch die, and what they watch come to life — are the real researchers. These teachers use their research abilities not only for graduate study but for professional reasons. These teachers have learned well the lessons of support and borrowed ideas. They readily give credit to ideas they use, and they eagerly receive the recognition for what they have discovered in their inquiry of teaching and learning. Teachers who actively engage in and write research have students who do the same.

Linda Ellis, formerly of Lovelady ISD, Lovelady, Texas, studied her middle school readers and writers. Her inquiry led her to a doctoral program at Texas A & M University. As she became more involved with the study of her students, she became more involved with her own study and learning. One fed the other. These are the kinds of lessons teachers are learning of research.

Research is not so foreign to students. Middle school students are constantly studying and researching what it is to become teenagers. They are not immune or allergic to research. With the right direction, these students can understand the need for research and grow to respect it.

Research Loop for High School Students

A process that works with high school writers is one that starts in the reflexive mode and moves to the extensive mode. Starting with journals and prewritings, students and teachers can explore the interests recorded. Teachers then help the writer examine the issues found in the prewriting. Moving the writer to consider taking the issue out of the personal into a semiextensive mode is the next step. This process is similar to finding the best genre for a piece of writing, except that here the writer is encouraged to find support for the ideas presented in the writing.

For example, poet Jerry James wrote a reflexive piece about hitting a dog while driving down the street. It would be easy for the teacher to move Jerry into the extensive mode by suggesting he write a letter to the editor about leash laws and the value of dog tags. Once he has done that writing, the teacher could help Jerry identify the points that are true and those that are indecisive. At that point, Jerry will be ready to examine what others have discovered and recorded about his topic (see fig. 13.4 for the research loop on this process). He could interview someone in animal control, veterinarians, breeders, or pet owners. He could read statutes and opinions on the subject. During this process, the teacher will teach Jerry how to use a periodical index, how to paraphrase, and how to record findings. Jerry might then move his writing from the letter genre to the essay genre, while keeping his interest in the topic. (Requirements of 50 note cards are superfluous to this type of inquiry. Jerry might need audio tapes, video tapes, photocopies, or pictures. These are also tools of a good researcher — neatly copied note cards do not work for everyone or every type of research.) Jerry may be ready to consider writing a documented essay in which he expresses his views and the views of others. Depending on his purpose, he may want to present only the views that support his way of thinking, or he might want to present opposing views to make a better case for his own. There is no way Jerry or his teacher will know what the final form will be until Jerry has started to explore his writing, his thinking, and the impact his research has had on both.

After Jerry has completed his essay he should be ready to consider writing a thesis statement about his topic. By this time, Jerry is either "hot" on his topic or will want to find another. If Jerry were in a traditional classroom, he would have been asked to develop his thesis before he had done any type of inquiry. (And teachers wonder why students do poorly on research?) In doctoral research, it is common for the researcher to develop a hypothesis first, then write a proposal, conduct tests, do some preliminary research, and finally write a thesis that proves or disproves the hypothesis. In the research loop of the traditional classroom, the writers and the teacher skip this process and "cut to the chase." Students, not quite certain what is really happening, usually end up using someone else's thesis.

But Jerry does not have to say what someone else has already said. With more reading and study, he will be ready to document his sources and present a piece of writing that convincingly and coherently deals with his topic. Jerry moves from what he knows into what others help him know better, more deeply, or differently. He never has to leave the arena of his own knowledge. He never has to report on things about which he knows nothing. Jerry is learning a research process he can use over and over again, for everything from how to buy a car, to the effect of inflation on his net income.

Fig. 13.4. Advanced-level research loop.

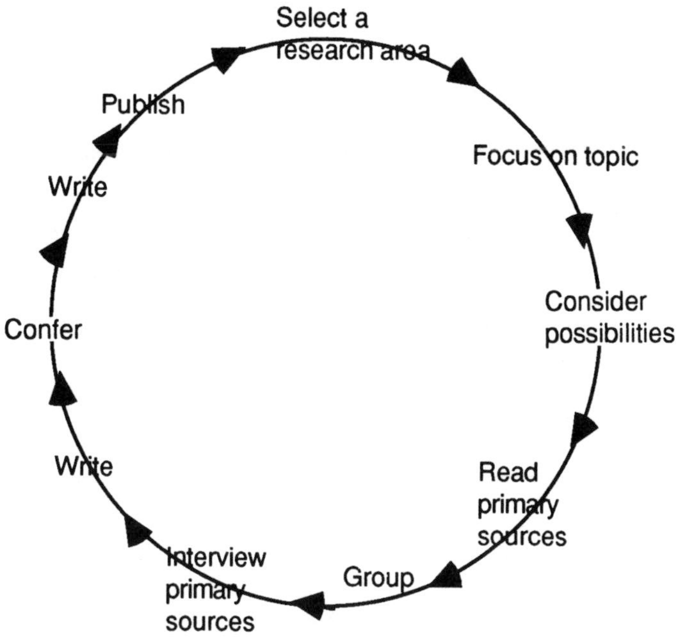

Again, research need not be the event of the year. In stark contrast, research can be an ongoing process. The student who incorporates research into many types of writing on many occasions will be better prepared to make research a lifelong skill, than the student who views research as a hurdle in the race to graduation.

What do students think of research? Mike Gill's essay, "The Eyes of the Beholder" (see pages 430-432), gives a glimpse of what he thinks. Satirical messages appear in phrases like, "dreaded Junior composition research paper," "total self abuse and mind wracking impossibilities," "writing failures," "possessed by the devil," and "total doom." His essay serves to remind all secondary teachers of the hazards of just doing "the research paper."

THE PERSONAL PRONOUN IN RESEARCH

A teacher once said, "Students cannot use the first-person pronoun in the research paper because they are not experts on what they are researching." In fact, this teacher held to this tenet so tightly that her grading policy reflected her strong belief—automatic failure on the entire paper. Because the school in which she taught required that the "junior research paper" on a current topic had to be mastered before a junior could receive credit for the year's course, the principal had initiated a review board made up of teachers and parents to arbitrate disputes about the grade.

(Text continues on page 433.)

⚕ The Eyes of the Beholder
Michael M. Gill, Senior

Christmas break was finally over and with the fond memories of my relatives and many gifts still rumbling through my mind, I grumpily walked up to the bleak, puke green doors that led into the academic halls. I stood there for a couple of minutes contemplating suicide, for on the other side of those doors was the most feared task my feeble human brain could ever conceive—the dreaded Junior composition research paper. I shrugged my shoulders, gave a small meaningless stone a kick, and flung the doors open; sadly committing myself to eight weeks of total self abuse and mind wracking impossibilities.

I walked down the corridor, entered room twenty-three twenty-three, and quickly took my seat by the trashcan. Coincidently, I knew I'd probably be having to use the recepticle either to vomit or to discard many writing failures. I looked around the room and noticed that everyone in the class looked as boring as they had last month. You see, nobody wears their new clothes they got for Christmas until later in the week because that's the "cool" thing to do.

But then my theory was totally ruined when Gary Emptyboat walked in wearing new everything—even bright red ropers. My theory was then further demolished as Mrs. Hildabroom walked into the room flaunting her new dress from Sax Sixth Street. She had undoubtedly purchased the dress with her slightly overused American Express Platinum card. She seemed so righteous as she walked up to the table where she began to pass out little neatly stacked pieces of paper. I thought, for a second, that I heard lightning and thunder along with a hideous laugh. "No, that's impossible." So I decided to forget the whole thing.

Mrs. Hildabroom then spoke in a tone that I had never heard her speak in before. It was as if she were possessed by the devil.

"As you all know, this semester we will be working on your Junior composition research papers. I hope that you've been thinking about what you are going to research, since we start taking note cards on Wednesday."

I could hear her laugh deep in her throat as she walked down the aisle. Then, as if the world were about to end, a moan went up over the entire room. Such was the noise, Mr. Fixitcorridor and his side kick Mr. Small would probably be down in the room in a minute having a cow in the hallway. Then I thought to myself, "Hmm, what can I do my research paper on? I'm not interested in anything but swimming and that would be boring." Then like a flash of lightning I thought, "Hey, I'm a party kinda guy and what kind of parties are the best? Fraternity parties! I'll do my paper on fraternities—yeah, that's the ticket."

Well, from that point on, I had nothing but pure hard work ahead of me and the subject seemed to beckon me like the sirens to Ulysses. It sounded great but I was headed towards total doom and a certain early grave. As my peers stood up and proudly told Hazel Hildabroom their subjects they had chosen, I gradually began to think my topic was not worthy enough to compete with the others in class. First of all, there was somebody researching brains and brain surgeons and another euthenasia. Then some dweeb actually wanted to learn about the effects of sugar substitutes on the body. Finally to top things off, Willy Snide wanted to find out if dreams and R.E.M. could ever be reality or something to that extent.

When it was my turn to speak, I felt my stomach knot up as I lifted myself from the chair.

"Fraternities," I said as I blended my words with a cough.

"What was that Michael?" She called me Michael, because she thought it was really a cute name.

I spoke again, "Fraternities and the benefits of the Greek way of life in college."

Apparently she was not impressed, but what really made me sick was when she said in a very bored voice, "Oh, that's very nice." And she went on, not bothering to ask why or anything.

I knew right then and there I was in Big Time Trouble. If she didn't think my subject was worthy of her class, she would probably just laugh at it when I turned the paper in. "I'll show her," I thought to myself, "I'm going to write the best damn research paper she's ever seen!" That very night I went down to the public library and began on my quest for information on my so called "great" subject. I looked and searched and searched some more. Nothing! Not one damn thing on fraternities. Then I figured, "Hey, college libraries must have something about fraternities. Right!"

Wrong. Not one of the libraries in town had anything I could use in my paper that would prove my thesis. That's when I really started to worry about how I could find the information I needed. Well, to make a long story short, the next six weeks were spent writing letters to colleges all over America, getting bits of information here or scrounging magazines from there. I wrote to so many Inter-Fraternity Councils that I figured it would be easier to just xerox the letters or better yet, not even do the whole thing. Just then the haunting figure of Mrs. Hilda-broom, dressed in her furs from Padre's came flashing into my mind.

"Oh, Michael Darling—" as if she were trying to imitate ZaZa Gabore, "if you don't receive a passing grade on this research paper, you won't ever graduate! Ha, Ha, Ha, Ha, Ha."

The laughs went right through my soul like Chinese food goes through a Wisconsin dairy farmer with a bad case of the runs. I was left standing in a cold sweat as I placed another letter into our little blue mailbox in the front yard. This was the same box, which I prayed would in a week or two bring me the massive amounts of letters, articles, or books thus saving me from another year of Junior composition. Well, to say the least, I received about three pieces of literature which I could actually use. The rest was kindling for the fire inside the mailbox. I guess I just started blaming that stupid box for it's inadequacy to pick up letters of the opposite sex, or something like that, and burned the little sucker to the ground.

I guess by now, you can tell that, yes, I was getting a little crazy about the whole gosh-darn thing. But just as I was getting ready to commit hara-kiri, my brother Larry, back from college, was reading something with great intensity. As he walked by, ignoring the fact that his only brother was about to sacrifice his body to the God of English, I noticed the book said something about Fraternities! I jumped up amid the candle and incense, threathened my brother's life, and grabbed the book from his shaking hands. I looked at the cover and cried tears of joy. The cover read: "A Modern Guide to Fraternities and Sororities."

("The Eyes of the Beholder" continues on page 432.)

I was saved. It was a gift from the great god of English, Neddy Wilso, who in his infinite wisdom had sent a miracle to a poor distressed sixteen year old. Now I was having more success than ever. By now miracles were happening daily. I was receiving books from people I had never even written and even got a phone call from a member of the Phi Theta Delta Fraternity in Lubbock, Texas. I don't think it really counted though, it was only my brother asking us to send him some clean underwear, and babbling about a little accident that happened during hell week.

The weeks went by very fast as I was writing and recopying. By now, the week before the paper was due, I had the whole thing ready to be sent to my father's trusty secretary. Yes, I was three days ahead of schedule and very proud of myself. I think I might have even impressed Mrs. Hildabroom ... just a little bit. Now all I had to do was take it easy. Relax. Let everyone else sweat it out. I was done with everything and those who weren't could go jump for all I cared. I actually enjoyed myself, in a sick kind of way, walking around the room telling people that they had typed their whole bibliography wrong. Or saying that we were supposed to use double space lines instead of single space.

But what really got me off was rubbing salt into the wounds of all those "brilliant" people who chose so called marvelous topics to write about. They just kept telling me things like.

"Oh, I'll get it done by tomorrow," or "Sure, I can type this in a couple of hours. No problem."

I just had to laugh out loud, and I'm sure those people got together after class and planned to beat me senseless on the way to school Friday morning. To my pleasure, everything went fine and I was not killed driving to school. In fact, everything from that day on seemed to be just a little bit better than they were eight weeks ago. I walked to those same puke colored doors, as I had done all year and before I opened them, I examined them even closer. To my surprise, they didn't at all look too badly discolored. In fact, the whole world looked better to me. The grass was greener, the people still looked the same, but they seemed a bit more friendly. I opened the doors, and to my amazement, they did not creak any longer.

On the way up to Mrs. Hildabroom's desk, I looked down at the manila envelope that held my hard work and hundreds of hours of research, and was very pleased with myself. Pleased was I, because I accomplished something that just a few weeks ago, seemed to be an almost impossible task. Not only had I increased my knowledge, but I felt that I had matured a great deal in this small period of time.

I still received an eightyseven. Oh, well, such is life.

One year a young woman who used the first-person pronoun and her mother met with this panel to complain that the teacher's dictum was unfair. The girl and parent both reluctantly agreed that the dictum had been posted in advance and that the writer had elected to disregard it. When the teacher was questioned about the rule, she reiterated, "Students are not experts on what they are researching." Sensing failure and frustration, the young writer exploded. No one could have predicted her vehement and impassioned response. "Have you had an abortion? I have, and I think I earned the right to be an expert on the topic." No student should ever be thrust into this kind of situation.

School is no place for rules that reflect the attitude that students cannot be experts. Russell Stovall, by the time he had reached Cooper High School, Abilene, Texas, had already syndicated his news column, "Whiz Kid," in national newspapers, appeared on Johnny Carson, and knew more about computers than 98 percent of the faculty. He was an acknowledged expert. Consider the expertise of this young writer:

⚕ Arthritis and Rheumatism: The Common Chronic Cripplers

"Twisted," "distorted," "grotesque": these are harsh words to say about someone I love, but they create an image of his body. I can see the pain in his eyes. He has trouble doing things that seem trivial to the rest of us. He seems like another man—feeble and old.

Although the memory is vague, I still remember when he was a strong, hard-working farmer. He used to lift me up to the tractor seat and let me help plow. After all the chores were finished, it was time for fun. On this farm was the world's best fishin' hole. When we would go there I got to ride in the back of the pickup. I did not really like fishing, but I would do anything to be with him. Perhaps he felt the same because he did not make me put those dirty worms on the hook or take those slimy fish off; he took care of that. Then something happened, he began to lose weight and his hands and feet became useless appendages. He would sit in his chair all day wringing his crippled hands, refusing any help. He had too much pride.

Once or twice after he became ill we went fishing—only this time it was different. Instead of riding in the back of the pickup, I drove. The truck had to be backed up to the porch so that he would only have to exert a minimum amount of effort. We would slowly drive to the tank, being careful not to hit any hard bumps. When there, he would slowly creep up the ramp that had been specially built. It took a great deal for me to bait his hook with worms and take the fish off, but being unable to do these things himself, it was up to me to do the dirty work.

What kind of illness could be so bad that it could totally disable my grandfather? A common disease. Usually not thought of as a chronic crippler, arthritis crippled him. Arthritis stole my grandfather.

Arthritis, rheumatism, and gout are among the oldest diseases known to affect human beings. Even before the time of Hippocrates, evidence of the occurrence of the disease had been found in mummies and other ancient civilizations....

The writer of this research has good reason to search for answers to her questions about arthritis. She considers them in her conclusion. "Will I become a victim like my grandfather?" How absurd it would be if she were to write, "Will *one* become a victim like *one's* grandfather?" Taking the first person out of research is to distance the discoverer from what she is discovering. Practices that promote this type of distanced writing are bound to produce perfectly bland papers, contested grades, hostility, and reluctance to or avoidance of research.

HOW IS RESEARCH USED IN EDUCATION AND TESTING?

In light of Bruner's work on the narrative being key to meaning and learning, one must continue to question what state departments of education and testing companies, with their isolated divisions devoted to assessment, read. Do they know Bruner? Do they care? How, in the light of such prestigious and credible scholarship, can they continue to test students in the manner that neuters the voice from the writing? These test-makers continue to produce tests that require elementary students to step outside their personal narratives to describe a clown with a bird on its shoulder in counterclockwise organization. Or worse yet, the topic a high school neighbor shared. "We were given the dumbest topic on the face of the earth. We were supposed to write about whether or not a teenage father should be responsible for his child. Some of the guys in my homeroom thought they were supposed to write about fathers of teenagers taking care of the kids. The only thing I could think of to write was that my father would kill me if I became a teenage father, so I wouldn't have to worry about it." Will the testing companies and state departments receive a score that genuinely reflects this young man's writing ability? Yet these scores affect his future. Will the students who do not master the writing prompt be considered poor writers when they are asked to write out of their contexts and contrary to all the research? There is no question whether to test students' writing abilities. Student and school accountability should be established, but questions need to be asked about the research upon which the testing is based. Perhaps it is fair to ask how these institutions do their research. What answers might they give teachers, students, and parents in response to these questions?

Don Graves said in a conversation, "Research is another form of fiction." He was speaking specifically about how the authorship of writing research affects the way the writer records such research. But consider his words out of context. Consider them in a literal sense — research is fiction. What fiction spawns a type of testing that does not allow students to write from themselves and their expertise?

Linda Rief knows this frustration. She describes what happened when her middle school received a test from a district-hired testing service.

> I read the "rules." ... I opened the booklet. There was a picture: two muskrats, one dressed as a man, one as a woman. The muskrats were posed on a hill, a castle in the background, a picnic blanket spread on the ground before them. The female muskrat was posed seductively on the blanket, the male muskrat standing over her. Both held what appeared to be champagne glasses, toasting each other....
>
> I was furious. My colleagues were appalled. We cut the picture and question out of each test booklet. On Monday morning we handed out the writing sample test and posed our own question: "Write about anything you care deeply about. Try to convince the reader how much you care." We complied with the other conditions.
>
> I don't know what happened at the scoring session. I was too angry to participate. We were not fired. Our students were not blocked from entering high school. I did write a letter to the testing company. I argued vehemently about the inadequacies and inappropriateness of such a test, with suggestions about better ways for testing actual instructional methods and beliefs of what real writers do. No one responded to my letter. (121)

No wonder Rief used Donald M. Murray's quote in her book, "We should be seeking diversity, not proficient mediocrity" (vi). No wonder she titled her book *Seeking Diversity*.

THE I-SEARCH PAPER

Ken Macrorie in *Searching Writing* details his steps for having students write the I-Search Paper. The I-Search Paper is an alternative to the research paper, which he feels "are bad jokes. They're funny because they pretend to be so much and actually are so little" (161). He says a search should be done when someone wants to answer a question. He feels that the I-Search is beyond the abilities of elementary and middle school students. Because this text is intended not only for elementary and middle school teachers, but also for high school teachers, it is recommended that those interested in learning more about the I-Search read his book.

PERSONAL INQUIRIES

Consider what students of all ages are capable of doing. They are capable of discovering information about a topic they already know something about, or want to discover. They are capable of asking questions and following leads—regardless of their ages.

No one really needs to write a "research" paper, instead they need to engage in personal inquiry. Students and teachers need to drop the adherence to outdated, unjustifiable ideas such as footnotes, errors, patient study, a specific number of sources, outlines, and notecards. Real inquiry is a way for students to discover, rediscover, uncover, and document. Figure 13.5 presents a step-by-step approach to conducting an inquiry.

Fig. 13.5. Inquiry in a box.

Teacher Steps	Student Steps
1. Begin by asking students to brainstorm or list what they know. After they have mulled their ideas around, ask students to consider what they want to know more about, basing their "curiosity to know" on real needs.	1. Record what you want to know more about and place in a box. (The box is also for storing other items, as described in the following steps.)
2. Teach students how to find the core issues of their inquiry. Encourage students to explore.	2. Find the core issues to record and place in the box.
	3. Make a list of people, experts, and places to find possible answers to inquiries.
4. Tell students that they may not yet know what they can or cannot use in their inquiry.	4. Interview the experts. Ask the experts where they go for answers. Ask which books, magazines, and tapes, for example, helped them know what they know. Record these and place in the box.
	5. Collect all the information possible and place in the box.
6. Teach students about hunches, how to follow a hunch, what to do if the hunch pays off, and what to do if the hunch is a dead end.	6. Record your hunches.
7. Invite students to go back and reinterview the experts. This time they will know more about their inquiry.	7. Reinterview experts.

(Figure 13.5 continues on page 436.)

Fig. 13.5 *(continued)*

Teacher Steps	Student Steps
8. Teach students how to observe and collect information. Place these in the box.	8. Place observation and information in the box.
9. Teach students how to make and conduct surveys and questionnaires.	9. Use surveys and questionnaires when your inquiry needs it.
10. Have students store all the information gathered in the box. Nothing should be dismissed as insignificant or trivial. The box at this point should be filling up with all types of information.	10. Test some of the information gathered to see if another person agrees or disagrees. Write down the results.
11. Encourage the use of people and books. Teach students to trust their inquiry. Show students how one definitive source may be all they need, but that if information is lacking, they need to inquire further.	11. Find your sources to record and place in the box. Copy articles, make tape recordings, and so on to go in the box.
	12. Tape the box shut.
	13. Take time to prewrite about your topic, leaving the box sealed. Write everything you now know about your inquiry.
14. Move students through the writing process. As they move into the process of revision, teach them how to use the information in the box to support what they have to say.	14. Open the box and use your research to help write and revise your inquiries.
15. Teach students how to document the source(s) used in their drafts.	15. Document your sources.
16. Move the students through the rest of the writing process.	
17. Encourage students to make this process a lifelong inquiry, one they can use for any personal inquiry they may have.	
18. Share your personal inquiry process with the students.	

A first-grader may need to know about the right kinds of fish for his fish tank, whereas a fourth-grader may need to know the types of dance and dance instructors available for lessons. A group of middle school students shared their list of need-to-know items:

How come if we don't feel good about ourselves we are told, "You have a poor self-concept." But if we do feel good about ourselves we're told, "You're being arrogant."

How do adults see us? They tell us to be responsible, but won't let us do anything.

Why is it easier for people to see what we do wrong, rather than what we do right?

Everyone asks, "What are you going to be when you grow up?" How do we find out this answer?

Ministers and parents tell us money isn't everything, but why do they want us to be doctors instead of working for the Peace Corps?

Where does racial tension come from?

Why are there homeless children in our city, and homeless children along the border of Texas and Mexico when our government spends millions and sends troops to foreign countries, but it doesn't send anyone to help us?

Why are there neglected and abused children?

Why do we have to be latchkey kids?

The government spends millions to save the savings in loans, but we see pictures on the news of schools in L.A. that are falling down. Isn't our future worth more than a failed savings in loan?

Why do adults think middle school students don't know anything?

When the principal asked our opinion about teaming and we gave it, why were we told it was wrong?

Encourage students to explore. Often it is a good idea to let students spend time looking at books. The personal inquiry does not have to be a dry, dull process. Instead it can be a lively exchange and discovery of ideas. Every brain engages in inquiry everyday—the brain does not care if it is in the body of a six-year-old or an eighteen-year-old. Because this activity is already happening daily, teachers can have their students participate in natural personal inquiry.

DOCUMENTATION FORMS

Currently the major method of documentation is internal documentation (this text, for example, uses internal documentation). It is easily recognizable by the author's name and page number between the parentheses, for example, (Carroll 93). Notice that some of the articles reprinted in this book use the older and more difficult to manage style of footnotes and endnotes. Nothing is as frustrating as typing a page only to have the last four words of the footnote hanging off the bottom. Internal documentation, whether the style of the MLA (Modern Language Association) or APA (American Psychological Association), eliminates much of the cumbersome mechanics of citing references. If the sole reason for having students do research is because they will need it "next year," then no wonder students throw up their hands in frustration. As Larson points out in the article reprinted on pages 441-449, different teachers and different disciplines have distinct documentation styles. Trying to second-guess what students will need next year is like throwing a handful of beans at a door hoping one will go into the keyhole. It is important that students learn that other documentation styles exist; they will be better served if they learn one consistent, workable documentation style. If they learn one style well, then they can master others independently. Then it becomes the students' responsibility to find out what style the teacher or the discipline requires and to use it.

SEXIST LANGUAGE

Generally, there is no place in writing for sexist language. Sexist language reflects attitudes that are better left unstated. The problem is that English has no singular neuter pronoun that refers to persons. "It" insults humanity; "he" ignores half the human race. Most writers try to rephrase in the plural to avoid this dilemma. Sometimes, however, rephrasing does not solve the sexist language reference and the singular pronoun must be used. When this occurs it is preferable to use "he or she" or "he/she." Occasionally, the use of "s/he" is found.

Some authors will cite the name of a student that clearly has a gender and use the pronoun accordingly (although persons with names like Joyce Kilmer become problematic with this approach). Literature is full of examples of women writers who have used male names for subtle and not-so-subtle reasons of sexism, e.g., George Eliot and Acton, Ellis and Clive Bell (the Brontes) to name a few. At a time when, as Tillie Olsen points out, one out of twelve published writers are men; at a time when intolerance to race, color, and creed is aberrant and undignified; at a time when cultural diversity is celebrated, there is little to gain by adhering to outdated language conventions as embodied in sexist language.

Authors who write about all principals as "he's," all teachers as "she's," and all students as "he's," need to change. Language changes. Just as the "thou" and "thee" of the Puritan era has been replaced, so should sexist language be replaced. (Of course, nonsexist language can be taken to extremes; as editorials and jokes remind readers, "humanhole covers" for "manhole covers" strike the reader or listener as humorous.) While laughter and the ability to laugh at ourselves are admirable human traits, it is not a laughing matter when sexist language bias becomes imbedded in the psyche of students.

Sexist attitudes, like cultural bias, are changing in schools, and the effective teacher and writer will want to stay informed of these changes by using a current grammar handbook or guidebook. For an excellent guide consider *The Handbook of Nonsexist Writing: For Writers, Editors and Speakers* by Casey Miller and Kate Swift. They state,

> The reason the practice of assigning masculine gender to neutral terms is so enshrined in English is that every language reflects the prejudices of the society in which it evolved, and English evolved through most of its history in a male-centered, patriarchal society. We shouldn't be surprised, therefore, that its vocabulary and grammar reflect attitudes that exclude or demean women. But we are surprised, for until recently few people thought much about what English — or any other language for that matter — was saying on a subliminal level. Now that

we have begun to look, some startling things have become obvious. What stan-dard English usage says about males, for example, is that they are the species. What it says about females is that they are a subspecies. From these two asser-tions flow a thousand other enhancing and degrading messages, all encoded in the language we in the English-speaking countries begin to learn almost as soon as we are born. (4)

Writers recognize the changes in language and the need for nonsexist writing. Margaret Donaldson writes in the preface of her book, *Children's Minds,*

While the word "child" does not convey any information as to sex, there is no similarly neutral personal pronoun in English. I have followed here, though not without some heart-searching, the tradition of using the masculine form *he* when a neutral sense is intended. It is particularly desirable when one is speaking of education not to suggest that boys are somehow more important. The arguments in this book apply equally to boys and to girls. (x)

Donaldson is keenly aware of the bias reflected in language. As educators move to the twenty-first century, as language continues to change, the need for changing with language becomes more and more apparent.

As teachers write for other audiences and as teachers have their students write for publication, they will want to teach precision of language. "To go on using in its former sense a word whose meaning has changed is counterproductive. The point is not that we should recognize semantic change, but that in order to be precise, in order to be understood, we must" (Miller and Swift 8). Nonsexist language is just that, more precise.

CONCLUSION

Earlier in this chapter, the work of Jerome Bruner was used to support the narrative in writing. Macrorie would agree. In *Searching Writing* he writes, "The most fundamental mode of human communication is telling stories" (98). Ending this chapter on research it seems appropriate to be reminded of the validity of the story. As Willa Cather says in *O Pioneers!*, "There are only two or three human stories, and they go on repeating themselves as fiercely as if they had never happened before." Inquiry is finding these stories—that's the truth in inquiry.

WORKS CITED

Bruner, Jerome. *Acts of Meaning.* Cambridge, MA: Harvard University Press, 1990.

Carroll, Joyce Armstrong. "Plagiarism: The Unfun Game." *English Journal* (September 1982): 92-95.

_____. "TV and Term Papers." *English Journal* (October 1985): 85-86.

Cather, Willa. *O Pioneers!* New York: Viking Penguin, 1989.

Donaldson, Margaret. *Children's Minds.* New York: W. W. Norton, 1978.

Gill, Michael. "The Eyes of the Beholder." In *Commentarius 1987*, edited by Megan Hawkins and Scott O'Hara. Pp. 62-64. Abilene, TX: O. H. Cooper High School, 1987.

Macrorie, Ken. *Searching Writing: A Contextbook.* Rochelle Park, NJ: Hayden Book, 1980.

_____. *Telling Writing.* New York: Hayden Book, 1970.

_____. *Writing to Be Read*. Rochelle Park, NJ: Hayden Book, 1968, 1976.

Miller, Casey, and Kate Swift. *The Handbook of Nonsexist Writing: For Writers, Editors and Speakers*. New York: Harper & Row, 1980, 1988.

Rief, Linda. *Seeking Diversity*. Portsmouth, NH: Heinemann Educational Books, 1992.

Romano, Tom. *Clearing the Way*. Portsmouth, NH: Heinemann Educational Books, 1987.

"The 'Research Paper' in the Writing Course: A Non-Form of Writing"

RICHARD L. LARSON

(From *College English*, December 1982. Copyright 1982 by the
National Council of Teachers of English. Reprinted with permission.)

Let me begin by assuring you that I do not oppose the assumption that student writers in academic and professional settings, whether they be freshmen or sophomores or students in secondary school or intend to be journalists or lawyers or scholars or whatever, should engage in research. I think they should engage in research, and that appropriately informed people should help them learn to engage in research in whatever field these writers happen to be studying. Nor do I deny the axiom that writing should incorporate the citation of the writer's sources of information when those sources are not common knowledge. I think that writers must incorporate into their writing the citation of their sources—and they must also incorporate the thoughtful, perceptive evaluation of those sources and of the contribution that those sources might have made to the writer's thinking. Nor do I oppose the assumption that a writer should make the use of appropriate sources a regular activity in the process of composing. I share the assumption that writers should identify, explore, evaluate, and draw upon appropriate sources as an integral step in what today we think of as the composing process.

In fact, let me begin with some positive values. On my campus, the Department of English has just decided to request a change in the description of its second-semester freshman course. The old description read as follows:

> This course emphasizes the writing of formal analytic essays and the basic methods of research common to various academic disciplines. Students will write frequently in and out of class. By the close of the semester, students will demonstrate mastery of the formal expository essay and the research paper. Individual conferences.

The department is asking our curriculum committee to have the description read:

Commentary

Teaching research does not happen only in the traditional sense of a research paper. Research should be an ongoing activity rather than an event undertaken once a year and usually during one entire marking period.

Remember, this is a college course description, and while the change in course description is significant, it is also developmentally appropriate for that level. Inclusion here does not mean to suggest it is equally appropriate for middle school or high school, although documentation in authentic ways may be adapted to various levels. Informed curricula writers adjust their scope and sequence to lay foundations rather than to engage students in watered-down versions of college courses.

This course emphasizes the writing of analytical essays and the methods of inquiry common to various academic disciplines. Students will write frequently in and out of class. By the close of the semester, students will demonstrate their ability to write essays incorporating references to suitable sources of information and to use appropriate methods of documentation. Individual conferences.

I applauded the department for requesting that change, and I wrote to the college curriculum committee to say so.

While thinking about this paper — to take another positive example — I received from the University of Michigan Press a copy of the proofs of a forthcoming book titled *Researching American Culture: A Guide for Student Anthropologists*, sent to me because members of the English Composition Board of the University of Michigan had decided that the book might be of use as a supplementary text at Michigan in writing courses that emphasize writing in the academic disciplines. Along with essays by professional anthropologists presenting or discussing research in anthropology, the book includes several essays by students. In these essays the students, who had been instructed and guided by faculty in anthropology, report the results of research they have performed on aspects of American culture, from peer groups in high school to connections between consumption of alcohol and tipping in a restaurant, to mortuary customs, to sports in America. If anyone was in doubt about the point, the collection demonstrates that undergraduate students can conduct and report sensible, orderly, clear, and informative research in the discipline of anthropology. I am here to endorse, indeed to applaud, such work, not to question the wisdom of such collections as that from Michigan or to voice reservations about the capacity of undergraduates for research.

Why, then, an essay whose title makes clear a deep skepticism about "research papers"? First, because I believe that the generic "research paper" as a concept, and as a form of writing taught in a department of English, is not defensible. Second, because I believe that by saying that we teach the "research paper" — that is, by acting as if there is a generic concept defensibly entitled the "research paper" — we mislead students about the

We have here a clear example of Vygotsky's zone of proximal development.

Again, learning research must take place within a context. Doing research because the curriculum guide says so is not helping students see the connections between research and what they are learning.

activities of both research and writing. I take up these propositions in order.

We would all agree to begin with, I think, that "research" is an activity in which one engages. Probably almost everyone reading this paper has engaged, at one time or another, in research. Most graduate seminars require research; most dissertations rely upon research, though of course many dissertations in English may also include analytical interpretation of texts written by one or more authors. Research can take many forms: systematically observing events, finding out what happens when one performs certain procedures in the laboratory, conducting interviews, tape-recording speakers' comments, asking human beings to utter aloud their thoughts while composing in writing or in another medium and noting what emerges, photographing phenomena (such as the light received in a telescope from planets and stars), watching the activities of people in groups, reading a person's letters and notes: all these are research. So, of course, is looking up information in a library or in newspaper files, or reading documents to which one has gained access under the Freedom of Information Act—though reading filed and catalogued documents is in many fields not the most important (it may be the least important) activity in which a "researcher" engages. We could probably define "research" generally as the seeking out of information new to the seeker, for a purpose, and we would probably agree that the researcher usually has to interpret, evaluate, and organize that information before it acquires value. And we would probably agree that the researcher has to present the fruits of his or her research, appropriately ordered and interpreted, in symbols that are intelligible to others, before that research can be evaluated and can have an effect. Most often, outside of mathematics and the sciences (and outside of those branches of philosophy that work with nonverbal symbolic notation), maybe also outside of music, that research is presented to others, orally or in writing, in a verbal language.

But research still is an activity; it furnishes the substance of much discourse and can furnish substance to almost any discourse except, possibly, one's personal reflections on one's own experience. But it is itself the subject—the substance—of no distinctively identifiable kind of writing. Research can inform

A challenge for English language arts teachers may be to brainstorm what would constitute research for the level they teach.

Preoccupation with card catalogs and guides to periodic literature is both antiquated and shortsighted. Teachers like Larson want to broaden the definition of research.

Consider the work of Donald Graves, Lucy McCormick Calkins, Tom Romano, and Nancie Atwell as examples of substantive research based primarily on personal observation taken systematically and organized in literate and interesting ways.

Consider, too, the difference between a research paper and research skills.

virtually any writing or speaking if the author wishes it to do so; there is nothing of substance or content that differentiates one paper that draws on data from outside the author's own self from another such paper—nothing that can enable one to say that this paper is a "research paper" and that paper is not. (Indeed even an ordered, interpretive reporting of altogether personal experiences and responses can, if presented purposively, be a reporting of research.) I would assert therefore that the so-called "research paper," as a generic, cross-disciplinary term, has no conceptual or substantive identity. If almost any paper is potentially a paper incorporating the fruits of research, the term "research paper" has virtually no value as an identification of a kind of substance in a paper. Conceptually, the generic term "research paper" is for practical purposes meaningless. We can not usefully distinguish between "research papers" and non-research papers; we can distinguish only between papers that should have incorporated the fruits of research but did not, and those that did incorporate such results, or between those that reflect poor or inadequate research and those that reflect good or sufficient research. I would argue that most undergraduate papers reflect poor or inadequate research, and that our responsibility ... should be to assure that each student reflect in each paper the appropriate research, wisely conducted, for his or her subject.

I have already suggested that "research" can take a wide variety of forms, down to and including the ordered presentation of one's personal reflections and the interpretations of one's most direct experiences unmediated by interaction with others or by reference to identifiably external sources. (The form of research on composing known as "protocol analysis," or even the keeping of what some teachers of writing designate as a "process journal," if conducted by the giver of the protocol or by the writer while writing, might be such research.) If research can refer to almost any process by which data outside the immediate and purely personal experiences of the writer are gathered, then I suggest that just as the so-called "research paper" has no conceptual or substantive identity, neither does it have a procedural identity; the term does not necessarily designate any particular kind of data nor any preferred procedure for gathering data. I would argue that the so-called "research paper," as ordinarily taught

At best, this is merely copying; at worse, it is plagiarism. Additionally, most elementary, middle, and high school libraries are inadequate. Sending students to university libraries results in either frustration on the students' part, or aggravation on the librarian's part, or both. Case in point: A high school student from an honors class was told to research every article in the Washington Post *related to the first 30 days of the Clinton presidency. The student sat at the microfilm reader in tears when she realized the enormity of the task. The college reference librarian finally walked off in disgust saying, "I don't know what your teacher wants."*

by the kinds of texts I have reviewed, implicitly equates "research" with looking up books in the library and taking down information from those books. Even if there [are goings on] in some departments of English instruction that [get] beyond those narrow boundaries, the customary practices that I have observed for guiding the "research paper" assume a procedural identity for the paper that is, I think, nonexistent.

As the activity of research can take a wide variety of forms, so the presentation and use of research within discourse can take a wide variety of forms. Indeed I cannot imagine any identifiable design that any scholar in rhetoric has identified as a recurrent plan for arranging discourse which cannot incorporate the fruits of research, broadly construed. I am not aware of any kind or form of discourse, or any aim, identified by any student of rhetoric or any theorist of language or any investigator of discourse theory, that is distinguished primarily — or to any extent — by the presence of the fruits of "research" in its typical examples. One currently popular theoretical classification of discourse, that by James Kinneavy (*A Theory of Discourse* [Englewood Cliffs, N.J.: Prentice-Hall, 1971]), identifies some "aims" of discourse that might seem to furnish a home for papers based on research: "referential" and "exploratory" discourse. But, as I understand these aims, a piece of discourse does not require the presence of results of ordered "research" in order to fit into either of these classes, even though discourse incorporating the results of ordered research might fit there — as indeed it might under almost any other of Kinneavy's categories, including the category of "expressive" discourse. (All discourse is to a degree "expressive" anyway.) The other currently dominant categorization of examples of discourse — dominant even over Kinneavy's extensively discussed theory — is really a categorization based upon plans that organize discourse: narration (of completed events, of ongoing processes, of possible scenarios), causal analysis, comparison, analogy, and so on. None of these plans is differentiated from other plans by the presence within it of fruits from research; research can be presented, so far as I can see, according to any of these plans. And if one consults Frank J. D'Angelo's *A Conceptual Theory of Rhetoric* (Cambridge, Mass.:

In this sentence Larson opens up research, which, unfortunately, has been too often viewed as a closed up activity.

Richard L. Larson is without peers as a scholar of integrity. He is equally respected by members of the Modern Language Association and the National Council of Teachers of English. That a professor of this caliber holds that the "research paper" has no formal, substantive, or procedural identity should give all teachers of English pause.

Once again, integration, not fragmentation, is the key.

First, it is interesting to note that Larson comfortably uses personal pronouns, and these personal pronouns in no way distract from the import of his meaning. Second, in 1990 I visited La Joya High School in La Joya ISD, La Joya, Texas. The students in Linda Garcia Perez's class had undertaken exciting research. They had interviewed the joyas *(jewels), that is, the older members of the*

Winthrop, 1975) one will not find, if my memory serves me reliably, any category of rhetorical plan or any fundamental human cognitive process—D'Angelo connects all rhetorical plans with human cognitive processes—that is defined by the presence of the fruits of research. If there is a particular rhetorical form that is defined by the presence of results from research, then, I have not seen an effort to define that form and to argue that the results of research are what identify it as a form. I conclude that the "research paper," as now taught, has no formal identity, as it has no substantive identity and no procedural identity.

For me, then, very little is gained by speaking about and teaching, as a generic concept, the so-called "research paper." If anything at all is gained, it is only the reminder that responsible writing normally depends on well-planned investigation of data. But much is lost by teaching the research paper in writing courses as a separately designated activity. For by teaching the generic "research paper" as a separate activity, instructors in writing signal to their students that there is a kind of writing that incorporates the results of research, and there are (by implication) many kinds of writing that do not and need not do so. "Research," students are allowed to infer, is a specialized activity that one engages in during a special course, or late in a regular semester or year, but that one does not ordinarily need to be concerned about and can indeed, for the most part, forget about. Designating the "research paper" as a separate project therefore seems to me to work against the purposes for which we allegedly teach the research paper: to help students familiarize themselves with ways of gathering, interpreting, drawing upon, and acknowledging data from outside themselves in their writing. By talking of the "research paper," that is, we undermine some of the very goals of our teaching.

We also meet two other, related difficulties. First, when we tend to present the "research paper" as in effect a paper based upon the use of the library, we misrepresent "research." Granted that a good deal of research in the field of literature is conducted in the library among books, much research that is still entitled to be called humanistic takes place outside the library. It can take place, as I mentioned earlier, wherever "protocol" research or writers' analyses of their composing processes take place: it can take place in the living room or study of an author who is being interviewed about his or her habits of working. It can take place in the home of an old farmer or rancher or weaver or potter who is telling a student about the legends or songs of his or her people, or about the historical process by which the speaker came from roots at home or abroad. Much research relies upon books, but books do not constitute the corpus of research data except possibly in one or two fields of study. If we teach the so-called "research paper" in such a way as to imply that all or almost all research is done in books and in libraries, we show our provincialism and degrade the research of many disciplines.

Second, though we pretend to prepare students to engage in the research appropriate to their chosen disciplines, we do not and cannot do so. Faculty in other fields may wish that we would relieve them of the responsibility of teaching their students to write about the research students do in those other fields, but I don't think that as teachers of English we can relieve them of that responsibility. Looking at the work of the students who contributed to the University of Michigan Press volume on *Researching American Culture*, I can't conceive myself giving useful direction to those students. I can't conceive myself showing them how to do the research they did, how to avoid pitfalls, assure representativeness of data, draw permissible inferences, and reach defensible conclusions. And, frankly, I can't conceive many teachers of English showing these students what they needed to know either. I can't conceive myself, or very many colleagues (other than trained teachers of technical writing) guiding a student toward a report of a scientific laboratory experiment that a teacher of science would find exemplary. I can't conceive myself or many colleagues guiding a student toward a well-designed experiment in psychology, with appropriate safeguards and controls and wise interpretation of quantitative and nonquantitative information. In each of these fields (indeed probably in each academic field) the term "research paper" may have some meaning—quite probably a meaning different from its meaning in other fields. Students in different fields do write papers reporting research. We in English have no

community, about their experiences. They were encouraged to note facial expressions and capture direct dialogue. Most students worked with tape recorders. The results were bound together in an anthology entitled Our Town, Nuestro Pueblo, which won 2d place in the national Arts and Entertainment 1990 Teacher Grant Competition, May 14, 1990, in Washington, D.C. As I read through Monica A. Gonzalez's account of her great aunt's memories of picking cotton, Miguel Ramos's interview with his grandfather who was paid seventy-five cents a day pruning orange trees, or Noralisa Leo's essay, "The Medicis of La Joya," I was struck with the individual style of each writer as he or she documented the data of their interviewee. The results were poignant, sometimes sad, often humorous, but always interesting. I couldn't put the anthology down. I even requested a copy to share with other teachers. Beside this rich book of heritage sat the students' other research. These papers were on such topics as John Donne's metaphysical poetry and the use of symbolism in the collected works of D. H. Lawrence. I randomly selected a few to read. Style, voice, and verve were gone. Lifeless prose, obviously copied from much too advanced scholarly works, rose up to greet me. At the end of the day, I stood with the anthology in one hand and the "research papers" in the other. "Do you see any difference?" I asked Linda. Of course she had. And it is doubtful that Linda as teacher-researcher will ever put her students through the generic research paper again.

If Julie as a third-grader (page 424) was able to research her name, and Audrey and Leah as first-graders (page 425) were able to research mice, most certainly students on all levels are capable of research and should, in Larson's words, "be required to say, from evidence, why they believe what they assert."

We have often said that this cogent article by Larson should be photocopied (with permission, of course) and dropped by crop dusters over schools across the nation.

business claiming to teach "research" when research in different academic disciplines works from distinctive assumptions and follows distinctive patterns of inquiry. Such distinctions in fact are what differentiate the disciplines. Most of us are trained in one discipline only and should be modest enough to admit it.

But let me repeat what I said when I started: that I don't come before you to urge that students of writing need not engage in "research." I think that they should engage in research. I think they should understand that in order to function as educated, informed men and women they have to engage in research, from the beginning of and throughout their work as writers. I think that they should know what research can embrace, and I think they should be encouraged to view research as broadly, and conduct it as imaginatively, as they can. I think they should be held accountable for their opinions and should be required to say, from evidence, why they believe what they assert. I think that they should be led to recognize that data from "research" will affect their entire lives, and that they should know how to evaluate such data as well as to gather them. And I think they should know their responsibilities for telling their listeners and readers where their data came from.

What I argue is that the profession of the teaching of English should abandon the concept of the generic "research paper"—that form of what a colleague of mine has called "messenger service" in which a student is told that for this one assignment, this one project, he or she has to go somewhere (usually the library), get out some materials, make some notes, and present them to the customer neatly wrapped in footnotes and bibliography tied together according to someone's notion of a style sheet. I argue that the generic "research paper," so far as I am familiar with it, is a concept without an identity, and that to teach it is not only to misrepresent research but also quite often to pander to the wishes of faculty in other disciplines that we spare them a responsibility that they must accept. Teaching the generic "research paper" often represents a misguided notion of "service" to other departments. The best service we can render to those departments and to the students themselves, I would argue, is to insist that students recognize their continuing responsibility for looking attentively at their experiences; for seeking out, wherever it can be found, the information they need for the development of their ideas; and for putting such data at the service of every piece they write. That is one kind of service we can do to advance students' humanistic and liberal education.

This kind of service best serves democracy.

CHAPTER

14

ASSESSING WRITING
Ways to Grade, Test, and Evaluate

> We are talking about two incompatible models of education.
> The difference between the factory model, which uses tests,
> and the "community of learners" model, which uses assessments,
> is like the difference between the Ptolemaic and the Copernican views
> of the universe. As in all paradigm shifts, changed relationships
> rearrange the value system.
> — Ruth Mitchell☐

As teachers change how they teach students, they need to change how they evaluate students. Making a paradigm shift from product to process in everything but evaluation will only set up disharmony and acrimony. Instead, as teachers make the shift to learning processes, not only in writing but also in reading, thinking, listening, speaking, and viewing, they need to shift how they judge and ultimately grade the work done by students. Evaluation is an extension of pedagogy and therefore should match its philosophy. If a teacher is learner-centered, then evaluation must also be learner-centered. There is no place in the new paradigm for "I gotcha." Of course, making such a shift in evaluation is just as demanding as making the shift in teaching.

But it can be done. It must be done. Grading practices from the old paradigm have established a host of myths that teachers, students, and parents have had to grapple with as pedagogy changes. Consider these myths.

MYTHS ABOUT GRADING, TESTING, AND EVALUATION

Grading practices are even harder to change than are teaching practices. It is often difficult for teachers to even begin to consider other ways of evaluating student knowledge, performance, and potential when for years testing and grading have been propelled by state assessments, textbooks, district mandates, and habit. Nowhere in education is the lament "But we've always done it this way!" more true.

Myth 1: Tests Tell What Students Know

In the big game show of life, the buzzer signals a resounding NO! to the first myth. Even the best tests can show only a portion of what a student knows. Considering the breakthroughs in cognition, brain theory, and multiple intelligences, not to mention the preponderance of rapidly growing and changing information, it seems myopic to think that a test, or even several tests, could produce an accurate picture of any one student's knowledge.

In addition, there are the problems of the tests themselves. Most tests successfully teach students how to fill in blanks, match items in a series, or bubble in a computer-readable grading sheet. These are often norm-referenced tests, i.e., the student taking the test is graded against a standard, usually derived by calculating an average from a pilot group. Some administrators — perhaps in imitation of commercially produced norm-referenced tests, or in an effort to develop so-called standards, or out of some misplaced notion that standardized testing will produce standardized teaching — require that blanket tests be given every six weeks on a designated day by every member of a department. These administrators seem to assume that all students learn the same way and that all teachers teach the same way. These tests are designed as if teaching is a pouring of information into students and that learning is exteriorized when the students regurgitate that information on paper. Many call this the "jug and mug" theory; others call it "sit and get." This attitude toward tests seems to ignore recent research that finds learning an active, distinctive, and incredibly complicated process.

Some of these tests are ancient relics left by a retired teacher who taught Shakespeare, Beowulf, or Chaucer. Some are testimonials to a group of dedicated teachers who worked hours pounding out items, quotes, and true or false statements (most of which were not quite true) to check students' comprehension of discrete bits of information — as if identifying Polyphemus as a member of the race of Cyclopes is somehow more important in the scheme of things than understanding the lesson Homer conveys in that section of *The Odyssey*, as if drawing a line from the letter *B* to a ball tells more about the student's knowledge of letters than if the student writes a story and uses the letter correctly. Proponents of these tests often use words like *standards, basics, scope and sequence, aligned curriculum*, and *core information* to support this type of testing.

How often are teachers surprised when a productive, spirited student does poorly on a test? How often, when scores are returned from outside agencies, are teachers shocked when the most intelligent student receives the lowest score?

> *When I taught fifth grade, I noticed a pattern with Diana. She was an eager learner, attentive, and smart, but she was absent every test-taking day. So I approached her mother. "Diana becomes physically ill if she knows she will have a test. I'm taking her to the doctor. He said he could prescribe tranquilizers."*
>
> *"That won't be necessary. Diana will not have to take any more tests in my classroom. I'll find another way to evaluate her." I talked to the school administration, arguing that we should not be in the business of causing students to take otherwise unnecessary medication. I won.*
>
> *And so, long before writing folders became commonplace, Diana kept one. In science she worked experiments, in social studies she worked projects, and in mathematics I took her daily work. It was not long before I began evaluating all the fifth-graders that way.*

Tests and what students know do not always coincide. Perhaps this could be remedied by combining norm-referenced tests and performance-based tests, tests that are ongoing and multi-dimensional. Consider the policy of the Canadian Council of Teachers of English: "The teacher's judgement must be the main determiner of the performance of his/her students, and he/she will employ a variety of measures and observations to inform that judgement. Tests or examinations extrinsic to the classroom should play only a subordinate role in any determination of student achievement" (27).

In truth, tests usually tell more about what the test maker knows, what the test maker got from the material, or what the test maker wants the students to know than they tell about what students have learned. One telling addition to test making might be gained by engaging students in the process to some degree.

Myth 2: Grammar Is Not Graded by Those Who Teach Writing as a Process

This myth seems to come from two groups. The first group is composed of those who were never secure with their own grasp of grammar. They are so insecure about usage and parts of speech that they avoid grammar instruction altogether. They do not even teach it in isolation. They use writing as a process to cover their insufficient knowledge. They know that if they teach writing as a process, they will have to interact spontaneously with the student on the matter of grammar. The second group objects to teaching writing as a process because it minimizes worksheets and exercises in grammar books. These are the ones who teach the 16-week grammar and usage unit in isolation. They bemoan the status of written expression and the fact that today's students cannot write. Yet, they continue to teach as they always have taught, failing or refusing to see the connection between students' failure to write and their teaching methods. Because they like their 16 weeks of grammar — easy to teach, easy to grade (there is only one possible answer in the key) — they attack writing as a process on the front line of grammar and grading, knowing this attack will garner the most attention. Grammar carries with it an aura of anxiety, and these teachers fail to understand that with writing as a process, grammar is taught within process as a part of the process. The logic of teachers in this group goes something like this: if grammar is not *the* instruction, then there must not be *any* instruction. They provide themselves, therefore, with a rationale for returning to worksheets and textbook exercises while claiming teachers who teach writing as a process do not teach or grade grammar.

Nothing can be farther from the truth. Of course grammar is graded in the writing process. But grammar is not the *only* thing graded. For too many years the only items marked on a paper were grammar mistakes. This history of marking up papers leads to the third myth.

Myth 3: Grading Means Marking Up a Paper

Teachers who hold to this myth liberally use the abbreviations, *awk, frag, sp, ww* with numerical equivalents for every mistake. In some instances the resulting grade can be a negative one. They play the game "take-away," subtracting not only points but self-esteem, security of expression, and love of writing.

Young students react to the papers joylessly, whereas older students react as if being turned down the third time for the prom. They generally do not even read the marks on the paper, unless it is to challenge a grade. They neither study the lexicon nor analyze the marks, nor do they seem to learn from the marks since they often repeat them on subsequent papers. Sometimes after a cursory glance at the grade, they demonstrate their hostility to the entire procedure by tossing their paper in the trash.

Research by the National Council of Teachers of English shows that teachers spend from five to twenty minutes correcting each paper, which adds up to weekends of drudgery. Because well-meaning teachers want students to benefit from their work, not trash it, they sometimes require a redo. "Rewrite the paper. Correct the mistakes, and I will raise your grade." Although some students choose this route, mechanically changing the writing according to all the teacher's marks, many refuse to do even that.

Some parents believe that teachers who mark all over papers are the skilled, dedicated teachers. That may have been true when learning was viewed as a discipline of the body as well as of the mind, but today these teachers are slightly out of step. They have not kept abreast of the latest research on how students learn. They do not realize that grammar is metalinguistic and abstract and cannot be learned until the brain is ready to process abstractions in certain ways. They do not realize that marking every grammar error on a paper is not teaching grammar concepts but creating subterfuge. All the marks lead students to think they are supposed to be learning grammar, which ultimately leads them to wonder why they are having difficulty, which finally leads them to say, "I'm no good in grammar. I hate writing." Because parents have only their own school experiences to gauge what they think should be happening at school, they sometimes make erroneous assumptions.

Consider the message a marked-up paper sends to the writer. If writing is self-exposure, as Murray contends; if writing is a sign of the mind at work; if writing is ownership; if writing is an outgrowth of a learning community; if writing shows the thought, dreams, and ideas of a writer, then what right does any other person have to mark the self, mind, thoughts, and dreams of that writer? Teachers rarely deface a student's artwork; why would they spoil a student's writing? Art and writing are just different symbolizing systems. Instead of a watercolor, still life, or pastel bucolic scene to express the artist's thoughts, the writer uses words. Are these words less valuable than brush strokes? Because each writer claims ownership of his or her words, the teacher does not have the right, duty, or mission to mark directly on the paper.

Alternatives to marking a student's paper include the conference and self-adhesive notes. The one-, two-, or three-minute conference with a student is often equal in value to all the red marginalia. Students better internalize help rendered in a conference because that help is usually clearer and more specific than cryptic notations on paper. Also, students have the opportunity after the one-on-one exchange to make changes while the changes still count for something. Self-adhesive notes are effective for pointing out certain things to students without marring their papers. Skilled teachers devise ways for students to retain the notes to prevent similar mistakes in ensuing papers.

Myth 4: It Takes Longer to Grade Writing

If the teacher insists on believing and practicing myth 3, then it does take a long time to grade each and every error. This grading is called "atomistic" because not even the tiniest slip-up or the most minute mistake escapes the watchful eye and red pen of the teacher.

But time does not have to be the ogre of grading writing. When teachers incorporate all the strategies and pedagogies associated with writing as a process, students' papers go through many drafts, peer grouping, teacher conferences, and some type of final editing, such as clocking. During that process, most, if not all, of the stylistic infelicities are corrected by the writer. This means the teacher may spend time considering the quality of content, the organization, and the rhetoric of the writing. Further, the teacher who grades the paper will interact with the paper's meaning. Instead of marking the paper, the teacher has a dialectic with the writer through the writing. The teacher responds to what is being said; the teacher and student work at appropriating each other's meaning.

Peter Elbow states, "It's not a question of whether we like evaluation.... Besides, we couldn't learn without feedback.... There are two purposes [of evaluation]. The first is to provide the audience with an accurate evaluation of the student's performance.... The second function of evaluation is to help the student to the condition where he can evaluate his own performance accurately: teacher grades should wither away in importance if not in fact" (167).

Myth 5: Evaluation Must Take Place in the Form of a Test

Adherents to this myth believe everything can be reduced to a test. Effort and processes become lost. Writing also suffers. Teacher observations, student self-evaluations, peer evaluations, and parent evaluations are unwarranted in this system—the test does it all.

This myth dismisses John Dewey's idea of reflection. Why reflect on what the student has done, how the student has done the task, or why the student embarked on the learning when a multiple-choice test can be graded in 15 minutes?

The believers of this myth also believe that tests tell what students know. As previously stated, a single test can never be an accurate judge of what a student knows. Nor is evaluation possible only through a test.

Myth 6: Standardized Tests Accurately Measure Students' Learning

Some state departments and legislative bodies believe that one test can prove whether a student has learned what is taught. They believe that the only way to evaluate the return on tax dollars is by administering tests, which, of course, cost tax dollars. They hire testing companies to make these tests, score them, and report the results. Testing companies, nonexistent 100 years ago, make millions because others believe this myth. Consider these two examples: (1) the state of Texas spent $23 million on student testing for the 1991-92 school year, and (2) the Educational Testing Service (ETS), which was founded in 1947, is the largest private testing service in the United States. Its revenues for the fiscal year ending June 30, 1992, were $342 million.

Professor S. Alan Cohen of the University of San Francisco, levels strong criticism on standardized tests in his provocative monograph *Tests: Marked for Life?* He repeatedly questions the reliability and validity of commercially published norm-referenced standardized tests (NRSTs), where scores are compared or referenced to some norm, and concludes, "They usually don't test what we think they test, and test users misinterpret their results: a *validity* problem. Or the scores are inaccurate, but test users act as if they're not: a *reliability* problem" (13). He believes that criterion-referenced tests (CRTs), where scores are referenced to what was actually taught, are more effective and humane.

Working from the perspective of reading assessment, researchers Hoopfer and Hunsberger list many criticisms resulting from studies of standardized tests. Concerns range from ambiguity, test bias, and lack of objectivity to lack of breadth and depth of content. They point out that thinking too deeply is often penalized and that usually there is a decontextualization of the test situation. And, like Cohen, they question the limits of the certainty of assessment and the foisting of adult reality on children and the assumption that learning is alike for all students (103-119).

Mike Dilena and Jane Leaker share what some teachers think of standardized tests. "These tests are often a test of test-taking skills (i.e., the ability to perform quite tricky tasks) as much as a test of authentic reading and writing" (36). In truth, one wonders at the validity and reliability of these tests when the only ones who seem to validate them are the testing companies themselves.

Howard Gardner writes, "The test is the ultimate scholastic invention, a 'decontextualized measure' to be employed in a setting that is itself decontextualized. Students learn about scientific principles or distant lands while sitting at their desks reading a book or listening to a lecture; then, at the end of the week, the month, the year, or their school careers, the same students enter a room and, without benefit of tests or notes, answer questions about the material that they are supposed to have mastered" (132-133). Gardner maintains that "formal testing has moved much too far in the direction of assessing knowledge of questionable importance in ways that show little transportability. The understanding that schools ought to inculcate is virtually invisible on such instruments; quite different forms of assessment need to be implemented if we are to document student understandings" (134).

Myth 7: Students Cannot Accurately Self-Assess

Because most students find tests a source of anxiety, as well as nonlearning events, they feel unempowered by the tests. In fact, tests often cause students to build a negative view of themselves in relation to evaluation. This negative view erodes the effectiveness of any classroom practice. However, if students were part of evaluation, they might not feel disenfranchised from the process. Madeline Hunter suggests that "students judge their achievement by comparison with their own past record or with comparable students who have the same learning task and probability of success" (5). And while more research is needed in self-assessment, the niggling question remains: Who has more right to a voice in their evaluation than the students themselves?

If students become involved in self-assessments, classrooms can become learning communities where everyone effectively affects the performance of the community of learners. In such a classroom the infrastructure will have been laid for a genuine partnership to develop between the learner and the teacher.

Peter Elbow says, "There are two sources of increased trustworthiness in student evaluations. First, the student knows more than the teacher does about what and how she learned—even if she knows less about what was taught. Second, even though the student's account *might* be skewed— by her failure to understand the subject matter, or by her self-interest, or (what is in fact more frequent) by her underestimation of self—if you read that account *in combination* with the teacher's account, you can usually draw a remarkably trustworthy conclusion about what the student actually learned and how skilled she is. Because there are two perceivers and because they are using natural language rather than numbers, there is remarkably rich internal evidence that usually permits the reader to see *through* any contradictions and skewings to what was really going on" (226).

WAYS TO EVALUATE WRITING

There is little if any real consensus by practitioners of English language arts regarding terms like *grading, testing, measuring, scoring,* and *assessing.* Lumped in most minds as evaluating, recent work in how these methods evaluate writing and the teaching of writing can help teachers differentiate the methods by definition and purpose. Books as comprehensive as *Evaluating Writing* by Charles Cooper and Lee Odell and *Teaching and Assessing Writing* by Edward M. White, and as specific as *Portfolio Portraits*, edited by Donald H. Graves and Bonnie S. Sunstein, help hone the theory of evaluating writing for practical application in the classroom. But evaluation of any kind consistently emerges as a problem.

Grading

Grading students' work is typically done by teachers and is usually numerical. Sometimes districts require a certain number of grades in a subject per marking period. These grades are determined subjectively, as it is usually the teacher who establishes the criteria and judges the work accordingly. Grades pose a dilemma for both teachers and students.

Consider what Jim Corder, professor at Texas Christian University, says of his dilemma:

> I have *not* learned what to do about grades. The chairperson, the dean, the registrar all think that there should be grades assigned at the end of the semester. So do the students. I do not. Especially in writing classes, I think that about all I should indicate at term's end is, "Hey, neat work, I've enjoyed reading it," or "Thoughtful work, there, keep at it," or "You're okay, and you'll see more to do as you go along," or "Why don't you practice some particular writing chores with me for a while longer?" ... Often early in the semester, I do not put grades on students' papers, but that makes them uneasy. It makes me uneasy if I do assign grades. I don't know what I'll do. While I'm still trying to learn, I would not be surprised if the grades in my composition classes are generally pretty high. I don't think I am going to worry about that too much. (97)

The dilemma for students is often, as Howard Gardner describes it, "stunning." In the sense of paralyzing findings, Gardner explains his term, "Researchers at Johns Hopkins, M.I.T., and other well-regarded universities have documented that students who receive honor grades in college-level physics courses are frequently unable to solve basic problems and questions encountered in a form slightly different from that on which they have been formally instructed" (3).

The truth about grades is that teachers need to change the way they go about assigning them. Teachers need to resist the obsessive-compulsive behavior of grading everything. Policies that dictate a certain number of daily grades and a certain number of major grades every six weeks are nothing more than edicts by a dictatorial management—they have little to do with learning and more to do with control. Some principals justify their proclamations by saying, "If I don't mandate grades, some teachers won't have a single grade all six weeks." Instead of taking care of such isolated cases, they use the military approach to take care of the problem—everyone must adhere to a controlling mandate. But there is no place in good schools for this type of grading policy. Giving 10 assignments and taking grades from those assignments cannot assure that the assignments (1) are anything more than busy work; (2) connect to any real learning; or (3) reveal what the learner is learning. When teachers are assigners, when they ask how they "should" get grades, when they do not have any other way of grading students than by "workshits," then it is obvious that these teachers need staff development, not mandates. Schools and students do not need more assigners; they need more teachers.

Skilled teachers, teachers who understand and practice a philosophy of education based upon current research and practices, always have an abundance of grades. They have classrooms where learning is rich and where students are excited and produce quality work. These teachers not only have more grades but they have grades that indicate achievement in many different ways. For example, they may have oral and silent reading grades, grades for prewriting, ratiocination, clocking, group work, the conference, participation grades, notes from debriefings, the status of the class, a grade on learning logs or writing folders, and perhaps an ongoing project grade to consider. For skilled teachers, students and their writing offer many opportunities to grade. For an example of this, see figure 14.1.

The other crucial aspect of grading is failure. Most students who fail do so because they refuse to do the work, not because they cannot do the work. When this occurs teachers must ask themselves the hard question, Why? Teachers who have high failure rates are failures themselves. They fail either at the types of assessment they devise, or they fail in their ability to teach. There is no place in school for failure in the traditional sense. When students do not achieve, that is the time to diagnose the problem, restructure the assignment or the class, reteach, and practice. School is a place for success, for learning. In the writing classroom, there is always more right with a student's writing than there is wrong. In fact, *failure, error,* and *wrong* are words that writing teachers need to replace with *reexamine, revise, edit,* and *next time.*

So what do grades really mean? William Glasser maintains that "high grades are a reward for quality work and are very satisfying to students' need for power. In a quality school, however, permanent low grades would be eliminated. A low grade would be treated as a temporary difficulty, a problem to be solved by the student and the teacher working together with the hope that the student would come to the conclusion that it is worth expending more effort" (107). Hunter believes that in the nongraded school, teachers would "expect all students to earn an 'A' or 'B,' but the time to do so will vary" (4).

Testing

Enormous amounts of academic time are spent in testing, both in the preparation and in the actual taking of tests. Test sales are at their peak; estimates suggest that students do over 2,000 test items per year; 91 percent of teachers give basal tests more than three times per year; 22 percent give them more than nine times per year; 64 percent give their own test more than three times per year; 37 percent give their own tests more than nine times per year (Tierney, Carter, and Desai 22-23).

In the name of accountability, testing is touted as *the* way to measure learning. In the writing classroom, the test is generally both an interruption and an interference. There is something illogical about a separate test for writing. Writing itself is the test. For instance, it would be absurd to create a test that contained multiple choice items about introductions, organizational patterns, or even the elements of a narrative. If students write appropriate introductions, use suitable organizational patterns, and include all the elements of narrative in their writings, those writings become the test. Even more illogical has been the multiple choice test of writing skills and conventions. Skills and conventions do not exist in some rarefied dimension; they exist as part of the larger context of communicating in the world. If students have poor skills, that shows in their speaking and writing. Therefore, those skills are best tested in their natural contexts.

(Text continues on page 458.)

Fig. 14.1. Model for grading student work in the writing-as-process classroom.

Where Grades Can Come From:
A Look at the Implementation Models

Refer to the language arts implementation model in chapter 15 (pages 491-494). Notice that grades could be taken from the following activities, though certainly everything need not be graded.

Day 1 — Grade for prewriting.

Day 2 — Grade for reader response.

Day 3 — Grade for reader response.

Day 4 — Grade for description based on mini-lesson criteria.

Day 5 — Grade for setting based on mini-lesson criteria.

Day 6 — Grade for reader-response.

Day 7 — Grade for reader-response.

Day 8 — Grade for independent reading.

Day 9 — Grade for independent writing.

Day 10 — Grade for reader response. (One grade could also be taken from day 1, day 2, day 3, day 6, and day 10 prewritings. Each prewriting would represent 20 percent.)

Day 11 — Analysis of narrative elements.

Day 12 — Grade the grid for accuracy and completion.

Day 14 — Grade leads based on mini-lesson criteria.

Day 15 — Grade section of writing for elaboration based on mini-lesson criteria.

Day 16 — Grade conclusions based on mini-lesson criteria.

Day 17 — Have students choose and write 10 sentences from their writing that require punctuation from mini-lesson. Grade these 10 sentences. Each paper will be unique.

Day 18 — Grade papers on the appropriate paragraphing of dialogue.

Day 19 — Grade written individual responses to grouping. Each student records her or his responses and the grade comes from depth of response.

Day 21 — Students write out 10 sentences that are ratiocinated for revision. Grade the adeptness of these revisions.

Day 22 — Grade completion of title and author's biography.

Day 23 — Grade completion of library check-out cards.

Day 24 — Students select 10 words from their writing they want to know how to spell. They look these up and record definitions as well as spelling. Grade for completion.

Day 28 — Grade quality of seriousness of clocking responses from editing sheets.

Day 29 — Test spelling of words gathered on day 24.

Day 30 — Grade books based on analytic scale devised on day 25.

Again, not all of these grades need to be taken. The example here is to show grading possibilities during the unit. If all the grades were garnered, they would reflect:

10 completion grades (days 1, 2, 3, 6, 7, 10, 12, 22, 23, 24)

8 grades for written expression (days 4, 5, 11, 14, 15, 16, 18, 30)

3 grades for grammar and spelling (days 17, 21, 29)

3 grades for independent reading and writing (days 8, 9, 11)

3 grades for group work (days 19, 28)

Second-graders proudly read their dinosaur stories. Each author settled into the author's chair and waited for respect. First Beth used a double negative, and the teacher jotted something on her clipboard. Then she noted Wayne doing it, too. When Una used the double negative twice, the teacher leaned over and whispered, "I have my mini-lesson for tomorrow." That teacher did not require a test to illuminate what his students needed; that need became apparent in the "test" of the author's chair. Indeed, I sometimes wonder whether, when teachers grade worksheets, they make note of who makes what mistakes, or do they simply plow onward through the basal, the curriculum, and their stack of blackline masters?

Testing companies, state departments, federal agencies, school districts, and teachers need to be very careful in the development of any test, whether it be given by one teacher in one class, or designed to evaluate an entire state. A case in point is the writing prompt on the Texas state mandated test. With regard to the Texas Assessment of Basic Skills (TABS) for the first five years of schooling, the Texas Educational Assessment of Minimum Skills (TEAMS) for the next five years, and even into the early years with the Texas Assessment of Academic Skills (TAAS), the prompts for students in grades three, five, seven, nine, and the exit level were based on the theory of James L. Kinneavy, a professor at the University of Texas. Yet as early as 1982, John D. O'Banion raised questions about applying Kinneavy's theory to composition, "Kinneavy clarifies the need for order in English studies, but—to use his own term for characterizing the field—his work is preparadigmatic in that his categories are static and his approach is too closely tied to literary criticism to be helpful in composition" (196). O'Banion goes on to say, "Though he intends to rescue composition from 'the present anarchy of the discipline,' his theory is unsatisfactory for many who teach composition, largely because he fails to account adequately for rhetorical choices and composing processes" (196). Yet students across the state have been tested on the modes and purposes of Kinneavy's theory for more than 10 years, even as teachers have been urged to teach writing as a process. While few would opt to return to the "anarchy of the discipline," most teachers trained in writing as a process, collaborative learning, and integrated language arts would appreciate prompts that truly evaluated their students' ability to write as a process.

As James T. English, head of the middle school of Moses Brown School in Providence, Rhode Island, says, "Tests have the power to be enormously damaging, and yet those who devise and administer them live mostly test-free lives" (27).

Clearly more research and study on tests and testing is needed. Priscilla Vail's *Smart Kids with School Problems* offers some options. Howard Gardner's *Frames of Mind*, which questions what can be measured by standardized tests, offers a broader definition of intelligence (that is, the theory of multiple intelligences). This theory, in turn, raises further questions about the manner in which these intelligences might be tested. Because so much is at stake—students' careers, futures, and their very quality of life—all concerned and connected with testing, from the teacher who makes a semester test to the psychometrician who creates items for students in culturally diverse classrooms across the nation, should proceed with the utmost caution.

Measuring

The term *measuring* usually refers to a unit or system that indicates the dimensions of learning. When measuring, evaluators most often use descriptors. For example, Lee Odell suggests that by systematically examining linguistic cues in students' writing, intellectual processes are illuminated. He uses the descriptors *focus, contrast, classification, change, physical context,* and *time sequence.* Odell maintains that by looking at students' initial efforts and final papers, an analysis of their intellectual processes can be described and therefore measured (106-132).

Measuring also may be performed using computer analysis. By allowing the computer to count word frequencies, word choices, spelling, and other descriptors, teachers may measure several aspects of students' growth.

A third means of measuring students' growth is through the descriptor coined by Kellogg W. Hunt. The T-Unit measures student's syntactic maturity, that is, their ability to write sentences with sophisticated levels of thoughts. Hunt defines his descriptor as "a single main clause (independent clause) plus whatever clauses and nonclauses are attached or embedded within that one main clause" (92). It is "the shortest grammatically complete unit that is not a fragment. The *T* stands for 'terminable.' Simply stated, a T-unit is a single main clause and whatever goes with it" (93). When marking passages for T-units, most scorers use a double virgule — // — much the way a line of poetry is marked. Hunt offers this example, which has been marked for T-units:

> I like the movie we saw about Moby Dick the white whale // the captain said if you can kill the white whale Moby Dick I will give this gold to the one that can do it // and it is worth sixteen dollars // they tried and tried // but while they were trying they killed a whale and used the oil for the lamps // they almost caught the white whale.// (92)

To compute the writer's average T-unit score, the number of T-units (6) is divided into the number of words (68). The result is a score of 11.3.

Hunt says, "The reason for defining a T-unit, as distinguished from a sentence, is simply that the T-unit turns out, empirically, to be a useful concept in describing some of the changes that occur in the syntax of the sentences produced by schoolchildren as they grow older. When we know what a T-unit is, we can understand certain measures of maturity that we could not understand without it" (93).

To standardize the measurement of T-units, the same prewriting and postwriting sample passage, composed of short, choppy sentences, is given to all students to rewrite. The general instructions are simple. At the beginning of the year or semester, students receive a sample passage, they read it, then rewrite it a better way. They may not leave out any important information. After students rewrite the passage, each student counts the number of words in his or her rewrite and records that number at the top of the paper. Students then exchange papers and check the number. The teacher marks the T-units and computes the students' average score. At the end of the year or semester, they are given the same sample, which they read and rewrite in a better way. Once the post-test is complete, the teacher may examine the numbers to get a measure of syntactic growth. Remember, while there are some published tables on syntactic rates, T-units provide a measure of student with self, not student in comparison with others in the class or on that grade level. For example, if a fifth-grade student has a 6.1 mean T-unit in September and a 7.2 T-unit in May, then the measure is clear — that student shows syntactic growth. If a tenth-grade student measures 11.5 in September and 11.5 in January, there is reason to analyze the lack of improvement.

Scoring

Scoring generally refers to large-scale evaluations. Scores enable evaluators to sort or rank written work quickly. Scoring may be done schoolwide, districtwide, statewide, or even nationwide, as with the writing section on the College Board Examinations. Scoring is done numerically. The most common scoring procedures for large-scale writing samples are Holistic Scoring, developed by the Educational Testing Service (ETS), and Primary Trait Scoring, developed by the National Assessment of Educational Progress.

HOLISTIC SCORING

At this time, holistic scoring may be the most reliable way to score, sort, and rank a large number of students' writing. Originally developed by Gertrude Conlan at ETS, it is a way to score a large number of writing samples in a relative short period of time.

Unlike atomistic scoring, where every detail or particular feature is noted, holistic scoring allows the scorer to quickly read and rate each paper. The key to success in holistic scoring is training. Holistic scoring is difficult work and demands that both those who lead the scoring sessions and those who do the actual scoring be well trained. There are two ways to score a paper holistically: general impression holistic scoring and focused holistic scoring.

In general impression scoring, a represented number of papers from the entire batch of papers to be scored are randomly selected, read, and scored. From among these, anchor papers are chosen. This part of the process is usually done by those accomplished and well trained. The anchor papers are used to train the other scorers. Through a procedure of reading and discussing the anchor papers, the scorers are calibrated, or socialized, so that there is a consistency of response. Occasionally a scorer emerges who does not calibrate, whose scores are always discrepant, that is, not in agreement with others who score the same papers. When that happens, that scorer is sometimes asked to act as a runner to help distribute and redistribute papers but not score them.

It is important to note that with general impression holistic scoring, new anchor papers are determined from each batch of papers to be scored. For example, a batch of papers from ninth-graders in 1990 have anchor papers chosen from that batch, whereas the papers from ninth-graders in 1992 have new anchor papers chosen from the 1992 batch. What this means is the papers are rated according to other papers in their batch. Therefore a high paper in 1990 may not be a high paper in 1992. Once the group has been trained, all the papers in that batch can be rated.

The anchor papers ascertain what constitutes a general impression of "high," "low high," "high low," and "low" papers. For example, if a four-point scale is being used, then the scorer is asked to make two decisions. The first decision determines if the paper is high or low. For example, if the paper is determined to be high, then the scorer asks, "Is this a high paper, or a low high paper?" If the paper is determined to be low, then the scorer asks, "Is this a high low paper or a low paper?" The high paper receives a 4, the low high paper receives a 3, and the high low paper receives a 2, and the low paper receives a 1. A four-point scale allows the scorer to avoid the easy way out—the middle score.

General impression is the older of the holistic methods and is not without its critics. To answer these critics, the National Assessment of Educational Progress and committees at ETS working on the Advanced Placement Program began the development of primary trait scoring or focused holistic scoring.

PRIMARY TRAIT SCORING

In this type of holistic scoring, a more precise and exact guide is established for the scorers to use while scoring the papers. There are six guidelines that are considered standard to conducting primary trait scorings. (1) Controlled essay reading—all the papers are scored at one time; (2) Scoring criteria guide—a rubric of descriptors is established by those controlling the readings; (3) Anchor papers—sample papers to illustrate the scoring criteria are selected and used to calibrate the scores; (4) Scoring checks—while the scoring or reading is being done the scores are checked to keep the scores on target to the rubric; (5) Multiple scoring—scorers from different tables rank the papers twice. With the exception of very few scoring guides, a one-point difference between the two readings is allowable. More than that is considered discrepant; (6) Scorer profiles—records of rankings are maintained on individual readers to maintain consistency and accuracy to the criteria. Readers who have discrepant scores are eliminated from the readings (White 23-27).

The major difference between general impression and primary trait scoring is the rubric. In the former, the criteria rise out of consensus based on close reading and discussion of the anchor papers. In the latter, certain criteria are developed before the papers are read; these items narrow the focus of the scorer, who ranks the papers accordingly.

Edward M. White, professor of English at California State University, in *Teaching and Assessing Writing*, urges teachers to share the scoring guides with students and even have students participate in the development of the scoring guides (122). Where holistic scoring is being used in large-scale assessment, real growth and understanding can never occur if the scoring guides are kept secret. Teachers and students are left with a certain amount of wonder about why a score is received and have no way of resolving questions of performance.

White goes on to consider the limitations of holistic scoring. "The first and most important limitation is that it gives no meaningful diagnostic information beyond the comparative ranking it represents.... The second implication of the limited value of the holistic score emerges from its connection to its particular test group: It cannot represent an absolute value in itself. This means that every time a holistic scoring is completed, those responsible for reporting scores need to make a fresh decision about where cutting levels should be" (28).

In the classroom, teachers and students adapt holistic scoring by devising their own rubrics and scoring their own papers. They may use holistic scoring on drafts to provide an indication of where the paper is at that time in the process. Or holistic scoring or primary trait scoring may be used on the final copy. When the guides are clearly communicated to the student, papers can be scored quickly and with a certain amount of reliability. Because most teachers do not have a second person to rate the paper, many teachers team with another teacher or invite students to be the second scorer. Because holistic scoring is done with the papers anonymous, this usually is not a problem. When instituting this type of grading, it is wise to communicate the guidelines and procedures to parents. Most parents are unfamiliar with holistic scoring and expect atomistic grading, so there will be questions and concerns the teacher may wish to discuss with them.

Assessing

The term *assessment* encompasses many of the more recent approaches to evaluation, from self-assessment to portfolios, from inventories to scales. Two major divisions of assessment will be covered in this chapter—self-assessment and teacher assessment.

SELF-ASSESSMENT OF WRITING

Having students engage in self-assessment does not necessarily mean that the teacher will have less grading to do. There are those who propose self-assessment as a way to diminish the teacher's grading time. While this certainly can happen, it is not the reason to implement self-assessment in the classroom.

Instead, self-assessment is meant to give students ways of knowing and evaluating their performance, their processes, and their achievement. What does it say about students when the only way they may receive affirmation of their learning is from the teacher? Nowhere is this injustice more apparent than during the first several debriefings held with a group of students. When asked, "What did you learn?" they appear dumbstruck. When asked, "How did you learn?" they become mute. When asked what the teacher could do to be more effective, they are thunderstruck. As debriefings continue, students become quite apt at assessing exactly what occurred; as with any skill, self-assessment takes practice and patience. If schools want independent thinkers, if schools want students to take the responsibility for their own learning, then schools will have to allow the learners to take some responsibility for assessment. No longer will students run to the teacher for confirmation; instead, the student will run to the teacher for celebration.

This premise is radical for many schools, many teachers, and most students. The process of making the writer into an assessor will not happen magically or by proclamation. The teacher or school that says, "All assessment in writing will be self-assessment" is doomed for failure. Instead, the teacher becomes the most important variable as the facilitator in the self-assessment process. Teachers will need to talk often and authentically with their students; they will need to read and respond to students' writings; they will need to provide models and ways for self-assessment. Ultimately, teachers will become another voice to be considered by the person for whom the assessment is most crucial—the student.

Nor will self-assessment necessarily be the only type of evaluation to occur in schools. When the right kinds of things happen with self-assessment, the other assessments will not be as crucial to the writer. Each evaluation will have its place and purpose—all will give a more total, more integrated picture of the student. As students become more secure in their self-assessments, then the other evaluations can become tools for students to gauge their conclusions.

Elbow identifies three problems in evaluation: "(1) What constitutes good student performance? (2) How do you communicate evaluation? (3) How do you produce in the student the ability to evaluate his own work?" (176). Students—not only teachers—should be involved in determining the answers to these questions.

When students self-assess their own writing, the teacher is provided with many opportunities for mini-lessons on the criteria of good writing, e.g., Is the vocabulary suited to the audience? What keeps the reader from becoming confused? How do authors keep readers reading? Janet Emig succinctly describes good writing as apt, clear, and lively. Other criteria may be established on William Irmscher's description: "intellectual and imaginative ... transforms the material and language in some unusual way" (156-157). Or still other criteria could be based on what Richard Lloyd-Jones says that good writing "should be—primarily related to aims (i.e., does the piece of writing fulfill its purpose?)" (33). Lessons on the nature of good writing should move students away from their most common definition of writing—it is error-free.

It seems reasonable that the more teachers read and write, the better they will know what is good writing. What is good writing this year may not do for next year. As the students change and as the teacher changes, their ideas and notions about "good" are bound to change. But teachers must read. Gardner points out, "It has been reported that the average schoolteacher reads a book a year" (188). To be a good evaluator of writing, the teacher must be more than just average.

Probably the best classroom will be the one in which teacher and students together discover what is good, what is quality. Glasser offers his definition of quality as "whatever we put into our quality world" (102). Extending that definition, writers achieve quality by whatever they put into their quality papers. And, according to Glasser,

> There is no doubt that they [students] know both what quality is and that to achieve it takes a great deal of hard work. When I ask them whether they have done much quality work in school, at first many say that they have. But when I ask them how many times they have actually worked hard enough to do the best work they possibly could, almost none, including the very good students, say that they have ever done as much as they are capable of doing. I think it is safe to say that very few students expend the effort to do quality work at school.... But for students to do quality work, it is crucial that they see that it is for their benefit, not the benefit of their teachers, school systems, or parents." (94, 96)

TYPES OF SELF-ASSESSMENT

Inventories. Inventories are a specific type of self-assessment. Students create and complete inventories to record the processes and progress in their writing. Inventories come in many forms; the best are always student produced with teacher guidance. The poorest are usually the mass produced, decontextualized inventories that are so generic that students and teachers are bound to wonder if they were produced to assess writing or the weather. Student produced inventories usually include all or some of these items:

- a chronicle of what the student wrote, categorized by mode, assignment, and genre;
- a list of the student's strengths;
- records of what needs improvement;
- logs that date starts and completions;
- feelings about what the student has written;
- analysis of what the student has written;
- comments; and
- future plans.

Movies. Movies of the writer's mind are based on an idea from Elbow (181-192). They are records kept by writers on the moment-by-moment readings of their minds. Students record what they think while engaged in the writing process. They step outside of self and record the what, when, how, and why of the writing. The results are significant in that they reveal to the students what they do or do not do in the writing. For the teacher, movies show an inside picture of the student's thinking. Sometimes what is not recorded is just as significant as what is.

Observation Profiles. This type of self-evaluation requires the writers to note observable behaviors. The evaluation centers around the actions of the writers. It is a type of self-diary and self-analysis. The writers record these items:

- what they observe themselves doing when they write;
- what they observe about the way they write;
- what they observe from others when they share their writing; and
- what they observe about the writing itself.

Performance Profiles. Students who keep performance profiles generally find them to be descriptive of not only the process but of the product. The performance profile looks for the items shown in figure 14.2. Comments on each item usually are kept as short narrative notes, for example, "I spent twenty minutes rewriting today."

Fig. 14.2. Matrix for performance profile.

	Duration	**Effort**	**Quality**	**Effectiveness**
Prewriting				
Writing				
Rewriting				
Publishing				

When the writer considers the duration of various processes, time becomes an evaluative indicator. More time spent on prewriting and less on rewriting might indicate that the getting started was difficult; it might also indicate excitement for the topic. One may understand and interpret duration, in light of effort, quality, and effectiveness. When considering effort, the writer needs to focus on what is done. The quality factor requires that the writer use the internal criteria of what the writer thinks is good. In evaluating the writing's effectiveness, the writer will want to interpret how others respond to the writing. As always, the best profiles always ask the follow-up question "Why?" Of course, as the writer records these profiles, the teacher will want to encourage and model responses using examples from the writing or the writer's attitudes and thinking.

Another type of performance profile asks the writer to record narrative answers to the following items:

- This is what I wrote.

- This is who I grouped with and what I learned in the group.

- This is what I learned from the conference.

- This is the process I used and when I did things.

- This is the organization I used in this writing.

- This is the rating I would give the writing.

- This is the rating I would give myself while doing this writing.

- This is why I wrote this piece.

- This is what I learned from writing this piece.

- This is what I want you to know about this writing.

TEACHER ASSESSMENT OF WRITING

Limited Marking Procedure. One approach many writing teachers take to assess writing is to limit the number of items marked on any given paper. Often they correct three to five items and leave the rest of the paper untouched. Some teachers inform their students that they will only correct three items and respond to the content of the paper. The idea is that these corrected errors are the ones the student should learn and work on first. Certainly these methods are better than copious marking of errors. This approach does not overwhelm the student and it also is better than giving the double grade — one for mechanics and one for content. Separating the mechanics from the content is akin to separating the dancer from the dance. It is ridiculous to think a paper can receive a 22/96. If the mechanics of a paper are that poor, how can it communicate effectively? The messages the students receive from this type of grading are mixed at best.

Many skilled teachers who use a limited marking approach also use self-adhesive, removable notepads. This allows students to remove the teacher's markings from the paper as it is corrected, leaving the paper unscarred and intact.

Analytic Scale. An analytic scale allows the teacher and students to develop a scoring system together. They decide on a list of the characteristics and features appropriate to the writing. Ideally, several days before the paper is due, the teacher asks the students what they were taught during the writing of this paper. This brainstormed list is written on the board. Students prioritize the list with the teacher. The teacher uses the prioritized list to create the scale.

One of the most well-known scales, the Diederich scale, was developed from an analysis of judgments of the writing of college freshmen (see fig. 14.3).

It is easy to see how teachers and students can devise their own scales based on the Diederich scale. The advantage of the analytic scale is that students have a say in the way their work is scored. There are no surprises in the grading, and students know beforehand what is expected. There are additional examples of analytic scales in appendix A.

Fig. 14.3. Diederich scale for evaluating writing.

	Low		**Middle**		**High**
General Merit					
Ideas	2	4	6	8	10
Organization	2	4	6	8	10
Wording	2	4	6	8	10
Flavor	2	4	6	8	10
Mechanics					
Usage	1	2	3	4	5
Punctuation	1	2	3	4	5
Spelling	1	2	3	4	5
Handwriting	1	2	3	4	5
				Total	_____

THE WRITING PORTFOLIO

Few ideas seem to have sparked the imagination and sense of fairness of English language arts teachers as have portfolios. They are one of the best methods to evaluate student writing. In a portfolio, examples of selected pieces of writing are stored. Unlike the writing folder, which serves as a storage file for *all* writing in a given marking period, portfolios are receptacles of what students, teachers, peers, and parents deem the best writing. Myriad journal articles and books explain various ways to establish and evaluate portfolios. While the portfolio has much to offer, unfortunately for many, the portfolio will be nothing more than a writing folder.

Portfolios should be like the student — individual and unique. No two portfolios should ever look the same. As no two students, nor any two classrooms, are the same, it is unrealistic to expect all portfolios to look the same, contain the same things, or reflect the same writings. Graves gives one of the most realistic views of portfolios.

> As educators we are mere infants in the use of portfolios. Artists have used them ... as a means of representing the range and depth of their best and most current work. Only in the last five years have educators latched on to the portfolio as an alternative to evaluating the literate work of students....
>
> But as young as this notion is, there are already signs that using portfolios in education is becoming a rigid process.... States and school systems have moved from reading about portfolios to mandating them as evaluation instruments for large school populations. Some small pilot studies were conducted to get some *minor* bugs removed, but sustained, long-term learning about the possibilities of portfolios as a learning/evaluation medium may be lost to us in the rush to mandate their use.
>
> Portfolios are simply too good an idea to be limited to an evaluation instrument. Early data that show their use as a medium for instruction is more than promising. (1)

Portfolios will require teachers to rethink the way they teach and the way they evaluate. Most certainly, portfolios will cause schools to reconsider how they use their time. Two formats can be adopted to facilitate the implementation of portfolios: the daily model and the weekly model.

Daily Model

The daily model begins with a mini-lesson. Divide the class into three groups. Each group applies the mini-lesson to its work, as shown in figure 14.4.

Fig. 14.4. Class assignments for the daily model.

Group 1	Group 2	Group 3
Reading workshop	Writing workshop	Portfolio assessment
Portfolio assessment	Reading workshop	Writing workshop
Writing workshop	Portfolio assessment	Reading workshop

Time is not the most important feature in this model—the learning is. Depending upon the teacher's need for intervention and the students' requirements for direct instruction, the teacher can work with one group or one strand. For example, if the students need a teacher conference, the teacher can confer with the groups during the writing workshop segments. Because assignment and discovery are more important than competing to finish first, groups determine the amount of time required for each segment.

Weekly Model

Similar to the daily model, the weekly model allows for greater depth and intensity (see fig. 14.5).

Fig. 14.5. Class assignments for the weekly model.

Monday	Tuesday	Wednesday	Thursday	Friday
Whole-group instruction	Group 1: Reading workshop	Group 1: Writing workshop	Group 1: Portfolio assessment	Testing Review Makeup
Establish goals	Group 2: Writing workshop	Group 2: Portfolio assessment	Group 2: Reading workshop	
	Group 3: Portfolio assessment	Group 3: Reading workshop	Group 3: Writing workshop	

In the December 16, 1992, issue of *Education Week*, Robert Rothman outlines the major problems with portfolio assessment. He writes, "A report analyzing Vermont's pioneering assessment system has found severe problems with it and raised serious questions about alternate forms of assessment.... But the report by the RAND Corporation ... found that the 'rater reliability' in scoring the portfolios was very low.... In examining possible reasons for the low levels of reliability, the RAND report suggests that the complex scoring scales may have contributed to the problem.... On a related point, the report also suggests that the training of the raters may have been inadequate" (1-20).

As teachers begin to use portfolios they will need training in them, just as they needed training in teaching writing. Giving teachers folders for portfolios and proclaiming "This year our school will do portfolios" is to flirt with failure.

Because the purpose of portfolios is to give a more accurate picture of students, educators will need to be slow and deliberate in their training and implementation of them. Joni Lucas writes in *ASCD Curriculum Update*, "With so many challenges inherent in scoring, analyzing, and evaluating portfolios on a large scale, portfolios might best be used as a diagnostic instrument and strong instructional tool helping classroom teachers to tap into the richness of student writing and learning and to reflect more clearly actual changes in instruction" (7).

Portfolio Profile of Student Capacities

During the past three years, NJWPT has developed the Portfolio Profile of Student Capacities (PPSC). This portfolio design heavily emphasizes student autonomy and student ability to engage in self-assessment. The PPSC invites students and teachers to look at the students' capacities for reading, writing, listening, viewing, and thinking, as the student decides what goes into the portfolio. The student, teacher, peers, and parents are involved in the evaluation of the work in the portfolio.

The PPSC asks students and teachers to focus on capacities rather than discreet skills, checklists of genre, writing prompts, or skills tests. The emphasis on students' capacities resulted from study of Howard Gardner, who wrote

> To declare oneself against the institution of the three R's in the schools is like being against motherhood or the flag. Beyond question, students ought to be literate and ought to revel in their literacy. Yet the essential emptiness of this goal is dramatized by the fact that young children in the United States are becoming literate in a *literal* sense; that is, they are mastering the rules of reading and writing, even as they are learning their addition and multiplication tables. What is missing are not the decoding skills, but two other facets: the capacity to read for understanding and the desire to read at all. Much the same story can be told for the remaining literacies; it is not the mechanics of writing nor the algorithms for subtraction that are absent, but rather the knowledge about when to invoke these skills and the inclination to do so productively in one's own daily life. (186-187)

Gardner hones in on why looking at student capacities is far more rewarding than a cursory examination of student work. A student's capacity reveals the depth of learning; thus the name *PPSC* reflects the idea of examining these capacities. The training the teachers receive in the PPSC encourages them to focus on the capacity of the student rather than the product of the old paradigm.

The PPSC is just as concerned with self-sponsored learning as it is with school-sponsored learning. As self-sponsored learning aligns itself with capacity and desire, real progress of learning can be easily recognized and therefore easily assessed.

Key to the development and implementation of the PPSC has been teacher training. Teachers are trained how to guide students and model self- and peer-assessment. The teachers receive training in various types of teacher assessment. Also, training sessions are conducted with parents.

After several districts piloted the PPSC, NJWPT conducted a study of NJWPT teachers (project group) and their colleagues (control group). The teachers in both groups implemented portfolios in at least one of their classes. The project group was trained in portfolio assessment and its rationale and was instructed in various research studies about portfolios. Also, these teachers met regularly with their trainers to discuss their students' portfolios. These were times when questions, concerns, and problems related to the portfolios were addressed. Additionally, these teachers formed a support group and met informally to share information and discoveries about their students' portfolios. In all but one case, these teachers also kept a portfolio and in that way reinforced its importance.

The teachers in the control group also implemented portfolios in at least one of their classes, but they received no training or direction, nor did they meet with others in the control group. Further, these teachers had not received training in the teaching of writing as a process.

At the conclusion of the academic year, the portfolios of both groups were examined. More than 88 percent of the portfolios of the control group emerged simply as writing folders, that is, places where writing was stored. Ten percent of these were filled with generic, mass-produced selections judged as written responses to specific writing prompts.

More than 90 percent of the portfolios from project group, however, evidenced an evolution of not only writing abilities and fluency, but an improvement in skills that moved from primitive starts and short bursts of writing coupled with hesitant explanations of choices to elaborated pieces, a wide array of selections, and securely worded descriptions of why each selection was made. These were clear demonstrations of the portfolio as a valuable assessment tool.

The PPSC starts with a basic design and allows teachers to tailor the portfolio to their individual students and classes. Training with the teachers, the students, and the parents becomes a vital part of the portfolio system. Initial results are promising and show real progress in student writing, reading, listening, viewing, and speaking.

Design of the PPSC

Students are asked to place evidence of reading, writing, listening, speaking, and viewing in the PPSC. This evidence may assume various forms. Not only are products considered, but the processes, efforts, improvements, and achievements are vital to the design. School- and self-sponsored evidence are encouraged and rewarded in the assessment. Preliminary results show a remarkable increase of self-sponsored reading and writing when using the PPSC.

The assignments of teachers evolve, as does the school- and self-sponsored writing of the students. The portfolio allows that growth to be preserved. This preservation captures the abilities of the students and projects their capabilities; therefore, it serves as a repository of evidence and potential. This potential increases as teachers and students become accustomed to the portfolio. Students realize that they control what goes into the PPSC, and therefore, their ownership increases. Often, students surprise teachers by what they place in the PPSC, but the reasons students give for their choices often illuminate more accurately what the learner learned.

The PPSC asks students to self-evaluate, have a peer evaluate, and have a parent, caregiver, or trusted adult evaluate what goes into the portfolio. Self-assessment is generally slow to begin and is uneven. As teachers and students become more comfortable with the assessment guides, their evaluations improve. Initially, student responses are vague and unresponsive. As the teacher models self-assessment instruments, then students begin to see the value of the portfolio. Self-assessment is difficult but valuable. The difficulty comes from asking students to metacognitively analyze that which they have placed in evidence. However, once students start to critically consider what and how they learn, processes of learning, reading, and writing are encoded neurologically; therein lies the value of the PPSC. Teachers who use the PPSC, and who are also researchers, record what Jane Healy describes: "What children do every day, the ways in which they think and respond to the world, what they learn and the stimuli to which they decide to pay attention — shapes their brains. Not only does it change the ways in which the brain is used (*functional change*), but it also causes physical alterations (*structural change*) in neural wiring systems" (51).

Peer evaluations are much like group responses to writing. Careful consideration is given to exactly what peers are to look for and to comment on. Again, it has been found that the more specific teachers are in the requests for the peer evaluations, the more precise and valuable are the responses.

Parent assessment is more difficult to control. In all cases, the teachers and students generally agree that some type of parent assessments are valuable, but some high school and junior high school students opt for a trusted adult (rather than a parent) to do the assessment. The assessment instruments given to parents request that they be positive and helpful. In some cases, parents do not assess the portfolio, rather they use it to send messages to the teacher. Attacks of this type are not acceptable, and in the parent training they are discussed. The parent assessments vary. Some parents spend a great deal of time looking at the PPSC, while others respond quickly. On occasion, this reflects on the attitude the student has about the work included in the portfolio. In some instances, in which parents involved in the PPSC were found to be illiterate and reluctant to participate in the assessment of their children's work, the students found remarkably imaginative ways to enlist their parents' cooperation. In one case, the daughter used her portfolio to teach her father to read. While this was not the student's overt goal, as she shared her writings with her father, his ability to recognize and decode increased. He proudly stated at the final assessment that he could read his daughter's work.

Heavy emphasis is placed on having the students record why they selected specific entries for the PPSC. Students also are asked to consider what they learned by doing a particular entry. Each self-assessment asks students to consider what they will do next. This self-directed goal setting is beneficial not only to the student, but to the teacher as well.

As teachers have implemented the PPSC, they have discovered that the portfolios become a mirror of the teaching and the curriculum. For example, teachers whose students did not have evidence of speaking and viewing for the PPSC discovered that little was done to teach these things in their classrooms.

The portfolio changes the way teachers and students regard what they do, because everything is looked at as evidence of reading, writing, listening, speaking, and viewing. As a result, a sense of community of learners increases with use of the portfolio. Students see the long-term advantages of the portfolio. They see that the PPSC is a collection of what they have learned, not just what they have done.

CONCLUSION

As portfolios develop, as alternative ways to evaluate and assess student writing proliferate, and as understanding of writing and the writer increases, the classroom will change. As brain theory becomes an exact science, the way teachers assess students' writing and learning also will change. As schools move to nongraded models, grading will evolve to evaluation. Grading or evaluation will continue to be difficult and demanding. But it is hoped that, as teachers and students begin to practice and understand writing as a process, they will align the way they judge and assess what they do accordingly.

While there is still much to know about learning to write and how to teach writing, it is clear the teacher needs to do more evaluation and assessment and less grading and testing. The nature of evaluation and assessment is based on student work and what students do or do not do. Evaluation allows teacher and student to work together rather than as polar entities. Assessment invites teacher, students, parents, and schools to look at the progress and products of students from a more global view. Assessment can be used to align curriculum. It can be used to evaluate teaching and learning.

Jim Corder suggests several things when evaluating:

> I have learned to consider the possibility that any essay turned in to me may be as good as it can be at the moment. Once again, I don't mean to suggest that I am pleading or recommending that all be forgiven in student writing. Hardly anyone, except my cousin Duane, gets up in the morning and decides, "I'm going to be evil today." Hardly anyone, not even some freshmen, gets up in the morning and decides, "I'm going to turn in a half-assed essay today." Most probably all believe that when they have turned in an essay, it's an okay essay. We probably ought to remember that. We probably ought to remember that any judgment we make of their writing may be rape of their judgment. All of us want justification, not denial; validation, not repudiation. If we are editors, not police officers, perhaps we can help them find their own authentication. (95-96)

APPLICATION

Choose a paper you have written. Exchange it with a partner. Evaluate it atomistically, that is, mark every mistake no matter how small. Then evaluate the paper another way discussed in this chapter. Write your findings and share them with your partner.

WORKS CITED

Bruner, Jerome. *The Process of Education*. New York: Vintage Books, 1963.

Canadian Council of Teachers of English. "Evaluation Policy." *Classmate* 16, no. 2 (1985): 27-30.

Cohen, S. Alan. *Tests: Marked for Life?* Toronto: Scholastic, 1988.

Cooper, Charles R., and Lee Odell. *Evaluating Writing: Describing, Measuring, Judging*. Urbana, IL: National Council of Teachers of English, 1977.

Corder, Jim W. "Asking for a Text and Trying to Learn It." In *Encountering Student Texts*, edited by Bruce Lawson, Susan Sterr Ryan, and W. Ross Winterowd. Urbana, IL: National Council of Teachers of English, 1989.

Diederich, Paul. *Measuring Growth in English*. Urbana, IL: National Council of Teachers of English, 1974.

Dilena, Mike, and Jane Leaker. "Literary Assessment: Assessing Achievements in Real Reading and Writing." In *The Literacy Agenda: Issues for the Nineties*, edited by Elaine Furniss and Pamela Green. Portsmouth, NH: Heinemann Educational Books, 1991.

Elbow, Peter. *Embracing Contraries*. New York: Oxford University Press, 1986.

English, James T. "Watching Parents React to Test Scores." *Education Week* (3 June 1992): 27.

Gardner, Howard. *Frames of Mind*. New York: Basic Books, 1985.

_____. *The Unschooled Mind: How Children Think and How Schools Should Teach*. New York: Basic Books, 1991.

Glasser, William. *The Quality School*. New York: Harper & Row, 1990.

Graves, Donald H., and Bonnie S. Sunstein, eds. *Portfolio Portraits*. Portsmouth, NH: Heinemann Educational Books, 1992.

Healy, Jane M. *Endangered Minds: Why Our Children Don't Think*. New York: Simon & Schuster, 1990.

Hoopfer, L., and M. Hunsberger. "An Ethnomethodological Perspective on Reading Assessment." *Forum in Reading and Language Education* 1, no. 1 (1986): 103-119.

Hunt, Kellogg W. "Early Blooming and Late Blooming Syntactic Structures." In *Evaluating Writing: Describing, Measuring, Judging*, edited by Charles R. Cooper and Lee Odell. Pp. 91-106. Urbana, IL: National Council of Teachers of English, 1977.

Hunter, Madeline C. *How to Change to a Nongraded School*. Alexandria, VA: Association for Supervision and Curriculum Development, 1992.

Irmscher, William F. *Teaching Expository Writing.* New York: Holt, Rinehart & Winston, 1979.

Kinneavy, James L. *A Theory of Discourse: The Aims of Discourse.* New York: Prentice Hall Press, 1971.

Lloyd-Jones, Richard. "Primary Trait Scoring." In *Evaluating Writing: Describing, Measuring, Judging*, edited by Charles R. Cooper and Lee Odell. Pp. 33-66. Urbana, IL: National Council of Teachers of English, 1977.

Lucas, Joni. "Teaching Writing." *ASCD Curriculum Update.* Alexandria, VA: Association for Supervision and Curriculum Development, January 1993.

Mitchell, Ruth. "Verbal Confusion." *The Council Chronicle* 2 (February 1993): 20.

O'Banion, John D. "A Theory of Discourse: Retrospective." *College Composition and Communication* 33 (May 1982): 196-201.

Odell, Lee. "Measuring Changes in Intellectual Processes as One Dimension of Growth in Writing." In *Evaluating Writing: Describing, Measuring, Judging*, edited by Charles R. Cooper and Lee Odell. Pp. 107-132. Urbana, IL: National Council of Teachers of English, 1977.

Richards, I. A. *The Principles of Literary Criticism.* New York: Harcourt, Brace, 1948.

Rothman, Robert. "RAND Study Finds Serious Problems in Vt. Portfolio Program." *Education Week* 12, no. 15 (16 December 1992): 1, 20.

Tierney, Robert J., Mark A. Carter, and Laura E. Desai. *Portfolio Assessment in the Reading-Writing Classroom.* Norwood, MA: Christopher-Gordon, 1991.

Vail, Priscilla. *Smart Kids with School Problems.* New York: E. P. Dutton, 1987.

White, Edward M. *Teaching and Assessing Writing.* San Francisco: Jossey-Bass, 1985.

15

LEARNING THROUGH WRITING
Teaching Writing
Across the Curriculum

We are all authors.
—Mikhail Bakhtin☐

When Mikhail Bakhtin, one of the great thinkers of the twentieth century, wrote that all people are authors, he was talking, among other things, about how people appropriate meaning. Further, he maintained that "the word is a two-sided act. It is determined equally by whose word it is and for whom it is meant.... A word is territory *shared* by both addresser and addressee" (Clark and Holquist 15). What he means is that when people use language to talk or write about a subject, they literally take ownership of that subject. Then, when others read or hear these words, they begin their own appropriation of meaning. In this way, the words belong in part to the authors and in part to the hearers or readers; the words are shared through meaning.

In a real sense this is what happens when students read and write across the curriculum. Words embedded in a context called "reading" or "mathematics" or "social studies" or some other discipline carry meaning. Students share that meaning as they read. Then, writing across the curriculum extends that sharing. As students write responses, they, in turn, become authors of meaning about or because of the words that have been shared. This appropriation of meaning and shared ownership is sometimes called writing to learn.

The importance of writing to learn is to help students get into the habit of writing, to understand writing as a representation of what they think, and to use writing to foster thinking and to integrate knowledge. If students believe writing only belongs in English or language arts classes, they may thwart the positive brain patterning that develops through writing often and for many purposes. In a sense they may be fragmenting their own learning. If writing in all contexts is a manifestation of appropriated information, why is there sometimes resistance to writing across the curriculum?

REASONS FOR RESISTANCE TO WRITING ACROSS THE CURRICULUM

One major reason for resistance to writing across the curriculum is a teacher's need for strategies that bring about in a classroom what writers seem to do naturally in life. They write letters to the editor when they feel strongly about issues. They tell stories that rise out of their experiences. They converse about family, sometimes telling a time-worn family story over and over again. They ask for clarifications; they demand examples. They persuade; they respond in genuine ways to the persuasion of others. They jot notes and memos. They record in journals, diaries, logs, and record books. They generate lists. They write personal letters, essays, poems, novels, treatises, problems, hypotheses, lab reports—all filled with uniquely appropriated meaning. Even when teachers do use strategies that enable students to become authentically engaged in writing, it may be difficult to convince them, as well as parents, colleagues, administrators, and the community, that they are indeed learning. Many people have been conditioned to think learning should be so arduous that it must be endured, not enjoyed, yet few things are as exciting as uncovering a meaning, giving words to thought, or discovering something new.

Another difficulty in writing across the curriculum lies in faulty perceptions on the part of both teachers and students. Some teachers, for example, may interpret the phrase "writing across the curriculum" to mean that they should now teach all the conventions of writing in their classrooms. This immediately sets off signals, and red flags go up. "That's the English teacher's job." "I can't even cover what I'm supposed to, and they want me to teach writing now." "I hate writing. That's why I didn't become an English teacher." "I don't have time to grade the writing." "I wouldn't know how to grade it." For students, the response is generally more straightforward. "This isn't English. Why do you want me to write in here?" So it seems three myths prevail: (1) Writing (implicit is teaching all the conventions and correcting all the grammar) would have to be taught in addition to the subject matter; (2) writing means students generate more papers and more papers mean more grading; and (3) writing should occur only in English and language arts classes. These myths are ubiquitous, pervasive, and sometimes debilitating.

It is time to reexamine these myths. Writing, one of the most rigorous intellectual activities, one that demands the writer take ephemeral, abstract thoughts and reconstitute them on a blank page in a comprehensible way, is both a manifestation and a mode of thought. With so much information bombarding students daily, they need strategies to cope with that information. Hazy or lazy thinking will not serve them well. So it seems prudent on every level that teachers in all disciplines come to grips with a definition of writing that includes thought and learning. When they do, they will be better able to use writing to maximize learning and enhance the intellectual rigor of their students.

Leon Botstein, president of Bard College, in the foreword to *Writing to Learn Mathematics and Science*, says, "Ordinary language, particularly in its notated forms—writing—must be construed as part of everyday experience. Even at low levels of general literacy, the complex cognitive and epistemological processes imbedded in everyday speech (as opposed to tacit experience) and action constitute a sufficient link to understanding mathematics and science. The act of writing in the process of learning these subject areas is essential to developing curiosity and comprehension in the learner" (Countryman xiv).

> *Sometimes people ask, "Not everyone will be employed in these higher-level thinking professions. What of the housekeeper or the gardener? Why do they need to learn to write?" While there are several responses to that line of thinking—one that questions whether these folks would teach to what they perceive to be the lowest common denominator, another that questions their touch with reality and what the future promises—the most tactful response is this parable of the gardener.*
>
> *Because we travel frequently, we have hired a young man to take care of our yard. We rarely see him. He sends us bills and we pay them. Recently we thought it would be nice to put in some bedding plants, so we wrote him a note explaining what we had in mind. He sent us back a note asking for more specifics—color, type, exact placement, and amount. We answered with more directions. He responded with questions about fertilizers, quotes of prices, and other pertinent information. Eventually the flowers were planted.*

Myth 1: Writing Would Have to Be Taught in Addition to the Subject Matter

First, maintaining that writing belongs in all disciplines is not an effort to turn all teachers into English language arts teachers, although, on a very basic level, all teachers do teach English because they model it daily. But in all practicality, it may be necessary to rethink exactly who teaches what. Perhaps English language arts teachers need to incorporate more information into their teaching of writing from other disciplines, while teachers in other disciplines need to incorporate more written responses into their class work. Perhaps teachers need to pool their efforts by team teaching, that is, two or more teachers collaborating and teaching smaller groups within larger groups. Perhaps, to borrow Madeline Hunter's term, lessons need to be designed with an "'educational wiggle' that will accommodate students who need different 'catch hold' points in a content area" (53). Perhaps time needs to be expanded so that teaching can be more sustained and take place within longer blocks. Perhaps students need to be grouped by phases and mastery of certain objectives, not solely by chronology—primary, lower elementary, middle elementary, upper elementary, lower high school, upper high school—in order to maximize the knowledge of skilled teachers and the learning of the students. If depth is the desired goal, then time must be allotted to plumb the depths. Madeline Hunter suggests that in the old paradigm *time* was the constant, but in the new paradigm *learning* has become the constant (2). Certainly this jibes with cognitive theory and brain research—as clearly, no two learners are exactly alike.

THREE EXAMPLES OF WRITING— SUBJECT MATTER INTEGRATION

Example 1: Math. Laurye Webb, a mathematics teacher in Alief ISD, opens her students to interesting writing assignments that connect to mathematics. Recently, all her middle school students worked in small groups designing games. Not only did the criteria of mathematical concepts have to be present in the final product, but also the directions had to be written in clear, appropriate English. Laurye checked the precision of their language as much as their mathematics as she monitored the groups, advised, probed, nudged, and facilitated.

Example 2: Science. Likewise, the third-graders of Dawn Mathews McLendon, Fernandez Elementary, Northside ISD, became deeply engaged in all aspects of earthquake investigation following the one that hit the San Francisco area. They role-played television interviewers, jotted notes, and wrote news articles; they researched the sites of prior earthquakes and predicted future earthquakes; they figured the projected costs for reclamation in areas hit by earthquakes; they had maps and globes and rulers and paper and pencils everywhere. Each cluster of students fine-tuned their area of expertise because they knew they would be sharing it with others in the class who also knew a great deal about the subject. Observing that class, it was difficult to see where one subject ended and another began. Students were writing their science and using science in their writing. They were reading, writing, calculating, and computing. They were listening, speaking, and thinking. They posed some problems and solved others. But no matter, because these students were totally immersed in their study, they understood the true nature of how knowledge crosses and criss-crosses itself in what Vygotsky calls a "web of meaning."

Example 3: History. In Abilene High School, the study of ballads in senior English led to a discussion of folklore and eventually to discussion of some specific local folklore—a phantom lady that supposedly appears on the local lake. In sharing their renditions of this lore, the students became intensely interested in the variations of the tale. They became so taken with the story that the history and English teacher combined classes to give students more time for deeper study. Thus began research into Fort Phantom, the supposed site of the story, which led next to discoveries about Fort Phantom Hill, ten miles or so from Abilene, Texas. That, in turn, ushered in history, most especially the mistaken geography of a Major General Smith who thought he was to build the fort to protect settlers on the Brazos and Trinity rivers.

After thorough investigations of local histories, old newspapers, and interviews with elderly residents, they decided they needed empirical data, so in caravans of cars, these twelfth-graders drove out to Fort Phantom. Later some even claimed to have seen the lady. They wrote their own versions of the ballad, which they performed at an all-school assembly. Subsequently, these seniors were written up in the local paper and interviewed on the local television station. It is not likely that these seniors, or their teachers, will soon forget ballads and how history envelops them. The entire experience echoed what Anne Ruggles Gere says, "Secondary education should provide students a way of thinking, not a set of facts" (3).

Admittedly, these examples indicate a longer, deeper, more intense study of mathematics, science, social studies, and literature, with writing as the thread that wound the learning events into a fabric with larger meaning. However, writing also may be used for shorter responses. Every class need not explore the entire lode in the mine; sometimes studying a nugget will do.

Strategies such as "Admit" and "Exit" slips, suggested by authors in Gere's *Roots in the Sawdust*, are brief written responses that can be collected as "tickets" in or out of any class. Learning logs, in which students write what they have learned each class period or at the end of the day, provide opportunities for students to capture their learning through writing. Instead of writing when they enter class or at the start of the day, they write as closure. These logs are then available as references to analyze their thinking processes or to see where they were so they may judge where they are going. They may wish to add, extend, alter, or elaborate upon what is there. What better way for teacher and student to see what was actually internalized?

Brainstorming as a class or listing in small groups are other ways to get students thinking, then writing. The old adage, "If you can't write it, you don't know it" holds.

In truth, teachers in any discipline who require writing should be ready to help their students through the process of that writing. Some training in the teaching of writing will be beneficial in order to do this effectively. The notion of teaming or clustering—English language arts teachers coupled with teachers from other disciplines—may present a viable option. Whatever the alternative, it is clear the old boundaries are crumbling. The days of standing in front of a class of row-upon-row of students, assigning a paper, and expecting that paper to happen are past. Vito Perrone, director of programs in teacher education at the Harvard Graduate School of Education and senior fellow of the Carnegie Foundation for the Advancement of Teaching, urges restructuring that is "within a framework of consequential purposes. Otherwise, what passes for restructuring will be formulaic and limited in substance, leading ultimately to greater cynicism" (132). He contends that "teachers need to construct for themselves a more powerful voice" (133). Teachers cannot construct a voice without very recent study in the ways students learn.

Myth 2: Writing Means Students Generate More Papers and More Papers Mean More Grading

Of course writing needs to be evaluated, but there are different purposes for evaluating, just as there are different purposes for writing. Reading prewriting and drafts holistically, for example, meets the need for a general impression of where the piece is in its rough form. Sometimes a student just needs assurance he or she is on the right track. Papers that have gone through the process require more deliberate assessment, perhaps through an analytic scale, but much of the writing that happens daily as reader-response is either shared immediately, is filed for further consideration, or is simply judged as work in progress.

Reconsider the three previous examples. The middle school students working on their game wrote reams. They filled pages with descriptions of their designs. They wrote problem cards, challenge cards, trivia cards to be used as part of the game. They wrote directions, mini "how-to" essays. They tested, corrected, revised, and reformulated what they had written. They wanted their game to "work." Laurye walked around, clipboard in hand, making notes, giving credit for work in progress, then she assessed the final product according to the criteria set out at the onset.

Another point: Because her students had worked in groups, she had six or seven games to evaluate per class, not twenty-five or thirty.

The third-graders were constantly writing. There was so much writing by the end of their study that Dawn asked them to gather it together "archaeologically," that is, what they did first was on the bottom; what they did last was on top. Then she led them quite brilliantly through some self-assessment (all the while taking notes in her grade book): What did they learn? How did they learn it? What would they do differently? What was best among their efforts? She did not read every word in every packet, but she knew exactly what each student had done. Grading for Dawn was easy.

The high school students' ballads were evaluated by the English teacher according to the characteristics of a ballad and the conventions of English; their historical research was evaluated by the history teacher. The history teacher then read the ballads for historical accuracy while the English teacher read the research for English conventions. Each student received a grade in each discipline; they also received a grade for process.

One additional example: Carolyn L. Johnson, a Deerpark Middle School teacher in Round Rock ISD, Round Rock, Texas, describes a workable classroom management strategy that provides for maximum reader-response without teacher burnout. (She describes the strategy in an article in process.) After studying the response theory of Robert Probst, Carolyn initiated readers' logs and literary letters in her classes. As an ongoing process, students respond in their readers' logs to whatever reading they accomplished that day. Sometimes she gives them questions as nudges, e.g., "How did what you read today make you feel?" At the conclusion of the week, students read through their logs and write a literary letter to her; to a classmate, a student in another class, or a friend; or to a caregiver, parent, or trusted adult. Carolyn's strategy works like this: Week 1: third period writes their letters to her; fifth period writes to a classmate; seventh period writes to their parents. Week 2: third period writes to a classmate; fifth to their parents, seventh to her. Week 3: third period writes to their parents, fifth to her, and seventh to a classmate. This rotation continues throughout the year with occasional scheduled breaks. In this way, Carolyn explains, there is a continuity of response, but she only responds to one class per week, not to every student every week.

Clearly, one implication is that students should be writing every day for many purposes, but every piece of that writing does not have to undergo traditional scrutiny. In the real world, people are judged on their best work, not on every attempt. Dancers practice for hours and make many mistakes, but audiences only see the final performance. Advertising agents create many concepts for clients, but they disregard all but their best for the final conference. Chefs experiment with sauces but serve only the most exquisite. Students should write, practice, create, and experiment, but they should be graded only on their best.

Myth 3: Writing Should Occur Only in English and Language Arts Classes

If writing occurs only in English language arts classes, students regard it as a limited tool, something perhaps associated with literature or isolated grammar. Indeed, some students (who grow up to be parents) think grammar *is* writing. In today's world, students probably are not exposed to much writing in their homes—the phone has replaced the letter in many households—and they certainly do not see evidences of it on television—the TelePrompTer has become so sophisticated, viewers do not even see speakers' notes or papers. Students most often do not see people generating notes, memos, lab reports, logs, and the other writing referenced earlier in this chapter. In addition, informal and formal surveys of teachers reveal that many do not write with their students (King). Therefore, it seems students have few models. No wonder students wonder at the brouhaha about writing. It must seem to many of them a worthless endeavor to learn—one created, no doubt, to bedevil them.

In truth, writing is an inextricably important skill in the world. Many business telephone calls are followed up with letters. Reports of all types on all levels are part of the work-a-day world.

Firefighters write reports; so do police officers, inspectors, insurance people, midmanagement, and C.E.O.'s. People who cannot write clearly and coherently are disadvantaged at best and, at worst, exploitable. In addition to the pragmatic application of writing, there is its aesthetic value. As a major symbolizing system, writing and an appreciation of writing enriches life through its levels of meaning and its nuances. As thinking on paper, it enables a person to clarify and refine thought. It also empowers people. Historically, one way to keep people in lower social strata was to limit their ability to write and read. The most effective way to communicate the importance of writing is by valuing it daily in the classroom.

> *I received a call from a C.E.O. of a large food chain. After the usual amenities, the distinguished-sounding voice on the other end asked, "Do you do for businesses what you do for teachers? Do you offer training in writing?"*
>
> *Before answering, I inquired about the reason for his call. He replied, "We like to encourage our people to work hard. And we reward them. We have some folks working for us who began as baggers, who were promoted to stockers, and who eventually worked their way into midmanagement positions. But I'm sitting here right now with three memos written by employees that make no sense to me; I can't understand them, and I'm the C.E.O."*

Robert J. Marzano, deputy director of training and development at the Midcontinent Regional Educational Laboratory in Aurora, Colorado, maintains that "a fundamental goal of schooling is for students to learn whatever is deemed important in a given subject—in other words, to acquire and integrate knowledge" (31). If students are to integrate knowledge, then schools should be structured and classes taught in a way that facilitates integration.

THE READING-WRITING CONNECTION ACROSS THE CURRICULUM

New Criticism

In order to gain a historical perspective on the reading-writing connection and how it applies across the curriculum, it is important to take a giant step or two back to the movement called New Criticism. This theory, primarily espoused by I. A. Richards, held that the text was central and primary to the learning experience, for it was the repository of truth and wisdom, and anything extraneous to the text was considered irrelevant. Teachers, considered authorities, albeit authorities by degree, were powerful. They were charged with transmitting this truth and wisdom to students, who, as neophyte readers-as-critics of the text, could never completely ascertain its truths or understand its wisdom without help. Clem Young of the Brisbane College of Advanced Education contends that New Criticism caught students in "a theory of deficits" (Young 11). By that he means that once the "true" or "correct" response had been postulated by professionals, any other response jarred the integrity of the work and was therefore considered "incorrect." So the job of the student became one of "learning the techniques of unlocking textual meanings and internalizing the canons of literary judgement and taste" (Young 11). Thus, the correctness of the response was judged according to its match with the postulations of the piece—the closer the match, the higher the grade. In this paradigm, the final critique was all important. Therefore, New Criticism stands as a product approach to teaching and learning that affected the way teachers have taught reading, literature, and other subjects since the 1920s.

Reader-Response Criticism

Reader-response criticism, or what is sometimes called transactional theory, grew out of Louise M. Rosenblatt's studies at the Sorbonne in the 1930s, and ran alongside the writings of William James, C. S. Peirce, George Santayana, and John Dewey. Rosenblatt succinctly states, "I rejected the notion of the poem-as-object, and the neglect of both author and reader" (1978, xii). In essence, Rosenblatt and those who followed her reintroduced the author and the reader back into the learning experience—the text belongs to the author, but the poem is what the reader creates from the text. In short, she returned the reader to the text as a cocreator of its meaning. Additionally, Wolfgang Iser, an adherent to the reader-response theory, posits that a painting or a sculpture or any text cannot be entirely taken in all at one time, so the understanding is dynamic, ever-changing, "a moving viewpoint which travels along *inside* that which is has to apprehend" (108-109). This makes sense. Most people will admit that they can read a passage one day and get certain meanings, but, upon rereading the same passage several days later, arrive at new and some different meanings. All that has transpired in the interim, plus mood, fatigue level, even the time of day, changes the reader's comprehension and response. Indeed, "Scientific research shows that there are a minimum of 500,000,000,000 possible different responses to a given text, that's at least 200 different responses for everybody in the world! And they are all related" (Purves 38-39). In light of recent brain research, that figure is probably conservative.

Reader-response theory invites the reader to call upon not just five senses, but what M. C. Richards identifies as "twelve senses: touch, life, movement, balance, smell, taste, sight, warmth, hearing, word, thought, and ego. The sense of ego is the highest. It is the sense one has of another" (146). In reading the work of others, no matter what discipline or what level, the reader must sense self and others in order to achieve what Rosenblatt calls understanding, which she defines as implying "the full impact of the sensuous, emotional, as well as intellectual force of the word" (1983, 112).

The way to help students develop this ability to participate in a text, according to Rosenblatt, is "to encourage them to engage in such imaginative writing. In this way they will themselves be involved in wrestling with the materials offered them by life or by their reaction to it; they will discover that problems of form and artistry are not separable from the problems of clarifying the particular sense of life or the particular human mood that the work of art is destined to embody" (1983, 48-49). With this theory, a teacher would not make the following comments to students: "No, that is wrong. You cannot feel that way." "No, World War II should not remind you of your uncle's death." "No, that mathematical problem can be solved only one way." Rather, the teacher receives the individual responses, lets them reverberate with each other, and then as Rosenblatt says, "the teacher will be able to lead him [the learner] to the various kinds of knowledge that will enable him to achieve the experiences offered by this particular text" (1983, 114). Because reader-response criticism as its very core validates the equality of personal meanings, esteems the both/all answer, and respects the primacy of individual responses and the plurality of meaning, it rests comfortably in the process paradigm.

Processes of Writing and Reading

Writing has been called the flip side of reading because composing and comprehending are so entangled that they really emerge as two sides of the same process. When composing, learners create meaning; when comprehending, learners recreate meaning. When writing, learners both compose and comprehend. First they write what they mean, then they return—sometimes over and over again—to understand what they have written, to develop it, to extend it, to reconsider it as a reader in an act of recreation. When reading, learners also compose and comprehend. First they read what someone has written, they compose that meaning for themselves (what Bakhtin calls "appropriating meaning"), then they comprehend that meaning (what it means to them and what it means to the writer).

This process best describes what writing across the curriculum does—it elicits responses from students after they have read a given text. These responses illuminate what meaning has been appropriated and what may be built upon for further learning. To begin the trek of writing across the curriculum, teachers might be served best by recognizing that composing is done by both writers and readers.

"Writing about reading is one of the best ways to get students to unravel their transactions so that we can see how they understand and, in the process, help them to elaborate, clarify, and illustrate their responses by reference to the associations and prior knowledge that inform them" (Petrosky 24). The following section describes a number of strategies to generate these responses from students in any discipline.

READING-WRITING STRATEGIES

Read and retell, shielding, the tri-fold, the dialectical notebook, text renderings, text tamperings, subtexting, sequence charts, writing walls, and "jackdaws" are among the reading-writing strategies that help nudge meaning out of literature, art and music, the performing arts, mathematics, science, social studies, physical education, computer study, English as a second language (ESL), and the industrial arts, and tease it onto the page. Also, most of the prewriting strategies described in chapter 3 may be used for reader-responses, for example, the pentad, hexagonal writing, trigger words, and so forth. Some of these strategies may offer a way into meaning just once; others may be repeated often. The pedagogy here is—repeat and vary.

Read and Retell

Explanation. This is a strategy developed by Hazel Brown and Brian Cambourne and has been adapted from their book *Read and Retell*. This strategy is easy to prepare, suitable across the curriculum, flexible, and provides practice over a range of skills that include reading, writing, listening, talking, thinking, interacting, comparing, matching, selecting, organizing, remembering, and understanding.

Implementation

1. Divide class into groups of four or five students.

2. Provide the title of the text to be studied.

3. On the basis of the title, students write a brief prediction of the text.

4. Share predictions in group.

5. Students comment on each other's predictions.

6. Teacher reads the text aloud.

7. Students read the text silently as many times as they need or wish to read it.

8. Students, not looking at the text, quickly write out what they remember.

9. Students share and compare what they have written.

10. Debrief.

Remarks. Read and retell begins with a level of surprise. Its novelty usually captures students' interest. It involves intensive reading and collaboration and demands intensive listening and attending. Writing engages the learner in a gamut of language processes. Sharing and comparing invites multiple readings and rereadings, shifts of focus, and metacognitive assessments. Brown and Cambourne claim observable growth in "knowledge of text forms; knowledge of text conventions; the conscious awareness of processes involved in text construction; the range and variety of text forms and conventions being employed in other writing tasks; control of vocabulary; reading flexibility; confidence" (11-12). When using read and retell, skilled teachers extend learners to levels beyond the paraphrasing level.

Shielding

The shielding strategy, developed by Edward Wilson, is fully explained in the reading following this chapter (pages 507-512). It is important to note that this strategy may be used in other than basic classes, and that it works particularly well when integrated with the study of medieval history or heraldry, or when taken in conjunction with any study related to King Arthur. Another effective way to use shielding is as an introduction—a project begun the very first day of class. Not only do teachers gain insights into students, but students gain insights into other students. It becomes a reflexive writing activity that can be called upon repeatedly throughout the grading period, semester, or year, for example, "We're going to study symbolism. Let's look at some of the symbols we put on our shields."

Projects

The notion of the ongoing use of the shield as a point of reference suggests the advantage of other ongoing projects, i.e., cooperative ventures undertaken by individuals or groups of students that expand the concepts taught and invite practical and immediate application of these concepts. Howard Gardner offers projects as one way to achieve performance-based education and assessment that go "beyond the bubble." He says that "students in these [Vermont, California, Connecticut] and some other states are being asked to carry out extended projects, often cooperatively, in which they demonstrate 'in practical situations' their understandings of concepts in mathematics, science, and other disciplines" (259). He cites examples in which students, while working on projects, argue controversial issues, design fiscally sound programs, assess toxic water supplies, and determine accurate media reporting. He portrays projects as a way around what can be faked because performance-based learning "requires sufficient mastery of concepts and principles so that students are able to bring them to bear appropriately on large multifaceted problems of the sort for which learnings ought to be mobilized" (259).

Tri-fold

Explanation. The tri-fold is a listening and thinking strategy that uses reader-response as its springboard. Workable with any discipline across the curriculum, it is a quick and nonthreatening way to involve all students, since they begin with what they consider important.

Implementation

1. Students use one sheet of paper, which they fold horizontally into thirds. (For elementary students, this may be a teachable moment for fractions.)

2. A story, poem, section from a text, or chapter is read aloud. Students are cautioned to listen carefully.

3. After the reading, students write in the center third what struck them most and why.

4. They write in the top third what came before what they wrote in the center section.

5. They write in the bottom third what came after what they wrote in the center section.

6. They divide into groups and share. They begin by reading their centers, then they share their before and after sections. After that they discuss the similarities and differences in their responses.

7. Conduct a debriefing on what was learned.

Remarks. This strategy gives students ownership over the material. They determine, in a truly reader-response way, what is important to them. Most often students will identify the main idea, but the point is *they* do the identifying. Through sharing, they hear the responses of others, which often extends their thinking. The strategy is also good for sequencing, with the focal point decided by the student. It makes class discussion more interesting as there will be differences in all sections of the tri-fold that permit the validation of diversity. Although tri-folds also serve as excellent prewriting for a longer piece of discourse, they may be an end unto themselves. Students often find that the center section offers the nugget for a thesis or a proposition that can be used with little refining, perhaps combining it with something gleaned from another student or from one of the other sections of their tri-fold.

This strategy was adapted to a pre-algebra class by Mary Ryan at Jefferson High School in San Antonio ISD, Texas. She invited her students to write three positive and three negative integers in the center section. In the top section they created a word problem using the integers from the center section. Then they exchanged papers. The recipient of the paper solved the problem in the bottom section and explained the process used to arrive at the solution. The papers were returned and checked by the originator of the problem. The teacher had only to double check these. Grading went quickly because Mary monitored the students during their work in process. Figure 15.1 is a sample from Maria Vasques, an ESL student. Maria clearly has difficulty with the English language, but not with the mathematical concepts of positive and negative integers. There can be no doubt that by writing in the mathematics class, and in other classes across the curriculum, she is receiving optimum practice using English as well as the opportunity to integrate it with other knowledge.

Dialectical Notebooks

Explanation. Ann E. Berthoff describes the dialectical notebook as a place for construing and constructing, that is, it is a double-entry notebook that invites the student to write notes on one side and notes about those notes on the other side. She says, "The important thing is to separate

Fig. 15.1. Maria Vasques's math tri-fold.

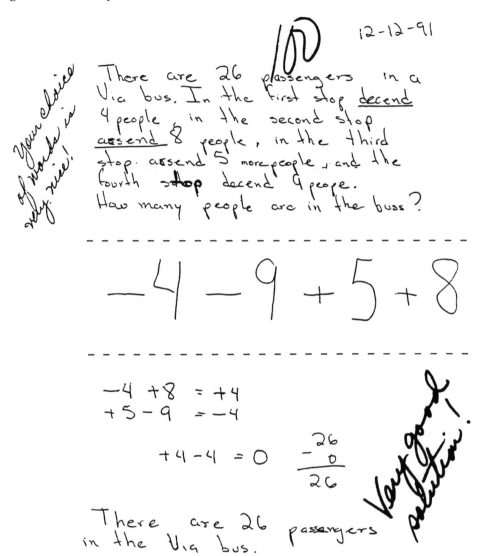

your notes from notes about notes so that you can carry on a dialogue between you-as-listener and you-as-reviewer, the One Who Listens and Looks Again" (26).

Implementation

1. Students draw a line vertically down the center of each page in a standard spiral note-book. They label the column on the left "Notes"; they label the column on the right "Notes on Notes."

2. Students use the left side of these pages to take notes from a source, for example, pacewalking in physical education, Copernicus in science, recent newspaper reports in social studies, and so forth. They may include reading or observational notes, direct quotations, sketches, passages, fragments, lists, images (verbal and visual), and paraphrases.

3. On the right side, students write commentary on the notes. They may include their own notes or observations, comments, responses, reactions, comparisons, contrasts, summaries, questions, suggestions, revisions, and aphorisms.

Remarks. Berthoff calls this activity the "audit of meaning," that is, a continuous effort to review thought and meaning. It is metacognitive because there is continual opportunity to "see" one's thinking and rethink its meaning.

Emily Flores, a Coke R. Stevenson Middle School teacher in Northside ISD, San Antonio, Texas, uses the dialectical notebook with her eighth-grade students. She says it benefits them in four ways: it strengthens notetaking and listening skills, it provides a valuable study and review tool, it serves as a writing to learn tool in other classes, and it works as a spark for future writing topic possibilities. Emily collects dialectical notebooks five times during a six-week marking period. Each check is worth a maximum of 20 points. Students receive 10 points for thoroughness and completion; 5 points for effort on both sides of the notebook; 5 points for conscientious upkeep of notes and responses, neatness, and practicality of notebook contents. Figure 15.2 is an excerpt from Richard Baisen's notebook.

Fig. 15.2. A page from Richard Baisen's dialectical notebook.

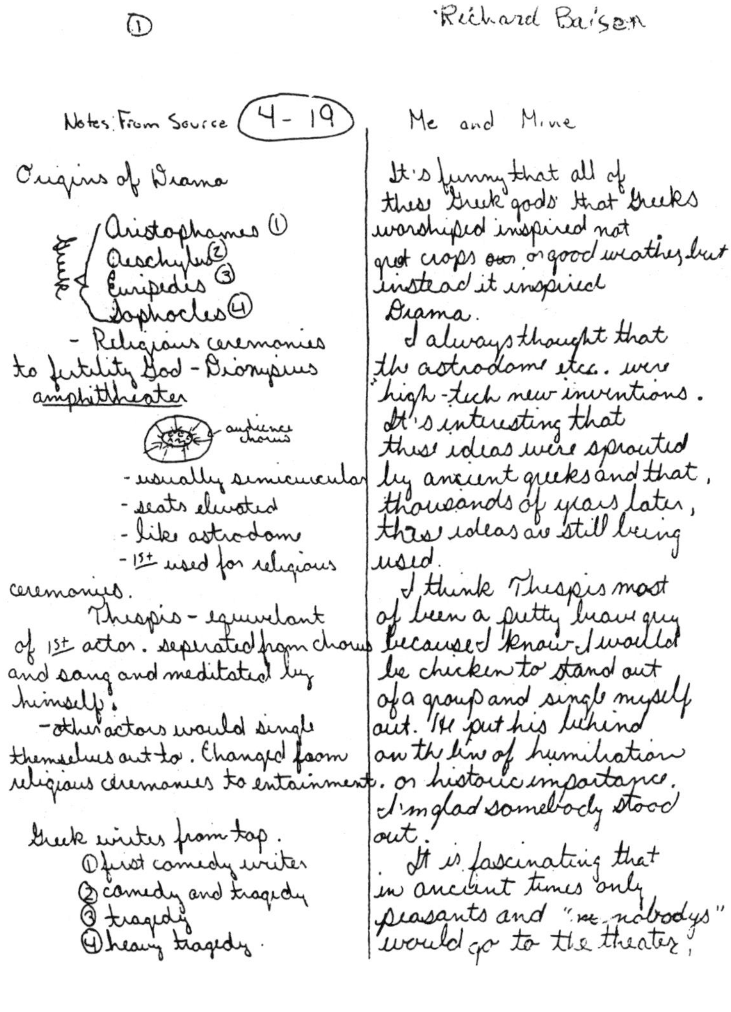

(1) Richard Baisen

Notes From Source (4-19)	Me and Mine
Origins of Drama Greek: Aristophanes (1), Aeschylus (2), Euripides (3), Sophocles (4) - Religious ceremonies to fertility God - Dionysius amphitheater audience, chorus - usually semicircular - seats elevated - like astrodome - 1st used for religious ceremonies. Thespis - equivalant of 1st actor. seperated from chorus and sang and meditated by himself. - other actors would single themselves out to. Changed from religious ceremonies to entainment. Greek writers from top. (1) first comedy writer (2) comedy and tragedy (3) tragedy (4) heavy tragedy.	It's funny that all of these Greek gods that Greeks worshiped inspired not great crops or good weather but instead it inspired Drama. I always thought that the astrodome etc. were high-tech new inventions. It's interesting that these ideas were sprouted by ancient greeks and that, thousands of years later, these ideas are still being used. I think Thespis must of been a pretty brave guy because I know I would be chicken to stand out of a group and single myself out. He put his behind on the line of humiliation or historic importance. I'm glad somebody stood out. It is fascinating that in ancient times only peasants and "nobodys" would go to the theater;

Richard records his connection between the Greek amphitheater, which he is studying, and contemporary amphitheaters, such as the Houston Astrodome, which is part of his experiential knowledge. That is an important association; he is linking ideas, he is making connections. The dialectical notebook has enabled him to integrate his knowledge. This subjective organization of information is key to memory. Richard also identifies with the bravery of Thespis, a typical and therefore genuine response from an adolescent. Perhaps most telling on the left side, however, is the way he organized the Greek writers, with numbers following their names. It is not apparent until the bottom of the column that Richard used them as an identification code. Does Richard know he needs space (and perhaps time) between received information so he can process it? Was Richard mimicking some model quiz he read or saw in a magazine? Was the information given this way in the source? Was Richard testing himself as he took the notes? Whatever the answers to these questions, it is clear that the dialectical notebook helped Richard appropriate meaning. It also gives Emily a clear picture of Richard's learning at this point.

Text Rendering

Explanation. Text rendering comes from the musical idea of rendition. When students "render" a text they interpret it; they create their version of it. Like the jazz greats, they may improvise on a theme, repeat chords, omit what seems extraneous—but they never lose the original melody, the harmonious relationships—they just play around with them.

Implementation

1. Divide students into groups. Assign a poem, story, passage, chapter, or section to be rendered.

2. Model a short text rendering.

3. Groups decide how they will render their assignment, but they must keep to the following guidelines:

    a. Convey the basic information;

    b. Repeat, interweave (as in counterpoint), rearrange, or improvise;

    c. Omit nothing important;

    d. Add nothing new—stay with the words in the text;

    e. Say parts singularly or in chorus, chant, rap, or in any combination;

    f. Words may be emphasized by drawing them out, by tone, pitch, or repetition;

    g. Groups may ask other groups to participate in all or part of their rendering.

4. Groups present their renderings orally to the class.

Remarks. This strategy electrifies a class. One, it is novel. Two, it is collaborative. Three, it allows, even encourages, different learning styles. Four, it is fun. Additionally and importantly, students who are aural learners benefit, as do kinetic learners. Perhaps most importantly, it demands close reading, and the repetition of the information during practice in groups helps students remember the material. This works with children's books, passages from texts, and rules for teams to remember. It reinforces musical concepts, encourages a transfer to art concepts, and assists ESL students who learn language by repeating and using it. What would happen in science, if students rendered their lab reports? What would happen in mathematics, if students rendered their word problems? What would happen in social studies, if students rendered a poignant passage on the issue of slavery, or a powerful section on war, or a somewhat dull chapter on various treaties?

At first students may render more like a chorus or a reader's theater, but the elegance of this strategy becomes apparent with additional implementations. Students borrow and use ideas for renderings after hearing each other. Callie Vassar, San Antonio ISD, used it successfully during her appraisal lesson to introduce her twelfth-graders to Chaucer. She confided that all the students became involved, and that she received high marks from her appraiser.

Text Tampering

Explanation. Building on Rosenblatt's concept of cocreating a text, Iser's concept of coming to a text from a moving viewpoint, and Jacques Derrida's theory of deconstruction, text tamperings actually invite students to take the text and manipulate it into meaning. Bill Corcoran, senior lecturer in English education at James Cook University of North Queensland, Australia, claims that tampering with texts has "long been in the repertoire of inspired teachers who have played with, distorted, and cut the texts to shape their students rather than contorting their students to the shape of the text" (66). And readers have always done this—who has not mentally rewritten the dialogue for a beloved character, created a different ending, predicted an outcome, put themselves into the text, or played "what if" while reading? This strategy simply asks students to do this tampering on paper.

Consider the implicit invitation to tamper with the text in this book. The articles have an accompanying commentary and wide margins, which bids readers to add their commentary—thereby together cocreating additional meanings.

Implementation. There are three major ways to tamper with a text. Each of these may be adapted in various ways, so that there are many possible permutations and innovations. The first is to find the gaps in a story, passage, or chapter, or even in a sentence or two. For example, take the first book in the *Chronicles of Narnia*. C. S. Lewis begins with these two sentences:

> Once there were four children whose names were Peter, Susan, Edmund and Lucy. This story is about something that happened to them when they were sent away from London during the war because of the air-raids.

Students (or teacher, but it is far better for students to do this) identify the gaps for them, places where they may insert their own projections. As they travel along the book, they may modify or change their projections. For instance, students may find a gap in not immediately knowing the ages of the children. They may, therefore, project what they think the ages to be. Before the opening paragraph is over, they will discover who is the youngest and next youngest. They may have to change their projection, or they may feel good about being correct.

Students may wonder what war the author means. Filling in that gap for most students probably would entail research and analysis of the clues in the text.

Students working in groups may collaborate on any subject using this strategy. There are gaps in other genre besides narratives, for example, rules, directions, and experiments, to name a few.

Young children do this almost naturally when they make predictions based on the pictures in the book. They also predict as the story is being read to them, "I think they will find the princess." Teachers help this along by stopping regularly while reading aloud to ask children to predict, project, identify, comment, or consider what the authors did not tell.

Another way to tamper with texts is by writing different beginnings or endings, or by extending the story with a sequel. While this is not a new notion, and, in fact, it can become somewhat trite, there are many stories and opportunities that lend themselves to this activity. Also, it provides an effective way for students to search out the seeds in a passage or story in order to make their changes fit. It is not enough to write a new ending to a story, for example. That ending must flow from the story, which assumes comprehension, and must bring events to a reasonable conclusion. Writing, for example, that all the children in Margaret Wild's *Let the Celebrations Begin!* lived happily ever after is to belie any knowledge of the survivors of concentration camps, their physical and mental health, their desire to locate parents, and so forth.

Writing self into a story or a passage is a third way to text tamper. Students may do this by becoming a new character, an observer, or the scientist or mathematician who is being studied. ESL students may conduct an interview using alternating languages with a character in the story. In the industrial arts, students may take some information, such as building a bookcase or roofing a house, and rewrite it for the television show "Home Improvement." Students may take great liberties as they cozy into a text, but they must remain faithful to its information.

Remarks. This strategy promotes risk taking, thinking, research, close reading, remembering, rereading, checking, cross-checking, integrating information, and writing. Students enjoy finding the gaps and filling them in, writing different parts, and placing themselves in the context. They experience self-satisfaction, gain confidence, and develop some aesthetic sense. Also, this skill of projecting and inferring is an important one for a future that promises rapid change and many unknowns; it will be the basic skill called upon to cope.

Sub-Texting

Explanation. Sub-texting is an idea used in drama by Roslyn Arnold of the University of Sydney, but it may be applied to other disciplines as well. Arnold defines sub-texting as a method of "articulating and bringing to the surface all the ideas and associations the reader has in response to the text" (220).

Implementation. (This implementation is adapted from Arnold 218-233.)

1.   Divide students into large groups. (Arnold suggests 10 in a group.)

2.   Distribute copies of the text, or assign sections of the text to each group.

3.   Model sub-texting for students.

4.   Students, in turn, read several lines or sentences as originally written, then they write those lines *in first person*, as if they were the character or as if they were present. Finally, they read their lines as a free translation.

5. Validate all responses, no matter how trivial, silly, or confused they may be. Responses often vary, but it is in the diversity that students begin to see what the text means when it is enacted by others.

6. After sub-texting once, the text may be reworked again. (Arnold claims that often in the reworking aberrant interpretations are excised for the more conventional ones.)

Figure 15.3 shows how a group of ninth-graders sub-texted a portion of *Romeo and Juliet*.

Fig. 15.3. Ninth-graders' sub-text exercise.

Romeo and Juliet, Act I, Scene i,
Lines 163-173

TEXT	SUB-TEXT
Enter Romeo	
Benvolio: Good morrow, cousin.	Romiester! What's going down?
Romeo: Is the day so young?	This day's a drag. Is it still only morning?
Benvolio: But new struck nine.	It's nine. What's your problem?
Romeo: Ay me! sad hours seem long.	I'm bummed out and tired of waiting.
Was that my father that went hence so fast?	Hey, was that Dad in the Porsche? Whoa!
Benvolio: It was. What sadness lengthens Romeo's hours?	Yeah. One more time, what's your problem?
Romeo: Not having that which having makes them short.	I'm not getting anywhere with Julie.
Benvolio: In love?	Man, are you falling for that chick?
Romeo: Out —	I'm out in left field, I think.
Benvolio: Of love?	Why her? You could have your pick.
Romeo: Out of her favor, where I am in love.	She doesn't even look my way, and I'm crazy about her.
Benvolio: Alas! that love, so gentle in his view, Should be so tyrannous and rough in proof!	That's a real bummer, man. She's neat, but she sure is making it rough on you.

Remarks. Perhaps more than any other reader-response, this strategy elicits engagement and ownership. In answer to those who may express concern that sub-texting is not authentic reading, Arnold states, "I reiterate the purpose of sub-texting as one of coming to terms with the author's language through a dynamic process of making it one's own. When the process has been experienced effectively, the author's language lives for the reader, in its own right, and as part of the reader's range of experienced language options" (232). Recently published textbooks have so many annotations for almost every line of Shakespeare, the pages look like a dialectical notebook. With sub-texting, at least the annotations are the students' own.

Sequence Charts

Explanation. Sequence charts, while not new, are ideal ways to incorporate writing into a temporal perspective. They may be used to chronicle some historical occurrence, the course of events in a story, stages in a problem, the arrangement of procedures for making or creating something, the steps for following directions, the proceedings of a meeting, or the succession of happenings. They work for any discipline.

Implementation

1. Divide students into small groups.

2. Assign text to be sequenced.

3. Distribute long sheets of butcher paper or long pieces of cash register tape (about 4 or 5 feet) to each group.

4. Students reenter what they are to sequence and trace it on the paper. They may write, draw, cut out suitable pictures, affix small symbolic objects, or use a combination of media, textures, and words.

5. Groups share their sequence charts by explaining them to the class and then displaying them somewhere in the room or hall.

Remarks. This strategy, because it is collaborative, enriches the knowledge of each student. It invites reexamination of the text for a particular purpose. It lends itself to variation and specificity. For example, one variation is to keep the sequence chart daily, that is, end each class period with 10 minutes or so of work on the chart so that students may add what they learned that day. Also, teachers often make sequence charts specific, for example, sequence events by people or chronicle events by dates. When the sequence chart is complete, students may go back to add labels, other data, and further explanations. This acts as a review.

Writing Walls

Explanation. This is an ongoing strategy that invites writing in bursts; it is visual, enables review, and almost demands a final product. It can be done in any discipline.

Implementation

1. Distribute "bricks" in the form of 3-inch-by-5-inch index cards (or paper cut that size) to students at the end of a week, every several days, or even daily—depending on the class.

2. Students quickly write the most significant thing they have learned on their cards. (For teachers with multiple classes, the cards may be color-coded to a class, for example, first period uses green cards; third period, blue.)

3. When they have completed their cards, they affix them to the wall. (Qwik-Tac or other reusable adhesives work well for this because they can be used again and usually do not mar walls.) Students begin at the bottom of the wall. In this way they quite literally build a writing wall.

4. At the end of the marking period, divide students into groups. Students retrieve their bricks and discuss in group what they have learned. This serves as a review.

5. Teachers may want students to use the information on their cards to synthesize what they have learned and to write that into a sustained paper.

Remarks. Not only does this strategy encourage writing for a purpose, but the writing becomes a visible entity in the room. Students begin writing more as the wall progresses and they see what others have written. The collaborative nature of the final sharing is a novel and interesting way for students to review what they have learned and to continue to learn from others in their group.

Jackdaws

Explanation. Jackdaws, named after the curious European crow that takes interesting objects back to its nest, is a strategy that integrates reading, writing, speaking, viewing, and thinking with some interesting object or artifact. Typically, students are focused on the lesson through a selection from children's literature, which, while brief, ensures the lesson's direction or purpose. For example, students in American literature may be introduced to Emily Dickinson through Michael Bedard's delightful book *Emily*; social studies students may be presented with the African-American experience through an excerpt from Walter Dean Myers nonfiction work *Now Is Your Time!*; or science students may quickly embark on a study of aerodynamics through Robert Burleigh's award-winning *Flight*. Usually the reading is followed by students making or receiving an artifact associated with the book, an artifact that also may serve as a prompt for writing. Often there is the same sense of discovery in the making or receiving of an artifact as there is in writing. As M. C. Richards so eloquently says, "The exchange between the crafts, the mergers and the interpenetrations, are also witnesses to this centering attitude, which cuts across the lines and allows the values of color and shape and texture and innerness and architecture and use and inspiration all to blow like different currents of air into a single breath through whatever object we make" (63).

Implementation

1. No matter what the level, gather the students around your chair as you read. This closeness generates an intensity of purpose and better focuses the lesson.

2. Read the book, selection, or excerpt.

3. Discuss, predict, raise questions.

4. Distribute or make the artifact, for example, for *Emily* it may be a flower or flower bulb.

5. Students write something that rises out of the text, the artifact, or both. For *Emily*, creating a poem would be natural, although writing description or conducting research also would be appropriate. Another approach may invite students to freewrite to the lines, "I brought you some spring," or, "No, you are poetry. This only tries to be."

6. This strategy usually concludes with some type of sharing.

Remarks. "There is a continuum between the child's earliest retelling of the familiar picture-book story and the critical article in a learned journal" (Protherough 79). Knowing that, teachers on every level may wish to rethink the viability of using children's literature from time to time as doors to deeper, more sophisticated concepts. In addition to the obvious literary connections, the promised artifact always generates anticipation and surprise. Using children's literature as a springboard into any discipline and on any level enables quick access into the purpose of the lesson. (Presently there are four books in Joyce Armstrong Carroll's Jackdaws series. Each contains many examples of reading-writing connections, suggested artifacts, and extensions to other disciplines.)

> *"I want to thank you for an idea you gave me,"* said Peggy Meathenia, then director of curriculum for the San Marcos ISD, Texas. *"What idea is that?"* I asked.
> *"Using a piece of children's literature to focus a presentation. Now whenever I have a staff meeting, I find a book that has the message I want to convey encapsulated in it. I use it to start the meeting. People love the books. It sets a comfortable tone and gets our meetings off on a positive note."*

IMPLEMENTATION MODELS

Overview

In an effort to help teachers incorporate writing as a process and reader-response in their disciplines, five implementation models are included in this chapter. Language Arts, Social Studies, Science, Mathematics, and one for Kindergarten. These outlines may be adapted to any level. A high school English teacher may take the kindergarten idea of working with a corpus of work by an author, or a science teacher may work with a genre, for example, the informative essay. Also, these models are meant to *suggest* time lines. Some students may require an accelerated adaptation, while other students may demand more time in certain areas. Skilled teachers may adapt these models to smaller groups or even to individual learners within the class.

The general approach is to decide upon a key concept or genre, choose children's books or other literature that illuminate that concept or genre, establish the skills to be covered, and progress through the six weeks in natural, reader-response ways. The grids that are part of all but the kindergarten implementation model provide students with a concrete way to analyze their prewriting. As they reread their prewriting, they mark their grids. These marks then help them find patterns, relationships, or foci. The point of using a grid is not the grid per se, but rather a visual strategy to help students establish a link between their writing and the elements, facts, principles, essentials, points, or details within the discipline they are studying. A sample or model grid may be that day's mini-lesson. The teacher makes then marks the grid according to what is in his or her prewriting, while explaining the connections made between the prewriting and the thinking processes. This is followed by the students making and marking their grids. Their subsequent writing then grows out of what they discover on their grids.

Regardless of the discipline, writing folders should be kept by each student. The students should retrieve the folders from their storage box or file at the beginning of the class, file any writing done during that class in the folders, and replace them in their proper place at the conclusion of the class. Each student should write his or her name on the file and be fully responsible for keeping its contents in order. If portfolios are part of the system, these writing folders will assume an even more important role as the repository of all students' written work.

Areas in the room for writing, the conference, and group work, as well as places for materials, should be clearly delineated on the first day of implementation. Having clear classroom procedures up front will save valuable instructional time in the long run, set the tenor and pace for more successful implementation, and place some responsibility upon the student. (All books suggested in the implementation models are fully cited in the bibliography.)

Language Arts Model

This model is based on six weeks of study and a 45- to 55-minute period of time. The genre is the narrative, but this model could be reworked for poetry, persuasive essays, drama, or any other genre. The reading-writing connection follows the Jackdaws format, i.e., read a related book or excerpt that embodies the genre, distribute or make an artifact, write a response that rises out of the reading and artifact, model that writing, share and debrief.

Day 1   General introduction to the narrative genre, perhaps from their language arts textbook. Read a story and discuss informally. Lead students through a warm up based on the story, such as trigger words or freewriting. Distribute writing folders. Talk about their purpose. File prewriting. Discuss classroom procedures.

Day 2   Reading-Writing Connection, e.g., read *Aunt Isabel Tells a Good One* by Kate Duke. Discuss. Distribute miniature mice (plastic ones available in the miniature section of craft stores) or have students make them from paper or felt. Pair students and have the pair write a story following the model in the book. The teacher writes, too. Students will not finish, but they have a start. Take a few moments at the end of the class to share story ideas. Debrief. File.

Day 3   Reading-Writing Connection, e.g., read *Cyclops* by Leonard Everett Fisher. Discuss. Distribute paper plates and one plastic eye (available at craft stores). Students quickly construct a Cyclops mask. Under the eye, they make a small hole. They take their masks, sit somewhere in the room, and write a description of what they see through their Cyclopian eye. The teacher writes, too. Several students share. Debrief. File.

Day 4   Mini-lesson on description as part of a good story. Build upon writing done the day before. Use textbook to augment lesson. Debrief.

Day 5   Mini-lesson on setting as part of a good story. Build upon writing done day 3. Discuss how that could be a setting for a story. Debrief.

Day 6   Reading-Writing Connection, e.g., read an excerpt from *Bearstone* by Will Hobbs. Discuss. Distribute clay. Students fashion their own "bearstones." They write about why they chose the animal or symbol they chose. The teacher writes, too. Several students share. Debrief.

Day 7   Reading-Writing Connection, e.g., Demi's *The Empty Pot*. Distribute or make tiny clay pots. Discuss. Students write about a time when they did the right thing and were rewarded (or they can make up a time). Several students share. Debrief.

Day 8   Free Reading/Free Writing—Student/Teacher Conferences. This day permits students to pursue independent reading, finish something that is in their folder, do other writing, or confer with the teacher about an unclear concept. This also allows the teacher to "catch up" any students who may have been absent.

Day 9   Free Reading/Free Writing – Student/Teacher Conferences.

Day 10   Reading-Writing Connection, e.g., "The People Could Fly," a story in the book by the same name, written by Virginia Hamilton. Distribute feathers. Students (and teacher) write a response to the sentence stub "If I could fly ...." Several students share. Debrief. (Students now have at least five pieces of prewriting in their folders.)

Day 11   Introduce the elements of the narrative. Use "Little Miss Muffet" (see fig. 15.4). Students write out these elements on a sheet of paper. Study a literary sample of the narrative, perhaps from the textbook or another piece of children's literature, such as Margaret Hodges's retelling of *Saint George and the Dragon*. Review the elements in the stories read in the reading-writing connections thus far.

Fig. 15.4. Elements of narrative in "Little Miss Muffet."

Day 12   Students review the elements (usually by reciting "Little Miss Muffet"). They turn over the sheet on which they listed the narrative elements (day 11). On the back, they make a grid like the one in figure 15.5. (Do not make these grids for the students. Remember: As they construct their grids, they are in the act of remembering. Their learning is being reinforced.)

Students reread all their prewriting and record the narrative elements *they* wrote from each prewriting onto the grid. For example, students may only check a protagonist and antagonist for their response to *Aunt Isabel*; they may only have a setting for *Cyclops*; but for the *Empty Pot*, they may have a protagonist, antagonist, setting, and problem. After they have recorded the narrative elements noted in prewritings on their grids, they examine what they have already written and make a decision. They must make a commitment to develop one prewriting into a narrative. That is their challenge. Students make their decisions. Discuss and debrief.

Day 13   The teacher uses one of his or her prewritings for a mini-lesson on moving that prewriting into a narrative, i.e., what has to be added, deleted, elaborated upon, what elements are missing, and so forth.

Day 14   Mini-lesson on ways to begin a narrative (see chapter 8). Students practice leads for their story. Share. Debrief.

Day 15   Mini-lesson on elaboration strategies for the narrative (see chapter 8). Work on the laminae of meaning. Use plenty of models from literature and from teacher and student work. Students practice. Share. Debrief.

Day 16   Mini-lesson on conclusions for the narrative (see chapter 8). Students practice. Share. Debrief. For days 14, 15, and 16, it is a good idea to incorporate examples from literature in the mini-lesson.

Fig. 15.5. Grid to analyze elements of narrative in students' prewriting.

Narrative Elements	Day 2 Prewriting	Day 3 Prewriting	Day 6 Prewriting	Day 7 Prewriting	Day 10 Prewriting
Protagonist	✔			✔	
Antagonist	✔				✔
Setting		✔		✔	
Action/Plot					
Conflict/Problem				✔	
Resolution					
Beginning					
Middle					
Ending					
Interest					

Day 17 Skills lessons: Teach quotation marks (see chapter 6), direct and indirect dialogue, the proper way to punctuate dialogue, or other skills appropriate for the narrative, the level and needs of the learner.

Day 18 Skills lessons: Teach the paragraph (see chapter 8) and when and how to indent dialogue. An effective way to teach indention is with a quick object lesson. Hold up an empty soda pop can. When all eyes are focused on the can, squeeze it. Ask students to offer words to describe what you have just done. They will suggest words such as "squeezed," "crushed," "squashed." Eventually someone will say, "You dented it!" When they do, draw a parallel between the dent in the can and the dent made with words. Show how there can be no dent if the words do not first go inward (like the part dented in) and then come outward (like the part not dented in). Explain how "indenting" is the same as "denting in." Make the concept concrete.

Day 19 Student grouping technique. Use the Say Back technique (see chapter 5). Student/ Teacher Conferences.

Day 20 Free Reading/Free Writing—Student/Teacher Conferences.

Day 21 Ratiocination. If quotation marks and paragraphing have been taken as skills lessons, students might take red markers and "put lipstick" on their quotation marks. This helps the students check that they have both opened and closed their quoted material. This also helps students double-check where they have placed the terminal marks. For paragraphs, they might check indentions with red arrows or mark their paragraphs as TRIPSQA (see pages 260-261), transitions, or paragraph blocs.

Day 22 Final publication will be in the format of an eight-page book. Fold books and identify the cover, title page, and dedication page. Number the pages and label the last page "All About the Author." Teach titles, strategies for getting a title, and how to write a title.

Day 23 Visit the library. Find the narrative section. Examine the books. Distribute library cards and envelopes. Each student makes a card and envelope to be affixed to his or her book.

Day 24 Students reenter their writing to check spelling.

Day 25 Analytic scale (see chapter 14, pages 464-465, and appendix A).

Day 26 Writing final copy.

Day 27 Writing final copy.

Day 28 Clocking (see chapter 9, pages 282-283).

Day 29 Free Reading/Free Writing—Student/Teacher Conferences.

Day 30 Publication Day—Celebration of the Publication—Read around.

Kindergarten Model

Day 1 General introduction/creating an environment for kindergarteners reading-writing. Explain classroom rules and management strategies. Create an author's corner, for example, for David McPhail. Consult Sharron L. McElmeel's *Bookpeople: A First Album.*

Day 2 Reading-Writing Connection, for example, talk about pets. Read McPhail's *Emma's Pet.* Students write (draw) a story (narrative) about a pet they had, have, or wish they had. Share from the author's chair.

Day 3 Reading-Writing Connection, for example, talk about something that broke and needed to be fixed. Read *Fix-It* by David McPhail. Students write (draw) a "how to" fix something. Share from the author's chair.

Day 4 Mini-lesson on the *B* sound, because Emma is a bear. Find objects in the room that begin with *B.* Work with that letter in a context.

Day 5 Mini-lesson on bears. Connect to animal study and science.

Day 6 Students do dramatic play activities on bears. Students walk like bears, make the sounds, and reenact the stories.

Day 7 Reading-Writing Connection, for example, talk about the family and the members of the family. List words associated with family, such as mother, father, brother, sister, aunt, and so forth. Read McPhail's *Sisters.* Students write about someone in their family. Share in the author's chair.

Day 8 Reading-Writing Connection, for example, talk about a time when students were lost or felt lost, for example, in the supermarket. Read McPhail's *Lost!* Students write about a time when they were lost or when someone they knew was lost. Share in the author's chair.

Day 9 Reading-Writing Connection, for example, talk about losing a tooth or having a toothache. Read David McPhail's *The Bear's Toothache.* Students write about a time when they lost a tooth or had a toothache. Share in the author's chair.

Day 10 Students do an art activity about bears.

Day 11 Reading-Writing Connection, for example, talk about a time it snowed, what to do in the snow, what snow feels like, and so forth. Read McPhail's *Snow Lion.* Students make snowflakes, paste them on paper, and display. Students do movement activities, such as snowflakes falling. Play the song "Winter Wonderland" or "Jingle Bells."

Day 12 Reading-Writing Connection, for example, talk about something special, what makes something special, and so on. Read McPhail's *Something Special*. Students make something special (provide materials). Share in the author's chair.

Day 13 Model/Mini-lesson. Review the *B* sound. Teach the *S* sound. Create a word bank of words that begin with the letter *S*.

Day 14 Reading-Writing Connection, for example, talk about airplanes, flying, and travel. Read McPhail's *First Flight*. Students write an informative paper about a kind of travel they know. Share in the author's chair.

Day 15 Reading-Writing Connection, for example, continue the work on locomotion and travel. Read McPhail's *The Train*. Students form groups. Each person makes part of a train. They write something on it (words of what trains do, a name, numbers, or letters). Display groups' trains in the room.

Day 16 Reading-Writing Connection, for example, continue the work on locomotion and travel. Read Emilie Warren McLeod's *The Bear's Bicycle*. Students decide if this book, illustrated by McPhail, should go in the author's corner.

Day 17 Look at all the books by David McPhail. Walk over to the author's corner and review the books. Invite students to tell what they remember about the books, which one they liked best and why. Perhaps reread a favorite.

Day 18 Count the number of bears in a book; in several books. Give the bears names. Distribute bear cookies or gummy bears.

Day 19 Rhythmic activity. Use Bill Martin, Jr.'s book *Brown Bear, Brown Bear, What Do You See?*

Day 20 Read a version of *Goldilocks and the Three Bears*. Students write a letter to Baby Bear.

Day 21 Bear habitats: Locate on a map places where bears live, such as wilderness areas and national parks.

Day 22 Library skills appropriate to bear habitats. Take students to the library to find other bear books. Teach proper behavior in the library.

Day 23 Rhythmic activity. Use Bill Martin, Jr.'s book *Polar Bear, Polar Bear, What Do You Hear?*

Day 24 Check out nonfiction bear books from the library, such as those in The Little Polar Bear series by Hans de Beer.

Day 25 Work with students on writing a book, how they would go about it, ideas.

Day 26 Students make an eight-page book about bears.

Day 27 Students group and read their books to peers.

Day 28 Students continue to write, edit, and confer with teacher.

Day 29 Students illustrate their books.

Day 30 Publication Day—celebration of the publication. Invite parents to a Bear Display.

Social Studies Model

Day 1   General introduction/create an environment for a social studies reading-writing classroom. Create a sense of how social scientists work, establishing the key concept, for example, the Holocaust.

Day 2   Reading-Writing Connection on the Holocaust, for example, read *Let the Celebrations Begin!* by Margaret Wild and Julie Vivas. Students begin a "Holocaust Notebook" of the key words, words of special interest, and Holocaust facts. Share several books. Keep books shared as resources in the classroom. Debrief.

Day 3   Reading-Writing Connection on the Holocaust, for example, Eve Bunting's *Terrible Things: An Allegory of the Holocaust*. Students write their reaction to the allegory in their notebooks. Share. Debrief.

Day 4   Mini-lesson on one aspect of the Holocaust, for example, the Nazi party, Adolf Hitler, concentration camps, boycott of Jewish businesses, book burnings, the political climate in Europe, and so forth. Consult social studies book information. Add to notebooks. Debrief.

Day 5   View nonfiction videos, such as those on Anne Frank, Alan Resnais's documentary *Night and Fog*, or portions of Leni Riefenstal's *Triumph of the Will*. Add information to notebooks. Share. Debrief.
(Note: Resnais's documentary is both poignant and graphic. It should be previewed. It is not appropriate for young children.)

Day 6   Reading-Writing Connection on the Holocaust, for example, read portions of Lois Lowry's *Number the Stars*. Students take the position of Annemarie and write what they would do for a friend in those circumstances. Share. Debrief.

Day 7   Reading-Writing Connection on the Holocaust, for example, read selected passages from Jane Yolen's *The Devil's Arithmetic*. Students assume the persona of Chaya and write how they feel about the numbers tattooed on their arms. Share. Debrief.

Day 8   Divide students into groups. Distribute long strips of butcher paper. Students create a timeline. This begins in 1919 when Adolf Hitler joined the German Workers' Party, which a year later became the National Socialist German Workers' party—the Nazi party—and ends on May 8, 1945, when Germany surrendered to the Allies.

Day 9   Free Reading/Free Writing—Student/Teacher Conferences.

Day 10   Reading-Writing Connection on the Holocaust, for example, share Inge Auerbacher's personal biography *I Am a Star: Child of the Holocaust*. Students write about innocent children as victims of the Holocaust in their notebooks. Share. Debrief.

Day 11   Introduce Art Spiegelman's *Maus*, a two-book graphic novel series on the Holocaust. In their notebooks, students express their reactions to the Holocaust through cartoons. Play some Jewish folk music; play some German folk music; play an opera by Wagner. Share. Debrief.

Day 12   Grid the Holocaust, for example, Auschwitz and other concentration camps, nonfiction accounts, fictionalized accounts, Hitler, wearing the Star of David, relocations, and so forth. Record responses to aspects of the Holocaust to use as a possible focus for a paper. Make decisions. Discuss. Based on the model graph (see fig. 15.6), this student might focus on children and the Holocaust.

Fig. 15.6. Grid to analyze elements of narrative in students' prewriting.

Narrative Elements	Day 2 Prewriting	Day 3 Prewriting	Day 6 Prewriting	Day 7 Prewriting	Day 10 Prewriting
Concentration camps	✔	✔		✔	✔
Hitler					
Star of David			✔		✔
Jewish and gentile friends			✔		
Tattooed numbers				✔	
Children and the Holocaust	✔		✔	✔	✔
Interest	✔		✔		

Day 13   Model/Mini-lesson an informative essay. Discuss, study, and work on the format of this type of essay for final publication.

Day 14   Teach the appropriate beginnings for an essay (although informative essays are usually formal, personal anecdotes or quotations are often as effective a lead as is a startling statistic or fact).

Day 15   Teach the appropriate elaboration for this essay (include ways to support information and references).

Day 16   Teach the appropriate endings (indication that further study is needed or what was learned is often better than a dull summary).

Day 17   Teach appropriate related social studies concepts.

Day 18   Teach appropriate related social studies concepts.

Day 19   Teach appropriate related social studies concepts.

Day 20   Teach appropriate related social studies concepts.

Day 21   Teach appropriate related social studies concepts.

Day 22   Teach library skills appropriate to the Holocaust in general and each student's focus specifically. Take students to the library to check data or find any additional support or information to add to their paper.

Day 23   Ratiocination.

Day 24   Student grouping—use Say Back (see chapter 5, page 157).

Day 25   Analytic scale, work with students (see chapter 14, pages 464-465, and appendix A).

Day 26   Students write final copy.

Day 27   Free Reading/Free Writing and/or make-up work. Student/Teacher Conferences.

Day 28   Clocking the final paper.

Day 29   Final six-week test

Day 30   Publication Day—celebration of the publication. Share a selected portion of the report in a read around.

Mathematics Model

Day 1   General introduction/create an environment for a mathematics reading-writing classroom. Give a sense of how mathematicians work. Establish the key concept, for example, problem solving. Share the following parallels with students:

Composing	**Problem Solving**
prewriting	experiencing the phenomenon
writing	stating the problem
revising	constructing a mathematical model
editing	manipulating algebraic statements and stating a solution
publishing	interpreting the solution in a mathematical context and in the real world.

(Adapted from Joan Countryman's *Writing to Learn Mathematics*.)

Day 2   Reading-Writing Connection, for example, read Margarette Reid's *The Button Box*. Students begin a "Math Notebook" by listing the kind of thinking involved in the story. Relate to thinking involved in a problem. Share several lists. Discuss.

Day 3   Reading-Writing Connection, for example, read *Let the Celebrations Begin!* by Margaret Wild and Julie Vivas. Pose the problem: Based on the information in the book and other information students may know about concentration camps and prisons, students estimate the area of the camp. Students add to notebooks their reasons for their size estimation. Share. Debrief.

Day 4   Mini-lesson on one aspect of area using problem solving. Teach how to figure the area of a circle. Formula states: Area = *pi* times (radius times radius), or $A = \pi r^2$. Conduct an experiment to reinforce the formula for area of a circle. Divide students into groups. Distribute circular lids. Students determine the area of the lid. Change to metric. Tell students the second hand of the clock is 6 inches (15 centimeters) long. Figure the area the hand sweeps in 1 minute. In their notebooks, students explain how they worked the problems. Consult mathematics book for information. Debrief.

Day 5   Mini-lesson on another aspect of area using problem solving. Teach how to figure surface area of a square or rectangle. Formula states: Area = length times width. Conduct an experiment to teach surface area. Divide students into groups. Give each group different size boxes, cereal boxes, open boxes, and so forth. Students compute the area. In their notebooks, students explain how they worked the problems. Consult mathematics book for more information. Debrief.

Day 6 Groups select an area in the school, e.g., classroom, cafeteria, outside playground, principal's office. Each group writes a problem involving area for another group to solve. Exchange problems. Solve. Share. Add to notebooks. Debrief.

Day 7 Reading-Writing Connection, for example, read Daniel Barbot's *A Bicycle for Rosaura.* Students working in groups determine the problem and offer possible solutions. Debrief.

Day 8 Reading-Writing Connection on the concept of estimating, e.g., read *A Million Fish ... More or Less* by Patricia C. McKissack. In their notebooks, students write what is necessary to estimate and what makes a good estimate. Share and discuss.

Day 9 Reading-Writing Connection on the concept of money, e.g., read David M. Schwartz's *How Much Is a Million?* and *If You Made a Million*; or read *The Go-Around Dollar* by Barbara Johnston Adams. Divide students into groups. Distribute catalogs. Students list what they would buy and compute other problems using money.

Day 10 Use Marilyn Burns's *Math for Smarty Pants* for other unique problems to solve.

Day 11 Use Janice Van Cleave's *Math for Every Kid* for additional problem-solving activities.

Day 12 Grid problem solving. Students reread their notebooks. Students mark the grid with possibilities for a report (see fig. 15.7) and make decisions about what they want to write for their part of the collaborative class book. Discuss.

Fig. 15.7. Problem-solving grid.

Narrative Elements	Day 2 Prewriting	Day 3 Prewriting	Day 7 Prewriting	Day 8 Prewriting	Day 9 Prewriting
Problem solving	✔	✔	✔		✔
Estimates		✔		✔	
Problem posing	✔		✔		✔
Computing problems		✔			✔
Format for problems	✔				✔
Interest		✔			✔

Day 13 Model/Mini-lesson for creating a class book of problems. Discuss, study, and work on the format for this type of book.

Day 14 Teach the appropriate format: introduction that explains the book's purpose; an organized way to categorize the problems, such as, fractions, subtraction, ratio; or word problems, number problems; or easy, difficult, almost impossible.

Day 15 Teach clarity of expression, appropriate word choice, and ways to illustrate complex problems. Use the mathematics textbook as a resource.

Day 16 Start draft of "Book of Problems."

Day 17 Teach appropriate related mathematics concepts.

Day 18   Teach appropriate related mathematics concepts.

Day 19   Teach appropriate related mathematics concepts.

Day 20   Teach appropriate related mathematics concepts.

Day 21   Teach appropriate related mathematics concepts.

Day 22   Teach library skills appropriate to the concepts. Take students to the library to check data, find any additional support or information to add to their book.

Day 23   Ratiocination.

Day 24   Student grouping—use Say Back (see chapter 5, page 157).

Day 25   Analytic scale, work with students (see chapter 14, pages 464-465, and appendix A).

Day 26   Students write final copy.

Day 27   Free Reading/Free Writing and/or make-up work. Student-teacher conferences.

Day 28   Clocking the final paper.

Day 29   Final six-week test.

Day 30   Publication Day—celebration of the publication. Share a selected portion of their "Book of Problems" in a read around.

Science Model

Day 1   General introduction/create an environment for a science classroom. Create the science area, including lab and supplies. Give a sense of how scientists work. Establish the key concept, e.g., space.

Day 2   Reading-Writing Connection, e.g., read "Our Launchpad" from *The Space Atlas* by Heather Couper and Nigel Henbest. Students begin a "Space Facts Notebook" of the key words, words of special interest, and space facts. Share several books. Keep books shared as resources in the classroom. Debrief.

Day 3   Reading-Writing Connection, e.g., read *My Place in Space* by Robin Hirst and Sally Hirst. Students add to notebooks. Share. Debrief.

Day 4   Mini-lesson on one aspect of space, e.g., spiral galaxy. Conduct an experiment to reinforce the concept. (1) Fill a jar about three-fourths full of water. (2) Sprinkle with about 20 paper circles cut from a hole punch. (3) Quickly stir water in a circular motion with a straw. (4) View the motion of the water and circles from top and sides when you stop. Compare to the Milky Way galaxy. Consult science book information. Add to notebooks. Debrief.

Day 5   Visit a planetarium or museum with a space display, or consult the annual *Film and Video Catalog* from The National Geographic Educational Service for excellent videos on space. Catalog is available from The National Geographic Society, Washington, D.C. Add to notebooks. Share. Debrief.

Day 6   Reading-Writing Connection, e.g., Ruth Young's *A Trip to Mars*. Students add to their notebooks. Share. Debrief.

Day 7   Reading-Writing Connection, e.g., Jeanne Willis's *Earthlets as Explained by Professor Xargl*. Students choose some things from their notebooks and, using *Earthlets* as their model, they write them up from a different point of view. Share. Debrief.

Day 8   Free Reading/Free Writing—Student/Teacher Conferences.

Day 9   Free Reading/Free Writing—Student/Teacher Conferences.

Day 10   Reading-Writing Connection, e.g., Laurence Santrey's *Discovering the Stars*. Students add to notebooks. Share. Debrief.

Day 11   Introduce Seymour Simon's books on planets. Play portions of Gustav Holst's *The Planets*. Students add to notebooks. Share. Debrief.

Day 12   Grid space (see fig. 15.8) (entering space, living in space, space suits, space travel, and so forth); galaxies (spiral, Milky Way, movement, exploding, and so forth); planets (Earth, Mercury, Venus, Mars, Jupiter, Saturn, Uranus, Neptune, Pluto, orbiting speed, rotations, heat shields, magnetic fields, and so forth); stars (brightness, nearest, shooting, size, twinkling, variable, and so forth). Students reread their notebooks. Mark grids with possibilities for a report and make decisions accordingly. Discuss.

Fig. 15.8. Space grid.

Narrative Elements	Day 2 Prewriting	Day 3 Prewriting	Day 6 Prewriting	Day 7 Prewriting	Day 10 Prewriting
Space facts	✔	✔		✔	
Space vocabulary	✔	✔		✔	✔
Feelings about space			✔		
Travelling in space*	✔		✔		
Interest	✔				✔

*More things may be added according to the students' level.

Day 13   Model/Mini-lesson a report. Discuss, study, and work on the format of a report for final publication.

Day 14   Teach the appropriate beginnings for a report (although a report is informative and usually formal, personal anecdotes or quotations are often as effective a lead as is a starting statistic or fact).

Day 15   Teach the appropriate elaboration for a report (include ways to support information and references).

Day 16   Teach the appropriate endings (indication that further study is needed or what was learned is often better than a dull summary).

Day 17   Teach appropriate related science concepts.

Day 18   Teach appropriate related science concepts.

Day 19   Teach appropriate related science concepts.

Day 20   Teach appropriate related science concepts.

Day 21   Teach appropriate related science concepts.

Day 22   Teach library skills appropriate to the concepts. Take students to the library to check data, find any additional support or information to add to their paper.

Day 23   Ratiocination.

Day 24   Student grouping—use Say Back (see chapter 5, page 157).

Day 25   Analytic scale, work with students (see chapter 14, pages 464-465, and appendix A).

Day 26   Students write final copy.

Day 27   Free Reading/Free Writing and/or make-up work. Student/Teacher Conferences.

Day 28   Clocking the final paper.

Day 29   Final six-week test.

Day 30   Publication Day—celebration of the publication. Share a selected portion of the report in a read around.

CONCLUSION

A final thought about writing to learn. Writing in the various disciplines ranges from the technical to the memo, from directions to reports, from plans to explanations. To teach only these specific modes limits students. The point is to teach writing in such a way that students learn how to write, so they may carry it with them and call upon it when necessary. If skilled teachers begin by teaching writing reflexively and move into more extensive writing, students will enter the world armed with viable strategies.

> *Recently a West Point cadet was interviewed on a local news report. In the course of the interview the cadet discussed his training. "When I was a plebe," he said, "we learned about combat. Now I am about to graduate and we are learning about humanitarian efforts. The world's changed, and so we changed. What I know is that when I am on any assignment, I will have both to call upon. But I am sure of what I know." The analogy seems clear: we learn different material in different disciplines, but above all, we need students to go out into whatever job or profession secure in what they know. With the world undergoing rapid and unprecedented change, students will have to have the knowledge that will enable them to change and to cope with the change. Writing makes learning visual, establishes a process by which to learn, and preserves that learning.*

APPLICATION

Text tampering includes underlining, highlighting, labeling, annotating, commentary, and questions. Reenter a text or book you have studied or read. Examine it for text tampering. Evaluate how the tampering helped the purpose of the study or reading. Be prepared to share your conclusions.

WORKS CITED

Adams, Barbara Johnston. *The Go-Around Dollar*. New York: Macmillan, 1992.

Arnold, Roslyn. "The Hidden Life of a Drama Text." In *Readers, Texts, Teachers*, edited by Bill Corcoran and Emrys Evans. Upper Montclair, NJ: Boynton/Cook, 1987.

Auerbacher, Inge. *I Am a Star: Child of the Holocaust*. New York: Prentice Hall, 1986.

Barbot, Daniel. *A Bicycle for Rosaura*. New York: Kane Miller, 1991.

Bedard, Michael. *Emily*. New York: Delacorte Press, 1992.

Berthoff, Ann E., with James Stephens. *Forming, Thinking, Writing*, 2d ed. Portsmouth, NH: Heinemann Educational Books, 1988.

Brown, Hazel, and Brian Cambourne. *Read and Retell*. Portsmouth, NH: Heinemann Educational Books, 1987.

Bunting, Eve. *Terrible Things: An Allegory of the Holocaust*. New York: The Jewish Publication Society, 1989.

Burleigh, Robert. *Flight*. New York: Philomel, 1991.

Burns, Marilyn. *Math for Smarty Pants*. Boston: Little, Brown, 1982.

Carroll, Joyce Armstrong. *Books for Special Days* (1993); *Chapter Books* (1992); *Picture Books* (1991); and *Story Books* (1992). Jackdaw series. Englewood, CO: Teacher Ideas Press.

Clark, Katerina, and Michael Holquist. *Mikhail Bakhtin*. Cambridge, MA: Harvard University Press, 1984.

Corcoran, Bill. "Teachers Creating Readers." In *Readers, Texts, Teachers*, edited by Bill Corcoran and Emrys Evans. Upper Montclair, NJ: Boynton/Cook, 1987.

Countryman, Joan. *Writing to Learn Mathematics and Science*. Portsmouth, NH: Heinemann Educational Books, 1992.

Couper, Heather, and Nigel Henbest. *The Space Atlas*. New York: Harcourt Brace Jovanovich, 1992.

de Beer, Hans. *Ahoy There, Little Polar Bear* (1988); *Little Polar Bear* (1987); *The Little Polar Bear Address Book* (1990); *The Little Polar Bear Birthday Book* (1990); *Little Polar Bear Finds a Friend* (1989). The Little Polar Bear series. New York: North-South Books.

Demi. *The Empty Pot*. New York: Henry Holt, 1990.

Duke, Kate. *Aunt Isabel Tells a Good One*. New York: Dutton Children's Books, 1992.

Fisher, Leonard Everett. *Cyclops*. New York: Holiday House, 1991.

Gardner, Howard. *The Unschooled Mind: How Children Think and How Schools Should Teach*. New York: Basic Books, 1991.

Gere, Anne Ruggles, ed. *Roots in the Sawdust: Writing to Learn Across Disciplines*. Urbana, IL: National Council of Teachers of English, 1985.

Hamilton, Virginia. *The People Could Fly*. New York: Knopf, 1985.

Hirst, Sally, and Robin Hirst. *My Place in Space*. New York: Orchard Books, 1988.

Hobbs, Will. *Bearstone*. New York: Atheneum, 1989.

Hodges, Margaret. *Saint George and the Dragon*. Boston: Little, Brown, 1984.

Holst, Gustav. *The Planets*. CD-Deutsch Gramaphone, No. 429730-2.

Hunter, Madeline C. *How to Change to a Nongraded School*. Alexandria, VA: Association for Supervision and Curriculum Development, 1992.

Iser, Wolfgang. *The Act of Reading: A Theory of Aesthetic Response*. Baltimore, MD: The Johns Hopkins University Press, 1978.

King, Barbara. "Two Modes of Analyzing Teacher and Student Attitudes Toward Writing: The Emig Attitude Scale and the King Construct Scale." Ed.D. diss., Rutgers University, New Brunswick, NJ, 1979.

Lewis, C. S. *The Lion, the Witch and the Wardrobe*. New York: Collier, 1950.

Lowry, Lois. *Number the Stars*. Boston: Houghton Mifflin, 1989.

Martin, Bill, Jr. *Brown Bear, Brown Bear, What Do You See?* New York: Henry Holt, 1983.

_____. *Polar Bear, Polar Bear, What Do You Hear?* New York: Henry Holt, 1991.

Marzano, Robert J. *A Different Kind of Classroom: Teaching with Dimensions of Learning*. Alexandria, VA: Association for Supervision and Curriculum Development, 1992.

McElmeel, Sharron L. *Bookpeople: A First Album*. Englewood, CO: Libraries Unlimited, 1990.

McKissack, Patricia C. *A Million Fish ... More or Less*. New York: Knopf, 1992.

McLeod, Emilie Warren. *The Bear's Bicycle*. David McPhail, illus. Boston: Little, Brown, 1975.

McPhail, David. *The Bear's Toothache*. Boston: Joy Street Books, 1988.

_____. *Emma's Pet*. New York: E. P. Dutton, 1985.

_____. *First Flight*. Boston: Little, Brown, 1987.

_____. *Fix-It*. New York: E. P. Dutton, 1984.

_____. *Lost!* Boston: Little, Brown, 1990.

_____. *Sisters.* New York: Harcourt Brace Jovanovich, 1984.

_____. *Snow Lion.* Boston: Parents Magazine Press, 1982.

_____. *Something Special.* Boston: Little, Brown, 1988.

_____. *The Train.* Boston: Little, Brown, 1977.

Myers, Walter Dean. *Now Is Your Time! The African-American Struggle for Freedom.* New York: HarperCollins Children's Books, 1991.

Perrone, Vito. *A Letter to Teachers: Reflections on Schooling and the Art of Teaching.* San Francisco: Jossey-Bass, 1991.

Petrosky, Anthony R. "From Story to Essay: Reading and Writing." *College Composition and Communication* 33 (1982): 24-25.

Probst, Robert E. *Adolescent Literature: Response and Analysis.* Columbus, OH: Charles E. Merrill, 1984.

Protherough, Robert. "The Stories That Readers Tell." In *Readers, Texts, Teachers*, edited by Bill Corcoran and Emrys Evans. Upper Montclair, NJ: Boynton/Cook, 1987.

Purves, Alan C., ed. *How Porcupines Make Love: Notes on a Response-Centered Curriculum.* Lexington, MA: Xerox College, 1972.

Reid, Margarette S. *The Button Box.* New York: E. P. Dutton, 1990.

Resnais, Alan. *Night and Fog.* Video. Skokie, IL: Films. (Also available in video stores.)

Richards, M. C. *Centering: In Pottery, Poetry, and the Person.* Middletown, CT: Wesleyan University Press, 1972.

Riefenstal, Leni. *Triumph of the Will.* Video. Skokie, IL: Films. (Also available in video stores.)

Rosenblatt, Louise M. *Literature as Exploration*, 4th ed. New York: Modern Language Association of America, 1983.

_____. *The Reader, the Text, the Poem: The Transactional Theory of the Literary Work.* Carbondale and Edwardsville, IL: Southern Illinois University Press, 1978.

Santrey, Laurence. *Discovering the Stars.* Mahwah, NJ: Troll, 1982.

Schwartz, David M. *How Much Is a Million?* New York: Lothrop, Lee & Shepard, 1989.

_____. *If You Made a Million.* New York: Lothrop, Lee & Shepard, 1989.

Simon, Seymour. *Jupiter.* New York: William Morrow, 1985.

_____. *Mars.* New York: Mulberry Books, 1987.

_____. *Neptune.* New York: Morrow Junior Books, 1991.

Spiegelman, Art. *Maus: A Survivor's Tale.* New York: Pantheon Books, 1973, 1980, 1981, 1982, 1983, 1984, 1985, 1986.

_____. *Maus: A Survivor's Tale II: And Here My Troubles Began.* New York: Pantheon Books, 1986, 1989, 1990, 1991.

Van Cleave, Janice Pratt. *Math for Every Kid: Easy Activities That Make Learning Fun.* New York: John Wiley & Sons, 1991.

Wagner, Richard. *Das Rheingold.* CD EMI No. 749853-2.

Wild, Margaret, and Judy Vivas. *Let the Celebrations Begin!* New York: Orchard Books, 1991.

Willis, Jeanne. *Earthlets as Explained by Professor Xargl.* New York: E. P. Dutton, 1988.

Yolen, Jane. *The Devil's Arithmetic.* New York: Viking Kestrel, 1988.

Young, Clem. "Readers, Texts, Teachers." In *Readers, Texts, Teachers,* edited by Bill Corcoran and Emrys Evans. Upper Montclair, NJ: Boynton/Cook, 1987.

Young, Ruth. *A Trip to Mars.* New York: Orchard Books, 1990.

"Shielding the Basic Student"

EDWARD E. WILSON

(From *English in Texas* 14, no. 3. Reprinted with permission.)

The note in my box invited me to the principal's office, and it vaguely alluded to next year's schedule. As a high school teacher, I have learned that anything about next year's schedule intensifies anxieties. These anxieties plus those associated with a fear of "the principal's office" connoted trouble; yet, I reluctantly obliged.

Imagine, there I was anxious about being called to the office, expectant about a new schedule, and Mr. B. greets me with a loaded question, "You're supposed to know something about writing?" When I heard that question, I should have found any excuse to immediately leave. My "Yes" to the question came out more as a confession of guilt rather than as an affirmation of knowledge or training. That's how it went one year ago when I found myself confronted with the "opportunity to really use my expertise"—my principal's concluding words.

The above is a condensed version of how I acquired two classes of tenth grade basic students, all of whom had failed the writing sample for TABS as ninth graders. The school judiciously informed these forty students they would be enrolled in basic classes because they did not meet satisfactorily the objectives on the TABS test. The students saw right through the carefully worded statement— (proving to me they were capable of getting the main idea—) "We're failures—we can't write."

Mina Shaughnessy's words haunted me as I prepared for those basic classes. "For the BW (basic writing) student, writing is a trap, not a way of saying something to someone ... writ-ing is but a line that moves haltingly across the page, exposing as it goes all that the writer doesn't know, then passing it to the hands of a stranger who reads it with a lawyer's eyes, searching for flaws" (*Errors and Expectations*, p. 7).

I wanted to concentrate on prewriting, writing and rewriting with these students. Feeling that if they could find their own process, then they could overcome all the negative attitudes and practices they had obviously developed about writing over the years. My purpose classified me as an idealist, or so said

Commentary

Those of us who taught in the "factory model" paradigm remember the dread of being "invited" to the principal's office.

Texas Assessment of Basic Skills (TABS), the first round of the five-year testing program, was instituted to improve the writing of students across the state. For some students, unfortunately, it merely reinforced low self-esteem when it came to writing.

To paraphrase Don Graves, the trouble with writing is not writing—it is not writing. Typically, students who are labeled "basic" get the mindless worksheets on which only a word or two is required, even though they are the very students who should be writing daily. They should become acquainted with making meaning on a page like one gets to know a friend, rather than regarding words and writing as enemies.

Sometimes what we write as lesson plans has little to do with students' real needs.

More and more we need developmental lesson plans — the skeletal outline that is fleshed out daily because of what really happens in the classroom.

When ordinary methods fail, it is time to regroup and try extraordinary methods. This is exactly where the teacher as researcher becomes crucial. Keen observations of learners, their attitudes, and processes help gear subsequent teaching to their needs. Otherwise, failure is simply reinforced.

my colleagues, but I had accepted my principal's challenge and proceeded to write a curriculum that looked beautiful. As an attempt at the realistic, I scheduled the first essay for the end of October. This would give the class six weeks of prewriting. I garnered every activity I could find, invent, or improvise. Anyone who has taught basic students is probably holding their sides laughing because with these plans I found out what every basic teacher knows: It doesn't work that way.

After the first week of following my immaculate lesson plans, some of my colleagues asked, "Are you sick?" Others, more direct, said, "You look awful." The dogs at home wouldn't come near me, sensing my foul mood. And my wife simply stopped talking to me. My options, as I saw them then, were: 1. It's going to be a long year; 2. I better do something else with my idealistic plans; 3. I could look for another job.

I figured the easier task of redoing the lesson plans outweighed the options of a long year or bagging groceries since by then I had discovered through my own learning process that reading about the basic student and teaching the basic student were totally different. But with two classes staring at me for one week, I reread what Shaughnessy had told me the first time, "Some writers, inhibited by their fear of error, produce but a few lines an hour or keep trying to begin, crossing out one try after another until the sentence is hopelessly tangled" (*E&E*, p. 7). She was right. The week of prewriting had failed miserably — free-writing came-out more as forced writing — and journals stayed empty.

I decided I had to regroup and reevaluate. I came up with the following suggestions for myself. Of course, there are exceptions to each one, but for my class's survival and because I didn't want another week like the first one, I admitted:

1. Basic Students have an attention span of about 12 minutes. A direct correlation to TV shows and commercials.
2. A basic student will not sustain work for a fifty minute period, regardless of how exciting that task may seem to the teacher.
3. When students fail the ninth grade TABS writing section their attitudes about writing are not good.

4. If the classroom assignments and activities don't have a ring of "is it practical" to the basic student, no amount of fear, anger, plea bargaining, or bribery can get them to even begin writing, and forget about finishing the writing.

5. Basic students' attitudes about writing are almost the same as their attitudes about themselves — again not good.

6. They tend to be very vocal, active, and have an unusual awareness of the opposite sex.

Learning far more that first week than my students, I felt a curriculum could be built around these generalizations. And even though it was still September, I had the claustrophobic feeling February and TABS would arrive too soon. With these assessments, I threw away my lesson plans and chose to focus only on fluency and prewriting for the first semester. An essay could be the culminating experience at the end of the semester. I then implemented the following strategies:

1. Integrate literature, grammar, writing, reading, communication with practical, job related, or personal experiences.

2. Have at least three different types of activities for each class period.

3. Forget about errors in writing until the students started feeling positive about what they have done.

4. Emphasize finishing a task.

5. Find something nice to say about everyone everyday.

6. Give time for the basic student to let the steam out of the pressure cooker.

With this new manifesto, I rewrote my lesson plans. Then on the second Monday in September I girded my loins and prepared for first period. The lesson was to make a shield. Shields had always been successful in regular classes since students enjoyed researching family names and crests in order to produce an artistic artifact. I gambled on the interest being there for the basic student. The format for the lesson followed the schedule of three fifteen to twenty minute activities. I kept this format for the rest of the year because I

Appropriate pedagogy rests on clear theory.

Although the classic terms plot, setting, and so forth were used, applying these literary terms to self made the difference. Beginning with the self was concrete, and it made sense to the students.

quickly discovered basic students like familiarity, set schedules and no big surprises. Their anxieties decreased as they became accustomed to patterns.

Monday's lesson contained prewriting, talking, instruction, abstract thinking on a concrete level, a usage rule, and reading. I scheduled three activities:

I.   Create the shield.
II. Discuss the shield.
III. Read a story and use the shield to discuss plot, theme, setting, irony, and symbols.

I knew if I defined the literary terms in regular English "teacherese," the basic students would either stare at me or comment with something like "Man, you gotta be kiddin'." I revised the shield concept to help my basic students so they could use concrete images for personal definitions of plot, theme, setting, irony and symbols. The day went something like the following.

I explained what a shield was.

We cut a shield design out of poster board (I, too, made a shield).

Then we divided the shield into four equal parts.

Next we drew a two to three inch circle in the exact center.

On the top left hand corner we wrote PLOT; on the top right hand corner we wrote SETTING; the lower left hand corner had IRONY; and in the lower right corner we wrote THEME.

At the top of the circle we wrote SYMBOL. Then I instructed the students to write in the PLOT space four or five sentences about the story of their life. For a basic student four or five sentences can be stretching what they consider to be a "nothing life." I wrote too. For the SETTING corner we wrote the places we had lived. I reminded them to capitalize all the names of towns/cities and states. If they had lived out of state, I told them to always place a comma between the town/city and state.

The THEME corner held a favorite quote that best described themselves or what they felt. They wrote quotes like: "Go for the gusto," or "Let's Party," and phrases from popular song lyrics.

The IRONY corner was hardest. They had to write about that what every one sees in a person may not be the way the person really

For younger students, IRONY may be replaced with CHARACTERS.

is—the old Shakespearean "appearances versus reality." In other words, I invited them to write what they were really like inside. I told them this part of the shield could be kept secret if they wished. A few opted for this, but they all got quiet when working on it.

For the center of their shield, the SYMBOL part, they drew an object that best identified themselves. We had crosses, pickups, doobies, rings, the typical teenager symbols—all for personal reasons.

After finishing this, we discussed each part in detail. The test for the exercise came when I distributed the short story "On a Commuter Train" by Willie Morris, which only takes about three minutes to read. Then I asked them to get out their shields and we found the plot, theme, setting, symbol(s), irony in the story. Because they had found those things in their own lives the transference to the story was incredibly successful.

With the lesson completed, I knew it had been a success. Constantly throughout all of the discussions I encouraged the students and gave them positive reinforcement. Errors weren't checked for because the completion of the shield mattered, not the correctness. Though I must add many of the students went home and remade their shields. They were proud of them. They felt good about what they had done. In one day these basic students had prewritten about themselves. Had had a discussion. Learned five abstract literary terms and used them in a discussion of a story that they had read. Incidentally, they had also learned a rule of capitalization and one of commas. And finally, they had finished all the task required for the lesson.

The shields became almost an everyday experience. When ever we would get confused about a meaning we would refer to them. They were useful to encourage fluency with writing. They became a tool for a starting place. They existed as a reminder to the students that errors were not going to be the only reason for a grade. Ideas written were more important. Communication and self expression of those ideas were valued more than correction, although rules taught "incidentally" did have some transference into their writing.

Needless to say the second week went by much faster and February arrived before any of us were totally ready. All of their writing anxieties started flaring up again because they

Talking after the composing process is completed is as important as talking before the process begins. Giving words to what happened helps many learners solidify the concepts in their minds. The leap to literature was not quantum; rather, it was a small step made easily by the students.

Shielding may be adapted to any grade level by changing the descriptors to meet the needs of that level. For instance, for primary students THEME may be changed to PROBLEM, and SYMBOL to SOLUTION.

knew they were going to have to pass the writing sample. I reassured them, "Just write. Write what you think." It worked. All but two of the forty passed the writing sample. Eventually, we got to a point where we could write an essay, albeit an elementary one.

One more time: Systematic teaching based on learners' needs and coupled with a sense of success works. In this case, shielding accomplished what the red penning did not.

At the conclusion of my first year of teaching the basic student I again regrouped and developed my own conclusions about teaching the basic student. Once the basic writer is "shielded" from the fear of errors, once the basic writer is "shielded" from the trap of writing anxiety they start to produce. Shield them, they need it.

Reference

Shaughnessy, Mina P. *Errors and Expectations.* New York: Oxford University Press, 1977.

A

SAMPLE ANALYTIC SCALES

Analytic scales (as explained in chapter 14, pages 464-465) are scoring sheets developed cooperatively by teacher and students. Students brainstorm to create a list of criteria on which the paper should be evaluated. This criteria is based on what was taught. The teacher and students prioritize the list. Finally, the teacher uses the prioritized list to create the scoring sheets, and ultimately uses them to evaluate the writing.

This appendix includes three sample analytic scales adapted from Diederich. The first is suitable for reflexive papers, the second for extensive papers, and the third is a sample of the scale adapted to the elementary level. Note that in all of the scales, content is weighted more heavily than mechanics and there is space for writing in comments.

Analytic Scale 1: For a Reflexive Paper

1 — Poor   2 — Weak   3 — Below Average   4 — Good   5 — Excellent

Section 1

Quality of development Concrete, sensory detail; specifics	1	2	3	4	5

Introduction
    First two sentences hook the reader; remainder of introduction
    prepares the reader
	1	2	3	4	5

Logical order Chronological; flashback	1	2	3	4	5
Point of narration is clear (or implied for stated thesis)	1	2	3	4	5
Writing matches audiences	1	2	3	4	5
Writing fulfills purpose	1	2	3	4	5

Subtotal for section 1

x   2

Total for section 1

Section 2

"To be" verbs Got rid of half	1	2	3	4	5
Commas Checked with chart	1	2	3	4	5
Sentence beginnings vary Adjusted for interest	1	2	3	4	5
Conversation Used when appropriate	1	2	3	4	5
Spelling	1	2	3	4	5
Word choice (diction) Carefully chose apt word	1	2	3	4	5
Format of final draft	1	2	3	4	5

Drafts
    Prewriting
    Trial rough draft — color coded
    Rough draft
    Any drafts
	1	2	3	4	5

Subtotal for section 2

Total for section 1   +

Total Grade

Comments:

(Adapted from Paul Diederich, *Measuring Growth in English*. Urbana, IL: National Council of Teachers of English, 1974.)

Analytic Scale 2: For an Extensive Paper

0 — Not in evidence   1 — Poor   2 — Below Average   3 — Good

Section 1

Writing matches audience	0	1	2	3
Writing fulfills purpose	0	1	2	3
Type of paper clear	0	1	2	3
Structure	0	1	2	3

Inductive (pyramid); deductive (funnel)

Coherence	0	1	2	3

Internal; external

Introduction	0	1	2	3

Hook; prepares the reader; thesis underlined

Subtotal for section 1 _____

x ____ 3

Total for section 1 _____

Section 2

Drafting process	0	1	2	3

Prewriting
Trial rough draft
Rough draft
Drafts
Final copy

Sentence variety	0	1	2	3

Length; beginnings

Documentation	0	1	2	3
TRIPSQA	0	1	2	3

Subtotal for section 2 _____

x ____ 2

Total for section 2 _____

Section 3

"To be" verbs	0	1	2	3
Commas	0	1	2	3
Punctuation	0	1	2	3
Spelling	0	1	2	3

Subtotal for section 3 _____

Total for section 1   + _____

Total for section 2   + _____

Total Grade _____

Comments:

(Adapted from Diederich, *Measuring.*)

Analytic Scale 3: For an Elementary Level Narrative

	Low		Middle		High
Section 1					
Ideas	1	2	3	4	5
Sequence	1	2	3	4	5
Beginning	1	2	3	4	5
Middle	1	2	3	4	5
End	1	2	3	4	5

Subtotal for section 1 _____

                                                          x   3
                                                        _____

Total for section 1 _____

	Low		Middle		High
Section 2					
Capitals	1	2	3	4	5
End marks	1	2	3	4	5
Spelling	1	2	3	4	5
Handwriting	1	2	3	4	5
Prewriting	1	2	3	4	5

Subtotal for section 2 _____

Total for section 1   +   1

Total for section 2 _____

Subtotal grade _____

Total Grade _____

Note: Sometimes the math doesn't come out exactly to 100. In that case the student gets the extra point as a bonus.

Comments:

(Adapted from Diederich, *Measuring.)*

B

PARTIAL LIST OF MODELS TO USE WITH STUDENTS

This appendix contains a partial list of literary models to be used by teachers and students. For example, a teacher may choose Guy de Maupassant's "An Old Man" as a literary model of descriptive writing. Students and teachers together would examine that selection, what makes it effective, its style, and the blending of its meaning and form. Then the students might read independently Wayne Greenhaw's "Meet Bubba Able." Armed with these two models, as well as mini-lessons on description and the teacher's writing as another model, students would reexamine their descriptive pieces, add, delete, rearrange, revise, correct, and reformulate accordingly.

These models may also be used to elicit a reader's response. These responses may be developed into any number of genres. Most of these selections are from different collections and many were published in one source and reprinted in another. Where the selections are readily available, only one source is given. In others, both the original source and the collection are given. This has been done because some of the collections may be difficult to find and some may even possibly be out of print, although the original sources usually can be found in most large library holdings. Usually, in those instances where page numbers are not given, the collections have a table of contents.

Many of the models listed here reflect cultural diversity in topic and ethnicity of writers. In all cases, when using literature with students, careful reading of the selection or selections by the teacher must precede classroom use. The following symbols are used to signal companion pieces for each category: †, ††, †††, and so on.

SELF-EXPRESSION

1. Personal Narrative

    Teacher Model

    †   Brynes, Carla. "The Last Task." *Literary Cavalcade* 37, no. 8 (May 1986): 9-11. Scholastic Writing Awards

    ††   Anderson, Sherwood. "Paper Pills." In *Winesburg, Ohio*. New York: Viking Penguin, 1947.

    Student Model

    †   Grace, Randall. "The Road Out of Eden." *Literary Cavalcade* 38, no. 8 (May 1987). Scholastic Writing Awards

    ††   Buxton, Jennifer. "Family Portrait." *Literary Cavalcade* 37, no. 8 (May 1986): 18-19. Scholastic Writing Awards

2. Poetry

   Teacher Model

   †   Hudgins, Andrew. "At the Piano." In *The Music of What Happens*, edited by Paul B. Janeczko. New York: Orchard Books, 1988.

   ††   Pettit, Michael. "Driving Lesson." In *The Music of What Happens*, edited by Paul B. Janeczko. New York: Orchard Books, 1988.

   †††   Merriam, Eve. "Reply to the Question: '*How Can You Become a Poet?*'" In *Don't Forget to Fly*, edited by Paul B. Janeczko. Scarsdale, NY: Bradbury Press, 1981.

   †††† Wilson, Edward E. "Autumnal Equinox." In *The Music of What Happens*, edited by Paul B. Janeczko. New York: Orchard Books, 1988.

   ††††† Djamikian, Gregory. "How I Learned English." In *The Music of What Happens*, edited by Paul B. Janeczko. New York: Orchard Books, 1988.

   Student Model

   †   Welch, Don. "Spade Scharnweber." In *Poetspeak*, edited by Paul B. Janeczko. New York: Bradbury Press, 1983.

   ††   Matthew, William. "In Memory of the Utah Stars." In *Poetspeak*, edited by Paul B. Janeczko. New York: Bradbury Press, 1983.

   †††   Holden, Jonathan. "First Kiss." In *Going Over to Your Place*, edited by Paul B. Janeczko. New York: Bradbury Press, 1987.

   †††† Zimmer, Paul. "Julian Barely Misses Zimmer's Brains." In *Going Over to Your Place*, edited by Paul B. Janeczko. New York: Bradbury Press, 1987.

   ††††† Wallace, Robert. "The Girl Writing Her English Paper." In *Poetspeak*, edited by Paul B. Janeczko. New York: Bradbury Press, 1983.

3. Journal

   Teacher Model

   †   Santini, Rosemarie. "An American Dream." In *The Dream Book: An Anthology of Writings by Italian American Women*, edited by Helen Barolini. New York: Schocken Books, 1985.

   ††   Cassettari, Rosa. "The Life of an Italian Immigrant." In *The Dream Book: An Anthology of Writings by Italian American Women*, edited by Helen Barolini. New York: Schocken Books, 1985.

   Student Model

   †   Grieco, Rose. "The Sunday Papa Missed Mass." In *The Dream Book: An Anthology of Writings by Italian American Women*, edited by Helen Barolini. New York: Schocken Books, 1985.

   ††   Segale, Sister Blandina. "At the End of the Santa Fe Trail." In *The Dream Book: An Anthology of Writings by Italian American Women*, edited by Helen Barolini. New York: Schocken Books, 1985.

4. Friendly Letters

    Teacher Model

    †   McInnes, Bruce. "Dear Mrs. Carlson." In *Dear America: Letters Home from Vietnam*, edited by Bernard Edelman. New York: Penguin Books, 1987.

    Student Model

    †   Dawson, Charles. "Dear Mom." In *Dear America: Letters Home from Vietnam*, edited by Bernard Edelman. New York: Penguin Books, 1987.

5. Memoir

    Teacher Model

    †   Davis, Lydia. "The Sock." In *The Available Press/PEN Short Story Collection*. New York: Ballantine, 1985. Also in *Sudden Fiction*, edited by Robert Shapard and James Thomas. Layton, UT: Gibbs M. Smith, 1986.

    Student Model

    †   Gildner, Gary. "Sleepy Time Gal." In *The Crush*. New York: The Ecco Press, 1983. Also in *Sudden Fiction*, edited by Robert Shapard and James Thomas. Layton, UT: Gibbs M. Smith, 1986.

LITERARY EXPRESSION

1. Describe a Place

    Teacher Model

    †   Momaday, N. Scott. "The Way to Rainy Mountain." In *The Way to Rainy Mountain*. Albuquerque: University of New Mexico Press, 1969.

    Student Model

    †   Hellman, Lillian. "Memoir of a New Orleans Boarding House." In *The Short Prose Reader*, edited by Gilbert Muller and Harvey S. Wiener. New York: McGraw-Hill, 1982.

2. Describe a Person

    Teacher Model

    †   Maupassant, Guy de. "An Old Man." In *Maupassant: Selected Short Stories*. New York: Penguin Books, 1971.

    Student Model

    †   Greenhaw, Wayne. "Meet Bubba Able." In *The Short Prose Reader*, edited by Gilbert Muller and Harvey S. Wiener. New York: McGraw-Hill, 1982.

3. Describe an Imaginary Person

    Teacher Model

    †   Tanner, Ron. "Garbage." In *The Pushcart Prize XIV*, edited by Bill Henderson. New York: Penguin Books, 1989.

Student Model

†   Shaik, Fatima. "Before Echo." In *Breaking Ice*, edited by Terry McMillan. New York: Penguin Books, 1990.

4. News Story

Teacher Model

†   Wilford, John Noble. "Men Walk on Moon." *The New York Times*, 21 July 1969, Sec. A, 1.

Student Model

†   Mailer, Norman. "The Ride Down." In *Of a Fire on the Moon*. New York: Little, Brown, 1971.

†   Ellison, Harlan. "The Moon and the Mudball." *Los Angeles Free Press*, 1 August 1969.

5. Narrative

Teacher Model

†   Williams, William Carlos. "The Use of Force." In *Short Stories*, edited by Irving Howe and Ilana Wiener Howe. New York: Bantam Books, 1982.

††   Williams, Randall. "Daddy Tucked the Blanket." In *The Short Prose Reader*, edited by Gilbert Muller and Harvey S. Wiener. New York: McGraw-Hill, 1982.

†††   Anderson, Sherwood. "The Untold Lie." In *Winesburg, Ohio*. New York: Viking Penguin, 1947.

Student Model

†   Weidman, Jerome. "My Father Sits in the Dark." In *Short Shorts*, edited by Irving Howe and Ilana Wiener Howe. New York: Bantam Books, 1982.

††   Bradbury, Ray. "Tricks! Treats! Gangway." In *The Short Prose Reader*, edited by Gilbert Muller and Harvey S. Wiener. McGraw-Hill, 1982.

†††   Orwell, George. "A Hanging." In *Shooting an Elephant and Other Stories*. New York: Harcourt Brace Jovanovich, 1974.

6. Character Sketch

Teacher Model

†   Wong, Jade Snow. "Uncle Kwok." In *Fifth Chinese Daughter*. New York: Harper & Row, 1950.

Student Model

†   Littlebird, Larry. "The Hunter." In *Earth Power Coming*, edited by Simon J. Ortiz. Tuba City, AZ: Navajo Community College Press, 1988.

7. Short Story

Teacher Model

† Cook-Lynn, Elizabeth. "The Power of Horses." In *Spider Woman's Granddaughters*, edited by Paula Gunn Allen. Boston: Beacon Press, 1989.

Student Model

† Martin, Bill, Jr., and John Archambault. *Knots on a Counting Rope*. New York: Henry Holt, 1989.

8. Readers Theatre

Teacher Model

† Bass, Mary Gettys. "The Teen Age." *Literary Cavalcade* 38, no. 8 (May 1986): 5-13. Scholastic Writing Award

Student Model

† Jackson, David. "Delicate Operation." *Literary Cavalcade* 37, no. 8 (May 1985): 6-8. Scholastic Writing Award

9. One Act Play

Teacher Model

† Hogan, Linda. "Amen." In *Earth Power Coming*, edited by Simon J. Ortiz. Tuba City, AZ: Navajo Community College Press, 1988.

Student Model

† Williams, John A. "Sissie." In *Breaking Ice*, edited by Terry McMillan. New York: Penguin Books, 1990.

10. Hexagonal Piece

Teacher Model

† Stambaugh, Allison. "A Place for Rosie." *Literary Cavalcade* 39, no. 8 (May 1987): 30-31.

Student Model

† Soto, Gary. "Growing Up." In *Baseball in April*. New York: Harcourt Brace Jovanovich, 1990.

INFORMATIVE

1. Comparison and Contrast

Teacher Model

† Baker, Russell. "The Boy Who Came to Supper." *The New York Times*, 1980: _____.

† Baker, Russell. "The Boy Who Came to Supper." *The New York Times Sunday Magazine*, 31 August 1980.

†† Tan, Amy. "Two Kinds." *The Atlantic Monthly*, February 1989, 53-57.

††† Zitkala-Sa. "A Warrior's Daughter." In *Spider Woman's Granddaughters*, edited by Paula Gunn Allen. Boston: Beacon Press, 1989.

Student Model

† Stengel, Richard. "No More Moon-June: Love's Out." *The New York Times*, Op Ed, 5 August 1979, Sec. 4 E, 21.

†† Bissinger, H. G. "The Plane That Fell from the Sky." In *Popular Writing in America*, edited by Donald McQuade and Robert Atwan. New York: Oxford University Press, 1988.

††† Ekwensi, Cyrian. "The Ivory Dancer." In *African Short Stories*, edited by J de Gradsaigne. New York: St. Martin's Press, 1985.

2. How-to Essay

Teacher Model

† Rudner, Ruth. "Body Surfing." In *Forgotten Pleasures*. New York: Viking Penguin, 1978.

†† Conroy, Pat. "Burial on Yamacraw." In *The Water Is Wide*. Boston: Houghton Mifflin, 1972.

Student Model

† Soto, Gary. "The Marble Champ." In *Baseball in April*. New York: Harcourt Brace Jovanovich, 1990.

†† Negri, Sam. "Loafing Made Easy." In *The Short Prose Reader*, edited by Gilbert Muller and Harvey S. Wiener. New York: McGraw-Hill, 1982.

3. Documented Essays

Teacher Model

† Stevens, Martin, and Jeffery Kluewer. "The Death of John Lennon." In *In Print*, edited by Stevens and Kluewer. Detroit: Longman, 1983.

Student Model

† Brody, Jane E. "Survey Finds Boys Preferred as the First-Born, Girls as Second." In *Writing from Sources*, edited by Brenda Spatt. New York: St. Martin's Press, 1983.

4. Consumer Research

Teacher Model

† Ogilvy, David. "How to Write Potent Copy." In *Confessions of an Advertising Man*. New York: Macmillan, 1963.

Student Model

† "Spot Removers." *Consumer Reports 1979 Buying Guide Issue*. Mount Vernon, NY: Consumers Union of US, 1979.

5. Interview

Teacher Model

† Gbadamosi, Rasheed A. "Death by Waterfall." In *African Short Stories*, edited by J de Gradsaigne. New York: St. Martin's Press, 1985.

Student Model

†   Turkel, Studs. "Miss U.S.A., Emma Knight." In *American Dreams: Lost & Found.* New York: Random House, 1980.

6.   Personal Inquiry

Teacher Model

†   Haley, Alex. "My Search for Roots." In *Roots.* New York: Doubleday, 1974.

Student Model

†   Macrorie, Joyce T. "A Gift from Xipelotec." In *Searching Writing: A Contextbook*, by Ken Macrorie. Rochelle Park, NJ: Hayden Books, 1980.

7.   Classification

Teacher Model

†   Atkinson, Jennifer. "Imagining the Ocean." In *The Pushcart Prize XIV*, edited by Bill Henderson. New York: Penguin Books, 1989.

Student Model

†   Viorst, Judith. "Friends, Good Friends, and Such Good Friends." In *The Short Prose Reader*, edited by Gilbert H. Muller and Harvey S. Wiener. New York: McGraw-Hill, 1982.

PERSUASIVE

1.   Persuasive Letter

Teacher Model

†   Goodman, Ellen. "The State's Nose in Family Life." *Newsday*, 8 August 1980, 9.

††   Church, Francis Pharcellus. "Is There a Santa Claus?" In *Popular Writing in America*, edited by Donald McQuade and Robert Atwan. New York: Oxford University Press, 1988.

Student Model

†   Will, George. "'The Littlest Defector'—Deserves Asylum." In *In Print*, edited by Martin Stevens and Jeffery Kluewer. Detroit: Longman, 1983.

††   Brown, Heywood. "There Isn't a Santa Claus." In *Popular Writing in America*, edited by Donald McQuade and Robert Atwan. New York: Oxford University Press, 1988.

2.   Cause and Effect

Teacher Model

†   Thiong'o, Ngugi wa. "The Return." In *African Short Stories*, edited by J de Gradsaigne. New York: St. Martin's Press, 1985.

††   Achebe, Chinua. "Civil Peace." In *African Short Stories*, edited by J de Gradsaigne. New York: St. Martin's Press, 1985.

Student Model

†   Yngve, Rolf. "The Quail." *Quarterly West* 5 (1978). Also in *Sudden Fiction*, edited by Robert Shapard and James Thomas. Layton, UT: Gibbs M. Smith, 1986.

††   Boll, Heinrich. "The Laughter." In *Heinrich Boll: 18 Stories*. New York: McGraw-Hill, 1966.

3.   Business Letter

Teacher Model

†   Nellen, Valerie C. "The Clarkville File." *Literary Cavalcade* 38, no. 8 (May 1987): 20-21.

Student Model

†   Moore, Marianne. "Correspondence with the Ford Motor Company." In *Popular Writing in America*, edited by Donald McQuade and Robert Atwan. New York: Oxford University Press, 1988.

4.   Book Review

Teacher Model

†   Paterson, Katherine. "Heart Strings and Other Attachments." *Washington Post Book World* XVI, no. 45 (9 November 1986), 17. Also in Paterson, Katherine. *The Spying Heart*. New York: E. P. Dutton, Lodestar Books, 1989.

††   Harrison, Barbara. "Godfather II: Of Families and Families." In *The Dream Book: An Anthology of Writings by Italian American Women*, edited by Helen Barolini. New York: Schocken Books, 1985.

Student Model

†   Paterson, Katherine. "Learning to Love." *Washington Post Book World* 13 (May 1979), Sec. K, 1, 4. Also in Patterson, Katherine. *Gates of Excellence*. New York: Elsevier/Nelson Books, 1981.

††   Paterson, Katherine. "Through the Valley of Death." *Washington Post Book World* XVI, no. 23 (8 June 1986), 18. Also in Paterson, Katherine. *The Spying Heart*. New York: E. P. Dutton, Lodestar Books, 1989.

5.   Television Commercial

Teacher Model

†   Will, George F. "The Case of Phillip Becker." *Newsweek*, 14 April 1980, 112.

Student Model

†   Kurth, Dawn Ann. "Bugs Bunny Says They're Yummy." *The New York Times*, 2 July 1972, Sec. D, 11.

6.   Problem and Solution

Teacher Model

†   Baker, Russell. "Waiting for Wyatt." *The New York Times*, 5 January 1985, Sec. I, 21.

Student Model

†   Grue, Wuther. "Ordeal by Cheque." *Vanity Fair*, March 1932.

7.   Editorial

Teacher Model

†   Hurston, Zora Neale. "Sweat." *Fire* I (November 1926).

Student Model

†   Hunter, Kristen. "Debut." *Negro Digest* XVII (June 1968), 62-69.

INDEX

ABOUT THE AUTHORS

Joyce Armstrong Carroll (Ed.D., Rutgers University; M.A., Hardin-Simmons University; B.A., Georgian Court College) has taught almost all grades in her 33 years in the profession. She was Professor of English and Writing at McMurry University for 18 years. She currently works as a consultant for various school districts conducting interactive inservice seminars in classrooms.

Dr. Carroll has authored the Jackdaws series for Teacher Ideas Press, edited *Fusing Form with Content: A Collection of Exemplary Lessons*, and has written numerous articles on writing for *English Journal, Language Arts, CEA Critic, The Texas Humanist, Curriculum Review, Media & Methods, Southwest Philosophical Studies, YOUth, Florida English Journal*, and other journals. She published a children's story, "God's Cinderella," in the *Church Herald* and several poems in *College Composition and Communication* and *English Journal*. Her chapter on the New Jersey Writing Project in Texas appears in Beach and Bridwell's *New Directions in Composition Research* (Guilford, 1984). She served on the National Council of Teachers of English (NCTE) Commission on Composition and has received myriad awards for professional service. Dr. Carroll is cochair of the NCTE Standing Committee Against Censorship and is codirector of the New Jersey Writing Project in Texas.

Edward E. Wilson received his B.S. degree *Cum Laude* from McMurry University and is completing his M.Ed. in Administration and Supervision from Sam Houston State University. He has taught at the elementary, secondary, and junior college levels. As Secondary Writing Consultant for the Spring Independent School District, Texas, he worked with teachers and students in grades 6-12. He edited *English in Texas*, the Texas affiliate journal for the National Council of Teachers of English (NCTE) for six years. His poem "Autumnal Equinox" appears in Paul Janeczko's *The Music of What Happens*. He served three years on the Texas Teachers Professional Practices Commission. He is a member of NCTE, Texas Council of Teachers of English, and the Association for Supervision and Curriculum Development and its Texas affiliate. Mr. Wilson works with teachers and students as an educational consultant modeling and practicing writing and is codirector of the New Jersey Writing Project in Texas.